BUSINESS STATISTICS

(Strictly According to Syllabus for B.Com./BBM/BBA of MG University Kottayam, MS University Tirunelveli, Kerala University, Madurai Kamaraj University and Other Indian Universities

BUSINESS STATISTICS

Dr. M. WILSON

M.Com., D.B.A., M.Phil., Ph.D.

Reader in Commerce, Scott Christian College, Nagercoil.

Himalaya Publishing House

ISO 9001:2015 CERTIFIED

First Edition : 2000
Second Edition : 2001
Reprint : 2003
Reprint : 2005
Reprint : 2006
Third Edition : 2007
Reprint : 2010
Reprint : 2012
Reprint : 2013
Edition : 2014, 2015, 2017
Edition : 2018, 2020, 2022
Edition : 2023, 2024
Edition : 2025

Published by : Mrs. Meena Pandey
for **Himalaya Publishing House Pvt. Ltd.,**
"Ramdoot", Dr. Bhalerao Marg, Girgaon, Mumbai - 400 004.
Phone: 022-23860170, 23863863; **Fax:** 022-23877178
E-mail: himpub@bharatmail.co.in; **Website:** www.himpub.com

Branch Offices :

New Delhi : "Pooja Apartments", 4-B, Murari Lal Street, Ansari Road, Darya Ganj, New Delhi - 110 002.
Phone: 011-23270392, 23278631; Fax: 011-23256286

Nagpur : Kundanlal Chandak Industrial Estate, Ghat Road, Nagpur - 440 018. Phone: 0712-2738731, 2721216

Bengaluru : Plot No. 91-33, 2nd Main Road Seshadripuram, Behind Nataraja Theatre, Bengaluru - 560 020.
Phone: 08041138821; Mobile: 09379847017, 09379847005

Hyderabad : No. 3-4-184, Lingampally, Besides Raghavendra Swamy Matham, Kachiguda, Hyderabad - 500 027.
Phone: 040-27560041, 27550139

Chennai : No. 34/44, Motilal Street, T. Nagar, Chennai - 600 017.
Mobile: 09380460419

Pune : First Floor, "Laksha" Apartment, No. 527, Mehunpura, Shaniwar Peth (Near Prabhat Theatre), Pune - 411 030.
Phone: 020-24496323, 24496333; Mobile: 09370579333

Cuttack : Plot No. 5F-755/4, Sector-9, CDA Markat Nagar, Cuttack - 753 014, Odisha. Mobile: 09338746007

Kolkata : 3, S.M. Bose Road, Near Gate No. 5, Agarpara Railway Station, North 24 Parganas, West Bengal - 700 109. Mobile: 09674536325

Printed at : M/s Sri Sai Art Printer Hyderabad. On behalf of HPH.

Preface

The development of economic and business activities has compelled the Government and businessmen to consider the statistical data as an integral part of their day-to-day activities. Statistical data, when analyzed properly, provide the much needed information for various business and policy decisions. Keeping this in mind, this text is written with the sole aim of providing the statistical techniques in a clear and simple form for the benefit of the academic community in general and the PG and UG students of Commerce in particular.

It also helps the businessmen to solve the various statistical problems they confronted with in their business activities. The book contains a lot of solved problems in each chapter, which are well structured and graded for the easy comprehension of the students. The Miscellaneous Illustrations given in each chapter, contain the solved problems of Kerala University and Mahatma Gandhi University and other Indian Universities. The exercises in each chapter contains, suitable and adequate theory questions and problems.

First of all I express my heartfelt thanks to more inescapable Guiding Power that prompted and guided me to undertake this venture to the best of my abilities. I am also deeply indebted to all of my well-wishers who directly or indirectly offered me strength and courage in writing this book. I express my thanks to the Management and Staff of Scott Christian College for providing me the academic base and encouraging me to write a textbook of this kind. My sincere thanks are also due to Mr. Niraj Pandey, Partner of Himalaya Publishing House for resposing confidence in me in bringing out this textbook. Let me also take this opportunity to thank the representatives of Himalaya Publishing House, but for their constant pesterings, this book would not have seen the light of the day. My sincere thanks to my parents and my family, Joy and Doyle for their encouragement in writing the book.

Suggestions for improvement are most welcome.

M. Wilson

CONTENTS

1. **Introduction** ... 1 - 10
Origin, Meaning and Definition, Functions, Scope, Limitations, Statistics in Business, Statistics in Government and Commerce.

2. **Collection of Data** ... 11 - 24
Primary and Secondary Data, Methods of Collecting Primary Data, Drafting the Questionnaire, Specimen Questionnaire, Sources of Secondary Data, Editing the Primary and Secondary Data.

3. **Classification and Tabulation of Data** ... 25 - 36
Meaning and Objectives of Classification, Types of Classification, Tabulation of Data, Parts of a Table, General Rule of Tabulation, Types of Table, Miscellaneous Illustrations.

4. **Diagrammatic And Graphic Presentation** ... 37 - 65
Meaning, Significance, Rules, Types of Diagrams, Techniques and Rules of construction of different types of Graphs, Types of Graphs, Limitations of Diagrams and Graphs.

5. **Sampling and Sample Design** ... 36 - 76
Census and Sample Method, Methods of Sampling, Size of a Sample, Merits and Limitations of Sampling, Sampling and Non-Sampling Errors.

6. **Measures of Central Tendency** ... 77 - 159
Meaning and Definitions, Objectives, Type of Averages, Arithmetic Mean, Median, Mode, Geometric Mean, Harmonic Mean, Limitations of Average, Miscellaneous Illustrations.

7. **Measures of Dispersion** ... 160 - 233
Meaning, Methods of Dispersion, Range, Mean Deviation, Standard Deviation, Lorenz Curve, Miscellaneous Illustrations.

8. **Skewness, Kurtosis and Moments** ... 234 - 280
Meaning of Skewness, Type of Skewness, Measures of Skewness, Meaning of Kurtosis, Types of Kurtosis, Measures of Skewness based on Moments, Miscellaneous Illustrations.

9. **Correlation Analysis** ... **281 - 330**

Meaning of Correlations, Karl Pearson's Coefficient of correlation, Rank Correlation Coefficient, Concurrent Deviation Method, Lag and Lead in Correlation, Miscellaneous Illustrations.

10. **Regression Analysis** ... **331 - 368**

Meaning, Uses, Difference between Correlation and Regression Analysis, Regression Equations, Limitations of Regression Analysis, Miscellaneous Illustrations.

11. **Index Numbers** ... **369 - 429**

Meaning and Definition, Uses, Problems in the Construction of Index Numbers, Methods of Constructing Index Numbers, Quantity Index Numbers, Tests of adequacy of Index Numbers, Chain Index Numbers, Base Shifiting, Splicing and Deflating the Index Numbers, Consumer Price Index Numbers, Limitations of Index Numbers, Miscellaneous Illustrations.

12. **Analysis of Time Series** ... **430 - 483**

Meaning of Time Series, Components of Time Series, Measurement of Trend, Shifting the Trend Origin, Measurement of Seasonal variations, Measurement of Cyclical variations, Measurement of Irregular variations, Miscellaneous Illustrations.

13. **Interpolation and Extrapolation** ... **484 - 522**

Meaning and Definitions, Methods of Interpolation, Methods of Extrapolation, Limitations of Interpolation and Extrapolation, Miscellaneous Illustrations.

14. **Probability** ... **523 - 568**

Origin, Meaning, Importance, Calculation of Probability, Theorems of Probability, Conditional Probability, Baye's Theorem, Miscellaneous Illustrations.

15. **Theoritical Distributions** ... **569 - 625**

Meaning, Binomial Distribution, Poisson Distribution, Normal Distribution, Fitting a Normal Curve, Miscellaneous Illustrations.

16. **Linear Programming** ... **626 - 648**

Meaning, Linear Inequalities, Formulation of Linear Programming Problems, Graphic Methods of Solutions Linear Programming Problems.

17. Set Theory ... **649 - 659**

Meaning, Representation of Sets, Types of Sets, Set operations, Properties of Set Union and Intersection.

18. Matrices and Determination ... **660 - 691**

Meaning, Types of Matrices, Algebra of Matrices, Determinants, Properties of Determinants, Solution of Simultaneous Equations by Cramer's Rule, Adjoint of a Square Matrix, Inverse of a Square Matrix.

Appendix I Formulaes ... **692 - 706**

Appendix II Tables ... **707 - 712**

(i) Logarithms

(ii) Antilogarithms

(iii) Binomial Coefficients, Values of e^{-m}

(iv) Area under Standard Normal Curve

◆ Chapter 1 ◆

Introduction

The word statistics is derived from the latin word '*Status*' or the Italian word '*Statista*' or German word '*Statistik*', which means a political state. It is termed as political state, since in early years 'Statistics' indicates a collection of facts about the people in the state for administration or political purpose. The state administration requires data regarding birth, death, income, employment etc. to measure the socio-economic condition of the people. Hence, the subject statistics was used knowingly or unknowingly from very old days onwards. There exists evidence that during 435 B.C. Roman administration took military census. The development of the theory of probability in 17th century added more importance for statistics. This theory was developed due to the popularity of gambling in France and England, at that time.

The science of statistics has been applied widely to other areas at present. Many theories have been formulated during the last century. The major contributors for the development of statistics are Galton, Bowley, Edgeworth and Karl Pearson.

The word statistics is used as singular or plural. Statistics as a singular noun refers to the various methods adopted for collection, classification, analysis and interpretation. As a plural noun statistics refers to data or facts. It means data relating to income, population, production, profit etc.

I Definition of Statistics

The definitions for statistics has been given by many authors for the two seperate concepts of statistics - (i) statistics as a numerical data and (ii) statistics as methods. There are many definitions of statistics available for these two concepts. The important definitions are given below.

1. *Definitions of Statistics in terms of numerical data*

(i) **Cornor** defines Stastics as

"Statistics are measurements, enumerations or estimates of natural or social phenomena, systematically arranged so as to exhibit their inter-relations".

(ii) **Yule** and **Kendall** defines that

"By statistics we mean quantitative data affected to a marked extent by a multiplicity of causes."

(iii) **Dr. A.N. Bowly** defined statistics as

"Statistics are numerical statements of facts in any department of enquiry, places in relations to each other."

(iv) **Webster** defines statistics as

"Stastics are classified facts representing the conditions of the people in a state...... espicially those facts which can be stated in number or in table or numbers or in any tabular or classified arrangement."

(v) **Prof. Horce Secrist** defines statistics as

"By statistics we mean aggregates of facts affected to a marked extent by multiplicity of causes numerically expressed, enumerated or estimated according to reasonable standards of accuracy, collected in a systematic manner for a predetermined purpose and placed in relation to each other."

From the above definitions it is clear that only the definition given by Prof. Horace Secrist covers, all the aspects of stastics as a numerical data. From this definition the following features of statistics can be generated.

(i) Statistics are aggregate of facts: Only data related to facts are termed as statistics. This data should be plural one. Single (or) unrelated figures are not statistics. Since single figure could not be compared it cannot be termed as statistics. *Eg.* Single sales, purchase, production etc. The figures without any relationship is also not called as statistics. *Eg.* figures lik 15, 35, 50, 70 etc. If these figures are related with production or sales etc, then it is called statistics *eg.* production – 15 tonnes, 35 tonnes, 50 tonnes, 70 tonnes etc. (or) sales 15 units, 35 units, 50 units, 70 units etc.

(ii) Statistics are affected to a marked extent by multiplicity of causes: The facts and figures, termed as statistics are due to so many causes. Generally single cause won't influence the statistical facts and figures. *Eg.* Statistics of sales of a product is

affected by so many causes like taste, sales promotion, measures, income, competition etc.

In the above example no individual fact is studied separately.

(iii) Statistics are numerically expressed: Facts and figures should be numerically expressed to be called as statistics. Hence quantitative expressions like production, sales, population, marks etc. are called statistics. Quatitative expressions like character, performance, intelligence, monotonus etc. are not statistics. But these quatitative expressions can be converted into quantitative terms. These quatitative characters in terms of quantitative expression is called as statistics.

(iv) Statistics should be enumerated or estimated according to reasonable standard of accuracy: The facts and figures presented should have a reasonable standard of accuracy. These facts and figures can either be collected from the field or can be estimated. The data collected from the field would be more accurate. But it is not always possible to collect the data from the field. This is due to the fact that the area of the field for study is very large. This estimation should be done with the reasonable standard of accuracy. This reasonable standard of accuracy varies according to the nature of the data, the importance of the data and the purpose of the data. *Eg.* the accuracy for measuring the marks scored by the students in entrance examinations should be more than the accuracy for measuring the population in a village.

(v) They should be collected in a systematic manner: The data collected would be a systematic one. Proper arrangement in a systematic manner would minimise the time, as well as provide accurate information.

2. Statistics as Methods

Statistics as Methods is concerned with the collection, classification and analysis of data. Statistics as methods define statistics as a singular noun.

A L. Bowley defines statistics as *'the science of counting'* and at another place he says it as *'the science of averages'*. This definition is narrow in the sense that it states, statistics is confined only with counting and average. The other aspects of analysis like dispersion, correlation etc. are ignored in the definition.

Boddington defines statistics as *"the science of estimates and probalities."* This definition also ignores the other functions of statistics. It states that statistics only explains about the probability theories.

The most suitable definition for statistics as methods is given by Croxton and Cowden.

According to Croxton and Cowden, *"Statistics may be defined as the collection, presentation, analysis and interpretation of numerical data."*

He rightly pointed out that

(i) collection of data, (ii) presentation of data, (iii) analysis of data and (iv) interpretation of data are the four important methods or stages in statistical investigation. Croxton and Cowden ignores one more stage *i.e.* organisation.

It is clear from the above definitions that statistics as a method means collection, organisation, presentation, analysis and interpretation of data.

II Statistical Investigation (Statistical Enquiry)

Statistical investigation is concerned with investigation of some problem with the help of statistical methods. Data related to the problem is the basic necessity for investigation. Hence the data related to the problem should be collected. These data so collected, should be analysed and processed with suitable statistical devices. The analysed data gives valuable information about the problem under investigation. For *example*, if we want to study about the average monthly income of families in a locality, statistical investigation must be conducted. The data related to monthly income of all the families in the locality should be collected. The data so collected should be analysed so that we can know the average monthly income and the average income for high, middle and low income classes.

III Stages in a Statistical Investigation

The important stages in statistical investigation are

(1) Planning the enquiry
(2) Planning of data
(3) Organisation of data
(4) Presentation of Data
(5) Analysis of data and
(6) Interpretation of data

(1) Planning the enquiry: The first step in statistical investigation is planning. The investigator should determine the objectives and scope of the investigation. He should decide in advance about the type of enquiry to be conducted, source of information and the unit of study.

(2) Collection of data: Collection of data is the first step in statistics. The data may be collected from primary source and from secondary source. Data collected from the primary source (from the field or from the respondents) is called primary data. Data collected from already published materials (magazines, text books, journals, Government statistics) is called secondary data. The data collected should be accurate. There should not be any bias in collecting the data.

(3) Organisation of data: Organisation of data means arrangement of the data. First of all the data collected should be edited to eliminate unnecessary data. Then it should be classified on the basis of some common characteristics. Then the classified data should be presented in a tablulated form. It should be clearly presented in proper rows and columns of the table.

(4) Presentation of data: Organised data may be presented in the form of diagrams and graphs. It helps for easy understanding of the characteristics and nature of the data.

(5) Analysis of Data: The data presented in table form should be analysed to draw conclusion. Various statistical methods like average, dispersion, correlation, regression, time-series etc. are available for analysing the data. The selection of a suitable method of analysis depends on the nature of data and nature of the study.

(6) Interpretation of Data: The last stage in the statistical investigation is the interpretation of data. Interpretation means drawing conclusions. It explains the inference about the whole statistical investigation. It requires high degree of skill and analytical mind. If interpretation is not properly done it may give wrong conclusion. Hence, much care should be taken for interpretation of data to get valid conclusion.

IV Functions of Statistics

The important functions of statistics are as follows:

(1) It presents facts in a proper form.

(2) It simplifies unwiedly and complex data

(3) It facilitates for comparision
(4) It enlarges individuals experience
(5) It facilitates for formulating policies
(6) It tests hypothesis
(7) It measures the trend behaviour

(1) It presents facts in a proper from: Statistics presents facts in a precise and definite form. Facts presented in quantitative term give more meaning and easy understanding than it is presented in statement form. For example, the performance of a company regarding profit and sales, if presented in statement form, gives little meaning. When it is presented as the profit increased from Rs. 2,50,000 to Rs. 3,10,000 gives clear idea about the fact.

(2) It simplifies unwieldly and complex data: Data presented in raw form are unwieldly and complex. If the number of data are huge, it further gives complication for getting an idea about the data. The important function of statistics is to simplify the data. Mean, median, mode are some of the important techniques adopted to simplify the data.

(3) It facilitates for comparision: When data are presented in simplified form it is easy to compare the data. It is possible to compare the data of one period to another as well as to compare the data of one company with other company.

For example (i) the sales of a company of various periods can be compared to find out the performance of the company. (ii) the sales of one company can be compared with the sales of other companies in order to find out the relative performance of the company.

(4) It enlarges individuals knowledge: When data are presented in a form of comparision, the individuals try to find out the reasons for the variation of two or more figures. It thereby helps to enlarge the individuals knowledge.

For example, when the profit of a company for two or more years are presented, it facilitates for comparision. Suppose the profit of the current year is low than the previous year the individuals try to find out the reasons for the decline in profit. It gives more idea to individuals about he cost of production, selling, price, inflation, competiton etc.

(5) It facilitates for formulating policies: Statistics helps for formulating policies for the companies, individuals, Government etc. It is possible only with the help of data presented in suitable

form. Statistics provides various techniques like correlation analysis, regression analysis, dispersion etc. to formulate policies.

(6) It tests hypothesis: Hypothesis is an important concept in research studies. Statistics provides various methods for testing the hypothesis. The important methods for hypothesis test are Chi-square, Z-test, T-test and F-test.

(7) It measures the trend behaviour: Statistics helps for projecting the future with the help of present and past data. Hence plans, programmes and policies are formulated in advance with the help of statistical techniques. The important techniques adopted for measuring the trend are Time series and Regression analysis.

V Scope of Statistics

Statistics was used in olden days by the state to collect information for public administration. Now its scope was not only in collection of information, but also analyse the data collected, to draw inferences or formulate a theory. Hence, it helps for planning and formulation of policies. The methods and techniques available in statistics helps people to solve various problems presented in statistical data. Hence, it has a good application and scope in the field of commerce, economics, physics, chemistry, botany, zoolozy, psychology etc.

Statistics in Business

Statistics is most commonly used in Business. It helps to take decision regarding whether a company can start a new business. The statistical data regarding the demand and the supply of products can be collected and analysed to take a decision regarding the new business. The company can also calculate the cost of production and then the selling price. The selling price can be compared with the selling price of competitive products to make a final decision for starting a new business. The existing companies can also make a comparative study about their performance with the performance of other companies through statistical analysis. The existing companies can also project their future with regression and correlation analysis.

Statistics in Management

Most of the managerial decisions are taken with the help of statistics. The data regarding the performance of a company for the inception period will facilitate to take decision regarding future. Statistical techniques like correlation analysis, regression analysis and time series technique can be used in this regard. The important managerial activities like planning, directing and controlling are properly executed with the help of statistical data and statistical analysis. Statistical techniques can also be used for the payment of wages to the employees of the company.

Statistics in Banking and Finance

Banking and Financial activities use statistics most commonly. In banks statistical data regarding the customer deposit, loans etc are represented in statistical data. Banks also applies the statistical techniques in calculating interests. Stock exchange, Financial institutions like Industrial Development Bank of India, State Financial Corporation of India also use statistics in projecting the future and to solve various statistical problems.

VI Limitations of Statistics

Though statistics has a wide scope and utility, it has certain limitations. The following are the important limitations of statistics.

(1) Statistics studies only quantitative characteristics: Statistics studies only the quantitative phenomenon. It won't deal with the phenomena which could not be expressed in quantitative value. Hence qualitative phenomenon like intelligency, honesty, study etc. cannot be dealt with by statistics unless they are expressed in quantitative values.

(2) Statistics deals with aggregates and not with individual measurements: Statistics deals with aggregate of facts. It requires a series of figures for calculating averages and for analysis. The individual measurement has no recognition. It could not be taken into consideration for any statistical analysis.

(3) The statistical results are not perfectly accurate: The statistical theories won't give accurate results. The results would be only approximate value. First of all the data collected for analysis may not be accurate also.

(4) Data must be uniform in statistics: Data used for statistical analysis must be uniform. For example, the data related with the income of people in a locality could not be mixed with the data related to expenditure of the people. These two phenomena should be studied separately.

(5) Statistics can be misused: Only experienced and efficient persons can handle statistics in a proper way. Untrained and inefficient persons may not produce accurate result with the help of statistical techniques.

VII Statistical Methods Vs Experimental Methods

In early period, human beings acquired knowledge by perception and intuition. It was a matter of chance. At present, people acquire knowledge through scientific methods rather than as a matter of chance. People are systamatically enlarging their knowledge through this method. There are two suitable methods for enlarging their knowledge. They are,

(i) Experimental Method and (ii) Statistical Method

(i) Experimental Method: Through experimental method people acquire knowledge by observation or experiments. In natural science, like physics, chemistry, various experiments are conducted to study a theory or prove a theory. The cause and effect relationship can be studied under a controlled set up of a laboratory.

Experimental Method can be applied in social science like commerce, economics, psychology, political science, sociology etc. In this method, two groups, namely controlled group and experimental group should be selectd. Treatments should be given to the experimental group in order to measure the cause and effect relationship. The effectiveness of a medicine, special coaching etc can be measured under this method.

(ii) Statistical Methods: In statistical method the cause and effect relationship is not measured. The variations among all the variable is measured. It is concerned with comparing the data of one period to another as well as data of one company to another. These comparative study also gives more knowledge to the individuals.

Exercises

1. Distingsuish between 'statistics as data' (Statistics as plural noun) and 'statistics method (statistics as singular noun).
2. Define statistics. State the important features of statistics.
3. State the important steps in statistical investigation.
4. Define statistics. Explain the important functions of statistics.
5. State the scope and limitations of statistics.

6. Distinquish between statistical method and experimental method.
7. Explain five functions of statistics (MGU, Section B, April 1998)
8. Explain five uses of statistics in business with illustration (MGU, Section B, April 1997)
9. Discuss the importance of statistics and show how it can help the extension of scientific knowledge, the establishment of sound business and the introduction of social and political reform. (MGU, Section C, April, 1995)
10. Mention four uses of statistical methods (MGU, Section A, September 1994)
11. Give the various meanings of the term statistics (MGU, Section B, September, 1994)
12. Write a critical note on the availability and scope of agricultural statistics in India. (MGU, Section C, September, 1994)
13. Give one meaning of the term 'statistics'. (MGU, Section A, September, 1993)
14. Give two uses of statistics. (MGU, Section A, September, 1993 and MGU, Section A, September 1992)
15. Explain the importance of statistics in arriving at policy decision in any economy. (MGU, Section B, September, 1993)
16. Explain the uses and limitations of statistical methods (MGU, Section B, September 1992)
17. 'Statistics may be regarded as an instrument of research of great value but having several limitations, which are not possible to overcome and such they need our careful attention' Examine the statement. (MGU, Section C, September 1992)
18. Give two meanings of Statistics.? (MGU, Section A, April, 1992)
19. The proper function of statistics is to enlarge individual experience.' Comment. (MGU, Section A, April 1992)
20. Bring out the importance of statistics in arriving at policy decisions in an economy. (MGU, Section C, April 1992)
21. What are the limitations of Statistics? (KU, Section B, April 1992)
22. What is statistical investigation? (MGU, Section A, April 1995 and MGU, Section A, September 1993)
23. What is a statistical investigation? Describe the preliminary steps you would take in planning on statistical investigation. (MGU, Section B, April 1992)

◆ Chapter 2 ◆

Methods of Collection of Data

There are two basic sources of collecting the data. They are primary source and secondary source. If the data are collected from the primary source, it is called primary data. If it is collected from the secondary source it is called secondary data. The data obtained from the field (from the individuals or institutions for which the data is related) is called primary data. Primary data may be collected by individuals for research purpose or by institutions for business purpose or by government for government policy decisions. The government may collect the data related to population, industrial production, agricultural production etc.

Secondary data are those data collected not from the original source. They are obtained from published or unpublished sources. This data can be obtained from various trade journals or from the government statistical departments. Example, data collected from the already collected data for population studies, studies related to agricultural production and industrial production.

I Methods of Collecting Primary Data

Following are the important methods of collecting primary data

(1) Direct interview method
(2) Indirect interview method
(3) Information collected from local agencies
(4) Questionnaire method
(5) Schedule sent through enumerators

(1) Direct interview method: In this method, the data is collected by the researcher, individuals or institutions directly from the respondents. Hence, the person who needs the data, directly came into contact with the individuals, from where the information is collected. The information gathered under this

method is original in nature. This method facilitates for personal contact with the respondents and thereby, to know the reactions of the respondents immediately.

Merits

(i) The data collected through this method is more reliable since the information are directly gathered from the original source.

(ii) The investigator can get more information than any other method.

(iii) Qualitative information like taste; preferences etc., can be determined very accurately.

(iv) The investigator can motivate the respondents and thereby, extract valuable and secret information from them.

(v) Under this method, it is easy to identify whether respondent is giving correct information or he is manipulating the data.

Demerits

(i) It is an expensive method of collection of data. In case the data is to be collected from distant place or the respondents are very large in numbers the researcher has to spent more money for collecting data.

(ii) This method is suitable only for intensive studies and not for extensive studies.

(iii) It is not suitable if data are to be collected within very short period.

(iv) Quality of the data through this method depends upon the skill and intelligence of the investigator. If the investigator is not able one, then the data collected by him may not be a reliable one.

(2) Indirect Interview Method: This method is otherwise called as indirect oral interview method. Under this method the information about a person is collected through his friends, relatives and neighbours. When the information like smoking habits, drinking habits, consumption of drugs etc. are to be collected this method is most suitable. This type of information could not be an accurate one compared to the direct interview method. This method can also be applied to find out the truth regarding theft, murder, kidnapping etc.

Merits

(i) This method gives accurate information since the investigator can contact any people.

(ii) Since the investigator can get information from friends or relatives of the individuals he need not spent time to search the individual for whom data are to be collected.

(iii) This method is most suitable to explore the truths about the social evils like theft, murder, consumption of liquors etc.

Demerits

(i) Since the data are collected from the relatives of the individual, the information may be a wrong one if the relatives are not in good terms with the particular individuals.

(ii) It is an expensive method, since the information about an individual is to be collected from many people.

(iii) Inability of the investigator may bring wrong information.

(iv) Sometimes the information gathered about an individual from two or more people may contradict each other. In such a situation the investigator has to conduct so many enquiries to find out the truth.

(3) Information collected from local agencies: Under this method the investigator does not directly collect the data from the respondents. He appoints local agency, in the places where he wants to collect the data. These local agents are otherwise called as correspondents. This method is normally adopted when the data is to be collected from various places. This type of data collection is normally adopted by publishers of Newspapers, Journals, Periodicals etc.

The government may also follow this method of data collection for getting information related to illiteracy, unemployment, agricultural production, industrial production etc.

A modified technique adopted in this method of information received from local agencies is called *"registration method"*. Under this method instead of the local agencies, visiting the respondents to collect information, the respondents visit the local agencies to supply information *(eg)* the data relating to deaths and births in India are collected through registration method by the local agencies like hospitals, health departments etc.

Merits

(i) This method is most suitable when the area from which data are to be collected is very large.

(ii) The cost of collecting data under this method is very low when part time agents are employed for this purpose.

(iii) The data can be collected within very short period.

Demerits

(i) If full time agents are appointed in various places, this method would be a costly one.

(ii) Since the way of collecting the information by various agents are not uniform one, then the information may not be uniform one. Information may contradict each other.

(iii) More accurate information could not be collected under this method.

(4) Questionnaire Method: Under this method readymade questionnaires are prepared which are sent to respondents through mails. The number of copies of the questionnaire depends on the number of respondents. The questionnaire should be prepared with much care so that it accommodates all the questions related to the information to be collected. The questionnaire should be very clear, accurate and brief. It should motivate the respondents to write the answers within short period, so that he can post it at an early date. It should contain indirect questions rather than direct one.

A specimen of questionnaire is given below.

Specimen of Questionnaire

A study about the Consumers Satisfaction with regard to the Transport Corporation Buses

QUESTIONNAIRE

1. Name: ______________________
2. Address: ______________________
3. (a) Sex: Male / Female
   (b) Age: ______________
   (c) Education: ______________
   (d) Occupation: ______________
   (e) Annual Income: ______________
4. (a) Do you own any vehicle: Yes / No
   (b) If 'Yes' specify the item: Bicycle/ Two wheeler/ Car
5. Average distance travelled (in Kms):
   (a) Per day: ______________
   (b) Per month: ______________

6. State the average distance travelled per month by:

   (i) Own vehicles:__________Kms

   (ii) Transport Corporation Buses:__________Kms

7. (a) State the average expenses per month for transport.

   (i) Own vehicles:

Vehicles	Petrol/Diesel (Rs.)	Maintenance (Rs.)	Depreciation (Rs.)	Total (Rs.)
2-wheelers				
Car				
Total				

   (ii) Transport Corporation Bus: Rs. ______

8. If you are getting buses at the schedule time: Yes/No

   If no state the waiting time for getting the bus: ______.

9. How do you feel about the rate of the ticket:

   (i) High (ii) Low (iii) Reasonable

10. Are you satisfied with the driver and conductors of the bus.

    Yes / No.

    If No state the reasons for that.

    ____

    ____

11. State about the overall performance of the transport corporation bus.

    (i) Good (ii) Average (iii) Poor

12. State about your satisfaction with regard to the transport corporation bus

    (i) High (ii) Average (iii) Low (iv) Very Low

13. Give your suggestions for the improvement in the performance of the transport corporation buses.

    (i) ____________________

    (ii) ____________________

    (iii) ____________________

    (iv) ____________________

    (v) ____________________

Normally the questionnaire should be sent to the respondents with a covering letter. The covering letter should request the respondents to return the filled up questionnaire within very short period. It should be written in a very pleasing manner. Also the respondent should be given the confidence that the information given by him should be kept in strict confident. The questionnaire should also be enclosed with the self addressed stamped envelope. This self addressed stamped envelop can be used for returning the filled up questionnaires to the investigator.

Merits

(i) This is the cheapest method of collecting primary data.

(ii) Under this method any number of respondents can be contacted, even they are residing at distant places.

(iii) Data can be collected within a very reasonable short period, since the investigator need not visit various places.

(iv) The data collected under this method are unbiased one, since personal contact is not required.

Demerits

(i) The chances of receiving all the questionnaires posted are very rare.

(ii) The respondents may delay in posting the filled up questionnaires.

(iii) Only educated people can be able to fill up the questionnaires.

(iv) The respondents may give wrong information. Hence, it could not be considered as an accurate one.

(v) Personal motivation is not possible under this method. Hence, the secret information could not be collected through this method.

(5) Schedule sent through enumerators: Under this method the questionnaire is prepared in advance which is to be sent through enumerators. These ensumerators explain the questions to the respondents and record the information about the questions in the questionnaire by themselves. These questionnaires is otherwise called Schedules, since it is to be filled up by the enumerators. The enumerators are otherwise called as agents or interviewers. They act as an agent of the investigators. Normally, this method is adopted by Research Departments, Federation of Indian Chambers of Commerce and Industries (FICCI), Central Government, State Government etc.

Merits

(i) Information collected under this method will be more accurates, since enumerators can explain the questions to the respondents.

(ii) Information from illiterates can also be collected under this method.

(iii) The reactions of the individual can be known immediately through this method.

(iv) The enumerators can easily find out whether the respondents are giving the correct information or not.

Demerits

(i) This method is an expensive one, since enumerators should be given remuneration for their work.

(ii) This method became ineffective when the enumerators are inefficient and not sincere.

(iii) The information collected from different enumerators may contradict each other. Hence, it is difficult to identify the fact.

(iv) If the schedule does not contain all the relevant questions the information collected would be incomplete one.

Drafting the questionnaire or Schedule

While drafting the questionnaire utmost care would be taken to get a good quality questionnaire. It should properly communicate the facts, to the respondents. It should be drafted in such a way that it should motivate the respondents. It should be prepared according to the taste of the respondents.

Qualities of a good questionnaire

A good questionnaire should have the following qualities.

(i) The questionnaire should be as small as possible: The number of questions in the questionnaire should be very minimum. If the size of the questionnaire is a big one, the respondents may hesitate to answer all the questions. It may also consume lot of time. The investigator may also not able to concentrate on the important questions if the number of questions are more.

(ii) The questions should be simple, clear and brief: If the questions are ambiguous and lengthy one, it may be difficult for the respondents to understand the questions. They will be motivated to give the correct answer only when the questions are simple and of direct nature.

(iii) The questions should be arranged in natural logical order: When the questions are arranged in a logical order, it would be easy for the investigator for further analysis. Also it helps the respondents to answer the questions spontaneously. *Example:* For a study on the topic, *"Consumption of tea among the people in a village"*, the questions should be asked in a logical order which have been stated as follows:

(1) Do you consume tea?

(2) How many cups of tea are you consuming daily?

(3) What brand of tea are you consuming?

(4) How much money are you spending daily for the consumption of tea?

If the fourth question in the example is written as a first question or any other changes in the sequence, it clearly reveals that the questions do not have any logical sequence.

(iv) The questions of personal nature should be avoided: Since personal questions hurt the feelings of respondents it should be avoided. *Example:* Do you smoke?, Do you drink alcohol? etc.

(v) Proper words should be used in the questions: Proper words only convey the right meaning to the respondents.

(vi) Questions of opinion in nature should be avoided: Instead of asking opinion, indirect questions may be asked to extract the opinion.

(vii) Avoid the questions for which the correct answers will never be got. This type of questions should be avoided, so that the investigator may save time. *Example* of such type of questions are, Do you consume liquor?.

(viii) Avoid questions for which the answers are not known to the respondents. It is a waste to ask unnecessary questions for which the informants won't know the answer. *Example:* questions about blood pressure, sugar content etc.

(ix) As far as possible the question should be of *'Yes'* or *'No'* type: This type of questions get a clear-cut answer. The respondents also like this type of questions than descriptive type of questions.

(x) Cross-checks questions should be framed, so that the reliability of an answer can easily be found out. Cross-check questions should be framed for important information.

(xi) Types of questions: The types of questions selected depend upon the nature of investigation and the type of respondents. Following are the important types of questions.

(a) Simple alternative question: This is otherwise called as dichotomous questions. This type of question can be answered as '*yes*' or '*no*'; '*right*' or '*wrong*'; '*either*' or etc. *Example:* Do you like coffee?

(b) Multiple choice questions: These questions contain number of answers. The respondents have to choose a correct answer according to his taste and put a tick mark corresponding to it.

Example 1. *Which of the following cool drinks do you consume?*

1. Limca ☐
2. Thumpsup ☐
3. Lehar pepsi ☐
4. Goldspot ☐
5. None of the above ☐

2. *What is your hobby?*

1. Reading books ☐
2. Drawing ☐
3. Cinema ☐
4. Gardening ☐
5. Television ☐

(c) Specific information questions: The types of questions which require specific information is called specific information questions. *Example:* What are you doing? What is your qualification? What is your age? etc.

(d) Open questions: In the open questions, the respondents have to answer in their own words. The questions won't accomodate answers. The answers are of descriptive in nature. *Example:* What is your opinion about the new economic policy? What are the drawbacks in the consumption of liquor? How do you spend your free time? etc.

(xii) Pre-testing of questionnaire: Before printing the questionnaire it should be tested with few selected respondents. This process is called pre-testing. It will help to find out the

defects in the questionnaires. These defects can be rectified, before printing the questionnaire.

(xiii) Covering Letter: When the questionnaires are sent to the respondents through post, it should accomodate with a covering letter. If the questionnaires are given directly, the purpose of the questionnaire can be stated orally to the respondents.

The questionnaire should explain the objectives and scope of the survey, the important concepts and technical terms used in the questionnaire.

The questionnaire should accomodate with a self addressed stamped envelope for returning the questionnaire. It may also accomodate with free gifts, to get an early reply.

(xiv) The questionnaire should be an attractive one: It should appeal the respondents to respond immediately. Hence, the layout of the questionnaire should be properly designed.

II Sources of Secondary Data

Data which had already collected is called secondary data. The data collected by one may be used by others for research work or for further investigation. It is otherwise called as second-hand information. There are various sources of secondary data. They can be classified into following two categories.

(i) Published sources and (ii) Unpublished sources

(i) Published sources

Secondary data are available through published sources from government and non-government organisations. Both central government and state governments are having their own published data. Non-government organisations like trade associations, chambers of commerce, etc. also have their own publications.

Types of Published sources

(1) Government publications: The state government and central government are publishing data relating to various economic activities periodically. These data are published by various ministries of the government. The government has its own organisation for collecting and publishing data related to various fields. Example of such kind of organisations are Central Statistical Organisation, Labour Bureau Directorate of Economics and Statistics, National Service Organisation etc. The main publications by these organisations are, Monthly Abstract of

Statistics, Statistical Abstract of India (Annual), Annual Survey of Industries, Agricultural Statistics of India, National Income Statistical Systems of India, Indian Trade Journal Population Bulletin (Bi-annual related with population) etc.

(2) Semi-Government Publications: The semi-government organisations like Reserve Bank of India, The Institute of Foreign Trade, The Institute of Economic Growth also publish data relating to trade and other business activities. The Reserve Bank of India publishes these data through Annual Report of the Bank, Currency and Finance, Reserve Bank of India Bulletin etc.

(3) Reports of Committees and Commissions: Special committees and commissions are usually appointed by the Government to conduct enquiries and investigation. These committees submit their reports. These reports contain valuable information for research and further investigation. *Example:* The Reports of Monopolies Commissions, National Labour Commission, National Agricultural Commission, Financial Commission etc.

(4) Publication of Research Institutions: The publications of Research Institutions are important source of secondary data. Example of the research institutes are Institute of Labour Research, Bombay, Indian Standard Institute, New Delhi, Indian Agricultural Statistical Institute, New Delhi etc. These institutions have their findings in the form of reports and thesis.

(5) Newspapers and Journals: Newspapers and journals are usually an important source of secondary data. Newspaper are supplying information related to all the areas like Industry, Agriculture, Sports, National events etc. *Example* of important newspapers are Economic Times, Times of India, Financial Express etc. Journals also provide information in the form of articles. Example: Commerce, Indian Journal of Marketing, Southern Economist, Economic and Political weekly etc.

(6) Publications of Trade Associations and Chambers of Commerce: These associations usually publish data relating to trade and business activities. *Example* of these associations are Paper Manufacturer Association, Federation of Indian Chambers of Commerce, Sugar Mill's Association, Jute Mill's Associations, Indian Cotton Mills Federation etc.

(7) International Publications: The International Associations and Foreign Governments also publish data relating to international events. This can be taken as a reliable secondary

data. *Example* of the international organisations which provide secondary data are World Health Organisation (WHO), United Nations Organisations (UNO), International labour Organisation (ILO), International Finance Corporation (IFC), International Monetary Fund (IMF) etc.

(ii) Unpublished Sources

There are various sources of unpublished data. *Example:* records maintained by private business concerns, the research work done by individual research scholars etc. They do not publish the data relating to their field, since they feel it as an unnecessary one and also they may want to maintain the secrets of their findings.

Precautions to be taken before using the secondary Data

Since the investigator is not collecting these data, from the primary source, utmost care should be taken before using the data. If these data are misrepresenting the fact, the investigator may be going to a wrong decision. Hence the investigator must see the reliability, accuracy, adequacy and suitability of data.

(1) Reliability of data: The reliability of data can be tested through the following techniques.

(a) The investigator should verify the honesty, experience and integrity of the agency which collects and maintains data.

(b) The sources from which information is collected also convey the reliability of the data.

(c) The researcher should also examine the methods of data collection.

(d) The sample collected should be adequate one.

(e) The sample should fairly represents their population.

(f) The technique adopted for analysing the data should be a standard one.

(g) The experience, integrity and quality of the persons who collected the data should be studied.

(2) Adequacy of data: The data collected from the secondary source should be adequate for the purpose of the investigation. Sometimes the data may be more reliable and accurate one, but it may not be adequate one. This will not satisfy the scope of the investigation. *Example:* The data collected for the purpose of "A

study on consumption of coffee in India", will not be an adequate one, if the data related to the consumption of coffee in Kerala are not available.

(3) Suitability of data: The data collected from the secondary source should be suitable for the present study. *Example:* For a study about the preference of college going students, the data related with the preferences of people below 17 years old are not suitable for the purpose of the study.

(4) Accuracy of the data: The data should not be a mere approximation and assumption. It should be more accurate. Otherwise, the analysis based on such data, will not give an accurate result.

Editing of the primary and secondary data

Editing of data means arranging the data in a proper form and eliminating the unnecessary data. Through editing, the errors and irregularities in the data can be detected and prevented. Editing the data gives accuracy and homogeneity of the data.

Exercises

1. Define Primary data. Briefly explain the important methods of collecting primary data.
2. Define Secondary data. Explain the important methods of collecting secondary data.
3. Distinguish between Schedule and Questionnaire.
4. Distinguish between Primary data and Secondary data.
5. Distinguish between direct interview method and indirect interview method of collecting primary data.
6. What are the important aspects to be considered by an investigator before using secondary data? (MGU, Section B, April 1998)
7. What do you understand by Secondary data?
8. What do you mean by Primary data? (MGU, Section A, April 1992)
9. What is a Questionnaire? (MGU, Section A, April 1992)
10. What are the essential qualities of a good questionnaire?
11. Distinguish between Primary and Secondary data.
(Kerala Section B April 1997; Kerala Section A April 1995)
12. Define and distinguish between "Primary" and "Secondary" data. Give illustrations. (Kerala Section B April 1994)
13. Mention the precautions to be taken before using the Secondary data. (Kerala Section A April 1989)

14. Explain the procedure for collecting data through Schedule and Questionnaires. (Kerala, Section B, April 1989)

15. Define Secondary data. (Kerala, Section A, April 1993)

16. Explain the various techniques of collection of data.

(Kerala Section B April 1993)

17. What are the Secondary Data? State the main sources from which secondary data are collected. (Kerala Section A September 1993)

18. State any two methods of collecting statistical data.

(Kerala Section A September 1990)

19. Explain the role of schedules and questionnaire in collection of data.

(Kerala Section B September 1990)

20. Explain the various techniques of collection of data.

(Kerala Section B April 1990)

◆ Chapter 3 ◆

Classification and Tabulation

The next process after the collection of data is classification and tabulation. If the data collected is not presented in a classified form, then it would be difficult for identifying the data and for further analysis. Also the figures collected are a complex and unorganised mass of figures. Classification and tabulation helps to reduce the complexity of the data and to reduce the volume of the mass of data. Hence, classification and tabulation provide structure of data. Due to this, further analysis can easily be done.

I Meaning and Objectives of Classification and Tabulation

Classification is the process of arranging the collected data into classes and to subclasses according to their common characteristics. Classification should be done on the basis of common features of the data. Prof. Connor defines classification as the process of arranging things (either actually or notionally) in the groups according to their resemblances and affinities and given expression to the unity of attibutes that mean subsist amongst a diversity of individuals.

Example: Data have been collected for a study about the saving habit of the people in a village. The study is conducted for a sample of 250 families. This study may contain huge number of data relating to income, expenses, excess income and excess expenses etc. Hence classification can be done for data related to income, expenses, savings separately. Further classification of income between Rs.100-500, 500-1000, 1000-1500, 1500-2000 can also be made. Expenses can also be classified on this basis.

Objectives of Classification

The important objectives of classification are stated below.

(1) Simple form of presentation of data: Classification groups the vast data in a very simple form. The complex vast data are presented in simple, brief, logical and understandable form.

(2) It facilitates comparison: Classification helps to compare the data of one period to another. When the data are compared one can get an idea about the growth of a phenomenon. For example, the sales of a company in various periods, if presented in a classified form, helps to compare the sales of different periods.

(3) The relationship of data can easily be understood: The cause and effect relationship of data can easily be known, when the data are presented in a classified form. For example, the effect of sales due to the cause of advertisement is well known when the data are presented in classified form.

(4) It facilitates for easy understanding: The classified data facilitates for easy perception and conception.

(5) It forms a basis for tabulation: Classified data form a basis for tabulation of data. It further helps for the statistical analysis of data.

II Characteristics of Classification

The important characteristics of classification are stated below.

(1) Exhaustive: The classification must be exhaustive. Each item of data must be presented in any one of the classes. The classified data must not give any doubt in the mind of the individual that a particular data is excluded.

(2) Mutually Exclusive: Each item of data must be presented in one class only. No item of data should be represented in more than one class.

(3) Flexibility: Classification should be flexible one, so that it have the facility of making adjustment to new situations.

(4) Homogenity: The variables included in all classes should be homogeneous.

(5) Suitability: The classification must be most suited to the objects of the study.

(6) Arithmetical Accuracy: A good classification must be prepared with arithmetical accuracy.

III Methods of Classification

Following are the important methods of classication.

(1) Geographical classification

(2) Chronological classification

(3) Qualitative classification

(4) Quantitative classification

(1) Geographical classification: When data are classified on the basis of states, regions, zones, cities, villages etc., it is called geographical classification.

Example: Number of small scale industries in different cities can be classified on the following basis.

Classification of Small Scale Industries

Name of cities	*Total number of small scale industries (in '000s)*
A	145
B	122
C	111
D	100
E	95
F	85

(2) Chronological classification: Chronological classification means classification of data on the basis of time, like months, years etc. Example for chronological classification is given below.

Profit of a Company for 1990-1997

Year	*Profit (Rs. '000)*
1990	18
1991	22
1992	25
1993	20
1994	39
1995	55
1996	60
1997	85

(3) Qualitative classification: Qualitative classification is based on some attributes or characteristics. It cannot be quantitatively measured. Under this classification, the presence or absence of an attribute is the basis of classification. This classification can be done by two methods. (i) Two-fold or Dichotomous classification and (ii) Manifold classification.

(i) Two-fold or dichotomous classification: In two-fold classification, only one attribute is taken into consideration. It can be classified on the basis of one possessing an attribute and other not possessing that attribute. For *example,* Literacy as an attribute. It can be studied on the basis of literates and illiterates.

(ii) Manifold classification: The classification of attributes of more than one is called manifold classification. Under this classification, the presence or absence of one attribute may further be classified by the presence or absence of another attribute.

The presence of attributes is termed by capital letters A, B, C, D etc., and the absence of the attribute is termed by small letters like a, b, c, d etc., or by Greek letters like Alpha, Beta, Gama etc. Example for manifold classification is given below.

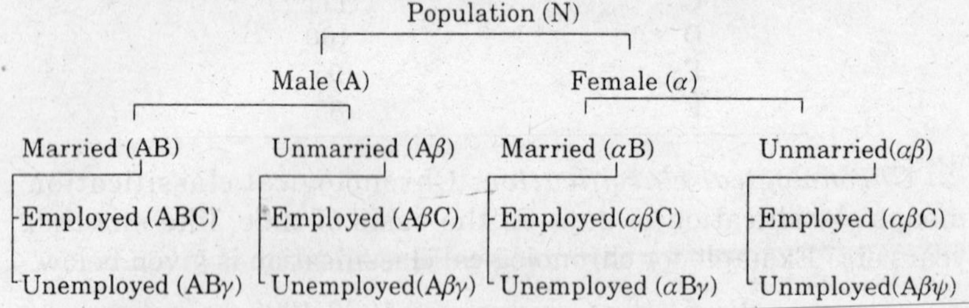

In the above example Male (A) Married (B) and Employed (C) are termed as presents of attributes. Female (Alpha), Unmarried (Beta), Unemployed (Gama) are termed as absence of attributes.

(4) Quantitative classification: When the data are collected on the basis of characteristics which can be quantitatively measured, it is called quantitative classification. *Example:* Income, expenses, production, weight etc. are grouped in Quantitative classification.

If the data are very small then the data can be presented without any classification. When the data are large then it may be classified for easy and convenient identification. There are two types of classification of data. They are (1` Classification for a Discrete Frequency Distribution (2) Classification for a Continuous Frequency Distribution.

(1) Classification for a Discrete Frequency Distribution: In Discrete Frequency Distribution data are classified on the basis of the number of times each data repeated. Hence, before classification, the number of times each item repeated should be counted. The counting can be done with the help of a technique

named Tally Table. The example, stated below explains the classification of data with the help of tally table.

Example: *The daily wages of 30 people in a locality are stated below.*

25, 75, 35, 30, 50, 55, 55 25, 30, 50, 60, 70, 75, 75 70, 55, 40, 45, 40, 35, 50, 55, 60, 75, 70, 40, 55, 75, 60, 55.

Classify the above data in the form of a discrete frequency distribution.

Solution: *Frequency Distribution of wages of people*

Wages per day (Rs.)	*Tallies*	*Frequency*
25	||	2
30	||	2
35	||	2
40	|||	3
45	|	1
50	|||	3
55	~~||||~~ |	6
60	|||	3
65	–	0
70	|||	3
75	||||	5
	Total	*30*

(2) Classification for a Continuous Frequency Distribution: Data are classified on the basis of continuous frequency distribution when the data are very large in number. The data are first grouped on the basis of class limits. For *example*, the daily income of people in a locality may range from Rs.20 to Rs.120. This may be grouped into Rs.20-30, 30-40, 40-50 etc. The class limits are the lowest and highest values of each class. The lowest value in a class is called *'lower limit'* and the highest value in the class is called the '*highest limit*'. The difference between the lowest value and the highest value of each class is called the *"class interval"*. The class interval depends upon the number of classes and the magnitude of data. There is a formula for calculating the class interval,

ie, $$i = \frac{L - S}{K}$$

where, i = class interval

L = Largest value of the data

S = Smallest value of the data

K = The required no. of classes.

For example, the monthly expenses of 200 families in a locality ranges between Rs.300 to Rs.2700. The total no. of classes required is 12. Find out the class interval.

$$i = \frac{L - S}{K}$$

$$= \frac{2700 - 300}{12} = \frac{2400}{12} = 200$$

According to Sturge's Rule the number of classes can also be determined with the help of the following formula,

$$K = 1 + 3.322 \text{ Log N}$$

Where N denotes, total number of observation.

With the help of the above formula the magnitude of the class interval can also be calculated through the following formula,

$$i = \frac{L - S}{1 + 3.322 \text{ Log N}}$$

After deciding the class interval and number of classes the class frequency can be derived. Class frequency is the number of items corresponding to each class.

Class frequency can be calculated with the help of Tally Table.

The important methods of classification of data according to class interval are (i) Exclusive Method and (ii) Inclusive Method.

(i) Exclusive Method: Under the exclusive method, the upper limit of a class interval is the lower limit of the next class interval. It car be known from the following example.

Daily Income (Rs.)	*No. of people*
20-40	4
40-60	7
60-80	10
80-100	5
100-120	3

In the above example the upper limit (*ie,* 40) of the first class interval is the lower limit of the second class interval (40-60). In this method an item valued 80 should be put in the class interval of 80-100 and not in the class interval 60-80.

The above example can be read as,

20 and under 40, 40 and under 60, 60 and under 80, 80 and under 100, 100 and under 120.

(ii) Inclusive Method: In this method the upper limit of a class interval is included in the class-interval itself. It can be known from the following example.

Daily Income (Rs.)	*No. of people*
21-40	4
41-60	7
61-80	10
81-100	5
101-120	3

In the above example the upper limit (*ie,* 60) of the second class interval is included in the class interval 41-60 itself.

Determination of frequency of each class

Frequency of each class can be determined with the help of tally table. Under this method the class groups should be written on a sheet of paper, known as tally sheet. For each item of the data, a small vertical line is marked against the class group in which it falls. When a class group contains more than 4 vertical lines then the fifth line should be a cross line over the 4 lines (卌).

A model tally sheet for determining the frequency of income of 100 peolple are stated below.

Income Rs.	*Tally mark*	*No. of people*
Below 500	卌 卌 ||	12
501-1000	卌 卌 卌 卌 ||||	24
1001-1500	卌 卌 卌 卌 卌	25
1501-2000	卌 卌 卌 |	16
2001 and above	卌 卌 卌 卌 |||	23
	Total	*100*

Tabulation

Tabulation is a process of systematic and scientific presentation of data in a compact form for further analysis. Tabulation is an orderly arrangement of data in columns and rows. Tabulation is the last stage in the collection and presentation of data. The further analysis of data for proving a theory, or for formulating a theory or inference depends on the presentation of a data in a tabulated form.

Objectives of Tabulation

The important objectives of tabulation are stated below.

(1) To present the data in a simplest possible form.

(2) To present the data in order to make it easy for further analysis.

(3) To facilitate for easy comparison of data.

Difference between Classification and Tabulation

(i) Classification is the process of grouping the data on the basis of some common characteristics. Tabulation is the process of placing the classified data in columns and rows.

(ii) Tabulation process starts only after the classification process is completed.

(iii) Classification is done for the purpose of Tabulation, whereas tabulation is done for the purpose of analysis of data.

Rules for Tabulation

Rules for Tabulation is otherwise called as principles of Tabulation. The important rules for Tabulation are stated below.

(1) Number: Table must be arranged with number, in order to identify the table.

(2) Title: Table must have a title. The title should be clear, brief and concise. It should convey the content and purpose of the table.

(3) Stubs and Captions: The details about the information available in each row are called stubs. Stubs should be very clear and brief. The details about the information available in each column are called captions. Captions should also be very clear and brief.

(4) Body of the Table: Body of the table must contain only relevant information. It should be comprehensive and consistent. The

data should be arranged very systematically. The arrangements may either be on ascending or descending order.

(5) Spacing: Proper space should be provided in between various data presented in the table. It helps for easy identification of data. Proper spacing gives good appearance for the table.

(6) Averages and Totals: If the data requires average and total it should be properly given. Totals may be given for each column or for each row.

(7) Footnotes: If any item presented in table needs further explanation, it should be given after the table. Special markings can be used in the respective places where explanation is needed. The explanation should follow with these markings.

(8) Source: Source is an important requirement for the table. Source indicates the place or person from whom information is collected. It gives more authenticity for the table.

Requisites for a Good Tabulation

The following are the requirements of a good Tabulation.

(1) Table must be simple. It should clearly convey the purpose for which it is prepared.

(2) Columns and rows should not be too narrow or too wide.

(3) Brief description should be given for the particulars of columns and rows. If more details are required, it should be given as footnotes.

(4) Table should clearly show the units of measurement.

(5) Table should be an optimum one. It should appeal the readers.

(6) Figures which are closely related should be kept together in columns or rows.

Types of Tables

Tables may be classified into two types. They are:

(1) Simple and Complex Tables and

(2) General purpose and Special purpose tables.

(1) Simple and Complex Tables: Simple table may be defined as a table showing only one characteristic. It is also called one way table.

Complex tables may be defined as tables showing two or more characteristics. If the table shows two characteristics, it is called *'two way table'* or *'double tabulation'*. If the table shows three characteristics, it is called *'trible tabulation'*. If the table shows four or more characteristics, it is called *'manifold tabulation'*.

The model of *'one-way table'* or simple table is shown as below.

Marks scored by students of a class

Marks in Statistics	*No. of students*
Below 20	5
20-40	8
40-60	13
60-80	12
80-100	7
Total	*45*

Model of Two-way table is given below.

Marks scored by students in 2 classes

Marks	*No. of students*		*Total*
	Class A	*Class B*	
Below 20	5	10	15
20-40	8	15	23
40-60	13	20	33
60-80	12	18	30
80-100	7	7	14
Total	*45*	*70*	*115*

(2) General and Special purpose table: General purpose tables are otherwise called reference tables or repository tables. It provides information for general use. *Examples* for this type of tables are tables published by the Statistical Department of Government like census, tables about the industrial and agricultural production in various periods etc.

Special purpose table is otherwise called summary tables or derivative tables. Special purpose tables are derived from the information of the general purpose tables. For *example*, when the data collected from the census report (which is general purpose table) for any study and presented in tables, it is called the special purpose table.

Exercises

1. Define classification. State the important objectives of classification.
2. Explain the important methods of classification.
3. Define Tabulation. State the important rules of classification.
4. What do you mean by tabulation? State the different types of tables.
5. Write short-notes of the following.
   (a) Stubs and Captions.
   (b) Exclusive and Inclusive method of Classification
   (c) Classification and Tabulation
6. Define tabulation. What are the characteristics of classification?
7. What is chronological classification of statistical data? Give an example. (MGU, Section A, April 1997)
8. Explain the term 'tabulation'. (MGU, Section A, April 1995)
9. What is meant by 'discrete series'?
   (MGU, Section A, April 1995 and M GU, Section A, April 1992)
10. What is class interval? (MGU, Section A, September 1994)
11. What is meant by 'tabulation' of data?
    (MGU, Section A, September 1994)
12. What are the requisites of a good table? State the rules that serve as a guide in tabulating statistical material.
    (MGU, Section B, September 1994)
13. Draw a blank table showing the distribution of students in university according to
    (a) Sex
    (b) Faculty (Arts, Commerce, Science and Law)
    (c) For two years (1992 and 1993)
    (d) Age groups (below 19 years, between 19 and 21 years, and above 21 years) (MGU, Section B, September 1994)
14. Explain class interval. (MGU, Section A, September 1993)
15. Distinguish between classification and tabulation.
    (MGU, Section B, September 1993)
16. What is meant by classification of data?
    (MGU, Section A, September 1992)
17. What is meant by 'continuous series'?
    (MGU, Section A, September 1992)
18. From the following data construct a continuous series whose class interval is 4 and the mid value of one of the class interval is zero.
    -8 , -7, 10, 12, 6, 4, 3, 0, 7, -4, -3, -2, 2, 8, 4, 7, 5, 6, 10, 21, -9, 13, 11, -10, -7, -1, 0, 5, 3, 2, 6, 10, -6, -4. (MGU, Section B, September 1992)

19. Classify the following data by taking class interval such that their mid-values are 17, 22, 27, 32 and so on.

30, 42, 30, 54, 40, 48, 15, 17, 51, 42, 25, 41, 30, 27, 42, 36, 28, 26, 37, 54, 44, 31, 36, 40, 36, 22, 30, 31, 19, 48, 16, 42, 32, 21, 22, 40, 33, 41, 21 (MGU, Section B, April 1992)

20. State the principle underlying classification of data (Kerala, Section A, April 1996, Kerala, Section A, April 1994, Kerala, Section A April 1990)

21. What is tabulation ? (Kerala, Section A, April 1992)

22. Draw a blank table to present the following information regarding the college students according to

(a) Faculty - Social Science, Commerce

(b) Class - Under graduate, Post Graduate

(c) Sex - Male, Female

(d) Year - 1985 and 1986. (MGU, Section B, April 1995)

◆ Chapter 4 ◆

Diagramatic & Graphic Representation

The data presented in tabulated form will not give meaning to layman. It will give an exact idea about the character of the data when it is presented in Diagram or Graph. It also helps to find out the increase or decrease of values over a period of time without any strain.

I Importance of Diagrams and Graphs

The Diagrams and Graphs attract common people. Hence the information reaches common people within a short period. People find it easy to get an idea from the diagram or graph than to read the whole information presented in the Tables. Moreover the diagrams have more memorising effect. It also facilitates for easy comparision of data from one period to another.

II Distinction between Diagrams and Graphs

Diagrams are prepared in a plain paper, whereas graphs should be prepared in graph paper. Since Diagrams are more attractive than Graph, it conveys the meaning very quickly. Graphs are more suited for presenting time series and frequcncy distribution.

III General Rules for preparing Diagrams

The important rules for the preparation of diagrams are stated below.

1.Heading: A suitable heading should be given to every diagran. The Heading should appropriately represent the content of the diagram. It is advisable to give short headings for diagram.

2. Scale: The scale should be mentioned in the diagram. The scale should convey the proportional magnitude of the data.

3. Drawing: Diagram should be drawn with the help of drawing instruments. In order to make the drawing attractive, colouring, dotting, crossing etc. should be done on the diagram.

4. *Index:* When different colours, dots or markings are given in diagram the index should be given. The index should properly convey the meaning of the colours, dots or markings.

5. *Attractiveness:* The diagram should be drawn attractively, so that it appeals the attention of the people.

6. *Accuracy:* The diagram should be drawn with accurate measurement. Inaccurate measurement will give wrong diagram.

7. *Size:* The diagram should neither too big nor too small. It should be of an optimum size. It should be presented in the middle of the page.

IV Types of Diagrams

The following are the important types of diagrams.

(1) One - dimensional diagrams

(2) Two - dimensional diagrams

(3) Three - dimensional diagrams

(4) Pictograms and Cartograms

(1) One dimensional diagram: One dimensional diagram is otherwise called as Bar diagrams. In a bar diagram only the length is considered as an important factor. The width of the bar is not given any importance.

Following are the important types of Bar Diagram.

(i) Simple Bar Diagrams

(ii) Sub-divided Bar Diagrams

(iii) Multiple Bar Diagrams

(iv) Percentage Bar Diagrams

(v) Deviation Bar Diagrams

(i) Simple Bar Diagram: Simple bar diagram represents only one variable. The figures like height, weight of students, sales, production in factories can be represented in this type of diagram. Bar diagram can either be prepared on vertical or horizontal position. The most common type of bar diagram is vertical type.

Illustration 1. *Prepare a bar diagram from the following data:*

Year	*1991*	*1992*	*1993*	*1994*	*1995*	*1996*
Sales (Rs. in '0000)	*42*	*55*	*65*	*70*	*72*	*60*

Solution:

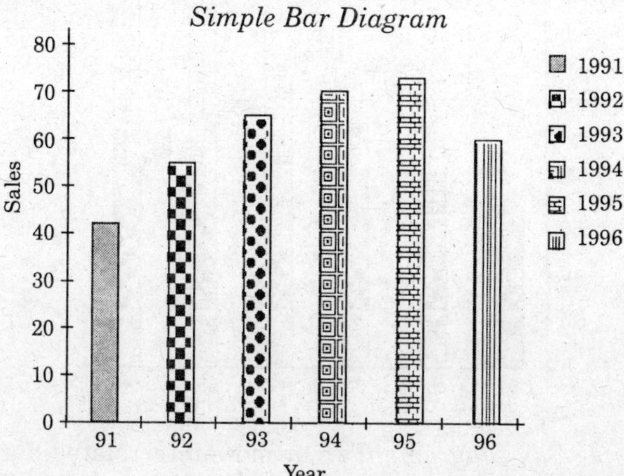

(ii) Sub-divided Bar Diagram: In the sub-divided bar diagram each bar explaining a phenomenon is sub-divided into two or more parts. Each part may explain different characters of the phenomenon. For example, the bar diagram explaining the sales of a company may further be subdivided according to regionwise sales.

Illustration 2. *The sales of a compnay for 1991-96 are stated below.*

Year	*Regoinwise Sales (Rs. '0000)*				
	North	*South*	*West*	*East*	*Total Rs. ('0000)*
1991	*15*	*20*	*18*	*12*	*65*
1992	*10*	*30*	*25*	*20*	*85*
1993	*20*	*25*	*30*	*25*	*100*
1994	*25*	*20*	*40*	*60*	*145*
1995	*25*	*30*	*45*	*50*	*150*
1996	*20*	*35*	*40*	*55*	*150*

Represent the data in a bar diagram.

Solution: *Sub-Divided Bar Diagram*

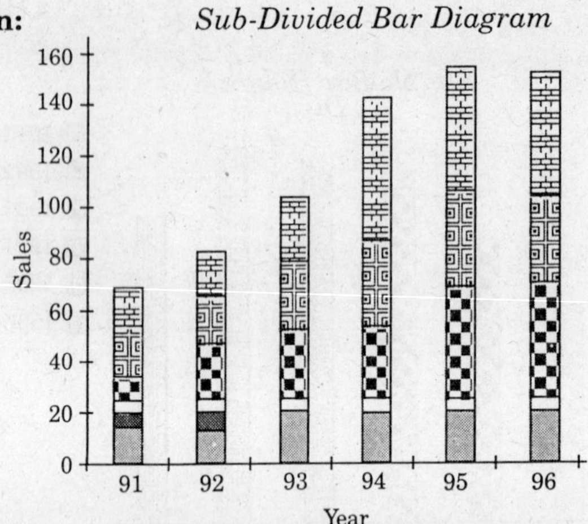

(iii) Multiple Bar Diagram: Two or more interrelated data are represented in a multiple bar diagram. In order to identify the interrelated data the bars should be differentiated with colours or shades.

Illustration 3 : *From the following data draw a suitable diagram.*

Year	*Production ('000 units)*		
	X	*Y*	*Z*
1992	*47*	*55*	*73*
1993	*32*	*60*	*79*
1994	*50*	*75*	*85*
1995	*55*	*87*	*98*
1996	*62*	*96*	*110*

Solution: *Multiple Bar Diagram*

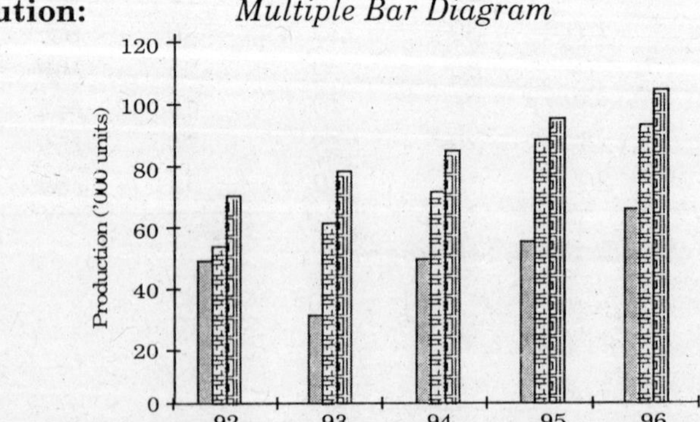

(iv) Percentage Bar Diagram: In percentage bar diagram the length of all the bars are equal. Various segments of each bar may change.

Illustration 4: *Prepare a sub-divided bar diagram drawn on the percentage basis.*

Year	*Direct cost Rs.*	*Indirect Cost Rs.*	*Profit Rs.*	*Sales Rs.*
1992	*35*	*15*	*10*	*60*
1993	*40*	*20*	*12*	*72*
1994	*32*	*22*	*8*	*62*
1995	*25*	*35*	*15*	*75*

Solution: Converted table according to percentage basis

Year	*Direct cost Rs.*	*Indirect Cost Rs.*	*Profit Rs.*	*Sales Rs.*
1992	58	25	17	100
1993	55	28	17	100
1994	52	35	13	100
1995	33	47	20	100

Percentage Bar Diagram

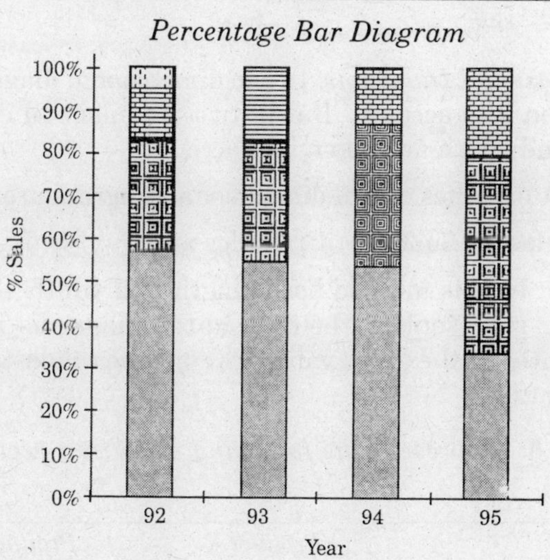

(v) Deviation Bar diagram: Deviation bar diagram represents data related to both positive and negative values. For example, data related to imports and exports; and profit or loss of a company can be represented in deviation bar diagram.

Illustration 5: *Represent the following data in a suitable bar diagram.*

Year	*Sales (Rs. in '0000)*	*Profit / Loss (Rs. in '000)*
1993	*44*	*15*
1994	*55*	*-8*
1995	*65*	*12*
1996	*79*	*-10*

Solution: *Deviation Bar Diagram*

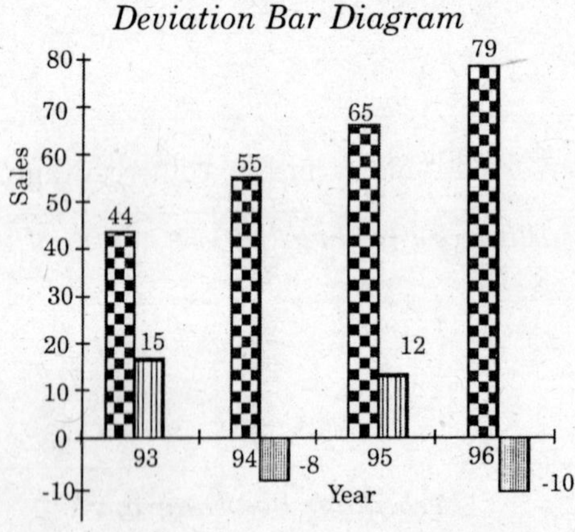

(2) Two Dimensional Diagrams: In one dimensional diagram only length is taken into account. But in two-dimensional diagrams both length and width are taken into account.

The important types of two-dimensional diagram are,

(i) Rectangles (ii) Squares (iii) Circles and (iv) Pie diagram

(i) Rectangles: In this method both length and width should be considered for representing the data in the diagrams.The data may be presented in the given value or it may be converted in the form of percentage.

Illustration 6: *Represent the following data in a rectangular diagram.*

Particulars	*Product X*	*Product Y*
Direct cost (Rs.)	*120*	*150*
Indirect cost (Rs.)	*50*	*70*
Profit (Rs.)	*30*	*20*
No. of units sold	*20*	*40*
Price per unit (Rs.)	*10*	*6*

Solution: Calculation of per unit cost of product X and Product Y.

Cost and Profit	*Product X (20 units)*		*Product Y (40 units)*	
	Total cost Rs.	*Per unit cost Rs.*	*Total cost Rs.*	*Per unit cost Rs.*
Direct Cost	120	6	150	3.75
Indirect Cost	50	2.5	70	1.75
Profit	30	1.5	20	0.50

Rectangular Diagram

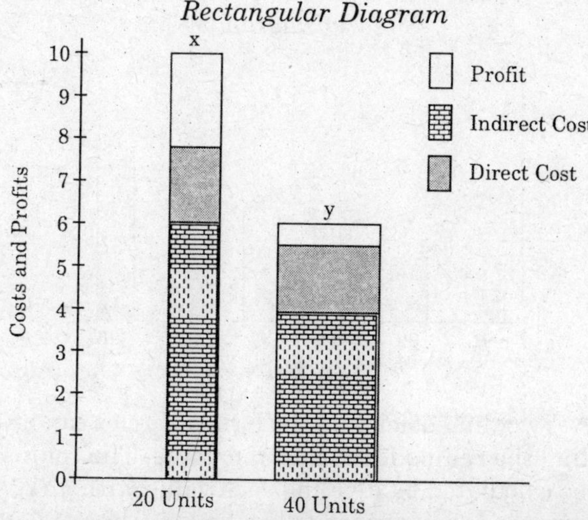

(ii) Squares: In the square type of two dimensional diagram each bar diagram is represented in the form of squares. For this purpose square-root of each value to be represented in the bar diagram should be calculated. Then the value should be represented in the form of bar diagram.

Illustration 7: *Represent the following data in a square form of two dimensional diagram*

Year	*Sales (Rs.)*
1991	*27,500*
1992	*62,850*
1993	*1,32,000*
1994	*1,62,000*
1995	*1,85,500*
1996	*2,50,000*

Solution: Calculation of square roots and side of squares for square diagrams.

Year	*Sales*	*Square root (in cms)*	*Side of the square*
1991	27,500	165.83	0.83
1992	62,850	250.70	1.25
1993	132,000	363.32	1.82
1994	162,000	402.49	2.01
1995	185,500	430.70	2.15
1996	250,000	500.00	2.50

Square Diagram

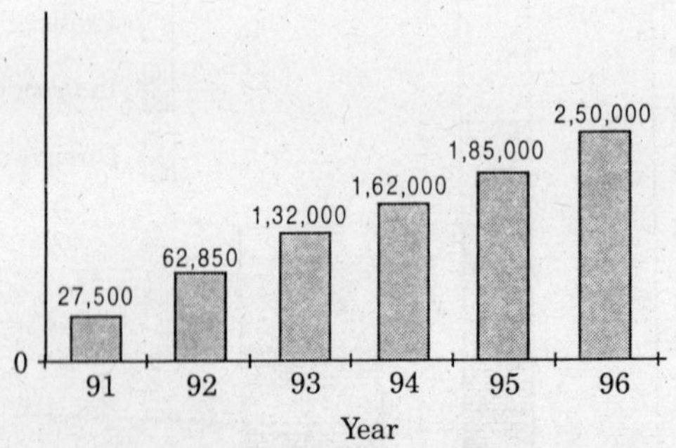

(iii) Circles: Two-dimensional in the form of circles can be drawn by calculating the radius for each given value. The radius of the value can be calculated by dividing each value with π (22/7) and then taking square-root of such value.

Illustration 8: *Represent the following data in circels in two-dimensional diagram.*

Year	*Profit (Rs.)*
1991	*8,000*
1992	*14,000*
1993	*75,000*
1994	*110,000*
1995	*150,000*
1996	*260,000*

Solution: Calculation of Radius

Year	*Profit*	*Dividing by* π *22/7*	*Square Root*
1991	8,000	2,545.45	50.45
1992	14,000	4,454.55	66.74
1993	75,000	23,863.64	154.48
1994	110,000	35,000.00	187.08
1995	150,000	47,727.27	218.47
1996	260,000	82,727.27	287.62

Circle Diagram

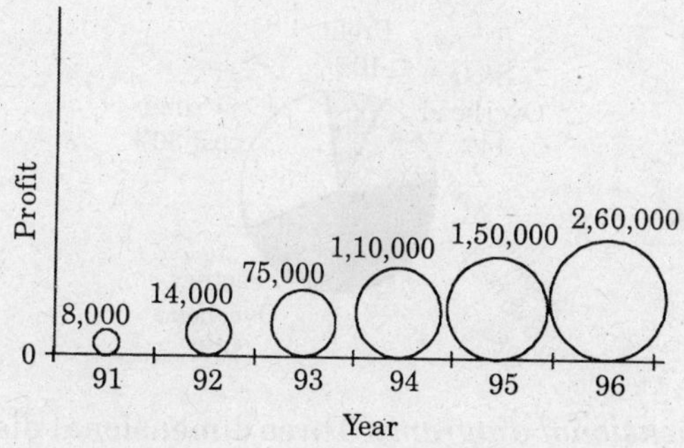

(iv) Pie diagram: Pie diagram is a representation of various data on the basis of different characters. For example, the selling price of a product can be divided into various segments like factory cost, administrative cost, selling cost and profit. These segments are converted into percentage form in order to represent in the pie diagram. It gives a clear idea about the percentage of the component of each item of cost spend for manufacturing the product.

In order to prepare the pie diagram each percentage outlay must be multiplied by 3.6, since the pie diagram contain 360^0 scale.

Illustration 9: *Draw a pie diagram from the following data. The selling price of a product contains the following elements of costs and profit.*

Prime cost	*30%*
Factory Overhead	*18%*
Administrative Overhead	*28%*
Selling and Distribution overhead	*14%*
Profit	*10%*

Solution: Calculations for the preparation of pie diagram.

Elements of costs & profit	*Percentage*	*Angles*
Prime cost	30	108^0
Factory overhead	18	65^0
Administrative overhead	28	101^0
Selling and Distribution overhead	14	50^0
Profit	10	36^0
Total	*100*	*360*

Pie Diagram

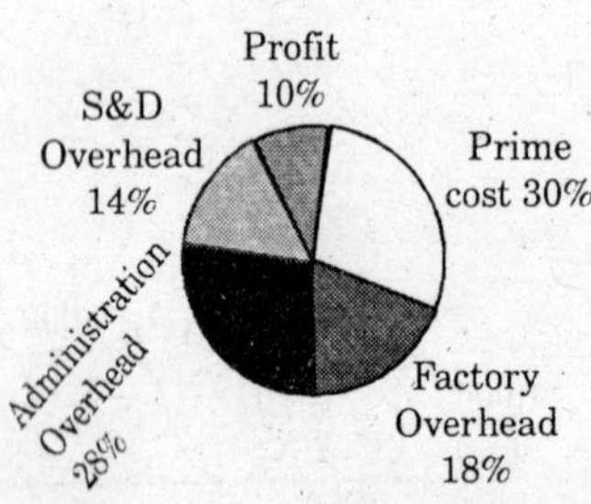

(3) Three dimensional diagrams: Three dimensional diagrams are prepared in the form of cubes, spheres, cylinders etc. In these diagrams, length, breadth and width are the three important things which are to be taken into consideration.

(4) Pictograms and Cartograms

(i) Pictograms: Pictograms convey more meaning than any other diagrams, especially for a lay man. Under the pictogram, data are represented in the form of appropriate pictures most suited for the data.

Illustration 10: *Present the following data in a pictogram*

Animals	*Forest A*	*Forest B*
Elephants	*12,000*	*10,000*
Horses	*6,000*	*4,000*
Deer	*3,000*	*5,000*
Monkeys	*11,000*	*14,000*
Giraffes	*1,500*	*2,000*
Lions	*750*	*500*
Bears	*600*	*400*

Solution:

Animals		*Forest A*	*Forest B*
Elephants		12,000	10,000
Camels		6,000	4,000
Deer		3,000	5,000
Monkeys		11,000	14,000
Giraffes		1,500	2,000
Lions		750	500
Bears		600	400

(ii) Cartograms: Cartogram means the presentation of data in a geographical basis. It is otherwise called as statistical maps. The quantities on the map may be shown through shades, dots, or colours, etc. The example for a cartogram representing the rivers and river valley project map of India is presented as below.

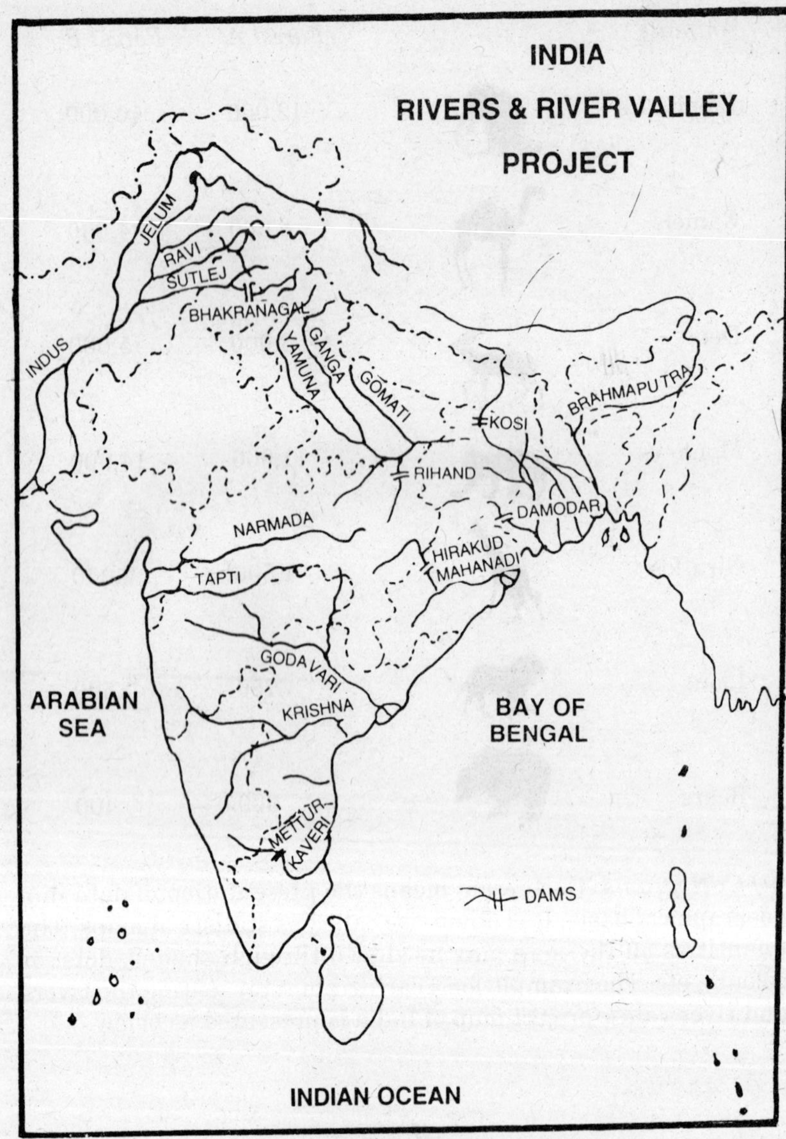

V Graphical Presentation

Graphic presentation is classified into two major head. They are (1) Graphs of frequency distribution and (2) Graphs of time series.

Frequency distribution related to discrete and continuous series can be well drawn in a graph. There are various methods for drawing graphs for frequency distribution. The most common methods are :

(1) Histogram (2) Frequency Polygon (3) Frequency Curve

(4) Ogives or Cumulative Frequency curve

(1) Histogram: Histogram is the most popular and widely used method of graphical representation of data. Histogram is a set of vertical bars. Frequencies representing the variables should be drawn in a graph in the form of vertical bars. In the construction of Histogram the X axis should be represented with variables (in the form of class intervals) and Y axis should be represented with corresponding frequencies for the variables. The frequencies corresponding to the variable should be plotted in the graph. These vertical bars from X axis corresponding to the class intervals should be drawn to the plotted points. This will give equal number of classes.

Distinction between Histogram and Bar diagram

Histogram is different from Bar Diagram. Bar digaram is one dimensional. It means, only length of the bar is important and not the width.

Histogram is two dimensional. In histogram length as well as width are important.

Steps for the construction of Histogram

Histogram are of two types - (a) Histogram for frequency distributions having equal class -intervals and (b) Histogram for frequency distribution having unequal class-intervals.

(a) Histogram for frequency distribution having equal class-intervals

Steps

(i) In the graph X axis should be conveniently divided, to represent the variables.

(ii) Y axis should be represented with frequencies.

(iii) Plot two points each for variables corresponding to the frequencies. These two points with equal distance is taken for the lower and upper limits of each class intervals.

(iv) Join all the plotted points towards the X axis to get rectangular adjacent bars.

Illustration 11: *Draw a histogrm from the following information.*

Marks	*No. of Students*
0-10	*7*
10-20	*12*
20-30	*15*
30-40	*17*
40-50	*20*
50-60	*18*
60-70	*14*
70-80	*10*
80-90	*4*

Solution: *Histogram*

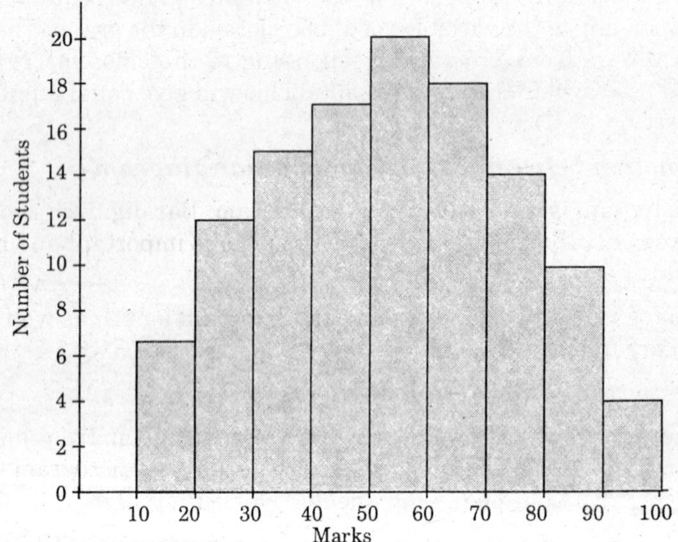

(b) Histogram for frequency distribution having unequal class-intervals: Following are the important steps for the construction of histogram when the class intervals are unequal.

(i) The unequal class intervals must be corrected first of all through relative frequency density method.

Correction of unequal class intervals.

$$\frac{\text{Frequency of unequal class interval}}{\text{Width of the unequal class interval}} \times \begin{array}{l}\text{Width of the lowest}\\ \text{class interval}\end{array}$$

(ii) In the graph X axis should be represented with variables.

(iii) Y axis should be represented with frequencies.

(iv) Plot two points each for variables corresponding to the frequencies. These two points with equal distance is taken for the lower and upper limits of each class intervals.

(v) Join all the plotted points towards the X-axis to get rectangular adjacent bars.

Illustration 12: *Draw a histogram from the following data*

Daily wages (Rs.)	*No of Workers*
15-20	*4*
20- 25	*9*
25-30	*12*
30-40	*20*
40-50	*16*
50-55	*7*
55-60	*6*
60-75	*15*
75-80	*4*
80-95	*9*
95-100	*2*

Solution: Since in this problem the class intervals are not equal, the frequencies should be adjusted for the purpose of drawing the histogram.

Calculation of Frequency Density

Daily Wages	*No. of Workers*	*Frequency Density*	
15-20	4		4
20-25	9		9
25-30	12		12
30-40	20	$20 / 10 \times 5$	10
40-50	16	$16 / 10 \times 5$	8
50-55	7		7
55-60	6		6
60-75	15	$15 / 15 \times 5$	5
75-80	4		4
80-95	9	$9 / 15 \times 5$	3
95-100	2		2

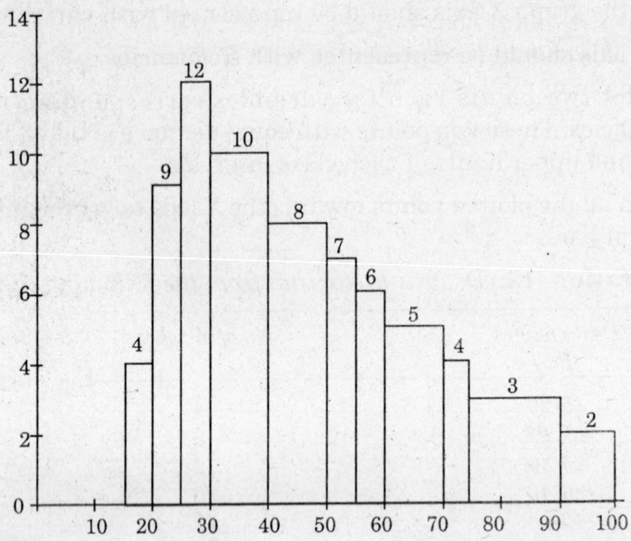

(2) Frequency Polygon: Frequency polygon is an improved method of histogram. It gives a curve instead of bars. There are two methods for constructing frequency polygon.

First of all, the histogram should be drawn from the given data by taking variables on X axis and frequencies on Y axis. Then mark mid-points of upper side of each bar of the histogram. After that join all the mark points to get frequency polygon curve.

In the second method, first of all plot the frequencies corresponding to mid-points of various class-intervals. Then join all the plotted points to get the frequency polygon curve.

Illustration 13: *Represent the following data in a histogram and frequency polygon.*

Daily Income	*No. of people*
0-10	*5*
10-20	*8*
20-30	*15*
30-40	*27*
40-50	*35*
50-60	*43*
60-70	*24*
70-80	*16*
80-90	*10*
90-100	*4*

Solution: *Histogram and Frequency Polygon*

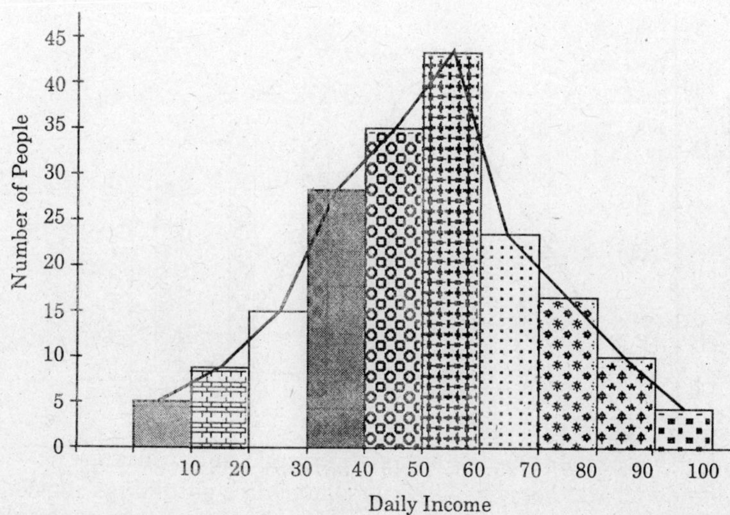

(3) Frequency Curve: Frequency polygon won't give a smooth frequency curve. It consists of sharp turns ups and downs. Hence, the curve should be smoothed with freehand, without sharp turns of ups and downs. First of all a frequency polygon should be drawn by joining the plotted points derived from the frequencies corresponding to the mid points of each class intervals. Then the frequency polygon should be smoothed. There is no need to draw histogram to draw a smoothed frequency curve.

Illustration 14: *Draw a frequency curve through frequency polygon from the data given below.*

Marks	*No. of students*
0-10	*4*
10-20	*12*
20-30	*18*
30-40	*25*
40-50	*30*
50-60	*20*
60-70	*16*
70-80	*10*
80-90	*5*
90-100	*2*

Solution: *Frequency Curve*

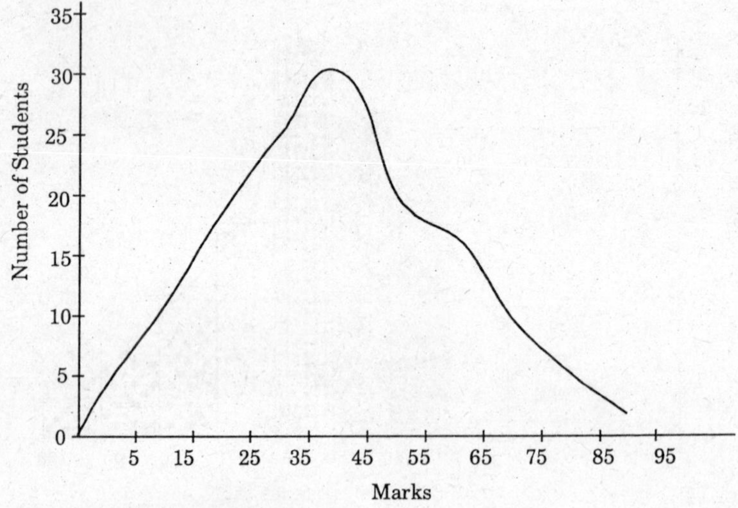

(4) Ogives or Cumulative Frequency Curve: Ogives are drawn on the basis of cumulative frequencies of the various class intervals. First of all cumulative frequencies should be calculated for all the class intervals. In the X axis class intervals should be represented and in the Y axis cumulative frequencies should be represented. Plot points corresponding to the cumulative frequencies representing each class intervals. Then join all the plotted line to get ogives. Ogives can be constructed through two methods,

(1) Less than method

and (2) More than method

(1) Less than method: Under this method cumulative frequencies from below are plotted against the upper class limits. Ogives under less than method, gives a positive curve.

(2) More than method: Under this method cumulative frequencies from above are plotted against the corresponding lower class limits. Ogive under this method gives a negative curve.

Illustration 15: *Draw less than and more than ogives from the following data.*

Marks	*No. of students*
10-20	*4*
20-30	*6*
30-40	*10*
40-50	*15*
50-60	*22*
60-70	*19*
70-80	*9*
80-90	*8*
90-100	*7*

Solution: Calculation for less than give

Marks	*No. of students*	*Cumulative Frequencies*
20	4	4
30	6	10
40	10	20
50	15	35
60	22	57
70	19	76
80	9	85
90	8	93
100	7	100

Calculation for more than ogive

Marks	*No. of students*	*Cumulative Frequencies*
10	4	100
20	6	96
30	10	90
40	15	80
50	22	65
60	19	43
70	9	24
80	8	15
90	7	7

Solution: *Ogive Curve*

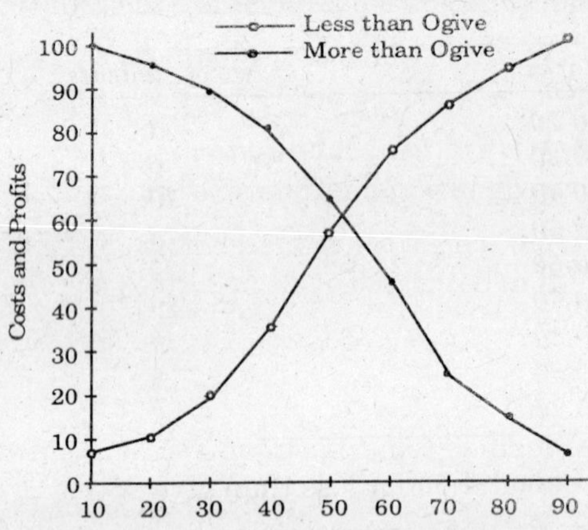

Graphs of Time-series: Time-series is concerned with the representation of data for different periods of time. If these data are represented graphically, it may convey more meaning. It also helps for easy comparison of the changes of variable at different periods of time. *X* axis of the graph for time series should represent various periods (year or months). *Y* axis should be denoted with variables. There are two methods for constructing graphs for time series. They are,

(i) Nature Scale Method and (ii) Ratio Scale Method

(i) Nature Scale Method: In nature scale method, time-series graph can be drawn on the basis of line graphs. They are of two types.

(a) Line Graph or Line Chart for one variables.

(b) Line Graph or Line Chart for two or more variables.

(a) Line Chart for one variable: Time series for one variable gives one variable for related periods. In line chart for one variable *X* axis should be represented with time and *Y* axis with variable. The variables corresponding to different periods should be plotted on the graph. Then the plotted points should be joined together to get the line chart.

Illustration 16: *Construct a line chart for the following data.*

Year	*Profit Rs. ('000)*
1990	*145*
1991	*173*
1992	*199*
1993	*215*
1994	*245*
1995	*275*
1996	*300*

Solution: *Line chart for one Variable*

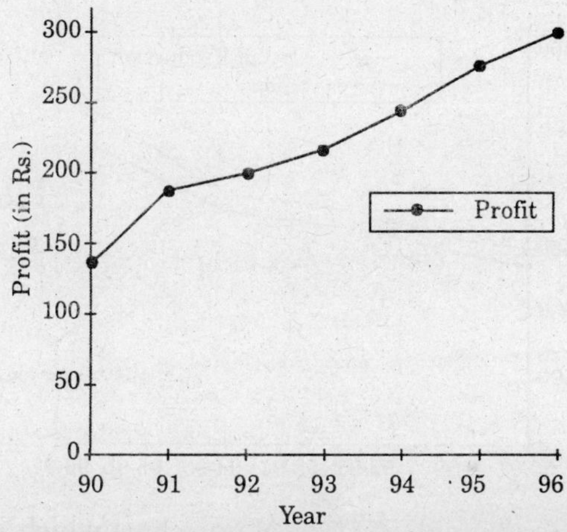

(b) Line chart for two or more variables: When two or more variables are available corresponding to various periods of time, line graph will show two or more line charts. X axis should be represented with time and Y axis should be represented with value of variables. First of all one variable corresponding to the year should be plotted on graph. Then the plotted points should be joined to get the line graph. The same procedure should be repeated for other variables also.

Illustration 17: *Represent the following data in line-graph.*

Year	*Cost of Production Rs. ('0000)*	*Sales Rs. ('0000)*
1990-91	*285*	*300*
1991-92	*300*	*320*
1992-93	*315*	*350*
1993-94	*325*	*360*
1994-95	*350*	*375*
1995-96	*410*	*450*
1996-97	*470*	*520*

Solution: *Line chart for two or more variables*

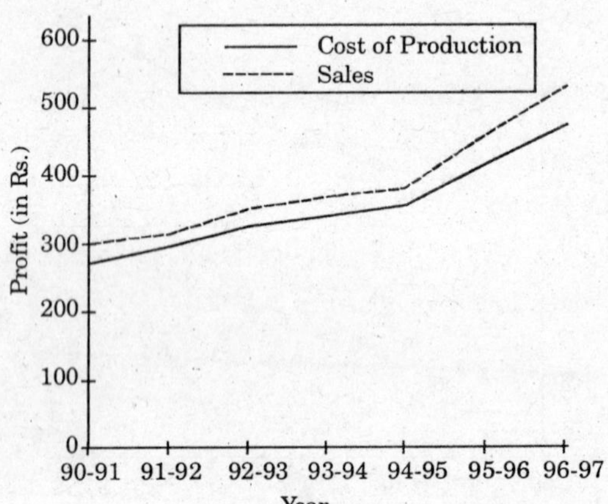

Band Graph: Band graph is a type of line chart which shows the different components of variables in the graph. For example, the production and sales of a factory for different periods may be represented with different cost elements and profit.

Illustration 18: *Prepare a Band Chart for the following data.*

Year	*Costs. (Rs.'000)*			*Profit (Rs '000)*	*Total (Rs. '000)*
	Factory cost	*Ad. cost*	*Selling & Dist.cost*		
1990	*29*	*12*	*8*	*3*	*52*
1991	*32*	*18*	*12*	*8*	*70*
1992	*45*	*22*	*18*	*11*	*96*
1993	*52*	*28*	*20*	*18*	*118*
1994	*60*	*35*	*25*	*20*	*140*
1995	*65*	*39*	*28*	*25*	*157*
1996	*70*	*42*	*24*	*30*	*166*

Solution: *Band Graph*

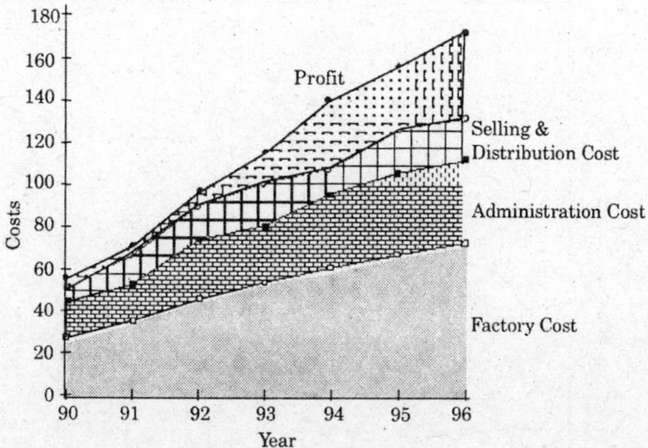

(ii) Ratio Scale: The graphs drawn with ratio scale are called ratio charts or logarithmic charts. Ratio scale shows the relative change in variables whereas the natural scale shows only the actual change in variables. In order to compare the relative change of variables over a period of time, logarithmic chart or ratio chart, is prepared. In the ratio chart, the X axis represents the values in natural scale. It represents year or month. Y axis represents the logarithm of the values of variables.

Logarithmic chart is also called "Semi - Logarithmic chart" since the vertical scales are logarithmic and the horizontal scales show the variables in absolute values.

Illustration 19: *Construct a ratio chart for the following data.*

Year	*1990*	*1991*	*1992*	*1993*	*1994*	*1995*	*1996*
Units of Production	*600*	*1100*	*1800*	*2600*	*3500*	*4800*	*6000*

Solution: Calculation for a Ratio chart

Year	*Limits of Production*	*Logarithmic value*
1990	600	2.7782
1991	1100	3.0414
1992	1800	3.2553
1993	2600	3.4150
1994	3500	3.5441
1995	4800	3.6812
1996	6000	3.7782

Solution:

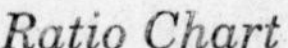

Ratio Chart

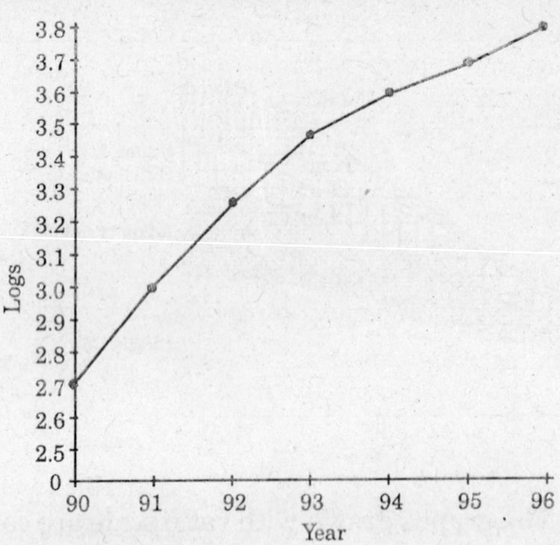

Exercise

1. Define Diagram. State the important rules for preparing diagrams.
2. Define Circle Diagram. State the procedure for drawing circle diagram.
3. Define Diagram. Explain briefly the important types of diagrams.
4. Write short-notes of the following.
   (a) Pie Diagram (b) Pictogram (c) Cartogram (d) Ogives
5. Define graphs. Explain briefly the different types of graphic presentation of frequency distribution.
6. Define graphs. Explain briefly the different types of graphs of time series.
7. What do you understand by a Frequency polygon?
   (MGU, Section A, April 1998)
8. Distinguish histogram and ogive. (MGU, Section B, April 1997)
9. What do you mean by scatter diagram? (MGU, Section A, April 1996)
10. Give two advantages of two dimensional diagram.
11. What is an ogive curve? (MGU,Section A, September 1994)
12. State briefly the purpose served by diagrammatic presentation.
    (MGU, Section B, September 1994)
13. What is a Scatter Diagram? Explain how do you infer the nature of relationship of the variables from the Scatter Diagram.
    (MGU, Section B, April 1994)

14. What is histogram?

(MGU, Section A, September 1993; MGU, Section A, April 1992)

15. Illustrate graphically the distinction between a frequency polygon, a histogram and an ogive curve.

(MGU, Section B, September 1993; MGU, Section B, April 1992)

16. What do you mean by a frequency curve? State the important characteristics of a frequency curve. (MGU, Section B September 1992)

17. What is an "Ogive"? (Kerala: Section A April 1998)

18. How do you determine median graphically?

(Kerala: Section B April 1997; Kerala: Section B April 1996)

19. What is Histogram? How do you construct it?

(Kerala: Section B April 1995)

20. Distinguish between Bar Diagram and Histogram.

(Kerala: Section B April 1989)

21. What is a Scatter Diagram? (Kerala: Section A April 1993)

22. State the two functions which are served by graphs and diagrams.

(Kerala: Section A September 1993)

23. What are Ogive? State their uses. (Kerala: Section B September 1993)

24. Describe any two methods of graphical representation of statistical data. (Kerala: Section B September 1990)

25. Prepare a Bar Diagram from the following data.

Year	1992	1993	1994	1995	1996	1997
Profit (Rs. '000)	32	55	63	70	89	95

26. Represent the following data in a Bar diagram.

Year	*Regionwise Sales (Rs. '0000)*				*Total*
	North	*South*	*West*	*East*	
1992	12	18	22	10	62
1993	18	25	32	25	100
1994	20	30	40	34	124
1995	22	34	45	36	137
1996	27	39	47	48	161
1997	25	42	50	55	172

27. Draw a multiple bar diagram from the following data.

Year	*Sales ('000 tonnes)*		
	A	*B*	*C*
1993	27	35	62
1994	35	47	70
1995	42	59	75
1996	55	65	82
1997	60	72	90

28. Prepare a sub-divided bar diagram on percentage basis, from the following data.

Year	*Direct Cost (Rs. '0000)*	*Indirect Cost (Rs. '0000)*	*Profit (Rs. '0000)*	*Sales (Rs. '0000)*
1994	20	10	5	35
1995	27	22	8	57
1996	35	30	6	71
1997	37	32	7	76

29. Represent the following data in a Deviation Bar Diagram.

Year	*Sales (Rs. in '0000)*	*Profit/Loss (Rs. in '0000)*
1994	37	3.5
1995	45	-4.5
1996	55	8.5
1997	60	-7.5

30. Draw a rectangular bar diagram from the following data.

Particulars	*Product A*	*Product B*
Direct Cost (Rs)	100	130
Indirect Cost (Rs)	45	70
Profit (Rs)	25	30
No. of units sold	50	100
Price per unit (Rs)	12	15

31. Draw a square form of two-dimensional diagram from the following data.

Year	*Production (units)*
1992	21,000
1993	60,000
1994	130,000
1995	160,000
1996	190,000
1997	260,000

32. Represent the following data in Circles of two-dimensional diagram.

Year	*Sales (units)*
1992	5,000
1993	15,000
1994	80,000
1995	120,000
1996	160,000
1997	250,000

33. The selling price of a product contains the following elements of costs and profit.

Prime Cost	32%
Factory Overhead	15%
Administration Overhead	28%
Selling and Distribution Overhead	16%
Profit	9%

34. Draw a histogram from the following data.

Marks	*No. of students*
0-10	8
10-20	12
20-30	16
30-40	18
40-50	25
50-60	20
60-70	15
70-80	8
80-90	7
90-100	5

35. Draw a histogram from the following data.

Daily wages (Rs.)	*No. of workers*
15-20	5
20-25	10
25-30	14
30-40	25
50-55	8
55-60	10
60-75	11
80-95	15
95-100	7

36. Represent the following data in a histogram and frequency polygon.

Marks	*No. of students*
0-10	7
10-20	8
20-30	14
30-40	29
40-50	34
50-60	40
60-70	25
70-80	15
80-90	10
90-100	6

37. Draw a frequency curve through Frequency Polygon from the data given below.

Marks	*No. of students*
0-10	7
10-20	12
20-30	15
30-40	18
40-50	25
50-60	20
60-70	14
70-80	12
80-90	9
90-100	4

38. Draw less than and more than ogives from the following data.

Marks	*No. of students*
10-20	6
20-30	10
30-40	15
40-50	30
50-60	35
60-70	20
70-80	17
80-90	10
90-100	7

39. Draw a Line chart from the following data.

Year	*Sales (Rs. '0000)*
1991	35
1992	49
1993	55
1994	75
1995	84
1996	97
1997	110

40. Represent the following data in a Line-graph.

Year	*Cost of Production (Rs. '0000)*	*Sales (Rs. '0000)*
1991	155	170
1992	185	200
1993	200	210
1994	220	235
1995	245	267
1996	260	288
1997	275	299

41. Prepare a Band chart from the following data.

Year	*Costs (Rs. '000)*			*Profit (Rs. '000)*	*Total (Rs. '000)*
	F.C.	*A.C*	*S&D. C*		
1991	20	12	5	3	40
1992	24	15	7	5	51
1993	30	18	8	7	63
1994	39	22	10	9	80
1995	45	25	12	13	95
1996	55	27	15	16	113
1997	60	32	18	17	127

F.C. - Factory Cost, A.C- Administrative Cost,
S&D. C- Selling and Distribution Cost.

42. Construct a ratio chart from the following data.

Year	1991	1992	1993	1994	1995	1996	1997
Sales (in units)	800	1200	1900	2200	4000	5500	7500

43. Present the following data by means of histogram and from it obtain the value of mode.

Weekly wages (Rs.)	*No. of workers*
10-15	7
15-20	9
20-25	27
25-30	15
30-35	12
35-40	12
40-45	8

[Ans: Mode = 20 - 25; MGU: Part B April 1995]

44. Draw an appropriate diagram to present the data given below.

Year	1965	1966	1967	1968	1969	1970	1971	1972	1973
Production (in tonnes)	212	220	235	257	289	263	250	283	290

[Ans: Line chart for one variable; MGU, Section B, September 1992]

45. Present the following data by a suitable graph.

Year	1	2	3	4	5	6	7	8
Import ('000 tonnes)	400	450	560	620	580	460	500	540
Value of Imports (Crores of Rs.)	22.0	23.5	38.5	42.0	42.0	38.0	36.0	40.0

[Ans: Line chart for two variables; MGU, Section B, April 1992]

◆ Chapter 5 ◆

Sampling Theories

I Population and Sample

Statistical data are usually gathered for the purpose of analysis and to draw inferences therefrom. These data may be collected in two ways - (1) Population method or Census method and (2) Sample method.

1. Population method or Census method: Population represents the whole area for which study is to be conducted; Complete enumeration of all terms in the selected area is known as population method or census method.

Example: All students of a college, all industries in a state, all industries in a district etc.

The term population means any collectivity or totality of objects.

According to Simpson and Kafka, "*population or a universe means an aggregate of items possessing a common trait or traits*".

According to Ya-lan-chou, *"the population is used to mean an aggregate of individual items, whether compared of people or things, that are to be observed in a given situation"*.

G. Kalton defines population as "*the term population does not necessarily refer to people but is a technical term used to describe the complete groups of person or objects for which the results are to apply. Hence, population may be defined as collectivity or totality of objects*".

The population may be classified into two types. They are (a) Finite or Infinite (b) Real or Hypothetical

(a) Finite or Infinite population: If the number of elements in the population can be counted, then it is called finite population.

Example : The number of students in a college, the number of people in a village, number of workers in a factory etc. Infinite population represents an infinitely large number of items. The elements in the population could not be counted.

Example : Stars in the sky, weight or health of newly born babies etc.

(b) Real or Hypothetical population: Real population indicates population in which the elements or items really exist. *Example,* The number of people in a locality, number of factories in a district etc. In the hypothetical universe or population, the items or elements may not really exist. *Example,* A hypothetical universe may be created by tossing a coin or throwing a die.

Merits of Census Method

The following are the merits of Census method.

(i) The character of all the limits of the population can be studied

(ii) The results derived under this method is more accurate and reliable.

(iii) This method is suitable for some type of study. (*e.g.*) (a) Study about the height of students in a college (b) Study about the average monthly income of families in a locality etc.

(iv) It provides more information which can be used for further research.

Demerits of Census Method

The following are the demerits of Census method.

(i) It requires more money and time.

(ii) Inexperience and inefficient researcher may collect wrong information by spending more money

(iii) Census method is not required for all type of research (*e.g.*) Study about consumer preference of a product.

(2) Sample Method: Sample means representative items of the population. Since it is difficult to study the whole population, samples can be drawn out from the population and the study can be conducted. For *example*, it is difficult to examine all the fruits by a merchant. He can take samples of few fruits and can come to the conclusion that the whole lo , can be accepted or rejected.

We examine a small portion of cloth and form an idea about the quality of the entire length of the cloth. The character of a person can be measured by meeting him for a shortwhile.

Merits of Sample Method

1. Sample method reduces cost. Since fewer item of the population are selected for the study, it reduces the cost.

2. It saves time. In this method since only fewer items are selected, the time for collection of data is saved.

3. Highly trained personnel or specialised equipments may be used to obtain the data. In census method it is difficult to use these techniques.

4. It gives accurate results. Since efficient people can be employed in the sample study, it would bring more accurate results.

5. It provides for detailed enquiry. Since in sample survey number of units to be studied is limited, it is possible to conduct a detailed study.

6. The organisation and administration of sample surveys are easy.

7. It is the only method in certain situations. If the universe is too large or infinite, it is difficult to conduct a census study.

Demerits of Sample Method

1. If the sample are selected with bias, the conclusions may not be correct.

2. The result of the sample investigation will be accurate only when the sample are representative sample.

3. Sample investigation requires specialised knowledge. Inefficiency of the investigator may bring wrong conclusions.

4. Sample method may not be suitable for all types of investigation.

5. If the universe is small it is difficult to select representative sample.

II Methods of Sampling

The important methods of sampling are stated below.

(I) Random Sampling Method: This method can be classified into

- (a) Simple or unrestricted random sampling
- (b) Restricted random sampling
  - (i) Stratified Sampling
  - (ii) Systematic Sampling, and
  - (iii) Cluster Sampling

(II) Non-Random Sampling

(a) Judgement or purposive Sampling

(b) Quota Sampling

(c) Convenience Sampling

(I) Random Sampling Method

A random sample is a method in which each item of the universe has the equal chance of being selected. The important types of random sampling are stated below.

(a) Simple or unrestricted random sampling: Simple random sampling are of two types. They are

(i) Lottery method and

(ii) Table of Random Numbers

(i) Lottery Method: Under this method all the items of the universe are numbered on separate slip of paper of same size and colour. These slips are folded and put in a box or container. Then the required number of slips are selected blindfold from the box or container.

(ii) Table of Random Numbers: When the size of the population is very large, Random Number Table is commonly used to select the sample. A table of random digits is a table of digits, which have been generated by a random process.

The following tables of random digits are available.

(a) Tibbett's Random Sampling Numbers.

It consists of 10400 numbers arranged in 4 digits at a time.

(b) M.G. Kendall and Babington Smith's Random Sampling Numbers containing 1 lakh digits.

(c) Rand Corporation's million random digits.

(d) Snedecor's 10,000 random numbers.

(b) Restricted Random Sampling

(i) Stratified Sampling: When the population is hetrogeneous then the population should be classified into different types of strata with common character. Each strata or sub-group will be homogeneous. From different stratas samples are to be drawn.

(ii) Systematic Sampling: Under the systematic sampling, the items of populations are arranged in a continuous order. Serial

number for the items should be assigned. Then required number of sample should be selected on a systematic basis. For *example*, in a population of 200 variables, if a sample of 10 variables are to be selected the following procedure should be adopted.

(a) First of all, arrange the variables of the population in a continuous order.

Assign Nos. from 1 to 200

(b) Find out the sample interval i.e.

$$K = \frac{N}{n}$$

N = Number of variabels in the population, n

n = samples size, k = sampling interval.

Hence $$K = \frac{200}{10} = 20$$

Therefore, under the systematic sampling every 20th item should be selected as 20th, 40th, 60th etc.

(iii) Cluster Sampling: Cluster sampling is a method of sampling which is carried out in several stages. For *example*, if one wants to select a sample of 1000 factory workers in a city, he has to identify all the industries in the locality. Then in the second stage the selection of factories should be done. In the third stage the workers may be selected.

(II) Non-Random Sampling Method

(a) Judgement Sampling: Under the judgement sampling the decision of the investigator alone decides the selection of sample. Investigator may select the sample as per his will and desire.

(b) Quota Sampling: Quota Sampling is just like the stratified sampling. The population is divided into various quota with some common character. Then the required sample are to be selected from these quotas.

(c) Convenience Sampling: The sample selected from the convenient population units is called convenience sampling. (*E.g.*) samples obtained from telephone directories, automobile registration etc.

III Sampling Distribution

We are often concerned with sampling distribution in sampling analysis. If we take certain number of sample and for each sample compute various statistical measures such as mean, standard deviation etc. then we find that each sample may give its own value for the statistic under consideration. All such values of particular statistic say mean, together with their relative frequencies will constitute the sampling distribution of the particular statistic, say, mean. Accordingly there are various sampling distribution, which are stated as follows.

(1) Sampling distribution of mean

(2) Sampling distribution of proportion

(3) Students '*t*' distribution

(4) '*F*' distribution and

(5) Chi-square distribution

The sampling distribution tends quite closer to the normal distribution if the number of samples is large. The significance of sampling distribution is the same as the mean of the universe. Thus the mean of the sampling distribution can be taken as the mean of the universe.

Sampling

Sampling may be defined as the selection of some part of an aggregate or totally on the basis of which a judgement or inference about the aggregate or totally is made. It is a process of obtaining information about an entire population by examining only a part of it.

Role of Sampling in Statistics

Sampling plays a significant role in statistics. The details of which are stated below.

1. Sampling minimises the time of the study: The sample is a representative of the population. Hence the number of variables to be studied is very minimum. So it requires minimum time for collection and analysis of data.

2. Sampling reduces the cost of the study: Since the sample study reduces the number of variables the expenses in collection and analyse of data are also reduced to a considerable extent. Expenses toward visiting various places, printing questionaires *etc.* are minimised due to sampling technique.

3. *Sampling helps in collecting detailed information:* Detailed information can be collected in sampling technique, since the number of respondents are very small. For example, a study is to be conducted with regard to the income and expenses of 5000 workers working in a village. Detailed information could not be collected if the study is conducted for all the 5000 workers. But the information would be in detail if a sample study is conducted by randomnly selecting 100 workers.

4. *Sample study gives more accurate results:* Sample study may give more accurate result than a population study. This is because of various reasons. Population study requires lot of time and money. Hence detailed information may not be collected. In addition to this the data once collected may become outmoded when the entire process of collection is over. In the sample study quality of data may be good since experts can be appointed to collect and process data.

5. *Population study may not be possible in all areas:* In some areas the population study may not be possible. Only sampling study could be conducted in these areas. When the population is infinite like the fishes in a sea, birds in a locality, number of trees in forest etc., it is impossible to conduct a population study. Only remedy is to select few samples of the population and to study the required character. In some areas though the population is finite it is difficult to conduct the study on Census Method. (eg) Study about the food habit of the people above 60 years old, in India.

IV Law of Inertia of large numbers

Law of large number is concerned with the selection of large samples, for study purpose. It also deals with relative merit of the selection of large numbers over selection of small numbers as sample. According to this law, when other things being equal, larger the size of the sample, more accurate the results are likely to be.

Example:

1. For studying the average weight of about 1500 students in a college, average weight of 50 sample students won't give accurate result. If the sample size is reasonably more, say 250 or more, it may give accurate result.

2. The probability of head or tail in tossing a coin is 1/2. If the coin is tossed for 20 times the outcomes may not be equal to 10 heads and 10 tails. It may even be 7 heads and 3 tails or vice

versa. To get equal number of heads and tail, the coin should be tossed 100 or more times. Hence, the increase in sample size, the decrease is the sampling error and vice versa. It can be graphically represented as follows:

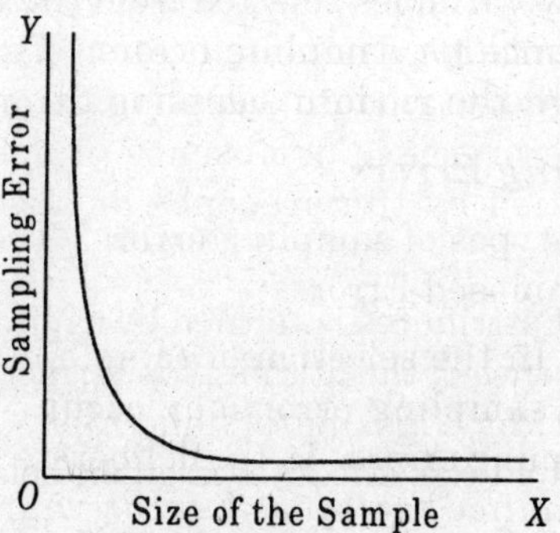

It is clear from the above diagram that the sampling error is very large when size of the sample is small. The sampling error may be reduced by increasing the sample size.

V Sampling and non-sampling errors

In complete enumeration and sample surveys there may be errors. These errors are classified into sampling errors and non-sampling errors. The errors arising in the study of sample is called sampling errors. This errors arise when inferences about the population is drawn on the basis of few observations *i.e.*, sample. Sampling error won't arise in the complete enumeration survey since the entire population is surveyed in this method. Non-sampling errors are those errors which arise at the stage of ascertainment and processing of data. This error may arise both in census method and sample method.

Distinction between sampling errors and Non-Sampling errors

1. Sampling errors arise in drawing inferences about the population on the basis of sample. But non-sampling error arise at the stage of ascertainment and processing of data.

2. Sampling error may occur only in sample study whereas non-sampling errors may occur both in sample study and population study.

Sampling Errors

The results derived from a sample study, may not be exactly equal to the true value in the population. This difference in value of the sample and population is called sampling errors. Since sample is only few variables selected from the whole population, there is more chance for sampling errors. These errors can be minimised through the modern sampling theories.

Types of Sampling Errors

There are two types of sampling errors. They are, (1) Biased Errors and (2) Unbiased Errors.

1. Biased Errors: In the selection of sample, if there is any bias on the selection, sampling error may occur. These errors are called biased sampling errors. In the deliberate sampling method, there is more chance for biased error than in the random sampling method of selection of sample.

2. Unbiased Errors: In the unbiased selection of the sample also, the result of the sample may vary with the actual result of the population. These difference in the result of population and the sample is called unbiased errors. Otherwise it means, the difference between the value of a statistic and that of the parameters.

Measurement of Errors

Statistical errors are of two types. They are

(1) Absolute error and (2) Relative error

1. Absolute error: The difference between the approximated figure and the original quantity is called absolute error.

Hence, Absolute Error = Actual value - Estimated value

i.e. $A.E. = a - e$

For example, the average estimated weight of students in a college is 54 Kgm and the actual average weight is 52.5.

Hence the Absolute Error = 52.5 – 54 = -1.5

2. Relative Error: Relative error is the ratio of absolute error to the estimated value

i.e. $$R.E. = \frac{a - e}{e}$$

For example, if the actual value is 450 and the estimated value is 400, the relative error,

$$R.E. = \frac{450 - 400}{400}$$

$$= \frac{50}{400}$$

$$= 0.125$$

Exercise

1. Distinguish between Population Method and Sample Method of Data collection.
2. State the merits and demerits of sample method.
3. Define Sampling. State the important methods of sampling.
4. What do you mean by Sampling Distribution?
5. State the role of Sampling in Statistics.
6. State the Law of Inertia of Large numbers.
7. Distinguish between Sampling Error and Non-sampling Error.
8. Write short notes of the following:
   (a) Stratified Sampling (b) Random Sampling
   (c) Hypothetical Population (d) Infinite Population
9. Write short notes of the following:
   (a) Absolute error vs Relative error (b) Sampling Distribution
10. What do you understand by the Law of Inertia of Large Number? (MGU, Section A, April 1997)
11. Explain briefly why a Sample survey is usually preferred to a Census Survey. (MGU, Section B, April 1995)
12. What is meant by "Biased Error" in Statistics? (MGU, Section A, September 1994)
13. What do you mean by Statistical units? What are the various types of Statistical units? Explain with example. (MGU, Section B, September 1994)
14. What is "Random Sample"? (MGU, Section A September 1993)
15. What do you understand by "Statistical units"? (MGU, Section A, September 1992)
16. Describe the various steps that are taken in conducting a Survey. (MGU: Section B, September 1992)
17. What is meant by "Sample Survey"? (MGU, Section A April 1992)
18. What is random Sampling? Name one method. (Kerala: Section A April 1998)

19. **State the uses of Survey method as compared to Census method.**
(Kerala: Section A April 1996)

20. **Explain the merits of Sampling techniques over the Census technique.** **(Kerala: Section B April 1995)**

21. **Enumerate the various steps in conducting a Sample Survey.**
(Kerala: Section B April 1994)

22. **Describe the method of conducting Sample Surveys.**
(Kerala: Section B September 1990)

23. **Distinguish between Sampling and Census method of Survey.**
(Kerala: Section A April 1990)

◆ Chapter 6 ◆

Measures of Central Tendency

Statistical data presented in tabular form would not give a clear picture for further analysis and comparison. If these data are presented in condensed form, it would facilitate for easy comparison with other data. For example, the marks obtained by 50 students in mathematics is not easy to compare with the marks obtained by them in science subject unless it is presented in one figure. Obtaining these 'one figure' is termed as the measure of central tendency, otherwise it is called as Averages.

Average represents the whole value and it lies between the minimum and maximum value of the data. Hence, it is a representative figure of the entire data. This figure can be used for comparing with other figures.

The definitions given by various authors, clearly exhibit the the meaning of central tendency.

I Definitions

Following are the important definitions of average.

(1) Bowley defines as *"an average is only a short way of expressing an arithmetical result"*.

(2) Leabo defines as *"The average is sometimes described as number which is typical of the whole group"*.

(3) Clark and Sekkade defines as *"average is an attempt to find one single figure to describe whole of figures"*.

(4) Murry R. Speigal defines as *"average is a value which is typical or representative of a set of data"*.

(5) Wallis and Roberts defines as *"an average is a single number describing some features of a set of data"*.

From the above definitions, average means a representative value of a group of data. It represents the character of the entire data.

II Objectives of average

The following are the important objectives of the measure of central tendency.

(i) To find out one single value which represents the entire data. The representative value explains the character of entire data. This one value may represent thousands or millions of values. From the single value one can get an idea about entire data. Example: The data related to income of the five hundred families in a village. If this data is presented as one representative item then it would be easy to know the character of the entire data. But it is difficult to get a clear picture about the data, if the data are presented in the form of individual values.

(ii) It facilitates for taking policy decisions. Policy decisions can be easily taken if the data are presented conveniently in one single value.

(iii) Average facilitates for easy comparison of data. It is difficult to compare the mass data with other group of data. When this data are presented in one single value, it helps for easy comparison. For example, the marks obtained by students of one class may compared with the students of other class, if the marks are available in single values rather than the mass values of marks.

III Characteristics of a good average

The average which represents the entire group of data should have the following characteristics.

(1) The average should be easy one to understand. If the single value is a complicated one, then it is meaningless of getting one single value.

(2) It should be simple to calculate. The technique adopted for obtaining the average should be a simple one to calculate.

(3) It should be rigidly defined. The average should be defined in such a way that it should give only one interpretation.

(4) It should represent all the data. The average should be taken for all the observations. If any item in the particular group of data is not taken into account, then such average wouldn't properly represent the entire group of data.

(5) It should not be affected by the extreme values. Sometimes the observations may contain either extremely low value or

extremely high values or both of them. This will affect the reliability of the single value as a true representative item. Hence proper descriptions should be given regarding the extreme values, while presenting the averages.

(6) Average should be eligible for further algebraic treatment. Further algebraic treatments mean comparison and analysis of the averages.

(7) Average should have sampling stability. The sample selected for the study should be capable of giving same data when approached by different group of people. Otherwise different values will be obtained from different observations from the same sample. It will defeat the very purpose of the average.

IV Types of Average

There are three major types of the Measures of Central Tendency (or Average). They are, (1) Mean (2) Median (3) Mode

Median and Mode are known as Average of position, while mean is known as Mathematical average.

Mean

Mean may further be classified into three types. They are,

(1) Arithmetic Mean (A.M.)

(2) Geometric Mean (G.M.)

(3) Harmonic Mean (H.M.)

(1) Arithmetic Mean: Arithmetic mean is the most popular method of measuring the representative value. It is otherwise called as an average. The arithmetic mean can be obtained by dividing the sum of all the observations by the total number of the observations.

There are two types of arithmetic mean. They are,

(1) Simple Arithmetic Mean and

(2) Weighted Arithmetic Mean

(1) Simple Arithmetic Mean

(A) Simple Arithmetic Mean for individual observation

(i) Direct Method

$$\text{Arithmetic Mean } \overline{X} = \frac{\text{Sum of all values}}{\text{Number of values}}$$

If values are represented as $X_1, X_2, X_3, X_4, X_5 .....X_n$, then,

$$\overline{X} = \frac{X_1 + X_2 + X_3 + X_4 .... X_n}{N}$$

or $$\overline{X} = \frac{\Sigma X}{N}$$

Where $\overline{X}$ represents arithmetic mean, ΣX represents sum of all values and N represents number of values.

Illustration 1: *Calculate arithmetic mean of the weight of 10 students in a class.*

Sl.No.	*1*	*2*	*3*	*4*	*5*	*6*	*7*	*8*	*9*	*10*
Weight (in Kg)	*42*	*56*	*49*	*50*	*49*	*53*	*52*	*48*	*47*	*54*

Solution: Calculation of Average Weight

Sl.No.	*Weight X (in Kg)*
1	42
2	56
3	49
4	50
5	49
6	53
7	52
8	48
9	47
10	54
N = 10	*ΣX = 500*

$$\text{Arithmetic mean } \overline{X} = \frac{\Sigma X}{N} = \frac{500}{10} = 50 \text{ kg}$$

(ii) Short-cut method: The short-cut method is based on assumed mean. The assumed mean should closely related with the data. Deviations of the data frøm the assumed mean should be ascertained and its sum of deviations should be calculated.

Formula, $\overline{X} = A \pm \frac{\Sigma d}{N}$ should then be applied to get the arithmetic mean.

In the formula, A represents Assumed Mean: Σd represents sum of the deviations from the assumed mean i.e. $\Sigma d = \Sigma(X - A)$

Illustration 2: *Marks obtained by 10 students in statistics are given below:*

Students	*1*	*2*	*3*	*4*	*5*	*6*	*7*	*8*	*9*	*10*
Marks	*62*	*43*	*31*	*75*	*55*	*59*	*45*	*42*	*45*	*90*

Calculate Arithmetic mean by short-cut method.

Solution: Calculation of Arithmetic Mean

Sl.No.	*Marks X*	*(X-50) (A = 50)*
1	62	+12
2	43	-7
3	31	-19
4	75	+25
5	55	+5
6	59	+9
7	45	-5
8	42	-8
9	45	-5
10	90	+40
N = 10		*Σd = 47*

$$\overline{X} = A \pm \frac{\Sigma d}{N} = 50 + \frac{47}{10} = 54.7$$

B. Simple Arithmetic Mean for Discrete Series

(i) Direct Method: Arithmetic Mean can be ascertained through direct method by applying the following formula:

$$\overline{X} = \frac{\Sigma fx}{N}$$

Where, f = represents frequency; x = represents variables and N represents total number of observations (i.e. Σf). Each variable should be multiplied with respective frequencies. The sum of the products thus obtained should be divided by the total number of frequencies to get the arithmetic mean.

Illustration 3: *Calculate the mean value of income per day of families in a village from the following data.*

Income (Rs.)	*20*	*30*	*40*	*50*	*60*	*70*	*80*
No. of Families	*12*	*15*	*10*	*13*	*20*	*14*	*16*

Solution: Calculation of Arithmetic Mean

Income Per day (Rs.) X	*Number of families* f	fX
20	12	240
30	15	450
40	10	400
50	13	650
60	20	1200
70	14	980
80	16	1280
	$\Sigma f = 100$	$\Sigma fx = 5,200$

$$\overline{X} = \frac{\Sigma fX}{\Sigma f} = \frac{5200}{100} = 52$$

Ans: Mean value of income of the families in the village is 52.

(ii) Short-cut Method: This method is an easy way of calculating the arithmetic mean. In this method assumed mean should be ascertained first. Then deviations from the assumed mean for all the data are to be calculated. These deviations should be multiplied with respective frequencies. The total of these figures (*i.e.*, the products of deviations and frequencies) should be divided by the total frequencies to get the arithmetic mean.

Formula for arithmetic mean under this method is,

$$\overline{X} = A \pm \frac{\Sigma fd}{N}$$

Where A = Assumed Mean; d = deviation of variables from Assumed Mean $(X - A)$; f = frequency.

Illustration 4: *Marks obtained by students of a class in mathematics are given below:*

Marks	*25*	*30*	*35*	*40*	*45*	*50*	*55*	*60*	*65*	*70*
No. of students	*3*	*8*	*12*	*9*	*4*	*7*	*15*	*5*	*10*	*7*

Calculate Arithmetic mean through short-cut method.

Solution: Calculation of Arithmetic Mean through short-cut method.

Marks *X*	*No. of students* *f*	*(A = 55)* *d = x - 55*	*fd*
25	3	-30	-90
30	8	-25	-200
35	12	-20	-240
40	9	-15	-135
45	4	-10	-40
50	7	-5	-35
55	15	0	0
60	5	+5	+25
65	10	+10	+100
70	7	+15	+105
	N = 80		*Σfd = -510*

$$\overline{X} = A \pm \frac{\Sigma fd}{N} = 55 - \frac{510}{80} = 55 - 6.375 = 48.625$$

Ans: Mean marks obtained by 80 students in mathematics is 49

C. Simple Arithmetic Mean for continuous series.

(i) Direct Method: In continuous series variables are represented by class intervals. Each class intervals has its own frequency. (Eg) Weight of students in a class between 50-60 K.gram is 12. Mid points of each class should be ascertained, first. (i.e the average of the highest value and lowest value in each class). These mid points should be multiplied with respective frequencies. Then sum of these figures is to be divided by the total frequencies, to get the arithmetic mean. It can be represented through the following formula.

$$\overline{X} = \frac{\Sigma fm}{N}$$

Where f = frequency; m = mid point and N = total no. of frequencies ($N = \Sigma f$)

Illustration 5: *Calculate Arithmetic Mean from the following data.*

Production in tonnes	*No. of factories*
10-20	*5*
20-30	*4*
30-40	*7*
40-50	*12*
50-60	*10*
60-70	*8*
70-80	*4*

Solution: Calculation of Arithmetic Mean

Production in tonnes X	*No. of factories* f	*Mid value* m	fm
10-20	5	15	75
20-30	4	25	100
30-40	7	35	245
40-50	12	45	540
50-60	10	55	550
60-70	8	65	520
70-80	4	75	300
	N = 50		*Σfm = 2,330*

$$\bar{X} = \frac{\Sigma fm}{N} = \frac{2{,}330}{50} = 46.6$$

Ans: Mean production of the factories is 46.6 tonnes.

(ii) Short-cut Method: This method is based on assumed arithmetic mean. Assumed arithmetic mean may be taken either from the mid points of the class intervals or not. Then deviations from the mid points with the assumed mean are to be calculated. The figures so calculated should be multiplied by the respective frequencies. Arithmetic mean can be calculated by dividing the sum of the figures so obtained (i.e., sum of the products of deviations and frequencies) with the total observations.

Following formula can be used for this calculation.

$$\bar{X} = A \pm \frac{\Sigma fd}{N}$$

Where A = Assumed Mean; f = frequencies; d = deviation from mid points ($d = M - A$); N = total no. of frequencies ($N = \Sigma f$)

Illustration 6: *Calculate arithmetic mean through short-cut method from the following data.*

Income Per day (Rs.)	*No. of families*
0-10	*6*
10-20	*12*
20-30	*15*
30-40	*10*
40-50	*8*
50-60	*4*
60-70	*11*
70-80	*9*
80-90	*14*
90-100	*11*

Solution: Calculation of arithmetic mean through short-cut method.

Income Per day Rs. X	*No. of families f*	*Mid points m*	*d = m - 45 (A = 45)*	*fd*
0-10	6	5	-40	-240
10-20	12	15	-30	-360
20-30	15	25	-20	-300
30-40	10	35	-10	-100
40-50	8	45	0	0
50-60	4	55	+10	+40
60-70	11	65	+20	+220
70-80	9	75	+30	+270
80-90	14	85	+40	+560
90-100	11	95	+50	+550
	Σf = 100			*Σfd = 640*

$$\overline{X} = A \pm \frac{\Sigma fd}{N} = 45 + \frac{640}{100} = 45 + 6.4 = 51.4$$

Mean Income of the 100 families is Rs. 51.4

Illustration 7: *Calculate arithmetic mean from the following data through short-cut method.*

Marks	*No. of students*
0-9	*3*
10-19	*4*
20-29	*7*
30-39	*4*
40-49	*5*
50-59	*7*
60-69	*8*
70-79	*6*
80-89	*4*
90-100	*2*

Solution: Calculation of arithmetic mean through short-cut method.

Marks X	*No. of students* *f*	*Mid points* *m*	*d = (A - 54.5)*	*fd*
0-9	3	4.5	-50	-150
10-19	4	14.5	-40	-160
20-29	7	24.5	-30	-210
30-39	4	34.5	-20	-80
40-49	5	44.5	-10	-50
50-59	7	54.5	0	0
60-69	8	64.5	+10	+80
70-79	6	74.5	+20	+120
80-89	4	84.5	+30	+120
90-99	2	94.5	+40	+80
		N = 50		*Σfd = -250*

$$\overline{X} = A \pm \frac{\Sigma fd}{N} = 54.5 - \frac{250}{50} = 54.5 - 5 = 49.5$$

Ans: Mean marks of 50 students is 49.5

(iii) Step Deviation Method: Step deviation method is used to simplify the calculation of arithmetic mean for continuous series. A common factor should be ascertained from the class intervals. The common factor can be used to divide the product of deviations from mid points of each observations. The total of the figures so obtained should be used in the formula to know the arithmetic mean. The formula for arithmetic mean under step deviation method is stated as below.

$$\overline{X} = A \pm \left(\frac{\Sigma fd}{N}\right) \times i$$

Where A = Assumed Mean; f = frequency, d = deviation from mid points divided by common factor, N = total no. of frequency, i = common factor.

Illustration 8: *Following are the data related with the production of a product during January in 100 factories*

Production in tonnes	*No. of factories*
0-100	*7*
100-200	*15*
200-300	*10*
300-400	*9*
400-500	*10*
500-600	*12*
600-700	*8*
700-800	*13*
800-900	*9*
900-1000	*7*

Calculate arithmetic mean by Step-deviation method.

Solution: Calculation of arithmetic mean through step-deviation method.

Production (in tonnes) X	*No. of factories f*	*m*	*(m - 550) d*	*d / 100 d'*	*fd'*
0-100	7	50	-500	-5	-35
100-200	15	150	-400	-4	-60
200-300	10	250	-300	-3	-30
300-400	9	350	-200	-2	-18
400-500	10	450	-100	-1	-10
500-600	12	550	0	0	0
600-700	8	650	+100	+1	+8
700-800	13	750	+200	+2	+26
800-900	9	850	+300	+3	+27
900-1000	7	950	+400	+4	+28
	N = 100				*Σfd' = -64*

$$\overline{X} = A \pm \left(\frac{\Sigma fd}{N}\right) \times i = 550 - \left(\frac{64}{100}\right) \times 100 = 550 - 64 = 486$$

Hence, mean production of the product in January 1993 for 100 factories is 486 tonnes.

Step Deviation method can also be applied in the direct method of calculating arithmetic mean of continuous series. The following formula can be applied for this purpose.

$$\overline{X} = \left(\frac{\Sigma fm'}{N}\right) \times i$$

Where f = frequency; m' = mid points divided by common factor $\left(m' = \frac{m}{i}\right)$; i = common factor.

Illustration 9: *Calculate arithmetic mean from the following data.*

Marks	*No. of students*
0-10	*4*
10-20	*3*
20-30	*6*
30-40	*11*
40-50	*7*
50-60	*2*
60-70	*2*

Solution: Calculation of arithmetic mean

Marks X	*No. of students* f	*Mid points* m	$m/5$ m'	fm'
0-10	4	5	1	4
10-20	3	15	3	9
20-30	6	25	5	30
30-40	11	35	7	77
40-50	7	45	9	63
50-60	2	55	11	22
60-70	2	65	13	26
	N = 35			$\Sigma fm' = 231$

$$\overline{X} = \left(\frac{\Sigma fm'}{N}\right) \times i = \frac{231}{35} \times 5 = 33$$

Ans: Average marks obtained by 35 students in a class is 33.

Illustration 10: *Following are the data related with the monthly income of 100 families in a village.*

Monthly Income (Rs.)	*No. of families*
Above 0	*100*
Above 100	*95*
Above 200	*80*
Above 300	*75*
Above 400	*60*
Above 500	*55*
Above 600	*40*
Above 700	*35*
Above 800	*25*
Above 900	*20*
Above 1000	*0*

Calculate arithmetic mean.

Solution: Calculation of arithmetic mean.

Monthly income X	*No. of families f*	*Mid points m*	*m-450 (A = 450) d*	*d / 100 d´*	*fd´*
0-100	5	50	-400	-4	-20
100-200	15	150	-300	-3	-45
200-300	5	250	-200	-2	-10
300-400	15	350	-100	-1	-15
400-500	5	450	0	0	0
500-600	15	550	+100	+1	+15
600-700	5	650	+200	+2	+10
700-800	10	750	+300	+3	+30
800-900	5	850	+400	+4	+20
900-1000	20	950	+500	+5	+100
	N = 100			*Σfd´ = +85*	

$$\overline{X} = A \pm \left(\frac{\Sigma fd'}{N}\right) \times i = 450 + \left(\frac{85}{100}\right) \times 100 = 450 + 85 = 535$$

Ans: Mean monthly income of 100 families is Rs. 535

Weighted Arithmetic Mean

The simple arithmetic mean gives equal importance to all the observations. Sometimes some observations got relatively more importance than other observations. For such kind of observations weighted arithmetic mean method should be applied to find out the average. In this method the weights for observations should be given on the basis of their relative importance. The formula under this method is

$$\bar{X}W = \frac{\Sigma Wx}{\Sigma W}$$

Where $\bar{X}W$ - indicates the weighted arithmetic mean, x - indicates the value of observations. *W* - indicates relative weights for the observations.

This method is normally used for construction of index numbers and for calculating standardised birth and death rates.

While assigning weights for the observations, maximum care should be taken to find out the relative importance of the variables. The weights assigned should be unbiased one.

Illustration 11: *Calculate the average mark scored by a student in 5 different subjects. The details of the marks are given below.*

English 85, Tamil 70, Mathematics 90, Science 60, Social 55. The weight given for these subjects are Mathematics 5, Science 4, Social 3, Tamil 2 and English 1.

Solution: Calculation of weighted arithmetic mean

Subject	*Weight* *W*	*Marks* *X*	*W X*
Mathematics	5	90	450
Science	4	60	240
Social	3	55	165
Tamil	2	70	140
English	1	85	85
	ΣW = 15		*ΣWx = 1080*

$$\bar{X}W = \frac{\Sigma W\text{X}}{\Sigma W} = \frac{1080}{15} = 72 \text{ marks}$$

Illustration 12: *The price of 6 products are stated below*

Products	*1*	*2*	*3*	*4*	*5*	*6*
Price (Rs.)	*25*	*15*	*40*	*12*	*17*	*20*

According to the importance of the products they are ranked a products 2,5,4,6,1,3.

Solution: Since the weights of the products have not been given, it should be assumed on the basis of the importance of the products.

Calculation of weighted arithmetic mean.

Products	*Weight* W	*Price (Rs.)* X	*WX*
1	2	25	50
2	5	15	75
3	4	40	160
4	6	12	72
5	1	17	17
6	3	20	60
	ΣW = 21		*ΣWX = 434*

$$\bar{X}W = \frac{\Sigma WX}{\Sigma W} = \frac{434}{21} = \text{Rs } 20.67$$

Correcting an Incorrect Arithmetic Mean

Sometimes the arithmetic mean may be wrongly calculated. This is due to the mistakes in copying, oversight and taking wrong values. It is easy to calculate the correct arithmetic mean from the incorrect one. First of all, from the sum of the observations (ΣX) deduct the wrong observations. Then add the correct observations and divide the correct sum of observations (ΣX) by the number of observations. This will give the correct arithmetic mean.

Illustration 13: *The arithmetic mean of the sales in 20 factories was calculated as Rs. 1320. Later it was found out that the sales for two factories were wrongly calculated as Rs. 1540 and Rs. 1260 instead of Rs. 1450 and Rs. 1870.*

Solution: $\bar{X} = \frac{\Sigma X}{N}$

Hence $\Sigma X = N\bar{X} = 20 \times 1320 = 26400$

Less incorrect figure (1540 + 1260)

i.e. 2800 from ΣX, 26400 - 2800 = 23,600

Add correct figure (1450 + 1870) = 3,320

Corrected Σx = 26,920

Correct $\overline{X} = \frac{26920}{20} = 1346$

Properties of arithmetic mean

(i) The sum of the deviations of all the observations from arithmetic mean is equal to zero $\Sigma(X - \overline{X}) = 0$

Example: *Calculate arithmetic mean of the following data and prove that sum of the deviations from arithmetic mean is zero.*

27, 32, 45, 63, 67, 71, 80

X	$X - \overline{X}$ *(X – 55)*
27	-28
32	-23
45	-10
63	8
67	12
71	16
80	25
$\Sigma X = 385$	$\Sigma(X - \overline{X}) = 0$

$$\overline{X} = \frac{\Sigma X}{N} = \frac{385}{7} = 55$$

Hence the sum of positive value (61) is equal to sum of the negative value (-61) of the deviations, it proves that sum of the deviations of all the observations from arithmetic mean is zero.

(ii) The sum of the squared deviation of all the variables from arithmetic mean is less than the squared observations of all the variables from any other value.

Example: X - 5, 7, 8, 12, 13

$$\Sigma X = 45$$

$$\overline{X} = \frac{\Sigma X}{N} = \frac{45}{5} = 9$$

To prove the second property deviations from 10 is taken

X	$X-\overline{X}$	$(X-\overline{X})^{-2}$	$(X-10)$	$(X-10)^{-2}$
5	-4	16	-5	25
7	-2	4	-3	9
8	-1	1	-2	4
12	3	9	+2	4
13	4	16	+3	9
	$\Sigma(X-\overline{X})^2 = 46$			$\Sigma(X-10)^2 = 51$

Hence, $\Sigma(X-\overline{X})^2 > (X-10)^2$ it is proved that sum of the squared deviations of all the observations from arithmetic mean is less than the sum of squared deviations of all the observations from any other value.

(iii) Calculation of combined arithmetic mean: Combined arithmetic mean of two or more related groups can be calculated if the arithmetic mean of these groups are available. The formula for calculating combined arithmetic mean is

$$\overline{X}_{12} = \frac{N_1\overline{X}_1 + N_2\overline{X}_2}{N_1 + N_2}$$

Where $\overline{X}_{12}$ means combined arithmetic mean

$\overline{X}_1$ means arithmetic mean of the first group

$\overline{X}_2$ means arithmetic mean of the second group

N_1 indicates number of observations in the first group

N_2 indicates number of observations in the second group

Illustration 14: *The arithmetic mean of marks obtained in statistics by the students of two classes are 83 and 67 respectively. The number of students in these two classes are 40 and 50 respectively. Calculate the mean marks obtained by 90 students of these two classes.*

Solution: The combined arithmetic mean,

$$\overline{X}_{12} = \frac{N_1\overline{X}_1 + N_2\overline{X}_2}{N_1 + N_2}$$

$N_1 = 40,\ N_2 = 50,\ X_1 = 83,\ X_2 = 67$

$$\overline{X}_{12} = \frac{(40 \times 83) + (50 \times 67)}{40 + 50} = \frac{3320 + 3350}{90} = \frac{6670}{90} = 74.11$$

Illustration 15: *The mean wages of 150 workers in a factory is Rs. 85/- If the arithmetic mean of 80 workers in one section is Rs. 92/ - calculate the arithmetic mean of wages for other section.*

Solution:

$\overline{X}_{12} = 85,\ \overline{X}_1 = 92,\ N_1 = 80,\ N_2 = 150 - 80 = 70$

$$\overline{X}_{12} = \frac{N_1\overline{X}_1 + N_2\overline{X}_2}{N_1 + N_2}$$

$$\overline{X}_{12} = \frac{(80 \times 92) + (70\overline{X}_2)}{80 + 70}$$

$$85 = \frac{7360 + 70\overline{X}_2}{150}$$

$$85 \times 150 = 7360 + 70\overline{X}_2$$

$$70\overline{X}_2 = 12750 - 7360$$

$$\overline{X}_2 = \frac{5390}{70} = 77$$

Calculation of Arithmetic mean for open-end classes

If the lower limit of the first class interval and upper limit of the last class interval are not known, it is called open-end classes. The types of open-end classes are as follows:

(i) Class intervals of equal intervals

(ii) Class intervals increase proportionately

(iii) No consistency in class intervals.

(i) Class intervals of equal intervals: If the class intervals are equal for all classes then the lowest value for the first class should be ascertained by deducting the value of intervals with the upper limit of the first class. The value of the upper limit of the last class can be calculated by adding the lower limit of the last class with class interval.

Example:

Below 20
20-40
40-60
60-80
80-100
above 100

In the above example the first class is 0-20 and the last class is 100-120.

(ii) Class intervals increases proportionately: If the class intervals increase proportionately, the proportionate value of increases should be taken into account for calculating the open-end classes.

Example:

Below 25
25-35
35-50
50-70
70-95
above 95

Here the first class would be 20-25 and the last class would be 95-125.

(iii) No consistency in class intervals: When there is no consistency in class intervals, the first class interval can be ascertained on the basis of the second class interval and the last class interval, on the basis of the last but one class interval.

Example:

Below 20
20-35
35-70
70-100
100-120
above 120

Here, the first class would be 5-20 and the last class would be 120-140

Merits of Arithmetic Mean

(i) Arithmetic mean is easy to calculate.

(ii) It is easy to understand.

(iii) It can be used for further mathematical analysis.

(iv) The nature of two or more groups of distribution can be easily compared through arithmetic mean.

(v) It represents the entire group of data in one single value.

Demerits of Arithmetic Mean

(i) It can be affected by extreme values.

Example: The mean for 5, 7, 250 and 475 is 184.5, which is not fairly representing any of the above data.

(ii) The qualities like intelligent, efficiency etc. could not be studied in this method.

(iii) It is difficult to calculate mean for open-end frequency distribution.

(iv) It will not represent the data in a reasonable manner, if the distribution is an abnormal one.

Geometric Mean

Meaning & Definition

Geometric mean may be defined as nth root of the product of n observations of a series. For two observations square root should be taken; for three observations third root should be taken; for four observations fourth root should be taken and so on.

It can be represented as,

$$\text{G.M.} = \sqrt[N]{x_1 + x_2 + x_3 + \ldots .. x_n}$$

Where N = number of items and $x_1 + x_2 + x_3 + \ldots .. x_n$ indicate the observations of the series.

If the number of observations are more, it would be complicated to calculate the geometric mean. In order to simplify the calculations the technique of logarithm can be applied. Hence, geometric mean can be calculated through the following formula.

$$\text{G.M.} = \text{Antilog} \frac{\log x_1 + \log x_2 + \log x_3 \ldots .. \log x_n}{N}$$

OR

$$\text{G.M.} = \text{Antilog} \left(\frac{\Sigma \log x}{N} \right)$$

Calculation of G.M for individual observations

$$G.M. = \text{Antilog}\left(\frac{\Sigma \log x}{N}\right)$$

Illustration 16: *Calculate the geometric mean for the following data. 25, 37, 356, 545, 976, 500, 750*

Solution: Calculation of Geometric Mean

X	*log X*
25	1.3979
37	1.5682
356	2.5515
545	2.7364
976	2.9894
500	2.6990
750	2.8751
	Σlog x = 16.8175

$$G.M. = \text{Antilog}\left(\frac{\Sigma \log X}{N}\right)$$

$$= \text{Antilog}\left(\frac{16.8175}{7}\right) = \text{Antilog } 2.4025 = 252.6$$

Calculation of G.M for Discrete Series

$$G.M. = \text{Antilog}\left(\frac{\Sigma f \log X}{N}\right)$$

Where f = frequency, $\log x$ = logarithms for variable X; $N = \Sigma f$.

Illustration 17: *Calculate geometric mean for the following data.*

Production (in tonnes)	*15.5*	*22.3*	*36.4*	*17.8*	*21.9*
No. of factories	*7*	*16*	*9*	*4*	*6*

Solution: Calculation of geometric mean.

Production (in tonnes) X	*No. of factories f*	*log X*	*f log X*
15.5	7	1.1903	8.3321
22.3	16	1.3483	21.5728
36.4	9	1.5611	14.0499
17.8	4	1.2504	5.0016
21.9	6	1.3404	8.0424
	N = 42		*Σf log X = 56.9988*

$$\text{G.M.} = \text{Antilog}\left(\frac{\Sigma f \log x}{N}\right)$$

$$= \text{Antilog}\left(\frac{56.9988}{42}\right)$$

$$= \text{Antilog } 1.3571 = 22.76$$

Calculation of G.M for Continuous Series

$$\text{G.M.} = \text{Antilog}\left(\frac{\Sigma f \log m}{N}\right)$$

Where, *f*-indicates frequencies; log *m*-indicates logarithms for the mid value of the classes and *N*- indicates the total number of frequencies.

Illustration 18: *Calculate geometric mean for the following data.*

Weekly Income (Rs.)	*No. of families*
0-100	*20*
100-200	*15*
200-300	*12*
300-400	*13*
400-500	*5*
500-600	*25*
600-700	*17*
700-800	*5*

Solution: Calculation of geometric mean.

Weekly . Income Rs. X	*No. of families f*	*Mid point m*	*log m*	*f log m*
0-100	20	50	1.6990	33.98
100-200	15	150	2.1761	32.6415
200-300	12	250	2.3979	28.7748
300-400	13	350	2.5441	33.0733
400-500	5	450	2.6532	13.266
500-600	25	550	2.7404	68.51
600-700	17	650	2.8129	47.8193
700-800	5	750	2.8751	14.3755
	N = 112			*Σf log m = 272.4404*

$$\text{G.M.} = \text{Antilog}\left(\frac{\Sigma f \log m}{N}\right)$$

$$= \text{Antilog}\left(\frac{272.4404}{112}\right)$$

$$= \text{Antilog } 2.4325 = 279.7$$

Illustration 19: *The geometric mean of five numbers 10, 12, 15, 20 and 25 is 14.5. If the frequencies of first three numbers and the last last number are 8, 6, 5 and 4, find out the frequency of the fourth number.*

Solution: Calculation of missing frequency.

X	*f*	*log X*	*f log X*
10	8	1	8
12	6	1.0792	6.4752
15	5	1.1761	5.8805
20	f_4	1.3010	$1.3010f_4$
25	4	1.3979	5.5916
Total	$23 + f_4$		$25.9473 + 1.3010f_4$

$$\text{G.M.} = \text{Antilog}\left(\frac{\Sigma f \log X}{N}\right)$$

$$\log \text{G.M.} = \frac{\Sigma f \log X}{N}$$

$$\log 14.5 = \frac{25.9473 + 1.3010 f_4}{23 + f_4}$$

$$(23 + f_4)(1.1614) = 25.9473 + 1.3010 f_4$$

$$26.7122 + 1.1614 f_4 = 25.9473 + 1.3010 f_4$$

$$26.7122 - 25.9473 = 1.3010 f_4 - 1.1614 f_4$$

$$0.1396 f_4 = 0.7649$$

$$f_4 = 5.479$$

$$\text{i.e.,} \quad = 6$$

Merits of Geometric mean

(i) It is rigidly defined.

(ii) It can be used for further statistical analysis.

(iii) Geometric mean can be used for averaging ratios, rates and percentages.

(iv) It is suitable for calculating index numbers.

Demerits of Geometric mean

(i) It is difficult to calculate and understand.

(ii) If any of the value in a series is zero geometric mean will also be zero. Hence it cannot be calculated for such kind of series.

(iii) It cannot be calculated when the distribution has open-end class.

Harmonic Mean

Harmonic mean may be defined as the total number of observations divided by the sum of reciprocals of the numbers. It may be represented as,

$$\text{H.M.} = \frac{n}{\frac{1}{x_1} + \frac{1}{x_2} + \frac{1}{x_3} + \frac{1}{x_4} \ldots\ldots \frac{1}{x_n}} = \frac{n}{\Sigma \frac{1}{x}}$$

Where n = total number of variables and $\Sigma \frac{1}{\text{x}}$ is the total number of the reciprocals of variables.

Calculation of Harmonic Mean for individual observations

Illustration 20: *Compute harmonic mean for the following data.*

2, 97, 150, 5, 285, 427, 550

Solution: Calculation of harmonic mean

X	*1 / X*
2	0.5
97	0.0103
150	0.0067
5	0.2
285	0.0035
427	0.0023
550	0.0018
N = 7	*Σ1 / x = 0.7246*

$$\text{H.M.} = \frac{N}{\Sigma\frac{1}{x}} = \frac{7}{0.7246} = 9.6605$$

Calculation of Harmonic Mean for Discrete Series

Formula for H.M under Discrete series is, $\text{H.M.} = \dfrac{N}{\Sigma\left(\dfrac{f}{X}\right)}$

Illustration 21: *Calculate harmonic mean from the following data.*

Wages (Rs.)	*60*	*45*	*25*	*75*	*80*	*15*	*30*
No. of workers	*4*	*9*	*7*	*21*	*6*	*3*	*2*

Solution: Calculation of harmonic mean.

Wages (Rs.) *x*	*No. of workers* *f*	*f / x*
60	4	0.0667
45	9	0.2
25	7	0.28
75	21	0.28
80	6	0.075
15	3	0.2
30	2	0.0667
	N = 52	*Σ(f / x) = 1.1684*

$$H.M. = \frac{N}{\Sigma\left(\frac{f}{x}\right)} = \frac{52}{1.1684} = 44.5053$$

Calculation of Harmonic Mean for Continuous Series

Formula for harmonic mean under continuous series is,

$$H.M. = \frac{N}{\Sigma\left(\frac{f}{m}\right)}$$

Where, N = total number of frequencies (Σf), m = mid value of class intervals and f = frequencies.

Illustration 22: *Calculate harmonic mean of the following data.*

Marks	*0-10*	*10-20*	*20-30*	*30-40*	*40-50*	*50-60*	*60-70*
No. of students	*7*	*8*	*20*	*11*	*9*	*3*	*4*

Solution:

Marks X	*No. of students* f	*Mid value* m	*f/m*
0-10	7	5	1.4
10-20	8	15	0.533
20-30	20	25	0.8
30-40	11	35	0.314
40-50	9	45	0.2
50-60	3	55	0.055
60-70	4	65	0.062
	N = 62		*Σ(f/m) = 3.364*

$$H.M. = \frac{N}{\Sigma\left(\frac{f}{m}\right)} = \frac{62}{3.364} = 18.43$$

Merits

(i) It is based on all the observations.

(ii) It can be used for further algebraic analysis.

(iii) It can be used for averaging rates and ratios.

(iv) It is rigidly defined.

Demerits

(i) It is difficult to understand and to calculate.

(ii) It can not be calculated if any one or more values of the variables is zero.

(iii) It can not be calculated if there exists both positive and negative values in a series.

Relation between Arithmetic Mean, Geometric Mean and Harmonic mean

The arithmetic mean would be greater than geometric mean and harmonic mean. Geometric mean would also be greater than harmonic mean.

Hence, $$A.M > G.M > H.M$$

If all the items of the data are of same value like, 25, 25, 25, 25, 25 then the arithmetic mean would be equal to geometric mean and harmonic mean.

i.e., $$A.M = G.M = H.M$$

Illustration 23: *Calculate A.M, G.M and H.M for the data 35, 24, 75, 50, 40 and prove that A.M > G.M > H.M*

Solution:

X	*log X*	*1/X*
35	1.5441	0.0286
24	1.3802	0.0417
75	1.8751	0.0133
50	1.6990	0.02
40	1.6021	0.025
ΣX = 224	*Σlog X = 8.1005*	*Σ1/X = 0.1286*

$$A.M. = \frac{\Sigma X}{N} = \frac{224}{5} = 44.8$$

$$G.M. = \text{Antilog}\left(\frac{\Sigma \log X}{N}\right) = \text{Antilog}\frac{8.1005}{5} = 41.70$$

$$H.M. = \frac{N}{\Sigma \frac{1}{X}} = \frac{5}{0.1286} = 38.88$$

44.8 > 41.70 > 38.88 Hence it is proved that A.M > G.M > H.M.

Illustration 24: *Calculate the A.M, G.M and H.M for the following data and prove that A.M = G.M = H.M Marks: 50, 50, 50, 50, 50*

Solution:

X	*log X*	*1/X*	
50	1.6990	02	0.02
50	1.6990	02	0.02
50	1.6990	02	0.02
50	1.6990	02	0.02
50	1.6990	02	0.02
ΣX = 250	*Σlog X = 8.495*	*Σ1/X = 0.1*	

$$\text{A.M.} = \frac{\Sigma X}{N} = \frac{250}{5} = 50$$

$$\text{G.M.} = \text{Antilog}\left(\frac{\Sigma \log X}{N}\right) = \text{Antilog}\,\frac{8.495}{1.699} = 50$$

$$\text{H.M.} = \frac{N}{\Sigma\frac{1}{X}} = \frac{5}{0.1} = 50$$

Hence it is proved that A.M = G.M = H.M.

Median

Median is the middle value of the group of data arranged in an order, either on an ascending order or descending order. It divides the entire group of data into two equal parts. The first part would be the observations which are smaller than median the second part are the observations which are greater than median.

If the total number of observations are in odd numbers then the median can be ascertained without any difficult.

Example: For the variables 5, 7, 9, 15, 20, 27, 32, 55, 60 median is, 20. But the median, for even number of observations, lies in two variables. Hence the average of such two variables can be taken as median.

Example: 5, 8, 12, 15, 20, 25, 32, 40

Median for the above observations lies in 15 and 20

Hence median $= \dfrac{15+20}{2} = 17.5$

Definitions: The important definitions of median are stated below.

(i) According to Croxtan and Cowder "*the median is that value which divides a series so that one half or more of the items are equal to or less than it and half or more of the items are equal to or greater than it*".

(ii) Yan Lun Chon defines "*the median, as its name indicates, is the value of the middle item in a series, when items are arranged according to magnitude*".

(iii) According to L.R. Connor "*the median is that value of the variable which divides the group into two equal parts, one part comprising all values greater and the other, all values less than median*".

Hence, it is very clear from the above definitions that median is the mid value of any series arranged in ascending or descending order. Moreover it divides the group of data into two equal parts.

Calculation of Median for Individual Observations

The data which are liable for calculating median should be arranged in ascending or descending order. Then the total number of data or observations should be added with one. This figure should be divided by 2 to get the value of median. It can be calculated through the following formula.

Formula for calculating median is

$$\text{Median, } M = \left(\frac{N+1}{2}\right)\text{th item.}$$

Illustration 25: *The weight of 15 students in a class is stated below:*

Sl. No.	*1*	*2*	*3*	*4*	*5*	*6*	*7*	*8*	*9*	*10*	*11*	*12*	*13*	*14*	*15*
Weight in	*49*	*52*	*47*	*48*	*42*	*55*	*56*	*54*	*50*	*52*	*51*	*59*	*57*	*41*	*43*

Find out the median weight of students.

Solution:

Sl. No.	*Weight in Kilograms*	*Weight in kilograms Ascending Order*
1	49	41
2	52	42
3	47	43
4	48	47
5	42	48
6	55	49
7	56	50
8	54	51
9	50	52
10	52	52
11	51	54
12	59	55
13	57	56
14	41	57
15	43	59

Median $M = \left(\frac{N+1}{2}\right)$th item

$= \left(\frac{15+1}{2}\right)$th = 8th item

Hence, Median weight is 51 Kilograms.

Illustration 26: *Calculate Median marks from the following data. 35, 46, 29, 57, 60, 73, 20, 59, 50, 70.*

Solution: Arrangement of data according to ascending order.

Sl. No.	*Marks in ascending order*
1	20
2	29
3	35
4	46
5	50
6	57
7	59
8	60
9	70
10	73
N = 10	

Median $M = \left(\frac{N+1}{2}\right)$th item

$$= \frac{10+1}{2}\text{th} = 5.5\text{th item}$$

$$5.5\text{th item} = \frac{5\text{th item} + 6\text{th item}}{2}$$

$$= \frac{50+57}{2} = 53.5 \text{ Marks}$$

Calculation of Median for Discrete Series

The observations should be arranged in ascending or descending order. Frequencies should also be placed for respective observations. Then cumulative frequencies should be calculated. Total number of items (i.e. the total of the frequencies) should be added with one and divided by 2. Then the figure so arrived should be found out in the cumulative frequency column. The figure may either equal to the cumulative frequency or just lower value. The data corresponding to such cumulative frequency is called Median.

Formula for median $M = \left(\frac{N+1}{2}\right)$th item.

Illustration 27: *From the following find out the median monthly income of families of a village.*

Monthly income Rs.	*No. of families*
500	4
600	6
700	5
800	7
900	15
1000	20
1100	9
1200	3
1300	6

Solution: Calculation of Median

Monthly Income Rs.	*No. of families*	*Cumulative frequency*
500	4	4
600	6	10
700	5	15
800	7	22
900	15	37
1000	20	57
1100	9	66
1200	3	69
1300	6	75
	N = 75s	

Median $M = \left(\frac{N+1}{2}\right)$th item $= \left(\frac{75+1}{2}\right)$th item = 38th item

Hence median of monthly income is Rs. 1000

Illustration 28: *Calculate median from the following data.*

Wages (Rs.)	*25*	*50*	*35*	*45*	*20*	*55*	*30*	*40*
No. of workers	*7*	*9*	*12*	*15*	*10*	*20*	*12*	*25*

Solution: Calculation of Median

Wages Rs.	*No. of workers* *f*	*Cumulative value* *C. f*
20	10	10
25	7	17
30	12	29
35	12	41
40	25	66
45	15	81
50	9	90
55	20	110
	N = 110	

Median $M = \left(\frac{N+1}{2}\right)$th item

$= \left(\frac{110+1}{2}\right)$th item = 55.5th item

Hence the median value of wages = Rs. 40

Calculation of Median for Continuous Series

Following formula may be applied for ascertaining median in continuous series.

$$\text{Median,} \qquad M = L + \left(\frac{N/2 - cf}{f}\right) \times i$$

Where, L - indicates lower value of the median class. The median class can be determined by tracing $N/2$ th item in the cumulative frequency. cf - indicates cumulative frequency of the class preceding the median class, f - indicates the frequency of the median class and i - indicates the class interval of the median class.

Illustration 29: *The monthly income of 100 families in a village are stated below:*

Monthly Income Rs.	*No. of families*
100-200	*7*
200-300	*5*
300-400	*15*
400-500	*22*
500-600	*14*
600-700	*12*
700-800	*8*
800-900	*9*
900-1000	*8*

Calculate the median.

Solution: Calculation of Median

Monthly Income Rs.	*No. of families f*	*Cumulative value cf*
100-200	7	7
200-300	5	12
300-400	15	27
400-500	22	49
500-600	14	63
600-700	12	75
700-800	8	83
800-900	9	92
900-1000	8	100
	N = 100	

Median $M = L + \left(\frac{N/2 - cf}{f}\right) \times i$

Hence, Median class = 500 - 600; L = 500; f = 14; cf = 49; i = 600-500 = 100

Median $M = 500 + \frac{50-49}{14} \times 100$

$= 500 + \frac{100}{14} = 500 + 7.14 = 507.14$

Hence, Median value of monthly income is Rs. 507.14

Illustration 30: *Compute the median from the following data.*

Mid value	*Frequency*
5	10
15	12
25	15
35	37
45	52
55	35
65	11
75	4

Solution:

Mid value *m*	*Class Intervals* *X*	*frequency* *f*	*Cumulative frequency f*
5	0-10	10	10
15	10-20	12	22
25	20-30	15	37
35	30-40	37	74
45	40-50	52	126
55	50-60	35	161
65	60-70	11	172
75	70-80	4	176
		N = 176	

Median $M = L + \left(\frac{N/2 - cf}{f}\right) \times i$

$N/2$ = 176/2 = 88. It lies in 126 of the cumulative frequency. Hence the median class intervals is 40-50. $L = 40$; $cf = 74$, $f = 52$; $i = 50 - 40 = 10$

Hence Median $$M = 40 + \left(\frac{88-74}{52}\right) \times 10$$

$$= 40 + \frac{140}{52} = 40 + 2.69 = 42.69$$

Hence, Median is 42.69

Illustration 31: *The details regarding the monthly production of 100 factories are stated in the following table.*

Production in tonnes	*No. of factories*
0-40	*25*
41-50	*15*
51-60	*11*
61-70	*20*
71-80	*13*
81-90	*6*
91-100	*10*

Find out the median.

Solution: Calculation of Median

Production in tonnes	*No. of factories* *f*	*Cumulative no. of factories cf*
0-40.5	25	25
40.5-50.5	15	40
50.5-60.5	11	51
60.5-70.5	20	71
70.5-80.5	13	84
80.5-90.5	6	90
90.5-100.5	10	100
	N = 100	

Median $$M = L + \left(\frac{N/2 - cf}{f}\right) \times i$$

$N/2$ = 100/2 = 50. It lies on 51 of the cumulative frequency. Hence, Median class = 50.5 - 60.5; $L = 50.5$; $cf = 40$; $f = 11$ and $i = 60.5 - 50.5 = 10$

Median $M = 50.5 + \left(\frac{50-40}{11}\right) \times 10$

$$= 50.5 + \frac{100}{11} = 50.5 + 9.09 = 59.59$$

Hence, mid value of production is 59.59 tonnes.

Illustration 32: *The marks obtained by 100 students in a class in the subject statistics are given below:*

Marks	*No. of students*
0-10	*3*
10-20	*9*
20-30	*10*
30-40	*20*
40-50	*16*
50-60	*18*
60-70	*9*
70-80	*4*
80-90	*1*

Calculate (a) Median and (b) the total number of students passed and the percentage of pass (c) the total number of students failed and its percentage, if the pass mark of the subject is 35.

Solution: Calculation of Median

Marks	*No. of students* *f*	*Cumulative no. of students* *cf*
0-10	3	3
10-20	9	12
20-30	10	22
30-40	20	42
40-50	16	58
50-60	18	76
60-70	9	85
70-80	4	89
80-90	1	90
	N = 90	

Median $M = L + \left(\frac{N/2 - cf}{f}\right) \times i$

Hence the median class in 40-50; $cf = 47; f = 16; L = 40; i = 10$

Median $$M = 40 + \left(\frac{45-42}{16}\right) \times 10$$

$$= 40 + \frac{30}{16} = 40 + 1.87 = 41.87$$

To calculate the total percentage, take 35 as Median value. It lies in the class interval 30-40; Hence $cf = 22; f = 20; i = 10$. The value of $N/2$ is the no of students and it is assumed as X. The formula for such calculation is,

$$35 = 30 + \left(\frac{x-22}{20}\right) \times 10$$

$$35 = 30 + \frac{10x - 220}{20}$$

$$\frac{10x - 220}{20} = 35 - 30$$

$$10x - 220 = 5 \times 20$$

$$10x = 100 + 220$$

$$x = \frac{320}{10} = 32$$

Percentage of fail $= \frac{32}{90} \times 100 = 35.5\%$

Hence total number of students passed in the examination is 90 - 32 = 58 students

Percentage of pass $= \frac{58}{90} \times 100 = 64.5\%$

Illustration 33: *Calculate median from the following data.*

Marks	*0-10*	*10-40*	*40-60*	*60-90*	*90-100*
No. of students	*3*	*9*	*20*	*12*	*3*

Solution:

Marks	*f*	*cf*
0-10	3	3
10-40	9	12
40-60	20	32
60-90	12	44
90-100	3	47
	N = 47	

Median $$M = L + \left(\frac{N/2 - cf}{f}\right) \times i$$

$N/2 = 47/2 = 23.5$ item, which lies in 40-60 class interval. Hence $L = 40$; $f = 20$; $cf = 12$; $i = 60 - 40 = 20$

Median $$M = 40 + \left(\frac{23.5 - 12}{20}\right) \times 20$$

$$= 40 + \frac{11.5 \times 20}{20} = 51.5$$

This problem can be solved by the following method also.

Marks	*f*	*cf*
0-10	3	3
10-20	3	6
20-30	3	9
30-40	3	12
40-50	10	22
50-60	10	32
60-70	4	36
70-80	4	40
80-90	4	44
90-100	3	47

$N/2 = 47/2 = 23.5$th item, which lies in class interval 50-60. Hence $L = 50$; $f = 10$; $cf = 22$; $i = 10$

Median $$M = 50 + \left(\frac{23.5 - 22}{10}\right) \times 10$$

$$= 50 + \frac{1.5}{10} \times 10 = 51.5$$

Graphic method of determination of Median

There are two methods of determining median, graphically. They are (a) One Ogive Method and (b) Two Ogives Method.

(a) One Ogive Method: Ogive means cumulative frequency curve. Under one ogive method cumulative frequency of raising trend (more than cumulative frequency method) should be plotted in the graph corresponding to the variables. Draw the ogive (curve) by joining all the plotted points. Normally variables should be marked on the 'X' axis and the cumulative frequencies, on the 'Y' axis. The middle item should be marked on the 'Y' axis. The middle item can be located through the formula *N*/2. Then from the middle item of the 'Y' axis, draw a parallel line to the 'X' axis, which will cut the ogive at any point. Then draw a parallel line of 'Y' axis from the 'X' point of ogive to *X* axis. Measure the distance from the origin to the point where parallel line cut the 'X' axis to find out the median.

(b) Two Ogives Method: Under the two ogives two curves in a graph, based on the cumulative frequencies should be drawn to locate median. Among these two curves, one curve is based on the cumulative frequencies of raising trend (more than cumulative frequency) and the other is based on the cumulative frequencies of decreasing trend (less than cumulative frequency method). Draw a perpendicular line to the 'X' axis from the point of intersection of these two ogives. The median is measured from the origin to the point where the perpendicular line cuts the 'X' axis.

Illustration 34: *Calculate median through graphic method from the following data.*

Income (Rs.)	*No. of workers*
0-10	*7*
20-40	*3*
40-60	*9*
60-80	*11*
80-100	*17*
100-120	*20*
120-140	*10*
140-160	*3*

Solution: Calculation of Median

Income (Rs.) (less than)	*No. of workers*	*Income (Rs.) (more than)*	*No. of workers*
0	0	0	80
20	7	20	77
40	10	40	67
60	19	60	47
80	30	80	30
100	47	100	19
120	67	120	10
140	77	140	7
160	80	160	0

Graphical Representation of Median

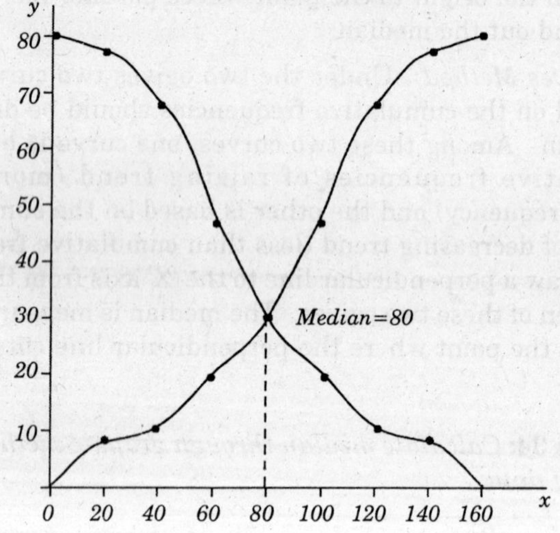

Advantages of Median

(i) Median can be used for further analysis of data.

Example: Mean deviation can be calculated through median.

(ii) It is easy to calculate and simple to understand. It will not be affected by the extreme values of the observations.

(iii) It can be calculated through graphical method.

(iv) It can be calculated eventhough the extremes of the variables are not known.

(v) It can be located even by mere inspection.

Disadvantages of Median

(i) Calculation of median for continuous series is a complicated one.

(ii) The use of median for further algebraic analysis is very limited.

(iii) Combined median cannot be calculated for two or more groups of data like arithmetic mean.

(iv) Sampling fluctuations affect the value of median.

(v) Arrangement of data on the basis of ascending order or descending order is a must for locating median.

Other Measures of Median

Median is termed as position measures of data. The data may be divided into 4 parts or 5 parts or 10 parts or 100 parts.

These types of dividing the distribution are called Quartiles (division into 4 parts), Quintiles (5 parts), Deciles (10 parts) and Percentiles (100 parts).

Quartiles: Quartiles may be defined as those values which divide the total frequencies into four equal parts. They are termed as Q1, Q2, Q3 and Q4. Formula for calculation of quartiles are,

$$Q_1 = \frac{N}{4} \text{ th item}$$

$$Q_2 = \frac{2N}{4} \text{ or } \frac{N}{2} \text{ th item (median)}$$

$$Q_3 = \frac{3N}{4} \text{ th item}$$

Q_2 is called median.

To find out the value of Q1 and Q3 the formula for calculating median should be applied by replacing N/2nd in the formula by N/4 or 3N/4.

For individual observation and discrete series $\frac{N+1}{4}$, $\frac{2(N+1)}{4}$ and $\frac{3(N+1)}{4}$ should applied instead of N/4, 2N/4 and 3N/4.

Illustration 35: *Calculate quartiles from the following data.*

36, 45, 29, 18, 30, 57, 43

Solution: Data: 18, 29, 30, 36, 43, 45, 57.

N = 7

$$Q_1 = \frac{N+1}{4} \text{ th item} = \frac{7+1}{4} = 2 \text{ th item} = 29$$

$$Q_2 = \frac{2(N+1)}{4} \text{ th item} = \frac{2(7+1)}{4} = 4 \text{ th item} = 36$$

$$Q_3 = \frac{3(N+1)}{4} \text{ th item} = \frac{3(7+1)}{4} = 6 \text{ th item} = 45$$

Illustration 36: *From the following data find out the quartiles.*

Wages Rs.	*30*	*40*	*50*	*60*	*70*	*80*
No. of workers	*4*	*8*	*10*	*9*	*6*	*3*

Solution:

Wages (Rs.) X	*No. of workers* f	*Cumulative value of No. of workers* cf
30	4	4
40	8	12
50	10	22
60	9	31
70	6	37
80	3	40
	N = 40	

$$Q_1 = \frac{N+1}{4} \text{ th item} = \frac{40+1}{4} = 10.25 \text{ th item} = 40$$

$$Q_2 = \frac{2(N+1)}{4} \text{ th item} = \frac{2(40+1)}{4} = 20.5 \text{ th item} = 50$$

$$Q_3 = \frac{3(N+1)}{4} \text{ th item} = \frac{3(40+1)}{4} = 30.75 \text{ th item} = 60$$

Illustration 37: *Find out the quartiles from the following data.*

Marks	*0-10*	*10-20*	*20-30*	*30-40*	*40-50*	*50-60*	*60-70*
No. of students	*8*	*12*	*10*	*15*	*11*	*9*	*5*

Solution:

Marks X	*No. of students* f	*Cumulative no. of students cf*
0-10	8	8
10-20	12	20
20-30	10	30
30-40	15	45
40-50	11	56
50-60	9	65
60-70	5	70

$$Q_1 = \frac{N}{4} \text{ th item } = \frac{70}{4} = 17.5 \text{ th item}$$

Hence $cf = 8,\ L = 10,\ f = 12,\ i = 10.$

$$Q_1 = L + \left(\frac{N/4 - cf}{f}\right) \times i = 10 + \left(\frac{17.5 - 8}{12}\right) \times 10$$

$$= 10 + \frac{9.5 \times 10}{12} = 10 + 7.9 = 17.9$$

$$Q_2 = \frac{2N}{4} \text{ th item } = \frac{2 \times 70}{4} = 35 \text{ th item}$$

Hence $L_1 = 30,\ cf = 30,\ f = 15,\ i = 10.$

$$Q_2 = L_1 + \left(\frac{2N/4 - cf}{f}\right) \times i = 30 + \left(\frac{35 - 30}{15}\right) \times 10$$

$$= 30 + \frac{50}{15} = 33.3$$

$$Q_3 = \frac{3N}{4} \text{ th item } = \frac{3 \times 70}{4} = 52.5 \text{ th item}$$

Hence, $L_1 = 40,\ cf = 45,\ f = 11,\ i = 10.$

$$Q_3 = L_1 + \left(\frac{3N/4 - cf}{f}\right)\times i = 40 + \left(\frac{52.5 - 45}{11}\right)\times 10$$

$$= 40 + \frac{75}{11} = 46.8$$

Formula for quintilies deciles and percentiles

$Qu_1 = \frac{N}{5}$ th item	$D_1 = \frac{N}{10}$ th item	$P_1 = \frac{N}{100}$ th item
$Qu_2 = \frac{2N}{5}$ th item	$D_2 = \frac{2N}{10}$ th item	$P_2 = \frac{2N}{100}$ th item
$Qu_3 = \frac{3N}{5}$ th item	•	•
$Qu_4 = \frac{4N}{5}$ th item	•	•
	•	•
	$D_8 = \frac{8N}{10}$ th item	$P_{98} = \frac{98N}{100}$ th item
	$D_9 = \frac{9N}{10}$ th item	$P_{99} = \frac{99N}{100}$ th item

Illustration 38: *Following are the informations relating to daily wages of workers in a factory.*

Wages (Rs.)	*0-20*	*20-40*	*40-60*	*60-80*	*80-100*
No. of workers	*7*	*12*	*9*	*18*	*4*

Calculate Qu_3, D_3, P_2, P_{22} and P_{74}

Solution: Calculation of Quantiles, Deciles and Percentiles.

Wages (Rs.) *X*	*No. of workers* *f*	*Cumulative no. of workers cf*
0-20	7	7
20-40	12	19
40-60	9	28
60-80	18	46
80-100	4	50

$$Qu_3 = \frac{3N}{5} \text{ th item } = \frac{3 \times 50}{5} = 30 \text{ th item}$$

Hence, $L = 60,\ f = 18,\ cf = 28,\ i = 20$

$$Qu_3 = L + \left(\frac{3N/5 - cf}{f}\right) \times i = 60 + \left(\frac{30 - 28}{18}\right) \times 20$$

$$= 60 + \frac{40}{18} = 60 + 2.22 = 62.22$$

$$D_3 = \frac{3N}{10} \text{ th item } = \frac{3 \times 50}{10} = 15 \text{ th item}$$

Hence, $L = 20,\ f = 12,\ cf = 7,\ i = 20$

$$D_3 = L + \left(\frac{3N/10 - cf}{f}\right) \times i = 20 + \left(\frac{15 - 7}{12}\right) \times 20$$

$$= 20 + \frac{8 \times 20}{12} = 20 + 13.33 = 33.33$$

$$P_2 = \frac{2N}{100} \text{ th item } = \frac{2 \times 50}{100} = 1\text{st item}$$

Hence, $L = 0,\ f = 7,\ cf = 0,\ i = 20$

$$P_2 = L + \left(\frac{2N/100 - cf}{f}\right) \times i = 0 + \left(\frac{1 - 0}{7}\right) \times 20 = \frac{20}{7} = 2.85$$

$$P_{22} = \frac{22N}{100} \text{ th item } = \frac{22 \times 50}{100} = 11\text{th item}$$

Hence, $L = 20,\ f = 12,\ cf = 7,\ i = 20.$

$$P_{22} = L + \left(\frac{22N/100 - cf}{f}\right) \times i = 20 + \left(\frac{11 - 7}{12}\right) \times 20$$

$$= 20 + \frac{4 \times 20}{12} = 20 + 6.67 = 26.67$$

$$P_{74} = \frac{74N}{100}\text{th item} = \frac{74 \times 50}{100} = 37\text{th item}$$

Hence, $L = 60$, $f = 18$, $cf = 28$, $i = 20$.

$$P_{74} = L + \left(\frac{74N/100 - cf}{f}\right) \times i = 60 + \left(\frac{37 - 28}{18}\right) \times 20$$

$$= 60 + \frac{9 \times 20}{18} = 60 + 10 = 70$$

MODE

Mode means the value that occurs most frequently in a statistical distribution. It is otherwise called as the value which occurs the greatest number of times in a series or group of data. Example: Marks obtained by 10 students in a class are 17, 42, 35, 42, 35, 80, 72 and 65. In this example the variable 42 occurred the maximum number of time. Hence 42 is called mode of the distribution.

Calculation of Mode for Individual Observation

In individual observation mode can be easily located without applying any formula. The data which appeared the maximum number of time can be treated as mode for that group of data. In individual observation there may be chance of obtaining one mode, two modes, three modes or more than three modes.

Illustration 39: *Calculate mode from the following data. 25, 36, 25, 33, 34, 25, 33*

Solution: In data 25, 36, 25, 33, 34, 25 and 33, 25 repeated 3 times and 33 repeated 2 times. Hence Mode = 25.

Illustration 40: *Calculate mode from the following data. 50, 40, 25, 45, 20, 25, 35, 55, 60*

Solution: In this data 50, 40, 25, 45, 20, 25, 35, 55 and 60; 25 and 45 repeated 2 times each. Hence both these data can be taken as modes.

Ans: Mode (i) = 25 and Mode (ii) = 45

Illustration 41: *Calculate mode from the following data. 60, 62, 73, 46, 27, 52, 45, 75*

Solution: In this group of data - 60, 62, 73, 46, 27, 52, 45 and 75, there is no mode since each item appeared once.

Calculation of Mode for Discrete Series

In the discrete series mode can be ascertained by mere inspection.

Example:

X -	10	15	20	25	30
f -	4	11	14	20	4

In the above distribution it is clearly known that mode is 25, since it repeated 20 times. But in some type of distribution it is very difficult to ascertain the mode.

Example:

X -	20	25	30	35	40	45
f -	3	7	20	19	10	9

In this distribution though it appears that mode is 30 since it repeated 20 times, it may not be correct. It may be 35 also since it repeated 19 times as well as the strength of the repetition of variables after the variable 35 is relatively more than that of the strength of the variables before the variables 30. In this type of information mode may be ascertained through a grouping table and analysis table.

Grouping table can be prepared with 7 columns. The first column should contain the variables. The second column should contain the no. of items. In column 3 the frequencies are grouped in two and total should be written there (i.e., 1 and 2, 3 & 4, 5 & 6, 7 & 8, etc.)

In column 4, the frequencies are grouped and totaled into two, leaving the first frequency (i.e., 2 & 3, 4 & 5, 6 & 7, 8 & 9 etc.)

In the 5th column the frequencies are grouped and totaled with 3 items (i.e., 1, 2 & 3, 4, 5 & 6, 7, 8 & 9 etc.)

In the 6th column the frequencies are grouped and totaled with 3 frequencies after leaving the first frequency (i.e., 2, 3 & 4, 5, 6 & 8, 9, 10 & 11 etc.)

The maximum number of frequencies obtained in the grouping table in respective columns, should be identified and then the respective variables should be allotted with one weight. Accordingly the variable which got the maximum weight should be traced out which is the mode or modal class.

Illustration 42: *Calculate mode from the data given below:*

Marks	*20*	*30*	*40*	*50*	*60*	*70*	*80*	*90*
No. of students	*3*	*2*	*1*	*15*	*14*	*8*	*9*	*12*

Solution: Grouping Table

Marks	*Frequency*					
	1	*2*	*3*	*4*	*5*	*6*
20	3	5				
30	2		3	6		
40	1	16			18	
50	15		29			30
60	14	22		37	31	
70	8		17			
80	9	21				29
90	12					

Analysis Table

Col. No.	*Size of item containing maximum frequency*					
	30	*40*	*50*	*60*	*70*	*80*
1			1			
2				1	1	
3			1	1		
4			1	1	1	
5				1	1	1
6		1	1	1		
Total		*1*	*4*	*5*	*3*	*1*

Hence mode = 60; In the mere inspection it appeared that mode in 50 but it is proved that Mode = 60

Calculation of Mode for Continuous Series

Mode can be ascertained in continuous series through the following formula.

Formula for Mode

$$Z = L + \left(\frac{f_1 - f_0}{2f_1 - f_0 - f_2} \right) \times i$$

Where, L indicates lower value of the model class f_1 indicates, frequency of the model class. f_2 indicates, frequency of the class succeeding the modal class, f_0 indicates frequency of the class preceding the model class and i - indicates class intervals of the model class.

This formula can otherwise be written as

$$Z = L + \left(\frac{\Delta_1}{\Delta_1 + \Delta_2}\right) \times i$$

where $\Delta_1 = f_1 - f_0$ and $\Delta_2 = f_1 - f_2$

In case it is difficult to ascertain the model class then the grouping table and analysis table should be prepared to identify the correct model class.

Illustration 43: *Calculate the mode from the following distribution.*

Marks	*No. of students*
0-10	*4*
10-20	*7*
20-30	*15*
30-40	*11*
40-50	*6*
50-60	*9*
60-70	*4*
70-80	*3*

Solution: Model class = 20-30 since it repeated the maximum number of time.

Hence $f_1 = 15; f_2 = 11; f_0 = 7; L = 20; i = 10.$

$$Z = L + \left(\frac{\Delta_1}{\Delta_1 + \Delta_2}\right) \times i$$

$$\Delta_1 = f_1 - f_0 = 15 - 7 = 8$$

$$\Delta_2 = f_1 - f_2 = 15 - 11 = 4$$

$$Z = 20 + \left(\frac{8}{8+4}\right) \times 10 = 20 + \frac{80}{12} = 26.67$$

Illustration 44: *Calculate mode from the following data.*

Daily Income (Rs.)	*No. of families*
0-10	*4*
10-20	*5*
20-30	*15*
30-40	*9*
40-50	*11*
50-60	*14*
60-70	*8*
70-80	*13*
80-90	*7*
90-100	*8*

Solution: Grouping table

Daily Income	*Frequency*					
(Rs.)	*1*	*2*	*3*	*4*	*5*	*6*
0-10	4	9				
10-20	5		20			
20-30	15			24	29	
30-40	9	24				35
40-50	11		20			
50-60	14	25		34		
60-70	8		22		33	
70-80	13	21		28		35
80-90	7		20		28	
90-100	8	15				

Analysis Table

Column	*Size of variable containing maximum frequency*					
	20-30	*30-40*	*40-50*	*50-60*	*60-70*	*70-80*
1	1					
2			1	1		
3				1	1	
4		1	1	1		
5			1	1	1	
6	1	1	1	1	1	1
Total	*2*	*2*	*4*	*5*	*3*	*1*

Though it appears that 20 - 30 is the model class, the real model class is 50-60.

Hence, $L = 50$; $f_1 = 14$; $f_2 = 8$; $f_0 = 11$; $i = 10$.

$$\Delta_1 = f_1 - f_0 = 14 - 11 = 3$$

$$\Delta_2 = f_1 - f_2 = 14 - 8 = 6$$

$$\text{Mode} = L + \left(\frac{\Delta_1}{\Delta_1 + \Delta_2}\right) \times i$$

$$Z = 50 + \left(\frac{3}{3+6}\right) \times 10$$

$$= 50 + \frac{30}{9} = 50 + 3.33 = 53.33$$

Location of Mode through Graphic Method

Mode can be located graphically for the frequency distribution. Draw histogram for the data. The highest rectangle should be taken as the model class. Then draw two lines diagonally from each upper corner of the model class bar. Each line should touch the upper corner of the adjacent rectangles. This two lines will intersect in one point. Draw a perpendicular line from the point to the '*X*' - axis. Mode is measured from the origin to the point where the perpendicular line cuts the '*X*' axis.

Illustration 45: *Calculate mode through graphic method for the following distribution.*

Wages (Rs.)	*No. of workers*
0-15	*12*
15-30	*7*
30-45	*15*
45-60	*20*
60-75	*9*
75-90	*7*
90-105	*5*

Graphical Method of Calculation of Mode

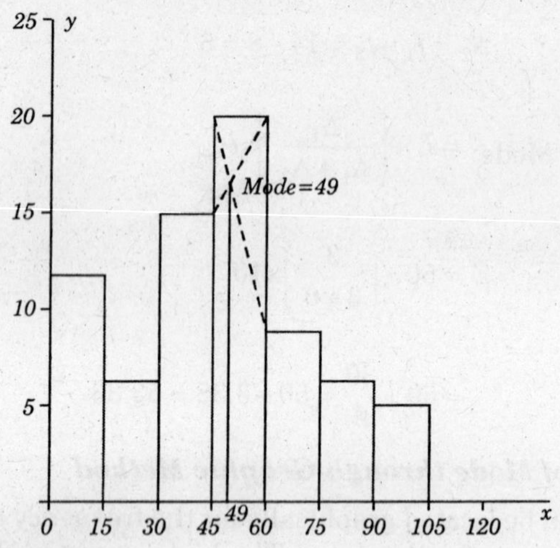

Advantages of Mode

(i) Mode can be located by mere inspection.

(ii) It can be ascertained graphically.

(iii) It would not be affected by extreme values.

(iv) It is simple to calculate and easy to understand.

(v) Sampling fluctuations would not affect the calculation of mode.

Disadvantages of Mode

(i) Mode may not be available for all the observation.

(ii) It is not suitable for further algebraic treatment.

(iii) It is not a rigidly defined measure.

(iv) It is difficult to locate mode for frequency distribution.

Relationship between Mean, Median and Mode

There exist a relationship between mean, median and mode since they deal with the measures of central tendency. In a symmetrical distribution, the values of mean, median and mode coincide. Hence in a symmetrical distribution mean equal to median equal to mode. In an assymmetrical distribution though the value of median and mode slightly varies, there exists a relation between them. Karl - Pearson studied this relationship and had given the following formula based on the relationship.

Mean - Median = 1/3 (mean - mode)

Mode = 3 Median - 2 Mean

Median = Mode + 2/3 (mean - mode)

$$\text{Mean} = \frac{3\ \text{median} - \text{mode}}{2}$$

Illustration 46: *In a distribution median and mean are 62.5 and 65.2 respectively, Calculate mode.*

Solution: Mode = 3 Median - 2 Mean

$$= (3 \times 62.5) - (2 \times 65.2)$$

$$= 187.5 - 130.4 = 57.1$$

Selection of the measure of Central Tendency

Suitable method of average should be selected based on the circumstances and nature of the data.

Arithmetic Mean: Arithmetic mean should not be used for measuring the central tendency in all circumstances. It should be avoided in the following circumstances.

(i) For uneven distribution.

(ii) For highly skewed distribution.

(iii) For distribution with open intervals.

(iv) For geometric progression (example 3, 9, 27, 81 etc.)

(v) For rate of growth and for averaging rates. Except for the above circumstances arithmetic mean is a good measure of central tendency.

Geometric Mean: It can be used for averaging ratios, percentages, rates of change and index numbers.

Harmonic Mean: It can be used for averaging rates, time, distance covered with in a specified time and quantity purchased or sold per unit.

Median: It can be used for measuring central tendency for open-end grouped distribution.

Mode: It is the best measure for discrete series and for a high frequency distribution.

Example: Number of children per household, number of person using a product etc.

Miscellaneous Illustrations

Illustration 47: *Calculate mean, median and mode from the following data relating to the production of a factory for 12 months.*

Months	*Jan*	*Feb*	*Mar*	*Apr*	*May*	*Jun*	*Jul*	*Aug*	*Sep*	*Oct*	*Nov*	*Dec*
Prodn.	*273*	*54*	*79*	*138*	*56*	*89*	*220*	*340*	*300*	*290*	*150*	*70*

Solution: Arrangement of the data for calculating mean, median and mode:

Sl. No.	*X*
1	54
2	56
3	70
4	79
5	89
6	138
7	150
8	220
9	273
10	290
11	300
12	340

$$\text{Mean} = \overline{X} = \frac{\Sigma X}{N} \qquad \text{Median} = \frac{N+1}{2} \text{ th item}$$

Mode = Most Repeatedone (or) = 3 Median - 2 Mean

$\Sigma X = 2059, \quad N = 12$

$$\text{Mean} = \overline{X} = \frac{\Sigma X}{N} = \frac{2059}{12} = 171.58$$

$$\text{Median} = \frac{N+1}{2} \text{th item} = \frac{12+1}{2} \text{th item}$$

$$= \frac{13}{2} \text{th item} = 6.5 \text{ th item}$$

i.e., $= \frac{6\text{ th item } + 7\text{th item}}{2} = \frac{138+150}{2} = 144$

$$\text{Mode} = 3\text{ Median} - 2\text{ Mean} = 3 \times 144 - 2 \times 171.58$$

$$= 432 - 343.16 = 88.84$$

Mean = 171.38, Median = 144, Mode = 88.84

Illustration 48: *Calculate the missing frequency from the following data.*

X	*0-10*	*10-20*	*20-30*	*30-40*	*40-50*	*50-60*	*60-70*
f	*4*	*7*	*12*	*?*	*22*	*11*	*3*

Arithmetic Mean is 37.

Solution: Let the missing frequency be *a*.

X	*f*	*m*	*fm*
0-10	4	5	20
10-20	7	15	105
20-30	12	25	300
30-40	a	35	35a
40-50	22	45	990
50-60	11	55	605
60-70	3	65	195
	$N = (59 + a)$		$\Sigma fm = (2215 + 35a)$

$$\text{Mean} = \bar{X} = \frac{\Sigma fm}{N}$$

$$\Sigma fm = 2215 + 35a$$

$$N = 59 + a$$

$$\bar{X} = 37 \text{ (given)}$$

$$\bar{X} = \frac{\Sigma fm}{N}$$

$$37 = \frac{2215 + 35a}{59 + a}$$

$$37(59+a) = 2215+35a$$

$$2183+37a = 2215+35a$$

$$37a-35a = 2215-2183$$

$$2a = 32$$

$$a = \frac{32}{2} = 16$$

Hence the missing frequency is 16.

Proof: $$37 = \frac{2215+35a}{59+a} = \frac{2215+35(16)}{59+16} = \frac{2775}{75} = 37$$

Missing frequency a = 16.

Illustration 49: *Calculate the average marks obtained by students in a class.*

Marks	*No. of students*
More than 10	*115*
More than 20	*112*
More than 30	*100*
More than 50	*84*
More than 60	*67*
More than 70	*53*
More than 80	*42*
More than 90	*30*
More than 100	*12*

Solution: Calculation of average marks

Marks	No. of students		(m-A) / c a=55 c=10	
	f	m	d	fd
10-20	3	15	-4	-12
20-30	12	25	-3	-36
30-40	16	35	-2	-32
40-50	17	45	-1	-17
50-60	14	55	0	0
60-70	11	65	1	11
70-80	12	75	2	24
80-90	18	85	3	54
90-100	12	95	4	48
	N = 115			Σfd = 40

$$\overline{X} = A + \frac{\Sigma fd}{N} \times c$$

$$A = 55,\ \Sigma fd = 40,\ N = 115,\ c = 10$$

$$\overline{X} = 55 + \frac{40}{115} \times 10$$

$$= 55 + 3.5 = 58.5 \text{ marks}$$

Illustration 50: *Calculate arithmetic mean from the following data.*

Weekly Income (Rs.)	No. of workers
Less than 20	4
Less than 30	9
Less than 40	15
Less than 50	32
Less than 60	45
Less than 70	52
Less than 80	60
Less than 90	67
Less than 100	75

Solution: Calculation of arithmetic mean

X	f	m	d=(m-A) A = 55; C = 10	fd
10-20	4	15	-4	-16
20-30	5	25	-3	-15
30-40	6	35	-2	-12
40-50	17	45	-1	-17
50-60	13	55	0	0
60-70	7	65	1	7
70-80	8	75	2	16
80-90	7	85	3	21
90-100	8	95	4	32
	N = 75			Σfd = 16

$$\overline{X} = A + \frac{\sum fd}{N} \times c$$

$$= 55 + \frac{16}{75} \times 10 = 55 + 2.13 = \text{Rs } 57.13$$

Illustration 51: *A company paid bonus to the workers on the following basis.*

Monthly Salary (Rs.)	*Bonus (Rs.)*
700-800	*500*
800-900	*580*
900-1000	*630*
1000-1100	*700*
1100-1200	*750*
1200-1300	*810*
1300-1400	*900*
1400-1500	*960*

The actual salary paid to the 40 workers are as follows.

725, 1450, 780, 1210, 1050, 910, 850, 930 820, 1320, 1070, 980, 720, 930, 1270, 1340, 1435, 1390, 890, 970, 770, 1020, 940, 910, 990, 1250, 870, 740, 1220, 1330, 1440, 950, 1490, 1115, 960, 1500, 700, 960, 1150, 920: Calculate the total bonus paid by the company and also calculate the average bonus paid.

Solution: Calculation of average bonus paid by the company.

Monthly Salary	*f*	*Bonus* *x*	*fx*
700-800	6	500	3000
800-900	4	580	2320
900-1000	12	630	7560
1000-1100	3	700	2100
1100-1200	2	750	1500
1200-1300	4	810	3240
1300-1400	4	900	3600
1400-1500	5	960	4800
	$N = 40$		$\Sigma fx = 28120$

Average bonus paid by the company per worker

$$\overline{X} = \frac{\Sigma fx}{N}$$

$$\Sigma fx = 28120, \quad N = 40$$

$$\overline{X} = \frac{28120}{40} = 703$$

Total bonus paid by the company = 703 x 40 = Rs. 28120.

Illustration 52: *The mean weight of all the students in a class is 54 Kgrams and the mean weight of the male students is 59 Kgs and the mean weight of the female students is 50 Kgs. Calculate the percentage of male and female in the class.*

Solution: $$\overline{X}_{12} = \frac{N_1X_1 + N_2X_2}{N_1 + N_2}$$

$$\overline{X}_{12} = 54, \ \overline{X}_1 = 59, \ \overline{X}_2 = 50, \ N_1 = x, \ N_2 = 100 - x$$

$$\overline{X}_{12} = 54 = \frac{x \times 59 + (100 - x)50}{x + 100 - x}$$

$$54 = \frac{59x + 5000 - 50x}{100}$$

$$9x = 5400 - 5000$$

$$x = \frac{400}{9} = 44.4\%$$

$$N_2 = 100 - x = 100 - 44.4 = 55.6\%$$

Percentage of male students = 44.4%

Percentage of female students = 55.6%

Illustration 53: *The average weekly wages of 150 literate workers in a factory is Rs. 500 and average weekly wages of 200 illiterate workers in the factory is Rs. 350. Calculate the average weekly wages of the workers in the factory.*

Solution: Calculation of average weekly wages of the workers in the factory.

$\overline{X}_1 = 500, \quad N_1 = 150 \qquad \overline{X}_2 = 350, \quad N_2 = 200$

$$\overline{X}_{12} = \frac{N_1\overline{X}_1 + N_2\overline{X}_2}{N_1 + N_2}$$

$$= \frac{150 \times 500 + 200 \times 350}{150 + 200} = \frac{75000 + 70000}{350}$$

$$= \frac{145000}{350} = 414.2857 = 414.29$$

Illustration 54: *The average monthly production in a factory is calculated as 575 tonnes. Later on it was discovered that the production of February, March and October are wrongly added as 400, 375 and 590 tonnes.instead of 420, 340 and 599 respectively. Calculate the correct arithmetic mean.*

Solution: Calculation of correct arithmetic mean

$N = 12$ (Total months in a year), $\overline{X} = 575$

$$\overline{X} = \frac{\Sigma X}{N}$$

$$575 = \frac{\Sigma X}{12}$$

$$\Sigma X = 12 \times 575 = 6900$$

Total production in the year = 6900

	Σx		6900
Less : Incorrect Items			
	Feb	400	
	March	375	
	Oct.	590	1365
			5535
Add : Correct Items			
	Feb.	420	
	March	340	
	Oct.	599	1359
			6894

Correct total production 6894

$$\text{Correct Mean} = \frac{6894}{12} = 574.5$$

Illustration 55: *Calculate the average increase in the income of the families of a town. The increase of income is 5% in 1988, 12% in 1989, 8% in 1990 and 9% in 1991.*

Solution: Calculation of geometric mean

Year	*% of icrease*	*Total income of the year taking the preceding year as 100*	*Log X*
1988	5	105	2.0212
1989	12	112	2.0492
1990	8	108	2.0334
1991	9	109	2.0374
			Σlog X = 8.1412

$$\text{G.M.} = \text{Antilog}\,\frac{\sum \log X}{N}$$

$\sum \log X = 8.1412,\ N = 4$

$$\text{G.M.} = \text{Antilog}\frac{8.1412}{4} = \text{Antilog}(2.0353) = 108.5$$

The average increase from year 1988 to 1991 is

$$= 108.5 - 100 = 8.5\%$$

Illustration 56: *Calculate geometric mean for the following data.*

Daily Income(Rs.)	*0-20*	*20-40*	*40-60*	*60-80*	*80-100*
No. of workers	*5*	*7*	*12*	*8*	*4*

Solution: Calculation of geometric mean.

Daily Income	*m*	*f*	*log m*	*f log m*
0-20	10	5	1.0000	5.0000
20-40	30	7	1.4771	10.3397
40-60	50	12	1.6990	20.3880
60-80	70	8	1.8451	14.7608
80-100	90	4	1.9542	7.8168
		$N = 36$		$\Sigma f log\ m = 58.3053$

When $N = 36$, $\Sigma f\ log\ m = 58.3053$

$$\text{Geometric Mean} = \text{Antilog}\ \frac{\Sigma \log m}{N}$$

$$= \text{Antilog}\frac{58.3053}{36} = \text{Antilog}\,(1.6195916)$$

$$= \text{Antilog}(1.6196) = 41.65$$

Geometric mean = 41.65.

Illustration 57: *A person walks 10 Kms at 3 Kms per hour. Again 6 Kms at 2 Km p.h and 5 Kms at 4 Km p.h. Calculate the average speed of the person.*

Solution: Harmonic Mean (Weighted)

$$\text{H.M.}_{(w)} = \frac{\Sigma w}{\left(\frac{1}{x_1}\times w_1\right)+\left(\frac{1}{x_2}\times w_2\right)+\left(\frac{1}{x_3}\times w_3\right)}$$

$x_1 = 3, \quad x_2 = 2, \quad x_3 = 4, \quad w_1 = 10, \quad w_2 = 6, \quad w_3 = 5$

$$\Sigma w = w_1 + w_2 + w_3 = 10 + 6 + 5$$

$$\Sigma w = 21$$

$$\text{H.M.}_{(w)} = \frac{\Sigma w}{\left(\frac{1}{x_1} \times w_1\right) + \left(\frac{1}{x_2} \times w_2\right) + \left(\frac{1}{x_3} \times w_3\right)}$$

$$= \frac{21}{\left(\frac{1}{3} \times 10\right) + \left(\frac{1}{2} \times 6\right) + \left(\frac{1}{4} \times 5\right)}$$

$$= \frac{21}{3.33 + 3 + 1.25} = \frac{21}{7.58} = 2.77$$

Thus, the average speed for the entire journey is 2.77 kmph.

Illustration 58: *A car driver travels to a distance of 150 Kms on an average of 60 Km p.h. On his return journey his average speed per hour is 67 Km p.h. Calculate the average speed per hour.*

Solution: Harmonic mean

$$\text{H.M.} = \frac{N}{\left(\frac{1}{x_1} + \frac{1}{x_1} \cdots \frac{1}{x_1}\right)}$$

$N = 2, \quad x_1 = 60, \quad x_2 = 67$

$$\text{H.M.} = \frac{N}{\left(\frac{1}{x_1} + \frac{1}{x_2}\right)} = \frac{2}{\frac{1}{60} + \frac{1}{67}} = 63.3$$

Average speed per hour is 63.3 Kms.

Illustration 59: *Calculate D_3, D_5, P_{27}, P_{32}, Q_1, Q_2, Q_3 and median from the following data.*

x	*120*	*140*	*145*	*169*	*180*	*195*	*200*
f	*4*	*13*	*15*	*27*	*32*	*15*	*2*

Solution: Calculation of Q_1, Q_2, Q_3, D_3, D_5, P_{27} and P_{32}.

X	f	cf
120	4	4
140	13	17
145	15	32
169	27	59
180	32	91
195	15	106
200	2	108
	N = 108	

$$Q_1 = \frac{N+1}{4} \text{ th item} = \frac{108+1}{4} \text{ th item}$$

$$= \frac{109}{4} = 27.25 \text{ th item} = 145$$

$$Q_2 = 2\frac{N+1}{4} \text{ th item} = (2 \times 27.25) \text{ th item}$$

$$= 54.5\text{th item} = 169$$

$$Q_3 = 3\frac{N+1}{4} \text{ th item} = (3 \times 27.25) \text{ th item}$$

$$= 81.75 \text{ th item} = 180$$

$$D_3 = 3\frac{N}{10} \text{ th item} = \left(3 \times \frac{108}{10}\right) \text{ th item}$$

$$= (3 \times 10.8) \text{ th item} = 32.4 \text{ th item} = 145$$

$$D_5 = 5\frac{N}{4} \text{ th item} = \left(5 \times \frac{108}{10}\right) \text{ th item}$$

$$= (5 \times 10.8) \text{ th item} = 54 \text{ th item} = 169$$

$$P_{27} = 27\frac{N}{100} \text{ th item} = \left(27 \times \frac{108}{100}\right) \text{ th item}$$

$$= (27 \times 1.08) \text{ th item} = 29.16 \text{ th item} = 145$$

$$P_{32} = 32\frac{N}{100} \text{ th item} = \left(32\times\frac{108}{100}\right) \text{th item}$$

$$= (32\times1.08)\text{th item} = 34.56 \text{ th item} = 169$$

Illustration 60: *The following data is related to the net profit of 75 factories located in a city. Calculate* Q_1, Q_2, Q_3, *Median* D_7, P_{80} *and* P_{67}

Net Profit (Rs. in '000s)	*0-25*	*25-35*	*35-45*	*45-55*	*55-65*
No. of factories	*12*	*18*	*30*	*8*	*7*

Solution: Calculation of Q_1, Q_2, Q_3, D_7, P_{80} and P_{67}

X '000s	*f*	*cf*
0-25	12	12
25-35	18	30
35-45	30	60
45-55	8	68
55-65	7	75
	$N = 75$	

$$Q_1 = \frac{N}{4} \text{ th item} = \frac{75}{4} = 18.75 \text{ th item}$$

Hence, $cf = 12, L = 25, f = 18, i = 10$

$$Q_1 = L + \left(\frac{N/4 - cf}{f}\right)\times i = 25 + \left(\frac{18.75 - 12}{18}\right)\times 10$$

$$= 25 + \frac{6.75}{18}\times 10 = 25 + (0.375\times 10)$$

$$= 25 + 3.75 = 28.75$$

$$Q_2 = \left(\frac{2N}{4}\right) \text{th item} = 2\times 18.75 \text{ th item} = 37.5\text{th item}$$

Hence, $L = 35$, $f = 30$, $cf = 30$, $c = 10$

$$Q_2 = L + \left(\frac{2N/4 - cf}{30}\right) \times c = 35 + \left(\frac{37.5 - 30}{30}\right) \times 10$$

$$= 35 + \frac{7.5}{30} \times 10 = 35 + (0.25 \times 10)$$

$$= 35 + 2.5 = 37.5$$

$$Q_3 = \left(\frac{3N}{4}\right) \text{th item} = 3 \times 18.75 \text{ th item} = 56.25\text{th item}$$

Hece, $L = 35,\ f = 30,\ cf = 30,\ c = 10$

$$Q_3 = L + \left(\frac{3N/4 - cf}{30}\right) \times c = 35 + \left(\frac{56.25 - 30}{30}\right) \times 10$$

$$= 35 + \frac{26.25}{30} \times 10 = 35 + 0.875 \times 10$$

$$= 35 + 8.75 = 43.75$$

$$D_7 = \left(\frac{7N}{4}\right) \text{th item} = \frac{7 \times 75}{10} \text{ th item} = 52.5\text{th item}$$

With $L = 35,\ cf = 30,\ f = 30,\ c = 10$

$$D_7 = 35 + \left(\frac{52.5 - 30}{30}\right) \times 10 = 35 + \frac{22.5}{30} \times 10$$

$$= 35 + (0.75 \times 10) = 35 + 7.5 = 42.5$$

$$P_{80} = \left(\frac{80N}{100}\right) \text{th item} = \frac{80 \times 75}{100} \text{ th item} = 60 \text{ th item}$$

Hence $L = 35,\ f = 30,\ cf = 30,\ c = 10$

$$P_{80} = 3L + \left(\frac{80N - cf}{f}\right) \times c = 35 + \frac{60 - 30}{30} \times 10$$

$$= 35 + \frac{30}{30}(10) = 35 + 10 = 45$$

$$P_{67} = \left(\frac{67N}{100}\right) \text{th item} = \frac{67 \times 75}{100} \text{ th item} = 50.25 \text{ th item}$$

Hence, $L = 35,\ f = 30,\ cf = 30,\ c = 10$

$$P_{67} = L + \left(\frac{67N/10 - cf}{f}\right) \times c = 35 + \frac{50.25 - 30}{30} \times 10$$

$$= 35 + \frac{20.25}{30} \times 10 = 35 + 0.675 \times 10$$

$$= 35 + 6.75 = 41.75$$

Illustration 61: *Find out the missing frequencies for the following data relating to the daily income of 60 families.*

Daily Income (Rs.)	*0-10*	*10-20*	*20-30*	*30-40*	*40-50*	*50-60*	*60-70*
No. of workers	*3*	*7*	*?*	*?*	*?*	*12*	*8*

The median and mode of the above distribution are 37.33 and 34 repectively.

Solution: Assume the missing frequencies as x_1, x_2 and x_3. Calculation of missing frequencies.

Daily Income (Rs.) X	*No. of families* f	*cf*
0-10	3	3
10-20	7	10
20-30	x_1	$10 + x_1$
30-40	x_2	$10 + x_1 + x_2$
40-50	x_3	$10 + x_1 + x_2 + x_3$
50-60	12	52 (i.e., 60 - 8)
60-70	8	60
	$N = 60$	

$$x_1 + x_2 + x_3 = 60 - (3 + 7 + 12 + 8) = 60 - 30 = 30$$

$$x_3 = 30 - (x_1 + x_2) = 30 - x_1 - x_2$$

Mode is 34 which lies in the model class 30-40.

$$\text{Mode} = L + \frac{f_1 + f_0}{2f_1 - f_0 - f_2} \times i$$

$f_0 = x_1,\ \ f_1 = x_2,\ \ f_2 = 30 - x_2 - x_2,\ \ L = 30,\ \ i = 10$

$$\text{Mode} = 34 = 30 + \frac{x_2 - x_1}{2x_2 - x_1 - (30 - x_1 - x_2)} \times 10$$

$$34 - 30 = \frac{10x_2 - 10x_1}{2x_2 - x_1 - 30 + x_1 + x_2}$$

$$4(3x_2 - 30) = 10x_2 - 10x_1$$

$$12x_2 - 120 = 10x_2 - 10x_1$$

$$10x_1 + 2x_2 = 120 \qquad \ldots \text{(i)}$$

$$\text{Median} = L + \frac{N/2 - cf}{f} \times i$$

$L = 30,\ N/2 = 60/2 = 30,\ \ cf = 10 + x_1,\ \ f = x_2,\ \ i = 10.$

$$\text{Median} = 37.33 = 30 + \frac{30 - (10 + x_1)}{x_2} \times 10$$

$$37.33 - 30 = \frac{200 - 10x_1}{x_2}$$

$$7.33x_2 = 200 - 10x_1$$

$$10x_1 + 7.33x_2 = 200 \qquad \ldots \text{(ii)}$$

$$10x_1 + 2x_2 = 120 \qquad \ldots \text{(i)}$$

(ii)- (i) $\quad 5.33x_2 = 80$

$$x_2 = 15$$

(i) $\quad 10x_1 + 2 \times 15 = 120$

$$10x_1 = 120 - 30$$

$$x_1 = \frac{90}{10} = 9$$

$$x_3 = 30 - x_1 - x_2 = 30 - 9 - 15 = 6$$

Hence the frequencies are, $x_1 = 9$; $x_2 = 15$ and $x_3 = 6$.

Illustration 62: *Calculate mode from the following data.*

X	*25*	*30*	*35*	*40*	*45*	*50*	*55*
f	*7*	*11*	*17*	*15*	*14*	*10*	*11*

Solution: Calculation of Mode.

X	*I*	*II*	*III*	*IV*	*V*	*VI*
25	7					
		18				
30	11			35		
			28			
35	17					
		32				
40	15				43	
			29			
45	14			39		46
50	10	24				
			21		35	
55	11					

Probable Model Value

Col. No.	*30*	*35*	*40*	*45*	*50*
I	-	1	-	-	-
II	-	1	1	-	-
III	-	-	1	1	-
IV	-	-	1	1	1
V	1	1	1	-	-
VI	-	1	1	1	-
	1	*4*	*5*	*3*	*1*

Mode = 40

Illustration 63: *Calculate mode from the following data.*

Average Monthly Sales (Rs. in '000s)	*No. of Factories*
Less than 20	7
Less than 30	15
Less than 40	22
Less than 50	30
Less than 60	42
Less than 70	53
Less than 80	59
Less than 90	70
Less than 100	80

Solution: Calculation of Mode

Monthly sales X '000s	*cf*	*f*	*m*	*(m-A) / c A = 55, c = 10 d*	*fd*
0-20	7	7	15	-4	-28
20-30	15	8	25	-3	-24
30-40	22	7	35	-2	-14
40-50	30	8	45	-1	-8
50-60	42	12	55	0	0
60-70	53	11	65	1	11
70-80	59	6	75	2	12
80-90	70	11	85	3	33
90-100	80	10	95	4	40
		N = 80			*Σfd = 22*

Mode = 3 Median - 2 Mean

Median = Size of N/2 th item

= 80/2 = 40 th item

Hence median lies in the class 50-60

$$\text{Median} = L + \frac{N/2 - cf}{f} \times c$$

where $L = 50$, $N/2 = 40$, $cf = 30$, $f = 12$, $c = 10$

$$\text{Median} = 50 + \frac{40-30}{12} \times 10 = 50 + 8.33 = 58.33$$

$$\text{Mean} \quad \overline{X} = A + \frac{\Sigma fd}{N} \times c$$

$A = 55$, $\Sigma fd = 22$, $N = 80$, $c = 10$

$$\overline{X} = 55 + \frac{22}{80} \times 10 = 55 + 2.75 = 57.75$$

$$\text{Mode} = 3 \ \text{Median} - 2 \ \text{Mean}$$

$$= 3 \times 58.33 - 2 \times 57.75$$

$$= 174.99 - 115.5 = 59.49$$

Hence model monthly sales is Rs. 59.49 Thousands.

Illustration 64: *Average rainfall of a city from Monday to Saturday is 3 cm. Due to heavy rainfall on Sunday the average for the week increased to 5 cm. What was the rainfall on Sunday.*

(Kerala: Section B April 1997)

Solution:

Average rainfall for 7 days	=	3 cms
Total rainfall for 7 days = 7 x 3	=	21 cms
Average rainfall for 7 days	=	5 cms
Total rainfall for 7 days = 7 x 5	=	35 cms
Rainfall for 6 days when the average rainfall is 3	=	18 cms
Rainfall on Sunday = 35 - 18	=	17 cms

Illustration 65: *The mean of 20 values is 45. If one of these values is taken as 64 instead of 46. Find the correct mean.*

(MGU: Section B September 1994)

Solution: Arithmetic mean

$$\overline{X} = \frac{\Sigma X}{N}$$

$$45 = \frac{\Sigma X}{20}$$

$$\Sigma X = 45 \times 20 = 900$$

Deduct : the wrong value 64 i.e., 900 - 64 = 836

Add : the correct value as 46 i.e., 836 + 46 = 882

\ Correct arithmetic mean = 882/20 = 44.1

Illustration 66: *The mean monthly pay to all employees in a company was Rs. 600. The mean monthly salary paid to the male and female employees were Rs. 620 and Rs. 520 respectively. Obtain the percentage of male and female employees in the company.* (Kerala: Section B September 1993)

Solution: Assume the total number of employees as 100; and number of male employees as x.

Number of female employees = $100 - x$

Arithmetic mean,

$$\overline{X} = \frac{N_1\overline{X}_1 + N_2\overline{X}_2}{N_1 + N_2}$$

$$600 = \frac{620 \times x + 520(100 - x)}{100}$$

$$620x + 52000 - 520x = 600 \times 100$$

$$52000 + 100x = 60000$$

$$100x = 60{,}000 - 52000$$

$$x = \frac{8000}{100} = 80$$

No. of female workers = $100 - x$ = 100 - 80 = 20

$\therefore$ Male employees = 80%

Female employees = 20%

Illustration 67: *The mean age of a combined group of men and women is 30 years. If the mean age of the group of men is 32 and that of the group of women is 27, find the percentage of men and women in the group.* (MGU: Section B April 1997)

Solution: Assume the total number of employees as 100 and the total number of men as x. Hence, the total number of women = 100 - x

Arithmetic mean,

$$\overline{X} = \frac{N_1\overline{X}_1 + N_2\overline{X}_2}{N_1 + N_2}$$

$$30 = \frac{32 \times x + 27(100 - x)}{100}$$

$$32x + 2700 - 27x = 30 \times 100$$

$$2700 + 5x = 3000$$

$$5x = 3{,}000 - 2700$$

$$x = \frac{300}{5} = 60$$

Number of women = 100 $- x$ = 100 - 60 = 40

Hence, Number of men = 60%

Number of women = 40%

Illustration 68: *In a moderately asymmetrical distribution the mode and mean are 32.1 and 35.4 respectively. Find the value of median.* (Kerala: Section B April 1998)

Solution:

Mode = 3 Median - 2 Mean

32.1 = 3 Median - 2 (35.4)

3 Median = 32.1 + 70.8

Median = 102.9/3 = 34.3

Illustration 69: *Find the median marks from the following marks of 9 students. 70, 60, 75, 90, 65, 80, 42, 65, 72.*

(Kerala: Section B April 1998)

Solution: Arrangement of marks is 42, 60, 65, 65, 70, 72, 75, 80, 90.

$$\text{Median} = \frac{N+1}{2} \text{ th item} = \frac{9+1}{2} = 5\text{th item}$$

Hence, Median = 70 marks

Illustration 70: *From the following data, calculate the value of harmonic mean.*

Income (Rs.)	*No. of Persons*
10-20	*4*
20-30	*6*
30-40	*10*
40-50	*7*
50-60	*3*

(MGU: Section B September 1993)

Solution: Calculation of Harmonic Mean.

Income (Rs.)	*f*	*m*	*1/m*	*f/m*
10-20	4	15	0.0667	0.2666
20-30	6	25	0.0400	0.2400
30-40	10	35	0.0286	0.2857
40-50	7	45	0.0222	0.1555
50-60	3	55	0.0182	0.0545
	$\Sigma f = 30$			$\Sigma f/m = 1.0023$

$$\text{H.M.} = \frac{N}{\Sigma\left(\frac{f}{m}\right)} = \frac{30}{1.0023} = 29.93$$

Illustration 71: *From the following data obtain the value of mode by using the formula Mean – Mode = 3 (Mean - Median)*

No. of day absent	*No. of workers*
Less than 5	*29*
Less than 10	*224*
Less than 15	*465*
Less than 20	*585*
Less than 25	*634*
Less than 30	*644*
Less than 35	*650*

Solution: Calculation of Mode

No. of days absent	*Class interval*	*f*	*cf*	*m*	*fm*
Less than 5	0 - 5	29	29	2.5	72.5
Less than 10	5 - 10	195	224	7.5	1462.5
Less than 15	10 - 15	241	465	12.5	3012.5
Less than 20	15 - 20	120	585	17.5	2100
Less than 25	20 - 25	49	634	22.5	1102.5
Less than 30	25 - 30	10	644	27.5	275.0
Less than 35	30 - 35	6	650	32.5	195.0
		$\Sigma f = 650$			$\Sigma fm = 8220$

Arithmetic mean,

$$\overline{X} = \frac{\Sigma fm}{\Sigma f} = \frac{8220}{650} = 12.65$$

Median: Size of N/2 th item i.e., 650/2 = 325th item which is the class interval 10-15.

Hence $L = 10,\ f = 241,\ cf = 224,\ c = 5$.

$$\text{Median} = L + \frac{N/2 - cf}{f} \times c = 10 + \frac{325 - 224}{241} \times 5$$

$$= 10 + \frac{101 \times 5}{241} = 10 + 2.095 = 12.1$$

Mean – Mode	=	3 (Mean – Median)
12.65 – Mode	=	3 (12.65 – 12.1)
Mode	=	12.65 – 3(.55)
	=	12.65 – 1.65 = 11

Illustration 72: *A train runs 25 miles at a speed of 30 m.p.h, another 50 miles at a speed of 40 m.p.h, then due to repair of track travels for 6 minutes at a speed of 10 m.p.h. What is the average speed of the journey.* (Kerala: Section B April 1998)

Solution: Total time taken

$$= \frac{25}{30} + \frac{50}{40} + 6 \text{ minutes}$$

$$= 0.83 + 1.25 + \frac{6}{60} = 2.18 \text{ hours.}$$

Distance for 6 min. travel $= \frac{10}{60} \times 6 = 1$ mile

Total distance $= 25 + 50 + 1 = 76$ minutes.

$$\text{Average Speed (H.M.)} = \frac{N}{\Sigma\left(\frac{1}{x}\right)} = \frac{76}{2.18} = 34.86 \text{ mph.}$$

Illustration 73: *Three persons P, Q, R can prepare a model in 20, 40 and 25 minutes respectively. What is their average speed?*

(MGU: Section A April 1998)

Solution:

$$\text{Average speed (H.M)} = \frac{N}{\Sigma\left(\frac{1}{x}\right)} = \frac{3}{\left(\frac{1}{20} + \frac{1}{40} + \frac{1}{25}\right)}$$

$$= \frac{3}{0.05 + 0.025 + 0.04} = \frac{3}{0.115} = 26 \text{ minutes}$$

Illustration 74: *Recast the following cumulative table into the form of an ordinary frequency distribution. Draw a histogram and calculate mode from the histogram.*

No. of days absent	*No. of students*
Less than 5	*29*
Less than 10	*224*
Less than 15	*465*
Less than 20	*582*
Less than 25	*634*
Less than 30	*644*
Less than 35	*650*
Less than 40	*653*
Less than 45	*655*

(MGU: Section B April 1998)

Solution: Conversion of ordinary frequency distribution.

No. of days	*No. of*	*No. of days*	*Frequency*
Less than 5	29	0-5	29
Less than 10	224	5-10	195
Less than 15	465	10-15	241
Less than 20	582	15-20	117
Less than 25	634	20-25	52
Less than 30	644	25-30	10
Less than 35	650	30-35	6
Less than 40	653	35-40	3
Less than 45	655	40-45	2
			Total 655

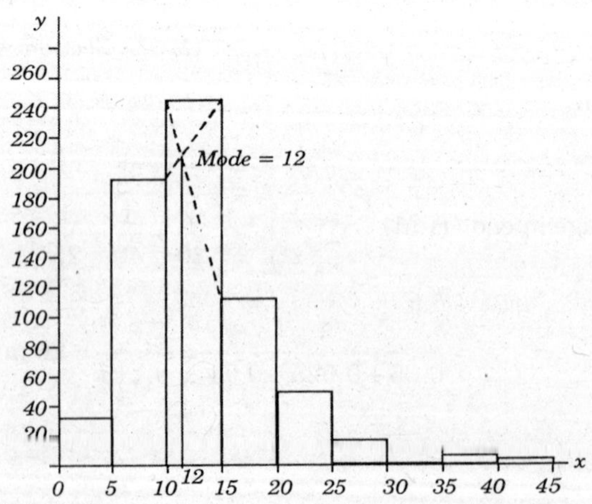

Illustration 75: *Draw a less than cumulative frequency polygon for the following distribution. Estimate graphically the number of persons between the age 27 and 42.*

Age (in years)	*No. of employees*
22.5	*50*
27.5	*70*
32.5	*100*
37.5	*180*
42.5	*150*
47.5	*120*
52.5	*70*
57.5	*59*

(MGU: Section B April 1997)

Solution: Less than Cumulative Series.

Age (in Years)	*No. of employees*
17.5	0
22.5	50
27.5	120
32.5	220
37.5	400
42.5	550
47.5	670
52.5	740
57.5	799

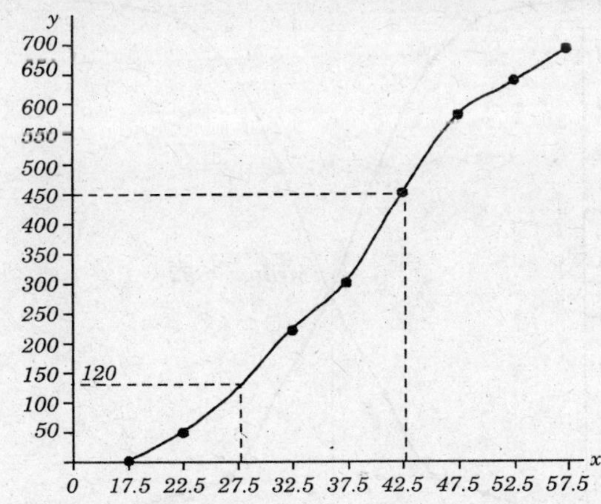

No. of employees between the age group of 27 and 42 = 550 – 120 = 430

Illustration 76: *Find the mode and median through graphical methods from the following data of marks obtained by 100 students.*

Class Interval	0-10	11-20	21-30	31-40	41-50	51-60	61-70	71-80	81-90	91-100
No. of students	2	3	5	15	18	26	20	8	2	1

(Kerala: Section C April 1994)

Solution: Calculation of Median

Calculation of Cumulative Frequencies.

Marks Less than	*No. of Students*	*Marks More than*	*No. of Students*
-	-	0	100
10	2	10	99
20	5	20	97
30	10	30	89
40	25	40	69
50	43	50	43
60	69	60	25
70	89	70	10
80	97	80	5
90	99	90	2
100	100	100	0

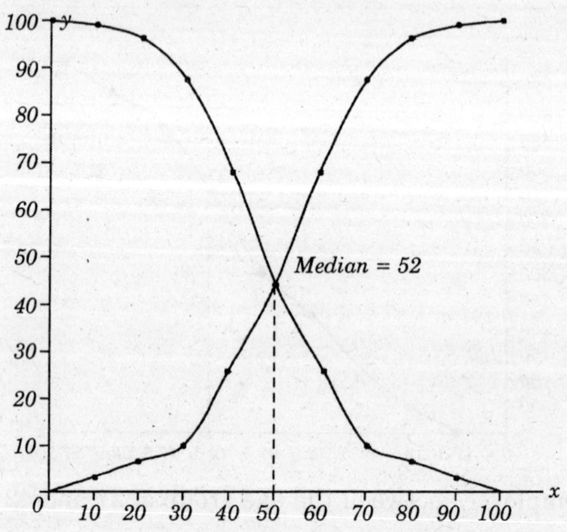

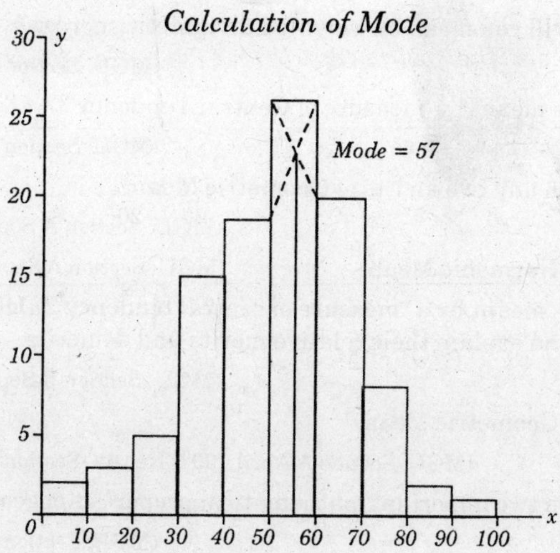

Exercises

1. Explain briefly, the different measures of central tendency.
2. What are the purposes of the measure of central tendency?
3. What are the objectives of calculating averages?
4. Define briefly the various M's of central tendency.
5. Define Statistical Average. What are the properties of an average?
6. What do you mean by A.M., G.M. and H.M? What are the differences between A.M and G.M and H.M?
7. What are the various measures of central tendency? Explain the merits and limitations.
8. Distinguish between median and quartiles. What are the circumstances for which median and quartiles can be applied?
9. Distinguish between weighted and unweighted mean.
10. Define different measures of central tendency. Which is the best measure of central tendency and why?
11. What is mode? Explain its importance as a measure of central tendency.
12. Explain the graphical method of locating the mode.
13. Prove with an example that A.M > G.M > H.M
14. Bring out the relative merits of various types of the central tendency. Define H.M.
15. Define H.M. Explain the situation where H.M can be applied as a measure of central tendency.
16. Give two properties of Median. (MGU: Section A April 1998)

17. What will you mean by weighted arithmetic agerage?

(MGU: Section A April 1998)

18. What is meant by 'measure of Central Tendency'?

(MGU: Section A April 1995)

19. Mention any two merits of Geometric Mean.

(MGU: Section A September 1994)

20. Define Harmonic Mean. (MGU: Section A September 1992)

21. What is meant by a "measure of central tendency"? Define median, mode and explain their relative merits and demerits.

(MGU: Section B September 1992)

22. Define Geometric Mean.

(MGU: Section A April 1992; Kerala: Section A April 1997)

23. Mention two important mathematical properties of geometic mean.

(MGU: Section A April 1992)

24. What is a measure of central tendency?

25. How is combined arithmetic mean calculated?

26. How would you determine median graphically?

(Kerala: Section B April 1996; Kerala: Section B April 1997)

27. How would you detemine mode graphically?

(Kerala: Section B April 1996)

28. Define and discuss the merits and limitation of the measure of central tendency. (Kerala: Section B April 1994)

29. Explain how arithmetic mean satisfies the various requirements of a good average. (Kerala: Section B April 1989)

30. Bring out arithmetic mean as a superior measure of central tendency. (Kerala: Section B September 1990)

31. State various measures of central tendency.

(Kerala: Section A April 1990)

32. State various measures of central tendency. Bring out relative merits of mean over others. (Kerala: Section B April 1990)

33. The following are the monthly expenditure in repees of 10 families in a city. Calculate arithmetic mean 750, 890, 1020, 690, 880, 1150, 1200, 1100, 990, 910. (Ans: 958)

34. Calculate arithmetic mean by (a) Direct method and (b) Short-cut method from the following data.

Class No.	1	2	3	4	5	6	7	8	9	10	11	12
Marks	74	32	56	40	79	84	92	27	30	41	52	67

(Ans: 56.17)

35. Calculate arithmetic mean for the following data.

(i) 1, 2, 3......upto 12th term.

(ii) 3, 6, 9......upto 8th term. (Ans: (i) 6.5 and (ii) 13.5)

36. Calculate arithmetic mean of the following data related to daily sales in rupees of a shop.

500, 690, 430, 670, 1200, 560, 860, 270, 340, 540, 360, 470, 590, 820, 210, 900, 700, 800, 910, 650, 520 (Ans: 618.57)

37. The probability of the appearance of heads in different tossing of coins were sudied. 9 coins were tossed for 370 times for this purpose. The apperance of heads in different toss was given below.

No. of heads x	0	1	2	3	4	5	6	7	8	9
Frequency	8	51	72	60	49	52	30	25	7	16

(Ans: A.M. = 4.5)

38. The following data are related to the daily wages of workers in a village. Calculate arithmetic mean.

Daily wages (Rs.)	32	37	42	44	47	50	55
No. of workers	4	7	9	20	15	9	3

(Ans: 44.25)

39. Calculate arithmetic mean from the following data.

x	0-10	10-20	20-30	30-40	40-50	50-60
f	27	32	57	73	61	46

(Ans: 33.34)

40. Find out arithmetic mean of the following data.

Marks	0-15	16-30	31-45	46-60	61-75	76-90
No. of students	4	7	12	9	6	2

(Ans: 42)

41. Calculate the missing variable of the following distribution.

Income (Rs.)	240	300	325	x	475	520	600
No. of people	3	2	9	12	15	4	2

Arithmetic mean of the above distribution is 395. (Ans: 326.25)

42. The arithmetic mean of the following distribution is 58.5 units. Find the missing frquency.

Sales (in units)	35-45	45-55	55-65	65-75	75-85	85-95
No. of factories	21	?	30	15	17	10

(Ans: 60)

43. The mean production of 10 factories is 145 tonnes. If the production in tonnes of 9 factories are 160, 190, 200, 85, 65, 170, 150, 100 and 115. Find the production of the 10th factory. (Ans: 205)

44. Prepare a frequency table with class intervals of 10 and calculate the arithmetic mean from the following data related with marks obtained by 60 students of a class.

42, 56, 72, 85, 30, 27, 15, 8, 5, 97, 80, 78

31, 27, 19, 29, 32, 45, 53, 67, 73, 79, 82, 91

95, 92, 35, 27, 57, 42, 32, 54, 79, 83, 81, 71

22, 18, 17, 16, 9, 7, 5, 4, 39, 2, 6, 4

54, 59, 63, 72, 89, 44, 32, 8, 11, 18, 93, 75 (Ans: 45.63)

45. Calculate arithmetic mean from the following data.

Income (Rs.)	*No. of families*
Below 200	12
Below 400	18
Below 600	27
Below 800	39
Below 1000	57
Below 1200	78
Below 1400	92
Below 1600	120

(Ans: 1093)

46. Compute arithmetic mean of the following data.

Production (in tonnes)	*No. of factories*
More than 50	150
More than 75	127
More than 100	115
More than 125	101
More than 150	97
More than 175	64
More than 200	53
More than 225	32
More than 250	17

(Ans: 163.5)

47. The mean marks of 60 students of a class is 55. Later on it was found that the marks of two students were wrongly entered as 34 and 67 instead of 43 and 76. Calculate the correct arithmetic mean.

(Ans: 55.3)

48. The mean production of a factory for 12 months is 1250 units. After verification of records it was found that the production for January, April and November are wrongly calculated as 1540, 1270 and 2000 units instead of 1450, 1720 and 1900 units. Calculate the correct arithmetic mean. (Ans: 1272)

49. The average marks scored by 42 male students in a class is 62.5 marks and the average marks scored by 33 female students in the same class is 64.2. Calculate the average mark scored by all the students in the class. (Ans: 63.25)

50. The average monthly sales in a shop for the first 7 months is Rs. 3250 and for the next 5 months is Rs. 4150. Calculate the average sales of the shop for the 12 months. (Ans: 3625)

51. The mean weekly wage of 200 workers in a factory is Rs. 320. The mean weekly wage of male workers is Rs. 360 and of female workers is Rs. 300. Find the number of male and female workers in the factory. (Ans: 67 & 133)

52. The mean weight of girls and boys in a class is 54.5. If the mean weight of boys is 56.2 and of girls is 52.3, calculate the percentage of boys and girls in the class. (Ans: 56.4% & 43.6%)

53. Compute geometric mean of the following data. 127, 39, 57, 94, 326, 515 (Ans; 128.3)

54. Calculate geometric mean of the following data related with the weight of 12 students in a class.

Class No.	1	2	3	4	5	6	7	8	9	10	11	12
Weight (in Kgm)	44	49	51	46	48	52	47	45	44	50	49	48

(Ans: 47.68)

55. Calculate geometric mean from the following data.

Income (Rs.)	45	52	59	62	75	80
No. of families	3	9	6	5	2	1

(Ans: 56.96)

56. Calculate geometric mean from the following data.

Marks	0-10	10-20	20-30	30-40	40-50	50-60	60-70
No. of students	5	7	12	8	9	5	4

(Ans: 27.15)

57. Calculate geometric mean and harmonic mean from the data given below. 42, 57, 21, 115, 127, 39, 55 (Ans: G.M = 55.25; H.M = 46.9)

58. Calculate harmonic mean and geometric mean from the data given below.

x	5	12	17	20	25	30
f	3	2	5	9	5	2

(Ans: H.M = 14.6; G.M = 17.1)

59. Calculate harmonic mean of the following data.

Marks	0-20	20-40	40-60	60-80	80-100
No. of students	4	5	12	8	6

(Ans: 35.4)

◆ Chapter 7 ◆

Measures of Dispersion

The measures of central tendency give one single value which represents the entire data. But it fails to give complete description of the data. It does not explain how the variables scatter around the central value. Though frequencies of data in the lowest values are more than highest value, the central value may be relatively highest value and vice verse. Hence, there is a need to know the complete character of the distribution. Measures of dispersion give a complete picture about the character and the degree of extenstion of the data from the central value.

I Definition of Dispersion

Dispersion is a measure of the degree of scatter of data from the central value. A.L. Bowley defines dispersion as, *"Dispersion is the measure of the variation of the items"*. According to Pro. L.R. Connor, dispersion is a measure of the extent to which the individual items vary.

John F. Griffin defines dispersion as, *"A measure of variation or dipersion describes the degree of scatter shown by value"*.

Spriegel states that the degree to which numerical data tend to spread about an average value is called the variation or dispersion of the data. According to W.F.L. Dick "*Dispersion or spread is the degree of the scatter or variation of the variables about a central value.*

It is noted from the definitions that dispersion means a measure of the degree of deviation or scatter of data from the central value.

II Objectives or Importance of the Measure of Dispersion

Following are the objectives of the measure of dispersion.

(1) To find out the reliability of an average: The data is more reliable when it is closely related with the central value. When

the scatter of data is more it could not be taken as a good measure. In order to know the reliability, dispersion technique can be applied. If the dispersion is of smaller value, then it means the data are more close to the central value; or it means the degree of deviation is small. When the dispersion is great, it indicates that the data are more deviated from the central value; or the degree of deviation is great. Hence, the data may be taken as a reliable one, when the dispersion is of smaller value.

(2) To control the variation of data from the central value: The measures of deviation helps to know the causes and nature of variation, so as to control the variations. It helps to measure the extent of variation from the standard quality, of various works carried in industries. Hence a corrective measure can be taken, after identifying the causes for the deviation. The Government can also take suitable policies to remove the inequalities in the distribution of income and wealth, after studying the dispersion of the income and wealth.

(3) To compare two or more set of data regarding their variability: Dispersion techniques can be applied to find out the uniformity of two or more set of data with regard to the degree of variation. The lowest degree of variation means the greatest uniformity, reliability and consistency of the data.

III Methods of Measuring Dispersion

The important methods of measuring dispersion are as follows.

(1) Range

(2) Quartile Deviation

(3) Mean Deviation

(4) Standard Deviation and

(5) Lorenz Curve.

(1) Range: Range is the difference between the largest value and the smallest value of the variables.

Hence, *Range = Largest Value – Smallest Value*

$$R = L - S$$

$$\text{Coefficient of Range} = \frac{L-S}{L+S}$$

Illustration 1. *Calculate Range from the following observation. Also find the value of coefficient of Range.*

75, 29, 96, 15, 7, 8, 11, 7, 4, 9

Solution: Range $= L - S$

$= 96 - 4 = 92$

$$\text{Coefficient of Range} = \frac{L-S}{L+S} = \frac{96-4}{96+4} = \frac{92}{100}$$

$= 0.92$

Advantages

It is very easy to calculate range. The result of range can be obtained within a very short period.

Drawbacks

It is not a correct measure since only two values of the variables are taken for calculation. If data are not evenly distributed then the range, as a measure of dispersion become a waste and meaningless.

(2) Quartile Deviation: Quartile deviation is otherwise called as Inter Quartile Range. It is the difference between the third quartile and the first quartile, divided by two

$$\text{Hence, Quartile Deviation, Q.D} = \frac{Q_3 - Q_1}{2}$$

Where Q_3 = third quartile and Q_1 = first quartile.

$$\text{Co-efficient of quartile deviation} = \frac{Q_3 - Q_1}{Q_3 + Q_1}$$

The values of Q_3 and Q_1 may also be obtained through the following equation.

$$Q_3 = \text{Median} + \text{Q.D}$$

$$Q_1 = \text{Median} - \text{Q.D}$$

Illustration 2. *Calculate quartile deviation from the following data.*

25, 15, 30, 45, 40, 20, 50

Also calculate co-efficient of quartile deviation.

Solution: Variables 15, 20, 25, 30, 40, 45, 50

$$Q_1 = \frac{N+1}{4} \text{ th item } = \frac{7+1}{4} = \text{ 2nd item } \quad i.e. \text{ 20}$$

$$Q_3 = \frac{3(N+1)}{4} \text{ th item } = \frac{3(7+1)}{4} = \text{ 6th item } \quad i.e. \text{ 45}$$

$$QD = \frac{Q_3 - Q_1}{2} = \frac{45-20}{2} = \frac{25}{2} = 12.5$$

$$\text{Co-efficient of Quartile Deviation} = \frac{Q_3 - Q_1}{Q_3 + Q_1}$$

$$= \frac{45-20}{45+20} = \frac{25}{65} = 0.385$$

Illustration 3. *Find out the value of quartile deviation and co-efficient of quartile deviation.*

Marks	*25*	*30*	*40*	*50*	*60*	*70*	*80*	*90*
No. of students	*4*	*7*	*12*	*8*	*9*	*15*	*7*	*3*

Solution: Calculation of Quartiles.

Marks X	*No. of students* *f*	*Cum. no. of students* *cf*
25	4	4
30	7	11
40	12	23
50	8	31
60	9	40
70	15	55
80	7	62
90	3	65

$$Q_1 = \frac{N+1}{4} \text{ th item } = \frac{65+1}{4} \text{ th item } = 16.5 \text{ th item}$$

i.e. = 40 marks

$$Q_3 = \frac{3(N+1)}{4} \text{ th item } = \frac{3(65+1)}{4} \text{ th item } = 49.5 \text{ th item}$$

i.e. = 70 marks

$$Q.D. = \frac{Q_3 - Q_1}{2} = \frac{70-40}{2} = 15 \text{ marks.}$$

Co-efficient of $Q.D. = \frac{Q_3 - Q_1}{Q_3 + Q_1} = \frac{70-40}{70+40} = \frac{30}{110} = 0.27$

Illustration 4. *Compute quartile deviation and co-efficient of quartile deviation from the following data.*

X	0-10	10-20	20-30	30-40	40-50	50-60
f	5	12	15	9	10	3

Solution: Calculation of Q.D.

X	f	cf
0-10	5	5
10-20	12	17
20-30	15	32
30-40	9	41
40-50	10	51
50-60	3	54

$$Q_1 = \frac{N}{4} \text{th item} = \frac{54}{4} \text{ th item} = 13.5 \text{ th item}$$

which lies in 10-20, Hence L = 10, cf = 5, f = 12, and i = 10.

$$Q_1 = L + \left(\frac{N/4 - cf}{f}\right) \times i = 30 + \frac{13.5-5}{12} \times 10$$

$$= 30 + \frac{85}{12} = 37.08$$

$$Q_3 = \frac{3N}{4} \text{th item} = \frac{3 \times 54}{4} = 40.5 \text{ th item}$$

Which lies in 30 - 40. Hence L = 30, cf = 32, f = 9, i = 10

$$Q_3 = L + \left(\frac{3N - cf}{f}\right) \times i = 30 + \left(\frac{40.5-32}{9}\right) \times 10$$

$$= 30 + \frac{85}{9} = 39.44$$

$$\text{Co-efficient of } Q.D = \frac{Q_3 - Q_1}{Q_3 + Q_1} = \frac{39.44 - 17.08}{39.44 + 17.08} = \frac{22.36}{56.52} = 0.396$$

Advantages

(1) Quartile deviation is superior to range as a measure of dispersion.

(2) It can be measured for open-end distribution.

(3) It cannot be affected by extreme values.

Drawbacks

(1) It is not capable of further algebraic analysis.

(2) Sampling fluctuations affect much of its value.

(3) It is not a good measure for distribution with greater degree of variation.

(3) Mean Deviation: Range and Quartile deviation are calculated with the help of two data of a series. In the calculation of range only 2 extreme values; and in quartile deviation only quartiles are taken into consideration, for the measurement of dispersion. They do not represent all the items of the series. But mean deviation is computed by taking into account all the items of the series.

Mean deviation, is otherwise called as Average deviation. It is a measure of deviation based on all the items in a distribution. Mean deviation may be defined as the arithmetic average of the series. While calculating the sum of the deviations, minus (-) should be ignored i.e., it should be treated as positive (+) value.

Calculation of Mean Deviation

(i) Mean Deviation for individual observations:

$$M.D. = \frac{\Sigma|D|}{N}$$

$\Sigma|D|$ indicates, the sum of deviations from the Mean or Median or Mode. $|D|$ can be read as modulus D. N indicates the total frequencies.

$$\text{Co-efficient of Mean Deviation} = \frac{\text{M.D}}{\text{Mean or Median or Mode}}$$

For calculating co-efficient of M.D., divide M.D by mean if deviations are taken from Arithmetic mean; or divide by Median if deviations are taken from median; or divide M.D by mode if it is taken from mode.

(ii) Mean Deviation for Discrete Series:

$$M.D. = \frac{\Sigma f\,|D|}{N}$$

Where, *f*- represents frequency. Here the deviations from mean or median or mode of the variables should be multiplied by respective frequencies.

(iii) Mean Deviation for Continuous Series:

$$M.D. = \frac{\Sigma f\,|D|}{N}$$

The deviations of the mid points of class intervals from mean or median or mode should be multiplied by the respective frequencies. Then the sum of these deviations should be divided by the total number of frequencies to get the mean deviation.

Illustration 5. *Find out the value of mean deviation and its co-efficient from the data given below:* 50, 70, 45, 20, 80, 90, 25, 30, 40, 10.

Solution: Calculation of mean deviation.

X	$\|D\| = (X - \overline{X})$ $x - 46$
10	36
20	26
25	21
30	16
40	6
45	1
50	4
70	24
80	34
90	44
$\Sigma x = 460$	$\Sigma\|D\| = 212$

$$\bar{x} = \frac{\Sigma x}{N} = \frac{460}{10} = 46$$

$$M.D. = \frac{\Sigma|D|}{N} = \frac{212}{10} = 21.2$$

$$\text{Co-efficient of M.D.} = \frac{\text{M.D}}{\text{Mean}} = \frac{21.2}{46} = 0.461$$

Illustration 6. *Calculate mean deviation from mean, median and mode from the following data. Also calculate the co-efficient of mean deviation.* 45, 5, 10, 45, 25, 45, 35

Solution: Calculation of M.D

X	$\lvert D \rvert = X - \bar{x}$ (X- 30)	$\lvert D \rvert = X$ - *Median* (X- 35)	$\lvert D \rvert = X$ - *Mode* (X- 45)
5	25	30	40
10	20	25	35
25	5	10	20
35	5	0	10
45	15	10	0
45	15	10	0
45	15	10	0
$\Sigma x = 210$	$\Sigma\lvert D \rvert = 100$	$\Sigma\lvert D \rvert = 95$	$\Sigma\lvert D \rvert = 105$

$$\bar{X} = \frac{\Sigma x}{N} = \frac{210}{7} = 30$$

$$\text{Median} = \frac{N+1}{2}\text{th item} = \frac{7+1}{2}\text{th item} = \text{4th item } i.e. = 35$$

$$\text{M.D. based on Mean} = \frac{\Sigma\lvert D \rvert}{N} = \frac{100}{7} = 14.3$$

$$\text{Co-efficient of M.D.} = \frac{\text{M.D.}}{\text{Mean}} = \frac{14.3}{30} = 0.48$$

$$\text{M.D. based on Median} = \frac{\Sigma\lvert D \rvert}{N} = \frac{95}{7} = 13.57$$

$$\text{Co-efficient of M.D.} = \frac{\text{M.D.}}{\text{Median}} = \frac{13.57}{35} = 0.388$$

$$\text{M.D. based on Mode} = \frac{\Sigma\lvert D \rvert}{N} = \frac{105}{7} = 15$$

$$\text{Co-efficient of M.D.} = \frac{\text{M.D.}}{\text{Mode}} = \frac{15}{45} = 0.33$$

Illustration 7. *The details regarding the production of goods in factories situated in a city are given below.*

Production (in tonnes)	*150*	*250*	*300*	*450*	*500*	*600*
No. of factories	*3*	*9*	*12*	*20*	*5*	*4*

Calculate the mean deviation and its co-efficient.

Solution: Calculation of M.D.

Porduction X	*No. of factories f*	*Deviations from Assumed mean d(X - 300)*	*fd*	$\|D\|$ $x-\overline{x}$ *(x - 372.64)*	$f\|D\|$
150	3	-150	-450	222.64	667.92
250	9	-50	-900	122.64	1103.76
300	12	0	0	72.64	871.68
450	20	+150	3000	77.36	1547.2
500	5	+200	1000	127.36	636.8
600	4	+300	1200	227.36	909.44
	N = 53		*Σfd = 3850*		$\Sigma f\|D\| = 5736.8$

$$\text{Arithmetic Mean } \overline{X} = A \pm \frac{\Sigma fd}{N} = 300 + \frac{3850}{53} = 372.64$$

$$= 300 + 72.64$$

$$M.D. = \frac{\Sigma f\,|D|}{N} = \frac{5736.8}{53} = 108.24$$

$$\text{Co-efficient of M.D.} = \frac{\text{M.D.}}{\text{Mean}} = \frac{108.24}{372.64} = 0.29$$

Illustration 8. *Calculate mean deviation and co-efficient of mean deviation from the following data.*

X	f
0-20	4
20-40	8
40-60	10
60-80	15
80-100	20
100-120	5
120-140	9
140-160	11

Solution: Calculation of mean deviation.

X	f	m	d' $\left(\frac{m-90}{20}\right)$	fd'	$\|D\|$ $(m - \overline{X})$ $m - 85.37$	$f\|D\|$
0-20	4	10	-4	-16	75.37	301.48
20-40	8	30	-3	-24	55.37	442.96
40-60	10	50	-2	-20	35.37	353.7
60-80	15	70	-1	-15	15.37	230.55
80-100	20	90	0	0	4.63	92.6
100-120	5	110	+1	5	24.63	123.15
120-140	9	130	+2	18	44.63	401.67
140-160	11	150	+3	33	64.63	710.93
	$N = 82$			$\Sigma fd' = -19$		$\Sigma f\|D\| = 2657.04$

$$\overline{X} = A \pm \frac{\Sigma fd'}{N} \times i = 90 - \frac{19 \times 20}{82} = 90 - 4.63 = 85.37$$

$$\text{M.D.} = \frac{\Sigma f\,|D|}{N} = \frac{2657.04}{82} = 32.403$$

$$\text{Co-efficient of M.D.} = \frac{\text{M.D.}}{\text{Mean}} = \frac{32.403}{85.37} = 0.3796$$

Advantages of Mean Deviation

(1) Mean deviation is easy to calculate.

(2) It shows the variation of all the items of the distribution. Hence, it is superior than range and quartile deviation.

(3) It would not be affected by the extreme values.

(4) The fluctuations of samples would not affect the calculation of mean deviation.

Disadvantages of Mean Deviation

(1) It is not suitable for further statistical analysis.

(2) It is a non-algebraic method since the positive and negative signs for the deviations are treated as positive only.

(3) It is not a popular method for measuring the dispersion.

(4) Standard Deviation: Standard deviation is a prominent and widely used measure of dispersion. It is the square root of the sum of squared deviations from average. Standard deviation has its own merits over other methods of dispersion, since it analyses the deviations by squairing it. In this method, deviations should be taken only from the arithmetic mean. It is denoted by the small Greek letter sigma (σ).

Calculation of Standard Deviation for Individual Observations

$$\text{S.D. } \sigma = \sqrt{\frac{\Sigma x^2}{N}} \quad \text{or} \quad \sqrt{\frac{\Sigma(x-\bar{x})^2}{N}}$$

Where, x-indicates deviation from arithmetic mean (*i.e.* $x-\bar{x}$); N = total number of variables.

If the observations are complicated one, or of very large size, then it takes time to find out the arithmetic mean. Further, it will be complicated to find out the deviations if the arithmetic mean is in fractional figures. To overcome these difficulties short-cut method can be adopted to calculate the standard deviation. Formula for standard deviation under short-cut method, is

$$\text{S.D. } \sigma = \sqrt{\frac{\Sigma d^2}{N} - \left(\frac{\Sigma d}{N}\right)^2}$$

d - refers to deviation from Assumed Mean (*i.e.* x - A)

Calculation of Standard Deviation for Discrete Series

$$\sigma = \sqrt{\frac{\Sigma fx^2}{N}}$$

Where, σ = Standard deviation

f = frequencies

x = deviations from arithmetic mean (*i.e.*, $x-\bar{x}$)

N = Total number of frequencies (*i.e.*, Σf)

If the calculation of A.M is difficult then the short-cut method can be applied to calculate the standard deviation. In the short-cut method assumed mean can be used instead of the actual mean. Formula for S.D under short-cut method is,

$$\sigma = \sqrt{\frac{\sum fd^2}{N} - \left(\frac{\sum fd}{N}\right)^2}$$

Where, d - indicates deviations from assumed mean. *i.e.,* (d = x – A); f = frequency; N = total number of frequencies, *i.e.,* Σf.

If the variables got common factor then the calculation for standard deviation may further be simplified through calculation under step deviation method.

Formula for S.D under Step-Deviation method is

$$\sigma = \sqrt{\frac{\sum fd'}{N} - \left(\frac{\sum fd'}{N}\right)^2} \times c$$

Where, d' indicates deviations from assumed mean divided by a common factor *i.e.,* $d' = \frac{\text{x - } A}{c}$, c indicates common factor for the observations, f-indicates frequencies; and N indicates the total number of frequencies (*i.e.,* N = Σf)

Calculation of Standard Deviation for Continuous Series

The formulas for standard deviation in the continuous series are almost same to the formulas for discrete series. In this series the mid points of the class intervals should be taken into account instead of the variable. Following formulas would be used for calculating the value of standard deviation.

(i) Direct Method:

$$\sigma = \sqrt{\frac{\sum fx^2}{N}}$$

Where, x - indicates deviation from arithmetic mean. (*i.e.,* $x = \text{x} - \bar{\text{x}}$), f - indicates frequency; N - indicates the total number of frequencies (*i.e.,* $N = \Sigma f$)

(ii) Short-Cut Method:

$$\sigma = \sqrt{\frac{\sum fd^2}{N} - \left(\frac{\sum fd}{N}\right)^2}$$

Where, d- indicates deviations of mid-points from the assumed mean (*i.e.*, $d = m - A$)

(iii) Step Deviation Method:

$$\sigma = \sqrt{\frac{\Sigma fd'^2}{N} - \left(\frac{\Sigma fd'}{N}\right)^2} \times c$$

Where, d' - indicates deviation of mid-points from assumed mean divided by a common factor (*i.e.*, $d' = \frac{x - A}{c}$), c - indicates the common factor.

Step deviation method is the most common method adopted for calculating standard deviation in continuous series.

Illustration 9. *Calculate standard deviation from the following data. 9, 27, 18, 54, 45, 72, 36, 63, 81.*

Solution: Calculation of standard deviation.

X	$x = (X - \bar{X})$ X - 45	x^2
9	-36	1296
27	-18	324
18	-27	729
54	9	81
45	0	0
72	27	729
36	-9	81
63	18	324
81	36	1296
$\Sigma X = 405$		$\Sigma x^2 = 4860$

$$\bar{X} = \frac{\Sigma x}{N} = \frac{405}{9} = 45$$

$$\sigma = \sqrt{\frac{\Sigma x^2}{N}} = \sqrt{\frac{4860}{9}} = \sqrt{540} = 23.24$$

Illustration 10. *Calculate standard deviation from the following data. 39, 46, 52, 75, 82, 93, 97.*

Solution: Calculation of standard deviation.

X	$d = (x - 60)$	d^2
39	-21	441
46	-14	196
52	-8	64
75	+15	225
82	+22	484
93	+33	1089
97	+37	1369
	$\Sigma d = 64$	$\Sigma d^2 = 3868$

$$= \sqrt{\frac{\sum d^2}{N} - \left(\frac{\sum d}{N}\right)^2} = \sqrt{\frac{3868}{7} - \left(\frac{64}{7}\right)^2}$$

$$= \sqrt{552.57 - 83.54} = \sqrt{469.03} = 21.657$$

Illustration 11. *Find out standard deviation for the following data.*

Production (in tonnes)	*No. of factories*
50	*2*
100	*5*
125	*7*
150	*12*
200	*9*
250	*5*
300	*3*

Solution: Calculation of standard deviation by Step Deviation Method.

Production (in tonnes) X	*f*	$d' = \frac{(X - 150)}{25}$	d'^2	fd'	fd'^2
50	2	-4	16	-8	32
100	5	-2	4	-10	20
125	7	-1	1	-7	7
150	12	0	0	0	0
200	9	+2	4	18	36
250	5	+4	16	20	80
300	3	+6	36	18	108
	$N = 43$			$\Sigma fd' = 31$	$\Sigma fd'^2 = 283$

$$\sigma = \sqrt{\frac{\sum fd'^2}{N} - \left(\frac{\sum fd'}{N}\right)^2} \times c = \sqrt{\frac{283}{43} - \left(\frac{31}{43}\right)^2} \times 25$$

$$= \sqrt{6.58 - 0.52} \times 25 = \sqrt{6.06} \times 25 = 2.46 \times 25 = 61.5$$

Illustration 12. *Calculate standard deviation from the following data.*

Marks	*10*	*20*	*30*	*40*	*50*	*60*	*70*	*80*	*90*
No. of students	*4*	*4*	*6*	*9*	*12*	*3*	*5*	*20*	*3*

Solution: Calculation of standard deviation through Direct Method

Marks X	*No. of students* *f*	*fx*	$X - \bar{X}$ *x - 49*	x^2	fx^2
10	4	40	-39	1521	6084
20	6	120	-29	841	5046
30	9	270	-19	361	3249
40	12	480	-9	81	972
50	3	150	+1	+1	3
60	5	300	+11	121	605
70	14	980	+21	441	6174
80	3	240	+31	961	2883
90	4	360	+41	1681	6724
	N = 60	*Σfx = 2940*			$\Sigma fx^2 = 31740$

$$\bar{X} = \frac{\Sigma fx}{N} = \frac{2940}{60} = 49$$

$$\sigma = \sqrt{\frac{\Sigma fx^2}{N}} = \sqrt{\frac{31740}{60}} = \sqrt{529} = 23$$

Illustration 13. *Calculate standard deviation for the information given below.*

Height (in Cms)	*157*	*160*	*162*	*164*	*166*	*168*
No. of students	*4*	*5*	*11*	*6*	*9*	*5*

Solution: Calculation of S.D through Short-Cut Method.

Height (in Cms) X	No. of students f	d = (X – A) = X – 162	d^2	fd	fd^2
157	4	-5	25	-20	100
160	5	-2	4	-10	20
162	11	0	0	0	0
164	6	+2	4	+12	24
166	9	+4	16	+36	144
168	5	+6	36	+30	180
	N = 40			Σfd = 48	Σfd^2 = 468

$$\sigma = \sqrt{\frac{\Sigma fd^2}{N} - \left(\frac{\Sigma fd}{N}\right)^2} = \sqrt{\frac{468}{40} - \left(\frac{48}{40}\right)^2}$$

$$= \sqrt{11.7 - 1.44} = \sqrt{10.26} = 3.2$$

Illustration 14. *Compute the standard deviation from the following data.*

Expenditure (Rs.)	*100-200*	*200-300*	*300-400*	*400-500*	*500-600*
No. of families	*30*	*20*	*40*	*5*	*10*

Solution: Calculation of standard deviation by Direct Method.

Expenditure Rs. X	No. of familites f	m	fm	$m - \overline{X}$ m - 297.6	x^2	fx^2
100-200	30	150	4500	-147.6	21785.76	653572.8
200-300	20	250	5000	-47.6	2265.76	45315.2
300-400	40	350	14000	+52.4	2745.76	109830.4
400-500	5	450	2250	+152.4	23225.76	116128.6
500-600	10	550	5500	+252.4	63705.76	637057.6
	N = 105		Σfm = 31,250			Σfx^2 = 1561904.6

$$X = \frac{\sum fm}{N} = \frac{31250}{105} = 297.6 = \sqrt{\frac{\sum fx2}{N}}$$

$$= \sqrt{\frac{1561904.6}{105}} = \sqrt{14875.28} = 122$$

Illustration 15: *Calculate standard deviation from the following data.*

X	0-25	25-50	50-75	75-100	100-125	125-150
f	13	12	19	11	15	17

Solution: Calculation of standard deviation by Short-Cut Method.

X	f	m	d = m-A m–87.5	fd	fd²
0-25	13	12.5	-75	-975	73125
25-50	12	37.5	-50	-600	30000
50-75	19	62.5	-25	-475	11875
75-100	11	87.5	0	0	0
100-125	15	112.5	+25	375	9375
125-150	17	137.5	+50	850	42500
N = 87			Σfd = -825		Σfd² = 166875

$$\sigma = \sqrt{\frac{\sum fd^2}{N} - \left(\frac{\sum fd}{N}\right)^2} = \sqrt{\frac{166875}{87} - \left(\frac{-825}{87}\right)^2}$$

$$= \sqrt{1918.10 - 89.87} = \sqrt{1828.23} = 42.76$$

Illustration 16. *Calculate standard deviation from the following distribution.*

X	0-50	50-100	100-150	150-200	200-250	250-300
f	12	15	10	20	9	6

Solution: Calculation of S.D by Step-Diviation Method.

X	f	m	d' = m - A / c (m-175 / c)	fd'	fd'²
0-50	12	25	-6	-72	432
50-100	15	75	-4	-60	240
100-150	10	125	-2	-20	40
150-200	20	175	0	0	0
200-250	9	225	+2	+18	36
250-300	6	275	+4	+24	96
	N = 72		Σfd' = -110		Σfd'² = 844

$$= \sqrt{\frac{\sum fd'^2}{N} - \left(\frac{\sum fd'}{N}\right)^2} \times c = \sqrt{\frac{844}{72} - \left(\frac{-110}{72}\right)^2} \times 25$$

$$= \sqrt{11.72 - 2.34} \times 25 = 3.1 \times 25 = 77.5$$

Mathematical Properties of Standard Deviation

The important mathematical properties of standard deviation are,

(1) Combined Standard Deviation

(2) Co-efficient of Variation and

(3) Variance

(1) Combined Standard Deviation: The combined standard deviation can be calculated by following the same method of calculating the combined mean of two or more than two groups. It may be denoted by σ_{12} Formula for combined standard deviation of two groups is,

$$\sigma_{12} = \sqrt{\frac{N_1\sigma_1^2 + N_2\sigma_2^2 + N_1d_1^2 + N_2d_2^2}{N_1 + N_2}}$$

or $$\sigma_{12} = \sqrt{\frac{N_1(\sigma_1^2 + d_1^2) + N_2(\sigma_2^2 + d_2^2)}{N_1 + N_2}}$$

Where,

σ_{12} - denotes, combined standard deviation

σ_1 - denotes standard deviation of the first group

σ_2 - denotes standard deviation of the second group.

d_1 - denotes the difference between the arithmetic mean of 1stgroup with the combined arithmetic mean of the two groups. (*i.e.*, $= \bar{x}_1 - \bar{x}_{12}$)

d_2 - indicates the difference between the arithmetic mean of the 2nd group with the combined arithmetic mean of the two groups *(i.e.,* $= \bar{x}_2 - \bar{x}_{12}$*)*

N_1 - indicates the total number of variables of the first group.

N_2 - indicates the total number of variables of the second group.

$$\bar{x}_{12} = \frac{N_1 \bar{x}_1 + N_2 \bar{x}_2}{N_1 + N_2}$$

Where, $\overline{X}_{12}$ is the combined arithmetic mean $\overline{X}_1$ is the arithmetic mean of the first group and $\overline{X}_2$ is the arithmetic mean of the second group.

The combined standard deviation of three or more groups can also be calculated by modifying the formula for σ_{12}.

Formula for combined standard deviation of three groups is,

$$\sigma_{123} = \sqrt{\frac{N_1\sigma_1^2 + N_2\sigma_2^2 + N_3\sigma_3^2 + N_1d_1^2 + N_2d_2^2 + N_3d_3^2}{N_1 + N_2 + N_3}}$$

$$\text{or} \quad = \sqrt{\frac{N_1\left(\sigma_1^2 + d_1^2\right) + N_2\left(\sigma_2^2 + d_2^2\right) + N_3\left(\sigma_3^2 + d_3^2\right)}{N_1 + N_2 + N_3}}$$

Illustration 17. *Following are the details regarding a study conducted by two groups, in a village about the monthly income of families.*

Groups	*Number of families studied*	*Mean Income (Rs.)*	*Standard Deviation (Rs.)*
I	30	2,500	9.3
II	40	1,800	6.4

Calculate the combined standard deviation.

Solution: $N_1 = 30$; $N_2 = 40$; $\bar{x}_1 = 2500$; $\bar{x}_2 = 1800$;

$\sigma_1 = 9.3$; $\sigma_2 = 6.4$

Hence,

$$\bar{X}_{12} = \frac{N_1\bar{X}_1 + N_2\bar{X}_2}{N_1 + N_2} = \frac{(30 \times 2500) + (40 \times 1800)}{30 + 40}$$

$$= \frac{75000 + 72000}{70} = \frac{147000}{70} = 2100$$

$$d_1 = \bar{x}_1 - \bar{x}_{12} = 2500 - 2100 = 400$$

$$d_2 = \bar{x}_2 - \bar{x}_{12} = 1800 - 2100 = -300$$

$$\sigma_{12} = \sqrt{\frac{N_1(\sigma_1^2 + d_1^2) + N_2(\sigma_2^2 + d_2^2)}{N_1 + N_2}}$$

$$= \sqrt{\frac{30\,(9.3^2 + 400^2) + 40\,(6.4^2 + 300^2)}{30 + 40}}$$

$$= \sqrt{\frac{30\,(86.49 + 160000) + 40\,(40.96 + 90000)}{70}}$$

$$= \sqrt{\frac{(30 \times 160086.49) + (40 \times 90040.96}{70}}$$

$$= \sqrt{\frac{4802594.7 + 3601638.4}{70}} = \sqrt{120060.47} = 346.5$$

Illustration 18. *The details regarding the marks obtained by students of 3 classes in a subject are stated below.*

Class	*No. of students*	*Mean Marks*	*Standard Deviation*
A	*50*	*75*	*9.2*
B	*40*	*48*	*7.8*
C	*60*	*55*	*8.7*

Calculate the combined standard deviation.

Solution: $N_1 = 50$; $N_2 = 40$; $N_3 = 60$, $\bar{x}_1 = 75$;

$\bar{x}_2 = 48$; $\bar{x}_3 = 55$; $\sigma_1 = 9.2$; $\sigma_2 = 7.8$;

$\sigma_3 = 8.7$.

$$\bar{x}_{123} = \frac{N_1\bar{x}_1 + N_2\bar{x}_2 + N_3\bar{x}_3}{N_1 + N_2 + N_3} = \frac{(50\times75)+(40\times48)+(60\times55)}{50+40+60}$$

$$= \frac{3750+1920+3300}{150} = \frac{8970}{150} = 59.8$$

$$d_1 = \bar{x}_1 - \bar{x}_{123} = 75 - 59.8 = 15.2$$

$$d_2 = \bar{x}_2 - \bar{x}_{123} = 48 - 59.8 = -11.8$$

$$d_3 = \bar{x}_3 - \bar{x}_{123} = 55 - 59.8 = -4.8$$

$$\sigma_{123} = \sqrt{\frac{N_1\left(\sigma_1^{\,2} + d_1^{\,2}\right) + N_2\left(\sigma_2^{\,2} + d_2^{\,2}\right) + N_3\left(\sigma_3^{\,2} + d_3^{\,2}\right)}{N_1 + N_2 + N_3}}$$

$$= \sqrt{\frac{50\left(9.2^2 + 15.2^2\right) + 40\left(7.8^2 + 11.8^2\right) + 60\left(8.7^2 + 4.8^2\right)}{50+40+60}}$$

$$= \sqrt{\frac{50\,(84.64 + 231.04) + 40\,(60.84 + 139.24) + 60\,(75.69 + 23.04)}{50+40+60}}$$

$$= \sqrt{\frac{50\times315.68 + 40\times200.08 + 60\times98.73}{150}}$$

$$= \sqrt{\frac{15784 + 8003.2 + 5923.8}{150}} = \sqrt{\frac{29711}{150}} = \sqrt{198.07} = 14.07$$

(2) Co-efficient of Variation: The relative measure of standard deviation is called the Co-efficient of Variation. Standard deviation is only an absolute measure of dispersion. The consistency, reliability, uniformity or stability of data cannot be known through the standard deviation. Hence, the co-efficient of variation technique is adopted to know whether the data is uniform, consistant, stable and reliable one. If the co-efficient of variation is greater, then the data are more variable and less consistant, less homogeneous, less uniform and less stable. If the value of co-efficient of variation is less, then the character of the data would be less variable and more consistant, more homogeneous, more uniform and more stable.

The co-efficient of variation can be measured through the following formula

$$C.V = \frac{\sigma}{\bar{x}}$$

Where, σ = Standard deviation;

$\bar{x}$ = Arithmetic mean and

c.v = Co-efficient of variation.

If it is termed in percentage then,

$$C.V = \frac{\sigma}{\bar{x}} \times 100$$

The formula for the co-efficient of variation was suggested by Karl Pearson.

(3) Variance: Variance is the square of standard deviation. Hence, variance is σ^2 or $ó = \sqrt{\text{Variance}}$

Relation between Standard Deviation and Other Measures of Dispersion

There exists a relationship between the standard deviation and quartile deviation; and between standard deviation and mean deviation. Of these deviations, quartile deviation is the smallest and standard deviation is the largest one. The mean deviation lies between the standard deviation and the quartile deviation.

$$Q.D = \frac{2}{3}\sigma \quad \text{and} \quad M.D = \frac{4}{5}\sigma$$

Hence, $$\sigma = \frac{3}{2}Q.D \quad \text{or} \quad \sigma = \frac{5}{4}M.D$$

Therefore $\frac{3}{2}$Q.D $=\frac{5}{4}$ M.D, M.D$=\frac{6}{5}$Q.D

Illustration 19. *The data relating to the monthly production of a product in 2 factories are given below.*

Factory	*Monthly Production in tonnes*											
	1	*2*	*3*	*4*	*5*	*6*	*7*	*8*	*9*	*10*	*11*	*12*
A	*30*	*50*	*45*	*54*	*49*	*53*	*60*	*46*	*41*	*56*	*59*	*45*
B	*70*	*120*	*20*	*15*	*150*	*100*	*90*	*80*	*10*	*25*	*95*	*85*

Find out which factory is more efficient and which factory is more consistant.

Solution: Calculation of co-efficient of variation for Factory A.

Production X	$X-\bar{X}$ *(x - 49) x*	x^2
30	-19	361
50	+1	1
45	-5	25
54	+4	16
49	0	0
53	+4	16
60	+11	121
46	-3	9
41	-8	64
56	+7	49
59	+10	100
45	-4	16
$\Sigma x^x = 588$		$\Sigma x^2 = 778$

$$\bar{X}=\frac{\sum x}{N}=\frac{588}{12}=49$$

$$\sigma=\sqrt{\frac{\sum x^2}{N}}=\sqrt{\frac{778}{12}}=\sqrt{64.83}=8.05$$

Co-efficient of variation $\frac{\sigma}{\bar{x}}=\frac{8.05}{49}=0.16$

Calculation of Co-efficient of Variation for Factory B.

X	$X - \bar{X}$ $(x - 70)$	x^2
70	0	0
120	+50	2,500
20	-50	2,500
15	-55	3,025
130	+60	3,600
100	+30	900
90	+20	400
80	+10	100
10	-60	3,600
25	-45	2,025
95	+25	625
85	+15	225
$\Sigma x = 840$		$\Sigma x^2 = 19,500$

$$\bar{X} = \frac{\sum x}{N} = \frac{840}{12} = 70$$

$$\sigma = \sqrt{\frac{\sum x^2}{N}} = \sqrt{\frac{19500}{12}} = \sqrt{1625} = 40.31$$

$$\text{Co-efficient of variation } \frac{\sigma}{\bar{x}} = \frac{40.31}{70} = 0.576$$

Ans: Factory *B* is more efficient than factory *A* in terms of production of the goods, since the average monthly production for Factory *B* is more than that of *A*. As for as consistant of production is concerned, factory A is more consistant than factory *B* since co-efficient of variation for Factory A is less than that of the Factory *B*.

Illustration 20. *Monthly expenditure of the sample families in two villages are given below.*

Monthly Expenditure (Rs.)	No. of families Village M	Village N
500	14	5
750	7	6
1000	3	7
1250	11	8
1500	9	7
1750	4	9
2000	2	8

Find out which village spend more and which one is spending more consistently.

Solution: Calculation of co-efficient of variation for Village *M*.

Monthly Income X	No. of families f	$d' = \frac{x-A}{c}$ $\left(\frac{x-1250}{250}\right)$	d'^2	fd'	fd'^2
500	14	-3	9	-42	126
750	7	-2	4	-14	28
1000	3	-1	1	-3	3
1250	11	0	0	0	0
1500	9	+1	1	+9	9
1750	4	+2	4	+8	16
2000	2	+3	9	+6	18
$N = 50$				$\Sigma fd' = -36$	$\Sigma fd'^2 = 200$

$$\bar{x} = A + \frac{\sum fd'}{N} \times c = 1250 - \frac{36}{50} \times 250 = 1250 - 180 = \text{Rs. } 1070$$

$$\sigma = \sqrt{\frac{\sum fd'^2}{N} - \left(\frac{\sum fd'}{N}\right)^2} \times c \quad = \sqrt{\frac{200}{50} - \left(\frac{36}{50}\right)^2} \times 250$$

$$= \sqrt{4 - 0.52} \times 250 \quad = \sqrt{3.48} \times 250 = 1.87 \times 250 = 467.5$$

$$\text{Co-efficient of variation} = \frac{\sigma}{\bar{x}} = \frac{467.5}{1070} = 0.437$$

Calculation of Co-efficient of Variation for village *N*.

Monthly Income Rs.	*No. of families f*	$d' = \frac{x - A}{c}$ $\frac{x - 1250}{250}$	*d'2*	*fd'*	*fd'2*
500	5	-3	9	-15	45
750	6	-2	4	-12	24
1000	7	-1	1	-7	7
1250	8	0	0	0	0
1500	7	+1	1	+7	7
1750	9	+2	4	+18	36
2000	8	+3	9	+24	72
	N = 50			*Σfd' = 15*	*Σfd' = 191*

$$X = A + \frac{\sum fd'}{N} \times c \;\; = 1250 + \frac{15}{50} \times 250 \;\; = 1250 + 75 = 1325 \text{ Rs.}$$

$$\text{S.D. } \sigma = \sqrt{\frac{\sum fd'^2}{N} - \left(\frac{\sum fd'}{N}\right)^2} \times c \;\; = \sqrt{\frac{191}{50} - \left(\frac{15}{50}\right)^2} \times 250$$

$$= \sqrt{3.82 - 0.09} \times 250 \;\; = 1.93 \times 250 = 482.5$$

$$\text{C.V.} = -\frac{\sigma}{\bar{x}} = \frac{482.5}{1325} = 0.3642$$

Ans: Village *B* spends more than *A*. Also village *B* is more Consistant than *A*.

Illustration 21. *Following are the information related with the marks obtained by 40 students of a class in 2 papers. Find out which one got the homogenity and which one got highest marks in the class.*

Marks	*0-10*	*10-20*	*20-30*	*30-40*	*40-50*	*50-60*	*60-70*
Paper I	*4*	*1*	*2*	*8*	*9*	*6*	*10*
Paper II	*5*	*7*	*6*	*6*	*7*	*5*	*4*

Solution: Calculation of co-efficient of variation.

Marks	Mid points m	f_1 paper I	f_2 paper II	$\left(\frac{x-35}{5}\right)$ d'		d'^2	f_1d'	$f_2d'^2$	$f_2d'^2$
0-10	5	4	5	-6	36	-24	-30	144	180
10-20	15	1	7	-4	16	-4	-28	16	112
20-30	25	2	6	-2	4	-4	-12	8	24
30-40	35	8	6	0	0	0	0	0	0
40-50	45	9	7	+2	4	+18	+14	36	28
50-60	55	6	5	+4	16	+24	+20	96	80
60-70	65	10	4	+6	36	+60	+24	360	144
		40	40			$\Sigma f_1d'$ = +70	$\Sigma f_2d'$ = -12	$\Sigma f_1d'^2$ = 660	$\Sigma f_2d'^2$ = 568

$$\bar{x}_1 = A \pm \frac{\sum f_1d'}{N} \times c = 35 + \frac{70}{40} \times 5 = 35 + 8.75 = 43.75$$

$$\text{S.D. } \sigma = \sqrt{\frac{\sum f_1d'^2}{N} - \left(\frac{\sum f_1d'}{N}\right)^2} \times c$$

$$= \sqrt{\frac{660}{40} - \left(\frac{70}{40}\right)^2} \times 5 = \sqrt{16.5 - 3.0625} \times 5$$

$$= \sqrt{13.4375} \times 5 = 3.67 \times 5 = 18.35$$

$$\text{C.V.} = \frac{\sigma}{\bar{x}} = \frac{18.35}{43.75} = 0.42$$

$$\bar{x}_2 = A \pm \frac{\sum f_2d'}{N} \times c = 35 - \frac{12}{40} \times 5 = 35 - 1.5 = 33.5$$

$$\text{S.D. } \sigma = \sqrt{\frac{\sum f_2d'^2}{N} - \left(\frac{\sum f_2d'}{N}\right)^2} \times c = \sqrt{\frac{568}{40} - \left(\frac{-12}{40}\right)^2} \times 5$$

$$= \sqrt{14.2 - 0.09} \times 5 = \sqrt{14.11} \times 5 = 3.756 \times 5 = 18.78$$

$$\text{C.V.} = \frac{\sigma}{\bar{x}} = \frac{18.78}{33.5} = 0.56$$

Therefore, Paper I got the homogenity and also got the highest mark in the class.

(5) Lorenz Curve: Lorenz curve is graphic method of measuring dispersion. This method was devised by Max 0. Lorenz, a famous economic statistician. It can be drawn by converting the value into percentages. It gives a clear picture about the dispersion of data from the central value.

Procedures for drawing Lorenz Curve

The procedures for drawing Lorenz Curve are given below.

1. Calculate the cumulative values of variables and frequencies.
2. Calculate the cumulative percentage of all the variables and frequencies.
3. X-axis should be represented with cumulative percentage of variables. Hence it should have a scale of 0 to 100.
4. Y-axis should be represented with cumulative percentage of frequencies. It should also have a scale of 0 to 100.
5. Plot the percentages of cumulative variables, against the percentages of corresponding cumulative frequencies. Join all the plotted points to get a curve.
6. Also draw a 45% straight line on the graph in order to know the extent of deviation of variables from the central value.

Illustration 22. *Draw a Lorenz Curve from the following data.*

Marks	*10*	*40*	*50*	*60*	*70*	*80*	*90*
No. of students	*4*	*11*	*15*	*10*	*4*	*2*	*4*

Solution: Calculation of Cumulative Percentages

Marks	*Cumulative marks*	*Cumulative %*	*No. of Stdts.*	*Cumulative No. of stdts.*	*Cumulative %*
10	10	2.5	4	4	8
40	50	12.5	11	15	30
50	100	25	15	30	60
60	160	40	10	40	80
70	230	57.5	4	44	88
80	310	77.5	2	46	92
90	400	100	4	50	100

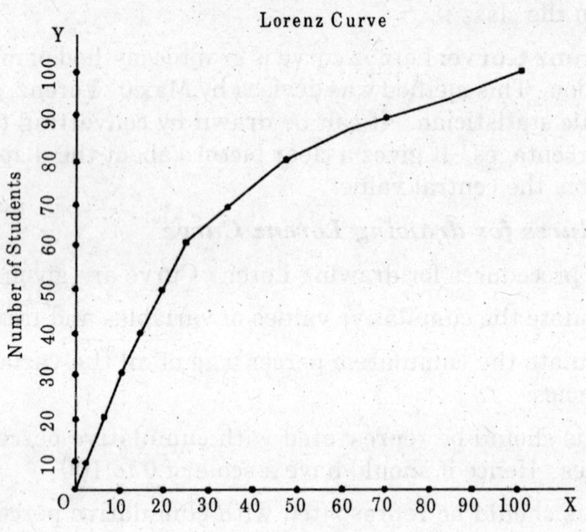

Illustration 23. *Draw a Lorenz Curve from the following data.*

Monthly Income	*No. of Persons*	
Rs.	*Village A*	*Village B*
100-200	*20*	*4*
200-300	*18*	*4*
300-400	*12*	*5*
400-500	*10*	*15*
500-600	*5*	*10*
600-700	*5*	*6*
700-800	*3*	*1*
800-900	*7*	*5*

Solution: Calculation of Cumulative Percentages

Monthly Income	*Mid value*	*Cumulative Mid value cf*	*Cumulative % cf*	*Village A f*	*cf*	*% of*	*Village B f*	*cf*	*% of*
100-200	150	150	4	20	20	25	4	4	8
200-300	250	400	10	18	38	47	4	8	16
300-400	350	750	19	12	50	62	5	13	26
400-500	450	1200	30	10	60	75	15	28	56
500-600	550	1750	44	5	65	81	10	38	76
600-700	650	2400	60	5	70	88	6	44	88
700-800	750	3150	79	3	73	91	1	45	90
800-900	850	4000	100	7	80	100	5	50	100

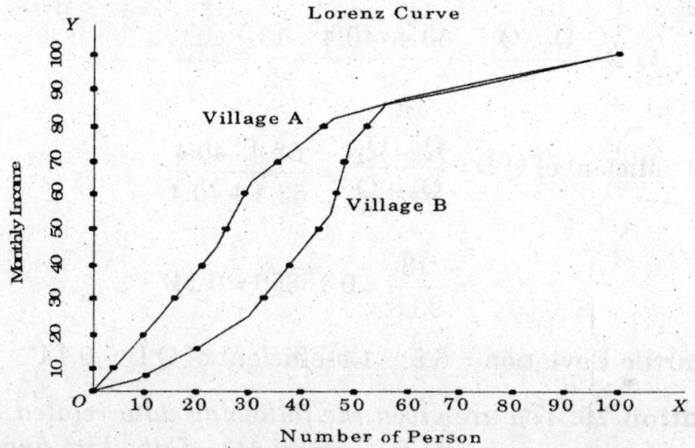

Miscellaneous Illustrations

Illustration 24. *Calculate range and co-efficient of range from the data. 150, 175, 35, 52, 73, 29, 86, 57*

Solution: Calculation of range and co-efficient of range.

$$\text{Range} = L - S$$

When, L = 175, S = 29

Range = 175 – 29 = 146

$$\text{Co-efficient of Range} = \frac{L - S}{L + S} = \frac{175 - 29}{175 + 29} = \frac{146}{204} = 0.72$$

Illustration 25. *Calculate quartile deviation and co-efficient of quartile deviation from the data given below. Weight of students in K.gms. 47.5, 42.2, 53.4, 59.4, 39.5, 40.4, 46.7*

Solution: Quartile deviation and its co-efficient.

Weight of students arranged in an order:

39.5, 40.4, 42.2, 46.7, 47.5, 53.4, 59.4.

$$Q_1 = \text{Size of } \frac{N+1}{4} \text{th item} = \frac{7+1}{4} \text{th item} = \text{2nd item}$$

Size of second item is 40.4 = Q_1

$$Q_3 = \text{Size of } 3\left(\frac{N+1}{4}\right)\text{th item} = 3\left(\frac{7+1}{4}\right)\text{th item} = \text{6 th item}$$

Size of sixth item is 53.4 = Q_3

$$Q.D = \frac{Q_3 - Q_1}{2} = \frac{53.4 - 40.4}{2} = \frac{13}{2} = 6.5$$

$$\text{Co-efficient of } Q.D = \frac{Q_3 - Q_1}{Q_3 + Q} = \frac{53.4 - 40.4}{53.4 + 40.4}$$

$$= \frac{13}{93.8} = 0.13859 = 0.14$$

Quartile Deviation = 6.5, Co-efficient of Q.D = 0.14

Illustration 26. *You are given the following data related with income of families in a city for one month. Calculate quartile deviation co-efficient of quartile deviation and Semi-Inter Quartile Range.*

Monthly Income (Rs.)	*350*	*475*	*590*	*670*	*890*	*950*
No. of families	*3*	*4*	*21*	*18*	*9*	*5*

Solution: Calculation of Quartile deviation.

X	*f*	*cf*
350	3	3
475	4	7
590	21	28
670	18	46
890	9	55
950	5	60
	N = 60	

$$Q_1 = \text{Size of } \frac{N+1}{4} \text{th item} = \frac{60+1}{4} \text{th item} = 15.25 \text{ item} = 590$$

$$Q_3 = \text{Size of } 3\left(\frac{N+1}{4}\right) \text{th item} = 3 \times 15.25 = 45.75 \text{ th item} = 670$$

$$Q.D. = \frac{Q_3 - Q_1}{2} = \frac{670 - 590}{2} = \frac{80}{2} = 40$$

$$\text{Co-efficient of } Q.D. = \frac{Q_3 - Q_1}{Q_3 + Q_1} = \frac{670 - 590}{670 + 590} = \frac{80}{1260} = 0.063$$

Inter Quartile Range $= Q_3 - Q_1 = 670 - 590 = 80$

Semi Inter Quarntile Range $= \dfrac{\text{Quartile Range}}{2} = \dfrac{80}{2} = 40$

Illustration 27. *Compute quartile deviation and co-efficient of quartile deviation from the following data.*

Marks	*15*	*25*	*35*	*45*	*55*	*65*	*75*
No. of students	*3*	*2*	*7*	*9*	*12*	*6*	*3*

Solution: Calculation of quartile deviation and co-efficient of Q.D

X	f	cf
15	3	3
25	2	5
35	7	12
45	9	21
55	12	33
65	6	39
75	3	42
	N = 42	

$$Q_1 = \frac{N+1}{4} \text{th item} = \frac{42+1}{4} \text{th item} = \frac{43}{4} \text{th item} = 10.75\text{th item.}$$

$$Q_1 = 10.75 \text{ th item} = 35$$

$$Q_3 = 3 \times \left(\frac{N+1}{4}\right) \text{th item} = 3 \times 10.75 \text{ th item} = 32.25 \text{ th item}$$

$$Q_3 = 32.25 \text{ th item} = 55$$

$$\text{Q.D.} = \frac{Q_3 - Q_1}{2} = \frac{55-35}{2} = \frac{20}{2} = 10$$

$$\text{Co-efficient of Q.D.} = \frac{Q_3 - Q_1}{Q_3 + Q_1} = \frac{55-35}{55+35} = \frac{20}{90} = 0.22$$

Quartile Deviation = 10, Co-efficient of Q.D. = 0.22.

Illustration 28: *Calculate the lower and upper quartiles, 6th and 85th percentile from the following data.*

X	7	21	28	35	42	49	56
f	4	5	6	10	3	7	2

Solution: Calculation of Q_1, Q_2, D_6 and P_{85}

X	*f*	*cf*
7	4	4
21	5	9
28	6	15
35	10	25
42	3	28
49	7	35
56	2	37
	N = 37	

$$Q_1 = \frac{N+1}{4} \text{ th item} = \frac{37+1}{4} \text{ th item} = \frac{38}{4} = 9.5 \text{ th item}$$

$$Q_1 = 9.5 \text{ th item} = 28$$

$$Q_3 = 3 \times \left(\frac{N+1}{4}\right) \text{th item} = 3 \times 9.5 \text{ th item} = 28.5 \text{ th item}$$

$$Q_3 = 28.5 \text{ th item} = 49$$

$$D_3 = 6\left(\frac{N+1}{10}\right) \text{th item} = 6\left(\frac{37+1}{10}\right) \text{th item} = 6 \times 3.8 \text{ th item}$$

$$= 22.8 \text{ th item} = 35$$

$$P_{85} = 85\left(\frac{N+1}{100}\right) \text{th item} = 85\left(\frac{37+1}{100}\right) \text{th item} = 87 \times 0.38$$

$$= 33.06 \text{ th item} = 49$$

Illustration 29. *Calculate co-efficient of quartile deviation from the following data.*

Marks	*0-10*	*10-20*	*20-30*	*30-40*	*40-50*	*50-60*	*60-70*
No. of students	*7*	*21*	*32*	*15*	*10*	*8*	*4*

Solution: Calculation of co-efficient of quartile deviation.

X	f	cf
0-10	7	7
10-20	21	28
20-30	32	60
30-40	15	75
40-50	10	85
50-60	8	93
60-70	4	97
	N = 97	

$$\text{Q.D.} = \frac{Q_3 - Q_1}{2} \qquad \text{Co-efficient of Q.D.} = \frac{Q_3 - Q_1}{Q_3 + Q_1}$$

Q_1 = Size of N/4 th item $= \frac{97}{4}$ th item = 24.25 th item

= 24.25 th items. Q_1 lies in the class 10-20

Q_3 = Size of 3N/4 th item $= 3 \times 24.25 = 72.75$ th item

Q_3 = lies in the class 30-40

$$Q_1 = L \pm \frac{N/4 - cf}{f} \times c, \text{ L=10, N/4=24.25, cf=7, f=21, c=10}$$

$$Q_1 = 10 + \frac{24.25 - 7}{21} \times 10 = 10 + \frac{17.25}{21} \times 10$$

$$= 10 + 0.821 \times 10 = 10 + 8.21 = 18.21$$

$$Q_3 = L + \frac{3N/4 - cf}{f} \times c, \text{ L=30, 3N/4=72.75, cf=60, f=15, c=10.}$$

$$Q_3 = 30 + \frac{72.75 - 60}{15} \times 10 = 30 + \frac{12.75}{15} \times 10$$

$$= 30 + 0.85 \times 10 = 30 + 8.5 = 38.5$$

$$\text{Q.D.} = \frac{Q_3 - Q_1}{2} = \frac{38.5 - 18.21}{2} = \frac{20.29}{2} = 10.145$$

$$\text{Co-efficient of Q.D.} = \frac{Q_3 - Q_1}{Q_3 + Q_1} = \frac{38.5 - 18.21}{38.5 + 18.21} = \frac{20.29}{56.71} = 0.36$$

Illustration 30: *Compute first quartile 3rd quartile, 45th percentile and the co-efficient of quartile deviation from the following data.*

Advertisement	*0-500*	*500-1000*	*1000-1500*	*1500-2000*	*2000-2500*
No. of factories	*25*	*39*	*46*	*40*	*30*

Solution: Calculation of Q_1, Q_3, P_{45} and co-efficient of quartile deviation.

X	*f*	*cf*
0-500	25	25
500-1000	39	64
1000-1500	46	110
1500-2000	40	150
2000-2500	30	180
	N = 180	

$$Q_1 = \text{N/4th item} = \frac{180}{4} \text{ th item} = \text{45th item} = 500 - 1000$$

$$Q_3 = 3N/4 \text{ th item} = 3 \times 45 = 135 \text{ th item} = 1500 - 2000$$

$$Q_1 = L + \frac{N/4 - cf}{f} \times c$$

$L = 500, N/4 = 45, cf = 25, f = 39, c = 500$

$$Q_1 = 500 + \frac{45 - 25}{39} \times 500 = 500 + \frac{20}{39} \times 500$$

$$= 500 + 0.5128 \times 500 = 500 + 256.4 = 756.4$$

$$Q_1 = L + \frac{3N/4 - cf}{f} \times c$$

$L = 1500, 3N/4 = 135, cf = 110, f = 40, c = 500$

$$Q_3 = 1500 + \frac{135 - 110}{40} \times 500 = 1500 + \frac{25}{40} \times 500$$

$$= 1500 + 0.625 \times 500 = 1500 + 312.5 = 1812.5$$

$$P_{45} = 45 \text{ N/100 th item} = 45 \times \frac{180}{100} \text{ th item}$$

$$= 45 \times 1.8 \text{ th item} = 81 \text{ th item}$$

P_{45} lies in the class 1000 – 1500.

$$P_{45} = L + \frac{45N/100 - cf}{f} \times c$$

$L = 1000$, $45N/100 = 81$, $cf = 64$, $f = 46$, $c = 500$.

$$P_{45} = 1000 + \frac{81-64}{46} \times 500 = 1000 + \frac{17}{46} \times 500$$

$$= 1000 + 0.369565 \times 500 = 1000 + 184.78 = 1184.78$$

Co-efficient of Q.D. $= \dfrac{Q_3 - Q_1}{Q_3 + Q_1}$ $Q_3 = 1812.5$, $Q_1 = 756.4$

Co-efficient of Q.D. $= \dfrac{1812.5 - 756.4}{1812.5 + 756.4} = \dfrac{1056.1}{2568.9}$

$= 0.4111 = 0.41$

Illustration 31: *The following data are related with the daily income of workers in a factory. Calculate mean deviation and its co-efficient.*

Daily Income (Rs.)	*15*	*25*	*35*	*45*	*55*	*65*
No. of workers	*17*	*12*	*5*	*3*	*10*	*13*

Solution: Calculation of co-efficient of mean deviation.

X	f	$\lvert D \rvert$ X - median	$f\lvert D \rvert$	cf
15	17	20	340	17
25	12	10	120	29
35	5	0	0	34
45	3	10	30	37
55	10	20	200	47
65	13	30	390	60
	$N = 60$		$\Sigma f\lvert D \rvert = 1080$	

Median = size of $= \left(\dfrac{N+1}{2}\right)$ th terms $= \dfrac{60+1}{2} = \dfrac{61}{2} = 30.5$ th term

Median = 35

$$\text{Mean Deviation} = \frac{\Sigma f|D|}{N}$$

$$\Sigma f\ |D| = 1080, N = 60.$$

$$\text{M.D.} = \frac{1080}{60} = 18$$

$$\text{Co-efficent of M.D.}\ \frac{\text{Mean Deviation}}{\text{Median}} = \frac{18}{35} = 0.5$$

Illustration 32: *Calculate arithmetic mean and mean deviation from median and mean from the data given below. 32, 56, 72, 29, 15, 7, 3, 9, 11.*

Solution: Calculation of mean deviation from median.

X	32	56	72	29	15	7	3	9	11	$\Sigma x = 234$
In order X	3	7	9	11	15	29	32	56	72	
$\|D\|$	12	8	6	4	0	14	17	41	57	$\Sigma\|D\| = 159$

$$\text{Median} \equiv \frac{N+1}{2} \text{ th term}$$

$$N = 9$$

$$= \frac{9+1}{2} \text{ th item} = \frac{10}{2} = 5 \text{ th item} = 15$$

Median = 15

$$\text{Mean} = \frac{\Sigma X}{N}, \quad \Sigma X = 234, N = 9$$

$$\text{Mean} = \frac{234}{9} = 26$$

Mean deviation from the Median

$$= \frac{\Sigma|D|}{N}, \ \Sigma|\text{D}| = 159, \quad \text{N} = 9$$

$$= \frac{159}{9} = 17.67$$

Calculation of mean deviation from mean

X	3	7	9	11	15	29	32	56	72	
D (x – 26)	23	19	17	15	11	3	6	30	46	$\Sigma \mid D \mid = 170$

$$\text{M.D.} = \frac{\Sigma \mid D \mid}{N}, \qquad \Sigma \mid D \mid = 170, \quad N = 9$$

$$= \frac{170}{9} = 18.9$$

Mean deviation from the mean = 18.9

Illustration 33: *The following data are related with the daily expenses of the families in a village. Calculate arithmetic mean and mean deviation from mean, median and mode.*

Expenses (Rs.)	*35*	*45*	*55*	*65*	*75*	*85*	*95*
No. of families	*8*	*20*	*25*	*35*	*18*	*9*	*5*

Solution: Calculation of mean deviation.

X	f	cf	d X - A	fd
35	8	8	-30	-240
45	20	28	-20	-400
55	25	53	-10	-250
65	35	88	0	0
75	18	106	10	180
85	9	115	20	180
95	5	120	30	150
	N =120			*Σfd = -380*

$$\text{Mean} = A \pm \frac{\Sigma fd}{N}, \quad A = 65, \quad \Sigma\text{fd} = -380, \quad \text{N} = 120$$

$$\text{Mean} = 65 + \left(\frac{-380}{120}\right) = 65 - 3.17$$

$$\overline{X} = 61.83$$

$$\text{Median} = \frac{N+1}{2}\text{th item} = \frac{120+1}{2}\text{th item} = \frac{121}{2}\text{th item}$$

$$= 60.5 \text{ th item} = 65$$

Median = 65

Mode = 3 Median – 2 Mean. Median = 65, Mean = 61.83

$$\text{Mode} = 3\times 65 - 2\times 61.83 = 195 - 123.66 = 71.34$$

Calculation of mean deviation

X	*f*	*From Mean = 61.83* |*D*|	*f*|*D*|	*From Median = 65* |*D*|	*f*|*D*|	*From Mode = 71.34* |*D*|	*f*|*D*|
35	8	26.83	214.64	30	240	36.34	290.72
45	20	16.83	336.60	20	400	26.34	526.80
55	25	6.83	170.75	10	250	16.34	408.50
65	35	3.17	110.95	0	0	6.34	221.90
75	18	13.37	237.06	10	180	3.66	65.88
85	9	23.17	208.53	20	180	13.66	122.94
95	5	33.17	165.85	30	150	23.66	118.30
	N = 120		*Σf|D| = 1444.38*		*Σf|D| = 1400*		*Σf|D| = 1755.04*

Mean Deviation from Mean

$$\text{M.D.} = \frac{\Sigma f\,|D|}{N}, \quad \Sigma f\,|D| = 1444.38, \quad N = 120$$

$$= \frac{1444.38}{120} = 12.04$$

Mean Deviation from Median

$$\text{M.D.} = \frac{\Sigma f\,|D|}{N}, \quad \Sigma f\,|D| = 1400, N = 120$$

$$= \frac{1400}{120} = 11.7$$

Mean Deviation from Mode

$$\text{M.D.} = \frac{\Sigma f|D|}{N}, \quad \Sigma f|D| = 1755.04, \quad N = 120$$

$$= \frac{1755.04}{120} = 14.6$$

Illustration 34: *Calculate standard deviation and co-efficient of variation from the data given below.*

Class Intervals	*Frequency*
0-5	*14*
5-10	*26*
10-15	*32*
15-20	*45*
20-25	*39*
25-30	*12*
30-35	*9*
35-40	*2*

Solution: Calculation of standard deviation.

X	*m*	*f*	*d*	*fd*	*fd²*
0-5	2.5	14	-4	-56	224
5-10	7.5	26	-3	-78	234
10-15	12.5	32	-2	-64	128
15-20	17.5	45	-1	-45	45
20-25	22.5	39	0	0	0
25-30	27.5	12	1	12	12
30-35	32.5	9	2	18	36
35-40	37.5	2	3	6	18
		N = 179		*Σfd = -207*	*Σfd² = 697*

$$\text{Standard deviation} = \sqrt{\frac{\Sigma \text{fd}^2}{N} - \left(\frac{\Sigma fd}{N}\right)^2} \times c$$

$\Sigma fd^2 = 697,\quad \Sigma fd = -207,\quad N = 179,\quad c = 5.$

$$\sigma = \sqrt{\frac{697}{179} - \left(\frac{-207}{179}\right)^2} \times 5$$

$$= \sqrt{3.89 - (-1.156)^2} \times 5$$

$$= \sqrt{3.89 - 1.34} \times 5$$

$$= 1.597 \times 5 \;\; = 7.98$$

Co-efficient of Variation $C.V. = \frac{\sigma}{\bar{x}} \times 100$

$$\bar{x} = A + \frac{\Sigma fd}{N} \times c, \quad A = 22.5, \quad \Sigma fd = -207, \quad N = 179, \quad c = 5$$

$$A = 22.5 + \frac{(-207)}{179} \times 5 = 22.5 - (1.156 \times 5) = 22.5 - 5.78 = 16.72$$

$$\bar{x} = 16.72$$

When, $\bar{x} = 16.72, \ \sigma = 7.98$

$$C.V. = \frac{\sigma}{\bar{x}} \times 100 = \frac{7.98}{16.72} = 0.48$$

Illustration 35: *You are given the heights of 60 students in a class. Calculate the standard deviation and also calculate the lowest and highest height through mean* ± 3 *technique.*

Height (in C.ms)	*No. of students*
62.5	*4*
63.0	*7*
63.5	*5*
64.0	*21*
65.0	*8*
65.5	*6*
67.5	*4*
68.0	*2*
69.5	*3*

Solution: Calculation of standard deviation.

X	*f*	*d (X - A, A = 65)*	*fd*	*fd²*
62.5	4	-2.5	-10.0	25.00
63.0	7	-2	-14.0	28.00
63.5	5	-1.5	-7.5	11.25
64.0	21	-1	-21.0	21.00
65.0	8	0	0	0
65.5	6	0.5	3.0	1.50
67.5	4	2.5	10.0	25.00
68.0	2	3	6	18.00
69.5	3	4.5	13.5	60.75
	$N = 60$	$\Sigma fd = -20$		$\Sigma fd^2 = 190.5$

$\Sigma fd = -20, \quad \Sigma fd^2 = 190.5, \quad N = 60$

$$\bar{x} = A + \frac{\Sigma fd}{N}$$

$$A = 65, \quad \Sigma fd = -20, \quad N = 60$$

$$\bar{x} = 65 + \left(\frac{-20}{60}\right) = 65 - 0.33 = 64.67$$

$$\text{S.D.} \quad \sigma = \sqrt{\frac{\Sigma fd^2}{N} - \left(\frac{\Sigma fd}{N}\right)^2}$$

$\Sigma fd^2 = 204, \quad \Sigma fd = -20, \quad N = 60$

$$\text{S.D.} \quad \sigma = \sqrt{\frac{190.5}{60} - \left(\frac{-20}{60}\right)^2} = \sqrt{3.2 - (-0.33)^2}$$

$$= \sqrt{3.2 - 0.11} = \sqrt{3.09} = 1.76$$

Calculation of Lowest and Highest Height

$$\bar{x} = 64.67, \quad \sigma = 1.76$$

Highest Height $= \bar{x} + 3\sigma = 64.67 + 3 \times 1.76 = 64.67 + 5.28 = 69.95$

Lowest Height $= \bar{x} - 3\sigma = 64.67 - 3 \times 1.76 = 64.67 - 5.28 = 59.4$

Illustration 36: *Calculate the missing information of the following data.*

	Item I	*Item II*	*Item III*	*Combined*
Total number	*?*	*150*	*100*	*300*
Mean	*125*	*?*	*136*	*129*
Standard deviation	*5.2*	*4.7*	*?*	*4.25*

Solution: Let N_1, N_2, N_3 denotes total numbers in the 1st, 2nd and 3rd items repectively.

We are given, $N_1 = ?$, $N_2 = 150$, $N_3 = 100$

$$N_1 + N_2 + N_3 = 300$$
$$N_2 + N_3 = 150 + 100 = 250$$
$$N_1 = 300 - (N_2 + N_3) = 300 - 250 = 50$$

Finding Mean of 2nd item

Let $\overline{X}_1$, $\overline{X}_2$, $\overline{X}_3$, denotes mean of 1st, 2nd and 3rd items repectively.

$$\overline{X}_{123} = \frac{N_1\overline{X}_1 + N_2\overline{X}_2 + N_2\overline{X}_3}{N_1 + N_2 + N_3}$$

$X_{123} = 129, N_1 + N_2 + N_3 = 300,\ \overline{X}_1 = 125,\ \overline{X}_2 = ?,\ \overline{X}_3 = 136,$
$N_1 = 50,\ N_2 = 150, N_3 = 100$

$$\therefore 129 = \frac{50 \times 125 + 150 \times \overline{X}_2 + 100 \times 136}{50 + 150 + 100}$$

$$129 = \frac{6250 + 150\overline{X}_2 + 13600}{300}$$

$$129 \times 300 = 19850 + 150\overline{X}_2$$

$$38700 = 19850 + 150\overline{X}_2$$

$$38700 - 19850 = 150\overline{X}_2$$

$$18850 = 150\overline{X}_2$$

$$150\overline{X}_2 = 18850$$

$$\overline{X}_2 = \frac{18850}{150} = 125.67$$

Calculation of standard deviation of 3rd item

$$\sigma_{123} = \sqrt{\frac{N_1\sigma_1 + N_2\sigma_2 + N_3\sigma_3 + N_1 d_1^2 + N_2 d_2^2 + N_3 d_3^2}{N_1 + N_2 + N_3}}$$

$\overline{X}_{123} = 129, N_1 = 50,\ s_1 = 5.2\text{m},\ \overline{X}_1 = 125, N_2 = 150,\ s_2 = 4.7,$

$\sigma_{123} = 4.25,\ \overline{X}_2 = 125.67,\ \overline{X}_3 = 136, N_3 = 100, \sigma_3 = ?,$

$d_1 = \overline{X}_1 - \overline{X}_{123} = 125 - 129 = -4,\ d_2 = 125.67 - 129 = -3.33,$
$d_3 = 136 - 129 = 7$

$$123 = \sqrt{\frac{50\times5.2^2 + 150\times4.7^2 + 100\times\sigma_3^2 + 50\times(-4)^2 + 150\times(-3.33)^2 + 100\times7^2}{50+150+100}}$$

$$4.25 = \sqrt{\frac{50\times27.04 + 150\times22.09 + 100\times\sigma_3^2 + 50\times16 + 150\times11.09 + 100\times49}{300}}$$

$$4.25 = \sqrt{\frac{1352 + 3313.5 + 100\sigma_3^2 + 800 + 1163.5 + 4900}{300}}$$

$$4.25 = \sqrt{\frac{11529 + 100\,\sigma_3^2}{300}}, \quad (4.25)^2 = \sqrt{\frac{11529 + 100\sigma_3^2}{300}}$$

$$18.0625\times300 = 11529 + 100\ \sigma_3^2,\ 5418.75 = 11529 + 100\,\sigma_3^2$$

$$5418.75 - 11529 = 100\ \sigma_3^2,\ +6110.25 = 100\,\sigma_3^2,\ 100\sigma_3^2 = +6110.25$$

$$= \sigma_3^2 = \frac{+6110.25}{100} = 61.1025 = 7.82$$

Illustration 37: *The following are the run-scores of two cricketers in 12 innings. Find which batsman is more consistant in scoring.*

I	*20*	*12*	*24*	*95*	*60*	*52*	*40*	*15*	*74*	*96*	*10*	*29*
II	*50*	*45*	*37*	*60*	*65*	*75*	*80*	*44*	*37*	*29*	*55*	*60*

Solution: Calculation of co-efficient of variation.

I (*X*)	(*X* - 44) *x*	x^2	*II* (*Y*)	(*Y* - 53) *y*	y^2
20	-24	576	50	-3	9
12	-32	1024	45	-8	64
24	-20	400	37	-16	256
95	51	2601	60	7	49
60	16	256	65	12	144
52	8	64	75	22	484
40	-4	16	80	27	729
15	-29	841	44	-9	81
74	30	900	37	-16	256
96	52	2704	29	-24	576
10	-34	1156	55	2	4
29	-15	225	60	7	49
527		10763	637		2701

Co-efficient of variation I

$$\bar{x} = \frac{\Sigma x}{N} = \frac{527}{12} = 43.9166 = 44$$

$$\sigma = \sqrt{\frac{\Sigma x^2}{N}} = \sqrt{\frac{10763}{12}} = \sqrt{896.9166} = 29.948 = 30$$

$$\text{C.V.} = \frac{\sigma}{\bar{x}} \times 100 = \frac{30}{44} \times 100 = 0.68 \times 100 = 68$$

Co-efficient of variation II

$$\bar{y} = \frac{\Sigma y}{N} = \frac{637}{12} = 53.0833 = 53$$

$$\sigma = \sqrt{\frac{\Sigma y^2}{N}} = \sqrt{\frac{2701}{12}} = \sqrt{225.0833} = 15.002 = 15$$

$$\text{C.V.} = \frac{\sigma}{\bar{y}} \times 100 = \frac{15}{53} \times 100 = .28 \times 100 = 28$$

Co-efficient of variation I = 68

Co-efficient of variation II = 28

Since the co-efficient of variation is more in case of Batsman I compared to II, Batsman II is more consitant in scoring.

Illustration 38: *The arithmetic mean of 6 observations is 55 and the variation is 3.4. If 4 of the observations are 47, 59, 62 and 32. Calculate the other two observations.*

Solution: Calculation of missing observations.

$$\bar{x} = \frac{\Sigma x}{N} \quad \therefore \; \Sigma x = N\bar{x}$$

Hence, $N = 6, \; \bar{x} = 55$

$$\Sigma x = N\bar{x} = 6 \times 55 = 330$$

Let the two missing items be x_1 and x_2.

$$47+59+62+32+x_1+x_2=330$$

$$200+x_1+x_2=330$$

$$x_1+x_2=330-200$$

$$x_1+x_2=130$$

(Variance) = 3.4

$$\sigma^2=\frac{\sum x^2}{N}-(\bar{x})^2$$

$$3.4=\frac{\sum x^2}{6}-(55)^2$$

$$6\times 3.4=\sum x^2-3025\times 6$$

$$20.4=\sum x^2-18150$$

$$\sum x^2=18150+20.4=18170.4$$

$$\sum x^2=x_1^2+x_2^2+47^2+59^2+62^2+52^2$$

$$\sum x^2=x_1^2+x_2^2+2209+3481+3844+1024$$

$$\sum x^2=x_1^2+x_2^2+10558$$

Where, $\sum x^2=18170.4$ then

$$18170.4=x_1^2+x_2^2+10558$$

$$18170.4-10558=x_1^2+x_2^2$$

$$x_1^2+x_2^2=7612.4$$

$$(x_1+x_2)^2=x_1^2+x_2^2+2x_1x_2$$

$$130^2=7612.4+2x_1x_2$$

$$16900=7612.4+2x_1x_2$$

$$2x_1x_2=9287.6$$

$$x_1x_2=\frac{9287.6}{2}=4643.8$$

$$(x_1-x_2)^2=x_1^2+x_2^2-2x_1x_2=7612.4-2\times 4643.8$$

$$=7612.4-9287.6=-1675.2$$

$$x_1-x_2=-40.9292=\pm 41$$

$$x_1 + x_2 = 130 \quad \ldots \text{(i)}$$

$$x_1 - x_2 = -41 \quad \ldots \text{(ii)}$$

(i) + (ii) $$2x_1 = 89$$

$$x_1 = \frac{89}{2} = 44.5$$

$$x_1 + x_2 = 130, \quad x_1 = 44.5$$

$$44.5 + x_2 = 130$$

$$x_2 = 130 - 44.5 = 85.5$$

$$x_1 = 44.5 \text{ and } x_2 = 85.5 \text{ OR } x_1 = 85.5 \text{ and } x_2 = 44.5$$

Illustration 39: *The mean of 10 observations is 69 and its standard deviation is 5.4. Later on it was found that an item with value 75 is wrongly calculated as 65. Calculate the correct arithmetic mean and standard deviation.*

Solution: Calculation of correct arithmetic mean and standard deviation.

$$\bar{x} = \frac{\Sigma x}{N}$$

$$\Sigma x = N\bar{x}, \; N = 10, \; \bar{x} = 69$$

$$\Sigma x = 10 \times 69 = 690$$

But this is not the correct Σx, because one items has been taken as 65 instead of 75.

$$\text{Correct } \Sigma x = 690 - 65 + 75 = 700$$

$$\text{Hence, Correct Mean } = \frac{700}{10} = 70$$

Correct Standard Deviation

(Variance) $$\sigma^2 = \frac{\Sigma x^2}{N} - \bar{x}^2$$

$$N = 10, \quad s = 5.4, \quad \bar{x} = 69$$

$$5.4^2 = \frac{\sum x^2}{10} - 69^2$$

$$29.16 = \frac{\sum x^2}{10} - 4761$$

$$29.16 \times 10 = \sum x^2 - 4761 \times 10$$

$$291.6 = \sum x^2 - 47610$$

$$\sum x^2 = 47610 + 291.6$$

$$\sum x^2 = 47901.6$$

Correct $\sum x^2 = 47901.6 - 65^2 + 75^2 = 47901.6 - 4225 + 5625$

$$= 47901.6 + 1400 = 49301.6$$

Correct Variance $= \frac{\sum x^2}{N} - \bar{x}^2$

$$\sum x^2 = 49301.6, \quad N = 10, \quad \bar{x} = 70$$

$$\sigma^2 = \frac{19301.6}{10} - 70^2 = \frac{49301.6}{10} - 4900$$

$$= \frac{49301.6 - 49000}{10} = \frac{301.6}{10} = 30.16$$

Standard Deviation $= \sqrt{30.16} = 5.49 = 5.5$

Correct Mean = 70.

Illustration 40: *The following informations are related with the marks scored by students of 3 classes. Calculate the arithmetic mean and standard deviation of the marks scored by all the 120 students of the 3 classes.*

	Class I	*Class II*	*Class III*
No. of students	*40*	*60*	*20*
Standard deviation of the marks	*4*	*3.2*	*5*
Average marks scored by the students	*45*	*52*	*65*

Solution: Calculation of combined standard deviation.

$$\sigma_{123} = \sqrt{\frac{N_1\sigma_2 + N_2\sigma_2 + N_3\sigma_3 + N_1d_1^2 + N_2d_2^2 + N_3d_3^2}{N_1 + N_2 + N_3}}$$

$$\overline{X}_{123} = \frac{N_1\overline{X}_1 + N_2\overline{X}_2 + N_3\overline{X}_3}{N_1 + N_2 + N_3}$$

$s_1 = 4$, $s_2 = 3.2$, $s_3 = 5$, $N_1 = 40$, $N_2 = 60$, $N_3 = 20$, $\overline{X}_1 = 45$, $\overline{X}_2 = 52$, $\overline{X}_3 = 65$

$$X_{123} = \frac{40 \times 45 + 60 \times 52 + 20 \times 65}{40 + 60 + 20} = \frac{1800 + 3120 + 1300}{120}$$

$$= \frac{6220}{120} = 51.83$$

$$d_1 = \overline{x}_1 - \overline{x}_{123} = 45 - 51.83 = -6.83$$

$$d_2 = \overline{x}_2 - \overline{x}_{123} = 52 - 51.83 = 0.17$$

$$d_3 = \overline{x}_3 - \overline{x}_{123} = 65 - 51.83 = 13.17$$

$$\sigma_{123} = \sqrt{\frac{40 \times 4 + 60 \times 3.2 + 20 \times 5 + 40 \times (-6.83) + 60 \times 0.17 + 20 \times 13.17}{40 + 60 + 20}}$$

$$\sigma_{123} = \sqrt{\frac{160 + 192 + 100 - 273.2 + 10.2 + 263.4}{120}}$$

$$= \sqrt{\frac{452.4}{120}} = \sqrt{3.77} = 1.94$$

Combined arithmetic mean = 51.83

Combined standard deviation = 1.94

Illustration 41: *Calculate mean deviation and standard deviation for the data given below :*

Profit or Loss	No. of companies (in '0000 rupees)
-6--4	7
-4--2	15
-2-0	20
+0-+2	12
+2-+4	7
+4-+6	9
+6-+8	4
+8-+10	3

Solution: Calculation of mean deviation and standard deviation.

Profit or loss X in '0000	m	f	A - 1 d = m - A	fd	fd^2
-6 to -4	-5	7	-6	-42	252
-4 to -2	-3	15	-4	-60	240
-2 to -0	-1	20	-2	-40	80
-0 to 2	1	12	0	0	0
2 to 4	3	7	2	14	28
4 to 6	5	9	4	36	144
6 to 8	7	4	6	24	144
8 to 10	9	3	8	24	192
		N = 77		Sfd = -44	Sfd^2 = 1080

$$\sigma = \sqrt{\frac{\Sigma fd^2}{N} - \left(\frac{\Sigma fd}{N}\right)^2} \times c$$

$$\Sigma fd^2 = 1080, \quad \Sigma \text{fd} = -44, \quad \text{N} = 77$$

$$\sigma = \sqrt{\frac{1080}{77} - \left(\frac{-44}{77}\right)^2} \times 1$$

$$= \sqrt{14.03 - (-.57)^2} \times 1$$

$$= \sqrt{14.03 - 0.33} \times 1$$

$$= \sqrt{13.7} \times 1$$

$$= 3.7 \times 1 = 3.7$$

Calculation of mean deviation.

m	f	cf	$\lvert D \rvert$ m-(-1.175)	$f\lvert D \rvert$
5	7	7	3.825	26.775
3	15	22	1.825	27.375
1	20	42	0.175	3.500
1	12	54	2.175	26.100
3	7	61	4.175	29.225
5	9	70	6.175	55.575
7	4	74	8.175	32.700
9	3	77	10.175	30.525
	$N = 77$			$\Sigma f\lvert D \rvert = 231.775$

Median = N/2 th item = $\frac{77}{2}$ th item = 38.5th item = 42.

Median lies in the class -2 to 0.

$$\text{Median} = L + \frac{N/2 - cf}{f} \times c$$

L = -2, $N/2$ = 38.5, cf = 22, f = 20, c =1.

$$\text{Median} = -2 + \frac{38.5 - 22}{20} \times 1 = -2 + \frac{16.5}{20} = -2 + 0.825 = -1.175$$

$$\text{Mean Deviation} = \frac{\Sigma f \lvert D \rvert}{N}$$

$$\Sigma f \lvert D \rvert = 231.775, \; N = 77$$

$$\text{M.D.} = \frac{231.775}{77} = 3$$

Standard deviation = 3.7, Mean deviation = 3

Illustration 42: *Calculate variance and co-efficient of variance from the data given below.*

Production (in tonnes)	*No. of factories*
0-15	*21*
15-30	*32*
30-45	*45*
45-60	*20*
65-75	*18*
75-90	*12*
90-105	*5*

Solution: Calculation of variance and its co-efficient.

Production X	*f*	*m*	*d=(m-52.5)/15*	*fd*	*fd*^{2}
0 - 15	21	7.5	-3	-63	189
15 - 30	32	22.5	-2	-64	128
30 - 45	45	37.5	-1	-45	45
45 - 60	20	52.5	0	0	0
60 - 75	18	67.5	1	18	18
75 - 90	12	82.5	2	24	48
90 - 105	5	97.5	3	15	45
				-115	*473*

$$\bar{X} = A + \frac{\sum fd}{N} \times c$$

A = 52.5, $\sum fd$ = - 115, N = 153, c = 15, $\sum fd^2 = 473$

$$\bar{X} = 52.5 + \frac{(-115)}{153} \times 15 \quad = 52.5 - 0.75 \times 15$$

$$= 52.5 - 11.25 = 41.25$$

$$\sigma = \sqrt{\frac{\sum fd^2}{N} - \left(\frac{\sum fd}{N}\right)^2} \times c$$

$$= \sqrt{\frac{473}{153} - \left(\frac{-115}{153}\right)^2} \times 15$$

$$= \sqrt{3.09 - (-0.75)^2} \times 15$$

$$= \sqrt{3.09 - 0.56} \times 15 = \sqrt{2.53} \times 15$$

$$= 1.59 \times 15 = 23.8589 = 23.86$$

Variance = Standard deviation square

$$\sigma = 23.86$$

$$\sigma^2 = 23.86^2$$

Variance $= 569.3$

Co-efficient of variation $= \frac{\sigma}{\bar{X}} \times 100$

$$= \frac{23.86}{41.25} = 0.58$$

i.e., $= 0.58 \times 100 = 58\%$

Co-efficient of variation = 58%

Illustration 43: *The average price of coffee in India for 1990 and 1991 are given below.*

Months	*1990 (Rs.)*	*1991 (Rs.)*
January	*32*	*35*
February	*40*	*49*
March	*30*	*52*
April	*29*	*26*
May	*42*	*25*
June	*45*	*29*
July	*49*	*31*
August	*35*	*45*
September	*37*	*30*
October	*30*	*32*
November	*29*	*27*
December	*28*	*24*

Calculate mean and standard deviation. Also find out in which year the prices are stable.

Solution: Computation of mean and standard deviation.

1990 X	*X-35.5* x	x^2	*1991* Y	*Y-33.75* y	y^2
32	-3.5	12.25	35	1.25	1.5625
40	4.5	20.25	49	15.25	232.5625
30	-5.5	30.25	52	18.25	333.0625
29	-6.5	42.25	26	-7.75	60.0625
42	6.5	42.25	25	-8.75	76.5625
45	9.5	90.25	29	-4.75	22.5625
49	13.5	12.25	31	-2.75	7.5625
35	-0.5	0.25	45	11.25	126.5625
37	1.5	2.25	30	-3.75	14.0625
30	-5.5	30.25	32	-1.75	3.0625
29	-6.5	42.25	27	-6.75	45.5625
28	-7.5	56.25	24	-9.75	95.0625
$\Sigma X = 426$		$\Sigma x^2 = 381$	$\Sigma y = 405$		$\Sigma y^2 = 1018.25$

Year 1990:

$$\bar{X} = \frac{\Sigma X}{N} = \frac{426}{12} = 35.5$$

$$\sigma = \sqrt{\frac{\Sigma x^2}{N}} = \sqrt{\frac{381}{12}} = \sqrt{31.75} = 5.63$$

Mean = 35.5

Standard deviation = 5.63

$$\text{C.V.} = \frac{\sigma}{\bar{X}} \times 100 = \frac{5.63}{35.5} \times 100 = 15.85$$

Year 1991:

$$\bar{Y} = \frac{\Sigma y}{N} = \frac{405}{12} = 33.75$$

$$\sigma = \sqrt{\frac{y^2}{N}} = \sqrt{\frac{1018}{12}} = \sqrt{84.83} = 9.21$$

Mean = 33.75

Standard deviation = 9.21

$$\text{C.V.} = \frac{\sigma}{\bar{Y}} \times 100 = \frac{9.21}{33.75} \times 100 = 27.28$$

Co-efficient of Variation: For 1990 = 15.85 %

For 1991 = 27.28 %

The co-efficient of variation is less for the price of coffee in the year 1990. Hence the year 1990 shows greater stability in the prices of coffee compared to 1991.

Illustration 44: *The following information is related with the daily expenses (in rupees) of 50 sample families in a locality. Prepare the class intervals of 10 duration and find out the standard deviation and co-efficient of variation.*

75	*45*	*32*	*75*	*105*	*100*	*60*	*42*	*30*	*90*
54	*79*	*82*	*92*	*77*	*67*	*42*	*89*	*100*	*110*
45	*33*	*45*	*33*	*79*	*64*	*47*	*49*	*54*	*73*
39	*32*	*39*	*27*	*35*	*47*	*59*	*64*	*67*	*72*
47	*35*	*29*	*39*	*44*	*48*	*54*	*67*	*75*	*80*

Solution: Computation of standard deviation and co-efficient of variation.

Class intervals X	*Tally Bars*	*f*	*m*	*m-65 / 10* d	*fd*	*fd²*
20-30	‖	2	25	-4	-8	32
30-40	𝍸 𝍸	10	35	-3	-30	90
40-50	𝍸 𝍸 I	11	45	-2	-22	44
50-60	𝍸	5	55	-1	-5	5
60-70	𝍸	5	65	0	0	0
70-80	𝍸 IIII	9	75	1	9	9
80-90	III	3	85	2	6	12
90-100	III	3	95	3	9	27
100-110	‖	2	105	4	8	32
		50			*-33*	*251*

$$\text{C.V.} = \frac{\sigma}{\bar{X}} \times 100$$

$$\bar{X} = A + \frac{\Sigma fd}{N} \times c$$

$$A = 65, \quad \Sigma fd = -33, \quad N = 50, \quad c = 10, \quad \Sigma fd^2 = 251$$

$$\bar{X} = 65 + \frac{(-33)}{50} \times 10 \;= 65 + (-6.6)$$

$$= 65 - 6.6 = 58.4$$

Mean = 58.4

$$\text{Standard deviation} = \sqrt{\frac{\Sigma fd^2}{N} - \left(\frac{\Sigma fd}{N}\right)^2} \times c$$

$$= \sqrt{\frac{251}{50} - \left(\frac{-33}{50}\right)^2} \times 10 = \sqrt{5.02 - (-.66)^2} \times 10$$

$$= \sqrt{5.02 - 0.44} \times 10 = \sqrt{4.58} \times 10 = 2.14 \times 10 = 21.4$$

Co-efficient of variation $= \frac{\sigma}{\bar{X}} \times 100 = \frac{21.4}{58.4} \times 100$

$$= .3664 \times 100 = 36.64\%$$

Co-efficient of variation = 36.64 %

Standard deviation = 21.4

Illustration 45: *The following information is related with the wages given for workers in two factories.*

	Factory I	*Factory II*
No. of workers	*200*	*450*
Average wage (Rs.)	*83*	*65*
Variance of wage	*54*	*23*

Calculate the combined standard deviation of the 2 factories. In which factory variation of wages is greater.

Solution: Computation of combined standard deviation and variation.

Combined Mean $\bar{X}_{12} = \frac{N_1 \bar{x}_1 + N_2 \bar{x}_2}{N_1 + N_2}$

$\bar{x}_1 = 83$, $N_1 = 200$, $\bar{x}_2 = 65$, $N_2 = 450$

$$\bar{X}_{12} = \frac{200 \times 83 + 450 \times 65}{200 + 450} = \frac{16600 + 29250}{650} = \frac{45850}{650} = 70.53$$

$$\sigma_{12} = \sqrt{\frac{N_1\sigma_1^2 + N_2\sigma_2^2 + N_1 d_1^2 + N_2 d_2^2}{N_1 + N_2}}$$

$\bar{x}_{12} = 70.54$, $\bar{x}_1 = 83$, $\bar{x}_2 = 65$,

$$d_1 = \bar{x}_1 - \bar{x}_{12} = 83 - 70.54 = 12.46$$

$$d_2 = \bar{x}_2 - \bar{x}_{12} = 65 - 70.54 = -5.54$$

$N_1 = 200,\ \sigma_1^2 = 54,\ d_1 = 12.46,\ N_2 = 450,\ \sigma_2^2 = 23,$

$d_2 = -5.54$

$$\sigma_{12} = \sqrt{\frac{200 \times 54 + 450 \times 23 + 200 \times 12.46 + 450 \times (-5.54)}{200 + 450}}$$

$$= \sqrt{\frac{10800 + 10350 + 2492 - 2493}{650}}$$

$$= \sqrt{\frac{21149}{650}} = \sqrt{32.54} = 5.7$$

Co-efficient of variation for factory I & II

Factory I	Factory II
$\text{C.V.} = \frac{\sigma}{\bar{x}} \times 100$	$\text{C.V.} = \frac{\sigma}{\bar{x}} \times 100$
$= \sqrt{\text{Variance}}$	$= \sqrt{\text{Variance}}$
$= \sqrt{54} = 7.35$	$= \sqrt{23} = 4.79$
$\text{C.V.} = \frac{7.35}{83} \times 100$	$\text{C.V.} = \frac{4.79}{65} \times 100$
$= 0.0886 \times 100 = 8.86\%$	$= 0.0737 \times 100 = 7.37\%$

Co-efficient of variation of wages in Factory I is greater.

Illustration 46: *Calculate arithmetic mean of the two series if their co-efficient of variation are 40% and 75% repectively. The standard deviations of the two series are 8 and 5 repectively.*

Solution: Calculation of arithmetic mean

$$\text{C.V.} = \frac{\sigma}{\bar{x}} \times 100$$

Series A

C.V = 40

$\sigma = 8$

$\bar{x} = ?$

$$40 = \frac{8}{\bar{x}} \times 100$$

$$40 = \frac{800}{\bar{x}}$$

$$40\bar{x} = 800$$

$$\bar{x} = \frac{800}{40} = 20$$

Mean of Series A = 20.

Series B

C.V = 75

$\sigma = 5$

$\bar{x} = ?$

$$75 = \frac{5}{\bar{x}} \times 100$$

$$75 = \frac{500}{\bar{x}}$$

$$75\bar{x} = 500$$

$$\bar{x} = \frac{500}{75} = 6.67$$

Mean of Series B = 6.67

Illustration 47: *The arithmetic mean and standard deviation of group of 20 variables are 450 and 9 respectively. If one more variable with 600 as value, is added with the group, find out the new arithmetic mean and the standard deviation.*

Solution: Computation of new arithmetic mean and standard deviation.

New Mean $\bar{x} = \frac{\sum x}{N}, \quad N\bar{x} = \sum x$

$$N = 20, \qquad \bar{x} = 450$$

$$20 \times 450 = \sum x$$

$$\sum x = 9000$$

This is old $\sum x$, the New $\sum x$ after adding the variable 600.

$$\text{New } \sum x = 9000 + 600 = 9600$$

$$\text{New Mean} = \frac{\sum x \text{ (New)}}{N \text{ (New)}} = \frac{9600}{21} = 457.14$$

New Standard Deviation

(Variance) $\sigma^2 = \frac{\sum x^2}{N} - \bar{x}^2$

$\sigma = 9, \quad N = 20, \quad \bar{x} = 450$ (given)

$$9^2 = \frac{\sum x^2}{20} - 450^2$$

$$81 = \frac{\sum x^2}{20} - 202500 \quad = \frac{\sum x^2 - 202500 \times 20}{20}$$

$$= \frac{\sum x^2 - 4050000}{20}$$

$$81 \times 20 = \sum x^2 - 4050000$$

$$1620 = \sum x^2 - 4050000$$

$$\sum x^2 = 4050000 + 1620 = 4051620$$

New $\sum x^2 = 4051620 + 600^2$

$$= 4051620 + 360000 = 4411620$$

(Variance) $\sigma^2 = \frac{\sum x^2}{N} - \bar{x}^2$

$\sum x^2 = 4411620, \quad N = 21, \quad \bar{x} = 457.14$

$$\sigma^2 = \frac{4411620}{21} - 457.14^2 \quad = \frac{4411620}{21} - 208977$$

$$= \frac{4411620 - 4388517}{21} = \frac{23103}{21} = 1100.14$$

$$\sigma = \sqrt{1100.14} = 33.168 = 33.17$$

New Mean = 457.14 New standard deviation = 33.17

Illustration 48: *Calculate semi-interquartile range and quartile co-efficient of the following data.*

Age in years	*No. of companies*
20	*3*
30	*61*
40	*132*
50	*153*
60	*140*
70	*51*
80	*3*

(MGU: Section B April '95)

Solution:

Age in years X	*No. of companies* f	cf
20	3	3
30	61	64
40	132	196
50	153	349
60	140	489
70	51	540
80	3	543

$Q_1 = \left(\frac{N+1}{4}\right)$th item $= \frac{543+1}{4} = 136$ th item which is in *cf* 196.

Hence $Q_1 - 40$

$Q_3 = \frac{(N+1)3}{4}$ th item $Q_3 = \frac{(543+1)3}{4} = 408$ th item which is in *cf* 489. Hence $Q_3 = 60$

Semi-intergreatile range $= \frac{Q_3 - Q_1}{2} = \frac{60-40}{2} = 10$

Quartile co-efficient $= \frac{Q_3 - Q_1}{Q_3 + Q_1} = \frac{60-40}{60+40} = \frac{20}{100} = 0.2$

Illustration 49: *The following figures related to the size of the capital of companies.*

Capital (in lakhs of Rs.)	*No. of companies*
1-5	*20*
6-10	*27*
11-15	*29*
16-20	*38*
21-25	*48*
26-30	*53*
31-35	*70*

Calculate Mean Deviation. (MGU: Section B April '95)

Solution: Calculation of mean deviation.

Capital X	*No. of Co. f*	*m*	*d'*	*fd'*	*|D| m - 22*	*f|D|*
1-5	20	3	-3	-60	19	380
6-10	27	8	-2	-54	14	378
11-15	29	13	-1	-29	9	261
16-20	38	18	0	0	4	152
21-25	48	23	1	48	1	48
26-30	53	28	2	106	6	318
31-35	70	33	3	210	11	770
	N = 285				*Σfd'=221*	*Σf|D|=2307*

$$\text{Mean} = A \pm \frac{\sum fd^1}{N} \times c = 18 + \frac{221 \times 5}{285}$$

$$= 18 + 3.9 = 21.9 \quad \text{i.e., } 22$$

$$\text{M.D.} = \frac{\sum f\,|D|}{N} = \frac{2307}{285} = 8.09$$

Illustration 50: *Calculate the standard deviation of the following frequency distribution of marks.*

Marks	*0-10*	*10-20*	*20-30*	*30-40*	*40-50*	*50-60*	*60-70*
No. of students	*5*	*12*	*30*	*45*	*50*	*37*	*21*

(Kerala: Section B April '98)

Solution: Calculation of standard deviation.

Marks *X*	*f*	*m*	*d=m-A / i* *m-35 / 10*	*d²*	*fd*	*fd²*
0-10	5	5	-3	9	-15	45
10-20	12	15	-2	4	-24	48
20-30	30	25	-1	1	-30	30
30-40	45	35	0	0	0	0
40-50	50	45	1	1	50	50
50-60	37	55	2	4	74	148
60-70	21	65	3	9	63	189
	Σf = 200				*Σfd = 118*	*Σfd² = 510*

$$\text{Standard Deviation} = \sqrt{\frac{\sum fd^2}{N} - \left(\frac{\sum fd}{N}\right)^2} \times i$$

$$= \sqrt{\frac{510}{200} - \left(\frac{118}{200}\right)^2} \times 10$$

$$= \sqrt{2.2} \times 10 = 1.48 \times 10 = 14.8$$

Illustration 51: *The arithmetic mean and standard deviation of a series of 20 items were calculated by a student as 20 cm and 5 cm respectively. But while calculating them an item 13 was misread as 30. Find the correct mean and standard deviation.*

(Kerala: Section B April '97)

Solution: Arithmetic Mean $= \frac{\sum x}{N} \qquad 20 = \frac{\sum x}{20}$

$$\therefore \sum x = 20 \times 20 = 400$$

$$\text{Correct } \sum x = 400 + 13 - 30 = 383$$

$$\text{Correct Mean } = \frac{383}{20} = 19.15 \text{ cms.}$$

$$\text{S.D.} = \sqrt{\frac{\sum x^2}{N} - \left(\frac{\sum x}{N}\right)^2}$$

$$5 = \sqrt{\frac{\sum x^2}{20} - \left(\frac{400}{20}\right)^2}$$

$$25 = \frac{\sum x^2}{20} - 20^2$$

$$\frac{\sum x^2}{20} = 25 + 400$$

$$\sum x^2 = 425 \times 20 = 8500$$

$$\text{Correct } \sum x^2 = 8500 - 30^2 + 13^2 = 8500 - 900 + 169 = 7769$$

$$\text{Correct S.D.} = \sqrt{\frac{\sum x^2}{N} - \left(\frac{\sum x}{N}\right)^2} = \sqrt{\frac{7769}{20} - \left(\frac{383}{20}\right)^2} = 4.66$$

Illustration 52: *An operator of a fleet of trucks purchases 100 new tyres - 50 of Brand A and 50 of Brand B at the same price under substantially similar driving condition, he gets the following results.*

	Tyre A	*Tyre B*
Arithmetic Mean	*16,000 miles*	*20,000 miles*
Standard Deviation	*4,000 miles*	*8,000 miles*

Which brand you would advise him to buy in future and why?

(MGU: Section B September '94)

Solution: *Tyre A*

$$\text{Coefficient of Variation} = \frac{\text{S.D.}}{\text{A. Mean}} \times 100 = \frac{4000}{16000} \times 100 = 25\%$$

Tyre B

$$\text{Coefficient of Variation} = \frac{\text{S.D.}}{\text{A. Mean}} \times 100 = \frac{8000}{20000} \times 100 = 40\%$$

Since, co-efficient of variation for Tyre B is more, it is more variable. Hence, it is advisable to buy Tyre A.

Illustration 53: *Two samples of size 40 and 60 have 25 and 30 as their respective mean values. If their standard deviation are 4 and 5 respectively, find the mean and standard deviation of the combined group of size 100.* (MGU: Section B April '92)

Solution: Combined Mean $= \dfrac{n_1 \bar{x}1 + n_2 \bar{x}2}{n_1 + n_2} = \dfrac{40 \times 25 + 60 \times 30}{40 + 60}$

$$= \frac{1000 + 1800}{100} = 28$$

$$\text{Combined S.D.} = \sqrt{\frac{n_1\sigma_1^{\ 2} + n_2\sigma_2^{\ 2} + n_1 d_1^{\ 2} + n_2 d_2^{\ 2}}{n_1 + n_2}}$$

$$\sigma_1 = 4; \qquad \sigma_2 = 5$$

$$d_1 = \overline{X}_{12} - \overline{X}_1 = 28 - 25 = 3$$

$$d_2 = \overline{X}_{12} - \overline{X}_2 = 28 - 30 = -2$$

$$\text{Combined S.D.} = \sqrt{\frac{(40 \times 4^2) + (60 \times 5^2) + (40 \times 3^2) + (60(-2)^2}{40 + 60}}$$

$$= \sqrt{\frac{640 + 150 + 360 - 240}{100}}$$

$$= \sqrt{\frac{910}{100}} = \sqrt{9.1} = 3.02$$

Illustration 54: *Show that the standard deviation of the natural numbers 1 to 5 is 2.* (Kerala: Section B April '96)

Solution: Calculation of S.D.

X	*d* (x-3)	d^2
1	-2	4
2	-1	1
3	0	0
4	1	1
5	2	4
$\Sigma X = 15$		$\Sigma d^2 = 10$

$$\overline{X} = \frac{\Sigma x}{N} = \frac{15}{5} = 3$$

$$\text{S.D.} = \sqrt{\frac{\Sigma d^2}{N}} = \sqrt{\frac{10}{5}} = \sqrt{2} \quad \text{Variance} = 2$$

Illustration 55: *Mean of 100 items is 50 and the S.D is 4. Find the sum of square of all items.* (MGU: Section A April '98)

Solution: $\text{A.M.} = \frac{\Sigma x}{N}$

$$50 = \frac{\Sigma x}{100} \qquad \therefore \Sigma x = 100 \times 50 = 5000$$

$$\text{S.D.} = \sqrt{\frac{\Sigma x^2}{100} - \left(\frac{\Sigma x}{n}\right)^2}$$

$$4 = \sqrt{\frac{\Sigma x^2}{100} - \left(\frac{5000}{100}\right)^2}$$

$$16 = \frac{\Sigma x^2}{100} - 2500$$

$$\frac{\Sigma x^2}{100} = 2500 + 16 \qquad \therefore \Sigma x^2 = 2516 \times 100 = 251600$$

Illustration 56: *Calculate arithmetic mean, standard deviation and co-efficient of variation for the following data.*

Temperature 0 'C	*No. of days*
-40 to -30	*10*
-30 to -20	*28*
-20 to -10	*30*
-10 to 0	*42*
0 to 10	*65*
10 to 20	*180*
20 to 30	*10*

(Kerala: Section C April '97)

Solution:

Temperature X	*No. of days* *f*	*m*	*d* *m-d/10*	*fd*	d^2	fd^2
-40 to -30	10	-35	-4	-40	16	160
-30 to -20	28	-25	-3	-84	9	252
-20 to -10	30	-15	-2	-60	4	120
-10 to 0	42	-5	-1	-42	1	42
0 to 10	65	5	0	0	0	0
10 to 20	180	15	1	180	1	180
20 to 30	10	25	2	20	4	40
	$\Sigma f = 365$			$\Sigma fd = -26$		$\Sigma fd^2 = 794$

$$\text{Arithmetic Mean} = A \pm \frac{\Sigma fd}{N} \times c = 5 - \frac{26}{365} \times 10 = 5 - 0.7 = 4.3$$

$$\text{S.D.} = \sqrt{\frac{\Sigma fd^2}{N} - \left(\frac{\Sigma fd}{N}\right)^2} \times c = \sqrt{\frac{794}{365} - \left(\frac{26}{365}\right)} \times 10$$

$$= \sqrt{2.18 - 0.01} \times 10 = 1.47 \times 10 = 14.7$$

$$\text{Coefficient of Variance} = \frac{\text{S.D.}}{\bar{x}} = \frac{14.7}{4.3} = 3.41$$

C.V. should be less than one.

Exercises

1. Define Dispersion. Explain briefly the different methods of measuring dispersion?
2. What do you mean by dispersion? What are the purpose for calculating dispersion?
3. Define Dispersion. What are the characteristics of a good measure of dispersion?
4. Explain the merits and demerits of the measures of dispersion.
5. What are the different methods of calculating dispersion? Explain any one method you think the most important one and also state the reason for it.
6. Distingiush between the absolute and the relative measure of dispersion.
7. What do you mean by dispersion? What are the relative merits and demerits of various measures of dispersion?

8. Define Quartile Deviation. What are the objectives of quartile deviation?
9. What is Mean Deviation? Explain its objectives, merits and demerits.
10. Define Mean Deviation. Distingiush mean deviation from standard deviation.
11. What do you mean by Standard Deviation? State the reasons for the superiority of standard deviation over other measures of dispersion.
12. What is Co-efficient of Variation? What are the major objectives of variation?
13. Define Variance Distingiush co-efficient of variation from variance.
14. Define Lorenz Curve. Explain its objectives and merits.
15. What do you mean by Lorenz Curve? What are the steps for drawing a Lorenz curve.
16. Define Co-efficient of Variation. (MGU: Section A April '98)
17. What are the objectives of measuring dispersion?
    (MG U: Section B April '97)
18. Define Dispersion. (MGU: Section A September '93)
19. Define Quartile Deviation. (MGU: Section A September '92)
20. What do you mean by relative measure of dispersion?
    (Kerala: Section A April '97 & '98)
21. Distinguish between Mean Deviation and Standard Deviation.
    (Kerala: Section B April '98)
22. Define Standard Deviation. (Kerala: Section A April '93)
23. What is meant by relative measure of dispersion? State any two such measure. (Kerala: Section A September '93)
24. State the rank correlation co-efficient formula according to Spearman if there are ties and if there is no tie in the bivariate data. (Kerala: Section A September '93)
25. Calculate Range and Co-efficient of Range from the data given below.
    17, 25, 32, 69, 109, 165, 7, 4, 39
    (Ans: Range = 161; Co-efficient of Range = 0.95)
26. Calculate Quartile Deviation and Co-efficient of quartile deviation from the following data. 55, 49, 56, 72, 89, 39, 73, 54, 102, 90, 85
    (Ans: 17.5 and 0.24)
27. The following data are related with the income of families in a village for one month. Calculate quartile deviation co-efficient of quartile deviation and semi-inter quartile range.

Monthly Income (Rs.)	200	400	600	800	1000	1200
No. of families	4	16	19	18	12	7

(Ans: 300; 0.43; 300)

28. You are given the following data related with marks obtained by 75 students in a class. Calculate quartile deviation and co-efficient of quartile deviation.

Marks	10	20	30	40	50	60	70	80
No. of students	7	12	13	4	15	12	9	3

(Ans: 20 and 0.5)

29. Compute the co-efficient of quartile deviation from the following data.

Daily wages	0-10	10-20	20-30	30-40	40-50	50-60	60-70
No. of workers	11	15	17	19	20	5	4

(Ans; 0.42)

30. Calculate the lower and upper quartiles, 8 th Decile and 65 th Percentile from the following distribution.

x	12	18	24	30	36	42	48	54
f	3	5	7	12	13	6	5	4

(Ans: $Q_1 = 24$; $Q_3 = 42$; $D_8 = 42$; $P_{65} = 36$)

31. You are given the data related with the average monthly expenditure of sample families of a locality calculate first quartile, 3rd quartile, and co-efficient of quartile deviation.

Monthly Expenses	0-300	300-600	600-900	900-1200	1200-1500	1500-1800
No. of families	15	20	10	5	25	10

(Ans: $Q_1 = 393.8$; $Q_3 = 1365$; Co-efficient of Q. D = 0.55)

32. Calculate mean deviation and its co-efficient from the data given below.

x	10	20	30	40	50	60	70	80	90
f	35	47	52	69	78	57	43	32	15

(Ans: 17.59; 0.35)

33. The co-efficient of quartile deviation in a symmetrical distribution is 0.7. The first and 3rd quartiles are 21 and 42. Calculate the value of median. (Ans: 31.5)

34. Calculate arithmetic mean, mean deviation from median and mean from the data given below. 92, 45, 62, 38, 46, 72, 59, 40, 32

(Ans: 50; 14.88; 14.44)

35. The following data are related with the daily income of the families in a village. Calculate mean deviation from mean, median and mode. Also calculate co-efficient of mean deviations.

Income (Rs.)	25	35	45	55	65	75	85	95	105
No. of families	4	6	9	5	3	2	7	10	4

(Ans: M.D = 23.88; 23.8; 30.6; Co-efficient of M.D = 0.36; 0.37; 0.32)

36. Calculate standard deviation and co-efficient of variation from the data given below.

X	*f*
0-10.5	11
10.5-20.5	6
20.5-30.5	9
30.5-40.5	3
40.5-50.5	2
50.5-60.5	8
60.5-70.5	15
70.5-80.5	12
80.5-90.5	7

(Ans: S.D = 27.98; Co-efficient of Variation = 0.58)

37. Calculate the missing information from the following data.

	Variable A	*Variable B*	*Variable C*	*Combined*
Total Number	175	?	225	500
Mean	220	240	?	235
Standard Deviation	?	6.3	5.9	5.4

(Ans: 100; 244.4; 18.36)

38. The following information is related with the weight of 70 students of a class, calculate the standard deviation. Also calculate the lowest and highest weight of the students through mean technique.

Weight (in K.grams)	*No. of students*
42.5	4
45.5	9
47.5	3
49.5	7
51.5	15
54.5	12
56.5	9
58.5	11

(Ans: 4.74; 37.6; 66)

39. Calculate the S.D from the information given below.

d	-5	-4	-3	-2	-1	0	+1	+2	+3	+4
f	3	9	12	5	7	4	8	7	5	2

(Ans: 2.69)

40. You are given the details of runs scored by two batsmen in different innings. Find out who is the best batsman and who is more consistant in scoring runs.

A	22	80	10	72	97	32	25	120	30	92
B	52	45	39	47	39	57	44	46	40	51

(Ans: A is best batsman; B is more consistant)

41. The following information is extracted from the book of a company related with the work performance of 2 workers in term of their production in number of units for 10 days. Calculate the coefficient of variation of the two variables and find out who is more consistant in the performance.

Worker I	162	150	165	155	140	154	160	169	157	152
Worker II	160	95	170	182	87	105	97	69	173	150

(Ans : (1) 0.049, 0.303 (ii) Worker I is more consistant)

42. The arithmetic mean of 12 observations is 115 and its standard deviation is 3.7. Later on it was found out that a variable with value 127 is wrongly calculated as 172. Calculate the correct arithmetic mean and standard deviation. (Ans. X = 111.25, S.D. = 1648)

43. The coefficient of quartile deviation of 2 quartiles is 2.4. If Q1 is 39 calculate Q3. (Ans : 94.7)

44. The details regarding the weight of students in three classes of a school are given below.

	Class I	*Class II*	*Class III*
No. of Students	50	75	60
S.D. of the weights (kgms)	3.9	5.2	4.5
Average weight (kgms)	49	51	55

Calculate the combined arithmetic mean and the standar deviation.

(Ans. 51.76, 5.23)

45. The purchase of a company in various days are given below:

Mid values of intervals	125	135	145	155	165	175
No. of days	7	18	29	31	10	15

Calculate the arithmetic mean and standard deviation.

(Ans : 150.82; 14.1)

46. Calculate the mean deviation and standard deviation from the data given below.

Profit (Rs. in '000)	*No. of companies*
Above 10	100
Above 20	95
Above 30	82
Above 40	71
Above 50	57
Above 60	39
Above 70	22
Above 80	17
Above 90	9

(Ans : M.D. = 1854, S.D. 228.3)

47. The sales of various shops in a town are given below. Calculate variance and co-efficient of variation.

Sales (in '00 of rupees)		*No. of shops*
Less than	25	3
Less than	35	11
Less than	45	28
Less than	55	36
Less than	65	45
Less than	75	59
Less than	85	65

(Ans : 29600, 0.033)

48. The monthly income of people in two cities are given below.

Monthly Income (Rs.)	*No. of families*	
	Village I	*Village II*
300 - 350	120	12
350 - 400	93	32
400 - 450	109	43
450 - 500	57	72
500 - 550	110	50
550 - 600	65	62
600 - 650	72	54
650 - 700	44	65
700 - 750	60	70
Total	730	460

Calculate A.M, S.D; Combined A.M, S.D, and Variance.

(Ans. 126.5, 115.5; 524.92; 122.36 ; 14973)

49. The average daily expenses (in Rs.) for 60 families are given below.

32, 59, 12, 19, 27, 39, 57, 65, 79, 85, 93, 97, 17, 39, 54, 67, 79, 82, 87, 93, 21, 37, 52, 79, 82, 99, 75, 45, 42, 42, 47, 52, 53, 32, 52, 46, 45, 35, 67, 69, 71, 79, 82, 87, 86, 44, 47, 36, 53, 42, 48, 11, 87, 39, 45, 54, 67, 72, 82, 29, 37

Prepare the class intervals of 10 duration and calculate the standard deviation and coefficient of variation. (Ans. 22.86, 0.4)

50. Calculate standard deviation and co-efficient of variation from the following data.

X	0-20	20-40	40-60	60-80	80-100	100-120	120-140
f:	4	9	10	15	5	13	14

(Ans : 37.78, 0.48)

51. The average prices of tea and coffee in Inda for different months are given below.

Months	*Tea (Rs.)*	*Coffee(Rs.)*
January	32	53
February	39	59
March	42	41
April	36	37
May	34	57
June	37	36
July	41	39
August	39	40
September	37	55
October	41	37
November	40	35
December	35	54

Calculate mean and standard deviation separately for prices of tea and coffee. Find out which of the above is more consitant in prices.

(Ans. 37.75, 45.25; 2.98, 8.99; Tea is more consistant.)

52. From the following information calculate the combined standard deviation. Also find out in which factory variation of wage is great.

	Factory A	*Factory B*
No. of workers	500	750
Average wage (Rs.)	85	67
Variance of wage	22%	37%

(Ans. 31.72 Factory B)

53. The arithmetic mean and standard deviation of a distribution of 120 variables are 210 and 3.2 respectively. Calculate the sum of the deviation and the sum of the square of the deviation.

(Ans. 0, 1228.8)

54. The arithmetic mean and standard deviation of a distribution of 50 variables are 721 and 28 respectively. If two more variables of 820 and 800 are included with the distribution, find out the new arithmetic mean and standard deviation. (Ans. 724.42, 32.59)

55. Calculate the arithmetic mean of the two series if their coefficient of variations are 27% and 35% respectively. The standard deviation of the same series are 4.2 and 5.7 respectively. (Ans. 15.56, 16.29)

56. Calculate the mean deviation for the data

Marks	10 - 20	20 - 30	30 - 40	40 - 50	50 - 60	60 - 70
No. of Students	5	8	17	9	7	4

(Kerala: Section C April 96) (Ans: A.M = 38.4, M.D = 11.28)

57. Calculate Quartile deviation for the following data

Farm size (in acres)	*Number of farms*
0-40	394
40-80	461
80-120	391
120-160	334
160-200	169
200-240	113
240 and above	143

(Ans: 50.65)

58. The following table gives the data of income of 100 families in a village. Calculate Mean deviation and Standard deviation.

Income (Rs.)	*Number of families*
0-1000	18
1000-2000	26
2000-3000	30
3000-4000	12
4000-5000	10
5000-6000	4

(Kerala: Section C April 89) (MGU: Section B April 92)

(Ans: M.D = 1081.6, S.D. = 1353)

59. Find the standard devation of the following series.

Size of holding (Hectares)	*No. of farmers*
0-2	1000
2-4	2300
4-6	3600
6-8	2400
8-10	2700
10-12	3000
12-14	3300

What conclusion do you draw from your result (Ans: 3.54)

60. The annual salaries of a group of employes are given in the following tables

Salaries in Rs	45	50	55	60	65	70	75	80
No. of Persons	3	5	8	7	9	7	4	7

Calculate standard deviation of the salaries

(MGU: Section B Sep.93) (Ans: 7.55)

61. Calculate coefficient of quartile devation for the following data:

Wages in Rs per week	*No. of wage earners*
Less than 34	14
35-37	62
38-40	99
41-43	18
over-43	7

(MGU: Section C April 98) (Ans: 0.046)

62. Two cricketers scored the following runs in the several innings. Find who is better run getter and who is more consistant.

A:	42	17	83	59	72	76	64	45	40	32
B:	28	70	31	0	59	108	82	14	3	95

(MGU: Section B April 98) (Ans: A is better run getter and also more consistant Mean for A = 53 and B = 49)

63. From the data given below find which series is more consistant.

Variable	*Series A*	*Series B*
10-20	10	22
20-30	16	18
30-40	30	32
40-50	40	34
50-60	26	18
60-70	18	16

(Kerala: Section C April 95) (Ans: Series A is more constant, coefficinet of variance = 0.46 and 0.61)

64. Two sample size of 40 and 50 have the same mean 53, but different standard deviation 19 and 8 respectively find the standard deviation of combined sample of size 90. (Ans: Combined S.D = 14)

65. The following are the scores of two batsmen X and Y in a series of innings:

X:	12	115	6	73	7	19	119	36	84	29
Y:	47	12	76	12	4	54	37	48	13	8

Who is more consistant? Who is a better batman?

(Ans: Y is more cnsistant and X is a better batsman)

◆ Chapter 8 ◆

Skewness, Kurtosis, Moments

The measure of central tendency and dispersion do not explain all characteristics of frequency distribution. They explain only the central value, and to what extent the data are distributed from the central value. The measure of skewness and kurtosis explains the real characteristics of the distribution. They explain whether a distribution is symmetrical or not. If the distribution is not symmetrical the characteristics of the data are measured through skewness, kurtosis and moments.

I Skewness

Skewness means assymetrical distribution. If a distribution is assymmetrical one, it may be called as skewed distribution. In a symmetrical distribution (diagram No. 1) Mean, Median and Mode are equal. When the value of mean is more than the mode it is called positive skewness (diagram No. 2). When the value of mode is greater than mean, it is called negative skewness (diagram No. 3).

Diagram No. 1

Symmetrical Distribution

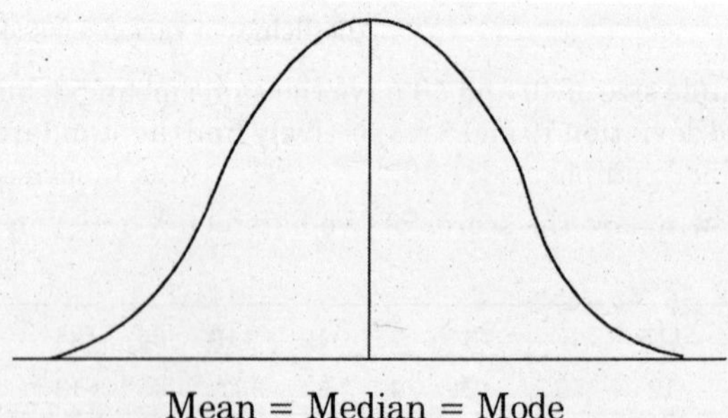

Mean = Median = Mode

Mean =Median = Mode

Diagram No.2

Positively Skewed Distribution

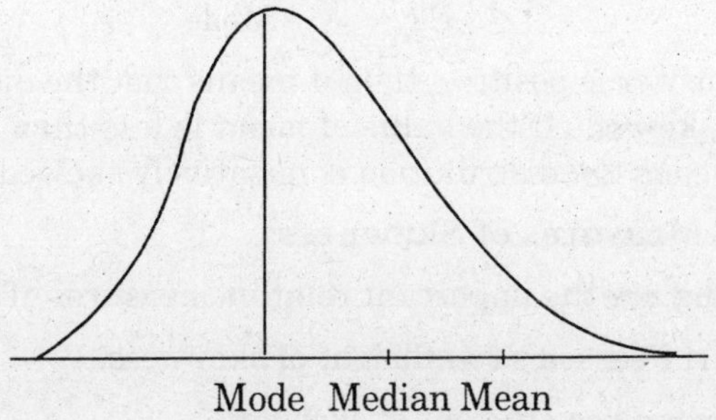

$\overline{X} > MED > MOD$

Diagram No.3

Negatively Skewed Distribution

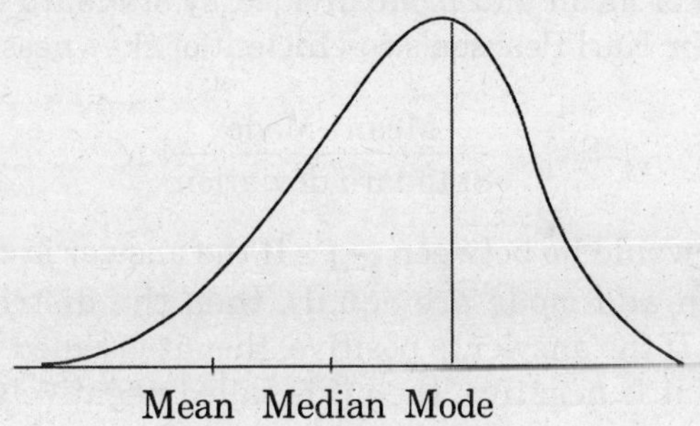

$\overline{X} < MED < MOD$

It is clear from the above diagrams that in a symmetrical distribution mean, median and mode are equal whereas in the assymmetrical distribution the value of mean, median and mode varies. The assymmetrical distribution is positively skewed if mean > median > mode. In the negatively skewed distribution mean < median < mode.

Measures of Skewness: Skewness may be measured either through absolute terms or through relative terms.

Absolute Measures of Skewness: In absolute terms, skewness may be measured by taking the difference between mode and mean. Hence the formula is,

$$\text{Sk.} = \bar{X} \text{ - Mode}$$

If the answer is positive, then it means that the distribution is positively skewed. If the value of mean is less than the value of mode, it means the distribution is negatively skewed.

Relatsive Measures of Skewness:

Following are the important relative measures of skewness.

1. Karl Pearson's co-efficient of skewness.
2. Bowley's co-efficient of skewness.
3. Kelly's co-efficient of skewness.
4. Measures of skewness based on moments.

1. Karl Pearson's co-efficient of Skewness: According to Karl Pearson the co-efficient of skewness woluld be measured through the difference of mean and mode divided by standard deviation. The formula for Karl Pearson's co-efficient of skewness is,

$$\text{Sk}_p = \frac{\text{Mean - Mode}}{\text{Standard deviation}}$$

The result would lie between ± 1. If the answer is zero (since mean, median and mode are equal), then the distribution is symmetrical. If the answer is positive, then it is called positively skewed and if it is negative, then it is called negatively skewed.

In the absence of mode the following formula may be applied by substituting the value of mode, as Mode = Median - 2 Mean,

$$\text{Sk}_p = \frac{3\left(\bar{X} \text{ - Median}\right)}{\text{Standard deviation}}$$

The result of the co-efficient of skewness through this formula, may vary between ± 3. But mostly it lies between ± 1.

Illustration 1: *From the following data calculate Karl Pearson's co-efficient of skewness.*

40, 36, 42, 53, 20, 65, 67, 20, 36

Solution: Calculation of mean and standard deviation.

X	d X - A (x - 40)	d^2
20	-20	400
20	-20	400
36	-4	16
36	-4	16
40	0	0
42	+2	4
53	+13	169
65	+25	625
67	+27	729
	$\Sigma d = 19$	$\Sigma d^2 = 2359$

$$\text{Mean} = A \pm \frac{\sum d}{N} = 40 + \frac{19}{9} = 42.11$$

$$\text{S.D.} = \sqrt{\frac{\sum d^2}{N} - \left(\frac{\sum d}{N}\right)^2} = \sqrt{\frac{2359}{9} - \left(\frac{19}{9}\right)^2} = \sqrt{262.11 - (2.11)^2}$$

$$= \sqrt{262.11 - 4.45} = \sqrt{257.66} = 16.05$$

$$\text{Median} = \frac{N+1}{2}\text{th item} = \frac{9+1}{2}\text{nd item}$$

= 5th item i.e., = 40

Since it is difficult to identify the mode the following formula may be applied for calculating the co-efficient of skewness.

Co-efficient of Skewness,

$$Sk_p = \frac{3\,(\text{Mean - Median})}{\text{Standard deviation}} = \frac{3(42.11 - 40)}{16.05} = \frac{3 \times 2.11}{16.05} = 0.39$$

Illustration 2: *The marks obtained by 100 students of a class are given below.*

Marks	*30*	*32*	*37*	*42*	*55*	*67*	*69*	*75*
No. of students	*9*	*11*	*17*	*20*	*10*	*13*	*9*	*11*

Calculate Karl Pearson's co-efficient of skewness.

Solution: Calculation of mean and standard deviation.

X	f	d x - A (x - 50)	d^2	fd	fd^2
30	9	-20	400	-180	3600
32	11	-18	324	-198	3564
37	17	-13	169	-221	2873
42	20	-8	64	-160	1280
55	10	+5	25	50	250
67	13	+17	289	221	3757
69	9	+19	361	171	3249
75	11	+25	625	275	6875
	100			$\Sigma fd = -42$	$\Sigma fd^2 = 25448$

$$\text{Mean} = A \pm \frac{\sum fd}{N} = 50 - \frac{42}{100} = 49.58$$

Mode = 42

$$\text{S.D.} = \sqrt{\frac{\sum fd^2}{N} - \left(\frac{\sum fd}{N}\right)^2} = \sqrt{\frac{25448}{100} - \left(\frac{-42}{100}\right)^2}$$

$$= \sqrt{254.48 - 0.1764} = \sqrt{254.3036} = 15.95$$

Karl Pearson's coefficient of skewness,

$$\text{Sk}_p = \frac{\text{Mean - Mode}}{\text{Standard deviation}} = \frac{49.58 - 42}{15.95} = 0.475$$

Illustration 3: *Calculate Karl Pearson's co-efficient of skewness from the following data.*

Marks	*No. of students*
0-10	*4*
10-20	*11*
20-30	*15*
30-40	*26*
40-50	*10*
50-60	*11*
60-70	*9*
70-80	*6*
80-90	*2*
90-100	*4*

Solution: Calculation of mean, mode and standard deviation.

X	f	cf	Mid value m	d (m - 55)/10	d^2	fd	fd^2
0-10	4	4	5	-5	25	-20	100
10-20	11	15	15	-4	16	-44	176
20-30	15	30	25	-3	9	-45	135
30-40	26	56	35	-2	4	-52	104
40-50	10	66	45	-1	1	-10	10
50-60	11	77	55	0	0	0	0
60-70	9	86	65	+1	1	9	9
70-80	6	92	75	+2	4	12	24
80-90	2	94	85	+3	9	6	18
90-100	4	98	95	+4	16	16	64
	N = 98					Σfd= -128	Σfd^2=640

$$\text{Mean} = A \pm \frac{\sum fd}{N} \times c = 55 - \frac{128}{98} \times 10 = 55 - 13.06 = 41.94$$

Calculation of Mode: Modal class is 30 - 40:

Hence, L = 30,

$$\Delta_1 = f_1 - f_0 = 26 - 15 = 11$$

$$\Delta_2 = f_1 - f_2 = 26 - 10 = 16$$

$$\text{Mode} = L + \frac{\Delta_1}{\Delta_1 + \Delta_2} \times i = 30 + \frac{11}{11+16} \times 10 = 30 + 4.07 = 34.07$$

$$\text{S.D.} = \sqrt{\frac{\sum fd^2}{N} - \left(\frac{\sum fd}{N}\right)^2} \times c = \sqrt{\frac{640}{98} - \left(\frac{-128}{98}\right)^2} \times 10$$

$$= \sqrt{6.53 - 1.72} \times 10 = 21.96$$

Karl Pearson's coefficient of skewness,

$$Sk_p = \frac{\text{Mean - Mode}}{\text{Standard deviation}} = \frac{41.94 - 34.07}{21.96} = \frac{7.87}{21.96} = 0.36$$

2. Bowley's Co-efficient of Skewness: Bowley's co-efficient of skewness is based upon the quartiles of the distribution. This measure is otherwise called as quartile measure of skewness. The formula under this method is stated as below.

$$Sk_B = \frac{(Q_3 - Q_2) - (Q_2 - Q_1)}{(Q_3 - Q_2) + (Q_2 - Q_1)} \text{ or } = \frac{Q_3 - Q_1 - 2\,\text{Median}}{Q_3 - Q_1}$$

where, Q_3 = third quartile;

Q_2 = second quartile or median and

Q_1 = first quartile.

The value of this co-efficient of skewness varies between ± 1.

Illustration 4: *Calculate Bowley's co-efficient of skewness for the data given below.*

Daily Income (Rs.)	*25*	*35*	*40*	*45*	*50*	*55*	*60*
No. of workers	*7*	*9*	*9*	*12*	*10*	*9*	*5*

Solution: Calculation of Bowley's co-efficient of skewness.

Income (Rs.) X	*No. of workers* *f*	*Cumulative No. of workers* *cf*
25	7	7
35	9	16
40	9	25
45	12	37
50	10	47
55	9	56
60	5	61

$$\text{Median } (Q_2) = \frac{N+1}{2} \text{ nd item } = \frac{61+1}{2} \text{ th item} = 31\text{st item}$$

i.e., = Rs. 45

$$Q_1 = \frac{N+1}{4} \text{ th item } = \frac{61+1}{4} \text{ th item} = 15.5 \text{ th item}$$

i.e., = Rs. 35

$$Q_3 = \frac{3(N+1)}{4} \text{ th item } = \frac{3(61+1)}{4} \text{ th item} = 46.5 \text{ th item}$$

i.e., = Rs. 50

Bowleys coefficient of skewness,

$$= \frac{Q_3 + Q_1 - 2\text{ Median}}{Q_3 - Q_1} = \frac{50 + 35 - (2 \times 45)}{50 - 35}$$

$$= \frac{85 - 90}{15} = \frac{-5}{15} = -0.33$$

Illustration 5: *Calculate Bowley's co-efficient of skewness from the following data.*

Expenses (Rs.)	*0-20*	*20-40*	*40-60*	*60-80*	*80-100*	*100-120*
No. of families	*4*	*21*	*18*	*27*	*37*	*5*

Solution: Calculation of co-efficient of skewness.

Expenses (Rs.) X	*No. of families* *f*	*Cumulative No. of families* *cf*
0-20	4	4
20-40	21	25
40-60	18	43
60-80	27	70
80-100	37	107
100-120	5	112

Median = N/2 th item = 112/2 th item = 56 th item. It lies in class interval 60 - 80;

Hence, L = 60, cf = 43, f = 27, i = 20 (80 - 60)

$$\text{Median} = L + \frac{N/2 - cf}{f} \times i = 60 + \frac{56 - 43}{27} \times 20 = 60 + 9.63 = 69.63$$

Q_1 = N/4 th item = 112/4 th item = 28th item. It lies in the class interval 40 - 60.

Hence, L = 40, cf = 25, f = 18, i = 20 (60 - 40)

$$Q_1 = L + \frac{N/4 - cf}{8} \times i = 40 + \frac{28 - 25}{18} \times 20 = 40 + \frac{60}{18} = 43.33$$

Q_3 = 3N/4 th item = (3 × 112)/4 th item = 84 th item. It lies in the class interval 80 - 100.

Hence, L = 80, cf = 70, f = 37, i = 100 - 80 = 20

$$Q_3 = L + \frac{3N/4 - cf}{f} \times i = 80 + \frac{84-70}{37} \times 20 = 80 + \frac{280}{37}$$

$$= 80 + 7.75 = 87.57$$

Bowley's coefficient of skewness,

$$Sk_B = \frac{Q_3 + Q_1 - 2\,\text{Median}}{Q_3 - Q_1} = \frac{87.57 + 43.33 - (2 \times 69.63)}{87.57 - 43.33}$$

$$= \frac{130.9 - 139.26}{44.24} = -0.189$$

3. Kelly's Co-efficient of Skewness: Kelly's co-efficient of skewness is based upon the percentiles or deciles of the distibution. It covers the beginning and end of the distribution. Here the distribution is analysed on the basis of the 10th and 90th percentiles. The formula is,

$$Sk_K = \frac{P_{90} + P_{10} - 2P_{50}}{P_{90} - P_{10}} \quad \text{(OR)} \quad = \frac{D_9 + D_1 - 2D_5}{D_9 - D_1}$$

where, P_{90} is 90th percentile; P_{10} is 10th percentile; P_{50} is 50th percentile or median; D_9 is decile9; D_1 is decile 1 and D_5 is decile 5 or median.

Illustration 6: *Calculate Kelly's co-efficient of skewness, from the following data.*

X	100	125	150	175	200	225	250
f	12	18	25	30	10	20	15

Solution: Calculation of Kelly's co-efficient of skewness.

X	*f*	*cf*
100	12	12
125	18	30
150	25	55
175	30	85
200	10	95
225	20	115
250	15	130

$$\text{Median } (P_{50}) = \frac{N+1}{2} \text{ th item} = \frac{130+1}{2} \text{ nd item} = 65.5 \text{ th item}$$

i.e., = 175

$$P_{90} = \frac{90(N+1)}{100} \text{th item} = \frac{90(130+1)}{100} \text{th item} = 117.9 \text{ th item}$$

i.e., = 250

$$P_{10} = \frac{10(N+1)}{100} \text{th item} = \frac{10(130+1)}{100} \text{th item} = 13.1 \text{ th item}$$

i.e., = 125

Kellys coefficient of skewness,

$$Sk_K = \frac{P_{90} + P_{10} - 2\,\text{Median}}{P_{90} - P_{10}} = \frac{250 + 125 - (2 \times 175)}{250 - 125}$$

$$= \frac{375 - 350}{125} = \frac{25}{125} = 0.2$$

Illustration 7: *Compute Kelly's co-efficient of skewness from the following data.*

Weekly Expenses (Rs.)	*No. of families*
0-25	*15*
25-50	*19*
50-75	*25*
75-100	*37*
100-125	*50*
125-150	*41*
150-175	*36*
175-200	*12*
200-225	*19*
225-250	*11*

Solution: Calculation of Kelly's co-efficient of skewness

Expenses (Rs.) X	*No. of families* f	*Cumulative No. of families* cf
0-25	15	15
25-50	19	34
50-75	25	59
75-100	37	96
100-125	50	146
125-150	41	187
150-175	36	223
175-200	12	235
200-225	19	254
225-250	11	265

Median = N/2 th item $= \frac{265}{2}$ th item = 132.5 th item. It lies in class interval 100 - 125;

Hence, L = 100, cf = 96, f = 50, i = 125 - 100 = 25.

$$\text{Median} = L + \frac{N/2 - cf}{f} \times i = 100 + \frac{132.5 - 96}{50} \times 25$$

$$= 100 + 18.25 = 118.25$$

$$P_{90} = \frac{90N}{100} \text{ th item} \qquad P_{90} = \frac{90 \times 265}{100} \text{ th item} = 238.5 \text{ th item}$$

It lies in class interval 200-225

Hence, L = 200, cf = 235, f = 19, i = 225 - 200 = 25

$$P_{90} = L + \frac{90N/100 - cf}{f} \times i = 200 + \frac{238.5 - 235}{19} \times 25$$

$$= 200 + 4.605 = 204.605$$

$$P_{10} = \frac{10N}{100} \text{ th item} = \frac{10 \times 265}{100} \text{ th item} = 26.5 \text{ th item}$$

It lies in the class interval 25-50.

Hence, L = 25, cf=15, f = 19, i = 50 - 25 = 25.

$$P_{10} = L + \frac{10N/100 - cf}{f} \times i = 25 + \frac{26.5 - 15}{19} \times 15$$

$$= 25 + 15.13 = 40.13$$

Kelly's coefficient of skewness,

$$Sk_K = \frac{P_{90} + P_{10} - 2\,\text{Median}}{P_{90} - P_{10}} = \frac{204.605 + 40.13 - (2 \times 118.25)}{204.605 - 40.13}$$

$$= \frac{8.235}{164.475} = 0.05$$

II Moments

The term moment is generally used in physics which means *"movement of a force"* that turn a pivoted lever. But in statistics, it has been used to measure the characters of deviations from arithmetic mean of a distribution.

Moment is related with the deviation of distribution from the arithmetical mean. The arithmetical mean of these deviations should be analysed to find out the various moments. Various powers to these mean of the deviation are called moments. The mean of the first power is called first moment; mean of the second power is called second moment and so on. Moment is denoted by Greek letter μ (Pronounced as mu). Hence, the first moment is called μ_1, second moment as μ_2 and so on.

Calculation of moments for individual observation.

$$\mu_1 = \frac{\sum\left(X - \bar{X}\right)}{N} \text{ or } \frac{\sum x}{N}, \quad \mu_2 = \frac{\sum\left(X - \bar{X}\right)^2}{N} \text{ or } \frac{\sum x^2}{N}$$

$$\mu_3 = \frac{\sum\left(X - \bar{X}\right)^3}{N} \text{ or } \frac{\sum x^3}{N}, \quad \mu_4 = \frac{\sum\left(X - \bar{X}\right)^4}{N} \text{ or } \frac{\sum x^4}{N}.$$

Where, $x = \left(X - \bar{X}\right)$ μ_1 will always be equal to zero since the sum of deviations of the data from arithmetic mean is always zero.

Calculation of mean for frequency distribution: (i.e., for discrete series and continuous series)

$$\mu_1 = \frac{\sum f\left(X-\bar{X}\right)}{N} \quad \text{or} \quad \frac{\sum fx}{N}$$

$$\mu_2 = \frac{\sum f\left(X-\bar{X}\right)^2}{N} \quad \text{or} \quad \frac{\sum fx^2}{N}$$

$$\mu_3 = \frac{\sum f\left(X-\bar{X}\right)^3}{N} \quad \text{or} \quad \frac{\sum fx^3}{N}$$

$$\mu_4 = \frac{\sum f\left(X-\bar{X}\right)^4}{N} \quad \text{or} \quad \frac{\sum fx^4}{N}$$

where, $x = \left(X - \bar{X}\right)$

For the continuous series, mid value '*m*' should be taken instead of '*X*'.

Calculation of skewness and kurtosis from moments:

1. Skewness: $\beta_1 = \frac{\mu_3^{\,2}}{\mu_2^{\,3}}$

(β_1 is called Beta one which indicates skewness)

2. Kurtosis: $\beta_2 = \frac{\mu_4}{\mu_2^{\,2}}$

(β_2 is called Beta two which indicates Kurtosis)

Moments based on Arbitrary Origin

The Assumed Mean can also be used for calculating moments, instead of Actual Mean. The moments calculated through assumed mean is called raw moments which can be denoted as μ^1. It should be converted into real moments through other formulae. The details regarding these formulae are given below:

For individual observation:

$$\mu_1' = \frac{\sum (X-A)}{N} \text{ or } \frac{\sum d}{N}, \quad \mu_2' = \frac{\sum (X-A)^2}{N} \text{ or } \frac{\sum d^2}{N}$$

$$\mu_3' = \frac{\sum (X-A)^3}{N} \text{ or } \frac{\sum d^3}{N}, \quad \mu_4' = \frac{\sum (X-A)^4}{N} \text{ or } \frac{\sum d^4}{N}$$

For frequency distribution

$$\mu_1' = \frac{\sum f(X-A)}{N} \text{ or } \frac{\sum fd}{N} \text{ or } \frac{\sum fd'}{N} \times c$$

$$\mu_2' = \frac{\sum f(X-A)^2}{N} \text{ or } \frac{\sum fd^2}{N} \text{ or } \frac{\sum fd'^2}{N} \times c$$

$$\mu_3' = \frac{\sum f(X-A)^3}{N} \text{ or } \frac{\sum fd^3}{N} \text{ or } \frac{\sum fd'^3}{N} \times c$$

$$\mu_4' = \frac{\sum f(X-A)^4}{N} \text{ or } \frac{\sum fd^4}{N} \text{ or } \frac{\sum fd'^4}{N} \times c$$

where, $d' = \frac{X-A}{c}$, c = common factor

For continuous series mid-value, ('*m*') should be used instead of *X*. Conversion of moments based on arbitrary origin (assumed mean) into moments based on arithmetic mean.

$$\mu_1 = \mu_1' - \mu_1' = 0, \qquad \mu_2 = \mu_2' - (\mu_1')^2$$

$$\mu_3 = \mu_3' - 3\mu_1'\mu_2' + 2(\mu_1')^3$$

$$\mu_4 = \mu_4' - 4\mu_1'\mu_3' + 6(\mu_1')^2(\mu_2') - 3(\mu_1')^4$$

Illustration 8: *Calculate the first four moments from the data given below. 11, 18, 9, 10, 7, 6, 5, 4, 8, 2*

Solution: Calculation of Moments.

X	$(X-\bar{X})$ d (x - 8)	$(X-\bar{X})^2$ d^2	$(X-\bar{X})^3$ d^3	$(X-\bar{X})^4$ d^4
11	3	9	27	81
18	10	100	1000	10000
9	1	1	1	1
10	2	4	8	16
7	-1	1	-1	1
6	-2	4	-8	16
5	-3	9	-27	81
4	-4	16	-64	256
8	0	0	0	0
2	-6	36	-216	1296
$\Sigma x = 80$	$\Sigma d = 0$	$\Sigma d^2 = 180$	$\Sigma d^3 = 720$	$\Sigma d^4 = 11748$

$$\text{Arithmetic mean} = \frac{\sum X}{N} = \frac{80}{10} = 8$$

$$\mu_1 = \frac{\sum d}{N} = \frac{0}{8} = 0, \qquad \mu_2 = \frac{\sum d^2}{N} = \frac{180}{10} = 18$$

$$\mu_3 = \frac{\sum d^3}{N} = \frac{720}{10} = 72, \qquad \mu_4 = \frac{\sum d^4}{N} = \frac{11748}{10} = 1174.8$$

Illustration 9: *Compute the first four moments from the particulars given below:*

x	*10*	*20*	*30*	*40*	*50*	*60*	*70*
f	*3*	*3*	*2*	*5*	*4*	*2*	*1*

Solution: Calculation of Moments.

X	f	fX	(X- 37) d	fd	fd^2	fd^3	fd^4
10	3	30	-27	-81	2187	-59049	1594323
20	3	60	-17	-51	867	-14739	250563
30	2	60	-7	-14	98	-686	4802
40	5	200	+3	15	45	135	405
50	4	200	+13	52	676	8788	114244
60	2	120	+23	46	1058	24334	559682
70	1	70	+33	33	1089	35937	1185921
	$\Sigma f = 20$	$\Sigma fX = 740$		$\Sigma fd = 0$	$\Sigma fd^2 = 6020$	$\Sigma fd^3 = -5280$	$\Sigma fd^4 = 3709940$

$$\text{Arithmetic mean} = \frac{\sum fX}{N} = \frac{740}{20} = 37$$

$$\mu_1 = \frac{\sum fd}{N} = \frac{0}{20} = 0, \qquad \mu_2 = \frac{\sum fd^2}{N} = \frac{6020}{20} = 301$$

$$\mu_3 = \frac{\sum fd^3}{N} = \frac{-5280}{20} = -264, \quad \mu_4 = \frac{\sum fd^4}{N} = \frac{3709940}{20} = 185497$$

Illustration 10: *Compute the first 4 moments from the data given below.*

X	0-10	10-20	20-30	30-40	40-50	50-60	60-70
f	5	3	2	5	4	4	2

Solution: Calculation of moments.

X	f	m	fm	(m - 33) d	fd	fd^2	fd^3	fd^4
0-10	5	5	25	-28	-140	3920	-109760	3073280
10-20	3	15	45	-18	-54	972	-17496	314928
20-30	2	25	50	-8	-16	128	-1024	8192
30-40	5	35	175	+2	10	20	40	80
40-50	4	45	180	+12	48	576	6912	82944
50-60	4	55	220	+22	88	1936	42592	937024
60-70	2	65	130	+32	64	2048	65536	2097152
	$\Sigma f = 25$	$\Sigma fm = 825$			$\Sigma fd = 0$	$\Sigma fd^2 = 9600$	$\Sigma fd^3 = -13200$	$\Sigma fd^4 = 6513600$

$$\text{Arithmetic mean} = \frac{\sum fm}{N} = \frac{825}{25} = 33$$

$$\mu_1 = \frac{\sum fd}{N} = \frac{0}{25} = 0, \qquad \mu_2 = \frac{\sum fd^2}{N} = \frac{9600}{25} = 384$$

$$\mu_3 = \frac{\sum fd^3}{N} = \frac{-13200}{25} = -528$$

$$\mu_4 = \frac{\sum fd^4}{N} = \frac{6513600}{25} = 260544$$

Illustration 11: *Calculate the first four moments from the following data.*

X	*0-20*	*20-40*	*40-60*	*60-80*	*80-100*	*100-120*
f	*7*	*11*	*15*	*9*	*12*	*6*

Solution: Calculation of moments through assumed mean.

X	*f*	*m*	*(m-70)/20* d^1	fd^1	fd^2	fd^3	fd^4
0-20	7	10	-3	-21	63	-189	567
20-40	11	30	-2	-22	44	-88	176
40-60	15	50	-1	-15	15	-15	15
60-80	9	70	0	0	0	0	0
80-100	12	90	1	12	12	12	12
100-120	6	110	2	12	24	48	96
	Σf = 60			*Σfd = -34*	*Σfd² = 158*	*Σfd³ = -232*	*Σfd⁴ = 866*

Moments based on Arbitrary Mean

$$\mu_1' = \frac{\sum fd}{N} \times i = \frac{-34}{60} \times 20 = -11.3$$

$$\mu_2' = \frac{\sum fd^2}{N} \times i^2 = \frac{158}{60} \times 20^2 = 1053.3$$

$$\mu_3' = \frac{\sum fd^3}{N} \times i^3 = \frac{-232}{60} \times 20^3 = -30933.3$$

$$\mu_4' = \frac{\sum fd^4}{N} \times i^4 = \frac{866}{60} \times 20^4 = 2309333.2$$

Conversion of the moments based on Arbitrary mean into moments based on Arithmetical mean:

$$\mu_1 = \mu_1' - \mu_1' = 11.3 - 11.3 = 0$$

$$\mu_2 = \mu_2' - (\mu_1')^2 = 1053.3 - 127.7 = 925.6$$

$$\mu_3 = \mu_3' - 3\mu_1'\mu_2' + 2(\mu_1')^3$$

$$= -30933.3 - 3 \times (-11.3)(1053.3) + 2(-11.3)^3$$

$$= -30933.3 + 35706.9 - 2885.8 = 1887.8$$

$$\mu_4 = \mu_4' - 4\mu_1'\mu_3' + 6(\mu_1')^2(\mu_2') - 3(\mu_1')^4$$

$$= 2309333.2 - 4 \times (-11.3)(-30933.3)$$

$$+ 6(-11.3)^2(1053.3) - 3(-11.3)^4$$

$$= 2309333.2 + 1398185 + 806975.3 - 48914.2 = 4465579.3$$

III Kurtosis

Kurtosis is a Greek word, which means bulginess. Kurtosis refers to the measure of the peakness or flatness of the distribution of data. The extent of the peakness of the distribution from the normal distribution can be measured through kurtosis. If the curve is more peaked than the normal curve, then it is called '*Leptokurtic*'. If the curve is more flat-topped than the normal curve, it is called '*Platykurtic*'. The normal curve is called '*Mesokurtic*'. The diagramatical representation of these kurtics are shown in the following diagrams.

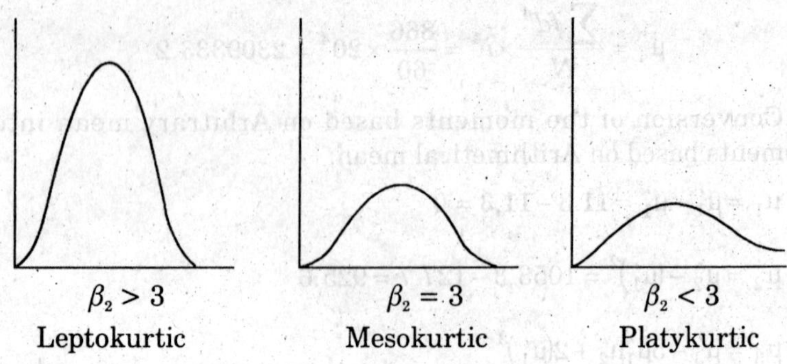

The kurtosis can be calculated through the following formu

$$\beta_2 = \frac{\mu_4}{\mu_2^{\ 2}}$$

where β_2 means kurtosis; μ_4 indicates 4th moment; μ_2 indic 2nd moment.

β_2 would equal to 3 for a normal curve i.e., mesokurtic. If value of $\beta_2 > 3$, then the curve is more peaked than the nor curve which is called Leptokurtic. If the value of $\beta_2 < 3$, t the curve is less peaked than the normal curve, which is ca platykurtic.

Illustration 12: *Calculate kurtosis from the following data.*

9, 18, 7, 11, 4, 6, 8

Solution: Calculation of kurtosis.

X	*d* (X - 9)	d^2	d^4
9	0	0	0
18	9	81	6561
7	-2	4	16
11	2	4	16
4	-5	25	625
6	-3	9	81
8	-1	1	1
$\Sigma x = 63$ $N = 7$		$\Sigma d^2 = 124$	$\Sigma d^4 = 7300$

Arithmetic mean, $\frac{\sum x}{N} = \frac{63}{7} = 9$

$\mu_2 = \frac{\sum d^2}{N} = \frac{124}{7} = 17.71$, $\mu_4 = \frac{\sum d^4}{N} = \frac{7300}{7} = 1042.86$

Kurtosis, $\beta_2 = \frac{\mu_4}{{\mu_2}^2} = \frac{1042.86}{(17.71)^2} = 3.33$

Since, $\beta_2 > 3$ it is Leptokurtic.

Illustration 13: *Calculate kurtosis from the following data.*

X	*5*	*11*	*15*	*17*	*20*	*35*
f	*2*	*1*	*4*	*10*	*3*	*2*

Solution: Calculation of kurtosis.

X	*f*	*(x - 15)* *d*	*fd*	*fd²*	*fd³*	*fd⁴*
5	2	-10	-20	200	-2000	20000
11	1	-4	-4	16	-64	256
15	4	0	0	0	0	0
17	10	2	20	40	80	160
20	3	5	15	75	375	1875
35	2	20	40	800	16000	320000
	N = 22		*Σfd = 51*	*Σfd² = 1131*	*Σfd³ = 14391*	*Σfd⁴ = 342291*

$\mu_1' = \frac{\sum fd}{N} = \frac{51}{22} = 2.32$, $\mu_2' = \frac{\sum fd^2}{N} = \frac{1131}{22} = 51.41$

$\mu_3' = \frac{\sum fd^3}{N} = \frac{14391}{22} = 654.14$

$\mu_4' = \frac{\sum fd^4}{N} = \frac{342291}{22} = 15558.68$

$\mu_2 = \mu_2' - (\mu_1')^2 = 51.41 - (2.32)^2 = 51.41 - 5.38 = 46.03$

$$\mu_4 = \mu_4' - 4\mu_1'\mu_3' + 6(\mu_1')^2(\mu_2') - 3(\mu_1')^4$$

$$= 15558.68 - (4 \times 2.32 \times 654.14) + 6(2.32)^2 \times 51.41 - 3(2.32)^4$$

$$= 15558.68 - 6070.42 + 1660.26 - 86.91 = 11061.61$$

Kurtosis, $\beta_2 = \frac{\mu_4}{\mu_2^2} = \frac{11061.61}{(46.03)^2} = 5.22$

Since, $\beta_2 > 3$ it is called Leptokurtic.

Illustration 14: *Calculate kurtosis from the following data.*

X	0-10	10-20	20-30	30-40	40-50	50-60
f	*11*	*7*	*9*	*20*	*2*	*4*

Solution: Calculation of kurtosis.

X	*f*	*m*	*(m -35)/10* *d*	*fd'*	*fd'²*	*fd'³*	*fd'⁴*
0-10	11	5	-3	-33	99	-297	891
10-20	7	15	-2	-14	28	-56	112
20-30	9	25	-1	-9	9	-9	9
30-40	20	35	0	0	0	0	0
40-50	2	45	1	2	2	2	2
50-60	4	55	2	8	16	32	64
	N = 53			*Σfd¹ = - 46*	*Σfd'² = 154*	*Σfd'³ = -328*	*Σfd'⁴ = 1078*

$$\mu_1' = \frac{\sum fd}{N} \times i = \frac{-46}{53} \times 10 = -8.7$$

$$\mu_2' = \frac{\sum fd^2}{N} \times i = \frac{154}{53} \times 10^2 = 290.6$$

$$\mu_3' = \frac{\sum fd^3}{N} \times i = \frac{-328}{53} \times 10^3 = -6188.7$$

$$\mu_4' = \frac{\sum fd^4}{N} \times i = \frac{1078}{53} \times 10^4 = 203396.2$$

$$\mu_2 = \mu_2' - (\mu_1')^2 = 290.6 - (-8.7)^2 = 290.6 - 75.7 = 214.9$$

$$\mu_4 = \mu_4' - 4\mu_1'\mu_3' + 6(\mu_1')^2(\mu_2') - 3(\mu_1')^4$$

$$= 203396.2 - 4(-8.7)(-6188.7) + 6(-8.7)^2(290.6) - 3(-8.7)^4$$

$$= 203396.2 - 215366.8 + 131973.1 - 17187 = 202815.5$$

Kurtosis, $\beta_2 = \dfrac{\mu_4}{\mu_2{}^2} = \dfrac{202815.5}{214.9^2} = 4.4$

Miscellaneous Illustrations

Illustration 15: *Calculate Karl Pearson's co-efficient of skewness from the following data.*

Daily Income (Rs.)	*12.5*	*15.5*	*18.5*	*21.5*	*24.5*	*27.5*
No. of workers	*27*	*32*	*11*	*15*	*5*	*10*

Solution: Calculation of co-efficient of skewness

X	*f*	*d* (X- 18.5)/3	*fd*	*fd*²
12.5	27	-2	-54	108
15.5	32	-1	-32	32
18.5	11	0	0	0
21.5	15	1	15	15
24.5	5	2	10	20
27.5	10	3	30	90
	N = 100		*Σfd = -31*	*Σfd² = 265*

Co-efficient of skewness, $= \dfrac{\text{Mean} - \text{Mode}}{\sigma}$

$\text{Mean} = A \pm \dfrac{\sum fd}{N} \times i$ A = 18.5, Σfd = -31, N = 100, i = 3

$$\bar{X} = 18.5 + \frac{(-31)}{100} \times 3 = 17.57$$

Mode: Since the highest frequency is 32, the corresponding value of x, i.e., 15.5 is the mode.

$$\text{S.D.} = \sqrt{\frac{\sum fd^2}{N} - \left(\frac{\sum fd}{N}\right)^2} \times i$$

$\Sigma fd^2 = 265$ N = 100 $\Sigma fd = -31$ i = 3

$$= \sqrt{\frac{265}{100} - \left(\frac{-31}{100}\right)^2} \times 3 = \sqrt{2.65 - 0.0961} \times 3$$

$$= \sqrt{2.5539} \times 3 = 4.79428$$

Coefficient of skewness, $= \frac{17.57 - 15.5}{4.79428} = 0.432$

Illustration 16: *Compute Karl Pearson's co-efficient of skewness from the data given below.*

Marks	*No. of students*
0-10	*4*
10-20	*11*
20-30	*21*
30-40	*32*
40-50	*15*
50-60	*13*
60-70	*5*
70-80	*7*
80-90	*3*

Solution:

Marks	*Mid point m*	*f*	*(m-45)d / 10*	*fd*	*fd²*
0-10	5	4	-4	-16	64
10-20	15	11	-3	-33	99
20-30	25	21	-2	-42	84
30-40	35	32	-1	-32	32
40-50	45	15	0	0	0
50-60	55	13	1	13	13
60-70	65	5	2	10	20
70-80	75	7	3	21	63
80-90	85	3	4	12	48
		N = 111		*Σfd = -67*	*Σfd² = 423*

Co-efficient of skewness, $= \frac{\text{Mean} - \text{Mode}}{\sigma}$

Mean $\bar{X} = A \pm \frac{\sum fd}{N} \times i$, A = 45, Σfd = -67, N = 111, i = 10

$$\bar{X} = 45 \pm \frac{(-67)}{111} \times 10 = 39$$

Mode: By inspection, mode lies in the class 40-50

$$M_O = L + \frac{\Delta_1}{\Delta_1 + \Delta_2} \times i = 40 + \frac{13}{45} \times 10 = 40 + \frac{11}{28} \times 10 = 43.9$$

(L = 40, Δ_1 = 32 - 21 = 11, Δ_2 = 32 - 15 = 17, i = 10)

$$\text{S.D.} = \sqrt{\frac{\sum fd^2}{N} - \left(\frac{\sum fd}{N}\right)^2} \times i = \sqrt{\frac{423}{111} - \left(\frac{-67}{111}\right)^2} \times 10$$

$$= \sqrt{3.8108 - 0.36434} \times 10 = \sqrt{3.44646} \times 10$$

$$= 1.8565 \times 10 = 18.6$$

Coefficient of skewness $= \frac{39 - 43.9}{18.6} = -0.26$

Illustration 17: *Calculate Karl Pearson's co-efficient of skewness from the data given below.*

X	*f*
25-50	*6*
50-75	*6*
75-100	*10*
100-125	*15*
125-150	*7*
150-175	*1*

Solution:

Range	*m.p* *m*	*f*	*(m - 112.5)/25* *d*	*fd*	*fd²*	*cf*
25-50	37.5	6	-3	-18	54	6
50-75	62.5	6	-2	-12	24	12
75-100	87.5	10	-1	-10	10	22
100-125	112.5	15	0	0	0	37
125-150	137.5	7	1	7	7	44
150-175	162.5	1	2	2	4	45
		N = 45		*Σfd =-31*	*Σfd² = 99*	

Karl Pearson's co-efficient of skewness,

$$Sk_P = \frac{3\left(\bar{X} - \text{Median}\right)}{\text{Standard deviation}}$$

$$\text{Mean } \bar{X} = A \pm \frac{\sum fd}{N} \times i = 112.5 - \frac{31}{45} \times 25 = 95.3$$

$$\text{S.D.} = \sqrt{\frac{\sum fd^2}{N} - \left(\frac{\sum fd}{N}\right)^2} \times i = \sqrt{\frac{99}{45} - \left(\frac{-31}{45}\right)^2} \times 25$$

$$= \sqrt{2.2 - 0.48} \times 25 = 1.3 \times 25 = 32.5$$

Median = Size of N/2 th item = 45/2 th item = 22.5 th item

It lies in class interval 100-125

Hence, L = 100, N/2 = 22.5, cf = 22, f = 15, i = 25

$$\text{Median} = L + \frac{N/2 - cf}{f} \times i = 100 + \frac{22.5 - 22}{15} \times 25$$

$$= 100 + 0.8 = 100.8$$

$$\text{Coefficient of skewness} = \frac{3(95.3 - 100.8)}{32.5} = -0.5$$

Illustration 18: *Calculate co-efficient of skewness on the basis of quartiles from the following distribution.*

Sales	*No. of factories*
0-20	*20*
20-40	*32*
40-60	*47*
60-80	*52*
80-100	*17*
100-120	*9*
120-140	*5*

Solution: Co-efficient of skewness $= \dfrac{Q_3 + Q_1 - 2\,\text{Median}}{Q_3 - Q_1}$

Calculation of Bowley's co-efficient of skewness.

Sales	*f*	*cf*
0-20	20	20
20-40	32	52
40-60	47	99
60-80	52	151
80-100	17	168
100-120	9	177
120-140	5	182
	N = 182	

Q_1 = N/4 th item = 182/4 th item = 45.5 th item

It lies in the class interval 20-40

L = 20, cf = 20, f = 32, i = 20, N/4 = 45.5

$$Q_1 = 20 + \frac{45.5 - 20}{32} \times 20 = 20 + 15.9 = 35.9$$

Q_3 = Size of 3N/4 th item = $(3 \times 182)/4$ th item = 136.5 th item

It lies in the class interval 60-80 $\therefore$ L = 60, cf = 99, f = 52

$$Q_3 = L + \frac{3N/4 - cf}{f} \times i = 60 + \frac{136.5 - 99}{52} \times 20$$

$$= 60 + 14.42 = 74.42$$

Median = Size of N/2 th item = 182/2 = 91 th item

It lies in the class 40-60

L = 40, cf = 52, f = 47, i = 20, N/2 = 91

$$\text{Median} = L + \frac{N/2 - cf}{f} \times i = 40 + \frac{91-52}{47} \times 20$$

$$= 40 + 16.5957 = 56.6$$

Coefficient of skewness

$$= \frac{74.42 + 35.9 - 2(56.6)}{74.42 - 35.9} = \frac{-2.88}{38.52} = -0.07$$

Illustration 19: *Compute Bowley's co-efficient of skewness, from the data given below.*

Mid value	*15*	*25*	*35*	*45*	*55*	*65*	*75*
Frequency	*3*	*9*	*6*	*12*	*4*	*8*	*2*

Solution: Calculation of Bowley's co-efficient of skewness.

Values	*f*	*cf*
10-20	3	3
20-30	9	12
30-40	6	18
40-50	12	30
50-60	4	34
60-70	8	42
70-80	2	44
	N = 44	

Q_1 = Size of N/4 th item = 44/4 th item = 11th item

It lies in the class interval 20-30

L = 20, cf = 3, f = 9, i = 10, N/4 = 11

$$Q_1 = L + \frac{N/4 - cf}{f} \times i = 20 + \frac{11-3}{9} \times 10 = 20 + 8.889 = 28.889$$

Q_3 = Size of 3N/4 th item = (3 × 44)/4 th item = 33 th item

It lies in the class interval 50-60

L = 50, cf = 30, f = 4, i = 10, 3N/4 = 33

$$Q_3 = L + \frac{3N/4 - cf}{f} \times i = 50 + \frac{33-30}{4} \times 10 = 57.5$$

Median = Size of N/2 th item = 22th item

It lies in class interval 40-50

L = 40, cf = 18, f = 12, i = 10, N/2 = 22

$$\text{Median} = L + \frac{N/2 - cf}{f} \times i = 40 + \frac{22-18}{12} \times 10 = 43.333$$

Coefficient of skewness,

$$= \frac{Q_3 + Q_1 - \text{Median}}{Q_3 - Q_1} = \frac{57.5 + 28.889 - 2(43.333)}{57.5 - 28.889}$$

$$= \frac{86.389 - 86.666}{28.611} = \frac{-0.277}{28.611} = -0.01$$

Illustration 20: *Calculate Kelly's co-efficient of skewness from the following data.*

X	*12*	*18*	*24*	*30*	*36*	*42*	*48*
f	*2*	*9*	*12*	*17*	*5*	*3*	*2*

Solution: Calculation of co-efficient of skewness on the basis of Kelly's Method.

x	f	cf
12	2	2
18	9	11
24	12	23
30	17	40
36	5	45
42	3	48
48	2	50

Kelly's co-efficient of skewness, $= \dfrac{P_{90} + P_{10} - 2\,\text{Median}}{P_{90} - P_{10}}$

$$\text{Median } (P_{50}) = \frac{N+1}{2} \text{ th item} = \frac{50+1}{2} \text{ th item} = 25.5 \text{ th item}$$

i.e., = 30

$$P_{90} = \frac{90(N+1)}{100} \text{ th item} = \frac{90(50+1)}{100} \text{ th item} = 45.9 \text{ th item}$$

i.e., = 42

$$P_{10} = \frac{10(N+1)}{100} \text{ th item} = \frac{10(50+1)}{100} \text{ th item} = 5.1 \text{ th item}$$

i.e., = 18

$$\text{Hence skewness} = \frac{42+18-(2\times30)}{42-18} = \frac{60-60}{24} = 0$$

Hence, it shows that the above data is symmetrically distributed.

Illustration 21: *Calculate co-efficient of skewness based on percentile from the following data.*

X	0-10	10-20	20-30	30-40	40-50	50-60
f	*12*	*20*	*35*	*45*	*10*	*8*

Solution: Skewness based on percentile is nothing but the Kelly's co-efficient of skewness.

Calculation of co-efficient of skewness.

x	*f*	*cf*
0-10	12	12
10-20	20	32
20-30	35	67
30-40	45	112
40-50	10	122
50-60	8	130

$$\text{Co-efficient of skewness} = \frac{P_{90}+P_{10}-2P_{50}}{P_{90}-P_{10}}$$

Median (P_{50}) = N/2 th item = 130/2 th item = 65 th item

It lies in class interval 20-30, L = 20, Cf = 32, f = 35.

$$\text{Median} = L + \frac{N/2 - cf}{f} \times i = 20 + \frac{65-32}{35} \times 10$$

$$= 20 + \frac{330}{35} = 29.43$$

$$P_{90} = \frac{90N}{100} \text{ th item} = \frac{130\times90}{100} \text{ th item} = 117 \text{ th item}$$

It is in class 40-50 $\quad \therefore$ L = 40, cf = 112, f = 10

$$P_{90} = L + \frac{90N/100 - cf}{f} \times i = 40 + \frac{117-112}{10} \times 10 = 40 + 5 = 45$$

$$P_{90} = \frac{10N}{100} \text{ th item} = \frac{10 \times 130}{100} \text{ th item} = 13 \text{ th item}$$

It lies in the class interval 0-10 $\quad \therefore$ L = 0, cf = 0, f = 12

$$P_{10} = L + \frac{10N/100 - cf}{f} \times i = 0 + \frac{13-0}{12} \times 10 = \frac{130}{12} = 10.8$$

Coefficient of skewness,

$$= \frac{P_{90} + P_{10} - 2P_{50}}{P_{90} - P_{10}} = \frac{45 + 10.8 - (2 \times 29.43)}{45 - 10.8} = \frac{-3.06}{34.2} = -0.089$$

Illustration 22: *The co-efficient of skewness based on quartiles for a distribution is 0.35. If the sum of the lower and upper quartiles is 42, and the median is 20, calculate the value of lower and upper quartiles.*

Solution: Given, $\frac{Q_3 + Q_1 - 2 \text{ Med}}{Q_3 - Q_1} = 0.35$

$$Q_3 + Q_1 = 42 \qquad \ldots (1)$$

$$\frac{42 - 2 \times 20}{Q_3 - Q_1} = 0.35, \qquad \frac{2}{0.35} = Q_3 - Q_1$$

$$Q_3 - Q_1 = 5.7143 \qquad \ldots (2)$$

Add (1) and (2)

$$Q_3 + Q_1 = 42, \qquad Q_3 - Q_1 = 5.714, \qquad 2Q_3 = 47.714$$

$$Q_3 = 23.857$$

$$23.8572 + Q_1 = 42,$$

$$Q_1 = 42 - 23.8572 = 18.1428$$

Upper Quartiles = 24, Lower Quartiles = 18.

Illustration 23: *Calculate the co-efficient of skewness through a suitable method from the data given below.*

Daily Expenses (Rs.)	*No. of families*
Below 30	*32*
30-40	*55*
40-50	*73*
50-60	*92*
60-70	*29*
70-80	*39*
80-90	*43*
Above 90	*20*

Solution: Calculation of Bowley's co-efficient of skewness.

Daily Expenditure (Rs.) X	*f*	*cf*
Below 30	32	32
30-40	55	87
40-50	73	160
50-60	92	252
60-70	29	281
70-80	39	320
80-90	43	363
Above 90	20	383
	N = *383*	

$$Sk_B = \frac{Q_3 + Q_1 - 2 \text{ Median}}{Q_3 - Q_1}$$

Q_1 = size of N/4th item = 383/4 th item = 95.75th item

It lies in the class interval 40-50.

$L = 40,\ cf = 87,\ f = 73,\ i = 10,\ N/4 = 95.75$

$$Q_1 = L + \frac{N/4 - cf}{f} \times i = 40 + \frac{95.75 - 87}{73} \times 10 = 41.2$$

Q_3 = size of 3N/4th item = (3 x 383)/4th item= 287.25th item.

It lies in the class interval 70-80.

$L = 70,\ cf = 281,\ f = 39,\ i = 10,\ 3N/4 = 287.25$

$$Q_1 = L + \frac{3N/4 - cf}{f} \times i = 70 + \frac{287.25 - 281}{39} \times 10 = 71.6$$

Median = size of N/2th item = 383/2th item = 191.5th item

It lies in class interval 50 - 60

$L = 50,\quad cf = 160,\quad f = 92,\quad i = 10,\quad N/2 = 191.5$

$$Q_1 = L + \frac{N/2 - cf}{f} \times i = 50 + \frac{191.5 - 160}{92} \times 10 = 53.4$$

$$Sk_B = \frac{71.6 + 41.2 - 2(53.4)}{71.6 - 41.2} = \frac{112.8 - 106.8}{30.4} = 0.2$$

Illustration 24: *The following data are related with the average daily production of workers in a factory.*

Production (in units)	*No. of workers*
20-30	*5*
30-40	*7*
40-50	*12*
50-60	*20*
60-70	*18*
70-80	*15*
80-90	*7*
90-100	*4*
100-110	*2*

Calculate the first four moments from the point 60 and convert the results into moments about mean. Also compute the values of β_1 *and* β_2.

Solution: Calculation of Moments.

Production	*m.p m*	*f*	*(m - 60)\10 d*	*fd*	*fd²*	*fd³*	*fd⁴*
20-30	25	5	-3.5	-17.5	61.25	-214.38	750.31
30-40	35	7	-2.5	-17.5	43.75	-109.38	273.44
40-50	45	12	-1.5	-18	27	-40.5	60.75
50-60	55	20	-0.5	-10	5	2.5	1.25
60-70	65	18	0.5	9	4.5	2.25	1.13
70-80	75	15	1.5	22.5	33.75	50.63	75.94
80-90	85	7	2.5	17.5	43.75	109.38	273.44
90-100	95	4	3.5	14	49	171.5	600.25
100-110	105	2	4.5	9	40.5	182.25	820.13
	N = 90			*0*	*308.5*	*154.25*	*2856.64*

$$\mu_1' = \frac{\Sigma fd}{N} \times i = \frac{0}{90} \times 10 = 0$$

$$\mu_2' = \frac{\Sigma fd^2}{N} \times i^2 = \frac{308.5}{90} \times 10^2 = 342.8$$

$$\mu_3' = \frac{\Sigma fd^3}{N} \times i^3 = \frac{154.25}{90} \times 10^3 = 1713.9$$

$$\mu_4' = \frac{\Sigma fd^4}{N} \times i^4 = \frac{2856.64}{90} \times 10^4 = 317404.4$$

Since $\Sigma fd = 0$ $A.M = 60$, when μ' is converted into μ, the same value will be available

For example: $\mu_1 = \mu_1' - \mu' = 0 - 0 = 0$

$$\mu_2 = \mu_2' - (\mu_1')^2 = 342.8 - 0 = 342.8$$

$$\mu_3 = \mu_3' - 3\mu_1'\mu_2' + 2(\mu_1')^3 = 1713 - 3 \times 0 \times 342.8 + 2(0)^2 = 1713$$

$$\mu_4 = \mu_4' - 4\mu_1'\mu_3' + 6(\mu_1')^2(\mu_2') - 3(\mu_1')^4$$

$$= 317404.4 - 4 \times 0 \times 1713.9 + 6 \times (0)^2 \times 342.8 - 3(0)^4 = 317404.4$$

$$\beta_1 = \frac{\mu_3^2}{\mu_2^3} = \frac{(1713.9)^2}{(342.8)^3} = 0.07, \quad \beta_2 = \frac{\mu_4}{\mu_2^2} = \frac{317404.4}{(342.8)^3} = 2.7$$

Illustration 25: *Calculate co-efficient of skewness and kurtosis through the method of moments from the data given below.*

Sales (Rs. in '00s)	*0-20*	*20-40*	*40-60*	*60-80*	*80-100*
No. of companies	*12*	*15*	*25*	*18*	*10*

Solution: Calculation of co-efficient of skewness and kurtosis

Sales	*m.p*	*f*	*(m - 50)/20*	*fd*	*fd²*	*fd³*	*fd⁴*
0-20	10	12	-2	-24	48	-96	192
20-40	30	15	-1	-15	15	-15	15
40-60	50	25	0	0	0	0	0
60-80	70	18	1	18	18	18	18
80-100	90	10	2	20	40	80	160
	N = 80			*-1*	*121*	*-13*	*385*

$$\mu_1' = \frac{\Sigma fd}{N} \times i = \frac{-1}{80} \times 20 = \frac{-20}{80} = -0.5$$

$$\mu_2' = \frac{\Sigma fd^2}{N} \times i^2 = \frac{121}{80} \times 20^2 = \frac{48400}{80} = 605$$

$$\mu_3' = \frac{\Sigma fd^3}{N} \times i^3 = \frac{-13}{80} \times 20^3 = \frac{-104000}{80} = -1300$$

$$\mu_4' = \frac{\Sigma fd^4}{N} \times i^4 = \frac{385}{80} \times 20^4 = \frac{61600000}{80} = 770000$$

$$\mu_2 = \mu_2' - (\mu_1')^2 = 605 - (-0.5)^2 = 604.75$$

$$\mu_3 = \mu_3' - 3\mu_1'\mu_2' + 2(\mu_1')^3 = -1300 - 3(-0.5)(605) + 2(-0.5)^3$$

$$= -1300 + 907.5 - 0.25 = -392.75$$

$$\mu_4 = \mu_4' - 4\mu_1'\mu_3' + 6(\mu_1')^2(\mu_1') - 3(\mu_1')^4$$

$$= 770000 - 4(-0.5)(-1300) + 6(-0.5)^2(605) - 3(-0.5)^4$$

$$= 770000 - 2600 + 907.5 - 0.2 = 768307.3$$

Coefficient of skewness $\beta_1 = \frac{\mu_3^2}{\mu_2^3} = \frac{(-392.75)^2}{(604.75)^3} = 0.42$

Kurtosis $\beta_2 = \frac{\mu_4}{\mu_2^2} = \frac{768307.3}{(604.75)^2} = 2.1$

Illustration 26: *Calculate S.D, mode and median when A.M is 125 C.V in 30% and co-efficient of skewness is + 0.24*

Solution: Given, $A.M = 125$, $C.V = 30\%$

Co-efficient of skewness = 0.24

$$C.V. = \frac{\sigma}{\bar{x}} \times 100 \qquad i.e. \quad 30 = \frac{\sigma}{125} \times 100 = 37.5$$

i.e. S.D. $= 37.5$

Also, coefficient of skewness,

$$= \frac{\bar{X} - Mode}{\sigma}, \quad 0.24 = \frac{125 - Mode}{37.5}, \quad \text{Mode} = 116$$

Again, Mode = 3 Median – 2 A.M

i.e, 116 = 3 Median – 2 x 125

3 Median = 366

Median = 122

Illustration 27: *Calculate S.D, when co-efficient of skewness is 0.8, A.M is 75 and Median is 70.*

Solution: Given, co-efficient of skewness = - 0.4, $A.M = 80$

Median = 70

Mode = 3 Median – 2 A.M = 3(70) – 2(75) = 210 – 150 = 60

$$\text{Co-efficient of skewness} = \frac{\bar{X} - Mode}{\sigma}$$

$$0.8 = \frac{75 - 60}{\sigma}, \quad S.D. = 8.75$$

Illustration 28: *You are given A.M = 140, median 135 and co-efficient of skewness = 0.42, calculate mode and co-efficient of variation.*

Solution: Given co-ef. of skewness = -0.42

Arithmetic mean = 140, Median = 135

Mode = 3 Med. – 2 $\bar{X}$ = 3 x 135 – 2 × 140 = 405 – 280 = 125

$$\text{Co-efficient of variation} = \frac{\bar{X} - Mode}{\sigma}, \quad -0.42 = \frac{140 - 125}{\sigma}$$

$$\sigma = \frac{15}{0.42} = 35.7$$

$$C.V. = \frac{\sigma}{\bar{X}} \times 100 = \frac{35.7}{140} \times 100 = 25.5\%$$

Illustration 29: *The S.D of a distribution is 3.4. Its A.M is 33.5 and Karl Pearson's co-efficient of skewness is +0.12. Calculate mode and median of the distribution.*

Solution: Given, S.D. = 3.4, $\bar{x}$ = 33.5, Sk_p = 0.12

$$Sk_p = \frac{\bar{X} - Mode}{\sigma} \qquad i.e., \qquad 0.12 \times 3.4 = 33.5 - Mode$$

$$Mode = 33.5 - 0.408 = 33.092$$

Also, Mode = 3 Median – 2x

i.e. 33.092 = 3 Median – 2 x 33.5

3 Median = 100.092

Median = 33.364

Illustration 30: *Using moments, calculate a measure of relative skewness and a measure of relative kurtosis for the following distribution and comment on the result obtained:*

Monthly wages (in Rs.)	*No. of workers*
70-90	*8*
90-110	*11*
110-130	*18*
130-150	*9*
150-170	*4*

(MGU: Section D April 1998)

Solution: Calculation of Moments.

X	*f*	*m*	*d*	*fd*	*fd²*	*fd³*	*fd⁴*
70-90	8	80	-2	-16	32	-64	128
90-110	11	100	-1	-11	11	-11	11
110-130	18	120	0	0	0	0	0
130-150	9	140	1	9	9	9	9
150-170	4	160	2	8	16	32	64
	50			*-10*	*68*	*-34*	*212*

$$\mu_1' = \frac{\Sigma fd}{N} \times i = \frac{-10}{50} \times 20 = -4 \qquad \mu_2' = \frac{\Sigma fd^2}{N} \times i^2 = \frac{68}{50} \times 20^2 = 544$$

$$\mu_3' = \frac{\Sigma fd^3}{N} \times i^3 = \frac{-34}{50} \times 20^3 = -5440$$

$$\mu_4' = \frac{\Sigma fd^4}{N} \times i^4 = \frac{212}{50} \times 20^4 = 678400$$

$$\mu_1 = \mu_1' - \mu_1' = 0$$

$$\mu_2 = \mu_2' - (\mu_1')^2 = 544 - (-4)^2 = 544 - 16 = 528$$

$$\mu_3 = \mu_3' - 3\mu_2'\mu_1' + 2(\mu_1')^3 = -5440 - 3 \times 544(-4) + 2(-4)^3$$

$$= -5440 + 6528 - 128 = 960$$

$$\mu_4 = \mu_4' - 4\mu_3'\mu_1' + 6\mu_2'(\mu_1')^2 - 3(\mu_1')^4$$

$$= 678400 - 4(-5440)(-4) + 6(544)(-4)^2 - 3(-4)^4$$

$$= 678400 - 87040 + 52224 - 768 = 642816$$

$$\text{Co-efficeint of Skewness} = \frac{\mu_3^2}{\mu_2^3} = \frac{(960)^2}{(528)^3} = 0.01$$

$$\text{Measure of Kurtosis} = \frac{\mu_4}{\mu_2^2} = \frac{642816}{(528)^2} = 2.3$$

Illustration 31: *From the following data, calculate the four moments (a) about the value 15; (b) about mean; (c) skewness based on moments and (d) Kurtosis.*

Class Interval	*0-10*	*10-20*	*20-30*	*30-40*
Frequency	*1*	*3*	*4*	*2*

(MGU: Section C April 1997)

Solution: Calculation of Moments about the value 15

X	*f*	*m*	*d*	*fd*	*fd²*	*fd³*	*fd⁴*
0-10	1	5	-1	-1	1	-1	1
10-20	3	15	0	0	0	0	0
20-30	4	25	1	4	4	4	4
30-40	2	35	2	4	8	16	32
	10			*7*	*13*	*19*	*37*

$$\mu_1' = \frac{\sum fd}{N} \times i = \frac{7}{10} \times 10 = 7 \qquad \mu_2' = \frac{\sum fd^2}{N} \times i^2 = \frac{13}{10} \times 10^2 = 130$$

$$\mu_3' = \frac{\sum fd^3}{N} \times i^3 = \frac{19}{10} \times 10^3 = 1900$$

$$\mu_4' = \frac{\sum fd^4}{N} \times i^4 = \frac{37}{10} \times 10^4 = 37000$$

$$\mu_1 = \mu_1' - \mu_1' = 0$$

$$\mu_2 = \mu_2' - (\mu_1')^2 = 130 - (7)^2 = 130 - 49 = 81$$

$$\mu_3 = \mu_3' - 3\mu_2'\mu_1' + 2(\mu_1')^3 = 1900 - 3(130)(7) + 2(7)^3$$

$$= 1900 - 2730 + 686 = -144$$

$$\mu_4 = \mu_4' - 4\mu_3'\mu_1' + 6\mu_2'(\mu_1')^2 - 3(\mu_1')^4$$

$$= 37000 - 4(1900)(7) + 6(130)(7)^2 - 3(7)^4$$

$$= 37000 - 53200 + 38220 - 7203 = 14817$$

Calculation of moments based on mean.

X	*f*	*m*	*fm*	*(X - x)*	*fd*	fd^2	fd^3	fd^4
0-10	1	5	5	-17	-17	289	-4913	83521
10-20	3	15	45	-7	-21	147	-1029	7203
20-30	4	25	100	3	12	36	108	324
30-40	2	35	70	13	26	338	4394	57122
	10		*220*		*0*	*810*	*-1440*	*148170*

$$\bar{X} = \frac{\Sigma fm}{N} = \frac{220}{10} = 22$$

$$\mu_1 = \frac{\sum fd}{N} = \frac{0}{10} = 0 \qquad \mu_2 = \frac{\sum fd^2}{N} = \frac{810}{10} = 81$$

$$\mu_3 = \frac{\sum fd^3}{N} = \frac{-1440}{10} = -144 \qquad \mu_4 = \frac{\sum fd^4}{N} = \frac{148170}{10} = 14817$$

$$\beta_1 = \frac{\mu_3^2}{\mu_2^3} = \frac{-144^2}{81^3} = 0.04, \qquad \beta_2 = \frac{\mu_4}{\mu_2^2} = \frac{14817}{81^2} = 2.26$$

Illustration 32: *From the data given below calculate skewness by using Pearson's measure.*

X	12.5	17.5	22.5	27.5	32.5	37.5	42.5	47.5
f	28	42	54	108	129	61	45	35

(MGU: Section C April 1996)

Solution: Calculation of skewness

X	*f*	*d'*	*fd'*	*fd'*^{2}
12.5	28	-3	-84	252
17.5	42	-2	-84	168
22.5	54	-1	-54	54
27.5	108	0	0	0
32.5	129	1	129	129
37.5	61	2	122	244
42.5	45	3	135	405
47.5	35	4	140	560
		N = 502	$\Sigma fd' = 304$	$\Sigma fd'^2 = 1812$

$$\text{Arithmetic Mean} = A \pm \frac{\Sigma fd'}{N} \times i = 27.5 + \frac{304}{502} \times 5$$

$$= 27.5 + 3.03 = 30.58$$

$$S.D. = \sqrt{\frac{fd'^2}{N} - \left(\frac{\Sigma fd'}{N}\right)^2} \times i = \sqrt{\frac{1812}{502} - \left(\frac{304}{502}\right)^2} \times 5$$

$$= \sqrt{3.61 - 0.37} \times 5 = 1.8 \times 5 = 9$$

Mode = 32.5

Karl Pearsons' Co-efficient of skewness

$$= \frac{\text{Mean} - \text{Mode}}{\text{Standard Deviation}} = \frac{30.58 - 32.5}{9} = \frac{-1.92}{9} = -0.21$$

Illustration 33: *Find out from the following data, Bowley's co-efficient of skewness.*

Marks in Hindi *90, 50, 52, 87, 76, 80, 85, 58, 61, 65.*

(MGU: Section B April 1994)

Solution: Arrangement of the data 50, 52, 58, 61, 65, 76, 80, 85, 87, 90

$$\text{Bowley's co-efficient of skewness} = \frac{Q_3 + Q_1 - 2 \text{ Med}}{Q_3 - Q_1} = 0.35$$

$$Q1 = \frac{N+1}{4} \text{th item} = \frac{10+1}{4} \quad \text{i.e., 2.75th item} = 58$$

$$Q3 = \frac{(N+1)^3}{4} \text{th item} = \left(\frac{10+1}{4}\right)^3 \quad \text{i.e., 8.25th item} = 85.$$

$$\text{Median} = \frac{\text{N}+1}{2} \text{th item} = \frac{10+1}{2} = 5.5 \text{ th item}$$

$$\text{i.e.} \quad \frac{65+76}{2} = 70.5$$

$$\text{Skewness} = \frac{85+58-2(70.5)}{85-58} = \frac{2}{27} = 0.07$$

Illustration 34: *For a moderately skewned distribution, arithmetic mean = 160, mode = 157 and standard deviation = 50. Find: (i) Co-efficient of variation; (ii) Pearson's co-efficient of skewness and (iii) Median* (Kerala: Section B April 1997)

Solution:

$$\text{Co-efficient of Variation} = \frac{\text{S.D}}{\text{Mean}} \times 100 = \frac{50}{160} \times 100 = 31.25\%$$

$$\text{Karl Pearson's Coefficient of Skewness} = \frac{\text{Mean} - \text{Mode}}{\text{S.D.}}$$

$$= \frac{160-157}{50} = \frac{3}{50} = 0.6$$

$$\text{Karl Pearson's Coefficient of Skewness} = \frac{3(\text{Mean} - \text{Median})}{\text{S.D.}}$$

$$0.06 = \frac{3(160 - \text{Median})}{50}$$

$$3(160 - \text{Median}) = 0.06 \times 50 = 3$$

$$160 - \text{Median} = \frac{3}{3} = 1, \quad \text{Median} = 160 - 1 = 159$$

Illustration 35: *Calculate Karl Pearson's co-efficient of skewness based on median from the following data.*

Marks above	0	10	20	30	40	50	60	70	80	90
No. of students	100	98	95	90	80	50	35	23	13	5

(Kerala: Section C April '97)

Solution: Calculation of skewness

Marks X	*f*	*Class interval*	*f*	*cf*	*m*	$d' = \frac{(m-45)}{10}$	*fd'*	fd'^2
0	100	0-10	2	2	5	-4	-8	32
10	98	10-20	3	5	15	-3	-9	27
20	95	20-30	5	10	25	-2	-10	20
30	90	30-40	10	20	35	-1	-10	10
40	80	40-50	30	50	45	0	0	0
50	50	50-60	15	65	55	1	15	15
60	35	60-70	12	77	65	2	24	48
70	23	70-80	10	87	75	3	30	90
80	13	80-90	8	95	85	4	32	128
90	5	90-100	5	100	95	5	25	125
							89	*495*

$$\text{Median} = \frac{N}{2} = \frac{100}{2} = 50 \text{ th item}$$

which is in class interval 40-50 $\therefore$ L = 40, cf = 20, f = 30

$$\text{Median} = L + \frac{N/2 - cf}{f} \times i$$

$$= 40 + \frac{50-20}{30} \times 10 = 40 + 10 = 50$$

$$\text{Arithmetic mean} = A \pm \frac{\sum fd'^2}{N} + i = 45 + \frac{89}{100} \times 10$$

$$= 45 + 8.9 = 53.9$$

$$\text{S.D.} = \sqrt{\frac{\sum fd'^2}{\text{N}} - \left(\frac{\sum fd'}{\text{N}}\right)^2} \times i = \sqrt{\frac{495}{100} - \left(\frac{89}{100}\right)^2} \times 10$$

$$= \sqrt{4.95 - 0.89^2} \times 10 = \sqrt{4.16} \times 10 = 20.4$$

$$\text{Skp} = \frac{3(\text{Mean - Median})}{\text{S.D}} = \frac{3(53.9 - 50)}{20.4} = 0.57$$

Illustration 36: *If the three quartiles of the distribution are respectively 14, 21, 26 find (i) the quartile deviation (ii) the co-efficient of quartile deviation and (iii) Bowley's co-efficient of skewness.* (Kerala: Section B April '95)

Solution: $Q_1 = 14$; Q_2 is median = 21; $Q_3 = 26$.

$$\text{Quartile Deviation} = \frac{Q_3 - Q_1}{2} = \frac{26 - 14}{2} = 6$$

$$\text{Coefficient of Quartile deviation} = \frac{Q_3 - Q_1}{Q_3 + Q_1}$$

$$= \frac{26 - 14}{26 + 14} = \frac{12}{40} = 0.3$$

$$\text{Bowleys coefficient of skewness} = \frac{Q_3 + Q_1 - 2\,\text{Median}}{Q_3 - Q_1}$$

$$= \frac{26 + 14 - 2(21)}{26 - 14} = \frac{40 - 42}{12} = \frac{-2}{12} = -0.17$$

Illustration 37: *The first three moments about 3 are 2, 10, 30. Find the mean, variance and third central moment.*

(Kerala: Section B September 93)

Solution: A = 3, $\mu_1{}^1 = 2 \quad \mu_2{}^1 = 10 \quad \mu_3{}^1 = 30$

$$\mu_1 = 0$$

$$\mu_2 = \mu_2{}^1 - (\mu_1{}^1)^2 = 10 - 2^2 = 10 - 4 = 6$$

$$\mu_3 = \mu_3{}^1 - 3\mu_1{}^1\mu_2{}^1 + 2\mu_2{}^{1^2} = 30 - 3 \times 2 \times 10 + 2(2)^3$$

$$= 30 - 60 + 16 = -14$$

$\text{Mean} = A + \mu_1^{\ 1} = 3 + 2 = 5$

$\text{Variance} = \mu_2 = 6$

$\text{Third central moment} = \mu_3 = -14$

Illustration 38: *Find the co-efficient of variation and Pearson's co-efficient of skewness of a frequency distribution of the number of children in 100 families.*

No. of children in a family	*0*	*1*	*2*	*3*	*4*	*5*
No. of families	*11*	*22*	*31*	*24*	*10*	*2*

(Kerala: Section C September 93)

Solution:

No. of children X	*No. of families* *f*	*cf*	*d* *(3 - x)*	*fd*	*fd²*
0	11	11	-3	-33	99
1	22	33	-2	-44	88
2	31	64	-1	-31	31
3	24	88	0	0	0
4	10	98	1	10	10
5	2	100	2	4	8
	100			*-94*	*236*

$$\text{Arithmetic Mean} = A \pm \frac{\sum fd}{N} = 3 - \frac{94}{100} = 2.06$$

$$\text{Median} = \frac{N}{2} \text{ th item} = \frac{100}{2} = 50 \text{ th item}$$

i.e., = 2

Mode = 2

$$\text{S.D.} = \sqrt{\frac{\sum fd'^2}{\text{N}} - \left(\frac{\sum fd'}{\text{N}}\right)^2} = \sqrt{\frac{236}{100} - \left(\frac{-94}{100}\right)^2}$$

$$= \sqrt{2.36 - 0.94^2} = \sqrt{1.48} = 1.21$$

$$\text{co - efficient of variation} = \frac{\text{S.D}}{\text{Mean}} \times 100$$

$$= \frac{1.21}{2.06} \times 100 = 58.7\% \quad \text{or} \quad 0.59$$

Karl Pearsons Co-efficient of skewness

$$= \frac{\text{Mean} - \text{Mode}}{\text{S.D}} = \frac{2.06 - 2}{1.21} = \frac{0.06}{1.21} = 0.05$$

Exercise

1. Define Skewness. What are the measures of skewness?
2. What is Kurtosis? State the methods of measuring kurtosis.
3. What is Moments? Explain the different types of moments and the methods of measuring moments.
4. Distinguish between skewness and kurtosis.
5. State the relationship of moments with skewness and kurtosis. How can skewness and kurtosis be measured through moments?
6. State diagramatically the different types of skewness.
7. State the different types of kurtosis through diagram.
8. Define skewness. (MGU: Section A April 97)
9. Define kurtosis.

   (MGU: Section A April 96; Kerala: Section A September 93)
10. Mention two tests to know the presence of skewness in a given series.

    (MGU: Section A April 95)
11. What is skewness?

    (MGU. Section A April 95; Kerala: Section A April 93 & 98)
12. What is Pearson's co-efficient of skewness?

    (MGU: Section A April 94)
13. What is kurtosis? (MGU: Section A April 93)
14. Explain positive skewness and negative skewness in a distribution. (Kerala: Section B April 98)
15. Define skewness and Kurtosis. (Kerala: Section A April 94 & 96)
16. Calculate Karl Pearson's co-efficient of skewness from the following data. 5, 7, 12, 15, 25, 35, 40, 45, 50 (Ans: 0.19)
17. From the following data compute co-efficient of skewness through Karl Pearson's method.

Daily Expenses (Rs.)	15	25	35	45	55
No. of families	4	8	10	6	2

(Ans: 0.18 (or) 0.54)

18. Compute co-efficient of skewness through Karl Pearson's method for the following data.

Marks	0-10	10-20	20-30	30-40	40-50	50-60	60-70
No. of students	4	7	8	10	6	4	1

(Ans: -0.17)

19. Calculate co-efficient of skewness by Bowley's method for the following data.

Daily wages (Rs.)	40	50	65	70	85	95
No. of workers	4	6	12	8	7	3

(Ans: -0.5)

20. Calculate co-efficient of skewness by Quartile and Median from the following data.

X	0-0	10-20	20-30	30-40	40-50	50-60
f	7	8	10	5	9	6

(Ans: 0.15)

21. Compute co-efficient of skewness by Kelly's method from the following data.

X	7	14	21	28	35	42
f	3	6	9	5	4	3

(Ans: 0.07)

22. From the following data calculate co-efficient of skewness through Kelly's method.

X	25-30	30-35	35-40	40-45	45-50
f	12	18	20	16	4

(Ans: -0.23)

23. Find out the value of co-efficient of skewness through percentile method for the following data.

Marks	35-45	45-55	55-65	65-75	75-85	85-95
No. of Students	2	4	18	16	7	3

(Ans: 0.11)

24. Compute the first 4 moments from the following data.

25 35 40 55 65

(Ans: $\mu_2 = 204$, $\mu_3 = 588$, $\mu_4 = 69252$)

25. Compute the first 4 moments from the following data. Calculate standard deviation also.

X	4	8	12	16	20	24
f	1	4	6	8	9	4

(Ans: $\mu_2 = 28$, $\mu_3 = -48$, $\mu_4 = 1792$, S.D = 5.3)

26. Find out the moments from the data given below.

Wages	30-40	40-50	50-60	60-70	70-80	80-90
No. of workers	4	8	12	6	3	2

(Ans: $\mu_2 = 187$, $\mu_3 = -77$, $\mu_4 = 83033$)

27. Calculate moments through indirect method from the following data.

X	12	15	21	30	42	45
f	8	4	7	5	3	2

(Ans: $\mu_2 = 119.3$, $\mu_3 = -4965.1$, $\mu_4 = 134789.3$)

28. Calculate kurtosis and co-efficient of skewness through moments from the following data. Also calculate standard deviation.

X	5	10	15	20	25	30	35
f	6	13	18	15	13	12	3

(Ans: Kurtosis = 2.08; Skewness = 0.01; S.D = 8.1)

29. Calculate S.D, mode and median, when A.M is 55, C.V is 20% and co-efficient of skewness is 0.12.

(Ans: S.D = 16.5; Mode = 53.02; Median = 48.4)

30. Compute S.D, when co-efficient of skewness is 2.4, A.M is 50 and median is 45. (Ans: S.D = 6.25)

31. You are given A.M as 120, median 115 and co-efficient of skewness 0.4. Calculate mode and co-efficient of variation.

(Ans: Mode = 115; C.V = 10.4%)

32. The S.D of a distribution is 6.8, the A.M is 62 and Karl Pearson's co-efficient of skewness is 0.8. Calculate mode and median of the distribution. (Ans: Mode = 56.56; Median = 60.2)

33. Find co-efficient of skewness, when the sum of two quartiles is 126.62, their difference is 18.8 and the median is 55.4. (Ans: 0.88)

34. Calculate β_1 and β_2 when $\mu_2 = 28$, $\mu_3 = 136$ and $\mu_4 = 1450$.

(Ans: $\mu_1 = 0.84$, $\mu_2 = 1.85$)

35. Calculate Pearson's co-efficient of skewness from the table given below.

Life of tube light (House)	*No. of tubes*
300-400	14
400-500	46
500-600	58
600-700	76
700-800	68
800-900	62
900-1000	48
1000-1100	22
1100-1200	6

(MGU: Section B September 94) (Ans: 0.24)

36. Find out Bowley's co-efficient of skewness from the following data.
Marks in Accountancy

Not more than	15	25	35	45	55	65	75	85
No. of students	3	10	40	55	65	72	75	80

(MGU: Section B September 93) (Ans: –1)

37. Find out the kurtosis of the data given below.

Income (Rs.)	20-40	40-60	60-80	80-100
No. of workers	3	4	3	1

(MGU: Section B September 92) (Ans: 30.73)

38. Calculate Karl Pearson's co-efficient of skewness from the following data.

X	0	1	2	3	4	5	6	7
f	12	27	29	19	8	4	1	0

(MGU: Section B September 93) (Ans: Co-efficient of skewness = 0)

39. Find out the skewness and kurtosis of the following series by the method of moments.

Measurement	0-10	10-20	20-30	30-40
Frequency	1	3	4	2

(MGU: Section B April 92) (Ans: Skewness = -0.2; Kurtosis = 2.26)

40. In a distribution Mean = 67, Median = 62 and Standard Deviation = 6, find skewness. (Kerala: Section B April 98) (Ans: 2.5)

◆ Chapter 9 ◆

Correlation Analysis

Correlation analysis is an analysis of the relationship of two or more variables. It measures whether the variables are correlated or not. It also measures the degree of correlation between two or more variables. The degree of correlation states about the extent of the closeness of two set of variables.

I Definition of Correlation Analysis

The important definitions of correlation analysis are stated below.

(1) According to Simpson and Kofka, correlation analysis deals with the association between two or more variables.

(2) Croxton and Cowden states when the relationship is of quantitative nature, the appropriate statistical tool for discovering and measuring the relationship and expressing it in brief formula is known as correlation.

(3) Ya Lum Chou defines 'Correlation analysis attempts to determine the degree of relationship between variables'. Hence, correlation analysis is defined as the study of the relationship of two or more variables.

Types of Correlation

There are three important types of correlation. They are,

(i) Positive or Negative Correlation

(ii) Simple, partial and multiple correlation

(iii) Linear and non-linear correlation.

(i) Positive or Negative Correlation: The correlation may either be positive or negative if, there exists correlation between two variables. If the increase in one variable influences the increase in the corresponding variables (or if the decrease in one variable, influences the decrease in other variables), then it is called positive correlation. If the increase in one variable decreases the value of

other variables or if the decrease in one variable increases the other variables, it is called negative correlation.

Example: Positive Correlation

(i)	x	:	10	20	30	40	50	60	70
	y	:	35	45	75	95	105	120	140
(ii)	x	:	48	40	32	24	16	8	
	y	:	30	25	20	15	10	5	

Negative Correlation

(i)	x	:	2	5	8	11	14	17
	y	:	20	25	20	15	10	5
(ii)	x	:	60	50	40	30	20	10
	y	:	12	24	36	48	60	72

(ii) Simple Partial and Multiple Correlation: Simple correlation means association of only two variables. It is a study of the relationship of only two set of variables. Partial and multiple correlation means the correlation of two or more set of variables. Sometimes one dependent variable may be influenced by two or more set of independent variables. *(e.g.)* Marks of students in a test paper may depend on teaching, tuition and study of students. Partial correlation is a study of correlation between one dependent variables with one independent variable by keeping the other independent variables as constants. *(e.g.)* The profit of companies depends on advertisement, volume of sales and seasonal selling. In partial correlation analysis, one can study the correlation between profit and advertisement by keeping sales and seasonal selling as constants. Multiple correlation is a study of three or more variables simultaneously.

(iii) Linear and Non-Linear Correlation: Linear and Non-linear correlation can be distinguished on the basis of the ratio of change of one variable with other variable. If the ratio of change between two set of variables is same, then it is called linear correlation.

Example for linear correlation is stated below.

x	5	10	15	20	25	30	35	40
y	8	16	24	32	40	48	56	64

The above data gives a straight line if plotted in a graph.

If the rate of change in one variable does not bear the constant ratio to the rate of change in the other variables, then it is called non-linear correlation. Non-linear correlation is otherwise called curvilinear correlation. The example for non-linear correlation is stated below.

x	5	10	15	20	25	30	35	40
y	3	6	12	10	15	21	28	35

II Methods of Correlation Analysis

Following are the important methods of calculating correlation.

I. Graphic Method

1. Scatter Diagram Method   2. Graphic Method

II. Statistical Method

1. Karl Pearson's Co-efficient of Correlation
2. Rank Method   3. Concurrent Deviation Method
4. Method of Least Squares

I Graphic Method

1. Scatter Diagram Method: This method is an important method in measuring the relationship of two variables. Under this method the data relating to the two variables should be plotted in a graph paper in the form of dots. The data relating to one variable should be plotted in x axis and the other variable in y axis. The number of dots plotted in the graph would equal to the number of observation of both the variables.

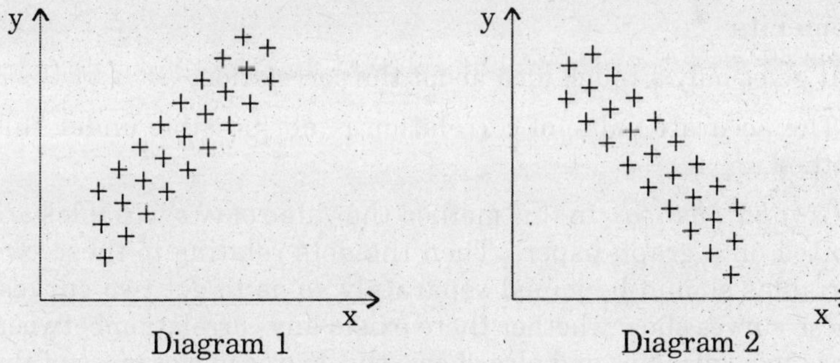

Diagram 1   Diagram 2

These plotted dots may show some trend either upward (Diagram 1) or downward (Diagram 2). If the trend of the dots are moving upward from left to right, then the correlation between these two variables is positive. It can be denoted as r = +1 (where r means correlation). If the trend of the dots are moving downward from left to right then also there exists a correlation between these variables. This correlation is called negative correlation, which can be stated as r = –1.

Sometimes there may not be any correlation between two variables. For such variables there may not be any trend either upward or downward.

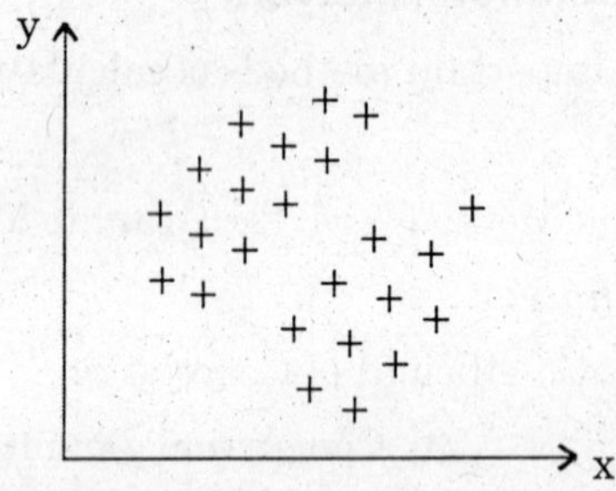

Hence, it is called absence of correlation (Diagram No. 3) which can be denoted as, r = 0.

Merits

1. It is a simple method of knowing the correlation.

2. It does not require any mathematical calculation.

3. It gives a rough idea about the correlation even to a lay men.

4. The extreme item of the variables may not affect this method of calculating the correlation.

Demerits

1. It gives only a rough idea about the correlation.

2. The accurate value of correlation is not possible under this method.

2. Graphic Method: In this method the value of two variables are plotted on a graph paper. Then the dots relating to these two variables should be joined separately so as to get two curves. These curves show whether there exists any correlation between these two variables and also shows the degree of closeness of the two variables. If the two curves move either upward or downward in the same direction, then the correlation between the two variables is positive. If the curves, move in the opposite direction then it is called negative correlation.

Illustration 1: *Draw a correlation graph from the following data.*

Months	*Jan*	*Feb*	*March*	*April*	*May*	*June*	*July*
Income (Rs.)	*1000*	*1200*	*1400*	*1800*	*1900*	*2000*	*2200*
Expenses	*900*	*1200*	*1300*	*1600*	*1700*	*1900*	*2000*

Solution: Correlation Graph

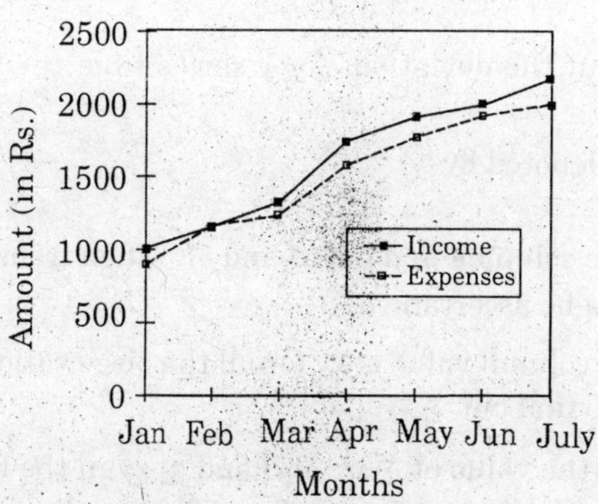

It is observed from the above graph that there exists a very close positive correlation between income and expenses.

II Statistical Method

1. Karl Pearson's Co-efficient of Correlation: Karl Pearson's co-efficient of correlation is the most popular method among the various methods for measuring the co-efficient of correlation. The co-efficient of correlation, under this method can be calculated as follows:

(a) Arithmetic Mean Method

$$r = \frac{\sum xy}{\sqrt{\sum x^2 \cdot \sum y^2}}$$

where, $x = \left(X - \bar{X}\right)$; $y = \left(Y - \bar{Y}\right)$

$X = X$ series, $Y = Y$ series N = Number of pairs of the variables,

r = Co-efficient of correlation

Steps

(i) Calculate arithmetic mean for x series and y series separately $(\bar{X}$ and $\bar{Y})$.

(ii) Find out the deviations for x series from the mean i.e.,

$\left(X-\bar{X}\right)$ It is denoted by 'x'.

Then find out the deviations for y series from the mean i.e.,

$\left(Y-\bar{Y}\right)$. It is denoted by 'y'.

(iii) In separate columns find out x^2 and y^2. Then from that $\sum x^2$ and $\sum y^2$ should be ascertained.

(iv) In another column value of xy for all the observations should be calculated to find out $\sum xy$.

(v) Substitute the value of $\sum x^2$, $\sum y^2$ and $\sum xy$ in the formula to get the Karl Pearson's co-efficient of correlation.

The value obtained by the formula normally lies within ± 1. If the correlation co-efficient value is +1, then there exists perfect positive correlation. If the value is -1, then it is called perfect negative correlation. If r = 0, then it means there is no relationship between the two variables. Practically, it is very rare to get the value for r as +1, -1 and 0. It normally lies between ± 1.

(b) Assumed Mean Method

$$r = \frac{\sum dxdy - \frac{(\sum dx)\times(\sum dy)}{N}}{\sqrt{\sum dx^2 - \frac{(\sum dx)^2}{N}}\ \sqrt{\sum dy^2 - \frac{(\sum dy)^2}{N}}} \qquad \text{OR}$$

$$r = \frac{N\sum dxdy - (\sum dx)\times(\sum dy)}{\sqrt{N\sum dx^2 - (\sum dx)^2}\ \sqrt{N\sum dy^2 - (\sum dy)^2}}$$

$\sum dx\,dy$ denotes sum of the product of deviations of x and y series from the assumed mean. $dx = (X-A)$ i.e., deviations taken from the assumed mean from the variables of x series.

$dy = (Y - A)$ i.e., deviations taken from the assumed mean from the variables of y series.

Steps

(i) First of all fix assumed means for X variables and Y variables.

(ii) Calculate the deviations for X variable from the assumed mean $(X - A)$ called dx. Also calculate square of these deviations (dx^2) in separate column. Then find out $\sum dx$ and $\sum dx^2$.

(iii) Calculate the deviations for Y variables from the assumed mean $(Y - A)$ called dy. Also calculate square of these deviations dy^2 in separate column. Then find out $\sum dy$ and $\sum dy^2$.

(iv) Also find out $dx\, dy$ for each pair in another column to get $\sum dx\, dy$.

(v) Substitute the values of $\sum dx.dy$, $\sum dx^2$, $\sum dy^2$, $\sum dx$ and $\sum dy$ in the formula to get the value of Karl Pearson's co-efficient of correlation.

(c) Actual Mean and Assumed Mean Method

$$r = \frac{\sum dxdy - N\left(\bar{X} - Ax\right)\times\left(\bar{Y} - Ay\right)}{N\sigma x\sigma y}$$

$\sum dx\, dy$ denotes sum of the product of deviations taken from assumed mean for the two variables X and Y.

$\bar{X}$ indicates actual mean for the X series

$\bar{Y}$ indicates actual mean for the Y series

Ax indicates assumed mean for X series

Ay indicates assumed mean for Y series

(d) Direct Method

Under this method correlation co-efficient can be calculated without taking actual mean and assumed mean. The formula for such kind of calculation is,

$$r = \frac{N\sum XY - (\sum X)\times(\sum Y)}{\sqrt{NX^2 - (\sum X)^2}\ \sqrt{NY^2 - (\sum Y)^2}}$$

Steps

(i) Take the square of variables in X series i.e., x^2 and find out $\sum x^2$.

(ii) Calculate the square of variables in Y series i.e., y^2 and find out $\sum y^2$.

(iii) Also find out $\sum x$ and $\sum y$.

(iv) Calculate the product of corresponding X variables and Y variables i.e., xy and find out $\sum xy$.

(v) Substitute the values of $\sum x$, $\sum y$, $\sum xy$, $\sum x^2$ and $\sum y^2$ in the formula to know the value of co-efficient of correlation.

(a) Arithmetic Mean Method

Illustration 2: *Compute co-efficient of correlation for the following data through Karl Pearson's co-efficient of correlation method.*

X	*25*	*35*	*45*	*52*	*20*	*33*	*40*	*30*
Y	*20*	*15*	*10*	*14*	*23*	*18*	*22*	*30*

Solution: Calculation of co-efficient of correlation.

X	Y	$X-\overline{X}$ $(X-35)$ x	$Y-\overline{Y}$ $(Y-19)$ y	x^2	y^2	xy
25	20	-10	+1	100	1	-10
35	15	0	-4	0	16	0
45	10	+10	-9	100	81	-90
52	14	+17	-5	289	25	-85
20	23	-15	+4	225	16	-60
33	18	-2	-1	4	1	+2
40	22	+5	+3	25	9	+15
30	30	-5	+11	25	121	-55
$\sum X =$ *280*	$\sum Y =$ *152*			$\sum x^2$ *=768*	$\sum y^2$ *= 270*	$\sum xy$ *=-283*

$$\overline{X} = \frac{\sum X}{N} = \frac{280}{8} = 35$$

$$\overline{Y} = \frac{\sum Y}{N} = \frac{152}{8} = 19$$

$\sum x^2 = 768$ $\sum y^2 = 270$ $\sum xy = -283$

Karl Pearson's Co-efficient of Correlation,

$$r = \frac{\sum xy}{\sqrt{\sum x^2 \sum y^2}} = \frac{-283}{\sqrt{768 \times 270}} = \frac{-283}{207360}$$

$$= \frac{-283}{455.37} = -0.621$$

(b) Assumed Mean Method

Illustration 3: *Calculate Karl Pearson's co-efficient of correlation from the following data.*

Income (Rs.)	*230*	*560*	*490*	*360*	*270*	*480*	*580*	*600*
Expenses (Rs.)	*200*	*440*	*350*	*250*	*240*	*300*	*420*	*550*

Solution:

X	*Y*	*dx* *(x-400)*	*dy* *(y-300)*	dx^2	dy^2	*dxdy*
230	200	-170	-100	28900	10000	17000
560	440	+160	+140	25600	19600	22400
490	350	+90	+50	8100	2500	4500
360	250	-40	-50	1600	2500	2000
270	240	-130	-60	16900	3600	7800
480	300	+80	0	6400	0	0
580	420	+180	+120	32400	14400	21600
600	550	+200	+250	40000	62500	50000
		$\sum dx =$ 370	$\sum dy =$ 350	$\sum dx^2 =$ 159900	$\sum dy^2 =$ 115100	$\sum dxdy =$ 125300

Karl Pearson's Co-efficient of Correlation,

$$r = \frac{\sum dxdy - \frac{(\sum dx)(\sum dy)}{N}}{\sqrt{\sum dx^2 - \frac{(\sum dx)^2}{N}} \sqrt{\sum dy^2 - \frac{(\sum dy)^2}{N}}}$$

$$= \frac{125300 - \frac{370 \times 350}{8}}{\sqrt{159900 - \frac{(370)^2}{8}} \times \sqrt{115100 - \frac{(350)^2}{8}}}$$

$$= \frac{125300 - \frac{129500}{8}}{\sqrt{159900 - \frac{136900}{8}} \times \sqrt{115100 - \frac{122500}{8}}}$$

$$= \frac{125300 - 16187.5}{\sqrt{159900 - 17112.5} \times \sqrt{115100 - 15312.5}}$$

$$= \frac{109112.5}{\sqrt{142787.5 \times 99787.5}} = \frac{109112.5}{377.87 \times 315.89}$$

$$= \frac{109112.5}{119365.35} = 0.914$$

Illustration 4: *Calculate co-efficient of correlation between rainfall and agricultural production through Karl Pearson's co-efficient of correlation method.*

Rainfall	*22*	*24*	*26*	*28*	*30*	*32*	*34*
Agricultural Production	*40*	*36*	*25*	*50*	*48*	*46*	*38*

Solution: Calculation of co-efficient of correlation.

Rainfall *X*	*(X - A)* *X - 28* *dx*	*dx^2*	*Agricultural Production* *Y*	*(Y - A)* *Y - 38* *dy*	*dy^2*	*dxdy*
22	-6	36	40	2	4	-12
24	-4	16	36	-2	4	8
26	-2	4	25	-13	169	26
28	0	0	50	12	144	0
30	2	4	48	10	100	20
32	4	16	46	8	64	32
34	6	36	38	0	0	0
	$\sum dx = 0$	$\sum dx^2 = 112$		$\sum dy = 17$	$\sum dy^2 = 485$	$\sum dxdy = 74$

$$r = \frac{N \sum dxdy - (\sum dx)\,(\sum dy)}{\sqrt{N \sum dx^2 - (\sum dx)^2}\ \sqrt{N \sum dy^2 - (\sum dy)^2}}$$

$$= \frac{7 \times 74 - (0 \times 17)}{\sqrt{7 \times 112 - (0)^2} \times \sqrt{7 \times 485 - (17)^2}}$$

$$= \frac{518}{\sqrt{784} \times \sqrt{3395 - 289}} = \frac{518}{28 \times 55.73}$$

$$= \frac{518}{1560.44} = 0.332$$

(c) Actual Mean and Assumed Mean Method

Illustration 5: *Calculate Karl Pearson's co-efficient of correlation through Actual Mean and assumed mean method from the following data.*

X	25	10	20	32	50	28	26	14	12	13
y	15	12	19	26	23	22	13	10	15	5

Solution: Calculation of co-efficient of correlation.

X	Y	$X - \overline{X}$ (X - 23)	$Y - \overline{Y}$ (Y - 16)	x^2	y^2	dx (X - 20)	dy (Y - 15)	$dxdy$
25	15	+2	-1	4	1	+5	0	0
10	12	-13	-4	169	16	-10	-3	30
20	19	-3	+3	9	9	0	+4	0
32	26	+9	+10	81	100	+12	+11	132
50	23	+27	+7	729	49	+30	+8	240
28	22	+5	+6	25	36	+8	+7	56
26	13	+3	-3	9	9	+6	-2	-12
14	10	-9	-6	81	36	-6	-5	30
12	15	-11	-1	121	1	-8	0	0
13	5	-10	-11	100	121	-7	-10	70
$\sum X$ = 230	$\sum Y$ = 160			$\sum x^2$= 1328	$\sum y^2$= 378			$\sum dxdy$ = 546

$$\overline{X} = \frac{\Sigma X}{N} = \frac{20}{8} = 23$$

$$\overline{Y} = \frac{\Sigma Y}{N} = \frac{160}{8} = 16$$

Karl Pearson's Coefficient of Correlation,

$$r = \frac{\Sigma dxdy - N\left(\bar{X} - Ax\right) \times \left(\bar{Y} - Ay\right)}{N\sigma x\sigma y}$$

$$\Sigma dxdy = 546, \quad Ax = 20, \quad Ay = 15$$

$$\sigma x = \sqrt{\frac{\Sigma x^2}{N}} = \sqrt{\frac{1328}{10}} = \sqrt{132.8} = 11.52$$

$$\sigma y = \sqrt{\frac{\Sigma y^2}{N}} = \sqrt{\frac{378}{10}} = \sqrt{37.8} = 6.15$$

$$r = \frac{546 - 10(23-20) \times (16-15)}{10 \times 11.5 \times 6.15} = \frac{546 - 30}{707.25} = 0.73$$

Calculation of Karl Pearson's co-efficient of correlation for Grouped Data.

When the observations are presented in the form of discrete series or continuous series, the following formula should be used to calculate the co-efficient of correlation.

$$r = \frac{\Sigma fdxdy - \frac{(\Sigma fdx)(\Sigma fdy)}{N}}{\sqrt{\Sigma fdx^2 - \frac{(\Sigma fdx)^2}{N}}\sqrt{\Sigma fdy^2 - \frac{(\Sigma fdy)^2}{N}}}$$

Steps

(i) Ascertain assumed means for variable x and variable y.

(ii) Take either deviations (d) or step deviations (d/c) for the values of x from the assumed mean and find out the products of the deviations with the frequencies *i.e.*, fdx then calculate Σfdx.

(iii) Calculate the deviations or step deviations for the variable of y from the Assumed Mean and find out the products of the deviations with the frequencies *i.e.*, fdy then calculate Σfdy.

(iv) Calculate the square of the dx and multiply with respective frequencies to get fdx^2 and then find out Σfdx^2.

(v) Calculate the product of square of dy with the corresponding frequencies to get fdy^2, then calculate Σfdy^2.

(vi) Find out *dxdy* multiplied with respective frequencies to know fdxdy to calculate $\sum fdxdy$.

(vii) Substitute the values of $\sum fdx^2$, $\sum fdy^2$, $\sum fdx$, $\sum fdy$ and $\sum fdxdy$ in the formula to know the value of co-efficient of correlation.

Illustration 6: *Calculate co-efficient of correlation for the following data relating to the weekly income and expenses of 50 families in a town.*

Weekly Income (Rs.)	*Weekly Expenses (Rs.)*						
	100-120	*120-140*	*140-160*	*160-180*	*180-200*	*200-220*	*Total*
125-150	*2*	*2*	*3*	*3*	*1*	*1*	*12*
150-175	-	*4*	*4*	*1*	-	-	*9*
175-200	*2*	*2*	-	*2*	*2*	*3*	*11*
200-225	-	*1*	*2*	*2*	*3*	-	*8*
225-250	*1*	-	*3*	*2*	-	*4*	*10*
	5	*9*	*12*	*10*	*6*	*8*	*50*

Solution: Calculation of Karl Pearsons Coefficient of Correlation.

$$\sum fdxdy = 175, \quad \sum fdx = -12.5, \quad \sum fdy = -46,$$

$$\sum fdx^2 = 656.25, \quad \sum fdy^2 = 524, \quad N = 50$$

$$r = \frac{\sum fdxdy - \frac{(\sum fdx)(\sum fdy)}{N}}{\sqrt{\sum fdx^2 - \frac{(\sum fdx)^2}{N}}\sqrt{\sum fdy^2 - \frac{(\sum fdy)^2}{N}}}$$

$$= \frac{175 - \frac{(-12.5 \times -46)}{50}}{\sqrt{656.25 - \frac{(-12.5)^2}{50}} \times \sqrt{524 - \frac{(-46)^2}{50}}}$$

$$= \frac{175 - \frac{575}{50}}{\sqrt{656.25 - \frac{156.25}{50}} \times \sqrt{524 - \frac{2116}{50}}}$$

X \ Y	M	M / dy/dx	100-120 110	120-140 130	140-160 150	160-180 170	180-200 190	200-220 210				
		dy/dx	-6	-4	-2	0	+2	+4	f	fdx	fdx^2	$fdxdy$
125-150	M 137.5	-5	2(60)	2(40)	3(30)	3(0)	1(-10)	1(- 20)	12	-60	300	100
150-175	162.5	-2.5	-	4(40)	4(20)	1(0)	-	-	9	-22.5	56.25	60
175-200	187.5	0	2(0)	2(0)	-	2(0)	2(0)	3(0)	11	0	0	0
200-225	212.5	+2.5	-	1(-10)	2(-10)	2(0)	3(15)	-	8	+20	50	-5
225-250	237.5	+5	1(-30)	-	3(-30)	2(0)	-	4(80)	10	+50	250	20
		f	5	9	12	10	6	8	N =50	Σfdx = -12.5	Σfdx^2 =656.25	$\Sigma fdxdy$ =175
		fdy	-30	-36	-24	0	+12	+32	Σfdy =-46			
		fdy^2	180	144	48	0	24	128	Σfdy^2 =524			
		$fdxdy$	30	70	10	0	5	60	$\Sigma fdxdy$ =175			

* $60 = 2(-5)(-6)$

$$= \frac{175 - 11.5}{\sqrt{656.25 - 3.125} \times \sqrt{524 - 42.32}}$$

$$= \frac{163.5}{\sqrt{653.125}\sqrt{481.68}} = \frac{163.5}{25.56 \times 21.95}$$

$$= \frac{163.5}{561.042} = +0.2914$$

2. Rank Correlation Co-efficient: This method of calculating the co-efficient of correlation is developed by a British psychologist named Charles Edward Spearman in the year 1904. This method can be applied where the population is not normal and the shape of distribution is not known. Unlike the Karl Pearson's co-efficient of correlation, it requires no assumption about the parameter of the population. The formula given by Spearman to calculate rank correlation co-efficient is given below.

$$r_R = 1 - \frac{6 \sum D^2}{N^3 - N}$$

Where r_R indicates rank co-efficient of correlation, D indicates the difference of ranks between the two variables and N indicates the total number of the pairs.

(a) Calculation of Rank Correlation co-efficient when the ranks are given.

Steps

(i) Find out the difference of the two ranks (i.e., D) for the two variables.

(ii) Take the square of these differences (*i.e.* D^2) and find out $\sum D^2$.

(iii) Substitute the values in the formula,

$$r_R = 1 - \frac{6 \sum D^2}{N^3 - N}$$

Illustration 7: *Calculate rank co-efficient of correlation for 12 students in 2 different subjects.*

Students No.	*1*	*2*	*3*	*4*	*5*	*6*	*7*	*8*	*9*	*10*	*11*	*12*
Subject I	*8*	*7*	*10*	*1*	*4*	*5*	*3*	*6*	*9*	*11*	*12*	*2*
Subject II	*2*	*4*	*9*	*3*	*12*	*11*	*8*	*1*	*7*	*6*	*5*	*2*

Solution: Calculation of rank co-efficient of correlation.

Class No. of students	*Rank in (R_1) Subject I*	*Rank in (R_2) Subject II*	*D (R_1 - R_2)*	*D^2*
1	8	2	+6	36
2	7	4	+3	9
3	10	9	+1	1
4	1	3	-2	4
5	4	12	-8	64
6	5	11	-6	36
7	3	8	-5	25
8	6	1	+5	25
9	9	7	+2	4
10	11	6	+5	25
11	12	5	+7	49
12	2	2	0	0
N = 12				*$\sum D^2 = 278$*

Rank co-efficient of correlation,

$$r_R = 1 - \frac{6\sum D^2}{N^3 - N} = 1 - \frac{6 \times 278}{12^3 - 12}$$

$$= 1 - \frac{1668}{1728 - 12} = 1 - \frac{1668}{1716} = 1 - 0.97 = 0.03$$

(b) Calculation of Rank Co-efficient of Correlation when ranks are not given

When the ranks are not available for the observations ranks should be calculated for both the series. While assigning ranks either highest value or the lowest value may be given the rank 1. But same technique should be followed for both the variables. If rank 1 is given for the highest value in one series, then the rank 1 should also be given to the highest value in the other series also.

Illustration 8: *Following are the data related to the marks obtained by 10 students in two different subjects. Calculate the rank correlation co-efficient.*

Class No. of students	*1*	*2*	*3*	*4*	*5*	*6*	*7*	*8*	*9*	*10*
Marks in Subject I	*37*	*52*	*75*	*11*	*69*	*78*	*90*	*40*	*32*	*50*
Marks in Subject II	*60*	*48*	*80*	*15*	*49*	*70*	*95*	*16*	*21*	*25*

Solution: Calculation of rank correlation co-efficient.

Class No.	Marks in Subject I	Marks in Subject II	Rank in Subject I	Rank in Subject II	D (x - y)	D^2
1	37	69	8	4	+4	16
2	52	48	5	6	-1	1
3	75	80	3	2	+1	1
4	11	15	10	10	0	0
5	69	49	4	5	-1	1
6	78	70	2	3	-1	1
7	90	95	1	1	0	0
8	40	16	7	9	-2	4
9	32	21	9	8	1	1
10	50	25	6	7	-1	1
	$N = 10$					$\Sigma D^2 = 26$

Rank Correlation Co-efficient,

$$r_R = 1 - \frac{6\sum D^2}{N^3 - N} = 1 - \frac{6 \times 26}{10^3 - 10}$$

$$= 1 - \frac{156}{990} = 1 - 0.158 = 0.842$$

Equal Ranks: There may be chances of obtaining same rank for two or more observations. In such a situation it is required to give average rank for all such observations. *(e.g.)* (i) If two observations got 4th rank, each of these observations should be given the rank (4+5)/2 *i.e.,* 4.5. (ii) If three observations should be given the same rank then each of these observations should be given the rank (7+8+9)/3, *i.e.*, 8th rank.

When equal ranks are available in the observations the following formula should be used for calculating rank correlation co-efficient,

$$r_R = 1 - \frac{6\left[\sum D^2 + \frac{1}{12}(m^3 - m) + \frac{1}{12}(m^3 - m) .....\right]}{N^3 - N}$$

Where, D indicates differences of the rank in the two observations, N indicates total number of pairs, m indicates number of observations which got equal rank.

$(m^3 - m)$ should be used in the equation on the following basis. *(e.g.)* If rank 4 repeated two times, rank 8 repeated 3 times and 10 repeated 2 times then $(m^3 - m)$ would be $(2^3 - 2)$, $(3^3 - 3)$ and $(2^3 - 2)$.

Illustration 9: *The data relating to the marks obtained by 15 students in a class, for two subjects are given below.*

Roll No. of students		*1*	*2*	*3*	*4*	*5*	*6*	*7*	*8*	*9*	*10*	*11*	*12*	*13*	*14*	*15*
Subject	*A*	*90*	*75*	*30*	*56*	*45*	*90*	*27*	*32*	*90*	*30*	*50*	*52*	*56*	*40*	*49*
Subject	*B*	*39*	*46*	*52*	*75*	*79*	*76*	*50*	*45*	*49*	*50*	*52*	*50*	*73*	*43*	*73*

Solution: Calculation of rank co-efficient of correlation

Roll No.	*Marks in Subject A*	*Marks in Subject B* R_1	*Rank in Subject I* R_2	*Rank in Subject II* $(R_1 - R_2)$	*D*	D^2
1	90	39	1	15	-14	196
2	75	46	4	12	-8	64
3	30	52	13.5	7	+6.5	42.25
4	56	75	5.5	3	+2.5	6.25
5	45	79	10	1	+9	81
6	90	76	1	2	-1	1
7	27	50	15	9	+6	36
8	32	45	12	13	-1	1
9	90	49	1	11	-10	100
10	30	50	13.5	9	+4.5	20.25
11	50	54	8	6	+2	4
12	52	50	7	9	-2	4
13	56	73	5.5	4.5	+1	1
14	40	43	11	14	-3	9
15	49	73	9	4.5	+4.5	20.25
						$\sum D^2 = 586$

$$r_R = 1 - \frac{6[\sum D^2 + \frac{1}{12}(m^3 - m) + \frac{1}{12}(m^3 - m) + \frac{1}{12}(m^3 - m) + \frac{1}{12}(m^3 - m) + \frac{1}{12}(m^3 - m)]}{N^3 - N}$$

$$= 1 - \frac{6[586 + \frac{1}{12}(3^3 - 3) + \frac{1}{12}(3^3 - 3) + \frac{1}{12}(2^3 - 2) + \frac{1}{12}(2^3 - 2) + \frac{1}{12}(2^3 - 2)]}{15^3 - 15}$$

$$= 1 - \frac{6\left[586 + \frac{24}{12} + \frac{24}{12} + \frac{6}{12} + \frac{6}{12} + \frac{6}{12}\right]}{3375 - 15}$$

$$= 1 - \frac{6\left(586 + 2 + 2 + \frac{1}{2} + \frac{1}{2} + \frac{1}{2}\right)}{3360}$$

$$= 1 - \frac{6(586 + 2 + 2 + 0.5 + 0.5 + 0.5)}{3360}$$

$$= 1 - \frac{6 \times 591.5}{3360} = 1 - \frac{3549}{3360} = 1 - 1.05 = -0.05$$

3. Concurrent Deviation Method: This method is based upon the increase or decrease of the variables. The trend of the ups and downs of the variables in both series should be ascertained. The increase in the trend is marked by '+' (plus) symbol and the decrease in the trend should be marked by '-' (minus) symbol. Then the symbol got in each pair should be multiplied so as to get a + or - symbol. *(e.g.)* (i) - symbol multiplied by - symbol will give + symbol (ii) + symbol multiplied by + symbols will give + symbol and (iii) - and + symbols multiplied will give - symbol. The total number of + symbols so ascertained should be calculated which is called concurrents (C). The value of 'C' should be substituted in the following formula to get the co-efficient of correlation.

$$r_C = \sqrt{\frac{2C - N}{N}}$$

Where, r_C denotes concurrent co-efficient of correlation, C denotes concurrents and N denotes total number of pairs of observations compared (or total number of pairs of symbol ascertained).

Illustration 10: *Compute the co-efficient of correlation through concurrent deviation method from the following data.*

X	36	42	59	45	47	44	49	57
Y	49	53	72	80	21	29	39	30

Solution: Calculation of co-efficient of correlation.

x	Dx	y	Dy	DxDy
36		49		
42	+	53	+	+
59	+	72	+	+
45	-	80	+	-
47	+	21	-	-
44	-	29	+	-
49	+	39	+	+
57	+	30	-	-
				C = 3

Co-efficient of concurrent correlation,

$$r_C = \sqrt{\frac{2C-N}{N}} = \sqrt{\frac{2\times 3-7}{7}} = \sqrt{-\frac{1}{7}} = -0.378$$

Illustration 11: *Compute the co-efficient of concurrent correlation from the following data.*

Months	*Jan*	*Feb*	*March*	*April*	*May*	*June*	*July*	*Aug*
Advertisement Expenses (Rs.)	*2750*	*3000*	*2900*	*4200*	*4000*	*3500*	*4700*	*4400*
Sales (Rs.)	*13000*	*20000*	*18000*	*16000*	*17000*	*16500*	*17700*	*15000*

Solution: Calculation of concurrent co-efficient of correlation.

Months	*Advertisement Expenses x*	*Dx*	*Sales (Rs.) y*	*Dy*	*DxDy*
Jan	2750		13,000		
Feb	3000	+	20,000	+	+
March	2900	-	18,000	-	+
April	4200	+	16,000	-	-
May	4000	-	17,000	+	-
June	3500	-	16,500	-	+
July	4700	+	17,700	+	+
August	4400	-	15,000	-	+
					C = 5

$$r_C = \sqrt{\frac{2C-N}{N}} = \sqrt{\frac{2\times5-7}{7}} = \sqrt{\frac{3}{7}} = 0.655$$

Illustration 12: *Compute co-efficient of correlation through concurrent deviation method.*

Months	*1*	*2*	*3*	*4*	*5*	*6*	*7*	*8*	*9*	*10*
Income (Rs.)	*2700*	*3000*	*2900*	*3100*	*3400*	*4000*	*3700*	*4100*	*3900*	*4200*
Expenditure (Rs.)	*1900*	*2800*	*2500*	*2400*	*3200*	*3100*	*3000*	*2900*	*2800*	*3000*

Solution: Calculation of co-efficient of concurrent deviation.

Months	*Income (Rs.)*	*Dx*	*Expenses (Rs.)*	*Dy*	*DxDy*
1	2700		1900		
2	3000	+	2800	+	+
3	2900	-	2500	-	+
4	3100	+	2400	-	-
5	3400	+	3200	+	+
6	4000	+	3100	-	-
7	3700	-	3000	-	+
8	4100	+	2900	-	-
9	3900	-	2800	-	+
10	4200	+	3000	+	+
					C = 6

$$r_C = \sqrt{\frac{2C-N}{N}} = \sqrt{\frac{2\times6-9}{9}} = \sqrt{\frac{1}{3}} = +0.577$$

Lag and Lead in Correlation

While calculating correlation in time series, there may exist a time gap between the cause and effect. This time gap is called Lag and Lead in correlation.

(e.g.) (i) The effect of income has an impact on expenditure in the next month.

(ii) The supply in one month may have the impact of demand only after few months.

(iii) The advertisement expenses spent in one year may have the effect on sales after two years etc. Hence, while comparing the two sets of variables, the variables of one period related to cause should be compared with the other period which gives effect.

Example:

Period	*Jan*	*Feb*	*March*	*April*	*May*	*June*	*July*
Advertisement Expenses (Rs.)	2500	1800	790	900	1000	1200	1500
Sales (Rs.)	15000	17000	14000	15500	14000	13000	14200

In the above example, if advertisement expenses have the impact on sales only after 2 months, then the data should be arranged in the following manner,

Period	Jan	Feb	March	April	May
Advertisement	2500	1800	790	900	1000
Sales (Rs.)	14000	15500	14000	13000	14200

Hence, the periods June and July for X could not be compared due to inavailability of data in Y series for the months August and September.

Illustration 13: *Following are the details regarding the expenses on advertisement and sale. The expenditure incurred on advertisement got an impact on sales after 3 months. Calculate co-efficient of correlation with the provision for lag time.*

Months	*Advertisement (Rs)*	*Sales (Rs)*
January	*500*	*20,000*
February	*800*	*60,000*
March	*950*	*50,000*
April	*1,500*	*15,000*
May	*1,050*	*25,000*
June	*1,200*	*30,000*
July	*850*	*32,000*
August	*750*	*40,000*
September	*500*	*35,000*
October	*450*	*19,000*
November	*950*	*15,000*
December	*1,000*	*14,000*

Solution: Calculation of co-efficient of correlation.

Months	Advertise-ment Exp. X (Rs.)	$\frac{(X-900)}{10}$	x^2	Sales Y (Rs.)	$\frac{(Y-25000)}{1000}$	y^2	xy
January	500	-40	1600	15000	-10	100	400
February	800	-10	100	25000	0	0	0
March	950	5	25	30000	5	25	25
April	1500	60	3600	32000	7	49	420
May	1050	15	225	40000	15	225	225
June	1200	30	900	35000	10	100	300
July	850	-5	25	19000	-6	36	30
August	750	-15	225	15000	-10	100	150
September	500	-40	1600	14000	-11	121	440
	8100		*8300*	*225000*		*756*	*1990*

$\Sigma x = 8100 \quad \Sigma y = 225000$

$$\overline{X} = \frac{\Sigma X}{N} = \frac{8100}{9} = 900$$

$$\overline{Y} = \frac{\Sigma Y}{N} = \frac{225000}{9} = 25000$$

$\Sigma xy = 1990 \qquad \Sigma x^2 = 8300 \qquad \Sigma y^2 = 756$

$$r = \frac{\Sigma xy}{\sqrt{\Sigma x^2 . \Sigma y^2}} = \frac{1990}{\sqrt{8300 \times 756}} = \frac{1990}{2505} = 0.79$$

There exists a positive correlation between Advertisement expenses and Sales. The degree of correlation is also high.

Co-efficient of Correlation and Probable Error

The technique of probable error should be applied to know the reliability of the co-efficient of correlation. The probable error of the co-efficient of correlation can be calculated through the following formula,

$$\text{P.E} = 0.6745 \ \frac{1-r^2}{\sqrt{N}}$$

Where, *r* indicates co-efficient of correlation, *N* indicates the total number of pairs of the observations and 0.6745 is a constant number.

If the value of r is less than 6 times of probable error ($r < 6\,P.E$) then, the value of r is insignificant one and hence, there should be no correlation between the two variables. If the value of r is more than six times of the probable error ($r > 6\,P.E$) then, the value of r is significant and hence, the correlation between the two variables are very certain.

The upper and lower limits of the co-efficient of correlation of the population can be ascertained by adding as well as deducting the co-efficient of correlation with the probable error. It can be stated as, $P = r \pm P.E$

P denotes correlation of the population.

Illustration 14: *Find out the significance of correlation co-efficient when r = 0.23 for 25 observations.*

Solution: Significance of correlation co-efficient can be tested through probable error.

$$P.E = 0.6745 \times \frac{1-r^2}{\sqrt{N}} = 0.6745 \times \frac{1-0.23^2}{\sqrt{25}}$$

$$= 0.6745 \times \frac{1-0.0529}{\sqrt{25}} = \frac{0.6745 \times 0.9471}{5}$$

$$= \frac{0.63882}{5} = 0.1278$$

If $r > 6\,P.E$, then there exists the significance for the correlation co-efficient.

$$6\ P.E = 6 \times 0.1278 = 0.7668$$

Hence, this value is greater than the correlation co-efficient, the calculated value of correlation co-efficient is not significant.

Co-efficient of Determination

The square of the co-efficient of correlation is called co-efficient of determination *i.e.*, r^2.

The value of co-efficient of determination is always with positive value. (*e.g.*) (i) when $r = -0.7$, co-efficient of determination $r^2 = (-0.7)^2 = +0.49$. (ii) When r = + 0.12 then, co-efficient of determination, $r^2 = +0.12^2 = 0.0144$

It may also be calculated through the following formula,

$$\text{Coefficient of Determination} = \frac{\text{Explained Variance}}{\text{Total Variance}}$$

Co-efficient of non-determination is calculated through the ratio of unexplained variance to total variance. It can be denoted by 'K^2'.

The square root of the co-efficient of non-determination is called co-efficient of alienation. It may be denoted by "K". Hence, co-efficient of non-determination,

$$= \frac{\text{Unexplained Variance}}{\text{Total Variance}}$$

$$= 1 - \frac{\text{Explained Variance}}{\text{Total Variance}} = 1 - r^2$$

Illustration 15: *Calculate co-efficient of determination and co-efficient of non-determination for the following data.*

X	*10*	*12*	*14*	*16*	*18*	*20*
Y	*10*	*15*	*20*	*25*	*30*	*38*

Solution:

X	*Y*	$X - \overline{X}$ *(X - 15)* *x*	$Y - \overline{Y}$ *(Y - 23)* *y*	x^2	y^2	*xy*
10	10	-5	-13	25	169	65
12	15	-3	-8	9	64	24
14	20	-1	-3	1	9	3
16	25	+1	+2	1	4	2
18	30	+3	+7	9	49	21
20	38	+5	+15	25	225	75
$\Sigma X =$ *90*	$\Sigma Y =$ *138*			Σx^2 *= 70*	Σy^2 *= 520*	Σxy *= 190*

$\Sigma X = 90$ $\qquad \Sigma Y = 138$

$$\overline{X} = \frac{\Sigma x}{N} = \frac{90}{6} = 15$$

$$\overline{Y} = \frac{\Sigma y}{N} = \frac{138}{6} = 23$$

$\Sigma xy = 190$ $\Sigma x^2 = 70$ $\Sigma y^2 = 520$

$$r = \frac{\Sigma xy}{\sqrt{\Sigma x^2 . \Sigma y^2}} = \frac{190}{\sqrt{70 \times 520}} = \frac{190}{190.79} = 0.996$$

Co-efficient of determination = $r^2 = (0.996)^2 = 0.9920$

Co-efficient of non-determination = $1 - r^2 = 1 - 0.9920 = 0.008$

Merits

(i) It is the most simple method of calculation of co-efficient of correlation.

(ii) This method is most suitable when the number of observations are very large.

Demerits

(i) This method gives only a rough idea about the presence or absence of correlation.

(ii) The degree of correlation is not accurately measured through this method.

(iii) It just measures only the increase or decrease of the value of the variables. The strength of the decrease and increase of the variables are not taken into account in this method.

Calculation of Correlation in Time Series

If the variables observed are based on time, then it is called time series. The variables based on time may either be a variable of short period and or of long period. Correlation of two sets of variables can be studied on the basis of time. But the correlation based on time series should be studied both for the short period as well as for long period. The reason for this is, that the correlation for short period may be positive while for the long period for the same variables may be neagative or vice versa. Hence, the study of correlation co-efficient based on time series, should be,

(i) Correlation co-efficient for long term period

(ii) Correlation co-efficient for short term period

(i) Calculation of correlation co-efficient for long term period: To know the correlation co-efficient for observations based on long term, trend value for all the observations should be ascertained. The trend value for the observations can be ascertained either through moving average method or through least square method. The trends so obtained should be utilised to calculate the deviations from the mean of the trends. Then the following common formula for co-efficient of correlation should be applied to ascertain the value of correlation co-efficient,

$$r = \frac{\sum xy}{\sqrt{\sum x^2 . \sum y^2}}$$

(ii) Calculation of correlation co-efficient for short period: Co-efficient of correlation for short period is also based on trends. Trends for the two sets of observations should be calculated either through the method of least square or through the method of moving average. The trend so calculated should be compared with the corresponding variables and the deviations should be ascertained. Then the sum of the square of such deviations ($\sum x^2$ and $\sum y^2$) for the two sets of variables should be calculated $\sum xy$, should also be calculated. These values should be substituted in the correlation co-efficient formula, which is,

$$r = \frac{\sum xy}{\sqrt{\sum x^2 . \sum y^2}}$$

The only difference in the calculation of co-efficient of correlation for short period and for long periods is in the calculation of deviations for the trend values. To calculate correlation co-efficient for long period, deviations of the trend should be taken from the mean of trend [$x = (Tx - \overline{Tx})$, $y = (Ty - \overline{Ty})$, where $\overline{Tx}$ is mean trends for x series, Tx is trend value for x series, $\overline{Ty}$ is mean value of trends for y series; Ty is trend values for y series. x = deviations for x series and y = deviation for y series]. To calculate correlation co-efficient for short period deviation of the trend should be taken from the corresponding variable itself. [$x = (X - Tx)$, $y = (Y - Ty)$, where, x = deviation for x series, y = deviations for y series, Tx = trends for x series, Ty = trends for y series, x = variables in x series and y = variables in y series].

Illustration 16: *Following are the data related to the index of supply and index of demand. Calculate co-efficient of correlation for the short term variations through Karl Pearson's Method.*

Year	*Index of Supply*	*Index of Demand*
1980	*115*	*85*
1981	*120*	*88*
1982	*117*	*92*
1983	*125*	*97*
1984	*123*	*98*
1985	*125*	*100*
1986	*135*	*108*
1987	*137*	*107*
1988	*145*	*112*
1989	*148*	*113*
1990	*145*	*115*
1991	*140*	*118*
1992	*147*	*122*

Solution:

Year	*Index of supply*	*Five Yearly moving average* *X*	*Deviations of actual values from moving average* *x*	*Square of Deviations* x^2	*Index of Demand*	*5 yearly moving average* *Y*	*Deviations of actual values from moving average* *y*	*Square of Deviation* y^2	*xy*
1980	115				85				
1981	120				88				
1982	117	120	-3	9	92	92	0	0	0
1983	125	122	3	9	97	95	2	4	6
1984	123	125	-2	4	98	99	-1	1	2
1985	125	129	-4	16	100	102	-2	4	8
1986	135	133	2	4	108	105	3	9	6
1987	137	138	-1	1	107	108	-1	1	1
1988	145	142	3	9	112	111	1	1	3
1989	148	143	5	25	113	113	0	0	0
1990	145	145	0	0	115	116	-1	1	0
1991	140				118				
1992	147				122				
				$\sum x^2 = 77$				$\sum y^2 = 21$	$\sum xy = 26$

$$r = \frac{\sum xy}{\sqrt{\sum x^2 . \sum y^2}} = \frac{26}{\sqrt{77 \times 21}} = 0.65$$

Partial Correlation and Multiple Correlation

Partial Correlation: Correlation analysis deals with the relationship between a dependent variable with that of an independent variable.

Normally, a dependent variable may be affected by more than one independent variables. (*e.g.*) (i) The result of students depends on the teaching, study and tuition (ii) The agricultural production depends on rainfall, fertilizer applied and quality of seed.

Partial correlation for three independent variables can be calculated as follows.

$$r_{12.3} = \frac{r_{12} - r_{13}r_{23}}{\sqrt{1-r_{13}^2}\ \sqrt{1-r_{23}^2}}$$

$$r_{13.2} = \frac{r_{13} - r_{12}r_{23}}{\sqrt{1-r_{12}^2}\ \sqrt{1-r_{23}^2}}$$

$$r_{23.1} = \frac{r_{23} - r_{12}r_{13}}{\sqrt{1-r_{12}^2}\ \sqrt{1-r_{13}^2}}$$

Illustration 17: *The rubber production in Kanyakumari District (x_1) depends on the rainfall (x_2) and the quantity of fertilizers applied (x_3). It is found that correlation of rubber production and rainfall, $r_{12} = 0.74$, rubber production and fertilizers, $r_{13} = 0.55$; rainfall and fertilizer $r_{23} = 0.6$. Calculate partial correlation co-efficient, excluding the effct of fertilizer.*

Solution:

$$r_{12.3} = \frac{r_{12} - r_{13}r_{23}}{\sqrt{1-r_{13}^2}\ \sqrt{1-r_{23}^2}} = \frac{0.74-(0.55\times0.6)}{\sqrt{1-0.55^2}\ \sqrt{1-0.6^2}}$$

$$= \frac{0.74-0.33}{\sqrt{1-0.3025}\ \sqrt{1-0.36}} = \frac{0.41}{\sqrt{0.6975}\ \sqrt{0.64}}$$

$$= \frac{0.41}{0.835\times0.8} = \frac{0.41}{0.668} = 0.614$$

Illustration 18: *A study shows that the sales of a company for the* *past 5 years depends on advertisement, low price and high quality. Find the partial correlation between sales (x_1) and high quality (x_4) keeping advertisement (x_2) and low price (x_3) constant. The study revealed the following data.* $r_{14.3} = 0.54$; $r_{12.3} = 0.46$ *and* $r_{24.3} = 0.65$

Solution: Partial correlation between sales (x_1) and high quality (x_4) keeping advertisement (x_2) and low price (x_3) as constant,

$$r_{14.23} = \frac{r_{14.3} - r_{12.3} r_{24.3}}{\sqrt{1 - r_{12.3}^{\ 2}}\ \sqrt{1 - r_{24.3}^{\ 2}}} = \frac{0.54 - (0.46 \times 0.65)}{\sqrt{1 - 0.46^2}\ \sqrt{1 - 0.65^2}}$$

$$= \frac{0.54 - 0.299}{\sqrt{1 - 0.2116}\ \sqrt{1 - 0.4225}} = \frac{0.241}{0.888 \times 0.76} = 0.357$$

Multiple Correlation: Multiple correlation is a study on the relationship between 2 or more variables. (*e.g.*) The relationship between the profit of company with sales, high price and low competition can be studied through multiple correlation.

If X_1 is denoted as dependent variable, and X_2 and X_3 are independent variables of X_1, the multiple correlation can be calculated as follows.

$$r_{1.23} = \sqrt{\frac{r_{12}^{\ 2} + r_{13}^{\ 2} - 2r_{12} r_{13} r_{23}}{1 - r_{23}^{\ 2}}}$$

If x_2 is treated as dependent variable; x_1 and x_3 as independent variables,

$$r_{2.13} = \sqrt{\frac{r_{21}^{\ 2} + r_{23}^{\ 2} - 2r_{21} r_{23} r_{13}}{1 - r_{13}^{\ 2}}}$$

If x_3 is treated as dependent variable: x_1 and x_2 as independent variables,

$$r_{3.12} = \sqrt{\frac{r_{31}^{\ 2} + r_{32}^{\ 2} - 2r_{31} r_{32} r_{12}}{1 - r_{12}^{\ 2}}}$$

Illustration 19: *Calculate multiple correlation for profit earned with sales and advertisement, from the following data.*

Profit and Sales $r_{12} = 0.43$

Profit and Advertisement $r_{13} = 0.54$

Sales and Advertisement $r_{23} = 0.36$

Solution: Multiple correlation between profit earned and, Sales and Advertisement is,

$$r_{1.23} = \sqrt{\frac{r_{12}^{2} + r_{13}^{2} - 2r_{12}r_{13}r_{23}}{1 - r_{23}^{2}}}$$

$$= \sqrt{\frac{(0.43)^2 + (0.54)^2 - 2(0.43)(0.54)(0.36)}{1 - (0.36)^2}}$$

$$= \sqrt{\frac{0.1849 + 0.2916 - 0.1672}{1 - 0.1296}} = \sqrt{\frac{0.3093}{0.8704}} = 0.596$$

Miscellaneous Illustrations

Illustration 20: *Calculate the co-efficient of correlation of advertisement and sales from the data given below.*

Advertisement Expenses (Rs. in '000)	*Sales (Rs. in '00000)*				
	10-20	*20-30*	*30-40*	*40-50*	*50-60*
10-15	-	-	2	3	5
15-20	2	6	-	4	3
20-25	2	3	5	-	-
25-30	6	-	4	5	-

Solution: Let the Sales be denoted as X and Advertisement Expenses be Y.

Calculation of co-efficient of correlation.

$$r = \frac{N\sum fdxdy - (\sum fdx) \times (\sum fdy)}{\sqrt{N\sum fdx^2 - (\sum fdx)^2}\ \sqrt{N\sum fdy^2 - (\sum fdy)^2}}$$

$$= \frac{50 \times (-34) - (-1)(30)}{\sqrt{50 \times 93 - (-1)^2} \times \sqrt{50 \times 80 - (30)^2}}$$

$$= \frac{-1700+30}{\sqrt{4650-1}\times\sqrt{4000-900}} = \frac{-1670}{\sqrt{4649}\times\sqrt{3100}}$$

$$= \frac{-1670}{68.18\times 55.68} = \frac{-1670}{3796.26} = -0.44$$

Illustration 21: *There are 10 participants for an interview. They are in different age groups. The marks scored by them are ranked according to their age which are stated as below.*

Ranking according to age	*1*	*2*	*3*	*4*	*5*	*6*	*7*	*8*	*9*	*10*
Ranking according to marks	*3*	*4*	*1*	*5*	*10*	*8*	*7*	*2*	*6*	*9*

State whether there exists any correlation between age and marks.

Solution: Calculation of Rank correlation.

Ranking according to age R_1	*Ranking according to marks* R_2	$R_1 - R_2$ D	D^2
1	3	-2	4
2	4	-2	4
3	1	2	4
4	5	-1	1
5	10	-5	25
6	8	-2	4
7	7	0	0
8	2	6	36
9	6	3	9
10	9	1	1
N = 10			$\sum D^2 = 88$

Rank correlation co-efficient,

$$R = 1 - \frac{6\sum D^2}{N(N^2-1)} = 1 - \frac{6\times 88}{10(10^2-1)} = 1 - \frac{528}{10\times 99}$$

$$= 1 - \frac{528}{990} = 1 - 0.53 = 0.47$$

There exists a low degree of correlation between age and marks.

Illustration 22: *The ranks of 12 students in 2 different subjects are stated below.*

Class No. of students	*1*	*2*	*3*	*4*	*5*	*6*	*7*	*8*	*9*	*10*	*11*	*12*
Rank in Subject I	*3*	*10*	*5*	*4*	*9*	*11*	*1*	*12*	*2*	*6*	*7*	*8*
Rank in Subject II	*5*	*7*	*6*	*11*	*8*	*4*	*3*	*9*	*1*	*2*	*12*	*10*

Solution: Calculation of Rank Correlation.

Class No.	*Rank in (R_1) Paper I*	*Rank in (R_2) Paper II*	*D (R_1 - R_2)*	*D^2*
1	3	5	-2	4
2	10	7	3	9
3	5	6	-1	1
4	4	11	-7	49
5	9	8	1	1
6	11	4	7	49
7	1	3	-2	4
8	12	9	3	9
9	2	1	1	1
10	6	2	4	16
11	7	12	-5	25
12	8	10	-2	4
N = 12				$\sum D^2 = 172$

Rank co-efficient of correlation,

$$R = 1 - \frac{6\sum D^2}{N(N^2-1)} = 1 - \frac{6\times172}{12(12^2-1)}$$

$$= 1 - \frac{172}{2(144-1)} = 1 - \frac{172}{286} = 1 - 0.6 = 0.4$$

Illustration 23: *Calculate the correlation co-efficient between age and exercising habits of teachers in a district.*

Age	30	31	32	33	34	35
No. of teachers	300	250	200	400	450	350
Teachers doing exercise daily	240	100	180	200	180	140

Solution: The percentage of teachers doing regular exercise should be calculated and it should be compared with age.

Calculation of correlation co-efficient.

Age X	X - 33 dx	dx^2	No. of Teachers	Teachers doing exercise	% of Teachers doing exercise	(y-50) dy	dy^2	dxdy
30	-3	9	300	240	80	30	900	-90
31	-2	4	250	100	40	-10	100	20
32	-1	1	200	180	90	40	1600	-40
33	0	0	400	200	50	0	0	0
34	1	1	450	180	40	-10	100	-10
35	2	4	350	140	40	-10	100	-20
	Σdx = -3	Σdx^2 = 19				Σdy = 40	Σdy^2 =2800	$\Sigma dxdy$ =-140

$$r = \frac{N\Sigma dxdy - (\Sigma dx)\times(\Sigma dy)}{\sqrt{N\Sigma dx^2 - (\Sigma dx)^2}\ \sqrt{N\Sigma dy^2 - (\Sigma dy)^2}}$$

$$= \frac{6(-140)-(-3)(40)}{\sqrt{6\times 19-(-3)^2}\ \sqrt{6\times 2800-(40)^2}}$$

$$= \frac{-840+120}{\sqrt{114-9}\ \sqrt{16800-1600}} = \frac{-720}{\sqrt{105}\ \sqrt{15200}}$$

$$= \frac{-720}{10.25\times 123.29} = \frac{-720}{1263.7} = -0.57$$

It is clear that there exists only negative correlation between age and exercise. The degree of negative correlation is also relatively greater.

Illustration 24: *Calculate Karl Pearson's co-efficient of correlation from the following data.*

Year	*1990*	*1991*	*1992*	*1993*	*1994*
Sales (Rs. '0000)	*37*	*42*	*48*	*52*	*61*
Profit (Rs. '000)	*28*	*32*	*37*	*45*	*38*

Solution: Calculation of co-efficient of correlation

Sales X	*Profit* Y	$X-\overline{X}$ *(X - 48)* *x*	$Y-\overline{Y}$ *(Y - 36)* *y*	x^2	y^2	*xy*
37	28	-11	-8	121	64	88
42	32	-6	-4	36	16	24
48	37	0	1	0	1	0
52	45	4	9	16	81	36
61	38	13	2	169	4	26
$\sum X =$ *240*	$\sum Y =$ *180*			$\sum x^2=$ *342*	$\sum y^2=$ *166*	$\sum xy=$ *174*

$\sum X = 240$ $\quad\sum Y = 180$

$$\overline{X} = \frac{\Sigma X}{N} = \frac{240}{5} = 48$$

$$\overline{Y} = \frac{\Sigma Y}{N} = \frac{180}{5} = 36$$

$$r = \frac{\sum xy}{\sqrt{\sum x^2 . \sum y^2}} = \frac{174}{\sqrt{342 \times 166}} = \frac{174}{238.27} = 0.73$$

Illustration 25: *Find out whether there exists any correlation between Income and Savings from the following data.*

Income (Rs. in '000)	*50*	*60*	*70*	*80*	*90*	*100*	*110*
Savings (Rs. in '00)	*3*	*4*	*12*	*18*	*20*	*15*	*13*

Solution: Calculation of correlation co-efficient.

Income	(X - A)		Saving	(Y - A)		
	X - 80			Y - 18	dy^2	dxdy
X	dx	dx^2	Y	dy		
50	-30	900	3	-15	225	450
60	-20	400	4	-14	196	280
70	-10	100	12	-6	36	60
80	0	0	18	0	0	0
90	10	100	20	2	4	20
100	20	400	15	-3	9	-60
110	30	900	13	-5	25	-150
	$\Sigma dx = 0$	$\Sigma dx^2 = 2800$		$\Sigma dy = -41$	$\Sigma dy^2 = 495$	$\Sigma dxdy = 600$

$$r = \frac{N\sum dxdy - (\sum dx)\times(\sum dy)}{\sqrt{N\sum dx^2 - (\sum dx)^2}\ \sqrt{N\sum dy^2 - (\sum dy)^2}}$$

$$= \frac{7\times 600 - 0\times(-41)}{\sqrt{7\times 2800 - (0)^2}\ \sqrt{7\times 495 - (-41)^2}}$$

$$= \frac{4200}{\sqrt{19600}\ \sqrt{3465 - 1681}} = \frac{4200}{140\times 42.24}$$

$$= \frac{4200}{5913.6} = 0.71$$

It is clear that there existed high degree of correlation between income and savings.

Illustration 26: *Calculate co-efficient of correlation and probable errors from the data given below.*

Village	% of Educated	% of Employed
1	55	30
2	45	25
3	65	20
4	80	40
5	75	35
6	60	25
7	70	45

Solution: Calculation of co-efficient of correlation.

% of Educated x	(X - 80)/5 dx	dx^2	% of Employed y	(Y - 40)/5 dy	dy^2	dxdy
55	-5	25	30	-2	4	10
45	-7	49	25	-3	9	21
65	-3	9	20	-4	16	12
80	0	0	40	0	0	0
75	-1	1	35	-1	1	1
60	-4	16	25	-3	9	12
70	-2	4	45	1	1	-2
	$\sum dx = -22$	$\sum dx^2 = 104$		$\sum dy = -12$	$\sum dy^2 = 40$	$\sum dxdy = 54$

$$r = \frac{N\sum dxdy - (\sum dx)\times(\sum dy)}{\sqrt{N\sum dx^2 - (\sum dx)^2}\ \sqrt{N\sum dy^2 - (\sum dy)^2}}$$

$$= \frac{7\times 54 - (-22)\times(-12)}{\sqrt{7\times 104 - (-22)^2}\ \sqrt{7\times 40 - (-12)^2}}$$

$$= \frac{378 - 264}{\sqrt{728 - 484}\ \sqrt{280 - 144}} = \frac{114}{15.62\times 11.66}$$

$$= \frac{114}{182.13} = 0.63$$

$$\text{Probable Error} = 0.6745\times\frac{1-r^2}{\sqrt{N}}$$

$$= 0.6745\times\frac{1-0.63^2}{\sqrt{7}} = 0.6745\times\frac{1-0.4}{2.65}$$

$$= \frac{0.6745\times 0.6}{2.65} = 0.15$$

Illustration 27: *The correlation co-efficient is 0.64 and its probable error is 0.1312. What was the value of N.*

(MGU: Section A April 97)

Solution: Probable Error $= 0.6745 \dfrac{1-r^2}{\sqrt{n}}$

$$0.1312 = 0.6745 \frac{1-0.64^2}{\sqrt{n}}$$

$$0.1312 \cdot \sqrt{n} = 0.6745 - 0.6745(0.64)^2$$

$$\sqrt{n} = \frac{0.3983}{0.1312} = 3 \quad \therefore n = 9$$

Illustration 28: *From the table given below, calculate the co-efficient of correlation between the ages of husbands and wives.*

Age of wives Y-series	*Age of husbands X-series*					*Total*
	20-30	*30-40*	*40-50*	*50-60*	*60-70*	
15-25	5	9	3	-	-	17
25-35	-	10	25	2	-	37
35-45	-	1	12	2	-	15
45-55	-	-	4	16	5	25
55-65	-	-	-	4	2	6
Total	5	20	44	24	7	100

(MGU: Section C April 98)

Solution: $\Sigma dxdy = 88$, $\Sigma fdx = 8$, $\Sigma fdy = -34$;
$\Sigma fdx^2 = 92$, $\Sigma fdy^2 = 154$, $N = 100$

Karl Pearson's co-efficient of correlation,

$$r = \frac{N\sum fdx \cdot dy - (\sum fdx \cdot \sum fdy)}{\sqrt{N\sum fdx^2 - (\sum fdx)^2} \cdot \sqrt{N\sum fdy^2 - (\sum fdy)^2}}$$

$$= \frac{(100\times 88) - 8(-34)}{\sqrt{100\times 92 - 8^2} \cdot \sqrt{100\times 154 - (-34)^2}}$$

$$= \frac{8800 + 272}{95.58\times 119.34} = \frac{9072}{11408.5} = 0.795$$

Illustration 29: *Find Karl Pearson's co-efficient of correlation between X and Y series.*

X series:	*17*	*18*	*19*	*19*	*20*	*20*	*21*	*21*	*22*	*23*
Y series:	*12*	*16*	*14*	*11*	*15*	*29*	*22*	*16*	*15*	*20*

(MGU: Section C April 95)

Solution:

X	*Y*	*dx* *X–20*	*dy* *Y–15*	*dxdy*	*dx²*	*dy²*
17	12	-3	-3	9	9	9
18	16	-2	1	2	4	1
19	14	-1	-1	1	1	1
19	11	-1	-4	4	1	16
20	15	0	0	0	0	0
20	29	0	14	0	0	196
21	22	1	7	7	1	49
21	16	1	1	1	1	1
22	15	2	0	0	4	0
23	20	3	5	15	9	25
	N = 10	*0*	*20*	*39*	*30*	*298*

$$r = \frac{N\Sigma dx \cdot dy - \Sigma dx \cdot \Sigma dy)}{\sqrt{N\Sigma dx^2 - (\Sigma dx)^2} \cdot \sqrt{N\Sigma dy^2 - (\Sigma dy)^2}}$$

$$= \frac{(10\times 39) - (0\times 20)}{\sqrt{10\times 30 - 0^2} \cdot \sqrt{10\times 298 - (20)^2}}$$

$$= \frac{390}{\sqrt{300}\times\sqrt{2580}} = \frac{390}{17.32\times 50.8} = 0.44$$

Illustration 30: *Calculate the co-efficient of rank correlation of 10 students in two subjects.*

Statistics:	*3*	*5*	*8*	*4*	*7*	*10*	*2*	*1*	*6*	*9*
Economics:	*6*	*4*	*9*	*8*	*1*	*2*	*3*	*10*	*5*	*7*

(Kerala: Section B April 98)

Solution: Calculation of co-efficient of rank correlation.

Rank in Statistics	*Rank in Economics*	*Difference D*	D^2
3	6	-3	9
5	4	1	1
8	9	-1	1
4	8	-4	16
7	1	6	36
10	2	8	64
2	3	-1	1
1	10	-9	81
6	5	1	1
9	7	2	4
			$\Sigma D^2 = 214$

$$\text{Rank Correlation Co-efficient} = 1 - \frac{6\sum D^2}{n(n^2 - 1)}$$

$$= 1 - \frac{6 \times 214}{10(10^2 - 1)}$$

$$= 1 - \frac{1284}{990} = 1 - 1.3 = -0.3$$

Illustration 31: *The competition in a beauty contest was ranked by three judges in the following order.*

First Judge:	*1*	*6*	*5*	*10*	*3*	*2*	*4*	*9*	*7*	*8*
Second Judge:	*3*	*5*	*8*	*4*	*7*	*10*	*2*	*1*	*6*	*9*
Third Judge:	*6*	*4*	*9*	*8*	*1*	*2*	*3*	*10*	*5*	*7*

Use the method of rank correlation to determine which pair of judge has the nearest approach to common taste in beauty.

(Kerala: Section C April 98)

Solution: Calculation of co-efficient of rank correlation.

Judge I	*Judge II*	*Judge III*	*I & II* D_1	*II & III* D_2	*I & III* D_3	D^2_1	D^2_2	D^2_3
1	3	6	-2	-3	-5	4	9	25
6	5	4	1	1	2	1	1	4
5	8	9	-3	-1	-4	9	1	16
10	4	8	6	-4	2	36	16	4
3	7	1	-4	6	2	16	36	4
2	10	2	-8	8	0	64	64	0
4	2	3	2	1	1	4	1	1
9	1	10	8	-9	-1	64	81	1
7	6	5	1	1	2	1	1	4
8	9	7	-1	2	1	1	4	1
						200	*214*	*60*

$$\text{Rank correlation co-efficient} = 1 - \frac{6\Sigma D^2}{n(n^2-1)}$$

$$\text{For Judge I and II} = 1 - \frac{6 \times 200}{10(10^2-1)}$$

$$= 1 - \frac{1200}{990} = 1 - 1.21 = -0.21$$

$$\text{For Judge II \& III} = 1 - \frac{6 \times 214}{10(10^2-1)}$$

$$= 1 - \frac{1284}{990} = 1 - 1.3 = -0.3$$

$$\text{For Judge I \& III} = 1 - \frac{6 \times 60}{10(10^2-1)}$$

$$= 1 - \frac{360}{990} = 1 - 0.36 = 0.64$$

Hence, Judge I & III have the nearest approach to common taste of beauty.

Illustration 32: *Calculate rank correlation co-efficient from the following data.*

X :	*22*	*28*	*31*	*23*	*29*	*31*	*27*	*22*	*31*	*18*
Y :	*18*	*25*	*25*	*37*	*31*	*35*	*31*	*29*	*18*	*20*

(MGU: Section B April 96)

Solution: Calculation of rank correlation co-efficient.

X	*Y*	*Rank x*	*Rank y*	*D*	D^2
22	18	8.5	9.5	-1	1.00
28	25	5	6.5	-1.5	2.25
31	25	2	6.5	-4.5	20.25
23	37	7	1	6	36.00
29	31	4	3.5	0.5	0.25
31	35	2	2	0	0
27	31	6	3.5	2.5	6.25
22	29	8.5	5	3.5	12.25
31	18	2	9.5	-7.5	56.25
18	20	10	8	2	4.00
					$\Sigma D^2 = 138.50$

X 31 repeated - 3 times

22 repeated - 2 times

Y 31 repeated - 2 times

25 repeated - 2 times

18 repeated - 2 times

Hence, 5 times m should be repeated,

Rank Correlation Co-efficient,

$$= 1 - \frac{6\left[\sum D^2 + \frac{(m^3 - m)}{12} + \frac{(m^3 - m)}{12} + \ldots\right]}{N^3 - N}$$

$$= 1 - \frac{6\left[138.5 + \frac{(3^3 - 3)}{12} + \frac{(2^3 - 2)}{12} + \frac{(2^3 - 2)}{12} + \frac{(2^3 - 2)}{12} + \frac{(2^3 - 2)}{12}\right]}{10^3 - 10}$$

$$= 1 - \frac{6[138.5 + 2 + 0.5 + 0.5 + 0.5 + 0.5]}{990}$$

$$= 1 - \frac{6 \times 142.5}{990} = 1 - 0.86 = 0.14$$

Illustration 33: *Compute the co-efficient of correlation between the number of licenced vehicles and the number of motor accidents from the following data. Interpret the values you obtain.*

Number of licenced vehicles (in '000)	*5.2*	*5.6*	*5.8*	*6.5*	*4.5*	*5.0*	*3.5*
Motor vehicle	*11.6*	*12.0*	*12.3*	*12.4*	*15.0*	*14.2*	*11.7*

(Kerala: Section C Sep 90)

Solution: Calculation of co-efficient of correlation.

No. of vehicles ('000) X	*No. of accidents ('000) Y*	*dx (X-5)*	*dy (Y-12)*	*dxdy*	*dx²*	*dy²*
5.2	11.6	0.2	-0.4	-0.08	0.04	0.16
5.6	12.0	0.6	0	0	0.36	0
5.8	12.3	0.8	0.3	0.24	0.64	0.09
6.5	12.4	1.5	0.4	0.60	2.25	0.16
4.5	15.0	-0.5	3.0	-1.50	0.25	9.00
5.0	14.2	0	2.2	0	0	4.84
3.5	11.7	-1.5	-0.3	0.45	2.25	0.09
		1.1	*5.2*	*-0.29*	*5.79*	*14.34*

$\Sigma dx = 1.1$; $\Sigma dy = 5.2$; $\Sigma dxdy = -0.29$; $\Sigma dx^2 = 5.79$; $\Sigma dy^2 = 14.34$; $N = 7$

Karl Pearson's co-efficient of correlation,

$$= \frac{N\sum dx \cdot dy - (\sum dx \cdot \sum dy)}{\sqrt{N\sum dx^2 \quad (\sum dx)^2} \cdot \sqrt{N\sum dy^2 - (\sum dy)^2}}$$

$$= \frac{(7 \times 0.29) - (1.1 \times 5.2)}{\sqrt{7 \times (5.79) - 1.1^2} \cdot \sqrt{7 \times (14.34) - (5.2)^2}}$$

$$= \frac{-2.03 - 5.72}{\sqrt{40.53 - 1.21} \quad \sqrt{100.38 - 27.04}}$$

$$= \frac{-3.69}{6.3 \times 8.6} = \frac{-3.69}{54.18} = -0.07$$

Hence, there is negative correlation between number of licenced vehicles and the number of road accidents. The degree of negative correlation is very thin.

Illustration 34: Let $n = 10$; $\Sigma x = 100$; $\Sigma y = 150$

$\Sigma(x-10)^2 = 180$ $\Sigma(y-15)^2 = 25$

$\Sigma(x-10)(y-15) = 60.$

Compute Karl Pearson's co-efficient of correlation.

(Kerala: Section B April 96)

Solution: $\Sigma x = 100$; $n = 10$; $x = 100/10 = 10$

$\Sigma y = 150$; $n = 10$; $y = 150/10 = 15$

$\Sigma(x-10)^2 = \Sigma dx^2$; $\Sigma(y-15)^2 = \Sigma dy^2$

$\Sigma(x-10)(y-15) = \Sigma dxdy$

Karl Pearson's co-efficient of correlation $= \frac{\Sigma dx.dy}{\sqrt{\Sigma dx^2} \cdot \sqrt{\Sigma dy^2}}$

$$= \frac{60}{\sqrt{180} \cdot \sqrt{25}} = \frac{60}{13.5 \times 5} = \frac{60}{67} = 0.896$$

Exercise

1. What is Correlation? Explain with example its significance in business.
2. Distinguish between positive and negative correlation.
3. What is linear and non-linear correlation?
4. Distinguish between co-efficient of correlation and co-efficient of variation.
5. Define correlation. Explain briefly the different methods of measuring correlation.
6. What is co-efficient of correlation? What are the diagramatical methods of measuring the co-efficient of correlation?
7. Define co-efficient of correlation. Explain briefly the different algebra methods of measuring the co-efficient of correlation.
8. What is scatter diagram? How does it help on measuring the correlation between two variables?

9. What is lag and lead in correlation?
10. Define rank correlation. Explain the steps of calculating rank correlation co-efficient.
11. Write short notes of the following:

    (a) Correlation Co-efficient (b) Scatter Diagram

    (c) Rank Correlation Co-efficient (d) Lag and Lead in Correlation
12. What is co-efficient of determination? (MGU: Section A April 97)
13. Define Rank Correlation. Write down Spearman's formula for rank correlation co-efficient. State the advantages of Spearman's rank co-efficient over Karl Pearson's correlation co-efficient. (MGU: Section B April 97)
14. What is a linear correlation? (MGU: Section A April 95)
15. What do you understand by 'zero' correlation? (MGU: Section A April 95)
16. What do you mean by limited degree of correlation? (MGU: Section A April 94)
17. What do you mean by Spurious Correlation? Explain the uses of correlation in business. (MGU: Section B Sep 93)
18. What is negative correlation? (Kerala: Section A April 98)
19. Explain the uses of correlation. (Kerala: Section B April 89)
20. State the measures of the concept of partial correlation. (Kerala: Section A Sep 90)
21. Draw a scatter diagram for the following variables.

X	5	10	15	20	25	30	35
Y	12	15	18	16	32	40	53

22. The rainfall and agricultural production in a district for 8 years are stated as follows.

Rainfall (mm)	22	26	24	20	18	26	30	28
Agricultural Production (1000 tonnes)	7	12	15	13	11	25	27	29

Draw a scatter diagram and find out whether the correlation is positive or negative.

23. The height and weight of 9 students in a M.com class is as follows:

Height (cms)	161	162	163	164	165	166	167	168	169
Weight (kg)	47	49	50	48	53	55	52	59	61

Construct a scatter diagram and fit a straight line by free - hand method.

24. Calculate Karl Pearson's co-efficient of correlation from the following data.

X	3	6	9	12	15	18	21
Y	25	19	14	11	10	12	7

[Ans: 0.11]

25. Calculate Karl Pearson's co-efficient of correlation between the marks scored by students in statistics and Accountancy.

Class No.	1	2	3	4	5	6	7	8	9	10	11	12
Marks in Statistics	80	45	36	75	70	45	30	52	60	28	47	55
Marks in Accountancy	90	50	25	70	60	40	40	60	50	15	40	35

[Ans: 0.87]

26. The average income and expenditure of workers in a factory are stated below.

Months:	Jan	Feb	March	April	May	June	July
Income:	500	650	720	800	950	980	1000
Expdre.:	450	590	700	690	750	770	790

Calculate co-efficient of correlation. [Ans: 0.953]

27. Calculate the co-efficient of correlation of the ages of husband and wife.

Age of husband:	25	27	30	32	35	37	40	45	48
Age of wife:	19	21	24	26	29	31	34	39	42

[Ans: 1.0]

28. Find out the correlation co-efficient from the following data.

X	5	10	15	20	25	30	35	40	45
Y	8	15	32	30	7	6	5	20	3

[Ans: -0.344]

29. Calculate co-efficient of correlation between family income and the percentage of saving.

Family Income (Rs.)	*Saving (in percentage)*				
	5-10	*10-15*	*15-20*	*20-25*	*25-30*
1000-1200	3	5	1	3	-
1200-1400	4	-	3	2	5
1400-1600	2	6	-	-	4
1600-1800	-	5	4	3	-
1800-2000	3	2	1	-	4

30. Calculate co-efficient of correlation for the following bivariate frequency distribution.

Marks in Accountancy	*Marks in Statistics* 0-20	20-40	40-60	60-80	80-100
0-20	2	-	-	3	4
20-40	3	2	-	-	2
40-60	-	-	4	5	-
60-80	1	2	-	4	6
80-100	-	3	4	-	5

[Ans: 0.096]

31. Calculate the co-efficient of correlation between investment and profit from the data given below.

Investment (Rs. in '0000)	*Profit (Rs. in '000)* 5-10	10-15	15-20	20-25	25-30
10-20	4	7	-	2	1
20-30	3	4	2	-	-
30-40	1	3	4	-	5
40-50	-	-	5	6	4
50-60	-	-	-	4	5
60-70	-	2	3	-	4
70-80	2	-	-	4	5

[Ans: 0.48]

32. Calculate Karl Pearson's co-efficient of correlation from the following particulars.

Sum of squares of deviations from arithmetic mean for x series is 2400 and y series is 3600. Sum of products of deviations of x series and y series from their respective arithmetic mean is 1100. No. of pairs of observation is 12. [Ans: 0.374]

33. The study concerned with the correlation of income and expenses of selected 10 families revealed that the sum of deviations from assumed mean for x series is -12, and y series is -24, sum of squares of deviations from assumed mean for x series is 5,650 and y series is 6,760 sum of products of deviations from their respective assumed mean is 1,950.

Calculate Karl Pearson's co-efficient of correlation. [Ans: 0.313]

34. Find out whether the rankings of 10 candidates in an interview by the judges are correlated. Calculate the degree of correlation also. The rankings are stated as follows:

Candidates	*A*	*B*	*C*	*D*	*E*	*F*	*G*	*H*	*I*	*J*
Judge I	4	5	1	3	10	9	8	6	7	2
Judge II	3	6	2	4	9	10	7	5	8	1

35. Two intelligent students, ranked their 8 subject teachers as follows:

Teachers	*A*	*B*	*C*	*D*	*E*	*F*	*G*	*H*
Student I	4	3	2	5	1	6	8	7
Student II	3	5	1	6	2	7	4	8

Find out the extent of ranking of these two students. [Ans: 0.69]

36. Calculate rank correlation co-efficient for the marks of 10 students in two different subjects.

Roll No. of Students	1	2	3	4	5	6	7	8	9	10
Marks in Statistics	75	90	60	45	30	25	55	84	70	68
Marks in costing	70	95	50	35	25	30	60	65	68	45

[Ans: 0.903]

37. Calculate rank correlation co-efficient for the marks of 10 students in two different subjects.

Roll No. of Students	1	2	3	4	5	6	7	8	9	10
Marks in Costing	75	60	35	45	60	35	85	35	50	65
Marks in Accountancy	68	72	43	49	43	54	73	82	79	83

[Ans: 0.236]

38. State whether rank of service and rank of efficiency for 10 staffs of a company is correlated. Calculate the degree of rank correlation. The rank of service and efficiency are stated below:

Ranking according to length of service	1	2	3	4	5	6	7	8	9	10
Ranking according to efficiency	4	3	2	8	5	9	7	10	1	6

[Ans: 0.273]

39. Calculate the co-efficient of concurrent deviation for the following data.

X	32	36	34	30	38	40	20	18
Y	15	17	19	18	15	20	14	10

[Ans: 0.65]

40. Calculate the co-efficient of concurrent deviation between sales and profit of a company for 9 years.

Year	1985	1986	1987	1988	1989	1990	1991	1992	1993
Sales (Rs. in '0000)	110	115	135	140	120	150	140	148	145
Profit (Rs. in '000)	68	70	65	72	70	74	76	80	78

[Ans: 0.5]

41. The following table shows the frequency distribution of 100 couples classified according to the ages:

Wife's Age (in years)	*Husband's Age (in years)* 20-25	25-30	30-35	35-40
15-20	20	10	3	2
20-25	4	18	6	4
25-30	-	5	11	-
30-35	-	-	2	-
35-40	-	-	-	5

(MGU: Section D April 97) [Ans: 0.19]

42. Find the co-efficient of correlation between the sale and expenses of ten firms (figures in '000 Rs).

Sales:	50	50	55	60	65	65	60	60	50
Expenses:	11	13	14	16	16	15	15	14	13

(MGU: Section C Sep 94) [Ans: 0.85]

43. Calculate the value of Pearson's co-efficient of correlation for the following series *A* and *B*:

A:	105	104	102	101	100	99	98	96	93	92
B:	101	103	100	98	95	96	104	92	97	94

Is there correlation between A and B?

(MGU: Section C Sep 92) [Ans: 0.73]

44. Calculate Karl Pearson's co-efficient of correlation between price, and supply of commodity from the following data.

Price (in Rs.)	17	18	19	20	21	22	23	24	25	26
Supply (in Kg)	38	37	38	33	32	33	34	29	26	23

(MGU: Section C April 92) [Ans: -0.92]

45. From the following data, calculate the co-efficient of correlation between *x* and *y*.

X	32	55	49	60	43	37	43	49	10	20
Y	40	30	70	20	30	50	72	60	45	25

(MGU: Section C April 92) [Ans: 0.37]

46. Compute the correlation co-efficient from the following data and comment on the value obtained. Also draw the scatter diagram.

Marks in Commerce:	35	60	45	57	45	52	55	18	27	70
Marks in Economics:	30	65	50	60	42	50	49	25	16	68

(Kerala: Section C April 94) [Ans: 0.94]

47. Calculate Karl Pearson's co-efficient of correlation and the probable error from the following data of imports and exports.

Year	*Imports*	*Exports*
1975	908	620
1976	1036	625
1977	904	575
1978	590	640
1979	1122	642
1980	1092	661
1981	1131	665
1982	1190	793
1983	1314	806
1984	1350	805

(Kerala: Section C April 89)

48. Calculate the correlation co-efficient between cost of living indices of two cities from the following data giving these indices for 10 years.

Year:	1982	1983	1984	1985	1986	1987	1988	1989	1990	9991
City A:	148	145	141	116	96	91	87	89	91	91
City B:	137	117	133	108	95	99	97	96	99	102

(Kerala: Section C April '93) [Ans: 0.93]

49. Compute the Karl Pearson's co-efficient of correlation between marks obtained in Commerce and Economics subjects by 10 students, and Comment.

Marks in Commerce:	48	50	55	60	45	60	75	80	51	60
Marks in Economics:	42	46	50	60	41	55	67	73	35	50

(Kerala: Section C April 90) [Ans: 0.93]

50. Ten competitiors in a beauty contest are ranked by three judges in the following order:

1st Judge:	1	5	4	8	9	6	10	7	3	2
2nd Judge:	4	8	7	6	5	9	10	3	2	1
3rd Judge:	6	7	8	1	5	10	9	2	3	4

(Kerala: Section C April 97) [Ans: Judge II & III; r = 0.55 (I & II); 0.73 (II & III); 0.05 (I & III)]

51. Obtain Rank Correlation Co-efficient from the following data.

X	68	64	75	50	64	80	75	40	55	64
Y	62	58	68	45	81	60	68	48	50	70

(MGU: Section B April 95) [Ans: 0.55]

◆ Chapter 10 ◆

Regression Analysis

Sir Fransis Galton was the first mathematician to use the term regression in the year 1877. He used this term while conducting a study based on the relationship between the height of fathers and sons. He selected a Sample of about 1000 fathers and sons for the study and the study revealed that (i) The tall fathers have tall sons, (ii) Short fathers have short sons, (iii) The average height of the sons of tall fathers was less than the average height of their fathers and (iv) The average height of the sons of short fathers are more than the average height of their fathers.

Regression analysis became most popular after the period of Galton. This analysis is used to find out an unknown variable from the known variable. If two variables are correlated then, the estimation of one variable from the corresponding known variable is possible. (eg) (i) If price and demand for a particular product is correlated, then one would easily ascertain the demand of the product if the price is further increased or decreased in future. (ii) If there exists a relationship between inflow of foreign investment and economic development, then it is possible to find out how much further foreign investment would be required to get a further, say, 25% increase in the economic development. Hence, estimation or prediction is possible through the regression analysis.

I Meaning and Definitions

The dictionary meaning of the term regression is *'the act of returning or going back'*. Regression is a statistical technique, through which the estimation of unknown variable from the known variable can be done. The curve for known variable can be drawn in a graph, to find out an unknown variable. This line was called as "*Regression line*" by Galton. This line has the tendency to regress or going back. The known variable which is used to estimate an unknown variable is called "*independent variable*" or "*explanatory variable*". The unknown variable or the variable for which the value is to be predicted is called "*dependent variable*" or '*explained variable*'.

The analysis used to find out an unknown variable from the known variable is called *"simple linear regression analysis"*. It is called simple linear, since only one set of independent variables are used to find out a dependent variable. Since the analysis is based on the linear relationship between the dependent and independent variables, it is termed as linear regression analysis.

The important definitions for the terms regression and regression analysis are stated as follows.

Ya Lun Chow defines that *"Regression analysis attempts to establish the nature of relationship between variables that is to study the functional relationship between the variables and thereby provide a mechanism for prediction or forecasting"*.

According to Blair, Regression is the measure of the average relationship between two or more variables in term of original units of the data.

The above definitions clearly explain that regression analysis is an important statistical method to find out the value of an unknown variable from a known variable.

II Regression Lines

There are two regression lines for two set of variables. If these two variables are termed as '*X*' on '*Y*', the two regression lines are the regression line of *X* and *Y* and the regression line of '*Y*' on '*X*'. If there exists perfect positive correlation between these two variables then the two regression lines are coinciding each other to give one line. When there is no perfect correlation then there would be two different regression lines. If the degree of correlation is high, the two lines are very close to each other. When the degree of correlation is low the two regression lines will keep distance with each other.

Difference between Correlation and Regression

The important differences between correlation and regression are stated below.

(i) The correlation analysis deals with the measure of the degree of relationship, but regression analysis deals with the nature of relationship.

(ii) Correlation analysis explains only the degree of relationship between two variables, whereas regression analysis explains the cost and effect relationship of the two variables.

Importance of Regression Analysis

The importance of regression analysis are stated below.

(1) The regression analysis helps to find out an unknown variable from the group of known variables.

(2) It can be applied in companies for quality control.

(3) It can also be used to find out co-efficient of correlation and co-efficient of determination.

III Regression Equations

Regression analysis studies the relationship of two sets of variables. These two set of variables can be plotted in a graph to give two regression curves, or regression lines. These regression lines can be expressed in algebra terms, which is known as regression equations. Hence these two lines will give two different regression equations, they are called the regression equation of x on y and the regression equation of y on x.

Regression Equation X on Y

The regression equation X on Y is used to find out the values of X for given value of Y.

This equation may be stated as, $X = a + bY$

This equation assumes X as dependent variable and Y as independent variable, a and b are two constants which determine the position of the regression line. If the value of these constants are ascertained, then the value of X for a given value of Y can easily be calculated

Following two equations are derived from the regression equation X on Y to find out the values of the two constants a and b,

$$\Sigma X = Na + b\Sigma Y,$$

$$\Sigma XY = a\Sigma y + b\Sigma Y^2$$

Regression Equation Y on X

The regression equation Y on X is used to ascertain the value of Y for a given value of X. It can be stated as, $Y = a + bX$

This equation states Y as dependent variable and X as independent variable, a and b are the two constants. The two constants determine the degree of the regression line Y on X. The value of Y can be ascertained for a given value of X if the values of a and b are known. The values of a and b are calculated through the following two equations. These equations have been derived from the regression equation Y on X,

$$\Sigma Y = Na + b\Sigma X$$

$$\Sigma XY = a\Sigma X + b\Sigma X^2$$

Illustration 1. *Find out the regression equations, X on Y and Y on X from the following data.*

X	25	30	35	40	45	50	55
Y	18	24	30	36	42	48	54

Solution: Calculation of regression equations.

X	Y	X^2	Y^2	XY
25	18	625	324	450
30	24	900	576	720
35	30	1225	900	1050
40	36	1600	1296	1440
45	42	2025	1764	1890
50	48	2500	2304	2400
55	54	3025	2916	2970
$\Sigma X = 280$	$\Sigma Y = 252$	$\Sigma X^2 = 11900$	$\Sigma Y^2 = 10080$	$\Sigma XY = 10920$

$\Sigma X = 280$, $\Sigma Y = 252$, $\Sigma X^2 = 11900$,

$\Sigma Y^2 = 10080$, $\Sigma XY = 10920$

Regression equation X on Y is X = a + bY

Hence, $\Sigma X = Na + b\Sigma Y$

$$\Sigma XY = a\Sigma Y + b\Sigma Y^2$$

$$280 = 7a + 252b \quad \ldots (1)$$

$$10920 = 252a + 10080b \quad \ldots (2)$$

Multiplying equation (1) by 36,

$$10080 = 252a + 9072b \quad \ldots (3)$$

$$10920 = 252a + 10080b \quad \ldots (4)$$

Deducting equation (3) from (2)

$$1008\ b = 840$$

Therefore, $b = \dfrac{840}{1008} = 0.83$

Substituting the value of b in equation (1)

$$280 = 7a + (252 \times 0.83)$$

$$280 = 7a + 209.16$$

$$7a + 209.16 = 280$$

$$7a = 280 - 209.16$$

$$7a = 70.84$$

$$a = 10.12$$

Hence, $X = a + bY$

$$X = 10.12 + 0.83Y$$

Reg. equ of Y on $X : Y = a + bX$

Hence, $\Sigma Y = Na + b\Sigma X^2$

$$252 = 7a + 280\text{ b} \qquad \ldots (1)$$

$$10920 = 280a + 11900b \qquad \ldots (2)$$

Multiplying equ (1) by 40

$$10080 = 280a + 11200b \qquad \ldots (3)$$

$$10920 = 280a + 11900b \qquad \ldots (4)$$

Deducting equation (4) from (3)

$$700b = 840 \qquad \therefore b = \frac{840}{700} = 1.2$$

Substituting the value of b in equ (1)

$$252 = 7a + (280 \times 1.2)$$

$$252 = 7a + 336$$

$$7a + 336 = 252$$

$$7a = 252 - 336$$

$$7a = -84$$

$$a = -12$$

Therefore $Y = -12 + 1.2X$

Calculation of Regression Equations through Arithmetic Mean Method.

The calculation of regression equation through the simple linear equation is not easy when the variables are large and complicated. Hence, the regression equations can be calculated through arithmetic mean method for such kind of variables. The following are the two regression equations under this method.

(a) Regression Equation X on Y,

$$X - \overline{X} = r\frac{\sigma x}{\sigma y}(Y - \overline{Y})$$

where, $\overline{X}$ indicates arithmetic mean of *X* series, $\overline{Y}$ indicates, arithmetic mean of *Y* series. $\frac{\sigma x}{\sigma y}$ indicates regression coefficient of *X* on *Y*. $\frac{\sigma x}{\sigma y}$ may be denoted as *bxy*.

Hence, $$bxy = r\frac{\sigma x}{\sigma y} = \frac{\Sigma xy}{N.\sigma x.\sigma y} \times \frac{\sigma x}{\sigma y} = \frac{\Sigma xy}{\Sigma y^2}$$

(b) Regression Equation Y on X,

$$Y - \overline{Y} = r\frac{\sigma y}{\sigma x}(X - \overline{X})$$

where $\frac{\sigma y}{\sigma x}$ indicates regression coefficient of *Y* on *X*. $\overline{X}$ indicates arithmetic mean of *X* series and $\overline{Y}$ indicates arithmetic mean of *Y* series. $\frac{\sigma y}{\sigma x}$ may be called as *byx*.

Hence, $$bxy = r\frac{\sigma y}{\sigma x} = \frac{\Sigma xy}{N.\sigma x.\sigma y} \times \frac{\sigma y}{\sigma x} = \frac{\Sigma xy}{\Sigma x^2}$$

Illustration 2. *Find out the regression equation X on Y and Y on X from the following data.*

X	20	30	40	50	60	70	80
Y	21	35	45	53	70	77	84

Solution: Computation of the regression equations.

X	Y	$X-\bar{X}$ (X - 50) x	$Y-\bar{Y}$ (Y - 55) y	x^2	y^2	xy
20	21	-30	-34	900	1156	1020
30	35	-20	-20	400	400	400
40	45	-10	-10	100	100	100
50	53	0	-2	0	4	0
60	70	+10	+15	100	225	150
70	77	+20	+22	400	484	440
80	84	+30	+29	900	841	870
$\Sigma X =$ 350	$\Sigma Y =$ 385			$\Sigma x^2 =$ 2800	$\Sigma y^2 =$ 3210	$\Sigma xy =$ 2980

$$\bar{X} = \frac{\Sigma X}{N} = \frac{350}{7} = 50 \qquad \bar{Y} = \frac{\Sigma Y}{N} = \frac{385}{7} = 55$$

$$\Sigma x^2 = 2800, \ \Sigma y^2 = 3210, \ \Sigma xy = 2980$$

Regression Equation X on Y.

$$X - \bar{X} = \frac{\sigma x}{\sigma y}(Y - \bar{Y}) \qquad r\frac{\sigma x}{\sigma y} = \frac{\Sigma xy}{\Sigma y^2} = \frac{2980}{3210} = 0.93$$

Hence, $X - 50 = 0.93\,(Y - 55)$

Regression equation Y on X,

$$Y - \bar{Y} = r\frac{\sigma y}{\sigma x}(X - \bar{X}) \qquad r\frac{\sigma y}{\sigma x} = \frac{\Sigma xy}{\Sigma x^2} = \frac{2980}{2800} = 1.06$$

Hence, $Y - 55 - 1.06\,(X - 50)$

Regression equation of X on Y

$$(X - 50) = 0.93\,(Y - 55)$$
$$X - 50 = 0.93Y - 51.15$$
$$X = 0.93Y - 51.15 + 50$$
$$X = -1.15 + 0.93\,Y$$

Regression equation of Y on X:

$$(Y - 55) = 1.06\,(X - 50)$$
$$Y - 55 = 1.06X - 53$$
$$Y = 1.06X - 53 + 55$$
$$Y = 2 + 1.06\,X$$

Calculation of Regression Equation on the basis of Assumed Mean

The calculation of regression equation is further simplified, if the deviations are taken from the assumed mean. The formula for the calculation of regression equation under this method is as follows.

(i) Regression equation of X on Y $X-\overline{X}=r\frac{\sigma x}{\sigma y}(Y-\overline{Y})$; $\frac{\sigma x}{\sigma y}$ can be calculated through the following formula.

(a) For Individual observations: $\frac{\sigma x}{\sigma y}=\frac{\Sigma dx\cdot dy-\frac{\Sigma dx\cdot\Sigma dy}{N}}{\Sigma dy^2-\frac{(\Sigma dy)^2}{N}}$

Where, dx = variables, X – Assumed mean, $(X - A)$; dy = variables Y - Assumed mean, $(Y - A)$; N = Total number of pairs of variables X and variables Y.

(b) For Discrete Series: $\frac{\sigma x}{\sigma y}=\frac{\Sigma fdx\cdot dy-\frac{\Sigma fdx\cdot\Sigma fdy}{N}}{\Sigma fdy^2-\frac{(\Sigma fdy)^2}{N}}$ Here, f indicates frequency.

(c) For Continuous Series: $\frac{\sigma x}{\sigma y}=\frac{\Sigma fdx\cdot dy-\frac{\Sigma fdx\cdot\Sigma fdy}{N}}{\Sigma fdy^2-\frac{(\Sigma fdy)^2}{N}}\times\frac{iX}{iY}$

where, iX - indicates difference of the class intervals of X series;
iY - indicates difference of the class intervals of Y series.

(ii) Regression equation Y on X : $Y-\overline{Y}=r\frac{\sigma y}{\sigma x}(X-\overline{X})$

(a) For Individual observations: $\frac{\sigma y}{\sigma x}=\frac{\Sigma dx\cdot dy-\frac{\Sigma dx\cdot\Sigma dy}{N}}{\Sigma dx^2-\frac{(\Sigma dx)^2}{N}}$

(b) *For Discrete Series:* $\frac{\sigma y}{\sigma x} = \frac{\sum fdx \cdot dy - \frac{\sum fdx \cdot \sum fdy}{N}}{\sum fdx^2 - \frac{(\sum fdx)^2}{N}}$ where, f indicates frequency.

(c) *For Continuous Series:* $\frac{\sigma y}{\sigma x} = \frac{\sum fdx \cdot dy - \frac{\sum fdx \cdot \sum fdy}{N}}{\sum fdx^2 - \frac{(\sum fdx)^2}{N}} \times \frac{iY}{iX}$

where, iX - indicates difference between the class intervals of X series; iY - indicates difference between the class intervals of Y series.

Illustration 3: *Find out the regression equation from the following data.*

X	*27*	*32*	*39*	*41*	*47*	*52*	*61*
Y	*18*	*35*	*24*	*37*	*23*	*27*	*47*

Solution: Calculation for regression equations.

X	*Y*	*dx (X-A)* *(X - 40)*	*dy (Y-A)* *(Y - 30)*	*dx^2*	*dy^2*	*dxdy*
27	18	-13	-12	169	144	+156
32	35	-8	+5	64	25	-40
39	24	-1	-6	1	36	+6
41	37	+1	+7	1	49	+7
47	23	+7	-7	49	49	-49
52	27	+12	-3	144	9	-36
61	47	+21	+17	441	289	+357
		$\Sigma dx = 19$	*$\Sigma dy = 1$*	*$\Sigma dx^2 = 869$*	*$\Sigma dy^2 = 601$*	*$\Sigma dxdy = 401$*

$$\overline{X} = A \pm \frac{\sum dx}{N} = 40 + \frac{19}{7} = 42.71$$

$$\overline{Y} = A \pm \frac{\sum dy}{N} = 30 + \frac{1}{7} = 30.14$$

$$\frac{\sigma x}{\sigma y} = \frac{\Sigma fdx \cdot dy - \dfrac{\Sigma fdx \cdot \Sigma fdy}{N}}{\Sigma fdy^2 - \dfrac{(\Sigma fdy)^2}{N}} = \frac{401 - \dfrac{19 \times 1}{7}}{601 - \dfrac{(1)^2}{7}}$$

$$= \frac{401 - 2.71}{601 - 0.14} = \frac{398.29}{600.86} = 0.66$$

$$\frac{\sigma y}{\sigma x} = \frac{\Sigma fdx \cdot dy - \dfrac{\Sigma fdx \cdot \Sigma fdy}{N}}{\Sigma fdx^2 - \dfrac{(\Sigma fdx)^2}{N}} = \frac{401 - \dfrac{19 \times 1}{7}}{869 - \dfrac{(19)^2}{7}}$$

$$= \frac{401 - 2.71}{869 - 51.57} = \frac{398.29}{817.43} = 0.49$$

Regression Equation X on Y, is

$$X - \overline{X} = r\frac{\sigma x}{\sigma y}(Y - \overline{Y}) \quad \text{i.e., } X - 42.71 = 0.66\ (Y - 30.14)$$

Regression equation Y on X is,

$$Y - \overline{Y} = r\frac{\sigma y}{\sigma x}(X - \overline{X}) \quad \text{i.e., } Y - 30.14 = 0.49\ (X - 42.71)$$

Regression equation of X on Y

$$(X - 42.71) = 0.66\ (Y - 30.14)$$

$$X - 42.71 = 0.66Y - 19.89$$

$$X = 0.66Y - 19.89 + 42.71$$

$$X = 22.82 + 0.66\ Y$$

Regression equation of Y on X

$$(Y - 30.14) = 0.49\ (X - 42.71)$$

$$Y - 30.14 = 0.49X - 20.93$$

$$Y = 0.49X - 20.93 + 30.14$$

$$Y = 9.21 + 0.49\ X$$

Graphical Representation of the Regression Equations

Regression equations can be drawn in a graph. The two axis (i.e, X axis and Y axis) of the graph can be used to identify the regression X on Y; or Y on X or vice versa. The values ascertained through the regression equations can be plotted in the graph so as to get two straight lines on the graph. If these two lines pass on the same points, there would be only one line exists for the two equations. It states that there is perfect positive correlation between these two set of variables. If these two lines take the same direction and keep a long distance, then the degree of correlation between these two variables is very low. If the two lines keep a very close distance and take the same direction, then the degree of correlation between these two variables is very high. There exists only a negative correlation between these two variables, when these two lines intersect each other.

Illustration 4: *Show graphically the regression equation with the data given in Illustration No. 3 by taking value of X as 50 and Y as 15.*

Solution: When $X = 50$

$$Y = 9.35 + 0.49\,X$$

$$= 9.35 + (0.49 \times 50) = 33.85$$

When $Y = 15$

$$X = 22.54 + 0.66\,Y$$

$$= 22.54 + (0.66 \times 15) = 32.44$$

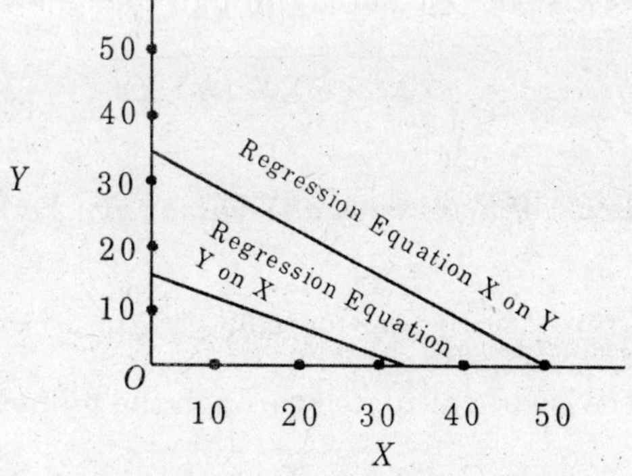

IV Standard Error of Regression

Standard error of regression is otherwise called as standard error of estimate. It is a statistical technique to know the reliability of the regression analysis. It is purely an estimate. It may not give the accurate data for the estimate. The prediction made by the regression analysis can be tested through the standard error of estimate. It can be ascertained through the following formula.

(a) Standard Error of Regression of X value from Y.

$$Syx = \sqrt{\frac{\Sigma(Y - YX)^2}{N}} \quad \text{or} \quad Syx = Y\sqrt{1-r^2}$$

If may be otherwise called as $= \sqrt{\frac{\text{Unexplained Variation}}{N}}$

Standard Error or estimate may otherwise be calculated as,

$$Sxy = \sqrt{\frac{\Sigma Y^2 - a\,\Sigma Y - b\,\Sigma XY}{N}}$$

(b) Standard Error of Regression of X value from Xe

$$Sxy = \sqrt{\frac{\Sigma(X - XY)^2}{N}} \quad \text{or} \quad Syx = X\sqrt{1-r^2}$$

It may be otherwise called as $= \sqrt{\frac{\text{Unexplained Variation}}{N}}$

It may otherwise be calculated through the following formula

$$Sxy = \sqrt{\frac{\Sigma X^2 - a\,\Sigma X - b\,\Sigma XY}{N}}$$

(c) Standard Error of Regression of Y value from Yc.

$$Syx = \sqrt{\frac{(Y - Yc)^2}{N}} \quad \text{or} \quad Syx = Y\sqrt{1-r^2}$$

It may otherwise be calculated through the following formula

$$Syx = \sqrt{\frac{\Sigma y^2 - a\,\Sigma y - b\,\Sigma xy}{N}}$$

Illustration 5. *From the following data find the two regression equations and calculate the standard error of the estimate.*

X	5	7	12	11	10
Y	4	5	8	3	5

Solution: Calculation of regression equation.

X	$X-\bar{X}$	x^2	Y	$Y-\bar{Y}$	y^2	xy
5	-4	16	4	-1	1	4
7	-2	4	5	0	0	0
12	3	9	8	3	9	9
11	2	4	3	-2	4	-4
10	1	1	5	0	0	0
$\Sigma x=45$	$x = 0$	$\Sigma x^2=34$	$\Sigma y=25$	$y=0$	$\Sigma y^2=14$	$\Sigma xy= 9$

Regression equation of X on Y,

$$X-\bar{X} = \frac{\sigma x}{\sigma y}(Y-\bar{Y})$$

$$r\frac{\sigma x}{\sigma y} = \frac{\Sigma xy}{\Sigma y^2} = \frac{9}{14} = 0.64$$

Regression Equation of Y on X

$$Y-\bar{Y} = \frac{\sigma y}{\sigma x}(X-\bar{X})$$

$$r\frac{\sigma y}{\sigma x} = \frac{\Sigma xy}{\Sigma x^2} = \frac{9}{34} = 0.26$$

Regression equation of X on Y

$$(X-9) = 0.64\,(Y-5)$$
$$X-9 = 0.64Y - 3.2$$
$$X = 0.64Y - 3.2 + 9$$
$$X = 5.8 + 0.64\,Y$$

Regression equation of Y on X

$$(Y-5) = 0.26\,(X-9)$$
$$Y-5 = 0.26X - 2.34$$
$$Y = 0.26X - 2.34 + 5$$
$$Y = 2.66 + 0.26\,X$$

Calculation of standard error of estimate

$Y = 2.66 + 0.26X; \quad X = 5.8 + 0.64Y$

X	Y	Yc	Xc	$(Y - Yc)^2$	$(X - Xc)^2$
5	4	3.96	8.36	0.0016	11.29
7	5	4.48	9.00	0.2704	4.00
12	8	5.78	10.92	4.9284	1.17
11	3	5.52	7.72	6.3504	10.76
10	5	5.26	9.00	0.0676	1.00
				$(Y - Yc)^2 = 11.6184$	$(X - Xc)^2 = 28.2$:

Calculations

Y	= 2.66 + 0.26 x		X	= 5.8 + 0.64 y
(X = 5) Y	= 2.66 + 0.26 x 5		(Y = 4) X	= 5.8 + 0.64 x 4
Y	= 2.66 + 1.3			= 5.8 + 2.56
Yc	= 3.96			= 8.36
(X = 7) y	= 2.66 + 0.26 x 7		(Y = 5) X	= 5.8 + 0.64 x 5
	= 2.66 + 1.82			= 5.8 + 3.2
	= 4.48			= 9
(X = 12) Y	= 2.66 + 0.26 x 12		(Y = 8) X	= 5.8 + 0.64 x 8
	= 2.66 + 3.12			= 5.8 + 5.12
	= 5.78			= 10.92
(X = 11) Y	= 2.66 + 0.26 x 11		(Y = 3) X	= 5.8 + 0.64 x 3
	= 2.66 + 2.86			= 5.8 + 1.92
	= 5.52			= 7.72
(X = 10) Y	= 2.66 + 0.26 x 10		(Y = 5) X	= 5.8 + 0.64 x 5
	= 2.66 + 2.6			= 5.8 + 3.2
	= 5.26			= 9

Standard Error of Regression of X value from Xc

$$Sxy = \sqrt{\frac{\Sigma(X - Xc)^2}{N}} = \sqrt{\frac{28.22}{5}} = \sqrt{5.644} = 2.38$$

Standard Error of Regression of Y value from Yc

$$Syx = \sqrt{\frac{\Sigma(Y - Yc)^2}{N}} = \sqrt{\frac{11.6184}{5}} = \sqrt{2.324} = 1.52$$

$$Syx = \sigma x\sqrt{1-r^2}, \quad \Sigma x^2 = 34, \quad \Sigma y^2 = 14, \quad N = 5$$

$$r = \sqrt{bxy \times byx}, \quad bxy \quad \text{(or)} \quad r \quad x/y = 0.64$$

$$= \sqrt{0.64 \times 0.26}, \quad byx \quad \text{(or)} \quad r \quad y/x = 0.26$$

$$= \sqrt{0.1664} = 0.41$$

$$\sigma x = \sqrt{\frac{\Sigma x^2}{n}} = \sqrt{\frac{34}{5}} = \sqrt{6.8} = 2.61$$

$$Sxy = \sigma x \times \sqrt{1-r^2}$$

$$Sxy = 2.61 \times \sqrt{1-(0.41)^2} = 2.61 \times \sqrt{1-0.1681}$$

$$= 2.611 \times \sqrt{0.8319} = 2.61 \times 0.91 = 2.38$$

$$Syx = \sigma y\sqrt{1-r^2}$$

$$\sigma y = \sqrt{\frac{\Sigma y^2}{n}} = \sqrt{\frac{14}{5}} = \sqrt{2.8} = 1.67$$

$$Syx = 1.67 \times 0.91 = 1.52$$

Regression Equations in Bivariate Grouped Distribution: Regression equation for Bivariate grouped frequency distribution, would be calculated by preparing the Bivariate correlation table. This correlation table would be used to find out the sum of deviations taken from assumed mean and the sum of the squares of the deviation etc. which are required for calculating the regression equation. The following formula can be applied to find out the regression equations.

Regression co-efficient of X on Y,

$$bxy = \frac{N\Sigma fdx.dy - \Sigma fdx.\Sigma fdy}{N\Sigma fdy^2 - (\Sigma fdy)^2} \times \frac{ix}{iy}$$

Regression co-efficient of Y on X,

$$byx = \frac{N\Sigma fdx.dy - \Sigma fdx.\Sigma fdy}{N\Sigma fdx^2 - (\Sigma fdx)^2} \times \frac{iy}{ix}$$

where, ix = width of the class interval of x variable;

iy = width of the class interval of y variable.

Illustration 6. *Find out the two regression equations from the following distribution.*

Sales	*Profit (in Rs.'000)*			
(Rs.'0000)	*0 - 10*	*10 - 20*	*20 - 30*	*30 - 40*
50-70	*4*	*3*	*5*	*8*
70-90	*6*	*7*	*4*	*9*
90-110	*5*	*3*	*5*	*6*
110-130	*3*	*2*	*6*	*4*

Calculate (i) The co-efficient of correlation (ii) The profit corresponding to sales of Rs. 1,50,000 and (iii) The sales corresponding to the profit of Rs. 60,000.

Solution: Let sales be denoted by x and profit by y.

Calculation of Regression Lines

y			0-10	10-20	20-30	30-40				
		m.p	5	15	25	35				
x		*dy / dx*	-2	-1	0	1	*f*	*fdx*	fdx^2	*fdxdy*
50-70	m.p 60	-1	[8] 4	[3] 3	[0] 5	[-8] 8	20	- 20	20	3
70-90	80	0	[0] 6	[0] 7	[0] 4	[0] 9	26	0	0	0
90-110	100	1	[-10] 5	[-3] 3	[0] 5	[6] 6	19	19	19	-7
110-130	120	2	[-12] 3	[-4] 2	[0] 6	[8] 4	15	30	60	-8
		f	18	15	20	27	*N* =80	*Σfdx* = 29	Σfdx^2 =99	*Σfdxdy* =-12
		fdy	-36	-15	0	27	*Σfdy* =-24			
		fdy^2	72	15	0	27	Σfdy^2 =114			
		fdxdy	-14	-4	0	6	*Σfdxdy* =-12			

Regression co-efficient of X on Y,

$$bxy = \frac{\sum fdx \cdot dy - \frac{\sum fdx \cdot \sum fdy}{N}}{\sum fdy^2 - \frac{(\sum fdy)^2}{N}} \times \frac{ix}{iy} = \frac{-12 - \frac{29 \times (-24)}{80}}{114 - \frac{(-24)^2}{80}} \times \frac{20}{10}$$

$$= \frac{-12 + \frac{696}{80}}{114 - \frac{576}{80}} \times 2 = \frac{-12 + 8.7}{114 - 7.2} \times 2 = \frac{-3.3}{106.8} \times 2$$

$$= \frac{-6.6}{106.8} = -0.06$$

Regression co-efficient of Y on X,

$$byx = \frac{\sum fdx \cdot dy - \frac{\sum fdx \cdot \sum fdy}{N}}{\sum fdx^2 - \frac{(\sum fdx)^2}{N}} \times \frac{iy}{ix} = \frac{-12 - \frac{29 \times (-24)}{80}}{99 - \frac{(29)^2}{80}} \times \frac{10}{20}$$

$$= \frac{-12 + \frac{696}{80}}{99 - \frac{841}{80}} \times \frac{1}{2} = \frac{-12 + 8.7}{99 - 10.51} \times \frac{1}{2}$$

$$= \frac{-3.3}{88.49} \times \frac{1}{2} = -0.0186$$

$$\overline{X} = A + \frac{\sum fdx}{N} \times c \qquad \overline{Y} = A + \frac{\sum fdy}{N} \times c$$

$$= 80 + \frac{29}{80} \times 20 \qquad = 25 + \frac{-24}{80} \times 10$$

$$= 80 + \frac{29}{4} = 87.25 \qquad = 25 - \frac{24}{8} = 22$$

Regression Equation of X on Y,

$$X - \overline{X} = r\frac{\sigma x}{\sigma y}(Y - \overline{Y})$$

$$X - 87.25 = -0.06\ (Y - 22)$$

$$X = -0.06Y + 1.32 + 87.25$$

$$X = 88.57 - 0.06Y$$

Regression equation of Y on X is

$$Y - \overline{Y} = r\frac{\sigma y}{\sigma x}(X - \overline{X})$$

$$Y - 22 = -0.0186\ (X - 87.25)$$

$$Y = -0.019X + 23.62$$

$$Y = 23.62 - 0.019X$$

(i) Co-efficient of Correlation

$$r = \sqrt{bxy \times byx} = \sqrt{(-0.06) \times (-0.0186)} = 0.03$$

(ii) The profit corresponding to sales of Rs. 1,50,000

$$Y_{150} = 23.62 - 0.019 \times 150 = 23.62 - 2.85 = 20.77$$

i.e., $20.77 \times 1000 = Rs.\ 20{,}770$

(iii) The sales corresponding to profit of Rs. 60,000

$$X_{60} = 88.57 - 0.06 \times 60 = 88.57 - 3.6 = 84.97$$

i.e., $84.97 \times 10000 = Rs.\ 8{,}49{,}700$

Second Degree Parabola: The equation for the second degree parabola for calculating non-linear trend is stated as,

$$Y_c = a + bX + cX^2$$

The trend value for any year may be computed with the help of this equation by substituting the value of a, b, c and X. The values of a, b and c can be calculated by solving the following three normal equations.

$$\Sigma Y = Na + b\Sigma X + c\Sigma X^2$$

$$\Sigma XY = a\Sigma X + b\Sigma X^2 + c\Sigma X^3$$

$$\Sigma X^2Y = a\Sigma X^2 + b\Sigma X^3 + c\Sigma X^4$$

If the origin is taken between two middle years ΣX and Σx^3 would be zero. Hence, the above equations can be reduced as follows.

$$\Sigma Y = Na + c\Sigma X^2$$

$$\Sigma XY = b\Sigma X^2$$

$$\Sigma X^2Y = a\Sigma X^2 + c\Sigma X^4$$

Hence, $a = \dfrac{\Sigma Y - c\Sigma X^2}{N}$; $\quad b = \dfrac{\Sigma XY}{\Sigma X^2}$

$$c = \frac{N\Sigma X^2Y - \Sigma X^2 \Sigma Y}{N\Sigma X^4 - (\Sigma X^2)^2}$$

Illustration 7. *Fit a parabola $Y = a + bX + cX^2$ from the following data. Estimate the price of the commodity for the year 1996.*

Year	*1990*	*1991*	*1992*	*1993*	*1994*
Price (Rs.)	*50*	*65*	*87*	*98*	*120*

Solution: Computation of second degree parabola.

Year	*Price Y*	*X*	*X^2*	*X^3*	*X^4*	*XY*	*X^2Y*	*Trend Yc*
1990	50	-2	4	-8	16	-100	200	49.82
1991	65	-1	1	-1	1	-65	65	66.49
1992	87	0	0	0	0	0	0	83.58
1993	98	1	1	1	1	98	98	101.09
1994	120	2	4	8	16	240	480	119.02
N = 5	*ΣY = 420*	*ΣX = 0*	*ΣX^2 = 10*	*ΣX^3 = 0*	*ΣX^4 = 34*	*ΣXY = 173*	*ΣX^2Y = 843*	*ΣYc = 420*

To calculate the value of a, b and c the following normal equations should be solved.

$$\Sigma Y = Na + b\Sigma X + c\Sigma X^2$$

$$\Sigma XY = a\,\Sigma X + b\,\Sigma X^2 + c\,\Sigma X^2$$

$$\Sigma X^2 Y = a\,\Sigma X^2 + b\,\Sigma X^3 + c\,\Sigma X^4$$

$$420 = 5a + 0 + 10c \qquad \ldots \text{(i)}$$

$$173 = 0 + 10b + 0 \qquad \ldots \text{(ii)}$$

$$843 = 10a + 0 + 34c \qquad \ldots \text{(iii)}$$

$$5a + 10c = 420 \qquad \ldots \text{(i)}$$

$$10b = 173 \qquad \ldots \text{(ii)}$$

$$10a + 20c = 843 \qquad \ldots \text{(iii)}$$

(i) × 2 $\quad 10a + 20c = 840 \qquad \ldots$ (iv)

(iv) - (iii) $\quad 14c = 3$

$$c = \frac{3}{14} = 0.21$$

(i) $\quad 5a + (10 \times 0.21) = 420$

$$5a = 420 - 2.1$$

$$a = \frac{417.9}{5} = 83.58$$

(ii) $\quad 10b = 173$

$$b = \frac{173}{10} = 17.3$$

Hence, $\;Yc = a + bx + cx^2$

$$Yc = 77.86 + 17.3x + 3.07x^2$$

Trend values can be calculated as follows.

$$Y_{1990} = 83.58 + 17.3(-2) + 0.21(-2)^2 = 83.58 - 34.6 + 0.84 = 49.82$$

$$Y_{1991} = 83.58 + 17.3(-2) + 0.21(-1)^2 = 83.58 - 17.3 + 0.21 = 66.49$$

$$Y_{1992} = 83.58 + 17.3(0) + 0.21(0)^2 = 83.58$$

$$Y_{1993} = 83.58 + 17.3(1) + 0.21(1)^2 = 83.58 + 17.3 + 0.21 = 101.$$

$$Y_{1994} = 83.58 + 17.3(2) + 0.21(2)^2 = 83.58 + 34.6 + 0.84 = 119.02$$

The price for 1996 can be calculated as follows.

For 1996 $X = 4$

$$Y = 83.58 + 17.3(4) + 0.21(4)^2 = 83.58 + 69.2 + 3.36 = 156.14$$

Miscellaneous Illustrations

Illustration 8. *From the following data obtain two regression equations.*

X	*6*	*9*	*12*	*5*	*8*	*14*
Y	*5*	*20*	*15*	*12*	*9*	*11*

Solution: Calculation of regression equations.

X	*Y*	$X-\overline{X}$ (X - 9)x	$Y-\overline{Y}$ (Y - 12)y	x^2	y^2	*xy*
6	5	-3	-7	9	49	21
9	20	0	8	0	64	0
12	15	3	3	9	9	9
5	12	-4	0	16	0	0
8	9	-1	-3	1	9	3
14	11	5	-1	25	1	-5
$\Sigma X = 54$	$\Sigma Y = 72$			$\Sigma x^2 = 60$	$\Sigma y^2 = 132$	$\Sigma xy = 28$

$$\overline{X} = \frac{\Sigma X}{N} = \frac{54}{6} = 9 \qquad \overline{Y} = \frac{\Sigma Y}{N} = \frac{72}{6} = 12$$

$$\Sigma X = 54 \quad \Sigma Y = 72 \qquad \Sigma x^2 = 60, \ \Sigma y^2 = 132, \ \Sigma xy = 28$$

Regression equation *X* on *Y*.

$$X - \overline{X} = r\frac{\sigma x}{\sigma y}(Y - \overline{Y}) \qquad \frac{\sigma x}{\sigma y} = \frac{\sum xy}{\sum y^2} = \frac{28}{132} = 0.21$$

Hence, $X - 9 = 0.21(Y - 12)$

$$X - 9 = 0.21y - 2.52$$

$$X = 9 - 2.52 + 0.21Y$$

$$X = 6.48 + 0.21Y$$

Regression equation Y on X.

$$Y-\overline{Y}=r\frac{\sigma y}{\sigma x}(X-\overline{X}) \qquad \frac{\sigma y}{\sigma x}=\frac{\Sigma xy}{\Sigma x^2}=\frac{28}{60}=0.47$$

$$(Y-12)=0.47(X-9)$$

$$Y-12=0.47X-4.23$$

$$Y=12-4.23+0.47X$$

$$Y=7.77+0.47X$$

Illustration 9. *Calculate the regression equations X on Y and Y on X from the following data.*

X	*8*	*7*	*10*	*9*	*6*
Y	*15*	*18*	*17*	*21*	*14*

Calculate, (i) The value of Y for a given value of X as 21. (ii) The value of X when the value of Y is 30.

Solution: Calculation of regression equations

X	*Y*	$X-\overline{X}$ *(X - 8)* *x*	$Y-\overline{Y}$ *(Y - 17)* *y*	*x2*	*y2*	*xy*
8	15	0	-2	0	4	0
7	18	-1	1	1	1	-1
10	17	2	0	4	0	0
9	21	1	4	1	16	4
6	14	-2	-3	4	9	6
$\Sigma X = 40$	$\Sigma Y = 85$			$\Sigma x^2 = 10$	$\Sigma y^2 = 30$	$\Sigma xy = 9$

$$\overline{X}=\frac{\Sigma X}{N}=\frac{40}{5}=8 \qquad \overline{Y}=\frac{\Sigma Y}{N}=\frac{85}{5}=17$$

$$\Sigma x^2=10, \quad \Sigma y^2=30, \quad \Sigma xy=9$$

Regression Equation X and Y

$$X-\overline{X}=r\frac{\sigma x}{\sigma y}(Y-\overline{Y}) \qquad \frac{\sigma x}{\sigma y}=\frac{\Sigma xy}{\Sigma y^2}=\frac{9}{30}=0.3$$

$$(X-8)=0.3(Y-17)$$
$$X-8=0.3Y-5.1$$
$$X=8-5.1+0.3Y$$
$$X=2.9+0.3Y$$

Regression Equation Y on X

$$Y-\overline{Y}=r\frac{\sigma y}{\sigma x}(X-\overline{X}) \qquad \frac{\sigma y}{\sigma x}=\frac{\sum xy}{\sum x^2}=\frac{9}{10}=0.9$$

$$(Y-17)=0.9(X-8)$$
$$Y-17=0.9X-7.2$$
$$Y=17-7.2+0.9X$$
$$Y=9.8+0.9X$$

(i) When value of X is 21, value of Y can be calculated as,

$$Y = 9.8 + 0.9(21) = 9.8 + 18.9 = 28.7$$

(ii) When value of Y is 30, value of X can be calculated as,

$$X = 2.9 + 0.3\,(30) = 2.9 + 9 = 11.9$$

Illustration 10. *From the following obtain two regression equations*

Sales (in '000)	*91*	*53*	*45*	*76*	*89*	*95*	*80*	*65*
Advertisement Expenses	*15*	*8*	*7*	*12*	*17*	*25*	*20*	*13*

Estimate the advertisement expenses for a sale of Rs. 1,20,000.

Solution: Calculation of regression equations

Sales X	*Adv.* Y	*dx* *X - A* *(X - 70)*	*dy* *Y - A* *(Y - 15)*	dx^2	dy^2	*dxdy*
91	15	21	0	441	0	0
53	8	-17	-7	289	49	119
45	7	-25	-8	625	64	200
76	12	6	-3	36	9	-18
89	17	19	2	361	4	38
95	25	25	10	625	100	250
80	20	10	5	100	25	50
65	13	-5	-2	25	4	10
		$\Sigma dx=$ 34	$\Sigma dy=$ -3	$\Sigma dx^2=$ 2502	$\Sigma dy^2=$ 255	$\Sigma dxdy=$ 649

The above calculations are based on Assumed Mean Method.

$\Sigma dx^2 = 2502$, $\Sigma dy^2 = 255$; $N = 8$, $\Sigma dx = 34$, $\Sigma dy = -3$

$\Sigma dxdy = 649$

Regression equation X on Y

$$X - \overline{X} = r\frac{\sigma x}{\sigma y}(Y - \overline{Y})$$

$$r\frac{\sigma x}{\sigma y} = \frac{\sum dx \cdot dy - \frac{\sum dx \cdot \sum dy}{N}}{\sum dy^2 - \frac{(\sum dy)^2}{N}} = \frac{649 - \frac{34(-3)}{8}}{255 - \frac{(-3)^2}{8}}$$

$$= \frac{649 + 12.75}{255 - 1.125} = \frac{661.75}{253.875} = 2.61$$

$$\overline{X} = A \pm \frac{\sum dx}{N} = 70 + \frac{34}{8} = 74.25$$

$$\overline{Y} = A \pm \frac{\sum dy}{N} = 15 - \frac{3}{8} = 14.63$$

$$X - 74.25 = 2.61\,(Y - 14.63)$$

$$X - 74.25 = 2.61Y - 38.18$$

$$X = 74.25 - 38.18 + 2.61\,Y$$

$$X = 30.07 + 2.61Y$$

Regression equation Y on X

$$Y - \overline{Y} = r\frac{\sigma y}{\sigma x}(X - \overline{X})$$

$$r\frac{\sigma y}{\sigma x} = \frac{\sum dx \cdot dy - \frac{\sum dx \cdot \sum dy}{N}}{\sum dx^2 - \frac{(\sum dx)^2}{N}} = \frac{649 - \frac{34(-3)}{8}}{2502 - \frac{(34)^2}{8}}$$

$$= \frac{649 + 12.75}{2502 - 144.5} = \frac{661.75}{2357.5} = 0.28$$

$$(Y - 14.63) = 0.28\,(X - 74.25)$$

$$Y - 14.63 = 0.28X - 20.79$$

$$Y = 14.63 - 20.79 + 0.28X$$

$$Y = -6.16 + 0.28X$$

Calculation of advertisement expenses for a sale of Rs. 1,20,000.

Variables x represent Sales and y represent Advertisement Expenses. Hence, regression equation y on x should be applied. Since the equation represent values in thousands x should be taken as 120.

$$Y = -6.16 + 0.28(120)$$

$$Y = -6.16 + 33.6 = 27.44$$

Hence, advertisement expenses = 27.44.

Illustration 11. *Calculate correlation co-efficient and regression co-efficient for the following data.*

X	*8*	*7*	*10*	*30*	*35*	*40*	*45*	*50*	*55*	*60*
Y	*4*	*3*	*7*	*10*	*15*	*17*	*18*	*20*	*22*	*24*

Find the estimate of Y when X is 70.

Solution: Calculation of regression equations.

X	Y	$X-\bar{X}$ (X-34) x	$Y-\bar{Y}$ (Y-14) y	x^2	y^2	xy
8	4	-26	-10	676	100	260
7	3	27	-11	729	121	297
10	7	-24	-7	576	49	168
30	10	-4	-4	16	16	16
35	15	1	1	1	1	1
40	17	6	3	36	9	18
45	18	11	4	121	16	44
50	20	16	6	256	36	96
55	22	21	8	441	64	168
60	24	26	10	676	100	260
$\Sigma X=340$	$\Sigma Y=140$			$\Sigma x^2=3528$	$\Sigma y^2=512$	$\Sigma xy=1328$

$$\overline{X} = \frac{\Sigma X}{N} = \frac{340}{10} = 34 \qquad \overline{Y} = \frac{\Sigma Y}{N} = \frac{140}{10} = 14$$

$$\Sigma x^2 = 3528, \quad \Sigma y^2 = 512, \quad \Sigma xy = 1328$$

Karl Pearson's co-efficient of correlation,

$$r = \frac{\Sigma xy}{\sqrt{\Sigma x^2 \times \Sigma y^2}} = \frac{1328}{\sqrt{3528 \times 512}} = \frac{1328}{1344} = 0.988$$

Calculation of Regression Coefficient

$$r\frac{\sigma x}{\sigma y} = \frac{\Sigma xy}{\Sigma y^2} = \frac{1328}{512} = 2.59, \qquad r\frac{\sigma y}{\sigma x} = \frac{\Sigma xy}{\Sigma x^2} = \frac{1328}{3528} = 0.38$$

In order to find out the estimate of y when x is 70, regression equation y on x should be calculated. It can be calculated as follows.

$$Y - \overline{Y} = r\frac{\sigma y}{\sigma x}(X - \overline{X})$$

$$(Y - 14) = 0.38(X - 34)$$

$$Y - 14 = 0.38X - 12.92$$

$$Y = 14 - 12.92 + 0.38X$$

$$Y = 1.08 + 0.38X$$

When, $x = 70$

$$Y = 1.08 + 0.38(70)$$

$$Y = 1.08 + 26.6 = 27.68$$

Illustration 12. *The test score and sales done by 10 selected salesman of a company shows the following.*

Test score	*55*	*65*	*75*	*60*	*74*	*85*	*70*	*73*	*80*	*65*
Sales (in 000)	*74*	*82*	*94*	*78*	*85*	*96*	*84*	*89*	*90*	*75*

Fit regression equation of test score on sales; and regression equation of sales on test score. Also estimate sales for test scorce of 50.

Solution: Calculate of regression equations.

Test Score X	Sales Y	dx X-A (X-70)	dx Y-A (Y-80)	dx^2	dy^2	dxdy
55	74	-15	-6	225	36	90
64	82	-6	2	36	4	-12
74	94	5	14	25	196	70
60	78	-10	-2	100	4	20
74	85	4	5	16	25	20
85	96	15	16	225	256	240
70	84	0	4	0	16	0
73	89	3	9	9	81	27
80	90	10	10	100	100	100
65	75	-5	-5	25	25	25
		$\Sigma dx = 1$	$\Sigma dy = 47$	$\Sigma dx^2 = 761$	$\Sigma dy^2 = 743$	$\Sigma dxdy = 580$

$$\sum dx^2 = 761; \ \sum dy^2 = 743; \ \sum dx = 1; \ \sum dy = 47; \ \sum dxdy = 580;$$

$$\overline{X} = A \pm \frac{\sum dx}{N} = 70 + \frac{1}{10} = 70 + 0.1 = 70.1$$

$$\overline{Y} = A \pm \frac{\sum dy}{N} = 80 + \frac{47}{10} = 80 + 4.7 = 84.7$$

Regression equation X on Y

$$X - \overline{X} = r\frac{\sigma x}{\sigma y}(Y - \overline{Y})$$

$$\frac{\sigma y}{\sigma x} = \frac{\sum dx \cdot dy - \dfrac{\sum dx \cdot \sum dy}{N}}{\sum dx^2 - \dfrac{(\sum dx)^2}{N}} = \frac{580 - \dfrac{1 \times 47}{10}}{743 - \dfrac{(47)^2}{10}}$$

$$= \frac{580 - 4.7}{743 - 220.9} = \frac{575.3}{522.1} = 1.1$$

$$X - 70.1 = 1.1(Y - 84.7)$$

$$X - 70.1 = 1.1Y - 93.17$$

$$X = -93.17 + 70.1 + 1.1Y$$

$$X = -23.07 + 1.1Y$$

Regression Equation Y on X

$$Y - \overline{Y} = r\frac{\sigma y}{\sigma x}(X - \overline{X})$$

$$\frac{\sigma y}{\sigma x} = \frac{\Sigma dx \cdot dy - \dfrac{\Sigma dx \cdot \Sigma dy}{N}}{\Sigma dx^2 - \dfrac{(\Sigma dx)^2}{N}} = \frac{580 - \dfrac{1 \times 47}{10}}{761 - \dfrac{(1)^2}{10}}$$

$$= \frac{580 - 4.7}{761 - 0.1} = \frac{575.3}{760.9} = 0.76$$

$$(Y - 84.7) = 0.76(X - 70.1)$$

$$Y - 84.7 = 0.76X - 53.28$$

$$Y = 84.7 - 53.28 + 0.76X$$

$$Y = 31.42 + 0.76X$$

Sales for test score 50 can be calculated by applying the equation Y on X.

$$Y = 31.42 + 0.76X$$

$$Y = 31.42 + 0.76 \times 50 = 31.42 + 38 = 69.42$$

i.e., Sales = Rs. 69,420

Illustration 13. *Find out the regression equation of incentives on production and production on incentives from the following data.*

	Average	*Standard Deviation*
Incentives (in thousand rupees)	*45.5*	*8.5*
Production (in thousand units)	*96.4*	*11.3*

$$r = 0.47$$

Also estimate the production for incentives 3.6.

Solution: Let X denotes incentives and Y denotes production.

$$X = 45.5 \qquad Y = 96.4$$

$$\sigma x = 8.5 \qquad \sigma y = 11.3$$

$$r = 0.47$$

Regression equation X on Y

$$X - \overline{X} = r\frac{\sigma x}{\sigma y}(Y - \overline{Y})$$

X - 45.5 = 0.47 (8.5/11.3) (Y - 96.4)

X - 45.5 = 0.35 (Y - 96.4)

X - 45.5 = 0.35Y - 0.35 x 96.4

X = 45.5 - 33.74 + 0.35Y

X = 11.76 + 0.35Y

Regression equation Y on X

$$Y - \overline{Y} = r\frac{\sigma y}{\sigma x}(X - \overline{X})$$

(Y - 96.4) = (0.47 x 11.3)/8.5 (X - 45.5)

Y - 96.4 = 0.62 (X - 45.5)

Y - 96.4 = 0.62X - 28.21

Y = 96.4 - 28.21 - 0.62X

Y = 68.19 + 62X

Illustration 14. *Estimate the production corresponding to the fertilizer application of 100kg per acre, from the following data.*

	Fertilizer application per acre (Kg)	*Production per acrc (tonnes)*
Average	*80*	*47*
S.D	*12.5*	*7.8*

r = *0.236*

Solution: Assume X as Fertilizer Application and Y as Production.

$X = 80$ $\quad Y = 47$

$\sigma x = 12.5$ $\quad \sigma y = 7.8$

$r = 0.236$

The estimate of production for fertilizer application is based on the regression equation Y on X. It can be calculated as follows.

$$Y - \overline{Y} = r\frac{\sigma y}{\sigma x}(X - \overline{X})$$

$$(Y - 47) = (0.236 \text{ x } 7.8)/12.5\ (X - 80)$$

$$Y - 47 = 0.15\ (X - 80)$$

$$Y - 47 = 0.15X - 12$$

$$Y = 47 - 12 + 0.15X$$

$$Y = 35 + 0.15X$$

When, $\quad X = 100$

$$Y = 35 + 0.15 \times 100 = 50 \text{ tonnes}$$

Illustration 15. *If the regression equations are 7X - 4Y - 28 = 0 and 12X - 10Y - 90 = 0. Find the correlation co-efficient between x and y.*

Solution: Let regression equation X on Y is,

$$7X - 4Y + 28 = 0$$

$$7X = 4Y - 28$$

$$X = (4/7)Y - (28/7)$$

i.e., $\quad r\frac{\sigma x}{\sigma y} = \frac{4}{7} = 0.57$

Let regression equation Y on X is,

$$12X - 10Y - 90 = 0$$

$$12X = 10Y + 90$$

i.e., $\quad 10Y = 12X - 90$

$$Y = 12X/10 - 90/10$$

$$r\frac{\sigma x}{\sigma y} = \frac{12}{10} = 1.2$$

Correlation coefficient $= \sqrt{bxy \times byx} = \sqrt{0.57 \times 1.2} = 0.83$

Illustration 16. *Following are the two regression equations with respect to a distribution of X and Y*

$$X = 5.7 - 0.32Y$$

$$Y = 8.4 - 0.52X$$

Calculate the arithmetic mean of X and Y and also calculate the co-efficient of correlation between X and Y.

Solution: Calculation of arithmetic mean.

$X = 5.7 - 0.32Y$ i.e., $X + 0.32Y = 5.7$ . . . (i)

$Y = 8.4 + 0.52X$ i.e., $Y - 0.52X = 8.4$ . . . (ii)

Multiply equation (i) by 0.52,

i.e., $0.52X + 0.17Y = 2.96$ . . . (iii)

$0.52X \times + Y = 8.4$ . . . (ii)

(ii - iii) $1.17Y = 11.36$

$$Y = 11.36/1.17 = 9.7$$

i.e., $\overline{Y} = 9.7$

Substitute the value in equation (i)

$$X + 0.32(9.7) = 5.7$$

$$X + 3.1 = 5.7$$

$$X = 5.7 - 3.1 = 2.6$$

i.e., $\overline{X} = 2.6$

Calculation of co-efficient of correlation,

$$X = 5.7 - 0.32Y$$

i.e., $r\dfrac{\sigma x}{\sigma y} = bxy = -0.32$

$$Y = 8.4 + 0.52X$$

i.e., $r\dfrac{\sigma x}{\sigma y} = byx = +0.52$

Coefficient of correlation $r = \sqrt{bxy \times byx} = \sqrt{(-0.32)\times(0.52)}$

$$= \sqrt{0.1664} = 0.41$$

Illustration 17. *Find the means of variables X and Y and the correlation co-efficient from the following regression equation.*

$$2Y - X - 50 = 0$$

$3Y - 2X - 10 = 0$ (MGU: Section C April '98)

Solution: $2Y - X = 50$ . . . (i)

$3Y - 2X = 10$ . . . (ii)

(i) × 2 $\qquad 4Y - 2X = 100 \qquad$ . . . (iii)

$2Y - 2X = 10 \qquad$ . . . (ii)

(iii) - (ii) $\qquad 2Y = 90$

$$Y = \frac{90}{2} = 45$$

(i) $\qquad 2 \times 45 - X = 50$

$$X = 90 - 50 = 40$$

Hence, Mean of variable X = 40 and Mean of variable Y = 45

Taking equ (i) as the regression of Y on X; $\quad 2Y = 50 + X$

$$Y = 25 + 1/2x$$

$$bxy = \frac{1}{2}$$

$$2X = -10 + 3y$$

$$X = -5 + \frac{3}{2}y$$

$$bxy = \frac{3}{2}$$

Correlation coefficient $r = \sqrt{bxy \times byx} = \sqrt{\frac{3}{2} \times \frac{1}{2}} = 0.87$

Illustration 18. *In a correlation analysis between production and price of a commodity, the following constants were obtained.*

	Production Index	*Price Index*
Arithmetic Mean	*110*	*98*
Standard Deviation	*12*	*5*

Correlation between production and price = -0.4

Write down the regression equation of price on production and calculate the price index when the production index is 116.

(MGU: Section B April '97)

Solution: Let production index be X and price index be Y.

$\bar{X} = 110; \quad \bar{Y} = 98; \quad \sigma x = 12; \quad \sigma y = 5; \quad r = -0.4.$

Regression equation Y on X

i.e., Price index as Production index.

$$Y-\overline{Y}=r\frac{\sigma x}{\sigma y}X-\overline{X}$$

$$Y-98=-0.4\times\frac{5}{12}(X-110)$$

$$Y-98=-0.17(X-110)$$

$$Y-98=-0.17X+18.7$$

$$Y=98+18.7-0.17X$$

$$Y=116.7-0.17X$$

When Production index is 116

Price Index $Y=116.7-0.17X$

$$Y=116.7-0.17(116)$$

$$Y=116.7-19.72$$

$\therefore$ Price Index = 97

Illustration 19. *Fit a linear regression line of Y on X for the following data. Hence, obtain the value of Y when X = 23. Verify the result graphically.*

X	10	15	35	40	50
Y	100	90	110	80	120

(Kerala: Section C April '96)

Solution: Calculation of regression equation Y on X.

X	$X-\overline{X}$ x (X-30)	x^2	Y	$Y-\overline{Y}$ y (Y-100)	xy
10	-20	400	100	0	0
15	-15	225	90	-10	150
35	5	25	110	10	50
40	10	100	80	-20	-200
50	20	400	120	20	400
$\Sigma X = 150$		$\Sigma x^2 = 1150$	$\Sigma Y = 500$		$\Sigma xy = 400$

$$\bar{X} = \frac{\Sigma X}{N} = \frac{150}{5} = 30 \qquad \bar{Y} = \frac{\Sigma Y}{N} = \frac{500}{5} = 100$$

Regression equation Y and X

$$Y - \bar{Y} = byx\,(X - \bar{X})$$

$$byx = \frac{\Sigma xy}{\Sigma x^2} = \frac{400}{1150} = 0.35$$

$$Y - 100 = 0.35\,(X - 30)$$

$$Y = 100 + 0.35X - 10.5$$

$$Y = 89.5 + 0.35X$$

Value of Y when $X = 23$

$$Y = 89.5 + 0.35 \times 23 = 97.6$$

Illustration 20. *The demand of TV set as obtained by sample survey on 7 towns are shown below:*

Population (in '000)	*11*	*14*	*14*	*17*	*17*	*21*	*35*
Demand of TV set	*15*	*27*	*27*	*30*	*34*	*38*	*46*

Fit linear regression equation of Y on X and find the demand of TV set in a town of population 30 thousand.

(Kerala: Section C April '95)

Solution: Calculation of regression equation.

X	Y	XY	X^2
11	15	165	121
14	27	378	196
14	27	378	196
17	30	510	289
17	34	578	289
21	38	798	441
35	46	1610	1225
$\Sigma x = 129$	$\Sigma y = 217$	$\Sigma xy = 4417$	$\Sigma x^2 = 2757$

Regression equation Y on X i.e., $Y = a + bX$

To determine the value of a and b` the following two normal equations are to be solved.

$$\Sigma Y = Na + b\Sigma X$$

$$\Sigma XY = a\Sigma X + b\Sigma X^2$$

Substituting the values,

$$217 = 7a + 129b \quad \ldots (i)$$

$$4417 = 129a + 2757b \quad \ldots (ii)$$

(i) × 129 $$27993 = 903a + 16641b \quad \ldots (iii)$$

(ii) × 7 $$30919 = 903a + 19299b \quad \ldots (iv)$$

(iv) - (iii) $$2926 = 2658b$$

$$b = \frac{2926}{2658} = 1.1$$

$$217 = 7a + 129(1.1)$$

$$217 = 7a + 141.9$$

$$7a = 217 - 141.9$$

$$a = \frac{75.1}{7} = 10.7$$

Regression equation Y on X is

$$Y = 10.7 + 1.1X$$

Demand of T.V. set for a population of 30,000 can be calculated as

$$Y = 10.7 + 1.1(30) = 10.7 + 33 = 44 \text{ sets}$$

Illustration 21. *The following results are given*

	x	y
A.M	*36*	*85*
S.D	*11*	*8*

Co-efficient of correlation between X and Y = 0.66.

Find (i) the two regression lines; (ii) the estimated value of X when Y = 75. (Kerala: Section C Sep '93)

Solution: $\bar{X} = 36, \quad \bar{Y} = 36, \quad \sigma x = 11, \quad \sigma y = 8, \quad r = 0.66$

Regression equation X on Y is

$$X - \bar{X} = r\frac{\sigma x}{\sigma y}(Y - \bar{Y})$$

$$X - 36 = 0.66\left(\frac{11}{8}\right)(Y - 85)$$

$$X - 36 = 0.91(Y - 85)$$

$$X - 36 = 0.91Y - 77.35$$

$$X = 0.91Y - 77.35 + 36$$

$$X = 41.35 + 0.91Y$$

(i) $X = -41.35 + 0.91Y$

Regression equation Y on X is

$$Y - \overline{Y} = r\frac{\sigma y}{\sigma x}(X - \overline{X})$$

$$Y - 85 = 0.66\left(\frac{8}{11}\right)(X - 36)$$

$$Y - 85 = 0.48X - (0.48 \times 36)$$

$$Y - 85 = 0.48X - 17.28$$

$$Y = 0.48X - 17.28 + 85$$

(i) $Y = 67.72 - 0.48X$

(ii) Estimated value of X when $Y = 75$

$$X = -41.35 + 0.92 \times 75$$

$$X = -41.35 + 68.25 = 26.9 \text{ i.e., } = 27$$

Exercises

1. Define Regression. State the advantages of regression equations.
2. Define Regression Lines. State the utilities of regression Lines.
3. What is Regression? State the difference between Correlation Analysis and Regression Analysis.
4. State the various methods of ascertaining the regression equations.
5. What do you mean by standard error of regression?
6. State the procedures for ascertaining regression equation in Bivariate Grouped Distribution.
7. Distinguish between correlation and regression.

(MG U: Section B April '98)

8. State any two differences between correlation and regression.

(MGU: Section A April '96)

9. Why are there in general two regression equations?

(MGU: Section A April '95)

10. What are regression co-efficients? Point out their properties.

(M GU: Section B April '95)

11. State the properties of regression co-efficients.

(Kerala: Section A April '95)

12. What is regression line? Write the equation of regression lines.

(Kerala: Section B Sep '93)

13. What do you understand by regression analysis? Illustrate its use in business management. (Kerala: Section B Sep '90)

14. Find out the regression equation from the following data.

X	8	14	22	26	30
Y	2	6	4	7	11

(Ans: X = 6.98 + 2.17Y; Y = -0.2 + 0.31X)

15. Fit a straight line trend by the method of least square from the following data.

X	5	10	15	20	25
Y	3	9	12	15	21

(Ans: X = 0.96 + 1.17Y; Y = -0.6 + 0.84X)

16. Calculate the regression equation X on Y and Y on X from the following data.

Income45 (Rs. '000)	45	40	59	65	89
Expenses (Rs. '000)	42	38	50	67	90

Also calculate (i) the expenses when the income is Rs. 50,000 and (ii) the income when the expenses is Rs. 100,000.

(Ans: X = 7.37 + 0.91Y; Y = -3.99 + 1.03X; (i) Rs. 47,510 (ii) 98,370)

17. Find out the regression equation from the following data.

X	92	90	85	63	57	40	30	22
Y	25	30	35	40	50	75	85	95

(Ans: X = 113.72 - 0.99Y; Y = 11.27 - 0.95X)

18. Find out the regression equation of sales on profit; and profit on sales, from the following data.

	Average	Standard Deviation
Sales (Rs. in '0000)	33	8.6
Profit (Rs. in '000)	42	17.4
r = 0.37		

Also estimate the profit when sales is Rs. 4,00,000.

(Ans: X = 25.31 + 0.18Y; Y = 17.25 + 0.75X; Rs. 47,250)

19. If the regression equations are, $10X - 5Y + 36 = 0$ and $16X - 6Y - 85 = 0$

Find the correlation co-efficient between x and y. (Ans: 0.73)

20. Following are the two regression equations with respect to a distribution of X and Y.

$X = 12.56 - 0.35Y, \quad Y = 13.7 + 0.26X$

Calculate the arithmetic mean of X and Y and also calculate the co-efficient of correlation between X and Y.

(Ans: $\overline{X} = 6.08$; $\overline{Y} = 18.5$; r = 0.3)

21. Find the two regression equations from the following data.

$\Sigma X = 69;\ \Sigma Y = 120;\ \Sigma X^2 = 675;\ \Sigma Y^2 = 960;\ \Sigma XY = 540;\ n = 6.$

(Ans: $X = -0.1 + 0.58Y$; $Y = -61.5 + 7.09X$)

22. The equation of two regression lines in a correlation analysis are as follows. $5X - 6X = 40$ and $2X + 2X = 123$

A student obtained $\overline{X} = 11$ and $\overline{Y} = 15$ and co-efficient of correlation $r = 0.32$. Do you agree with the answer? If not suggest your answers.

(Ans: No; x = 51; y = 36; r = 0.77)

23. A student obtained two regression lines as, $3X - 4Y - 9 = 0$ and $5X + 2Y - 6 = 0$ Do you agree with the answer?

(Ans: The answer is wrong since the equations give r as 1.83; r should never be greater than 1)

24. From the data given below find:

(a) The two regression equations, and

(b) The most likely marks is statistic when the marks in Economic is 30.

Marks in										
Economics	25	28	35	32	31	36	29	38	34	32
Statistics	43	46	49	41	36	32	31	30	33	39

(MGU: Section C April '95) (Ans: (a) $X = 41 + 0.24\,Y$; $Y = 60 + 0.69X$; (b) 39)

25. From the following data obtain two regression equations:

Sales	91	97	108	121	67	124	51	73	111	57
Purchase	71	75	69	97	70	91	39	61	80	47

(MGU: Section C Sep '93) (Ans: $X = -5 + 1.36Y$; $Y = 10 + 0.67X$)

26. Find the means of variables x and y and correlation co-efficient from the following regression equations. $2Y - X = 50,\ 3Y - 2X = 10$

(MGU: Section B April '96) (Ans: $\overline{X} = 40$; $\overline{Y} = 50$; $r = 0.87$)

◆ Chapter 11 ◆

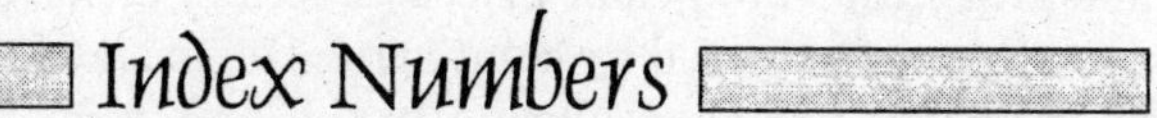

Index Numbers

I Meaning and Definition

Index numbers are first introduced in Italy in the year 1764. The first index was constructed to compare the Italian price index in 1750 with the price level of 1500. It spreaded to other countries later. At present the index number techniques are used for the measure of various economic and business activities in addition to the measure of prices.

Index number is a measure of studying the relationship between two variables. Taking one variable as a base, the relationship of the other variables as percentage, basis are calculated. Hence, it shows whether the particular variable is assuming an increasing trend or decreasing trend.

Definitions of Index number

The important definitions of Index number are stated below.

1. According to Croxtan and Cowden, *"Index numbers are devices for measuring difference in the magnitude of a group of related variables"*.
2. Clark and Schkode defines *"an index number is a percentage relative that compares economic measures in a given period with those same measures at a fixed period in the past"*.
3. Spiegal defines *"an index number is a statistical measure designed to show changes in a variable or a group of related variables with respect to time, geographical location or other characteristics"*.
4. Maslow defines *"Index Number is a numerical value characterising the change in complex economic phenomena over a period of time or space"*.

From the above definitions, index number means a measure of changes in one or two variables over a period of time.

Classification of Index Numbers

Index numbers can be classified on the basis of the nature of measurement. The most common types of index numbers are (i) Price index numbers, (ii) Quantity index numbers and (iii) Value index numbers.

(i) Price index numbers: Price index number is used for measuring the changes of prices of commodities over a period of time. It is constructed by comparing the price of commodities for two different periods. Normally the prices for past period are denoted as the prices of base period. There are two types of price index numbers. They are Wholesale Price Index Numbers and Retail Price Index Numbers. Wholesale Price Index Numbers deal with the wholesale or general price level of a commodity. Retail Price Index Number deals with the changes in the retail prices of the commodities.

(ii) Quantity index numbers: Quantity index numbers deal with the quantity of goods produced or consumed. It measures the rate of change of quantity of commodities produced and consumed between two different periods.

Example: Quantity of goods produced in industry, quantity of goods imported and exported, quantity of agricultural production etc.

(iii) Value index numbers: Value Index numbers are concerned with changes in the total value of products in a specific year compared with a past year. Value of product can be ascertained by multiplying the quantity with the price per unit.

Uses of Index Numbers

The following are the important uses in the construction of index numbers.

(i) Index numbers measure trend values: Index numbers are concerned with the measurement of changes of prices, quantity or value for different periods. Hence, trend values can be ascertained for these periods. This trend values may be upward or downward. The study of trend will help to find out the reasons for the upward or downward trends.

(ii) Index numbers facilitate for policy decisions: Index numbers help the government as well as non-government organisations to frame suitable policies. Example: The Government may fix the wages, salaries and dearness allowances for the workers on the

basis of cost of living index. The industries may take decisions for the future periods, with regard to quantity of goods to be produced, quantity of goods to be marketed, pricing policies etc., with the help of index numbers.

(iii) Index numbers are used for deflating: The original data can be adjusted according to the changes in prices with the help of index numbers. It also helps in transforming the normal income into real income and nominal sales into real sales.

(iv) Index numbers are economic barometers: The condition of the economy of a country can be known through construction of index numbers for different periods with regard to employment, literacy, agriculture, industry, commerce etc. Hence, it can be termed as economic barometers.

(v) Index numbers help in comparing the standard of living: The standard of living of people in various places of a country can be compared through index numbers. Hence, it facilitates the government to take suitable measures for the backward areas of the country.

Problems in the construction of Index numbers

The following factors should be taken into consideration before construction of the index numbers.

(i) The purpose of the index numbers: The purpose of construction of index number should be decided before construction of the index numbers. There are various types of index numbers on the basis of income, expenses, price level, production of various commodities etc. Example: In the construction of index number related to the small scale industrial production, only the production for small scale industries should be taken into account. The output of large scale industries should not be included for this purpose.

(ii) Availability of data: The areas selected for the construction of index numbers should provide adequate data. Sometimes, it is difficult to get data in some area which would prevent or delay in the construction of index numbers. Example: In the construction of index number for number of units produced by various factories of an industry the real data may not be supplied by the factories, in order to misappropriate in the payment of taxes.

The data should also be capable of comparison with other data. If the data collected could not be compared with other data the index numbers so constructed, could not be a quality one.

(iii) Selection of items: Selection of items for the construction of index numbers depends upon the nature of index numbers to be constructed. For the construction of cost of living index numbers for a specific income group, the representative items from the particular category of income group should be taken from that particular area. But for the construction of cost of living index numbers in general, the representative items from all income groups of the area must be selected.

(iv) Selection of base period: The construction of index number is based on base years. The comparison of changes in prices or quantity of production should be done on the basis of the base period. While selecting the base period care should be taken so that the period should be a normal one. The period had not experienced war, drought, famine etc. The base period should not be too long in the past.

Example: To compare the price level for 1993 it is not proper to select either 1940 or 1950 as base. It should be around 1970 or 1980.

The selection of base depends upon the nature of index numbers constructed and the availability of data. Following are the important types of bases.

(a) Fixed base: Under the fixed base the prices of the base year should be treated as 100. From this price of 100 the increase or decrease in price for the current year should be calculated.

(b) Chain base: Under the chain base, the base changes from period to period. In this method, prices of one year should be compared with another year, whereas, in the fixed base, the prices in various years should be compared with the particular fixed base year. For example under chain base method the prices of 1993 should be compared with 1992 by considering 1992 as base year. The prices of 1992 should be compared with the prices of 1991 by taking 1991 as base, etc.

(c) Average base: Under the average base the average prices of few years should be taken as base for comparison. This would reduce the abnormalities and fluctuations in the prices of commodities.

(v) Selection of average: Normally, in the construction of index numbers arithmetic mean is taken into account for calculation. Median and mode are not used in the construction of index numbers. But, geometric mean is also used to some extent. Geometric mean is considered as the best measure for the construction of index numbers. The reasons for the preference of geometric mean are, it gives equal weight to equal rate of change; it is a best measure when there is wide fluctuations in the variables; and it also satisfies time reversal test. Inspite of, its superiority over arithmetic mean, arithmetic mean is widely used in the construction of index numbers.

(vi) Selection of weights: It is practically difficult to assign weights while constructing index numbers. The question of assigning weight arises due to the fact that all items taken for construction of index numbers are not of equal important. According to the relative importance of one item with other, weights should be fixed. There are two most common methods adopted for assigning weights. They are (a) implicit weight and (b) explicit weight.

(a) Implicit weight: When a commodity is selected more than once for the construction of index numbers the weight should be given according to the number of times the particular commodity is selected. This type of weight is called implicit weight. *Example:* If three varieties of coffee, one variety of tea and two varieties of sugar are selected for the construction of price index numbers, weight three should be given for coffee and weight two should be given for sugar.

(b) Explicit weight: Under the explicit weight, weight should be given on the basis of the importance of the items selected, instead of the number of times it was selected. (*Eg*) The commodity rice is more important than edible oil. Hence, more weight should be assigned for rice than edible oil.

(vii) Selection of appropriate sources of data: There may be various sources for the data. It is very difficult to select the appropriate source. Hence, care should be taken in the selection of source. Different sources may charge different prices. Hence, the prices may be collected from the standard source.

(viii) Selection of suitable formula: The formula for the construction of index numbers depends upon the nature of index numbers to be constructed. An appropriate, standard formula should be selected for the construction of index numbers.

II Methods of construction of index numbers

Index numbers can be calculated through the following methods.

Methods of Calculating Index Numbers

- Unweighted (Simple)
  - Simple Aggregate
  - Simple average of price relatives
- Weighted
  - Weighted Aggregate
  - Weighted average of price relatives

(I) Unweighted Method

1. Simple Aggregate Method: In this method, the index numbers can be calculated by dividing the sum of the current year prices with the sum of the base year prices. It can be calculated by the following formula.

$$P_{01} = \frac{\sum P_1}{\sum P_0} \times 100$$

Where, P_{01} indicates, price index numbers

$\sum P_1$ indicates, sum of the prices for the current year

$\sum P_0$ indicates, sum of the prices of the base year

Steps:

(i) Calculate the sum of the prices of selected commodities for the current year. $(\sum P_1)$.

(ii) Find out the sum of the prices of the selected commodities for the base year $(\sum P_0)$.

(iii) Finally divide $\sum P_1$ by $\sum P_0$ and multiply it with 100 to get the index number based on simple aggregate method.

Merits:

(i) This method is the simplest method for constructing index numbers.

(ii) The result can be obtained within very short span of time.

Demerits:

(i) Importance of quantity is not taken into account in this method. Hence, it could not be claimed as an exact measure of construction of Index numbers.

(ii) The relative importance of items has not been taken into account in this method.

Illustration 1: *Construct the index numbers for 1992 on the basis of the prices of 1990, from the following data.*

Commodities	*Price in 1990* *Rs.*	*Price in 1992* *Rs.*
1	*115*	*130*
2	*72*	*89*
3	*54*	*75*
4	*60*	*72*
5	*80*	*105*

Solution: Calculation of Index numbers

Commodities	*Price in 1990* (P_0) *Rs.*	*Price in 1992* (P_1) *Rs.*
1	115	130
2	72	89
3	54	75
4	60	72
5	80	105
	$\Sigma P_0 = 381$	$\Sigma P_1 = 471$

$$P_{01} = \frac{\Sigma P_1}{\Sigma P_0} \times 100$$

$$= \frac{471}{381} \times 100 = 123.62$$

Illustration 2: *Calculate Index numbers based on the unweighted simple aggregate method for the year 1990, from the data given below.*

Commodities	*Price for 1989 Rs.*	*Price for 1990 Rs.*
Sugar	*5*	*7*
Tea	*45*	*52*
Coffee	*35*	*40*
Milk	*5*	*8*
Mutton	*50*	*60*
Beef	*20*	*25*
Chicken	*28*	*33*

Solution: Calculation of Price Index numbers

Commodities	*Price for 1989 Rs. (P_0)*	*Price for 1990 Rs. (P_1)*
Sugar	5	7
Tea	45	52
Coffee	35	40
Milk	5	8
Mutton	50	60
Beef	20	25
Chicken	28	33
	$\Sigma P_0 = 188$	$\Sigma P_1 = 225$

Price index numbers, $P_{01} = \frac{\Sigma P_1}{\Sigma P_0} \times 100$

$$= \frac{225}{188} \times 100 = 119.68$$

2. *Simple Average of Price Relative Method:* This method is based upon the price relative of each commodities used for constructing index numbers. The average of these price relatives of all commodities will give the price index numbers. While calculating the average of the price relatives either arithmetic mean or geometric mean can be applied.

Price relative for each commodities can be calculated as,

$$\frac{P_1 \times 100}{P_0}$$

Where, P_1 - denotes price for current year

P_0 - denotes price for base year.

Hence, index number can be calculated through the following formulas.

(i) Index number based on Arithmetic mean,

$$P_{01} = \frac{\sum \frac{P_1 \times 100}{P_0}}{N}$$

It can also be expressed as, $P_{01} = \frac{\sum P}{N}$

Where, $P = \frac{P_1}{P_0} \times 100$

(ii) Index number based on Geometric mean

$$P_{01} = \text{Antilog} \frac{\sum \log\left(\frac{P_1}{P_0} \times 100\right)}{N} = \text{Antilog} \frac{\sum \log P}{N}$$

Illustration 3: *Following data are related with the prices of 7 commodities for the years 1991 and 1992.*

Commodities	*A*	*B*	*C*	*D*	*E*	*F*	*G*
Price for 1991 (Rs.)	*150*	*110*	*170*	*200*	*50*	*80*	*10*
Price for 1992 (Rs.)	*160*	*100*	*190*	*220*	*90*	*50*	*15*

Calculate price index on the basis of simple average of price relative method through both arithmetic mean and geometric mean.

Solution: Calculation of Price Index Numbers

Commodities	*Price in 1991* (P_0)	*Price in 1992* (P_1)	$P = P_1/P_0 \times 100$	*Log P*
A	150	160	106.67	2.0281
B	110	100	90.90	1.9586
C	170	190	111.76	2.0484
D	200	220	110.00	2.0414
E	50	90	180.00	2.2553
F	80	50	62.50	1.7959
G	10	15	150.00	2.1761
			$\Sigma P = 811.83$	$\Sigma \log P = 14.3038$

(i) Price index based on arithmetic mean

$$P_{01} = \frac{\Sigma \frac{P_1}{P_0} \times 100}{N} \quad \text{or} \quad \frac{\Sigma P}{N}$$

$$= \frac{811.83}{7} = 116$$

(ii) Price index based on geometric mean

$$P_{01} = \text{Antilog} \frac{\Sigma \log P}{N} = \text{Antilog} \frac{14.3038}{7}$$

$$= \text{Antilog}\, 2.0434 = 110.5$$

Merits:

1. The extreme values will not affect the index numbers.
2. The index number will not be affected by the absolute level of individual prices.

Demerits:

1. It is difficult to select the appropriate average for the construction of index numbers. The arithmetic mean should not be used in all situations like changes in ratios.
2. The relative importance of each item has not been taken into account in this method.

(II) Weighted Index Numbers

This is the most accurate method for calculating index number. In this method, the quantity consumed is also taken into account, in addition to the prices of the commodities.

Weighted Index numbers can be calculated through,

(A) Weighted Aggregate Method and

(B) Weighted Average of Price Relatives

(A) Weighted Aggregate Method: This method is based on the weight of the prices of the selected commodities. The weight for the prices of the commodities can be ascertained by multiplying the quantity sold or consumed with the price of each commodity. It can be calculated through various methods. Following are the most common methods for calculating index under this method.

1. Laspeyre's Method.
2. Paasche's Method
3. Bowley - Darbish Method
4. Fisher's Ideal Method
5. Marshall - Edgeworth's Method and
6. Kelly's Method.

1. Laspeyres Method: In this method the weight for the price is calculated by multiplying both the current year prices and base year prices with base year quantities. Price index under this method is.

$$P_{01} = \frac{\sum p_1 q_0}{\sum p_0 q_0} \times 100$$

2. Paasche's Method: In this method current year quantities are taken as weight for the base year prices as well as current year prices. Price Index under this method is.

$$P_{01} = \frac{\sum p_1 q_1}{\sum p_0 q_1} \times 100$$

3. Bowley - Darbish Method: Price index under this method can be calculated by taking the average of the price indices calculated by Laspeyre's and Paasche's methods.

Hence price index is. $P_{01} = \frac{L+P}{2}$

Where, L indicates Laspeyre's method and P indicates Paasche's method

i.e., $$P_{01} = \frac{\frac{\sum p_1 q_0}{\sum p_0 q_0} + \frac{\sum p_1 q_1}{\sum p_0 q_1}}{2} \times 100$$

4. Fisher's Ideal Method: Price index number under this method can be calculated by the geometric mean of the index number under Laspeyre's and Paasche's method.

Hence the index number is.

$$P_{01} = \sqrt{L \times P}$$

i.e., $$= \sqrt{\frac{\sum p_1 q_0}{\sum p_0 q_0} \times \frac{\sum p_1 q_1}{\sum p_0 q_1}} \times 100$$

5. *Marshall Edgeworth Method:* Index number by Marshall Edgworth method is

$$P_{01} = \frac{\Sigma p_1(q_0 + q_1)}{\Sigma p_0(q_0 + q_1)} \times 100$$

i.e.,

$$= \frac{\Sigma p_1 q_0 + \Sigma p_1 q_1}{\Sigma p_0 q_0 + \Sigma p_0 q_1} \times 100$$

6. *Kelly's Method:* Index Number under Kelly's method is,

$$P_{01} = \frac{\Sigma p_1 q}{\Sigma p_0 q} \times 100, \qquad \text{where, } q = \frac{q_0 + q_1}{2}$$

Illustration 4: *Following are the data related with the prices and quantity consumed for 1990 and 1991.*

	1990		*1991*	
Commodity	*Price*	*Quantity*	*Price*	*Quantity*
Rice	*5*	*15*	*7*	*12*
Wheat	*4*	*5*	*6*	*4*
Sugar	*7*	*4*	*9*	*3*
Tea	*52*	*2*	*55*	*2*

Construct Price Index Numbers by,

(a) Laspeyre's Method (b) Paasche's Method

(c) Bowley - Darbish Method (d) Fisher's Method

Solution: Construction of Index Numbers

Commodity	*1990*		*1991*		p_1q_0	p_0q_0	p_1q_1	p_0q_1
	Price p_0	*Qnty* q_0	*Price* p_1	*Qnty* q_1				
Rice	5	15	7	12	105	75	84	60
Wheat	4	5	6	4	30	20	24	16
Sugar	7	4	9	3	36	28	27	21
Tea	52	2	55	2	110	104	110	104
					$\Sigma p_1q_0 = 281$	$\Sigma p_0q_0 = 227$	$\Sigma p_1q_1 = 245$	$\Sigma p_0q_1 = 201$

(a) Index number by Laspeyre's method:

$$P_{01} = \frac{\sum p_1 q_0}{\sum p_0 q_0} \times 100 = \frac{281 \times 100}{227} = 123.79$$

(b) Index number by Paasche's method:

$$P_{01} = \frac{\sum p_1 q_1}{\sum p_0 q_1} \times 100 = \frac{245 \times 100}{201} = 121.89$$

(c) Index number by Bowley - Darbish method:

$$P_{01} = \frac{L+P}{2} = \frac{123.79 + 121.89}{2} = 122.84$$

(d) Index number by Fisher's ideal method:

$$P_{01} = \sqrt{L \times P} = \sqrt{123.79 \times 121.89} = 122.84$$

Illustration 5: *Calculate Index numbers by (a) Marshal Edgeworth method and (b) Kelly's method from the following data.*

Commodity	*1991*		*1992*	
	Price	*Quantity*	*Price*	*Quantity*
A	*10*	*20*	*12*	*16*
B	*15*	*10*	*18*	*12*
C	*12*	*15*	*15*	*9*
D	*25*	*5*	*20*	*11*
E	*30*	*3*	*28*	*5*
F	*20*	*10*	*15*	*8*

Solution: Calculation of Index numbers

Commodity	*1990* p_0	q_0	*1991* p_1	q_1	$(q_0+q_1)/2$ q	p_1q_0	p_0q_0	p_1q_1	p_0q_1	p_1q	p_0q
A	10	20	12	16	18	240	200	192	160	216	180
B	15	10	18	12	11	180	150	216	180	198	165
C	12	15	15	9	12	225	180	135	108	180	144
D	25	5	20	11	8	100	125	220	275	160	200
E	30	3	28	5	4	84	90	140	150	112	120
F	20	10	15	8	9	150	200	120	160	135	180
						$\sum p_1q_0$ =979	$\sum p_0q_0$ =945	$\sum p_1q_1$ =1023	$\sum p_0q_1$ =1033	$\sum p_1q$ =1001	$\sum p_0q$ =989

(a) Index number under Marshal Edgeworth method:

$$P_{01} = \frac{\sum p_1 q_0 + \sum p_1 q_1}{\sum p_0 q_0 + \sum p_0 q_1} \times 100 = \frac{979 + 1023}{945 + 1033} \times 100 = 101.2$$

(b) Index number under Kelly's method:

$$P_{01} = \frac{\sum p_1 q}{\sum p_0 q} \times 100 = \frac{1001}{989} \times 100 = 101.2$$

Illustration 6: *Calculate price index numbers through. (a) Bowley - Darbish method and (b) Fisher's ideal method from the following data.*

Commodity	*1985* Price	*1985* Quantity	*1986* Price	*1986* Quantity
A	*21*	*15*	*20*	*17*
B	*70*	*10*	*75*	*12*
C	*60*	*14*	*62*	*15*
D	*32*	*10*	*30*	*10*
E	*36*	*12*	*38*	*8*

Solution: Calculation of Price Index Numbers

Commodity	1985 Price p_0	1985 Qnty q_0	1986 Price p_1	1986 Qnty q_1	p_1q_0	p_0q_0	p_1q_1	p_0q_1
A	21	15	20	17	300	315	340	357
B	70	10	75	12	750	700	900	840
C	60	14	62	15	868	840	930	900
D	32	10	30	10	300	320	300	320
E	36	12	38	8	456	432	304	288
					$\sum p_1q_0$ =2674	$\sum p_0q_0$ =2607	$\sum p_1q_1$ =2774	$\sum p_0q_1$ =2705

(a) Index number by Bowley - Darbish method:

i.e., $$P_{01} = \frac{\frac{\sum p_1 q_0}{\sum p_0 q_0} + \frac{\sum p_1 q_1}{\sum p_0 q_1}}{2} \times 100 = \frac{\frac{2674}{2607} + \frac{2774}{2705}}{2} \times 100 = 103$$

(b) Index number by Fisher's ideal method:

$$P_{01} = \sqrt{\frac{\Sigma p_1 q_0}{\Sigma p_0 q_0} \times \frac{\Sigma p_1 q_1}{\Sigma p_0 q_1}} \times 100 = 1.03 \times 100 = 103$$

(B) Weighted Average of Price Relatives Method: In this method, price relatives of each commodity should be taken into account for calculating the price index. The index number under this method can be calculated through arithmetic mean method and geometric mean method.

(a) Arithmetic mean method: Index number, under this method can be calculated as,

$$P_{01} = \frac{\Sigma PV}{\Sigma V}$$

Where, P means price relatives, i.e., equal to, $\frac{P_1}{P_0} \times 100$,

and V means value weights i.e., equal to p_0 q_0

Steps:

(i) Calculate the value weights of each commodity by multiplying the price for the base year with quantity for the base year. (*i.e.*, $V = p_0 q_0$) and ascertain ΣV.

(ii) Find out the price relatives for each commodity

i.e., $$P = \frac{P_1}{P_0} \times 100$$

(iii) Multiply the price relative with the value weights for each commodity (i.e., *PV*) and then compute the value ΣPV

(iv) Divide ΣPV with ΣV to find out the price index.

(b) Geometric mean method: The formula for the index number, under this method is,

$$P_{01} = \text{Antilog}\ \frac{\Sigma V \log P}{\Sigma V}$$

Steps:

(i) Calculate value weight for each commodity ($V = p_0 q_0$) and find out ΣV.

(ii) Find out the price relatives for each commodity,

$$P = \frac{P_1}{P_0} \times 100$$

(iii) Find out logarithm for the price relatives (log P) for each commodities.

(iv) Multiply the log price relatives with the value weights (*i.e.*, V log P). From this calculate $\sum$ log P.

(v) Then divide $\sum V$ log P with $\sum V$, and find out the antilog value for this, to get the price index number.

Illustration 7: *Calculate price index from the following data by weighted average of price relatives through (a) Arithmetic mean method and (b) Geometric mean method.*

	1991		*1992*	
Commodity	*Price*	*Quantity*	*Price*	*Quantity*
A	*12*	*20*	*14*	*18*
B	*14*	*15*	*16*	*15*
C	*10*	*10*	*8*	*8*
D	*15*	*12*	*12*	*10*
E	*20*	*8*	*25*	*10*
F	*8*	*7*	*10*	*9*

Solution: Calculation of Price Index Number

Commodity	*Price in 1991* p_0	*Qnty in 1991* q_0	*Price in 1992* p_1	*V* $p_0 q_0$	$p = p_1/p_0 \times 100$	*PV*	*Log P*	*V log P*
A	12	20	14	240	116.67	28001	2.0671	496.10
B	14	15	16	210	114.29	24001	2.0581	432.20
C	10	10	8	100	80	8000	1.9031	190.31
D	15	12	12	180	80	14400	1.9031	342.56
E	20	8	25	160	125	20000	2.0969	335.50
F	8	7	10	56	125	7000	2.0969	117.43
				ΣV = *946*		ΣPV = *101402*		$\Sigma PV \log P$ = *1914.1*

Price index under weighted average of price relatives

(a) Arithmetic mean method:

$$P_{01} = \frac{\Sigma PV}{\Sigma V} = \frac{101402}{946} = 107.19$$

(b) Geometric mean method:

$$P_{01} = \text{Antilog } \frac{\Sigma PV \log P}{\Sigma V} = \text{Antilog} \frac{1914.1}{946}$$

$$= \text{Antilog} 2.0234 = 105.5$$

III Quantity Index Numbers

Quantity index numbers measure the value or quantity of goods produced, sold or consumed. The quantities of goods produced or distributed from one period to another period is measured under this method. To construct quantity index numbers, the prices of the commodity either in the base year or in the current year should be taken into consideration.

The quantity index number can be calculated through the following methods.

(i) Laspeyre's method $$Q_{01} = \frac{\Sigma q_1 p_0}{\Sigma q_0 p_0} \times 100$$

(ii) Paasche's method $$Q_{01} = \frac{\Sigma q_1 p_1}{\Sigma q_0 p_1} \times 100$$

(iii) Fisher's method $$Q_{01} = \sqrt{\frac{\Sigma q_1 p_0}{\Sigma q_0 p_0} \times \frac{\Sigma q_1 p_1}{\Sigma q_0 p_1}} \times 100 \quad \text{OR}$$

$$= \sqrt{L \times P}$$

where L indicates Laspeyre's method and P indicates Paasche's method.

Illustration 8: *Calculate quantity index from the following data through (i) Laspeyre's method (ii) Paasche's method and (iii) Fisher's method.*

Commodity	1992 Price Rs.	1992 Quantity	1993 Price Rs.	1993 Quantity
A	30	10	28	12
B	34	15	35	16
C	25	12	30	10
D	20	14	25	15
E	40	8	45	10
F	32	6	35	6

Solution: Calculation of Quantity Index Numbers

Commodity	1992 Price p_0	1992 Qnty q_0	1993 Price p_1	1993 Qnty q_1	q_1p_0	q_0p_0	q_1p_1	q_0p_1
A	30	10	28	12	360	300	336	280
B	34	15	35	16	544	510	560	525
C	25	12	30	10	250	300	300	360
D	20	14	25	15	300	280	375	350
E	40	8	45	10	400	320	450	360
F	32	6	35	6	192	192	210	210
					$\sum q_1p_0 = 2046$	$\sum q_0p_0 = 1902$	$\sum q_1p_1 = 2231$	$\sum q_0p_1 = 2085$

Quantity index number under

Laspeyre's method, $Q_{01} = \frac{\Sigma q_1 p_0}{\Sigma q_0 p_0} \times 100 = \frac{2046}{1902} \times 100 = 107.57$

Quantity index number under

Paasche's method, $Q_{01} = \frac{\Sigma q_1 p_1}{\Sigma q_0 p_1} \times 100 = \frac{2231}{2085} \times 100 = 107$

Quantity index number under

Fisher's method, $Q_{01} = \sqrt{\frac{\Sigma q_1 P_0}{\Sigma q_0 P_0} \times \frac{\Sigma q_1 P_1}{\Sigma q_0 P_1}} \times 100$ OR $= \sqrt{L \times P}$

$$= \sqrt{107.57 \times 107} = 107.28$$

IV Value index number

Value index number is the ratio between the value of all commodities in the given period to the total value of all commodities in the base period. The formula under this method is,

$$\text{Value Index, } V = \frac{\sum p_1 q_1}{\sum p_0 q_0} \times 100 \quad \text{OR} \quad V = \frac{\sum V_1}{\sum V_0}$$

Where, $V_1 = p_1 \times q_1$

$V_0 = p_0 \times q_0$

p_1 = Price for current year

p_0 = Price for base year

q_1 = Quantity for current year

q_0 = Quantity for the base year

Test of Consistency of Index Numbers

Index numbers have been constructed through various formulas. Hence the consistency of index numbers so calculated should be found out. There are various tests available to find out the consistency of index numbers. The important among them are (1) Time reversal test (2) Factor reversal test (3) Circular test

(1) Time reversal test: This test is advocated by Prof. Irvin Fisher to test the consistency of the index number. According to him the formula for calculating the index number should be such that it will give the same ratio for one point of comparison and the other. It can be represented as $P_{01} \times P_{10} = 1$.

Where, p_{01} means the index number for time, "1" on time "0" as base and p_{10} means the index for time "0" on time "1" as base.

When this time reversal test is applied to all the method for calculating index numbers like Laspeyre's method, Paasche's method, Fisher's method etc. only Fisher's ideal method satisfies a time reversal test.

Index number under Fisher's method,

$$P_{01} = \sqrt{\frac{\sum p_1 q_0}{\sum p_0 q_0} \times \frac{\sum p_1 q_1}{\sum p_0 q_1}}$$

Hence,

$$P_{10} = \sqrt{\frac{\Sigma p_0 q_1}{\Sigma p_1 q_1} \times \frac{\Sigma p_0 q_0}{\Sigma p_1 q_0}}$$

$$P_{01} \times P_{10} = \sqrt{\frac{\Sigma p_1 q_0}{\Sigma p_0 q_0} \times \frac{\Sigma p_1 q_1}{\Sigma p_0 q_1} \times \frac{\Sigma p_0 q_1}{\Sigma p_1 q_1} \times \frac{\Sigma p_0 q_0}{\Sigma p_1 q_0}} = \sqrt{1} = 1$$

(2) Factor Reversal Test: This test is also recommended by Fisher to test the consistency of index number. According to this test the product of price index and the quantity index should be equal to the value index. It can be represented as $V = P_{01} \times Q_{01}$

$$V = \frac{\Sigma p_1 q_1}{\Sigma p_0 q_0}$$

$$P_{01} = \sqrt{\frac{\Sigma p_1 q_0}{\Sigma p_0 q_0} \times \frac{\Sigma p_1 q_1}{\Sigma p_0 q_1}}$$

$$Q_{01} = \sqrt{\frac{\Sigma q_1 p_0}{\Sigma q_0 p_0} \times \frac{\Sigma q_1 p_1}{\Sigma q_0 p_1}}$$

Hence, $$P_{01} \times Q_{01} = \sqrt{\frac{\Sigma p_1 q_0}{\Sigma p_0 q_0} \times \frac{\Sigma p_1 q_1}{\Sigma p_0 q_1} \times \frac{\Sigma q_1 p_0}{\Sigma q_0 p_0} \times \frac{\Sigma q_1 p_1}{\Sigma q_0 p_1}}$$

$$= \sqrt{\frac{(\Sigma p_1 q_1)^2}{(\Sigma p_0 q_0)^2}} = \frac{\Sigma p_1 q_1}{\Sigma p_0 q_0}$$

It is clear from the calculations, that only Fisher's ideal method satisfies the factor reversal test. (*i.e.*, $V = p_{01} \times q_{01}$).

(3) Circular Test: Circular test is applied for testing the consistency of index numbers especially for the index number of the changes in prices over a period of years.

According to the test,

$$P_{01} \times P_{12} \times P_{23} \ldots\ldots P_{(n-1)n} \times P_{no} = 1$$

It is proved that Laspeyre's method, Fishers method and Paasches method won't satisfy the circular test. Only simple

Aggregative method and the Fixed Weight Aggregative method satisfy the circular test. Hence, for calculating index number for the fluctuation of prices, over a period, this two methods are recommended.

The Circular test based on the simple aggregative method is calculated as follows,

$$\frac{\Sigma p_1}{\Sigma p_0} \times \frac{\Sigma p_2}{\Sigma p_1} \times \frac{\Sigma p_0}{\Sigma p_2} = 1$$

The circular test based on the fixed weight aggregative method is,

$$\frac{\Sigma p_1 q}{\Sigma p_0 q} \times \frac{\Sigma p_2 q}{\Sigma p_1 q} \times \frac{\Sigma p_0 q}{\Sigma p_2 q} = 1$$

Illustration 9: *From the following data calculate the price index number through Fisher's ideal method and find out the consistency of the index number by time-reversal test and factor - reversal test.*

Commodity	*1992*		*1993*	
	Price	*Quantity*	*Price*	*Quantity*
A	*7*	*10*	*9*	*12*
B	*8*	*15*	*10*	*13*
C	*5*	*21*	*7*	*20*
D	*11*	*30*	*12*	*35*
E	*9*	*20*	*11*	*21*

Solution: Calculation of Price Index Number

Commodity	*1992*		*1993*		p_1q_0	p_0q_0	p_1q_1	p_0q_1
	Price p_0	*Qnty* q_0	*Price* p_1	*Qnty* q_1				
A	7	10	9	12	90	70	108	84
B	8	15	10	13	150	120	130	104
C	5	21	7	20	147	105	140	100
D	11	30	12	35	360	330	420	385
E	9	20	11	21	220	180	231	189
					Σp_1q_0 = *967*	Σp_0q_0 = *805*	Σp_1q_1 = *1029*	Σp_0q_1 = *862*

Index number under Fisher's ideal method

$$P_{01} = \sqrt{\frac{\Sigma p_1q_0}{\Sigma p_0q_0} \times \frac{\Sigma p_1q_1}{\Sigma p_0q_1}} \times 100 = \sqrt{\frac{967}{805} \times \frac{1029}{862}} \times 100$$

$$= \sqrt{1.20 \times 1.19} \times 100 = 119.5$$

(a) Time - Reversal test: Index number is consistent, if Time Reversal test is equal to 1, *i.e.,* $P_{01} \times P_{10} = 1$.

$$P_{10} = \sqrt{\frac{\Sigma p_0q_0}{\Sigma p_1q_0} \times \frac{\Sigma p_0q_1}{\Sigma p_1q_1}} \times 100 = \sqrt{\frac{805}{967} \times \frac{862}{1029}} \times 100 = 83.51$$

$$P_{01} \times P_{10} = \sqrt{119.5 \times 83.51} = \frac{99.897}{100} = 1$$

(b) Factor - Reversal test: Index number is consistent, if factor reversal test,

$$P_{01} \times Q_{01} = \sqrt{\frac{\Sigma p_1q_1}{\Sigma p_0q_0}}$$

$$Q_{01} = \sqrt{\frac{\Sigma q_1p_0}{\Sigma q_0p_0} \times \frac{\Sigma q_1p_1}{\Sigma q_0p_1}} = \sqrt{\frac{862}{967} \times \frac{1029}{1029}} \times 100 = 1.07$$

$$P_{01} \times P_{10} = \sqrt{1.19 \times 1.07} = 1.13$$

i.e., equal to $\sqrt{\frac{\Sigma p_1q_1}{\Sigma p_0q_0}} = \sqrt{\frac{1029}{805}} = 1.13$

Hence, it satisfies Factor Reveral Test.

Illustration 10: *Calculate index number through Fisher's ideal index and test the consistency of it by (a) Time reversal test and (b) Factor reversal test.*

Commodity	1985 Price Rs.	1985 Quantity	1993 Price Rs.	1993 Quantity
Beef	15	25	25	20
Mutton	40	30	60	35
Chicken	30	40	50	38
Pork	10	10	20	12
Fish	30	15	40	12

Solution: Calculation of Index Numbers

Commodity	1985 Price p_0	1985 Qty q_0	1993 Price p_1	1993 Qty q_1	p_1q_0	p_0q_0	p_1q_1	p_0q_1
Beef	15	25	25	20	625	375	500	300
Mutton	40	30	60	35	1800	1200	2100	1400
Chicken	30	40	50	38	2000	1200	1900	1140
Pork	10	10	20	12	200	100	240	120
Fish	30	15	40	12	600	450	480	360
					$\Sigma p_1q_0 = 5225$	$\Sigma p_0q_0 = 3325$	$\Sigma p_1q_1 = 5220$	$\Sigma p_0q_1 = 3320$

Index number by Fisher's ideal index method:

$$P_{01} = \sqrt{\frac{\Sigma p_1q_0}{\Sigma p_0q_0} \times \frac{\Sigma p_1q_1}{\Sigma p_0q_1}} \times 100 = \sqrt{\frac{5225}{3325} \times \frac{5220}{3320}} \times 100 = 157$$

Test of consistency of index numbers

(a) Time Reversal Test

$$P_{10} \times P_{01} = 1$$

$$P_{10} \times P_{01} = \sqrt{\frac{\Sigma p_0q_0}{\Sigma p_1q_0} \times \frac{\Sigma p_0q_1}{\Sigma p_1q_1} \frac{\Sigma p_1q_0}{\Sigma p_0q_0} \times \frac{\Sigma p_1q_1}{\Sigma p_0q_1}}$$

$$= \sqrt{\frac{3325}{5225} \times \frac{3320}{5220} \frac{5225}{3325} \times \frac{5220}{3320}} = \sqrt{1} = 1$$

(b) Factor Reversal Test

$$P_{01} \times Q_{01} = \frac{\Sigma p_1q_1}{\Sigma p_0q_0}$$

$$P_{10} \times Q_{01} = \sqrt{\frac{\Sigma p_0 q_0}{\Sigma p_0 q_0} \times \frac{\Sigma p_1 q_1}{\Sigma p_0 q_1} \frac{\Sigma q_1 p_0}{\Sigma q_0 p_0} \times \frac{\Sigma q_1 p_1}{\Sigma q_0 p_0}}$$

$$= \sqrt{\frac{5225}{3325} \times \frac{5220}{3320} \frac{3320}{3325} \times \frac{5220}{5225}}$$

$$= \sqrt{\frac{5220 \times 5220}{3325 \times 3325}} = \frac{5220}{3325}$$

Hence, $$\frac{\Sigma p_1 q_1}{\Sigma p_0 q_0} = \frac{5220}{3325}$$

∴ The index number so calculated is consistent one.

V Chain Base Method

In the Fixed base index number, the base remains the same for all the series of the index. In practice, the base once selected may not be suitable for another period due to various reasons like changes in economic conditions, the changes in the social behaviour of people etc. The chain base method is most suitable method for calculating the index numbers in this circumstances. In this method, the index numbers should be constructed by treating the just previous year as the base year. Hence the base year will be changing year by year.

Steps for the construction of Chain indices

(1) Calculate the link relatives, which is equal to

$$\frac{\text{Current year price}}{\text{Previous year price}} \times 100$$

(2) Chain index can be calculated through the following formula,

$$\text{Chain Index} = \frac{\text{Current year link relative} \times \text{Previous year chain index}}{100}$$

Merits of Chain base index

(1) In this method the price of one year is compared with the price of just previous year. Hence, it helps the economist and businessmen to know the trend of the price level.

(2) It helps to take decisions for the management of a company.

(3) It won't be affected by seasonal fluctuations.

Demerits of Chain base index

(1) The long term changes in prices cannot be calculated under this method.

(2) It is difficult to exclude the abnormal period, in the calculation of chain base indices.

Illustration 11: *Calculate the chain base index numbers from the following fixed base index numbers.*

Year	*1987*	*1988*	*1989*	*1990*	*1991*	*1992*	*1993*
F.B.I	*210*	*340*	*560*	*450*	*540*	*620*	*734*

Solution: Calculation of Chain Base Index Numbers

Year	*F.B.I*	*Link Relatives*	*Chain Index*
1987	210		210
1988	340	$\frac{340}{210}\times 100 = 161.9$	$\frac{161.9\times 210}{100} = 340$
1989	560	$\frac{560}{340}\times 100 = 164.7$	$\frac{164.7\times 340}{100} = 560$
1990	450	$\frac{450}{560}\times 100 = 80.4$	$\frac{80.4\times 560}{100} = 450.2$
1991	540	$\frac{540}{450}\times 100 = 120$	$\frac{120\times 450.2}{100} = 540.24$
1992	620	$\frac{620}{540}\times 100 = 114.8$	$\frac{114\times 540.24}{100} = 620.2$
1993	734	$\frac{734}{620}\times 100 = 118.4$	$\frac{118.4\times 620.2}{100} = 734.3$

Conversion of Chain Base Index into Fixed Base Index

The fixed base index numbers can be calculated from the chain base index numbers. The following formula should be applied to convert the chain index into fixed index.

Current year's fixed base index (F.B.I)

$$= \frac{\text{Current years C.B.I} \times \text{Pervious years F.B.I}}{100}$$

(C.B.I = Chain Base Index)

Illustration 12: *Convert the following chain base index numbers into fixed base index numbers.*

Year	*1987*	*1988*	*1989*	*1990*	*1991*	*1992*
Chain Base Index Nos.	*75*	*120*	*115*	*95*	*150*	*170*

Solution: Conversion of C.B.I into F.B.I

Year	*Chain Base Index Nos.*	*Conversion of CBI Numbers with 1987 as base*	*F.B.I Numbers*
1987	75		75
1988	120	$\frac{75}{100}\times 120$	90
1989	115	$\frac{75}{100}\times\frac{120}{100}\times 115$	103.5
1990	95	$\frac{75}{100}\times\frac{120}{100}\times\frac{115}{100}\times 95$	98.34
1991	150	$\frac{75}{100}\times\frac{120}{100}\times\frac{115}{100}\times\frac{95}{100}\times 150$	147.5
1992	170	$\frac{75}{100}\times\frac{120}{100}\times\frac{115}{100}\times\frac{95}{100}\times\frac{150}{100}\times 170$	250.75

Base Shifting: Base Shifting means calculation of index number based on new base. The base has to be shifted from old one to new one due to the fact that old base may become outmoded. The base can be shifted through the following formula.

Index number based on New base year,

$$= \frac{\text{Current years old index number}}{\text{New base years old index number}} \times 100$$

Illustration 13: *From the following index numbers based on 1982, find out the new index numbers based on 1986.*

Year	*1982*	*1983*	*1984*	*1985*	*1986*	*1987*	*1988*	*1989*	*1990*
Index Number	*100*	*125*	*135*	*120*	*150*	*180*	*200*	*190*	*210*

Solution: Calculation of New Index Number

Year	*Old Index Number based on 1982*	*New Index Number based on 1986*
1982	100	$\frac{100}{150} \times 100 = 66.67$
1983	125	$\frac{125}{150} \times 100 = 83.33$
1984	135	$\frac{135}{150} \times 100 = 90$
1985	120	$\frac{120}{150} \times 100 = 80$
1986	150	$\frac{150}{150} \times 100 = 100$
1987	180	$\frac{180}{150} \times 100 = 120$
1988	200	$\frac{200}{150} \times 100 = 133.33$
1989	190	$\frac{190}{150} \times 100 = 126.67$
1990	210	$\frac{210}{150} \times 100 = 140$

Illustration 14: *Calculate the index number based on 1987 from the following Index number based on 1984.*

Year	*1984*	*1985*	*1986*	*1987*	*1988*	*1989*	*1990*	*1991*
Index Number	*100*	*145*	*175*	*190*	*200*	*215*	*230*	*250*

Solution: Calculation of Index numbers based on 1987

Year	*Old Index Number based on 1984*	*New Index Number based on 1987*
1984	100	$\frac{100}{190} \times 100 = 52.63$
1985	145	$\frac{145}{190} \times 100 = 76.32$
1986	175	$\frac{175}{190} \times 100 = 92.1$
1987	190	$\frac{190}{190} \times 100 = 100$
1988	200	$\frac{200}{190} \times 100 = 105.26$
1989	215	$\frac{215}{190} \times 100 = 113.16$
1990	230	$\frac{230}{190} \times 100 = 121$
1991	250	$\frac{250}{190} \times 100 = 131.58$

Illustration 15: *Calculate index numbers based on (i) 1985 and (ii) 1987 from the following index numbers based on 1980.*

Year	*1980*	*1981*	*1982*	*1983*	*1984*	*1985*	*1986*	*1987*	*1988*	*1989*	*1990*
Index Number	*100*	*120*	*132*	*144*	*148*	*152*	*167*	*175*	*182*	*195*	*200*

Solution: Calculation of New index numbers

Year	*For base 1980*	*Index numbers* *For base 1985*	*For base 1987*
1980	100	$\frac{100}{152}\times 100 = 65.79$	$\frac{100}{175}\times 100 = 57$
1981	120	$\frac{120}{152}\times 100 = 78.9$	$\frac{120}{175}\times 100 = 68.6$
1982	132	$\frac{132}{152}\times 100 = 86.8$	$\frac{132}{175}\times 100 = 75.4$
1983	144	$\frac{144}{152}\times 100 = 94.7$	$\frac{144}{175}\times 100 = 82.3$
1984	148	$\frac{148}{152}\times 100 = 97.4$	$\frac{148}{175}\times 100 = 84.6$
1985	152	$\frac{152}{152}\times 100 = 100$	$\frac{152}{175}\times 100 = 86.9$
1986	167	$\frac{167}{152}\times 100 = 109.9$	$\frac{167}{175}\times 100 = 95.4$
1987	175	$\frac{175}{152}\times 100 = 115$	$\frac{175}{175}\times 100 = 100$
1988	182	$\frac{182}{152}\times 100 = 119.7$	$\frac{182}{175}\times 100 = 104$
1989	195	$\frac{195}{152}\times 100 = 128.3$	$\frac{195}{175}\times 100 = 111.4$
1990	200	$\frac{200}{152}\times 100 = 131.6$	$\frac{200}{175}\times 100 = 114.3$

Splicing of two index numbers: Splicing means combination of two index numbers. The commodity included in an index number may become outmoded or out of fashion. New commodity may come into existence which replaces the old one. Hence, a new index number for the new article may be available. It should be combined with the existing index numbers. The procedure of combination of these two index numbers is called splicing.

The formula for splicing of index number is,

Spliced index number,

$$= \frac{\text{Index No. of current year} \times \text{Old Index No. of New base year}}{100}$$

Illustration 16: *Following are the two sets of index one with 1980 as base and the other with 1987 as base.*

Year I	*Index number*	*Year II*	*Index number*
1980	*100*	*1987*	*100*
1981	*115*	*1988*	*120*
1982	*125*	*1989*	*145*
1983	*120*	*1990*	*135*
1984	*135*	*1991*	*145*
1985	*130*	*1992*	*160*
1986	*140*		
1987	*150*		

The old index was discontinued in the year 1987 and new index number with 1987 base was calculated. Splice the second index numbers with the first index numbers to get a continuous series of index numbers from 1980 to 1992.

Solution: Splicing of Index Numbers

Year	*Index numbers with 1980 as base I*	*Index numbers with 1987 as base II*	*Index numbers II spliced to I with 1987 as base*
1980	100		
1981	115		
1982	125		
1983	120		
1984	135		
1985	130		
1986	140		
1987	150	100	$100 \times 150/100 = 150$
1988		120	$120 \times 150/100 = 180$
1989		145	$145 \times 150/100 = 217.5$
1990		135	$135 \times 150/100 = 202.5$
1991		145	$145 \times 150/100 = 217.5$
1992		160	$160 \times 150/100 = 240$

Deflating of Index Numbers

Deflating of index number means correction of index number according to changes in price level. It measures the decrease in the purchasing power of money due to the increase in price level. This technique is usually applied for calculating the real wages, in order to take suitable policies by the Government to raise the wages of employees. Wages earned by workers should be compared with the price index in order to find out the real wages. It can be calculated as follows.

$$\text{Real Wage} = \frac{\text{Money Wage}}{\text{Price Index}} \times 100$$

Real wage of income index number,

$$= \frac{\text{Money Wage}}{\text{Price Index}} \times 100 \quad \text{OR}$$

$$= \frac{\text{Real wage of the current year}}{\text{Real wage of the base year}} \times 100$$

Illustration 17: *Calculate (i) Index numbers for real wages and (ii) Real wages from the following data.*

Year	*1985*	*1986*	*1987*	*1988*	*1989*	*1990*	*1991*	*1992*
Wages (Rs.)	*800*	*900*	*1100*	*1200*	*1400*	*1500*	*1550*	*1800*
Consumer Price Index	*100*	*125*	*140*	*170*	*180*	*190*	*210*	*220*

Solution: Calculation of Real Wage Index Numbers

Year	*Wage Rs.*	*Price Index Numbers*	*Index of Wages*	*Real Wage Index*	*Real Wage*
1985	800	100	$\frac{100}{800}\times 800 = 100$	$\frac{100}{100}\times 100 = 100$	$\frac{800}{100}\times 100 = 800$
1986	900	125	$\frac{100}{800}\times 900 = 112.5$	$\frac{112.5}{125}\times 100 = 90$	$\frac{900}{125}\times 100 = 720$
1987	1100	140	$\frac{100}{800}\times 1100 = 137.5$	$\frac{137.5}{140}\times 100 = 98$	$\frac{1100}{140}\times 100 = 785.7$
1988	1200	170	$\frac{100}{800}\times 1200 = 150$	$\frac{150}{170}\times 100 = 88$	$\frac{1200}{170}\times 100 = 705.88$
1989	1400	180	$\frac{100}{800}\times 1400 = 175$	$\frac{175}{180}\times 100 = 97$	$\frac{1400}{180}\times 100 = 777.78$
1990	1500	190	$\frac{100}{800}\times 1500 = 187.5$	$\frac{187.5}{190}\times 100 = 99$	$\frac{1500}{190}\times 100 = 789.5$
1991	1550	210	$\frac{100}{800}\times 1550 = 193.75$	$\frac{193.75}{210}\times 100 = 92$	$\frac{1550}{210}\times 100 = 738.1$
1992	1800	220	$\frac{100}{800}\times 1800 = 225$	$\frac{225}{220}\times 100 = 102$	$\frac{1800}{220}\times 100 = 818.2$

Illustration 18: *Calculate Real wages and index number for real wages from the following.*

Year	*1986*	*1987*	*1988*	*1989*	*1990*	*1991*	*1992*	*1993*
Wages (Rs.)	*700*	*900*	*1100*	*1200*	*1400*	*1600*	*1800*	*1900*
Consumer Price Index	*100*	*120*	*150*	*175*	*195*	*200*	*210*	*220*

Solution: Calculation of Real Wage Index Number

Year	*Wage Rs.*	*Price Index Numbers*	*Index of Wages*	*Real Wage Index*	*Real Wage*
1986	700	100	$\frac{100}{700}\times700$ = 100	$\frac{100}{100}\times100$ = 100	$\frac{700}{100}\times100$ = 700
1987	900	120	$\frac{100}{700}\times900$ = 128.5	$\frac{128.5}{120}\times100$ = 107	$\frac{900}{120}\times100$ = 750
1988	1100	150	$\frac{100}{700}\times1100$ = 157.1	$\frac{157.1}{150}\times100$ = 105	$\frac{1100}{150}\times100$ = 733
1989	1200	175	$\frac{100}{700}\times1200$ = 171.5	$\frac{171.5}{175}\times100$ = 98	$\frac{1200}{175}\times100$ = 686
1990	1400	195	$\frac{100}{700}\times1400$ = 200	$\frac{200}{195}\times100$ = 103	$\frac{1400}{195}\times100$ = 718
1991	1600	200	$\frac{100}{700}\times1600$ = 228.6	$\frac{228.6}{200}\times100$ = 114	$\frac{1600}{200}\times100$ = 800
1992	1800	210	$\frac{100}{700}\times1800$ = 257.1	$\frac{257.1}{210}\times100$ = 122	$\frac{1800}{210}\times100$ = 857
1993	1900	220	$\frac{100}{700}\times1900$ = 271.5	$\frac{271.5}{220}\times100$ = 123	$\frac{1900}{220}\times100$ = 864

VI Consumer Price Index Numbers

Consumer price index number was also known as 'Cost of Living Index Number' or Price of Living Index Number. According to A.K. Konus (in 1924) the consumer price index number is the ratio of the monetary expenditures of an individual which secure for him the same 'standard of living' or 'total utility' in two situations differing only in respect of prices. It represents the average change in prices over a period of time, paid by the ultimate consumer for a fixed set of goods and services. It measures the relative changes over a period of time in the cost level required to maintain similar standard of living of a specified class of people. The consumption pattern of the specified class of the people and the retail prices of that region should not vary for calculating consumer price indices.

The items contributing for the construction of consumer price index are generally classified into (i) Food, (ii) Clothing, (iii) Fuel and light, (iv) Housing and (v) Miscellaneous items like Television, Radio etc.

Objectives of Constructing Consumer Price Index Numbers

The important objectives in the construction of consumer price index number are stated below.

1. It helps the Govt. to formulate wage policy, price policy and other economic policies.
2. The minimum wage and rate of Dearness Allowance can be fixed by the Govt. only through the construction of consumer price index number.
3. The purchasing power of money can be measured.
4. The real income of the money income can be measured.
5. It facilitates for the study of rate of changes of price of basic commodities over different periods of time.

Steps or precautions in the construction of consumer price index number

The important precautions to be taken in the construction of consumer price index number are stated below:

1. *Determination of the class of people for whom the index number is to be constructed:* The people living in the society may be classified into different groups as low income group, middle-income group and high-income group. These income groups may also further be classified into people living in urban areas and rural areas like, urban middle income group, rural middle income group etc. Hence, before constructing the index number, the class of people for whom the index number is to be constructed should be determined.

2. *Selection of Base Period:* The period selected as base shall be a period of economic stability. The consumption pattern over the long period should remain same. Base period should be taken as one complete year to avoid seasonal fluctuations in that year.

3. Conducting Family Budget Enquiry: The consumption pattern of the class of people for whom index number is to be calculated should be known. The expenses spent by the whole family for various important commodities should be enquired. Only those commodities which are commonly used by all families should be selected. (*Eg*) expenses spent on rice, vegetables, groceries, electricity, cloth etc. These enquiries are conducted through anyone of the different methods of data collection. Since the same class of people may be large in number sample study may be conducted. While selecting the sample random sampling technique may be adopted.

Problems in the construction of cost of living Index Number

1. Determination of the purpose for which index number is being constructed: Determination of the purpose and different class of people for whom the index number is to be constructed is a complicated one. There are various purposes for which index number may be constructed (eg) to fix wages, to know the rate of change of prices, to know the real income etc.

The class of people in the society may be grouped into the low income, middle income and high income groups. Identification of the group of people itself is a difficult task.

2. Problems in selection of the commodities: The commodities commonly used by the same group of people for whom study is to be conducted, should be selected. Since consumption pattern of each families are not identical it is difficult to choose the commodities. The commodities selected should remain uniform in quality from year to year.

3. Selection of sources of data: The markets selected for collection of data should be popular and well known in the localities selected for the study. The markets selected should charge uniform prices for all commodities selected for the study.

4. Methods of Collection of Data: The data may either be collected from primary source or secondary source. While data are collected from the primary source well qualified and experienced persons should be employed. Popular magazines, Statistical Department, Indian Chamber of Commerce and Industry are some of the source from which secondary data can be collected.

5. Problems in selection of Base Year: The base period shall be of a period of economic stability. It should not be too far in the past.

Base period should be taken as one complete year to avoid seasonal fluctuations in that year.

6. Problems in the method of combination data: The data collected are usually numerous in number due to the number of sample and the number of details. It remains a complicated task to combine these data. Hence, utmost care is needed for totaling and averaging the data so collected.

7. Problems in the system of weight: The system of weight depends upon the commodities, type of weight and time of weight. The economic importance of the commodities for which weight is to be conducted determines the type of weight. The type of weight may either be quantity weight or value weight. The quantity weight is the amount of commodity consumed. Value weight is the product of price and quantity consumed, The time of the weight is the different periods for which weight have to be taken *i.e.*, base period and current period.

Methods of Constructing Consumer Price Index

Consumer price index may be constructed through anyone of the following two methods.

(1) Aggregate Expenditure Method or Aggregative Method.

(2) Family Budget Method or Method of Weighted Relatives.

(1) Aggregate Expenditure Method or Aggregative Method: Aggregative method is based on the Laspeyre's method. In this method the quantities of commodities consumed by a particular group in the base year are fixed as weights.

The formula under this method is,

$$\text{Consumer Price Index Number} = \frac{\sum p_1 q_0}{\sum p_0 q_0} \times 100$$

Where, p_1 = Price of current year, p_0 = Price of base year, q_0= Quantity of base year.

(2) Family Budget Method or Method of Weighted Relatives: Family Budget method is based on the method of weighted average of price relatives.

The formula under this method is,

$$\text{Consumer Price Index} = \frac{\sum PV}{\sum V}$$

Where, $P = p_1/p_0 \times 100$; V = Value weight (P_0q_0), P_1 = Price of current year and P_0 = Price of base year.

1. Aggregative Method

Illustration 19: *Calculate index number through Aggregate Expenditure Method from the following data.*

Commodities	*Quantity consumed in 1982*	*Price per Unit in 1982*	*Price per unit in 1992*
A	120	20	22
B	150	15	17
C	160	30	25
D	80	10	20
E	70	5	15
F	40	12	24
G	30	7	18

Solution: Calculation of Index Number

Commodities	q_0	p_0	p_1	p_1q_0	p_0q_0
A	120	20	22	2640	2400
B	150	15	17	2550	2250
C	160	30	25	4000	4800
D	80	10	20	1600	800
E	70	5	15	1050	350
F	40	12	24	960	480
G	30	7	18	540	210
				$\Sigma p_1q_0 = 13340$	$\Sigma p_0q_0 = 11290$

$$P_{01} = \frac{\Sigma p_1q_0}{\Sigma p_0q_0} \times 100 = \frac{13340}{11290} \times 100 = 118.16$$

2. Family Budget method

Illustration 20: *Calculate index number on the basis of family budget method from the following data.*

Commodity	*weight*	*Price per unit 1983 (Rs)*	*Price per unit 1992 (Rs)*
A	30	27	35
B	20	15	30
C	10	13	28
D	15	11	52
E	25	22	60
F	10	30	70

Solution: Calculation of index number

Commodity	*Weights V*	*Price per unit in 1983*	*Price per unit in 1993*	$P = \frac{p_1}{p_0} \times 100$	*Weighted price P.V*
A	30	27	35	129.6	3888
B	20	15	30	200	4000
C	10	13	28	215.38	2154
D	15	11	52	472.72	7091
E	25	22	60	272.72	6818
F	10	30	70	233.33	2333
	$\sum V = 110$				$\sum PV = 26284$

Index number $$P_{01} = \frac{\sum PV}{\sum V} = \frac{26284}{110} = 239$$

Illustration 21: *Calculate consumer price index through Aggregate Expenditure method from the following data.*

Commodities	*Quantity consumed in 1983*	*Price per unit in 1983*	*Price per unit in 1993*
I	*50*	*15*	*29*
II	*40*	*20*	*40*
III	*80*	*12*	*20*
IV	*100*	*18*	*25*
V	*60*	*25*	*50*

Solution: Calculation of consumer price index number

Commodities	q_0	p_0	p_1	p_1q_0	p_0q_0
I	50	15	29	1450	750
II	40	20	40	1600	800
III	80	12	20	1600	960
IV	100	18	25	2500	1800
V	60	25	50	3000	1500
				$\sum p_1q_0 = 10150$	$\sum p_0q_0 = 5810$

$$P_{01} = \frac{\sum p_1q_0}{\sum p_0q_0} \times 100 = \frac{10150}{5810} \times 100 = 174.7$$

Illustration 22: *Calculate the consumer price index number through Family Budget method for the following data.*

Commodity	*Weight*	*Price per Unit 1985 Rs.*	*Price per Unit 1993 Rs.*
A	50	15	25
B	60	17	28
C	35	8	15
D	40	5	9
E	20	20	22
F	10	6	5

Solution: Calculation of consumer price index number

Commodity	*Weight*	*Price per unit in 1985 Rs.*	*Price Per unit in 1993 Rs.*	$P=\frac{p_1}{p_0}\times 100$ *Price*	*Weighted Relative P.V.*
A	50	15	25	166.66	833
B	60	17	28	164.7	9882
C	35	8	15	187 5	6562
D	40	5	9	180	7200
E	20	20	22	110	2200
F	10	6	5	83.33	833
	ΣV= 215				*ΣPV= 27510*

Index number $P_{01} = \frac{\sum PV}{\sum V} = \frac{27510}{215} = 128$

Miscellaneous Illustrations

Illustration 23: *From the following data calculate price index number by (i) Simple aggregate method and (ii) Average of price relative method.*

Commodity	*Price in 1985 Rs.*	*Price in 1992 Rs.*
A	34	39
B	52	50
C	47	52
D	74	75
E	60	65
F	45	53
G	50	55

Solution: Calculation of Index Numbers

Commodities	*Price in 1985* *(P_0)* *Rs.*	*Price in 1992* *(P_1)* *Rs.*	$\frac{p_1}{p_0}\times 100$
A	34	39	114.7
B	52	50	96.15
C	47	52	110.6
D	74	75	101.35
E	60	65	108.33
F	45	53	117.8
G	50	55	110
N = 7	$\Sigma P_0 = 362$	$\Sigma P_1 = 389$	$\Sigma P = 759$ *(approx)*

(i) $$P_{01} = \Sigma \frac{p_1}{p_0}\times 100 = \frac{389}{362}\times 100 = 107.5$$

(ii) $$P_{01} = \frac{\Sigma \frac{p_1}{p_0}\times 100}{7} = \frac{759}{7} = 108.43$$

Illustration 24: *The following data are related with the prices and quantity consumed for 1985 and 1992.*

Commodity	*1985*		*1992*	
	Price Rs.	*Quantity*	*Price*	*Quantity Rs.*
I	*12*	*30*	*15*	*35*
II	*7*	*12*	*10*	*15*
III	*9*	*10*	*7*	*12*
IV	*15*	*20*	*12*	*18*
V	*10*	*15*	*15*	*12*

Compute price index numbers through (a) Laspeyre's method (b) Paasche's method (c) Bowley - Darbish method (d) Fisher's method and (e) Kelley's method.

Solution: Calculate of price index numbers

Commodity	1985 p_0	1985 q_0	1992 p_1	1992 q_1	$(q_0+q_1)/2$ q	p_1q_0	p_0q_0	p_1q_1	p_0q_1	p_1q	p_0q
I	12	30	15	35	32.5	450	360	525	420	487.5	390
II	7	12	10	15	13.5	120	84	150	105	135	94.5
III	9	10	7	12	11	70	90	84	108	77	99
IV	15	20	12	18	19	240	300	216	270	228	285
V	10	15	15	12	13.5	225	150	180	120	202.5	135
						Σp_1q_0 1105	Σp_0q_0 984	Σp_1q_1 1155	Σp_0q_1 1023	Σp_1q 1130	Σp_0q 1003.5

(a) Laspeyre's method:

$$P_{01} = \frac{\Sigma p_1 q_0}{\Sigma p_0 q_0} \times 100 = \frac{1105}{984} \times 100 = 112.3$$

(b) Paasche's method:

$$P_{01} = \frac{\Sigma p_1 q_1}{\Sigma p_0 q_1} \times 100 = \frac{1155}{1023} \times 100 = 113$$

(c) Bowley - Darbish method:

$$P_{01} = \frac{\frac{\Sigma p_1 q_0}{\Sigma p_0 q_0} + \frac{\Sigma p_1 q_1}{\Sigma p_0 q_1}}{2} \times 100 = \frac{\frac{1105}{984} + \frac{1155}{1023}}{2} \times 100 = 112.6$$

(d) Fisher's method:

$$P_{01} = \sqrt{\frac{\Sigma p_1 q_0}{\Sigma p_0 q_0} + \frac{\Sigma p_1 q_1}{\Sigma p_0 q_1}} \times 100 = \sqrt{\frac{1105}{984} \times \frac{1155}{1023}} \times 100$$

$$= \sqrt{1.123 \times 1.129} \times 100 = 112.6$$

(e) Kelley's method:

$$P_{01} = \frac{\Sigma p_1 q}{\Sigma p_0 q} \times 100 = \frac{1130}{1003.5} \times 100 = 112.6$$

Illustration 25: *Compute Price index from the following data by weighted average of price relatives through (i) Arithmetic mean method and (ii) Geometric mean method.*

	1989		1992	
Commodity	*Price*	*Quantity*	*Price*	*Quantity*
I	55	110	64	120
II	49	105	57	100
III	75	90	85	85
IV	63	70	70	80
V	70	50	65	75

Solution: Calculation of index numbers

Commodity	*Price in 1989* p_0	*Qty in 1989* q_0	*Price in 1992* p_1	*V* $p_0\, q_0$	$p = \frac{p_1}{p_0} \times 100$	*PV*	*Log P*	*V log P*
I	55	110	64	6050	116.36	703978	2.066	12499.3
II	49	105	57	5145	116.32	598466.4	2.065	10624.4
III	75	90	85	6750	113.33	764977.5	2.054	13864.5
IV	63	70	70	4410	111.11	489995.1	2.046	9022.86
V	70	50	65	3500	92.9	325150	1.968	6888
				ΣV = 25855		*ΣPV = 2882567*		*ΣV log P 52899.06*

(a) *Arithmetic mean method:*

$$P_{01} = \frac{\Sigma PV}{\Sigma V} = \frac{2882567}{25855} = 111.5$$

(b) *Geometric mean method:*

$$P_{01} = \text{Antilog } \frac{\Sigma V \log P}{\Sigma V} = \text{Antilog } \frac{52899.06}{25855}$$

$$= \text{Antilog } 2.046 = 111.12$$

Illustration 26: *Calculate quantity index numbers from the following data by (a) Laspeyre's method (b) Paasche's method and (c) Fisher's method.*

Commodity	1990 Price	1990 Quantity	1993 Price	1993 Quantity
I	15	10	20	13
II	23	15	32	18
III	39	22	45	25
IV	17	12	15	10
V	25	11	32	15
VI	30	8	40	10

Solution: Calculation of quantity index numbers

Commodity	1990 Price P_0	1990 Qnty q_0	1993 Price P_1	1993 Qnty q_1	q_1p_0	q_0p_0	q_1p_1	q_0p_1
I	15	10	20	13	195	150	260	200
II	23	15	32	18	414	345	576	480
III	39	22	45	25	975	858	1125	990
IV	17	12	15	10	170	204	150	180
V	25	11	32	15	375	275	480	352
VI	30	8	40	10	300	240	400	320
					$\Sigma q_1p_0 = 2429$	$\Sigma q_0p_0 = 2072$	$\Sigma p_1q_1 = 2991$	$\Sigma q_0p_1 = 2522$

(a) *Laspeyre's method:*

$$Q_{01} = \frac{\Sigma q_1p_0}{\Sigma q_0p_0} \times 100 = \frac{2429}{2072} \times 100 = 117.23$$

(b) *Paasche's method:*

$$Q_{01} = \frac{\Sigma q_1p_1}{\Sigma q_0p_1} \times 100 = \frac{2991}{2522} \times 100 = 118.6$$

(c) *Fisher's method:*

$$Q_{01} = \sqrt{\frac{\Sigma q_1p_0}{\Sigma q_0p_0} \times \frac{\Sigma q_1p_1}{\Sigma q_0p_1}} \times 100 = \sqrt{\frac{2429}{2072} \times \frac{2991}{2522}} \times 100$$

$$= \sqrt{1.39} \times 100 = 117.9$$

Illustration 27: *Compute the price index number by Fisher's ideal method and find out the consistency of the index number by time-reversal test and factor-reversal test.*

Commodity	*1985* Price	*1985* Quantity	*1992* Price	*1992* Quantity
I	*9*	*15*	*15*	*20*
II	*15*	*25*	*25*	*30*
III	*12*	*20*	*18*	*25*
IV	*21*	*32*	*20*	*35*
V	*8*	*40*	*9*	*30*

Solution: Calculation of index numbers

Commodity	*1985* Price p_0	*1985* Qnty q_0	*1992* Price p_1	*1992* Qnty q_1	p_1q_0	p_0q_0	p_1q_1	p_0q_1
I	9	15	15	20	225	135	300	180
II	15	25	25	30	625	375	750	450
III	12	20	18	25	360	240	450	300
IV	21	32	20	35	640	672	700	735
V	8	40	9	30	360	320	270	240
					Σp_1q_0 = 2210	Σp_0q_0 = 1742	Σp_1q_1 = 2470	Σp_0q_1 = 1905

Index number under Fisher's ideal method:

$$P_{01} = \sqrt{\frac{\Sigma p_1q_0}{\Sigma p_0q_0} \times \frac{\Sigma p_1q_1}{\Sigma p_0q_1}} \times 100 = \sqrt{\frac{2210}{1742} \times \frac{2470}{1905}} \times 100 = 128.25$$

(a) *Time - Reversal Test:*

$$P_{10} = \sqrt{\frac{\Sigma p_0q_0}{\Sigma p_1q_0} \times \frac{\Sigma p_0q_1}{\Sigma p_1q_1}} \times 100$$

$$P_{01} \times P_{10} = \sqrt{\frac{\Sigma p_1q_0}{\Sigma p_0q_0} \times \frac{\Sigma p_1q_1}{\Sigma p_0q_1} \times \frac{\Sigma p_0q_0}{\Sigma p_1q_0} \times \frac{\Sigma p_0q_1}{\Sigma p_1q_1}}$$

$$= \sqrt{\frac{2210}{1742} \times \frac{2470}{1905} \times \frac{1742}{2210} \times \frac{1905}{2470}} = \sqrt{1} = 1$$

Since the value of $P_{01} \times P_{10}$ is 1, the index number is consistent.

(b) Factor - Reversal Test:

$$Q_{01} = \sqrt{\frac{\Sigma q_1 p_0}{\Sigma q_0 p_0} \times \frac{\Sigma q_1 p_1}{\Sigma q_0 p_1}}$$

$$P_{01} \times Q_{01} = \sqrt{\frac{\Sigma p_1 q_0}{\Sigma p_0 q_0} \times \frac{\Sigma p_1 q_1}{\Sigma p_0 q_1} \times \frac{\Sigma q_1 p_0}{\Sigma q_0 p_0} \times \frac{\Sigma q_1 p_1}{\Sigma q_0 p_1}}$$

$$= \sqrt{\frac{2210}{1742} \times \frac{2470}{1905} \times \frac{1905}{1742} \times \frac{2470}{2210}}$$

$$= \sqrt{\frac{(2470)^2}{(1742)^2}} = \frac{2470}{1742}$$

Hence, $\frac{\Sigma p_1 q_1}{\Sigma p_0 q_0} = \frac{2470}{1742}$

Since the value of, $P_{01} \times Q_{01} = \frac{\Sigma p_1 q_1}{\Sigma p_0 q_0}$ the index number is consistent.

Illustration 28: *Calculate Quantity Index numbers from the following data.*

	1985		*1992*	
Commodity	*Quantity*	*Price*	*Quantity*	*Price*
Tea	*12*	*25*	*15*	*60*
Coffee	*15*	*29*	*18*	*65*
Sugar	*90*	*5*	*110*	*9*
Wheat	*120*	*4*	*150*	*6*
Rice	*100*	*5*	*110*	*8*

Solution: Calculation of Quantity Index numbers

Commodity	1985 Price P_0	1985 Qty. q_0	1992 Price P_1	1992 Qty. q_1	q_1p_0	q_0p_0	q_1p_1	q_0p_1
Tea	25	12	60	15	375	300	900	720
Coffee	29	15	65	18	522	435	1170	975
Sugar	5	90	9	110	550	450	990	810
Wheat	4	120	6	150	600	480	900	720
Rice	5	100	8	110	550	500	880	800
					$\Sigma q_1p_0 = 2597$	$\Sigma q_0p_0 = 2165$	$\Sigma q_1p_1 = 4840$	$\Sigma q_0p_1 = 4025$

(i) Quantity index number under

Laspeyre's method

$$Q_{01} = \frac{\sum q_1 p_0}{\sum q_0 p_0} \times 100 = \frac{2597}{2165} \times 100 = 119.95$$

(ii) Quantity index number under

Paasche's method

$$Q_{01} = \frac{\sum q_1 p_1}{\sum q_0 p_1} \times 100 = \frac{4840}{4025} \times 100 = 120.25$$

(iii) Quantity index number under

Fisher's method

$$Q_{01} = \sqrt{\frac{\sum q_1 p_0}{\sum q_0 p_0} \times \frac{\sum q_1 p_1}{\sum q_0 p_1}} \times 100 = \sqrt{\frac{2597}{2165} \times \frac{4840}{4025}} \times 100$$

$$= 1.2 \times 100 = 120$$

Illustration 29: *Compute the chain base index number from the following fixed base index numbers.*

Year	*1985*	*1986*	*1987*	*1988*	*1989*	*1990*	*1991*
F.B.I.	*115*	*215*	*310*	*390*	*410*	*475*	*520*

Solution: Calculation of Chain Base index numbers

Year	*F.B.I*	*Link Relatives*	*Chain index*
1985	115		115
1986	215	$\frac{215}{115} \times 100 = 187$	$\frac{115 \times 187}{100} = 215$
1987	310	$\frac{310}{215} \times 100 = 144$	$\frac{215 \times 144}{100} = 310$
1988	390	$\frac{390}{310} \times 100 = 126$	$\frac{310 \times 126}{100} = 390$
1989	410	$\frac{410}{390} \times 100 = 105$	$\frac{390 \times 105}{100} = 410$
1990	475	$\frac{475}{410} \times 100 = 116$	$\frac{410 \times 116}{100} = 475.6$
1991	520	$\frac{520}{475} \times 100 = 109$	$\frac{475.6 \times 109}{100} = 518.4$

Illustration 30: *Compute the fixed base index number from the following chain base index numbers.*

Year	*1987*	*1988*	*1989*	*1990*	*1991*	*1992*	*1993*
Chain Base Index Numbers	*85*	*115*	*125*	*195*	*210*	*250*	*300*

Solution: Calculation of fixed base index numbers

Year	*C.B.I.*	*Fixed Base Index*
1987	85	85
1988	115	$115 \times 85/100 = 97.75$
1989	125	$125 \times 97.75/100 = 122.18$
1990	195	$195 \times 122.18/100 = 238.25$
1991	210	$210 \times 238.25/100 = 500.32$
1992	250	$250 \times 500.32/100 = 1250.8$
1993	300	$300 \times 1250.8/100 = 3752.4$

$$F.B.I. = \frac{\text{Current year C.B.I.} \times \text{Previous year F.B.I.}}{100}$$

Illustration 31: *From the following data of wholesale prices of a certain commodity construct index number by chain base method:*

Year:	*1979*	*1980*	*1981*	*1982*	*1983*	*1984*	*1985*	*1986*	*1987*	*1988*
Price:	*750*	*500*	*650*	*600*	*720*	*700*	*690*	*750*	*840*	*800*

(MGU: Section B April 98)

Solution: Calculation of index numbers by chain base method

Year	*Price*	*Index No. (Link relatives)*
1979	750	100
1980	500	66.67
1981	650	130
1982	600	92.31
1983	720	120
1984	700	97.22
1985	690	98.57
1986	750	108.66
1987	840	112
1988	800	95.24

Note: Link Relative for 1979 = 100; for 1980 $\frac{500}{750}\times 100$; for 1983 $= \frac{720}{600}\times 100$ etc.

Illustration 32: *From the following average price of three groups of commodities given in rupees per unit, find index number (a) by reference to 1986 as base year and (b) by the chain base method:*

Group	*1986*	*1987*	*1988*	*1989*	*1990*
I	*2*	*3*	*4*	*5*	*6*
II	*8*	*10*	*12*	*15*	*18*
III	*4*	*5*	*8*	*10*	*12*

(MGU Section D April 97)

Solution: Calculation of index numbers

Group	*1986*	*1987*	*1988*	*1989*	*1990*
I	2	3	4	5	6
II	8	10	12	15	18
III	4	5	8	10	12
	14	*18*	*24*	*30*	*36*

(a) Index No. for 1987 = 100

Index No. for 1987 $= \frac{\sum p_1}{\sum p_0} \times 100 = \frac{18}{14} \times 100 = 128.6$

Index No. for 1988 $= \frac{24}{14} \times 100 = 171.4$

Index No. for 1989 $= \frac{30}{14} \times 100 = 214.3$

Index No. for 1990 $= \frac{36}{14} \times 100 = 257.1$

(b) Calculation of index number by chain base method

Year	*Group I*	*Index No.*	*Group II*	*Index No.*	*Group III*	*Index No.*	*Total*	*Index No.*
1986	2	100	8	100	4	100	14	100
1987	3	150	10	125	5	125	18	128.6
1988	4	133	12	120	8	160	24	133
1989	5	125	15	125	10	125	30	125
1990	6	120	18	120	12	120	36	120

Note: Index No. based an chain base method - for 1986 = 0, 1987 group I $= \frac{3}{2} \times 100$ for 1988 $= \frac{4}{3} \times 100$ etc.

Illustration 33: *Calculate a suitable index number for the year 1992 with 1987 as the base using the following data.*

	1987		*1992*	
Commodity	*Price*	*Quantity*	*Price*	*Quantity*
A	*12*	*100*	*20*	*120*
B	*4*	*200*	*4*	*240*
C	*8*	*120*	*12*	*150*
D	*20*	*60*	*24*	*50*

(MGU: Section B April 95)

Solution: Marshall Edgeworth method can be applied for calculating index numbers.

Commodity	p_0	q_0	p_1	q_1	p_0q_0	p_1q_1	p_1q_0	p_0q_1
A	12	100	20	120	1200	2400	2000	1440
B	4	200	4	240	800	960	800	960
C	8	120	12	150	960	1800	1440	1200
D	20	60	24	50	1200	1200	1440	1000
					4160	*6360*	*5680*	*4600*

Index number by Marshal Edgeworth method

$$= \frac{\Sigma P_1 q_0 + \Sigma P_1 q_1}{\Sigma P_0 q_0 + \Sigma P_0 q_1} \times 100 = \frac{5680 + 6360}{4160 + 4600} \times 100$$

$$= \frac{12040}{8760} \times 100 = 137.4$$

Illustration 34: *Prepare index number for three years taking average price as base.*

Price per quintal in Rs

Year	*Wheat*	*Cotton*	*Oil*
1st year	*100*	*25*	*30*
2nd year	*90*	*20*	*25*
3rd year	*99*	*15*	*20*

(MGU: section B April 95 and Sep. 92)

Solution: Calculation of Index Numbers

	Price			*Index No.*			
Commodity	*I year*	*II year*	*III year*	*I year*	*II year*	*III year*	*Average price*
Wheat	100	90	99	103.8	93.5	102.8	96.3
Cotton	25	20	15	125	100	75	20
Oil	30	25	20	120	100	80	25

Note: Average price: Wheat $= \frac{100 + 90 + 99}{3} = 96.3$

Cotton $= \frac{25 + 20 + 15}{3} = 20$

$$\text{Oil} = \frac{30+25+20}{3} = 25$$

Index No. can be calculated by $\frac{P_1}{P_0} \times 100$

For wheat 1st year $= \frac{100}{96.3} \times 100 = 103.8$

2nd year $= \frac{90}{96.3} \times 100 = 93.5$ etc.

Illustration 35: *Calculate Fisher's ideal index number and test whether it satisfies time reversal test and factor reversal test*

	1993		*1994*	
Commodity	*Price*	*Quantity*	*Price*	*Quantity*
Rice	*12*	*75*	*30*	*90*
Milk	*3*	*22.5*	*9*	*15*
Fire wood	*1.5*	*30*	*3*	*37.5*
Sugar	*3*	*15*	*7.5*	*12*
Cloth	*1.5*	*60*	*4.5*	*4.5*

(Kerala: section C April 98)

Solution: Calculation of index numbers

Commodity	p_0	q_0	p_1	q_1	p_0q_0	p_1q_1	p_1q_0	p_0q_1
Rice	12	75	30	90	900	2700	2250	1080
Milk	3	22.5	9	15	67.5	135	202.5	45
Firewood	1.5	30	3	37.5	45	112.5	90	56.3
Sugar	3	15	7.5	12	45	90	112.5	36
Cloth	1.5	60	4.5	45	90	202.5	270	67.5
					$\Sigma p_0q_0 = 1147.5$	$\Sigma p_1q_1 = 3240$	$\Sigma p_1q_0 = 2925$	$\Sigma p_0q_1 = 1284.8$

Fisher's Ideal Index Number

$$= \sqrt{\frac{\sum p_1q_0 + \sum p_1q_1}{\sum p_0q_0 + \sum p_0q_1}} \times 100 = \sqrt{\frac{2925}{1147.5} \times \frac{3240}{1284.8}} \times 100$$

$$= \sqrt{2.55 \times 2.52} \times 100 = 2.53 \times 100 = 253$$

Fishers time reversal test

$$\sqrt{\frac{\sum p_1q_0}{\sum p_0q_0}\times\frac{\sum p_1q_1}{\sum p_0q_1}\times\frac{\sum p_0q_0}{\sum p_1q_0}\times\frac{\sum p_0q_1}{\sum p_1q_1}}=1$$

$$\sqrt{\frac{2925}{1147.5}\times\frac{3240}{1284.8}\times\frac{1147.5}{2925}\times\frac{1284.8}{3240}}=1$$

Hence time reversal test is satisfied.

Fishers factor reversal test

$$=\sqrt{\frac{\sum p_1q_0}{\sum p_0q_0}\times\frac{\sum p_1q_1}{\sum p_0q_1}\times\frac{\sum q_1p_0}{\sum q_0p_0}\times\frac{\sum q_1p_1}{\sum q_0p_1}}$$

$$=\sqrt{\frac{2925}{1147.5}\times\frac{3240}{1284.8}\times\frac{1284.8}{1147.5}\times\frac{1147.5}{2925}}$$

$$=\sqrt{\frac{3240\times3240}{1147.5\times1147.5}}=\frac{3240}{1147.5}\text{ which is }\frac{\sum p_1q_1}{\sum p_0q_0}$$

Hence factor reversal test is satisfied.

Illustration 36: *The following are the index number of prices, with base year taken as 1961 (= 100)*

Year:	*1970*	*1971*	*1972*	*1973*	*1974*	*1975*	*1976*
Index No.	*140*	*200*	*210*	*230*	*250*	*260*	*280*

Shift the base from 1961 to 1971 and then what are the index numbers? (Kerala Section B April 96)

Solution: Calculation of new index number based on 1971

Year	*Index no based on 1961*	*Index no based on 1971*
1970	140	$= 140/200\times100 = 70$
1971	200	$= 200/200\times100 = 100$
1972	210	$= 210/200\times100 = 105$
1973	230	$= 230/200\times100 = 115$
1974	250	$= 250/200\times100 = 125$
1975	260	$= 260/200\times100 = 130$
1976	280	$= 280/200\times100 = 140$

Illustration 37: *Construct cost of living index number from the following data*

Group :	*A*	*B*	*C*	*D*	*E*
Index :	*400*	*200*	*250*	*100*	*75*
Weight :	*4*	*3*	*1*	*2*	*3*

(Kerala Section B April 94)

Solution: Calculation of cost of living index numbers

Group	*Index no* *I*	*Weight* *W*	*Weight × index no* *W × I*
A	400	4	1600
B	200	3	600
C	250	1	250
D	100	2	200
E	75	3	225
		$\Sigma W = 13$	$\Sigma WI = 2875$

$$\text{Cost of living index number} = \frac{\sum WI}{\sum W} = \frac{2875}{13} = 221.2$$

Illustration 38: *Calculate Paasche's Index Number for the data*

	1986		*1985*	
Commodity	*Price*	*Quantity*	*Price*	*Quantity*
X	*6.8*	*24*	*7.3*	*30*
Y	*12.3*	*16*	*15.0*	*20*

(Kerala Section B April 89)

Solution: Calculation of Paasche's index number.

Commodity	p_0	q_0	p_1	q_1	p_1q_1	p_0q_1
X	6.8	24	7.3	30	219	204
Y	12.3	16	15.0	20	300	246
					$\Sigma p_1q_1 = 519$	$\Sigma p_0q_1 = 450$

$$\text{Paasche's index number} = \frac{\sum p_1q_1}{\sum p_0q_1} \times 100 = \frac{519}{450} \times 100 = 115.33$$

Illustration 39: *Contruct Laspeyres, Paasche's, Edgeworth - Marshals and Ideal Index Numbers from the following data*

Items	*Quantity*		*Price*	
	Base year	*Current year*	*Base year*	*Current year*
A	10	12	12	15
B	5	10	8	10
C	12	19	10	12

(Kerala Section C Sep. 93)

Solution: Calculation of index numbers

Commodity	p_0	q_0	p_1	q_1	p_0q_0	p_1q_1	p_1q_0	p_0q_1
A	12	10	15	12	120	180	150	144
B	8	5	10	10	40	100	50	80
C	10	12	12	19	120	228	144	190
					$\Sigma p_0q_0 = 280$	$\Sigma p_1q_1 = 508$	$\Sigma p_1q_0 = 344$	$\Sigma p_0q_1 = 414$

(i) Laspeyre's index number

$$= \frac{\Sigma p_1q_0}{\Sigma p_0q_0} \times 100 = \frac{344}{280} \times 100 = 122.9$$

(ii) Paasche's index number

$$= \frac{\Sigma p_1q_1}{\Sigma p_0q_1} \times 100 = \frac{508}{414} \times 100 = 122.7$$

(iii) Fisher's ideal index number

$$= \sqrt{\frac{\Sigma p_1q_0}{\Sigma p_0q_0} \times \frac{\Sigma p_1q_1}{\Sigma p_0q_1}} \times 100 = \sqrt{\frac{344}{280} \times \frac{508}{414}} \times 100$$

$$= \sqrt{\frac{174752}{115920}} \times 100 = 122.8$$

(iv) Marshal Edgeworth's index number

$$= \frac{\Sigma p_1q_0 + \Sigma p_1q_1}{\Sigma p_0q_0 + \Sigma p_0q_1} \times 100 = \frac{344 + 508}{280 + 414} \times 100 = \frac{852}{694} \times 100 = 122.8$$

Exercises

1. Define index numbers. State the utilities of Index numbers.
2. Distinguish between price index numbers, quantity index numbers and value index numbers.
3. What do you mean by index number? State the problems in the construction of index numbers.
4. Explain briefly the important methods of construction of index numbers.
5. Explain the different tests of consistency of index numbers.
6. What is chain base index number? State the procedures of construction of chain based index numbers.
7. State how chain base index number can be converted into fixed base index number.
8. Write short notes of the following.

   (a) Base shifting (b) Spliced index number

   (c) Deflating of index number
9. What is consumer price index number? State the important objectives of construction of consumer price index number.
10. Define consumer price index number. State the important precautions for the construction of consumer price index numbers.
11. What are the problems in the construction of cost of living index number?
12. Define consumer price index. State the important methods of constructing consumer price index.
13. What is base shifting? Why does it become necessary to shift base of index numbers? Give an example. (MGU Section B April 98)
14. What do you mean by splicing of index numbers? (MGU Section A April 97)
15. What is an index number? (MGU Section A April 95 and 92)
16. What is meant by unweighted index numbers? (MGU section A Sep. 94)
17. Explain the method of constructing an index number. What tests are usually applied to examine the suitability of index numbers? (MGU Section C Sep. 94)
18. Mention two limitations in the construction of index numbers. (MGU Section A April 94 and Sep. 93)
19. Define an index number (MGU: Section A sep. 93)
20. Explain how wholesale price index numbers are prepared. What are the points to be considered in the selection of the base year, prices and weights? (MGU: Section C Sep. 92)

21. What is meant by cost of living index number?

(MGU: Section A Sep. 92)

22. What is an index number? Discuss briefly the importance and the use of index numbers in business and industry

(MGU: Section C Sep 92)

23. Give a brief description of various types of index numbers. Explain in detail the method of construction of Fishers ideal index numbers.

(MGU: Section C April 92)

24. Define time reversal test. (Kerala Section A April 98)

25. State the index number which satisfy time reversal test.

(Kerala Section A April 95)

26. What are weighted index numbers? Explain any two methods of determining weights. (Kerala Section B April 95)

27. Distinguish between weighted and unweighted index numbers.

(Kerala Section B April 89 and 90)

28. What is an ideal index number ? (Kerala Section A April 93)

29. Explain the technique of deflating index numbers

(Kerala Section B April 93)

30. What is the cost of living index number? State any two uses of it.

(Kerala Section B Sep. 93)

31. Explain briefly the tests of index numbers

(Kerala Section B Sep. 93)

32. Explain how to construct cost of living index number

(Kerala Section B Sep. 90)

33. State the applicational uses of index numbers.

(Kerala Section A April 90)

34. Construct Index number for 1996 based on the prices of 1990.

Commodities	*A*	*B*	*C*	*D*	*E*	*F*	*G*
Price for 1990 Rs.	10	15	24	18	6	22	11
Price for 1996 Rs.	17	19	25	15	12	30	20

[Ans: 130]

35. The data related to the prices of 7 commodities for 1992 and 1997 are given below.

Commodities	*1*	*2*	*3*	*4*	*5*	*6*	*7*
Price for 1992 Rs.	35	48	50	20	15	44	65
Price for 1997 Rs.	45	55	62	29	26	40	60

Calculate price index on the basis of simple average of price relative method through A.M and G.M. [Ans: 124; 121.3]

36. Construct price index number by (a) Laspeyre's method (b) Paasche's method (c) Bowley-Darbish method and (d) Fisher's method from the data given below.

	1995		*1997*	
Commodity	*Price*	*Quantity*	*Price*	*Quantity*
A	12	8	15	10
B	16	10	25	11
C	10	15	16	14
D	5	6	8	5

[Ans: 151; 149.5; 150.3; 150.2]

37. Calculate price index from the following data by weighted average of price relatives through (a) Arithmetic mean method and (b) Geometric mean method.

Commodity	Quantity	Price in 1996	Price in 1997
A	12	7	8
B	10	14	15
C	8	20	24
D	15	50	48
E	5	12	20

[Ans: 105.3; 104.2]

38. Calculate quantity index number from the following data through (i) Laspeyre's method (ii) Paasche's method and (iii) Fisher's method.

	1996		*1997*	
Commodity	*Price Rs.*	*Quantity*	*Price Rs.*	*Quantity*
I	40	10	42	12
II	35	8	37	10
III	22	10	20	8
IV	64	15	66	12
V	28	8	30	10
VI	14	7	12	5

[Ans: 97.34; 98.02; 97.68]

39. Calculate price index number through Fisher's method and test the consistency of it by (a) time reversal test and (b) factor reversal test.

	1990		*1997*	
Commodity	*Price Rs.*	*Quantity*	*PriceRs.*	*Quantity*
Beef	30	20	40	25
Mutton	60	25	120	20
Chicken	25	18	40	20
Pork	15	10	25	8
Fish	30	30	50	32

[Ans: 172.07]

40. Calculate chain base index numbers from the following fixed base index numbers.

Year	1990	1991	1992	1993	1994	1995	1996
FBI	200	240	310	300	350	370	420

[Ans: 100; 120; 155; 150; 175; 185; 210]

41. Convert the following chain base index numbers into fixed base index numbers.

Year	1990	1991	1992	1993	1994	1995	1996
CBI	85	110	140	130	125	175	200

[Ans: 85; 110; 140; 130; 125; 175; 200]

42. Find out the new index numbers based on 1994 from the following index number based on 1988.

Year	1988	1989	1990	1991	1992	1993	1994	1995	1996	1997
Index number	100	140	155	150	165	177	184	195	210	240

[Ans: 54.3; 76.1; 84; 90; 96; 100; 106; 114; 130]

43. Find out the spliced index number for the following index numbers.

Year I	*Index number*	*Year II*	*Index number*
1984	100	1991	100
1985	120	1992	125
1986	125	1993	134
1987	129	1994	142
1988	135	1995	156
1989	140	1996	166
1990	150	1997	175
1991	160		

[Ans: 160; 200; 214; 227; 250; 266; 280]

44. Calculate (i) index numbers for real wages and (ii) real wages, from the following data.

Year	1990	1991	1992	1993	1994	1995	1996	1997
Wages Rs.	750	800	900	1000	1200	1400	1550	1800
Consumer price index	100	120	140	150	180	190	210	220

[Ans: (i) 100; 89; 86; 89; 89; 98; 98; 109

(ii) 750; 667; 643; 667; 667; 737; 738; 818]

45. Calculate index number through Aggregate Expenditure method from the following data.

Commodities	*Quantity consumed in 1986*	*Price per unit in 1986 Rs.*	*Price per unit in 1996 Rs.*
A	20	35	60
B	50	25	50
C	30	12	20
D	20	8	10
E	25	10	16
F	15	14	20
G	10	8	15

[Ans: 178]

46. Calculate index number on the basis of family budget method, from the following data.

Commodities	*Weight*	*Price per unit 1987*	*Price per unit 1997*
A	25	12	25
B	15	8	30
C	10	15	40
D	30	20	50
E	40	5	15
F	50	16	35

[Ans: 245]

47. The price quotations of four different commodities for 1981 and1985 are given below. Calculate the index for 1985 with 1981 as base by using. (a) The simple average of price relatives (b) The weighted average of price relatives

Commodities		*Unit (00 Rs.)*	*Weight 1981*	*Price in Rs 1985*
A	kg	6	2.00	4.5
B	kg	7	2.50	3.2
C	Dozen	6	3.00	4.5
D	kg	2	1.00	1.3

(MGU Section C April 95) [Ans: 158.25; 68.81]

48. Calculate Fishers ideal index from the following data and prove that it satisfies both the time reversal and factor reversal test

	1991		*1992*	
Commodity	*Price*	*Expenditure*	*Price*	*Expenditure*
A	8	80	10	120
B	10	12	120	96
C	5	40	5	50
D	4	56	3	60
E	20	100	25	150

(MGU Section C Sep. 93) [Ans: 223.9]

49. From the following prices, calculate index numbers with 1971 as base:

Year	1964	1965	1966	1967	1968	1969	1970	1971	1972
Price (Rs.)	4	5	6	9	11	7	13	14	9

(MGU Section B Sep. 93)

[Ans: price - 28.6, 35.7, 42.9, 64.3, 78.6, 50, 92.9, 100, 64.3]

50. The following figures relate to the price and quantities of correlation in business in base year and current year respectively. Construct an appropriate index using the following data.

Commodity	*Quantity*	*Price*	*Quantity*	*Price*
A	50	32	50	30
B	35	30	40	25
C	65	16	50	18

(MGU Section B Sep. 93) [Ans. Fisher's index number = 107.9]

51. On the basis of the following information, calculate the Fisher's ideal index number.

	Base year		*Current year*	
Commodity	*Price*	*Quantity*	*Price*	*Quantity*
A	2	40	6	50
B	4	50	8	40
C	6	20	9	30
D	8	10	6	20
E	10	10	5	20

(Kerala Section B April 97) [Ans. 149.2]

52. Compute Fisher's ideal index number for the following:

	Base year		*Current year*	
Commodities	*Price (Rs.)*	*Quantity*	*Price (Rs.)*	*Quantity*
Wheat	2 Rs./kg	5 kgs.	3 Rs./kg	6 kgs
Milk	1 Rs./lit	2 lit.	2 Rs./lit.	4 lit.
Eggs	Rs 3/ Dozen	1 dozen	Rs 4/dozen	1.5 dozen

(Kerala Section C April 96) [Ans.154.7]

53. Compute Fisher ideal index number for the following

	1980		*1989*	
Commodities	*Price*	*Quantity*	*Price*	*Quantity*
A	14	15	24	12
B	20	5	27	4
C	4	10	7	8

(Kerala Section C April 95) [Ans. 161.4]

54. Construct the cost of living index number from the following:

Group	*Index*	*Weight*
A	350	5
B	200	2
C	240	3
D	150	1
E	250	2

(Kerala section B April 93) [Ans. 270.8]

55. From the fixed base index numbers given below, prepare the chain base index numbers,

Year	1956	1957	1958	1959	1960	1961
Fixed base Index No.	375	395	410	380	390	400

(Kerala Section C Sep 90) [Ans. 100, 105.3, 103.8, 92.7, 102.6, 102.6]

56. Compute (i) Paasche's (ii) Laspeyre's index numbers for quantity for the following data for the year 1989 taking 1986 as the base year

	1986		*1989*	
Commodity	*Price*	*Quantity*	*Price*	*Quantity*
X	7.5	25	8.2	22
Y	16.0	35	18.0	40
Z	12.3	29	14.4	25

(Kerala Section C April 90) [Ans. (i) 113.3 (ii) 113.5]

57. Construct an index number of prices from the following data:

Commodity	*Base year price Rs.*	*Current year price Rs.*	*Weights*
A	12	8	38
B	16	15	22
C	27	30	29
D	59	64	9
E	21	29	2

(MGU: Section B April 92)

◆ Chapter 12 ◆

Time Series

Time series is the arrangement of statistical data according to the time of occurrence. It helps to find out the variations in the values of data due to changes in time. The sales of a company for various periods, annual production of tea in India, export of coffee from India for various periods etc are data related to time series.

Meaning and Definitions: Werner *Z.* Hirsch, defines time series as time series is a sequence of values of some variate corresponding to successive points in time.

According to Ya-lun-chou, A time series may be defined as a collection of readings belonging to different periods of some economic variable or composite of variables.

Hence, time series means the data related to successive period of time.

Importance of time series

(1) It helps for understanding past behaviour: The data related to past years helps to understand the changes took place in those periods. It facilitates to understand the causes and circumstances of the changes during the past years.

(2) It facilitates for forecasting and planning: The data related to the past and present periods give more idea about the future. The businessmen, the govt and social organisation can take proper decisions about the future period, with the help of time series.

I Components of time series

The changes in the value of variables in different periods of time are due to so many factors. These factors are called the components of a time series. They are classified as (a) Trend (b) Seasonal changes, (c) Cyclical changes and (d) Irregular or Random fluctuations.

1. Trend: The trend may be defined as the changes over a long period of time. The longer period depends upon the nature of the study or nature of the data. It may be few years, or decade, or even centuries of time. The significance of trend is greater when the period of time is very longer. The data would eliminate the seasonal and cyclical variations if the period is very longer. For example, when one analyse the price level of agricultural commodities for a very short period (say 5 years), it can be noticed that the prices might have been decreased or increased over the period. If the data are analysed for a longer period, (say 20 years) one can notice the general trend of increasing the price level. Hence trend may be considered as an accurate measure for knowing the character of a phenomenon over a period of time.

2. Seasonal Variations: Seasonal variations are measured for one calender year. Most of the business and economic activities vary due to the natural factors and man-made convention. Natural factors are like, rainfall, winter, summer etc. Man-made conventions are like festivals. During the winter season the demand for woolen cloths and hot drinks are greater. In summer there would be a heavy demand for cool drinks, Air Conditions etc. In festival season the demand for clothes, sweets etc are greater. The study about the seasonal variations helps for short term planning for businessmen and economists. The production in a company can be well planned according to the seasonal fluctuations.

3. Cyclical Variations: Most of the economic and business activities follow the periods of business cycle. They are (i) Prosperity, (ii) Decline, (iii) Depression and (iv) Recovery. After recovery, the prosperity stage takes place. The prosperity period gives high profit for the company. Profit declines during the declining stage and gives heavy loss for the company. Appropriate measures during this period bring the company to a recovery stage. During this stage the company gradually recover from the loss position and starts giving low profit so as to reach a prosperity stage.

4. Irregular Movements: Irregular movements are otherwise called as random or erratic or unpredicatable variations. The changes in variable could not be predicted due to irregular movements. Irregular movements are like changes in technology, war, famine, flood, strike etc. The business and economic activities will be affected unexpectedly due to the irregular movements. Usually the effect of irregular movement exists only for a very short period.

II Mathematical model of time series

All type of variations may not affect all the time series. Most of the time series are affected by some of these variations, while some of the time series are affected by all of them.

According to the classical time series analysis, any particular observation in a time series is a product of trend, seasonal, cyclical and irregular movements.

It can be represented as,

$$O = T \times S \times C \times I$$

where , O denotes original data: T denotes Trend; S denotes seasonal variations; C denotes cyclical variations and I denotes irregular movements.

There also exists one more model called addictive model. In addictive model particular observation in a time series is the sum of the trend, seasonal, cyclical and irregular variations.

It can be represented as,

$$O = T + S + C + I$$

In multiplicative model S, C and I are represented in decimal percents. In addictive model S, C and I are represented as quadrative variations.

(*Eg*) In multiplicative model, $T = 300$

$$S = 1.2, \; C = 0.8 \; I = 1.3$$

$$O = 300 \times 1.2 \times 0.8 \times 1.3 = 374.4$$

In multiplicative model $T = 300$

$$S = 80, \text{C} = 50, \text{I} = -60$$

$$O = 300 + 80 + 50 - 60 = 370$$

Measurement of secular trend

The following are the important methods of measuring secular trend.

(1) Graphic method (2) Semi-average method

(3) Moving average method (4) Method of least squares.

(1) Graphic method: The graphic method is otherwise called as free hand method. This is the simplest method for measuring

trend. The following procedures should be adopted under this method.

(i) The original data should be plotted on a graph paper.

(ii) The plotted lines should be joined to give a curve.

(iii) A straight line should be drawn carefully through the middle area of the curve.

The straight line will either takes upward or downward position, on the basis of the nature of the curve.

Merits

1. It is the easiest method of measuring trend.

2. It is more flexible than any other methods of measurement.

3. It also gives the picture of the movement of data, in addition to the straight line.

Demerits

1. This method is highly subjective in nature. Different trend lines can be drawn from the curve. The trend line drawn by one person will not be the same, if drawn by another person.

2. It won't accurately project the furture.

3. The accuracy depends upon the skill of the analyst.

Illustration 1: *Fit a trend line to the following data related to the production in a factory.*

Year	*1979*	*80*	*81*	*82*	*83*	*84*	*85*	*86*	*87*
Production (in 000 of rupees)	*50*	*75*	*49*	*80*	*60*	*95*	*75*	*100*	*110*

Solution:

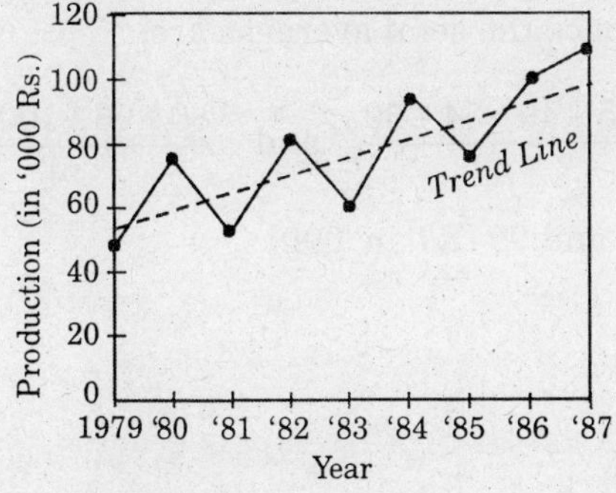

(2) Semi-average method: The whole data are to be divided into two equal parts and averages of these two equal parts are to be calculated. While calculating the averages the middle value should be eliminated, if the total number of observations are in odd number. The two averages are to be plotted in a graph. In the X axis the mid points of each intervals are to be used to plot these two points. Then the two points plotted in the graph should be joined so as to get a straight line. This line is called the trend line. The line should be extended backward or forward to know the past value or to predict the future value.

Merits

1. This method is a simple one to know the trend.

2. This method is an objective method of measuring trend. The trend line will be the same, though it is drawn by different people.

Demerits

1. This method assumes straight-line relationship whether such relationship exists or not.

2. It won't accurately estimate the character of phenomenon in future.

3. This method is subject to the limitation of arithmetic mean.

Illustration 2: *Fit a trend line through semi-average method for the following data.*

Year	*1985*	*86*	*87*	*88*	*89*	*90*	*91*	*92*
Income (Rs. in 000)	*45*	*49*	*54*	*60*	*80*	*96*	*100*	*120*

Solution: The eight observations related to years from 1985 to 1992 can be grouped into two parts as 45, 49, 54, 60 and 80, 96, 100, 120. Hence the semi averages are,

$$\frac{45+49+54+60}{4} \quad \text{and} \quad \frac{80+96+100+120}{4}$$

i.e., 52 and 99 (Rs. in '000).

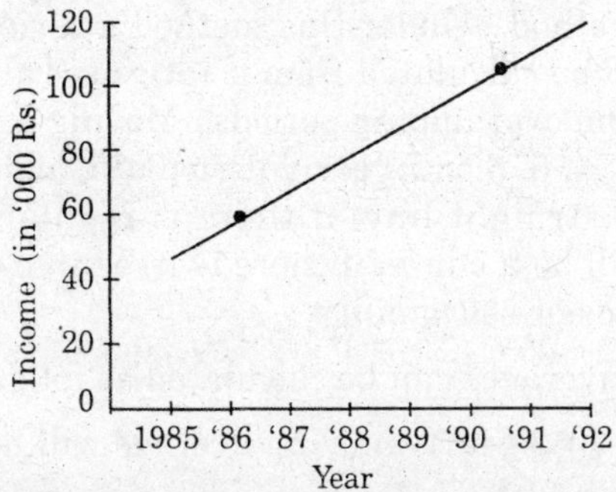

Illustration 3: *Draw a trend line to the following data by semi-average method.*

Year	*1984*	*85*	*86*	*87*	*88*	*89*	*90*	*91*	*92*
Sales (in 00 unit)	*47*	*62*	*73*	*70*	*80*	*85*	*87*	*94*	*98*

Solution: The nine observations related to the 9 years can be grouped into two parts, by leaving the middle value (i.e., value for the year 1988). Hence, the two parts are 47, 62, 73, 70 and 85, 87, 94 98 and the semi averages are,

$$\frac{47+62+73+70}{4} \quad \text{and} \quad \frac{85+87+94+98}{4}$$

i.e., 63 and 91 (in 00 units)

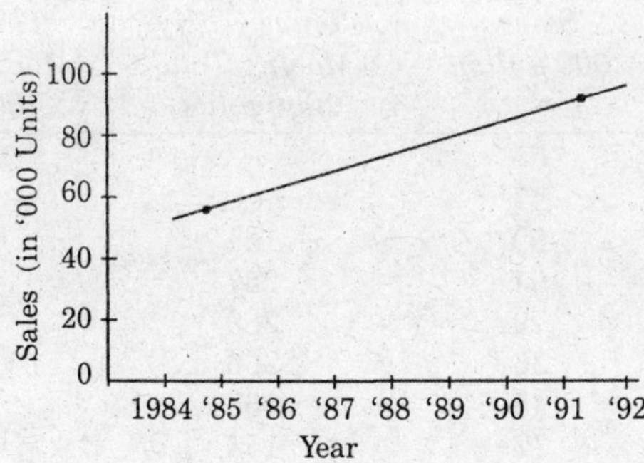

(3) Moving average method: This method is a logical extension of semi-average method. Under this method a series of successive averages should be calculated from a series of values. Averages can be taken from overlapping periods. Moving averages may be calculated for 3, 4, 5, 6 or 7 yearly periods. The moving average trend will be a straight line, if there is regular movement of variables. It will be a curve, if there is irregular movement due to business cycles or seasonality.

The moving averages can be calculated as follows.

The formula for 3 yearly moving average will be,

$$\frac{a+b+c}{3}, \frac{b+c+d}{3}, \frac{c+d+e}{3}, \frac{d+e+f}{3} \text{.... etc.}$$

The formula for 5 yearly moving average will be.

$$\frac{a+b+c+d+e}{5}, \frac{b+c+d+e+f}{5}, \frac{c+d+e+f+g}{5}$$

$$\frac{d+e+f+g+h}{5} \text{.... etc.}$$

(*a, b, c, d* . . . represent variables)

Illustration 4: *Compute 3 yearly moving averages from the following data.*

Year	*1982*	*83*	*84*	*85*	*86*	*87*	*88*	*89*	*90*	*91*	*92*
Sales (in 000 units)	*55*	*47*	*59*	*151*	*79*	*36*	*45*	*72*	*83*	*89*	*102*

Solution: Calculation of 3 yearly moving averages

Year	*Sales (000 units)*	*Three yearly Moving Total (000 units)*	*Three yearly Moving average (000 units)*
1982	55		
1983	47		
1984	59	161	53.67
1985	151	257	85.67
1986	79	289	96.33
1987	36	266	88.67
1988	45	160	53.33
1989	72	153	51
1990	83	200	66.67
1991	89	244	81.33
1992	102	277	91.33

Illustration 5: *Calculate 5 yearly moving averages from the following data.*

Year	1980	81	82	83	84	85	86	87	88	89	90
Income (in '000 rupees)	161	127	152	143	144	167	182	179	152	163	159

Solution: Calculation of 5 yearly moving averages

Year	*Income (Rs. in 000)*	*Five yearly Moving total (Rs. in 000)*	*Five yearly Moving average (Rs. in 000)*
1980	161		
1981	127		
1982	152	727	145.4
1983	143	733	146.6
1984	144	788	157.6
1985	167	815	163
1986	182	824	164.8
1987	179	843	168.6
1988	152	835	167
1989	163		
1990	159		

Illustration 6: *From the following data, related with average yearly expenditure of selected families in a village, calculate 7 years moving average.*

Year	*1977*	*78*	*79*	*80*	*81*	*82*	*83*	*84*	*85*	*86*	*87*
Expenses (Rs. in 00)	*97*	*87*	*102*	*115*	*122*	*130*	*142*	*140*	*147*	*153*	*160*

Solution: Calculation of seven yearly moving averages

Year	*Expenses (Rs. in 00s)*	*Seven yearly moving total (Rs. in 00s)*	*Seven yearly moving average (Rs. in 00s)*
1977	97		
1978	87		
1979	102		
1980	115	795	113.57
1981	122	838	119.71
1982	130	898	128.29
1983	142	949	135.57
1984	140	994	142
1985	147		
1986	153		
1987	160		

Calculation of moving averages for even periods

Moving averages may be calculated for the even periods also. While calculating moving averages for even periods like 2 years, 4 years or 6 years the placement of the moving average to a particular year is not possible. It lies between 2 years, say, between 3rd and 4th years. Hence to place the averages to respective years moving average for 2 years for the calculated moving averages for the even years should be calculated.

Illustration 7: *Calculate the four year moving average from the following data.*

Year	*Production (in tonnes)*	*Year*	*Production (in tonnes)*
1975	*33*	*1983*	*65*
1976	*44*	*1984*	*64*
1977	*57*	*1985*	*69*
1978	*20*	*1986*	*75*
1979	*15*	*1987*	*79*
1980	*39*	*1988*	*85*
1981	*35*	*1989*	*87*
1982	*55*	*1990*	*90*

Solution: Calculation of 4 yearly moving averages

Year	*Production (in tonnes)*	*4 yearly moving total*	*4 yearly moving average*	*Centred 4 yearly moving total*	*Centred 4 yearly moving average*
1975	33				
1976	44				
1977	57	154	38.5	72.5	36.25
1978	20	136	34	66.75	33.38
1979	15	131	32.75	60	30
1980	39	109	27.25	63.25	31.63
1981	35	144	36	84.5	42.25
1982	55	194	48.5	103.25	51.63
1983	65	219	54.75	118	59
1984	64	253	63.25	131.5	65.75
1985	69	273	68.25	140	70
1986	75	287	71.75	148.75	74.38
1987	79	308	77	158.5	79.25
1988	85	326	81.5	166.75	83.38
1989	87	341	85.25		
1990	90				

Illustration 8: *Calculate 6 yearly moving average from the following data and plot them in a graph paper.*

Year	*1980*	*81*	*82*	*83*	*84*	*85*	*86*	*87*	*88*	*89*	*90*
Demand (in tonnes)	*105*	*120*	*115*	*110*	*100*	*130*	*135*	*160*	*155*	*140*	*145*

Solution: Calculation of 6 yearly moving averages

Year	*Demand*	*6 yearly moving total*	*6 yearly moving average*	*Centred 6 yearly moving total*	*Centred 6 yearly moving average*
1980	105				
1981	120				
1982	115				
1983	110	680	113.3		
				231.6	115.8
1984	100	710	118.3		
				243.3	121.65
1985	130	750	125		
				256.67	128.34
1986	135	790	131.67		
				268.34	134.17
1987	160	820	136.67		
				280.84	140.42
1988	155	865	144.17		
1989	140				
1990	145				

Graph showing 6 yearly moving average

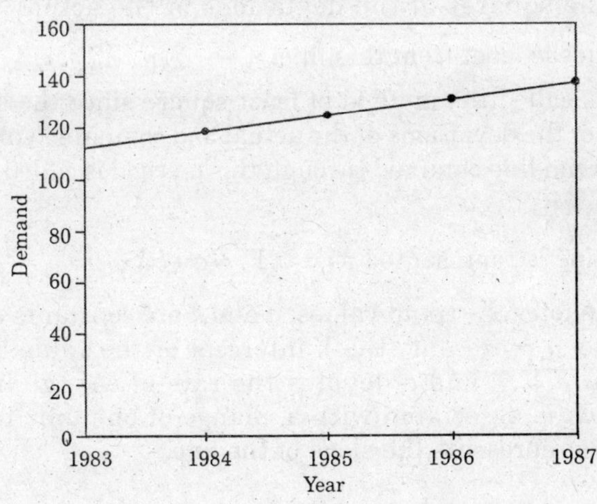

Merits

1. This method is the simplest method of measuring trend.

2. This method is flexible in nature. Eventhough few variables are added in the series the entire calculations are not changed.

3. Cyclical fluctuations are eliminated in this method due to overlapping of data for various periods.

4. The shape of the trend line is determined by data rather than the statistician.

5. This method is suitable even if the data of a series is very irregular.

Demerits

1. In this method trend values cannot be calculated for all the years. For example in 5 yearly moving average, 4 years are left out i.e., 2 years in the beginning and 2 years at the end.

2. There is no mathematical formula for selecting the period for calculating moving averages.

3. Moving average technique for calculating trend will not completely eliminate the cyclical fluctuation.

4. This method is of little use in forecasting since it is not represented by mathematical function.

(4) The method of least square: This is a popular method of obtaining trend line. Under this method, the trend line is fitted to the data so that (i) the sum of deviations of the actual value of Y and the computed values of Y is zero. *i.e.,* $\Sigma(Y - Y_c) = 0$ (ii) The sum of the squares of the deviations of the actual and computed values is least from this line. *i.e.,* $\Sigma(Y - Y_c)^2$ is least. This method is called the method of least square since the sum of the squares of the deviations of the actual and computed values is least. The trend line obtained through this method is called the line of best fit.

The trend line is represented as, $Y_c = a + bX$

Where Y_C denotes the trend values; a and b are constants and X denotes time; a represents the Y intercept or the value of Y variable when $X = 0$; and b denotes the rate of change in Y variables which is associated with a change of one unit in X variable; b also represents the slope of the line.

The value of a and b can be ascertained by solving the following two normal equations.

$$\Sigma Y = Na + b\Sigma x \qquad \ldots \text{(i)}$$

$$\Sigma XY = a\Sigma X + b\Sigma X^2 \qquad \ldots \text{(ii)}$$

Where X represents the time; Y represents the values; a and b represent constants and N represents the total number.

When the middle year is taken as the origin, then ΣX will be equal to zero. (i.e., $\Sigma X = 0$). Then the normal equations would be,

$$\Sigma XY = Na \qquad \ldots \text{(i)}$$

$$\Sigma XY = b\Sigma X^2 \qquad \ldots \text{(ii)}$$

Hence, $a = \dfrac{\Sigma Y}{N}$ and $b = \dfrac{\Sigma XY}{\Sigma X^2}$

a represents the arithmetic mean of Y, and b represents the rate of change.

When deviations are taken from the middle year as origin, ΣX would be zero, for the odd number of years. It is also possible to get $\Sigma X = 0$ for the even number of years when the origin is placed midway between two middle years. *(eg)* For even number of years like 1990, 1991, 1992, 1993, 1994, 1995 the origin should be fixed in between 1992 and 1993 as 1992.5.

Hence the deviations would be -2.5, -1.5, .5, 1.5, and 2.5.

Illustration 9: *Following are the data related with the output of a factory for 7 years.*

Year	*1980*	*1981*	*1982*	*1983*	*1984*	*1985*	*1986*
Output (in tonnes)	*47*	*64*	*77*	*88*	*97*	*109*	*113*

Calculate trend values through the method of least squares and also forecast the production in 1989 and 1991.

Solution: Calculation of trend value by the method of least squares

Year	*Production (in tonnes)* *Y*	*Deviation from 1983* *X*	*XY*	X^2	Y_C
1980	47	-3	-141	9	52
1981	64	-2	-128	4	63
1982	77	-1	-77	1	74
1983	88	0	0	0	85
1984	97	+1	+97	1	96
1985	109	+2	+218	4	107
1986	113	+3	+339	9	118
	$\Sigma Y = 595$	$\Sigma X = 0$	$\Sigma XY = 308$	$\Sigma X^2 = 28$	

$$\Sigma Y = Na + b\Sigma X$$

$$595 = 7a + 0$$

Hence, $$a = \frac{595}{7} = 85$$

$$\Sigma XY = a\Sigma X + b\Sigma X^2$$

$$308 = 0 + b \times 28$$

$$b = \frac{308}{28} = 11$$

Hence, $Y_C = a + bX$ i.e., $Y_C = 85 + 11X$

$$Y_{1980} = 85 + 11\,(-3) = 52$$

$$Y_{1981} = 85 + 11\,(-2) = 63$$

$$Y_{1982} = 85 + 11\,(-1) = 74$$

$$Y_{1983} = 85 + 11\,(0) = 85$$

$$Y_{1984} = 85 + 11\,(+1) = 96$$

$$Y_{1985} = 85 + 11\,(+2) = 107$$

$$Y_{1986} = 85 + 11\,(+3) = 118$$

Hence, the production in 1989 and 1991 can be calculated as follows.

$$Y_{1989} = 85 + 11\text{ X } = 85 + 11\,(6) = 151 \text{ units}$$

$$Y_{1991} = 85 + 11\,(9) = 184 \text{ units}$$

Illustration 10: Fit a straight line trend through the method of least squares for the following data. Also estimate the value for the year 1992.

Year	*1982*	*1983*	*1984*	*1985*	*1986*	*1987*	*1988*
Sales (in units)	*110*	*115*	*130*	*140*	*145*	*160*	*180*

Solution: Calculation of trend values

Year	*Sales* Y	*Deviations from 1985* X	XY	X^2
1982	110	-3	-330	9
1983	115	-2	-230	4
1984	130	-1	-130	1
1985	140	0	0	0
1986	145	+1	+145	1
1987	160	+2	+320	4
1988	180	+3	+540	9
	$\sum Y = 980$	$\sum X = 0$	$\sum XY = 315$	$\sum X^2 = 28$

$$Y = a + bX$$

$$\Sigma Y = Na + b\Sigma X$$

Since $\Sigma X = 0,$

$$a = \frac{\Sigma Y}{N} = \frac{980}{7} = 140$$

$$\Sigma XY = a\Sigma X + b\Sigma X^2$$

$$315 = 140 \times 0 + b \times 28$$

$$b = \frac{315}{28} = 11.25$$

Hence, $Y = 140 + 11.25X$

Estimated Sales for 1992 is, $Y_{1992} = 140 + 11.25\,(+7)$

$$= 140 + 78.75$$

$$= 219 \text{ units}$$

Calculation of straight line trend for even number of observation

Illustration 11: *From the following data, fit a straight line trend through the method of least square.*

Year	*1985*	*1986*	*1987*	*1988*	*1989*	*1990*	*1991*	*1992*
Expenditure (Rs. in '000)	*43*	*49*	*54*	*62*	*71*	*75*	*78*	*80*

Solution: Computation of a straight line trend

Year	*Expenditure (Rs. in '000)* Y	*Deviations from 1988.5* X	XY	X^2
1985	43	-3.5	-150.5	12.25
1986	49	-2.5	-122.5	6.25
1987	54	-1.5	-81	2.25
1988	62	-0.5	-31	.25
1989	71	+0.5	35.5	.25
1990	75	+1.5	112.5	2.25
1991	78	+2.5	195	6.25
1992	80	+3.5	280	12.25
	$\sum Y = 512$	$\sum X = 0$	$\sum XY = 238$	$\sum X^2 = 42$

$$\sum Y = Na + b\sum X$$

$$512 = 8a + 0$$

Hence, $$a = \frac{512}{8} = 64$$

$$\sum XY = a\sum X + b\sum X^2$$

$$238 = 0 + b \times 42$$

$$b = \frac{238}{42} = 5.67$$

Trend values are stated below.

$$Y_{1985} = 64 + 5.67\,(-3.5) = 44.15$$

$$Y_{1986} = 64 + 5.67\,(-2.5) = 49.82$$

$$Y_{1987} = 64 + 5.67\,(-1.5) = 55.5$$

$$Y_{1988} = 64 + 5.67\,(-0.5) = 61.16$$

$$Y_{1989} = 64 + 5.67\ (0.5) = 66.84$$
$$Y_{1990} = 64 + 5.67\ (1.5) = 72.5$$
$$Y_{1991} = 64 + 5.67\ (2.5) = 78.18$$
$$Y_{1992} = 64 + 5.67\ (3.5) = 83.85$$

III Measurement of seasonal variations

The economic and business activities mostly depend upon seasonal variations. The seasonal variations could not be identified when the data are expressed annually. It can be identified only when the data are expressed monthly or quarterly. For example, the sales of cool drinks for hot seasons are greater than the sales in other seasons. Hence, the sales for the whole one year compared with the sales of other years won't show much difference. It also won't explain the seasonal variations. Hence, the value for various seasons for different years should be calculated to find out the seasonal variations.

Methods of measuring seasonal variations

The important methods for measuring the seasonal variations are as follows.

(1) Simple averages method

(2) Ratio to trend method

(3) Ratio to moving average method

(4) Link relative method

(1) Simple averages method: This is the most easiest method for calculating seasonal variations. This method can be applied to monthly, bi-monthly, quarterly, half yearly etc. Under this method the individual totals for all the same months or period of all the given years should be obtained first (*Eg.*) If 4 years data are available for 12 months and, then the 12 months total for all the 4 years should be obtained. Then the average monthly total should be calculated by dividing these figures by the number of years (in the example it should be divided by 4).

Then the averages of the average of 12 months so obtained should be calculated. To ascertain the seasonal variations, index of each month or period of the individual averages connected with the month or season should be divided by the average of the averages; and then it can be multipled by 100.

To verify the correctness of the answer, find out the total of the seasonal indices so calculated and divide it by the total no. of periods (months or weeks etc). If the value is equal to 100, then the value of the seasonal indices are correct one.

Illustration 12: *Monthly sales of product X in a company for 4 years are given below.*

Months	*Production in tonnes*			
	1985	*1986*	*1987*	*1988*
January	*7*	*10*	*7*	*9*
February	*12*	*15*	*10*	*12*
March	*15*	*22*	*25*	*30*
April	*8*	*10*	*9*	*11*
May	*17*	*21*	*32*	*45*
June	*21*	*40*	*45*	*55*
July	*32*	*60*	*80*	*90*
August	*9*	*22*	*20*	*18*
September	*15*	*12*	*19*	*22*
October	*20*	*18*	*22*	*24*
November	*24*	*30*	*35*	*42*
December	*12*	*15*	*17*	*13*

Calculate seasonal variations through simple average method.

Solution: Calculation of monthly seasonal variations

Months	*1985*	*1986*	*1987*	*1988*	*Total*	*Average (col.6/4)*	*Seasonal Index*
January	7	10	7	9	33	8.25	34.23
February	12	15	10	10	47	11.75	48.75
March	15	22	25	30	92	23	95.43
April	8	10	9	11	38	9.5	39.4
May	17	21	32	45	115	28.75	119.29
June	21	40	45	55	161	40.25	167
July	32	60	80	90	262	65.5	271.78
August	9	22	20	18	69	17.25	71.57
September	15	12	19	22	68	17	70.54
October	20	18	22	24	84	21	87.14
November	24	30	35	42	131	32.75	135.89
December	12	15	17	13	57	14.25	59.13

Average of the averages = 289.25/12
= 24.1

Illustration 13: *Calculate seasonal index from the following data.*

Year	*Sales (in units)*			
	1st quarter	*2nd quarter*	*3rd quarter*	*4th quarter*
1987	*48*	*40*	*90*	*80*
1988	*77*	*35*	*100*	*90*
1989	*80*	*50*	*115*	*115*
1990	*100*	*60*	*125*	*118*
1991	*120*	*70*	*130*	*122*

Solution: Calculation of seasonal indices

Year	*Sales (in units)*			
	1st quarter	*2nd quarter*	*3rd quarter*	*4th quarter*
1987	48	40	90	80
1988	77	35	100	90
1989	80	50	115	115
1990	100	60	125	118
1991	120	70	130	122
Total	425	255	560	525
Average	85	51	112	105
Seasonal index	96.3	57.8	126.9	119

$$\text{Average of average} = \frac{85+51+112+105}{4} = \frac{353}{4} = 88.25$$

$$\text{Seasonal Index} = \frac{\text{Quarterly Average}}{\text{Average of averages}} \times 100$$

$$\text{Seasonal Index for the 1nd Quarter} = \frac{85}{88.25} \times 100 = 96.3$$

$$\text{Seasonal Index for the 2nd Quarter} = \frac{51}{88.25} \times 100 = 57.8$$

$$\text{Seasonal Index for the 3rd Quarter} = \frac{112}{88.25} \times 100 = 126.9$$

$$\text{Seasonal Index for the 4th Quarter} = \frac{105}{88.25} \times 100 = 119$$

The above table can also be represented through the following method.

Sales	Years					Five yearly Total	Five yearly average	Seasonal variation index
	1987	1988	1989	1990	1991			
1st quarter	48	77	80	100	120	425	85	96.3
2nd quarter	40	35	50	60	70	225	51	57.8
3rd quarter	90	100	115	125	130	560	112	126.9
4th quarter	80	90	115	118	122	525	105	119

Five yearly total of averages = 353

Five yearly average of averages = 353 / 4

= 88.25

Merits

This method is a simple and easiest method of measuring seasonal variation.

Limitations

1. The assumption that there is no trend component in the series, is not a reasonable assumption.

2. The effects of cyclical periods on the original values may or may not be eliminated by the process of averaging.

(2) Ratio to trend method: This method is an improvement over the method of simple average method. It assumes that seasonal variation for a given month is constant fraction of trend. Under this method the trend is eliminated when the ratios are calculated. This method isolates the seasonal factors as follows.

$$\frac{T \times S \times C \times I}{T} = S \times C \times I$$

where, T - Trend, S - Seasonal fractor

C - Cyclical factor I - Irregular factor

The steps for calculating seasonal index under this method are as follows.

1. First of all, the trend values should be calculated through the method of least squares.

2. Then, divide the actual data for all periods (months or quarter) by the corresponding trend values. These values must be multiplied with 100. These values are free from trend.

3. The next step is to free these values from irregular and cyclical movements also.

The values so obtained, for the various years of the periods (months or quarters) should be averaged either by mean or by median.

4. The sum of the average values of the periods should be equal to 1200 if the periods represent months. It should be equal to 400, if the periods represent quarters. If it is not equal to 1200, then each average value should be multiplied by,

$$\frac{1200}{\text{Sum of the 12 values}} \text{ (when the periods represent months)}$$

If it is not equal to 400, then each average values should be multiplied by,

$$\frac{400}{\text{Sum of the 4 values}} \text{ (when the periods represent quarters)}$$

Illustration 14: *Calculate seasonal index on the basis of ratio-to-trend method from the following data.*

Periods	*Production (in tonnes)*					
	1987	*1988*	*1989*	*1990*	*1991*	*1992*
I quarter	*100*	*110*	*104*	*110*	*115*	*150*
II quarter	*70*	*75*	*90*	*95*	*120*	*120*
III quarter	*30*	*50*	*80*	*90*	*105*	*130*
IV quarter	*40*	*85*	*86*	*105*	*140*	*160*

Solution: Calculation of trend through the method of least squares

Year	*Total yearly production*	*Quarterly average Y*	*Deviation from X*	*XY*	X^2	*Trend value*
1987	240	60	-2.5	-150	6.25	60
1988	320	80	-1.5	-120	2.25	76
1989	360	90	-0.5	-45	.25	91
1990	400	100	+0.5	50	.25	106
1991	480	120	+1.5	180	2.25	121
1992	560	140	+2.5	350	6.25	136
		$\sum Y = 590$	$\sum X = 0$	$\sum XY = 265$	$\sum X^2 = 17.5$	

$$Y = a + bX$$
$$\Sigma Y = Na + b\Sigma X$$
$$590 = 6a + 0$$
$$a = \frac{590}{6} = 98.33$$
$$\Sigma XY = a\Sigma X + b\Sigma X^2$$
$$265 = 0 + (b \times 17.5)$$
$$b = \frac{265}{17.5} = 15.14$$
$$Y = 98.33 + 15.14X$$

Calculation of yearly trend values

1987	Y = 98.33 + 15.14 (-2.5) = 60.48 = 60
1988	Y = 98.33 + 15.14 (-1.5) = 75.62 = 76
1989	Y = 98.33 + 15.14 (-0.5) = 90.76 = 91
1990	Y = 98.33 + 15.14 (0.5) = 105.9 = 106
1991	Y = 98.33 + 15.14 (1.5) = 121.04 = 121
1992	Y = 98.33 + 15.14 (2.5) = 136.18 = 136
	590

Calculation of Quarterly Trend Values

Quarterly increment = 12/4 = 3

(Eg) Trend value for 1987 = 60

Trend value for II quarter = 60 – 3/2 = 60 – 1.5 = 58.5

Trend value for III quarter = 60 + 3/2 = 60 + 1.5 = 61.5

Trend value for I quarter = 58.5 – 3 = 55.5

Trend value for IV quarter = 61.5 + 3 = 64.5

The quarterly trend values have been stated as below.

Trend values

Year	*1st Quarter*	*2nd Quarter*	*3rd Quarter*	*4th Quarter*
1987	55.5	58.5	61.5	64.5
1988	71.5	74.5	77.5	80.5
1989	86.5	89.5	92.5	95.5
1990	101.5	104.5	107.5	110.5
1991	116.5	119.5	122.5	125.5
1992	131.5	134.5	137.5	140.5

Quarterly Values as Percentage of Trend Values

Year	*1st Quarter*	*2nd Quarter*	*3rd Quarter*	*4th Quarter*
1987	180.1	119.7	48.8	62
1988	153.8	100.7	64.5	105.6
1989	120.2	100.6	86.5	90.1
1990	108.4	90.9	83.7	95
1991	98.7	100.4	85.7	111.6
1992	114	89.2	94.5	113.9
Total	775.2	601.5	463.7	578.2
Average	129.2	100.3	77.3	96.4
Adjusted Seasonal Index	128.2	99.5	76.7	95.6

Total of averages = 129.2 + 100.3 + 77.3 + 96.4 = 403.2

Since the total is not equal to 400 an adjustment is made by multiplying each average by 400/403.2

Merits

1. This method is more rational when compared to other methods of calculating seasonal indices.

2. Unlike the moving average method, this method won't exclude the extreme values.

3. This method gives trend values for all the seasons. Hence, it can be applied even for the calculation of trend values for a short period.

Demerits

1. This method requires complex mathematical calculations.

2. The cyclical variations affect the result obtained under this method.

(3) Ratio to Moving Average Method: This method is also known as the percentage of moving average method. This method is the most commonly used method for measuring seasonal variations. The important steps for measuring seasonal variations are as follows.

1. The seasonal variations should be eliminated by taking a centered moving average with a period of 12 months, if monthly data are available.

If quarterly data are available, a centered 4 quarter moving average must be used. This moving averages will also eliminate irregular movements.

2. Calculate the ratios of original data to the corresponding moving averages. It should be expressed in percentage i.e.,

$$\frac{\text{Actual value}}{\text{Moving Average}} \times 100$$

3. These percentages are then arranged by months and the average for each month is calculated. The total of these averages should be equai to 1200. If it is not equal to 1200 then each average value should be multiplied by, $\frac{1200}{\text{Sum of the 12 values}}$

If the periods represent quarters the total of the 4 averages should be equal to 400. If it is not equal to 400, then each average values should be multiplied by, $\frac{400}{\text{Sum of the 4 values}}$

Illustration 15: *Find out seasonal indices through the "ratio to moving average method" for the data given below.*

Year	*1st Quarter*	*2nd Quarter*	*3rd Quarter*	*4th Quarter*
1988	*25*	*13*	*14*	*18*
1989	*30*	*6*	*8*	*20*
1990	*36*	*4*	*12*	*25*
1991	*40*	*5*	*15*	*30*

Solution: Computation of Seasonal Indices.

Year	*Quarter*	*Variables*	*Moving Total for 4 figures*	*Moving Totals for 2 figures*	*Moving Average for 4 figure*	*% of Moving Average*
1988	I	25				
	II	13				
	III	14	70	145	18.13	77.22
	IV	18	75	143	17.88	100.67
1989	I	30	68	130	16.25	184.61
	II	6	62	126	15.75	38.1
	III	8	64	134	16.75	47.76
	IV	20	70	138	17.25	115.94
1990	I	36	68	140	17.5	205.71
	II	4	72	149	18.63	21.47
	III	12	77	158	19.75	60.76
	IV	25	81	163	20.38	122.67
1991	I	40	82	167	20.88	191.57
	II	5	85	175	21.88	22.85
	III	15	90			
	IV	30				

Computation of Seasonal Indices

Year	*Percentage to moving average*			
	1st Quarter	*2nd Quarter*	*3rd Quarter*	*4th Quarter*
1988	–	–	77.22	100.67
1989	184.61	38.1	47.76	115.94
1990	205.71	21.47	60.76	122.67
1991	191.57	22.85	–	–
Total	581.89	82.42	185.74	339.28
Average	193.96	27.47	61.91	113.09
Seasonal Index	195.7	27.7	62.5	114.1

$$\text{Total of averages} = 193.96 + 27.47 + 61.91 + 113.09$$
$$= 396.43$$

Since the total is not equal to 400 an adjustment is done by multiplying each average by, $\frac{400}{396.43} \times 100$

Merits

1. This method is the most widely used method for calculating seasonal variations.

2. The seasonal index calculated under this method does not fluctuate like other methods.

3. The cyclical variations won't affect much of the calculation of the seasonal index under this method.

Demerits

1. In this method the seasonal indices cannot be calculated for all the months even though the data are available.

2. The values of the months at the two extremes are left out, in this method.

(4) Link Relatives Method: This method is the most difficult one among the methods of measuring seasonal variation. The following are the important steps for calculating seasonal variations under this method.

1. Calculate the link relatives for the given values for different seasons. It can be calculated as, $\frac{\text{Current Season's figure}}{\text{Previous Season's figure}} \times 100$

These link relatives, link each month to preceding month, or link each quarter to preceding quarter.

2. Arrange the link relatives by months or quarters. Average value of the link relatives for the season (months or quarters) should be calculated, on the basis of mean or median.

3. Convert these averages into Chain Relatives on the basis of the first season (month or quarter). The chain relative of the 1st quarter will be equal to 100. The chain relative for the 2nd quarter will be,

$$\frac{\text{C.R of the 1st quarter} \times \text{L.R arithmetic mean of the 2nd quarter}}{100}$$

The chain relative of the third quarter will be,

$$\frac{\text{C.R of the 2nd quarter} \times \text{L.R arithmetic mean of the 3rd quarter}}{100}$$

The chain relative of the fourth quarter will be,

$$\frac{\text{C.R of the 3rd quarter} \times \text{L.R arithmetic mean of the 4th quarter}}{100}$$

4. Then calculate the chain relative of the first quarter, for correction, as,

$$\frac{\text{1st quarter L.R} \times \text{4th quarter C.R}}{100}$$

The difference between the chain relative of 1st quarter taken previously and calculated now should be divided by the number of seasons. The resulting figure should be multiplied by 1, 2 and 3 respectively. Then the product so obtained should be deducted respectively from the chain relatives of 2nd, 3rd and 4th quarters. These are called the corrected chain relatives.

5. The corrected chain relatives should be represented in percentage to give the seasonal indices.

Illustration 16: *Calculate seasonal indices by link relatives method, for the following data.*

Quarters	*Sales (Rs. in '000)*				
	1990	*1991*	*1992*	*1993*	*1994*
I Quarter	8.2	6.3	7.8	8.4	6.7
II Quarter	9.4	8.4	7.6	6.8	8.4
III Quarter	7.6	9.5	9.5	8.5	8.0
IV Quarter	9.8	8.3	7.7	9.5	9.0

Solution: Calculation of Seasonal Indices by Link Relatives Method.

Year	*Quarters*			
	1st Quarter	*2nd Quarter*	*3rd Quarter*	*4th Quarter*
1990	-	114.6	80.9	128.9
1991	64.3	133.3	113.1	87.4
1992	94.0	97.4	125.0	81.1
1993	109.1	81.0	125.0	111.8
1994	70.5	125.4	95.2	112.5
Total	337.9	551.7	539.2	521.7
Average	84.5	110.3	107.8	104.3
Chain Relative	100	$\frac{100\times110.3}{100}$ $= 110.3$	$\frac{110.3\times107.8}{100}$ $= 118.9$	$\frac{118.9\times104.3}{100}$ $= 124$
Corrected Chain Relatives	100	$110.3 - 1.2$ $= 109.1$	$118.9 - 1.2$ $= 117.7$	$124 - 1.2$ $= 122.8$
Seasonal Indices	$\frac{100}{112.4}\times100$ $= 88.9$	$\frac{109.1}{112.4}\times100$ $= 97.1$	$\frac{117.7}{112.4}\times100$ $= 104.7$	$\frac{122.8}{112.4}\times100$ $= 109.3$

The correction factor has been calculated as follows.

Chain relative of the first quarter

(on the basis of first quarter) = 100

Chain relative of the first quarter

(on the basis of the last quarter) $= \frac{84.5\times124}{100} = 104.78$

The difference between these chain relatives,

$$= 104.78 - 100 = 4.78$$

Hence, the difference per quarter, $= \frac{4.78}{4} = 1.195$ i.e., $= 1.2$

Seasonal variation indices have been calculated as follows.

Average of corrected chain relatives

$$= \frac{100+109.1+117.7+122.8}{4} = \frac{449.6}{4} = 112.4$$

$$\text{Seasonal variation index} = \frac{\text{Correct chain relatives} \times 100}{112.4}$$

IV Non - linear Trends

The linear trend is concerned with the measure of the nature of variable in future period, by taking into consideration of the increase or decrease of the variable over the period of past few years. It states that the variable in the future may increase or decrease on the basis of the same rate of increase or decrease in the past periods. But it does not take into account the long-term growth of an industry. The non-linear trend is a measure of trend value by taking into account of the long term growth of the industry.

Non-linear trend can be obtained with the help of **Second Degree Parabola.**

The equation for the second degree parabola is

$$y = a + bx + cx^2$$

The values of the constants a, b and c can be obtained by solving the following three normal equations.

$$\sum y = Na + b\sum X + c\sum X^2$$

$$\sum XY = a\sum X + b\sum X^2 = c\sum X^3$$

$$\sum X^2Y = a\sum X^2 + b\sum X^3 + c\sum X^4$$

Illustration 17: *The annual percentage of increse in a sales of a company is stated below.*

1990	*1991*	*1992*	*1993*	*1994*
20.5	*25.4*	*32.6*	*37.3*	*41.2*

Fit a parabolic curve to the data and also estimate the percentage increase for the year 1996.

Solution: Calculation of the equation for parabolic curve.

Year	*Values* *Y*	*X* *Year-1992*	*XY*	X^2	X^2Y	X^3	X^4
1990	20.5	-2	-41	4	82	-8	16
1991	25.4	-1	-25.4	1	25.4	-1	1
1992	32.6	0	0	0	0	0	0
1993	37.3	1	37.3	1	37.3	1	1
1994	41.2	2	82.4	4	164.8	8	16
N = 5	$\sum Y = 157.0$	$\sum X = 0$	$\sum XY = 53.3$	$\sum X^2 = 10$	$\sum X^2Y = 309.5$	$\sum X^3 = 0$	$\sum X^4 = 34$

The equation of parabola curve is, $y = a + bx + cx^2$

The value of constants can be calculated with the help of the following normal equation,

$$\sum Y = Na + b\sum x + cx^2$$

$$\sum XY = a\sum x + b\sum x^2 + c\sum x^3$$

$$\sum X^2Y = a\sum x^2 + b\sum x^3 + c\sum x^4$$

Hence, $157 = 5a + (0 \times b) + 10c$ .... (i)

$53.3 = (a \times 0) + 10b + (0 \times c)$ .... (ii)

$309.5 = 10a + (b \times 0) + 34c$ .... (iii)

i.e., $157 = 5a + 10c$ .... (i)

$53.3 = 10b$ .... (ii)

$309.5 = 10a + 34c$ .... (iii)

$$b = \frac{53.3}{10} = 5.33$$

(i) $\times$ 2 $314 = 10a + 20c$ . . . (iv)

$309.5 = 10a + 34c$ . . . (iii)

$4.5 = - 14c$

$$c = -\frac{4.5}{14} = -0.32$$

$314 = 10a + 20 (-0.32)$

$10a = 314 + 6.4$

$10a = 320.4$

$$a = \frac{320.4}{10} = 32.04$$

Therefore the parabolic curve equation is,

$$y = 32.8 + 5.33 \times - 0.32 \text{ x } 2$$

Increase in the year 1996 is (x = 1996 - 1992 = 4)

$$y = 32.8 + (5.33 \times 4) - 0.32(4)^2$$

$$= 32.8 + 21.32 - 5.12 = 49$$

Shifting the Origin

The origin of the linear and non-linear trend equations can be shifted backward or forward. When the base is shifted forward, in the place of X it should be $X + k$ (where k is the number of years from the original base to the new base). When the base is shifted backward, in the place of X it should be $X - k$.

Hence, the new trend equations for shifting the base are,

$$y = a + b(x + k) \quad \text{and} \quad y = a + b(x + k) + c(x + k)^2$$

Illustration 18: *When the trend equation, $y = 15 + 1.5x$ with 1990 as base, find the trend equation with 1993 as new base.*

Solution: $y = a + b(x+k) \qquad k = 1993 - 1990 = 3$

$y = 15 + 1.5(x+3)$

$y = 15 + 1.5x + 4.5$

$y = 19.5 + 1.5x$

Illustration 19: *Given the trend equation $y = 50 + 10x + 3x^2$; Origin is 1990; x unit = 1 year; Shift the origin of the equation to 1995.*

Solution: $k = 1995 - 1990 = 5$

$y = a + b(x+k) + c(x+k)^2$

$y = a + 10(x+k) + 3(x+5)^2$

$y = 50 + 10(x+5) + 3(x+5)^2$

$y = 50 + 10x + 50 + 3(x^2 + 10x + 25)$

$y = 50 + 10x + 50 + 3x^2 + 30x + 75$

$y = 175 + 40x + 3x^2$

Illustration 20: *Shift the origin for this following equation from 1990 to 1985, $y = 32 + 10X - 2X^2$ (x unit = 1 year)*

Solution: $k = 1985 - 1990 = -5$

$y = a + b(x+k) + c(x+k)^2$

$y = 32 + 10(x - 5) + 2(x - 5)^2$

$y = 32 + 10x - 50 + 2(x^2 - 10x + 25)$

$= 32 + 10x - 50 + 2x^2 - 20x + 50$

$= 32 - 10x + 2x^2$

V De-Seasonalisation

Deseasonalisation of data means elimination of the seasonal effects from the given values. Seasonal fluctuations are assumed that they won't occur in future. Deseasonalisation of data can be done for the Multiplication Model as well as Addition Model.

De-Seasonalisation of Data for Multiplication Model

$$\text{Deseasonalised Data} = \frac{0}{S} = \frac{TCSI}{S} = TCI$$

where, O represents any observed value

S represents seasonal variation

I represents irregular variation

T represents trend value

C represents cyclic variation.

De-Seasonalisation of data for Addition Model

The deseasonalisation data can be calculated by deducting the seasonal variation for the observed value.

Deseasonalised data = $O - S = T + C + I$

Illustration 21: *The seasonal indices of profit of a company are stated below:*

Quarter	*I*	*II*	*III*	*IV*
Seasonal Indices	*87*	*80*	*75*	*120*

If the profit of the company in the I Quarter is Rs 120,000. Find out the expected profit of the company in the remaining Quarters.

Solution: Profit in I Quarter = Rs 120,000

(When there is a seasonal index,)

The normal profit when there is no seasonal effect

$$= 120{,}000 \div 87/100 = \text{Rs } 137931$$

Hence, the estimated profit for other 3 quarters can be calculated as follows.

Quarter	*Seasonal Index*	*Seasonal Effect*	*Estimated Profit (Rs.)*
II	80	0.80	$137931 \times 0.8 = 110345$
III	75	0.75	$137931 \times 0.75 = 103{,}448$
IV	120	1.20	$137931 \times 1.2 = 165517$

Illustration 22: *The seasonal indices of sales of a company are as follows.*

Month	*Seasonal Index*
Jan	*77*
Feb	*80*
March	*85*
April	*90*
May	*120*
June	*127*
July	*130*
August	*135*
Sep	*102*
Oct	*105*
Nov	*90*
Dec	*80*

The estimated average monthly sales of the company is Rs 500,000. Find out the monthly sales budget of the company.

Solution: Monthly Sales Budget.

Month (1)	*Seasonal Index* (2)	*Seasonal Effect* (3)	*Estimated Sales (Rs.)* *(3)* X *500,000* (4)
Jan	77	0.77	385,000
Feb	80	0.80	400,000
March	85	0.85	425,000
April	90	0.90	450,000
May	120	1.20	600,000
June	127	1.27	635,000
July	130	1.30	650,000
August	135	1.35	675,000
Sep	102	1.02	510,000
Oct	105	1.05	525,000
Nov	90	0.90	450,000
Dec	80	0.80	400,000
Total	1221	12.21	61,05,000

Miscellaneous Illustrations

Illustration 23: *Draw a trend line by the method of semi-average method, from the following data.*

Year	*1990*	*1991*	*1992*	*1993*	*1994*	*1995*	*1996*
Sales in (tonnes)	*75*	*95*	*120*	*150*	*210*	*230*	*250*

Solution: Calculation of trend value by the method of semi-average.

Year		*Sales (in tonnes)*
1990	75	$\frac{290}{3} = 96.67$
1991	95	
1992	120	
1993	150	$\frac{690}{3} = 230$
1994	210	
1995	230	
1996	250	

Trend Line by Method of Semi-Average

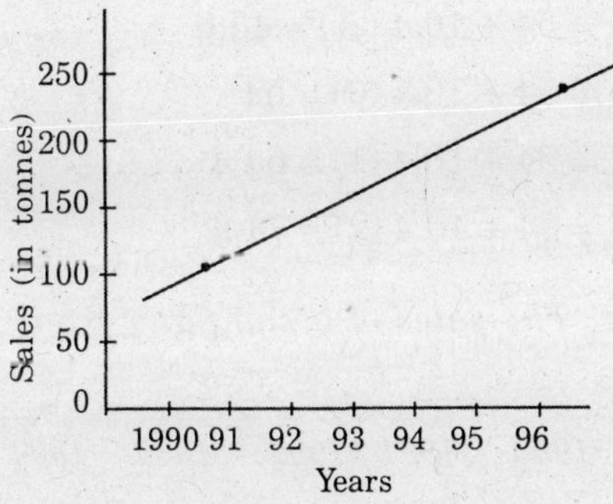

Illustration 24: *Fit a straight line trend for the following data.*

Year	*1992*	*1993*	*1994*	*1995*	*1996*
Profit (Rs. in '0000)	*32*	*45*	*55*	*63*	*75*

Solution: Fitting straight line trend.

Year	Profit (Rs. in '0000) Y	X	XY	X^2	Y_c	$Y - Y_c$
1992	32	-2	-64	4	33.2	-1.2
1993	45	-1	-45	1	43.6	1.4
1994	55	0	0	0	54	1
1995	63	1	63	1	64.4	-1.4
1996	75	2	150	4	74.8	0.2
$N = 5$	$\sum Y = 270$	$\sum X = 0$	$\sum XY = 104$	$\sum X^2 = 10$		

$$Y_c = a + bX$$

$$a = \frac{\Sigma Y}{N} = \frac{270}{5} = 54$$

$$b = \frac{\Sigma XY}{N} = \frac{104}{10} = 10.4$$

Hence, $Y = 54 + 10.4\,X$

$$Y_{1992} = 54 + 10.4\,(-2) = 33.2$$

$$Y_{1993} = 54 + 10.4\,(-1) = 43.6$$

$$Y_{1994} = 54 + 10.4\,(0) = 54$$

$$Y_{1995} = 54 + 10.4\,(1) = 64.4$$

$$Y_{1996} = 54 + 10.4\,(2) = 74.8$$

Illustration 25: *The sales of a company from 1990-1996 are stated below.*

Year	*1990*	*1991*	*1992*	*1993*	*1994*	*1995*	*1996*
Sales (in '000 tonnes)	*47*	*57*	*62*	*75*	*84*	*88*	*97*

Fit a straight line trend by the method of least square and tabulate the trend values. Also calculate (i) the sales for 1999 (ii) the monthly increase in sales of the company.

Solution: Fitting a Straight Line Trend.

Year	*Sales (in '000 tonnes)* Y	*Deviation from 1993* X	XY	X^2	*Trend Values*
1990	47	-3	-141	9	54.69
1991	57	-2	-114	4	60.47
1992	62	-1	-62	1	66.25
1993	75	0	0	0	72.03
1994	84	1	84	1	77.81
1995	88	2	176	4	83.59
1996	97	3	291	9	95.15
$N = 7$	$\sum Y = 510$	$\sum X = 0$	$\sum XY = 234$	$\sum X^2 = 28$	

The equation for straight line trend is, $Y_c = a + bX$

The values of a and b can be obtained by solving the two normal equations.

$$\sum Y = Na + b\sum X$$

$$510 = 7a + b0$$

$$\therefore \quad a = \frac{510}{7} = 72.86$$

$$\sum XY = a\sum X + b\sum X^2$$

$$234 = a.0 + b.28$$

$$\therefore \quad b = \frac{234}{28} = 8.4$$

Hence, $Y_c = 72.86 + 5.4X$

Trend Value, $Y_{90} = 72.86 + 5.4\,(-3) = 47.66$

$Y_{91} = 72.86 + 5.4\,(-2) = 56$

$Y_{92} = 72.86 + 5.4\,(-1) = 64.46$

$Y_{93} = 72.86 + 5.4\,(0) = 72.86$

$Y_{94} = 72.86 + 5.4\,(1) = 81.26$

$Y_{95} = 72.86 + 5.4\,(2) = 89.66$

$Y_{96} = 72.86 + 5.4\,(3) = 98.1$

Total 510

(i) Sales for 1999 is, $Y_{99} = 72.86 + 5.78\ (6) = 105.3$

(ii) Monthly increase in sales of the company is,

$$\frac{b}{12} = \frac{5.4}{12} = 0.45$$

Illustration 26: *Fit a straight line trend on the basis of a parabolic curve of the second degree for the following data.*

Year	*1993*	*1994*	*1995*	*1996*	*1997*
Profit (Rs. in '0000)	*12*	*18*	*20*	*25*	*30*

Also estimate the profit for the year 2000.

Solution: Calculation of Second Degree Parabola.

Year	*Profit*	*X*	*XY*	X^2	X^2Y	X^4
1993	12	-2	-24	4	48	16
1994	18	-1	-18	1	18	1
1995	20	0	0	0	0	0
1996	25	1	25	1	25	1
1997	30	2	60	4	120	16
N = 5	$\Sigma Y = 105$	$\Sigma X = 0$	$\Sigma XY = 43$	$\Sigma X^2 = 10$	$\Sigma X^2Y = 211$	$\Sigma X^4 = 34$

The second degree parabola equation is,

$$Y = a + bX + cX^2$$

The values of a, b and c can be calculated as follows.

$$b = \frac{\Sigma XY}{\Sigma X^2} = \frac{43}{10} = 4.3$$

$$c = \frac{N\Sigma X^2Y - \Sigma X^2\,\Sigma Y}{N\Sigma X^4 - \left(\Sigma X^2\right)^2} = \frac{5(211) - 10(105)}{5(34) - (10)^2} = 0.07$$

$$a = \frac{\Sigma Y - c\,\Sigma X^2}{N} = \frac{105 - 10(0.07)}{5} = 20.86$$

Hence, $Y = 20.86 + 4.3\,X + 0.07\,X^2$

Profit for the year 2000 is,

$$Y_{2000} = 20.86 + 4.3\,(5) + 0.07\,(5)^2$$

$$= 20.86 + 21.5 + 1.75 = 44.11$$

i.e., Rs. 441100

Illustration 27: *The seasonal indices of sales of a company for four quarters of a year are 100, 110, 90 and 160. Calculate sales for the year, if the sales in the first quarter is Rs. 45,000.*

Solution: Calculation of Sales in various quarters.

Quarter	*Seasonal Index*	*Estimated Sales (Rs.)*
I	100	45,000
II	110	49,500
III	90	40,500
IV	160	72,000

Sales for 2nd quarter,

$$= \frac{\text{Sales in I Quarter}}{\text{S.I for I Quarter}} \times \text{S.I in IInd Quarter}$$

$$= \frac{45000}{100} \times 100 = \text{Rs. } 49500$$

Sales for 3rd quarter,

$$= \frac{\text{Sales in I Quarter}}{\text{S.I for I Quarter}} \times \text{S.I in IIIrd Quarter}$$

$$= \frac{45000}{100} \times 90 = \text{Rs. } 40500$$

Sales for 4th quarter,

$$= \frac{\text{Sales in I Quarter}}{\text{S.I for I Quarter}} \times \text{S.I in IVrd Quarter}$$

$$= \frac{45000}{100} \times 160 = \text{Rs. } 72000$$

Illustration 28: *Find out, if there is any seasonality in the following data.*

Year	*I Quarter*	*II Quarter*	*III Quarter*	*IV Quarter*
1993	*4.3*	*5.2*	*3.2*	*4.8*
1994	*4.9*	*5.1*	*3.7*	*4.5*
1995	*5.2*	*4.9*	*3.9*	*4.3*
1996	*4.8*	*5.7*	*3.5*	*4.1*
1997	*4.7*	*5.9*	*4.1*	*3.9*

Also calculate the seasonal indices for various quarters.

Solution: Calculation of Seasonal Indices

Year	1st Quarter	2nd Quarter	3rd Quarter	4th Quarter
1993	4.3	5.2	3.2	4.8
1994	4.9	5.1	3.7	4.5
1995	5.2	4.9	3.9	4.3
1996	4.8	5.7	3.5	4.1
1997	4.7	5.9	4.1	3.9
Total	23.9	26.8	18.4	21.6
Average	4.78	5.36	3.68	4.32
Seasonal Index	105.4	118.2	81.14	95.26

$$\text{Average of averages} = \frac{4.78 + 5.36 + 3.68 + 4.32}{4}$$

$$= \frac{18.14}{4} = 4.535$$

$$\text{Seasonal Index} = \frac{\text{Quarterly Average}}{\text{General average}} \times 100$$

$$\text{Seasonal Index for 1st Quarter} = \frac{4.78}{4.535} \times 100 = 105.4$$

$$\text{Seasonal Index for 2nd Quarter} = \frac{5.36}{4.535} \times 100 = 118.2$$

$$\text{Seasonal Index for 3rd Quarter} = \frac{3.68}{4.535} \times 100 = 81.14$$

$$\text{Seasonal Index for 4th Quarter} = \frac{4.32}{4.535} \times 100 = 95.26$$

Illustration 29: *Fit a straight line trend for the following data.*

Year	*1990*	*1991*	*1992*	*1993*	*1994*	*1995*	*1996*
Production (in '000 tonnes)	*44*	*50*	*57*	*65*	*72*	*85*	*94*

Find out, (i) the estimated production in 2005, (ii) the revised trend equation by shifting the origin to 1995 and, (iii) the monthly trend equation.

Solution: Fitting straight line trend by the method of least square.

Year	*Production (in '000 tonnes)* *Y*	*X*	*XY*	X^2	*Trend Values* Y_c
1990	44	-3	-132	9	41.53
1991	50	-2	-100	4	49.92
1992	57	-1	-57	1	58.31
1993	65	0	0	0	66.7
1994	72	1	72	1	75.09
1995	85	2	170	4	83.48
1996	94	3	282	9	91.87
$N = 7$	$\sum Y = 467$	$\sum X = 0$	$\sum XY = 235$	$\sum X^2 = 28$	

$$Y = a + bX$$

$$a = \frac{\sum Y}{N} = \frac{467}{7} = 66.7$$

$$b = \frac{\sum XY}{\sum X^2} = \frac{235}{28} = 8.39$$

$$Y = 66.7 + 8.39\,X$$

$$Y_{90} = 66.7 + 8.39\,(-3) = 41.53$$

$$Y_{91} = 66.7 + 8.39\,(-2) = 49.92$$

$$Y_{92} = 66.7 + 8.39\,(-1) = 58.31$$

$$Y_{93} = 66.7 + 8.39\,(0) = 66.7$$

$$Y_{94} = 66.7 + 8.39\,(1) = 75.09$$

$$Y_{95} = 66.7 + 8.39\,(2) = 83.48$$

$$Y_{96} = 66.7 + 8.39\,(3) = 91.87$$

(i) Calculation of estimated production for 2005 is,

$$X = 2005 - 1993 = 12$$

$$Y_{2005} = 66.7 + 8.39\,(12) = 167.38$$

i.e., 167,380 tonnes.

(ii) Shifting the trend origin to 1995.

Trend equation for shifting the origin is,

$$Y_c = a + b(X+k)$$

When, the origin is shifted to 1995 from 1993 the new origin is 2 years forward i.e., $k = 2$.

Hence, the revised trend equation is,

$$Y_c = 66.7 + 8.39\,(X+2)$$

$$= 66.7 + 16.78 + 8.39\,X$$

$$Y_c = 83.48 + 8.39\,X$$

(iii) Conversion of annual trend equation to monthly trend equation.

The conversion formula is,

$$Y_c = \frac{a}{12} + \frac{b}{144}X$$

$$= \frac{66.7}{12} + \frac{8.39}{144}X = 5.56 + 0.06X$$

Illustration 30: *Calculate seasonal indices on the basis of Link Relative method from the following data.*

Quarters	*Years*				
	1990	*1991*	*1992*	*1993*	*1994*
I Quarter	*35*	*45*	*52*	*65*	*72*
II Quarter	*42*	*57*	*65*	*72*	*84*
III Quarter	*56*	*64*	*74*	*84*	*92*
IV Quarter	*75*	*80*	*90*	*95*	*98*

Solution: Calculation of Seasonal Indices by Link Relatives Method.

Year	Quarters 1st Quarter	2nd Quarter	3rd Quarter	4th Quarter
1990	–	120.00	133.33	133.93
1991	60.00	126.67	112.28	125.00
1992	65.00	125.00	113.85	121.62
1993	72.22	110.77	116.67	113.10
1994	75.79	116.67	109.52	106.52
Total	273.01	599.11	585.65	600.17
Average	68.25	119.82	117.13	120.03
Chain Relative	100	$\frac{119.82\times100}{100}$ = 119.82	$\frac{117.13\times119.82}{100}$ = 140.35	$\frac{120.03\times140.35}{100}$ = 168.46
Corrected chain Relatives	100	119.82 – 3.75 = 116.07	140.35 – 3.75 = 136.6	168.46 – 3.75 = 164.71
SeasonalIndex	$\frac{100}{129.35}\times100$ = 77.3	$\frac{116.07}{129.35}\times100$ = 89.7	$\frac{136.6}{129.35}\times100$ = 105.6	$\frac{164.71}{129.35}\times100$ = 127.3

$$\text{Link Relative} = \frac{\text{Current Quarters Value}}{\text{Previous Quarters Value}}\times100$$

$$\text{Chain Relative} = \frac{\text{Average Link Relative of a Quarters} \times \text{Chain Relative of Previous Quarter}}{100}$$

Calculation of Correction Factor

Chain Relative for I Quarter (on the basis of IV Quarter),

$$= \frac{68.25\times168.46}{100} = 115$$

Chain relative for I Quarter

(on the basis of I Quarter) = 100

The difference between these chain relatives,

$$= 115 - 100 = 15$$

Hence, correction factor, $= \frac{15}{4} = 3.75$

Average of corrected chain relatives,

$$= \frac{100 + 116.07 + 136.6 + 164.71}{4}$$

$$= \frac{517.38}{4} = 129.35$$

$$\text{Seasonal Index} = \frac{\text{Correct Chain Relatives}}{\text{Averages of Corrected Chain Relatives}} \times 100$$

Illustration 31: *Plot the following data on a graph paper and ascertain trend by the method of semi-average.*

Year	*1990*	*1991*	*1992*	*1993*	*1994*	*1995*	*1996*
Production(in million tonnes)	*100*	*120*	*95*	*105*	*108*	*102*	*112*

(MGU: Section B April 98)

Solution:

Year	*Production*	*Semi-Average*
1990	100	
1991	120	315/3=105
1992	95	
1993	105	
1994	108	
1995	102	322/3=107
1996	112	

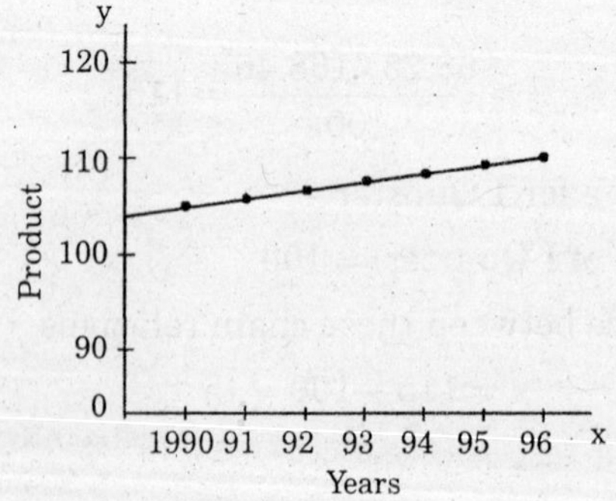

Trend values as per graph (Semi-Average Method)

Year	1990	1991	1992	1993	1994	1995	1996
Trend values	104	105	105.5	106	106.5	107	108

Illustration 32: *The following table gives the number of motor cars produced in a country over ten years.*

Year	*1*	*2*	*3*	*4*	*5*	*6*	*7*	*8*	*9*	*10*
Production (in '000)	*96*	*74*	*68*	*50*	*99*	*172*	*245*	*302*	*332*	*345*

Evaluate trend by the method of Moving Average. Explain how you would determine the period of Moving Average.

(MGU: Section B Sep 93)

Solution: Since the data are available for 10 years, it is ideal to calculate the trend values on the basis of 3 yearly Moving Average Method.

Calculation of Trend Values.

Year	*Production (in '000)*	*3 yearly Moving Total*	*3 yearly Moving Average (Trend Values)*
1	96	–	–
2	74	238	79
3	68	192	64
4	50	217	72
5	99	321	107
6	172	516	172
7	245	719	240
8	302	879	293
9	332	979	326
10	345	–	–

Illustration 33: *The following are the annual profits (in thousands of Rupees) in a certain business:*

Year	*1981*	*1982*	*1983*	*1984*	*1985*	*1986*	*1987*
Profits	*60*	*72*	*75*	*70*	*80*	*88*	*80*

Fit a straight line trend to the data by the method of least squares. Using the trend estimate the profit for the year 1988.

(MGU: Section C April 92)

Solution:

Year	*Production* Y	*Deviation for 1984* X	*Xy*	*X²*
1981	60	-3	-180	9
1982	72	-2	-144	4
1983	75	-1	-75	1
1984	70	0	0	0
1985	80	1	80	1
1986	88	2	176	4
1987	80	3	240	9
$N = 7$	$\Sigma y = 525$	$\Sigma X = 0$	$\Sigma Xy = 97$	$\Sigma X^2 = 28$

Equation to the straight line is, $Y = a + bX$

The value of a and b can be calculated with the help of the following normal equations.

$$\Sigma Y = Na + b\Sigma X \quad \text{and} \quad \Sigma XY = a\Sigma x + b\Sigma X^2$$

$$525 = 7a + 0$$

$$97 = a.0 + 28b$$

$$7a = 525; \quad a = \frac{525}{7} = 75$$

$$28b = 97; \quad b = \frac{97}{28} = 3.46$$

$$\therefore \quad Y = 75 + 3.46X$$

Trend values are calculated as follows:

1981	$(X = -3)$;	$Y = 75 + 3.46\ (-3)$	$= 64.62$
1982	$(X = -2)$;	$Y = 75 + 3.46\ (-2)$	$= 68.08$
1983	$(X = -1)$;	$Y = 75 + 3.46\ (-1)$	$= 71.54$
1984	$(X = 0)$;	$Y = 75 + 3.46\ (0)$	$= 75.00$
1985	$(X = 1)$;	$Y = 75 + 3.46\ (1)$	$= 78.46$
1986	$(X = 2)$;	$Y = 75 + 3.46\ (2)$	$= 81.92$
1987	$(X = 3)$;	$Y = 75 + 3.46\ (3)$	$= 85.38$
			525.00

Profit for 1988 $(X = 4)$; $Y = 75 + 3.46\ (4) = 88.84$

Illustration 34: *The sale of bicycle manufactured by a company for the last eight years are given below. Fit a straight line trend by the method of least squares.*

Plot the original data and trend line in a graph.

Year	*1970*	*1971*	*1972*	*1973*	*1974*	*1975*	*1976*	*1977*
No. of units Manufactured (in '000)	*12*	*13*	*13*	*16*	*19*	*23*	*21*	*23*

(MGU: Section C Sep 94)

Solution: Calculation of Straight Line Trend.

Year	*No. of units manufactured (in '000)* *Y*	*Deviation from 1973.5 x 2* *X*	*XY*	X^2
1970	12	-7	-84	49
1971	13	-5	-65	25
1972	13	-3	-39	9
1973	16	-1	-16	1
1974	19	1	19	1
1975	23	3	69	9
1976	21	5	105	25
1977	23	7	161	49
$N = 8$	$\Sigma Y = 140$		$\Sigma XY = 150$	$\Sigma X^2 = 168$

Equation for the straight line trend is $Y = a + bX$

When $\Sigma X = 0$,

$$a = \frac{\Sigma Y}{N} = \frac{140}{8} = 17.5$$

$$b = \frac{\Sigma XY}{\Sigma X^2} = \frac{150}{168} = 0.89$$

$$\therefore \quad Y = 17.5 + 0.89X$$

Hence, the trend values can be calculated as follows.

1970	(X = -7);	Y = 17.5 + 0.89 (-7)	= 11.27
1971	(X = -5);	Y = 17.5 + 0.89 (-5)	= 13.05
1972	(X = -3);	Y = 17.5 + 0.89 (-3)	= 14.83
1973	(X = -1);	Y = 17.5 + 0.89 (-1)	= 16.61
1974	(X = 1);	Y = 17.5 + 0.89 (1)	= 18.39
1975	(X = 3);	Y = 17.5 + 0.89 (3)	= 20.17
1976	(X = 5);	Y = 17.5 + 0.89 (5)	= 21.95
1977	(X = 7);	Y = 17.5 + 0.89 (7)	= 23.73
		Total	*140.00*

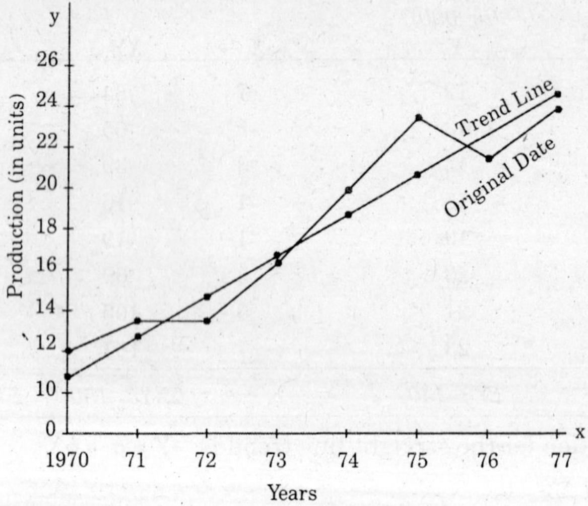

Illustration 35: *Fit a straight line trend by the method of least square from the following data. Also obtain trend for the year 1998*

Year	*1991*	*1992*	*1993*	*1994*	*1995*	*1996*	*1997*
Sales	*80*	*90*	*92*	*83*	*94*	*99*	*92*

(Kerala: Section C April 98)

Solution: Calculation of Trend Values.

Year	*Sales (Rs '000)* Y	*Deviation from 1994* X	XY	X^2
1991	80	-3	-240	9
1992	90	-2	-180	4
1993	92	-1	-92	1
1994	83	0	0	0
1995	94	1	94	1
1996	99	2	198	4
1997	92	3	276	9
$N = 7$	$\Sigma Y = 630$	$\Sigma X = 0$	$\Sigma XY = 56$	$\Sigma X^2 = 28$

Equation for straight line trend is $Y = a + bX$,

When $\Sigma X = 0$

$$a = \frac{\Sigma Y}{N} = \frac{630}{7} = 90$$

$$b = \frac{\Sigma XY}{\Sigma X^2} = \frac{56}{28} = 2$$

$$Y = 90 + 2X$$

Trend values can be calculated as follows:

1991	$(X = -3)$;	$Y = 90 + 2(-3)$	$= 84$
1992	$(X = -2)$;	$Y = 90 + 2(-2)$	$= 86$
1993	$(X = -1)$;	$Y = 90 + 2(-1)$	$= 88$
1994	$(X = 0)$;	$Y = 90 + 2(0)$	$= 90$
1995	$(X = 1)$;	$Y = 90 + 2(1)$	$= 92$
1996	$(X = 2)$;	$Y = 90 + 2(2)$	$= 94$
1997	$(X = 3)$;	$Y = 90 + 2(3)$	$= 96$
			630

Trend for the year 1998 is

$$X = 1998 - 1994 = 4$$
$$Y = 90 + 2(4) = 98$$

Illustration 36: *Fit a linear trend equation to the following data and estimate the value of sales for the year 1997.*

Year	*1992*	*1993*	*1994*	*1995*	*1996*
Sales (Rs.)	*100*	*120*	*140*	*160*	*180*

(Kerala: Section B April '97)

Solution: Calculation of Trend Values.

Year	*Sales* Y	*Deviation from 1994* X	XY	X^2
1992	100	-2	-200	4
1993	120	-1	-120	1
1994	140	0	0	0
1995	160	1	160	1
1996	180	2	360	4
$N = 5$	$\Sigma Y = 700$	$\Sigma X = 0$	$\Sigma XY = 200$	$\Sigma X^2 = 10$

Equation for straight line trend is, $Y = a + bX$,

when $\Sigma X = 0$

$$a = \frac{\Sigma Y}{N} = \frac{700}{5} = 140$$

$$b = \frac{\Sigma XY}{\Sigma X^2} = \frac{200}{10} = 20$$

$$\therefore \quad Y = 140 + 20X$$

The trend values can be calculated as follows:

1992	(x = -2);	y = 140 + 20 (-2)	= 100
1993	(x = -1);	y = 140 + 20 (-1)	= 120
1994	(x = 0);	y = 140 + 20 (0)	= 140
1995	(x = 1);	y = 140 + 20 (1)	= 160
1996	(x = 2);	y = 140 + 20 (2)	= 180
			700

Estimated value of sales for 1997 is, ($x = 1997 - 1994 = 3$)

$$Y = 140 + 20\ (3) = 200$$

Illustration 37: *Find trend for the following time data having a three year moving average method with weights 1, 2 and 1.*

Year	*1961*	*1962*	*1963*	*1964*	*1965*	*1966*	*1967*
Value	*2*	*4*	*5*	*7*	*8*	*10*	*13*

(Kerala: Section C April 96)

Solution: Calculation of Trend Values.

Year (1)	*Values* (2)	*3 yearly weighted moving total* (3)	*3 yearly weighted moving an average* (3)/4 (Trend Values)
1961	2		
1962	4	$(1 \times 2) + (2 \times 4) + (1 \times 5) = 15$	3.75
1963	5	$(1 \times 4) + (2 \times 5) + (1 \times 7) = 21$	5.25
1964	7	$(1 \times 5) + (2 \times 7) + (1 \times 8) = 27$	6.75
1965	8	$(1 \times 7) + (2 \times 8) + (1 \times 10) = 33$	8.25
1966	10	$(1 \times 8) + (2 \times 10) + (1 \times 13) = 41$	10.25
1967	13		

Illustration 38: *Compute the seasonal index for the following data assuming that there is no need to adjust the data for the trend.*

Quarter	*1986*	*1987*	*1988*	*1989*	*1990*	*1991*
1	*3.5*	*3.5*	*3.5*	*4.0*	*4.1*	*4.2*
2	*3.9*	*4.1*	*3.9*	*4.6*	*4.4*	*4.6*
3	*3.4*	*3.7*	*3.7*	*3.8*	*4.8*	*4.3*
4	*3.6*	*4.8*	*4.0*	*4.5*	*4.5*	*4.7*

(Kerala: Section C April 93)

Solution: Calculation of Seasonal Indices.

Quarter	*1986*	*1987*	*1988*	*1989*	*1990*	*1991*	*Quarterly Total for 6-yearly*	*6-yrly Average*	*Seasonal Variation Indices*
I	3.5	3.5	3.5	4.0	4.1	4.2	22.8	3.8	92.7
II	3.9	4.1	3.9	4.6	4.4	4.6	25.5	4.25	103.7
III	3.4	3.7	3.7	3.8	4.8	4.3	23.7	3.95	96.3
IV	3.6	4.8	4.0	4.5	4.5	4.7	26.1	4.35	106.1
						Total	98.1	16.35	398.8
						Average	24.53	4.1	100

Note: Second variation $= \dfrac{\text{6 yearly average}}{\text{Average}} \times 100$

for I Quarter $= \dfrac{3.8}{4.1} \times 100 = 92.7$

II Quarter $= \dfrac{4.25}{4.1} \times 100 = 103.7$

$$\text{III Quarter} = \frac{3.95}{4.1} \times 100 = 96.3$$

$$\text{IV Quarter} = \frac{4.35}{4.1} \times 100 = 106.1$$

Illustration 39: *The seasonal indices of sales of a firm are as under:*

Month	*Seasonal Index*
Jan	*106*
Feb	*105*
March	*101*
April	*104*
May	*98*
June	*96*
July	*93*
August	*89*
Sep	*92*
Oct	*102*
Nov	*106*
Dec	*108*

If the firm is expecting a total sale of Rs 42,00,000 during 1996, estimate the sale for the individual months of 1996.

(MGU: Section C April 97)

Solution: Monthly Sales Budget.

Month	*Seasonal Index*	*Seasonal Effect*	*Estimated Sales (Rs.)*
(1)	*(2)*	*(3)*	*(3)* X *42,00,000*
Jan	106	1.06	44,52,000
Feb	105	1.05	44,10,000
March	101	1.01	42,42,000
April	104	1.04	43,68,000
May	98	0.98	41,16,000
June	96	0.96	40,32,000
July.	93	0.93	39,06,000
August	89	0.89	37,38,000
Sep	92	0.92	38,64,000
Oct	102	1.02	42,84,000
Nov	106	1.06	44,52,000
Dec	108	1.08	45,36,000
Total	*1200*	*12.00*	*5,04,00,000*

Exercises

1. Define Time Series. State the importance of time series.
2. What is Time Series? State the components of time series.
3. Explain briefly the important measures of Secular Trend.
4. What do you mean by seasonal variations? State briefly the important methods of measuring seasonal variations.
5. Write short notes of the following:
   (a) Trend (b) Irregular Movements (c) Addictive Model
6. Write short notes of the following:
   (a) Cyclical Variations (b) Seasonal Variations
   (c) Link Relatives (d) Moving Average
7. Describe the different components of time series.
   (MGU: Section B April 97)
8. What is meant by Secular Trend?
   (MGU: Section A April 95 & Kerala: Section A April 97)
9. What are the different components of a time series? Describe briefly each of these components. (MGU: Section B April 95)
10. What is the purpose of time series analysis? Explain the moving average method of measuring the trend. (MGU: Section B April 94)
11. What is Trend? (MGU: Section A Sep 92)
12. What do you mean by de-seasonalisation of data.
    (MGU: Section A Sep 93)
13. Explain with few example the utility of the study of 'Seasonal Variation' in the time series. (MGU: Section B Sep 93)
14. What is time series? Name the components of the time series.
    (Kerala: Section B Sep 95)
15. State and define the various components in a time series.
    (Kerala: Section A April 94)
16. Explain any method of determining the trend value in a statistical time series data. Why should you determine trend to all in a time series? (Kerala: Section B April 94)
17. What are Irregular Variation? (Kerala: Section A April 89)
18. Distinguish between Cyclical and Seasonal Variation.
    (Kerala: Section B April 90 & 93)
19. Define Trend. What are the various methods of determining it?
    (Kerala: Section B April 93)
20. Give two examples of time series which consists seasonal variations.
    (Kerala: Section A Sep 93)

21. Explain the method of moving average for measuring the trend of the time series. (Kerala: Section B Sep 93)

22. Give a method of measurement of seasonal variations.
(Kerala: Section A Sep 90)

23. Explain the method of trend determination.
(Kerala: Section B Sep 90)

24. State two applications of time series analysis.
(Kerala: Section A April 90)

25. Explain how you compute the seasonal indices for a given data, indicating the necessary adjustments to be made, in detail.
(Kerala: Section C April 94)

26. Draw Trend Line by the method of Semi-Average from the following data.

Year	1991	1992	1993	1994	1995	1996
Profit (in '000)	34	47	52	73	89	95

27. Compute 3 yearly moving averages for the following data.

Year	1988	89	90	91	92	93	94	95	96	97
Production (in '000 tonnes)	33	55	72	56	35	89	95	73	44	96

28. Compute 4 yearly moving averages for the following data.

Year	1987	88	89	90	91	92	93	94	95	96	97
Profit (in '0000 of Rs)	12	15	35	25	30	45	47	52	55	59	65

29. Compute 5 yearly moving averages for the following data.

Year	1988	89	90	91	92	93	94	95	96	97
Sales (in '000 tonnes)	55	67	69	75	79	80	85	87	90	99

30. Compute 6 yearly moving averages for the following data.

Year	1987	88	89	90	91	92	93	94	95	96	97
Profit (Rs '000)	35	42	55	75	110	115	120	127	135	154	175

31. Compute 7 yearly moving averages for the following data.

Year	1987	88	89	90	91	92	93	94	95	96	97
Profit (in '000 Rs)	3	7	12	15	10	13	19	20	25	27	29

32. Fit a straight line trend for the following data by least square method.

Year	1990	1991	1992	1993	1994	1995	1996
Output (in '00 tonnes)	12	15	20	24	32	40	45

[Ans: y = 26.85 + 5.75 x]

33. Fit a straight line trend through the method of least square for the following data. Also estimate the sales for 1999 and 2004.

Year	1990	1991	1992	1993	1994	1995	1996
Sales (Rs. '0000)	25	29	32	35	50	54	55

[Ans: y = 40+5.64x; 73.8; 102.04]

34. Calculate Seasonal Index from the following data.

Year	*Sales (in '00 tonnes)*			
	I Quarter	*II Quarter*	*III Quarter*	*IV Quarter*
1993	30	22	15	45
1994	32	24	18	40
1995	35	29	20	37
1996	45	32	14	30
1997	50	30	12	35

[Ans: 129; 92; 53; 126]

35. Calculate Seasonal Index on the basis of ratio-to-trend method from the following data.

Quarters	*Profit (Rs. in '0000)*				
	1991	*1992*	*1993*	*1994*	*1995*
I Quarter	5	7	15	25	35
II Quarter	12	5	16	18	22
III Quatrer	15	20	24	26	29
IV Quarter	32	30	28	19	15

[Ans: 82; 75; 110.8; 132]

36. Find out Seasonal Indices through the ratio to moving average method for the data given below.

Year	*I Quarter*	*II Quarter*	*III Quarter*	*IV Quarter*
1993	7	9	12	18
1994	5	7	15	20
1995	12	6	5	4
1996	10	8	9	7

[Ans: 95.25; 76.4; 101.4; 126.9]

37. Calculate Seasonal Indices by Link Relative method for the following data.

Quarters	*Sales (Rs. in '0000)*				
	1992	*1993*	*1994*	*1995*	*1996*
I Quarter	4.7	5.4	7.8	3.4	8.4
II Quarter	6.7	8.9	7.4	7.8	9.7
III Quarter	3.6	4.7	5.8	6.9	9.8
IV Quarter	9.7	3.6	4.2	2.6	3.6

[Ans: 117; 150; 80; 53]

38. The sales of a company from 1990-96 are stated below.

Year	1990	1991	1992	1993	1994	1995	1996
Sales (in '000 tonnes)	32	45	49	50	55	59	65

Fit a straight line trend by the method of least square and tabulate the trend values. Also calculate (i) the sales for 2001 (ii) the monthly increase in sales of the company.

[Ans: y = 50.7 + 4.75y; 88.7; y = 4.2 + 0.33x]

39. Fit a straight line trend on the basis of a parabolic curve of the second degree for the following data.

Year	1993	1994	1995	1996	1997
Profit	24	36	40	50	60

[Ans: $Y = 41.72 + 8.6X + 0.14X^2$]

40. Fit a straight line trend for the following data.

Year	1990	1991	1992	1993	1994	1995	1996
Production (in '000 tonnes)	44	55	76	89	95	99	105

Find out

(i) the estimated production in 2005

(ii) the revised trend equation by shifting the origin to 1995 and

(iii) the monthly trend equation.

[Ans: $Y = 67.57 + 10.36X$; 191.89; $Y = 88.29 + 20.7Y$; $Y = 5.63 + 0.072X$]

41. The following table shows the number of salesmen working for a certain concern. Fit a straight line trend.

Year	1970	1971	1972	1973	1974	1975	1976
Number	28	38	46	40	56	63	62

(MGU: Section C April 92) [Ans: y = 47.57 + 5.79x; 30, 36, 42, 48, 53, 59, 65]

42. Fit a straight line by the method of least square to the data given below. Find the trend values and predict the sales of 1994.

Year	1986	1987	1988	1989	1990	1991	1992
Sales	35	42	44	48	46	49	51

(MGU: Section C Sep 93) [Ans: y = 45 + 2.29x; Trend values: 38, 40, 43, 45, 47, 50, 52, Sales of 1994 = 56,450]

43. Fit a straight line trend by the method of least squares from the following data.

Year	1	2	3	4	5	6	7	8	9	10
Value	110	125	115	135	150	165	155	175	180	200

[Ans: $Y = 151 + 4.76X$; 108, 118, 127, 137, 146, 156, 165, 175, 184, 194]

44. Compute the trend by four week moving average for the following data:

X (week)	1	2	3	4	5	6	7	8	9	10
y (production)	82	73	74	75	73	72	76	76	74	75
X (week)	11	12	13	14	15	16	17	18	19	20
y (production)	75	73	75	76	75	75	78	75	78	79

[Ans: 75, 74, 74, 74.4, 74.8, 75, 74.6, 74.4, 74.6, 74.8, 75, 75.6, 75.9, 76, 77]

45. Fit a straight line trend to the following data. Calculate the trend values.

Year	1951	1952	1953	1954	1955	1956
Electricity generated (million Kw)	101	107	113	121	136	148

46. From the following data, determine trend using 5-year moving average method.

Year	1948	1949	1950	1951	1952	1953	1954
Avg. monthly production of a commodity	50	37	43	45	39	38	33
Year	1955	1956	1957	1958	1959	1960	1961
Avg. monthly production of a commodity	39	42	41	34	35	48	42

[Ans: 42.8, 40.4, 39.6, 38.8, 38.2, 38.6, 37.8, 38.2, 40, 40]

47. For the following data on exports in a country (of a particular commodity) determine trend by:

(i) free hand curve method and (ii) 3-year moving average method and comment appropriately.

Year	1979	1980	1981	1982	1983	1984	1985	1986	1987	1988
Exports	950	1100	951	1002	1172	1125	1200	1350	1400	1400

(Kerala: Section C April 90) [Ans: 1000.33, 1018, 1042, 1100, 1166]

◆ Chapter 13 ◆

Interpolation and Extrapolation

Interpolation and Extrapolation are important statistical estimation of a variable when a set of variables are given. It is used to find out a missing figure for past or future period. Example The sales for the year 1990 can be estimated from the sales of 1985-89 and 1991-95 periods. If sales for 1985-95 are available, sale for 1983, 84, 96, 97 etc. can be estimated through interpolation and extrapolation techniques.

Definitions for interpolation and extrapolation

The important definitions of interpolation and extrapolation are stated as below:

1. Hirach defines interpolation as "*interpolation is the estimation of a most likely estimate in given conditions. The technique of estimating a past figure is termed as interpolation while that of estimating a probable figure for future is called extrapolation*".

2. According to Theile, Interpolations is "*the art of reading between the lines of the table*".

3. According to W.M. Harper, "*interpolation consists in reading a value which lies between two extreme points. Extrapolation means reading a value that lies outside to two extreme points*".

It is clear from the above definitions that interpolation is a measure of a value in between a set of variables. (*e.g.*) Calculation of the value of say, June 1995 when, the value of the other 11 months of the year are available.

Extrapolation is a measure to find out a value in future on the basis of the values of past.

(*e.g.*) Calculation of the value of 1998 when the values for 1990, 91, 92, 93, 94, 95 are available.

Assumptions

The following are the important assumptions for the interpolation and extrapolation method.

(i) The variables should not raise and fall over a period of time. It means that the variables should not assume sudden jump or fall period to period.

(ii) The rate of change of figures should be uniform from one period to another.

(iii) It is advisable that the time span for which data are available should be uniform one.

Methods of Interpolation and Extrapolation

The most common methods of interpolation and extrapolation are given below:

I Graphic Method and II Algebraic Method.

The important algebraic methods are as follows:

(1) Binomial Expansion Method

(2) Newton's Method

Newton's method may further be classified into:

(a) Newton's Gauss (Forward) Method

(b) Newton's Gauss (Backward) Method

(c) Newton's Method of Backward Differences

(d) Newton's Divided Difference Method

(3) Lagrange's Method and

(4) Parabolic Curve Method.

I Graphic Method: In this method the available data should be plotted on a graph paper. The plotted points should be joined so as to get a curve. If there are only two points, then a straight line can be drawn instead of a curve. The missing figure for a period can easily be obtained with the help of this curve or straight line.

Steps

(i) Draw '*X*' axis and '*Y*' axis in a graph paper.

(ii) On the '*X*' axis mark the periods conveniently.

(iii) Plot the points for respective variables corresponding to the periods.

(iv) The points should be joined to get a straight line (or) curve.

Merits

(i) This is the easiest method for measuring interpolation.

(ii) This method is less time consuming than any other method.

(iii) This method can be used for non linear situations also.

Demerits

(i) It is not an accurate method, particularly for extrapolation.

(ii) The shape of the curve may change due to the changes in the space provided for years and for variables.

(iii) This method could not be a clear one when the number of variables are more.

Illustration 1: *Find out the production of a factory for the year 1993 from the following data through graphic method*

Year	*1980*	*1982*	*1984*	*1986*	*1988*	*1990*	*1992*
Production (in tonnes)	*49*	*120*	*200*	*250*	*280*	*310*	*325*

Solution: Calculation of production of a factory.

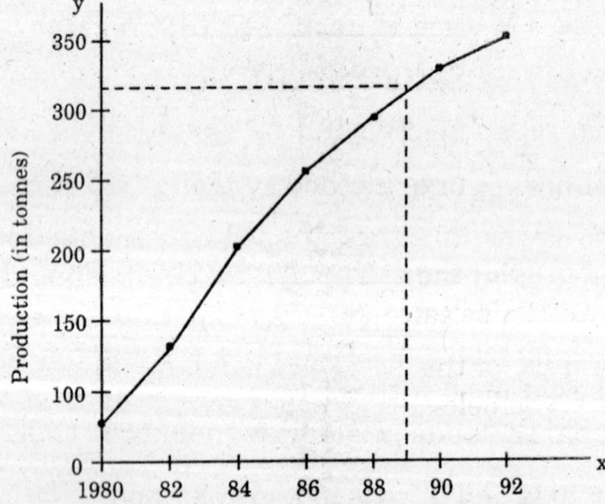

The estimated production for 1989 is 320 tonnes.

Illustration 2: *Interpolate literates in a village by graphic method for the year 1982 from the following data.*

Year	*1965*	*1970*	*1975*	*1980*	*1985*	*1990*
No. of literates (in '000)	*47*	*59*	*63*	*78*	*92*	*112*

Solution: Interpolation of literates for the year 1982.

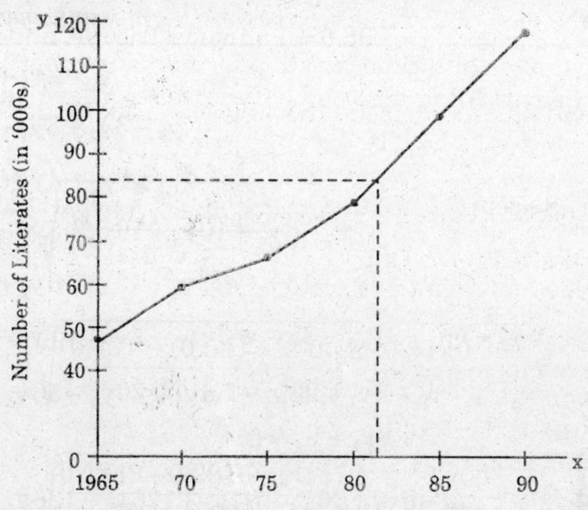

Ans: The estimated no. of literates in 1982 is Rs. 82,000.

II Algebraic Method

(1) Binomial Expansion Method: This method is one of the easiest method of interpolation. It can be applied only for specific type of problems. The independent variables (*X*) should advance by equal intervals (*e.g.*) 10, 20, 30, 40, 50. The value of *X* to the interpolated should be anyone of the variables in between the given values (*e.g.*). If the variables for '*X*' series are 10, 20, 30, 40, 50 then the value of y for any of the *x* variables can be calculated under this method. If all the values of '*y*' for the '*x*' variables are available except for variable 20. Then the value of '*y*' for the variable 20 can be calculated. But the value of '*y*' for 25 or 32 for *x*. (independent variable) cannot be calculated through this method.

The formula for the interpolation under the binomial expansion method is given below.

$$(y-1) = y^n - ny^{n-1} + \frac{n(n-1)}{2!}y^{n-2} - \frac{n(n-1)(n-2)}{3!}y^{n-3}$$

$$+ \ldots\ldots\ldots\ldots = 0$$

Where y is the dependent variable and 'n' is the number of known values of 'y'. The above equation is based on the number of known values of 'y'. Hence, the equations for the known values of 'y' can be framed as fallows.

No. of known values	Equation for determining the unknown values
2 or Δ_0^2	$y_2 - 2y_1 + y_0 = 0$
3 or Δ_0^3	$y_3 - 3y_2 + 3y_1 - y_0 = 0$
4 or Δ_0^4	$y_4 - 4y_3 + 6y_2 - 4y_1 + y_0 = 0$
5 or Δ_0^5	$y_5 - 5y_4 + 10y_3 - 10y_2 + 5y_1 - y_0 = 0$
6 or Δ_0^6	$y_6 - 6y_5 + 15y_4 - 20y_3 + 15y_2 - 6y_1 + y_0 = 0$
7 or Δ_0^7	$y_7 - 7y_6 + 21y_5 - 35y_4 + 35y_3 - 21y_2 + 7y_1 - y_0 = 0$
8 or Δ_0^8	$y_8 - 8y_7 + 28y_6 - 56y_5 + 70y_4 - 56y_3 + 28y_2 - 8y_1 + y_0 = 0$
9 or Δ_0^9	$y_9 - 9y_8 + 36y_7 - 84y_6 + 126y_5 - 126y_4 + 84y_3 - 56y_2 + 9y_1 - y_0 = 0$

Procedure

(i) Arrange the dependent variables in a continuous order and give symbol for it as y_1, y_2, y_3, y_4 etc.

(ii) The first value of the equation would be y_{n-1}.

(iii) After the first value, the second and subsequent values of the equation would be y_{n-2}, y_{n-3} etc.

(iv) The minus symbol should be given after the first value and subsequently (+) and (-) should be given, alternatively for all the values.

(v) The numerical co-efficients for the first value and last values of y in the equation are one. The other numerical coefficients of equations can be calculated through the pascals triangle which was given below.

Pascal's Triangle

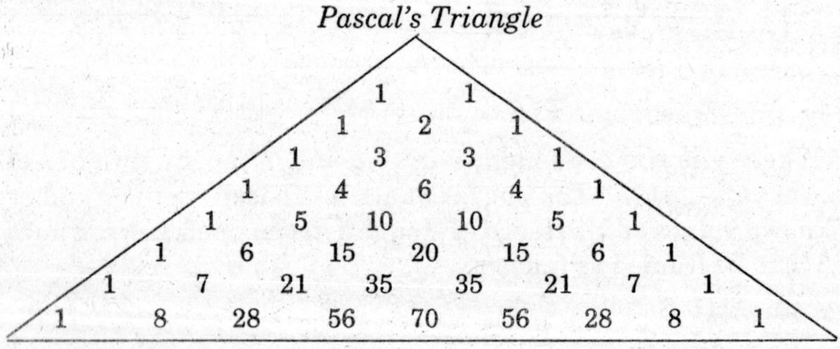

If the known variables of 'y' series are 8 in number then to know the unknown variable, the binomial equation $(y-1)^8 = 0$ should be applied. The co-efficient at 'y' can be found out from the above pascal's triangle which are 1, 8, 28, 56, 70, 56, 28, 8, 1.

Illustration 3: *Find out the missing item of the following data by binomial expansion method*

Year	*1985*	*1986*	*1987*	*1988*	*1989*	*1990*
Sales (in tonnes)	*40*	*49*	*52*	*?*	*73*	*89*

Solution: Calculation of the value for 1988.

X	Y	
1985	40	Y_0
1986	49	Y_1
1987	52	Y_2
1988	?	Y_3
1989	73	Y_4
1990	89	Y_5

The known variables are five. Hence, $\Delta_0^5 = 0$

$$\Delta_0^5 = y_5 - 5y_4 + 10y_3 - 10y_2 + 5y_1 - y_0 = 0$$

$$= 89 - (5 \times 73) + 10y_3 - (10 \times 52) + (5 \times 49) - 40 = 0$$

$$= 89 - 365 + 10y_3 - 520 + 245 - 40 = 0$$

$$10y_3 = -89 + 365 + 520 - 245 + 40 = 591$$

$$y_3 = 591/10 = 59.1$$

Calculation of two or more missing values through the Binomial Expansion Method

Binomial expansion method is the most suitable method to find out two or more missing values. The number of constants formed, for this purpose, should be equal to the number of missing variables, (*e.g.*) If two values are missing then the binomial equation $\Delta^n = 0$ and $\Delta^{n-1} = 0$ should be constructed, and the unknown values can be calculated by solving the equations.

Illustration 4: *From the following data, estimate the average profit of an industry for the years 1986 and 1989.*

Year	*1984*	*1985*	*1987*	*1988*	*1990*	*1991*
Profit (Rs in lakhs)	*35*	*42*	*49*	*56*	*63*	*84*

Solution:

Year	Profit (Rs in lakhs)	Y
1984	35	Y_0
1985	42	Y_1
1986	?	Y_2
1987	49	Y_3
1988	56	Y_4
1989	?	Y_5
1990	63	Y_6
1991	84	Y_7

Two equations should be framed, since there are 2 missing figures. They are, Δ_0^7 and Δ_0^6

$$\Delta_0^7 = y_7 - 7y_6 + 21y_5 - 35y_4 + 35y_3 - 21y_2 + 7y_1 - y_0 = 0.$$

$$\Delta_0^6 = y_6 - 6y_5 + 15y_4 - 20y_3 + 15y_2 - 6y_1 + y_0 = 0$$

Hence,

$$\Delta_0^7 = 84 - (7 \times 63) + 21y_5 - (35 \times 56) + (35 \times 49) - 21y_2 + (7 \times 42) - 35 = 0$$

$$84 - 441 + 21y_5 - 1960 + 1715 - 21y_2 + 294 - 35 = 0$$

$$21y_5 - 21y_2 = 343 \quad \text{. . . (i)}$$

$$\Delta_0^6 = 63 - 6y_5 + (15 \times 56) - (20 \times 49) + 15y_2 - (6 \times 42) + 35 = 0$$

$$63 - 6y_5 + 840 - 980 + 15y_2 - 252 + 35 = 0$$

$$-6y_5 + 15y_2 = 294 \quad \text{. . . (ii)}$$

(i) × 6 $\quad 126y_5 - 126y_2 = 2058$ . . . (iii)

(ii) × 21 $-126y_5 + 315y_2 = 6174$ . . . (iv)

(i) + (ii) $\quad 189y_2 = 8232$

$$y_2 = 8232/189 = 43.56$$

(i) $\quad 21y_5 - (21 \times 43.56) = 343$

$$21y_5 = 1257.76$$

$$y_5 = 1257.76/21 = 59.89$$

(2) Newton's Method

(a) Newton's Method of Advancing Differences: Sometimes the difference between 2 independent variables is a constant number

which is same for all the differences of the two adjacent independent variables.

(*e.g.*) (i) 25, 40, 55, 70, 85 (ii) 5, 10, 15, 20, 25, 30

In the example (i) difference between two variable is 15 which is same for all the differences and in example (ii) the difference is 5 which is same for all the differences.

When the differences in the independent variables are same, then Newton's method of advancing differences, can be used for interpolation and extrapolation.

The formula under this method to find out the value of a dependent variable (Y) for an independent variable (X) is,

$$y_x = y_0 + x\Delta_0 + \frac{x(x-1)}{1\times 2}\Delta_0{}^2 + \frac{x(x-1)(x-2)}{1\times 2\times 3}$$

$$\Delta_0{}^2 + \frac{x(x-1)(x-2)(x-3)}{1\times 2\times 3\times 4}\Delta_0{}^2 + \ldots\ldots +$$

where, y_x = Dependent variable to be calculated for a given independent variable.

y_0 = Value of y in the origin.

Δ = Difference between various values of y.

The value of x can be calculated through the following formula.

$$X = \frac{\text{The value to be interpolated} - \text{The value of } X \text{ in the origin}}{\text{The difference of two adjacent variables of } X}$$

If the value of X is given in years, then,

$$X = \frac{\text{Year of interpolation} - \text{Year of origin}}{\text{Difference between two adjoining year}}$$

The difference between the various value of $y(\Delta)$ can be calculated as follows.

$$\Delta_0{}^1 = y_1 - y_0$$

$$\Delta_1{}^1 = y_2 - y_1$$

$$\Delta_2{}^1 = y_3 - y_2 \quad \text{etc.}$$

$$\Delta_0^{\ 2} = \Delta_1^{\ 1} - \Delta_0^{\ 1}$$

$$\Delta_1^{\ 2} = \Delta_2^{\ 1} - \Delta_1^{\ 1} \quad \text{etc.}$$

$$\Delta_0^{\ 3} = \Delta_1^{\ 2} - \Delta_0^{\ 2}$$

$$\Delta_1^{\ 3} = \Delta_2^{\ 2} - \Delta_1^{\ 2} \quad \text{etc.}$$

$$\Delta_0^{\ 4} = \Delta_1^{\ 3} - \Delta_0^{\ 3}$$

$$\Delta_1^{\ 4} = \Delta_2^{\ 3} - \Delta_1^{\ 3} \quad \text{etc.}$$

Illustration 5: *From the following data, interpolate the value for the year 1979.*

Year	*1970*	*1975*	*1980*	*1985*	*1990*
Sales (in tonnes)	*195*	*215*	*260*	*280*	*310*

Solution: Calculation of the differences of *Y*.

Year	Sales	Difference			
X	Y	Δ_1	Δ_2	Δ_3	Δ_4
1970	195 Y_0				
		+ 20 Δ_0^{1}			
1975	215 Y_1		+ 25 Δ_0^{2}		
		+ 45 Δ_0^{2}		- 40 Δ_0^{3}	
1980	260 Y_2		- 15 Δ_1^{2}		+ 25 Δ_0^{4}
		+ 30 Δ_0^{2}		- 15 Δ_1^{3}	
1985	280 Y_3		- 30 Δ_2^{2}		
		+ 0 Δ_3^{1}			
1990	310 Y_4				

$$x = \frac{1979 - 1970}{5} = \frac{9}{5} = 1.8$$

$$y_{1979} = y_0 + x\Delta_0^{\ 1} + \frac{x(x-1)}{1 \times 2}\Delta_0^{\ 2} + \frac{x(x-1)(x-2)}{1 \times 2 \times 3}$$

$$\Delta_0^{\ 3} + \frac{x(x-1)(x-2)(x-3)}{1 \times 2 \times 3 \times 4}\Delta_0^{\ 4}$$

$$= 195 + 1.8 \times 20 + \frac{1.8(1.8-1)}{1 \times 2} \times 25 + \frac{1.8(1.8-1)(1.8-2)}{1 \times 2 \times 3} \times (-40)$$

$$+ \frac{1.8(1.8-1)(1.8-2)(1.8-3)}{1 \times 2 \times 3 \times 4} \times 25$$

$$= 195 + 36 + 18 + 1.92 + 0.36 = 251$$

Value for the year 1979 = 251

Illustration 6: *Interpolate the values of y for the value of x as 27, from the following data.*

X	*5*	*15*	*25*	*35*	*45*
Y	*47*	*52*	*74*	*82*	*95*

Solution:

X	Y	Δ_1	Δ_2	Δ_3	Δ_4
5	47 Y_0				
		+ 5 Δ_0^1			
15	52 Y_1		+ 17 Δ_0^2		
		+ 22 Δ_1^1		- 31 Δ_0^3	
25	74 Y_2		- 14 Δ_1^2		+ 50 Δ_0^4
		+ 8 Δ_2^1		+ 19 Δ_1^3	
35	82 Y_3		+ 5 Δ_2^2		
		+ 13 Δ_3^1			
45	95 Y_4				

$$x = \frac{27-5}{10} = 2.2$$

$$y_{27} = y_0 + x\Delta_0^{\ 1} + \frac{x(x-1)}{1 \times 2}\Delta_0^{\ 2} + \frac{x(x-1)(x-2)}{1 \times 2 \times 3}$$

$$\Delta_0^{\ 3} + \frac{x(x-1)(x-2)(x-3)}{1 \times 2 \times 3 \times 4}\Delta_0^{\ 4}$$

$$= 47 + \frac{2.2 \times 5}{47 + 2.2 \times 5} + \frac{2.2(2.2-1)}{1 \times 2} \times 17 + \frac{2.2(2.2-1)(2.2-2)}{1 \times 2 \times 3} \times (-31)$$

$$+ \frac{2.2(2.2-1)(2.2-2)(2.2-3)}{1 \times 2 \times 3 \times 4} \times 50$$

$$= 47 + 11 + 22.4 - 2.73 - 0.88 = 77$$

Illustration 7: *Find out the total number of students who got less than 54 marks from the following data.*

Marks	*0-30*	*30-50*	*50-70*	*70-90*
No. of students	*25*	*15*	*13*	*18*

Solution:

X	*f*	*Y*	Δ_1	Δ_2	Δ_3
30	25	25 y_0			
			+ 15 Δ_0^1		
50	15	40 y_1		- 3 Δ_0^2	
			+13 Δ_1^1		+ 8 Δ_0^3
70	13	53 y_2		+ 5 Δ_1^2	
			+ 18 Δ_2^1		
90	18	71 y_3			

$$x = \frac{54-30}{20} = 1.2$$

$$y_{54} = y_0 + x\Delta_0^{\,1} + \frac{x(x-1)}{1\times 2}\Delta_0^{\,2} + \frac{x(x-1)(x-2)}{1\times 2\times 3}\Delta_0^{\,3}$$

$$= 25 + 1.2\times 15 + \frac{1.2(1.2-1)}{1\times 2}\times(-3) + \frac{1.2(1.2-1)(1.2-2)}{1\times 2\times 3}\times 8$$

$$= 25 + 18 - 0.36 - 0.256 = 42$$

(b) Newton-Gauss (Forward) Method: This method can be applied only when the independent variable (*X*) increases by equal intervals and the variable to be interpolated lies in the middle of the series. The formula under this method is,

$$y_x = y_0 + x\Delta^1{}_{y-0} + \frac{x(x-1)}{1\times 2}\Delta^2{}_{y-1} + \frac{x(x-1)(x-2)}{1\times 2\times 3}$$

$$\Delta^3{}_{y-1} + \frac{x(x-1)(x-2)(x-3)}{1\times 2\times 3\times 4}\Delta^4{}_{y-2}$$

$$x = \frac{\text{Variable } X \text{ to be interpolated - Preceeding variable to the item to be interpolated}}{\text{Difference between any two adjoining Variables } X}$$

Steps

(i) The next preceeding variable to the item to be interpolated of the x series should be denoted by x_0.

(ii) The previous variables to X_0 should be denoted as X_{-1}, X_{-2}, X_{-3}, etc.

(iii) The succeeding variables to X_0 should be denoted as X_1, X_2, X_3, etc.

(iv) The corresponding values of Y variables to X variables should be denoted by Y_0, Y_{-1}, Y_{-2}, Y_{-3}, etc (for X_0, X_{-1}, X_{-2}, X_{-3}, etc) and Y_1, Y_2, Y_3, etc (for X_1, X_2, X_3, etc).

(v) Prepare the difference table and find out the value of X_{y0}.

Illustration 8: *Calculate the value of y when the value of X is 14, from the following data.*

X	*4*	*8*	*12*	*16*	*20*	*24*
Y	*12*	*18*	*22*	*36*	*45*	*62*

Solution:

X	*Y*	Δ_1	Δ_2	Δ_3
4 x_{-2}	12 y_{-2}			
		+ 6 Δ^1_{y-2}		
8 x_{-1}	18 y_{-1}		- 2 Δ^2_{y-2}	
		+ 4 Δ^1_{y-1}		+ 12 Δ^3_{y-2}
12 x_0	22 y_0		+ 10 Δ^2_{y-1}	
		+ 14 Δ^1_{y0}		- 15 Δ^3_{y-1}
16 x_1	36 y_1		- 5 Δ^2_{y0}	
		+ 9 Δ^1_{y1}		+ 13 Δ^3_{y0}
20 x_2	45 y_2		+ 8 Δ^2_{y1}	
		+ 17 Δ^1_{y2}		
24 x_3	62 y_3			

Here, 12 is selected for x_0 since it is the next preceding item to 14.

$$x = \frac{14-12}{4} = 0.5$$

$$y_x = y_0 + x\Delta^1{}_{y0} + \frac{x(x-1)}{1\times2}\Delta^2{}_{y-1} + \frac{x(x-1)(x-2)}{1\times2\times3}\Delta^3{}_{y-1}$$

$$y_{14} = 22 + (0.5\times14) + \frac{0.5(0.5-1)}{1\times2}\times10 + \frac{0.5(0.5-1)(0.5-2)}{1\times2\times3}\times(-15)$$

$$= 22 + 7 - 1.25 - 0.94 = 26.8$$

(c) Newton-Gauss (Backward) Method: This method of interpolation can be applied only when, the variable to be interpolated lies at the end of the series and the differences between all the two adjoining variable X are the same. In this method, the next succeeding item of the X series to the item to be interpolated should be taken as X_0.

Steps

(i) The next succeeding variable to the item to be interpolated of the X series should be denoted by x_0.

(ii) The previous variables to x_0 should be denoted as x_{-1}, x_{-2}, x_{-3}, etc.

(iii) The succeeding variables to x_0 should be denoted as x_1, x_2, x_3, etc.

(iv) The corresponding value of Y variables to X variables should be denoted by y_0, y_{-1}, y_{-2}, y_{-3}, etc. (for x_0, x_{-1}, x_{-2}, x_{-3}, etc) and y_1, y_2, y_3, etc (for x_1, x_2, x_3, etc).

(v) Prepare the difference table and find out, the value of Y_x

Then the value so calculated should be substituted in the following formula.

$$y_x = y_0 + x\Delta^1{}_{y-1} + \frac{x(x+1)}{1\times2}\Delta^2{}_{y-1} - \frac{x(x+1)(x-1)}{1\times2\times3}$$

$$\Delta^3{}_{y-2} + \frac{x(x+1)(x-1)(x-2)}{1\times2\times3\times4}\Delta^4{}_{y-2}$$

$$x = \frac{\text{Variable } X \text{ succeeding the item to be interpolated} - \text{variable } X \text{ to be interpolated}}{\text{Difference between any two adjoining Variables } X}$$

Illustration 9: *From the following data find out the sales for the month of August.*

Months	*Jan*	*March*	*May*	*July*	*Sept*	*Nov*
Sales (in units)	*250*	*310*	*450*	*570*	*680*	*750*

Solution:

Months	*X*	*Y*	Δ_1	Δ_2	Δ_3	Δ_4	Δ_5
Jan	1 x_{-4}	250 y_{-4}					
			+ 60 Δ^1_{y-4}				
March	3 x_{-3}	310 y_{-3}		+ 80 Δ^2_{y-4}			
			+ 140 Δ^1_{y-3}		- 100 Δ^3_{y-4}		
May	5 x_{-2}	450 y_{-2}		- 20 Δ^2_{y-3}		+ 110 Δ^4_{y-4}	
			+ 120 Δ^1_{y-2}		+ 10 Δ^3_{y-3}		- 150 Δ^5_{y-4}
July	7 x_{-1}	570 y_{-1}		- 10 Δ^2_{y-2}		- 40 Δ^4_{y-3}	
			+ 110 Δ^1_{y-1}		- 30 Δ^3_{y-2}		
Sept	9 x_0	680 y_0		- 40 Δ^2_{y-1}			
			+ 70 Δ^1_{y}				
Nov	11 x_1	750 y_1					

$$x = \frac{\text{Variable } X \text{ succeeding the item to be interpolated - variable } X \text{ to be interpolated}}{\text{Difference between any two adjoining Variables } X}$$

$$= \frac{\text{September} - \text{August}}{\text{January} - \text{March}} = \frac{1}{2} = 0.5$$

$$y_x = y_0 - x\Delta^1_{y-1} + \frac{x(x+1)}{2!}\Delta^2_{y-1} - \frac{x(x+1)(x-1)}{3!}$$

$$\Delta^3_{y-2} + \frac{x(x+1)(x-1)(x-3)}{4!}\Delta^4_{y-2}.$$

$$= 680 - (0.5 \times 110) + \frac{0.5(0.5+1)}{1 \times 2} \times (-40)$$

$$- \frac{0.5(0.5+1)(0.5-1)}{1 \times 2 \times 3} \times (-30)$$

$$= 680 - 55 - 15 - 1.875 = 680 - 71.875 = 608.125$$

Sale in August = 608 units

(d) Newton's Method of Backward Differences: This method is most suitable when the figure to be interpolated is at the end of the tabulated values.

The formula under this method is,

$$y_x = y_0 + x\Delta^1{}_0 + \frac{x(x-1)}{1\times 2}\Delta^2{}_0 + \frac{x(x-1)(x-2)}{1\times 2\times 3}$$

$$\Delta^3{}_0 + \frac{x(x-1)(x-2)(x-3)}{1\times 2\times 3\times 4}\Delta^4{}_0$$

Illustration 10: *Calculate the value of y, when x is 55 from the following data.*

X	20	30	40	50	60
Y	115	128	135	145	175

Solution: Calculation of Backward Differences.

X	Y	Δ_1	Δ_2	Δ_3	Δ_4
20 x_4	115 y_4				
		13 Δ_3^1			
30 x_3	128 y_3		-6 Δ_2^2		
		7 Δ_2^1		+9 Δ_1^3	
40 x_2	135 y_2		+3 Δ_1^2		+8 Δ_0^4
		10 Δ_1^1		+17 Δ_0^3	
50 x_1	145 y_1		+20 Δ_0^2		
		30 Δ_0^1			
60 x_0	175 y_0				

$$x = \frac{55-60}{10} = 0-0.5$$

$$y_x = y_0 + x\Delta^1{}_0 + \frac{x(x-1)}{1\times 2}\Delta^2{}_0 + \frac{x(x-1)(x-2)}{1\times 2\times 3}$$

$$\Delta^3{}_0 + \frac{x(x-1)(x-2)(x-3)}{1\times 2\times 3\times 4}\Delta^4{}_0$$

$$y_x = 175 + (-0.5\times 30) + \frac{-0.5(-0.5-1)}{1\times 2}\times 20$$

$$+\frac{-0.5(-0.5-1)(-0.5-2)}{1\times 2\times 3}\times 17$$

$$+\frac{-0.5(-0.5-1)(-0.5-2)(-0.5-3)}{1\times 2\times 3\times 4}\times 8$$

$$= 175 - 15 + 7.5 - 5.31 + 2.19 = 164.38$$

(e) Newton's Divided Difference Method: When the value of independent variable 'X' advances by unequal intervals, this method can be adopted to find out the missing figures. To calculate the missing figure first of all, the "Table of Divided Differences" should be prepared before applying the formula. Following is the method of preparing the table of divided differences.

Table of Divided Differences.

X	Y	*Divided Difference*		
		Δ^1	Δ^2	Δ^3
x_0	y_0			
		$\dfrac{y_1 - y_0}{x_1 - x_0}$ $\Delta_0^{\ 1}$		
x_1	y_1		$\dfrac{\Delta_1^{\ 1} - \Delta_0^{\ 1}}{x_2 - x_0}$ $\Delta_0^{\ 2}$	
		$\dfrac{y_2 - y_1}{x_2 - x_1}$ $\Delta_1^{\ 1}$		$\dfrac{\Delta_1^{\ 2} - \Delta_0^{\ 2}}{x_3 - x_0}$ $\Delta_0^{\ 3}$
x_2	y_2			
			$\dfrac{\Delta_1^{\ 2} - \Delta_0^{\ 2}}{x_3 - x_1}$ $\Delta_1^{\ 3}$	
		$\dfrac{y_3 - y_2}{x_3 - x_2}$ $\Delta_2^{\ 1}$		
x_3	y_3			

After calculating the differences it should be applied in the following formula,

$$y_x = y_0 + (x - x_0)\Delta^1{}_0 + (x - x_0)(x - x_1)\Delta^2{}_0$$
$$+ (x - x_0)(x - x_1)(x - x_2)\Delta^3{}_0 + \ldots.$$

Where, $\Delta^1{}_0, \Delta^2{}_0, \Delta^3{}_0$ are the first, second and third leading divided differences respectively.

Illustration 11: *Following are the details relating to the production in a factory for various months. Estimate the production for the month September.*

Months	*January*	*March*	*July*	*December*
Production	*220*	*250*	*390*	*480*

Solution:

x	y	*Differences* Δ^1	Δ^2	Δ^3
Jan 1 x_0	220 y_0			
		$\frac{250-220}{3-1}$ $\Delta_0{}^1$ 15		
Mar 3 x_1	250 y_1		$\frac{35-15}{7-1}$ $\Delta_0{}^2$ 3.3	
		$\frac{390-250}{7-3}$ $\Delta_1{}^1$ 35		$\frac{-1.89-3.3}{12-1}$ $\Delta_0{}^3$ -0.47
July 7 x_2	390 y_2		$\frac{18-35}{12-3}$ $\Delta_1{}^2$ -1.89	
		$\frac{480-390}{12-7}$ $\Delta_2{}^1$ 18		
Dec 12 x_3	480 y_3			

X is September i.e., 9

$$y_x = y_0 + (x - x_0)\Delta^1{}_0 + (x - x_0)(x - x_1)\Delta^2{}_0 + (x - x_0)(x - x_1)(x - x_2)\Delta^3{}_0$$

$$= 220 + (9-1)15 + (9-1)(9-3)(3.3) + (9-1)(9-3)(9-7)(-0.47)$$

$$= 220 + (8 \times 15) + (8 \times 6 \times 3.3) + (8 \times 6 \times 2 \times (-0.47))$$

$$= 220 + 120 + 158.4 - 45.12 = 453.28$$

(3) Lagrange Method: A famous mathematician named Lagrange advocated this method for interpolation. This method can be applied both for regular and irregular intervals of the independent variable 'x'. This method can also be applied both for interpolation in the beginning and in the end.

The formula under this method is,

$$y_x = y_0 \frac{(x-x_1)(x-x_2)(x-x_3)(x-x_n)}{(x_0-x_1)(x_0-x_2)(x_0-x_3)(x_0-x_n)}$$

$$+y_1 \frac{(x-x_0)(x-x_2)(x-x_3)(x-x_n)}{(x_1-x_0)(x_1-x_2)(x_1-x_3)(x_1-x_n)}$$

$$+y_2 \frac{(x-x_0)(x-x_1)(x-x_3)(x-x_n)}{(x_2-x_0)(x_2-x_1)(x_2-x_3)(x_2-x_n)} + y_3 \quad \text{etc.....}$$

$$+y_n \frac{(x-x_0)(x-x_1)(x-x_2)(x-x_{n-1})}{(x_n-x_0)(x_n-x_1)(x_n-x_2)(x_n-x_{n-1})}$$

Illustration 12: *From the following data find out the number of employed below 40 years of age in a village based on Lagrange Method.*

Age	*No. of employed*
Upto 15 years	*45*
Upto 25 years	*64*
Upto 35 years	*79*
Upto 45 years	*85*

Solution: Calculation of number of employed below 40 years of age.

Age		*No. of employed*	
Upto 15 years	x_0	45	y_0
Upto 25 years	x_1	64	y_1
Upto 35 years	x_2	79	y_2
Upto 45 years	x_3	85	y_3

$x = 40$ years.

$$y_x = y_0 \frac{(x-x_1)(x-x_2)(x-x_3)}{(x_0-x_1)(x_0-x_2)(x_0-x_3)} + y_1 \frac{(x-x_0)(x-x_2)(x-x_3)}{(x_1-x_0)(x_1-x_2)(x_1-x_3)}$$

$$+y_2 \frac{(x-x_0)(x-x_1)(x-x_3)}{(x_2-x_0)(x_2-x_1)(x_2-x_3)} + y_3 \frac{(x-x_0)(x-x_1)(x-x_2)}{(x_3-x_0)(x_3-x_1)(x_3-x_2)}$$

$$y_{40} = 45\frac{(40-25)(40-35)(40-45)}{(15-25)(15-35)(15-45)} + 64\frac{(40-15)(40-35)(40-45)}{(25-15)(25-35)(25-45)}$$

$$+79\frac{(40-15)(40-25)(40-45)}{(35-15)(35-25)(35-45)}$$

$$+85\frac{(40-15)(40-25)(40-35)}{(45-15)(45-25)(45-35)}$$

$$= 45\frac{(+15)(+5)(-5)}{(-10)(-20)(-30)} + 64\frac{(+25)(+5)(-5)}{(+10)(-10)(-20)}$$

$$+79\frac{(+25)(+15)(-5)}{(+20)(+10)(-10)} + 85\frac{(+25)(+15)(+5)}{(+30)(+20)(+10)}$$

$$= 45\frac{-375}{-6000} + 64\frac{-625}{+2000} + 79\frac{-1875}{-2000} + 85\frac{+1875}{+6000}$$

$$= 45 \times 0.0625 + 64 \times -0.3125 + 79 \times 0.9375 + 85 \times 0.3125$$

$$= 2.81 - 20 + 74.06 + 26.5 = 83$$

Illustration 13: *Calculate the number of students who obtained marks upto 45 from the following data, on the basis of Lagrange's Method.*

Marks	*0-10*	*10-20*	*20-30*	*30-40*	*40-50*	*50-60*
No. of students	*4*	*8*	*5*	*9*	*6*	*8*

Solution: Calculation of no. of students who obtained upto 45 marks.

Marks	*X*		*No. of students*	*Cumulative No. of students*	*Y*
0-10	10	x_0	4	4	y_0
10-20	20	x_1	8	12	y_1
20-30	30	x_2	5	17	y_2
30-40	40	x_3	9	26	y_3
40-50	50	x_4	6	32	y_4
50-60	60	x_5	8	40	y_5

$$y_x = y_0 \frac{(x-x_1)(x-x_2)(x-x_3)(x-x_4)(x-x_5)}{(x_0-x_1)(x_0-x_2)(x_0-x_3)(x_0-x_4)(x_0-x_5)}$$

$$+y_1 \frac{(x-x_0)(x-x_2)(x-x_3)(x-x_4)(x-x_5)}{(x_1-x_0)(x_1-x_2)(x_1-x_3)(x_1-x_4)(x_1-x_5)}$$

$$+y_2 \frac{(x-x_0)(x-x_1)(x-x_3)(x-x_4)(x-x_5)}{(x_2-x_0)(x_2-x_1)(x_2-x_3)(x_2-x_4)(x_2-x_5)}$$

$$+y_3 \frac{(x-x_0)(x-x_1)(x-x_2)(x-x_4)(x-x_5)}{(x_3-x_0)(x_3-x_1)(x_3-x_2)(x_3-x_4)(x_3-x_5)}$$

$$+y_4 \frac{(x-x_0)(x-x_1)(x-x_2)(x-x_3)(x-x_5)}{(x_4-x_0)(x_4-x_1)(x_4-x_2)(x_4-x_3)(x_4-x_5)}$$

$$+y_5 \frac{(x-x_0)(x-x_1)(x-x_2)(x-x_3)(x-x_4)}{(x_5-x_0)(x_5-x_1)(x_5-x_2)(x_5-x_3)(x_5-x_4)}$$

$$y_{45} = 4\frac{(45-20)(45-30)(45-40)(45-50)(45-60)}{(10-20)(10-30)(10-40)(10-50)(10-60)}$$

$$+12\frac{(45-10)(45-30)(45-40)(45-50)(45-60)}{(20-10)(20-30)(20-40)(20-50)(20-60)}$$

$$+17\frac{(45-10)(45-20)(45-40)(45-50)(45-60)}{(30-10)(30-20)(30\ \ 40)(30-50)(30-60)}$$

$$+26\frac{(45-10)(45-20)(45-30)(45-50)(45-60)}{(40-10)(40-20)(40-30)(40-50)(40-60)}$$

$$+32\frac{(45-10)(45-20)(45-30)(45-40)(45-60)}{(50-10)(50-20)(50-30)(50-40)(50-60)}$$

$$+40\frac{(45-10)(45-20)(45-30)(45-40)(45-50)}{(60-10)(60-20)(60-30)(60-40)(60-50)}$$

$$= 4\frac{(+25)(+15)(+5)(-5)(-15)}{(-10)(-20)(-30)(-40)(-50)} + 12\frac{(+35)(+15)(+5)(-5)(-15)}{(+10)(-10)(-20)(-30)(-40)}$$

$$+17\frac{(+35)(+25)(+5)(-5)(-15)}{(+20)(+10)(-10)(-20)(-30)}$$

$$+26\frac{(+35)(+25)(+15)(-5)(-15)}{(+30)(+20)(+10)(-10)(-20)}$$

$$+32\frac{(+35)(+25)(+15)(+5)(-15)}{(+40)(+30)(+20)(+10)(-10)}$$

$$+40\frac{(+35)(+25)(+15)(+5)(-5)}{(+50)(+40)(+30)(+20)(+10)}$$

$$= 4\frac{+140625}{-12000000} + 12\frac{+19685}{+2400000} + 17\frac{+328125}{-1200000}$$

$$+26\frac{+984375}{+1200000} + 32\frac{-984375}{-2400000} + 40\frac{-328125}{+12000000}$$

$$= 4\times -0.012 + 12\times 0.08 + 17\times -0.27 + 26\times 0.82$$

$$+32\times 0.41 + 40\times -0.027$$

$$= -0.048 + 0.96 - 4.59 + 21.32 + 13.12 - 1.08 = 30 \quad \text{students}$$

Illustration 14: *Find out the number of students who obtained marks from 40 to 55 through Lagrange Method, from the data given below.*

Marks	*0-30*	*30-40*	*40-50*	*50-60*	*60-70*
No. of students	*12*	*8*	*5*	*9*	*7*

Solution: Calculation of the number of students who got 40-55 marks in a class.

Marks	*X*		*No. of students*	*Cumulative No. of students*	*Y*
0-30	30	x_0	12	12	y_0
30-40	40	x_1	8	20	y_1
40-50	50	x_2	5	25	y_2
50-60	60	x_3	9	34	y_3
60-70	70	x_4	7	41	y_4

$$y_x = y_0 \frac{(x - x_1)(x - x_2)(x - x_3)(x - x_4)}{(x_0 - x_1)(x_0 - x_2)(x_0 - x_3)(x_0 - x_4)}$$

$$+ y_1 \frac{(x - x_0)(x - x_2)(x - x_3)(x - x_4)}{(x_1 - x_0)(x_1 - x_2)(x_1 - x_3)(x_1 - x_4)}$$

$$+ y_2 \frac{(x - x_0)(x - x_1)(x - x_3)(x - x_4)}{(x_2 - x_0)(x_2 - x_1)(x_2 - x_3)(x_2 - x_4)}$$

$$+ y_3 \frac{(x - x_0)(x - x_1)(x - x_2)(x - x_4)}{(x_3 - x_0)(x_3 - x_1)(x_3 - x_2)(x_3 - x_4)}$$

$$+ y_4 \frac{(x - x_0)(x - x_1)(x - x_2)(x - x_3)}{(x_4 - x_0)(x_4 - x_1)(x_4 - x_2)(x_4 - x_3)}$$

$$y_{55} = 12 \frac{(55-40)(55-50)(55-60)(55-70)}{(30-40)(30-50)(30-60)(30-70)}$$

$$+20 \frac{(55-30)(55-50)(55-60)(55-70)}{(40-30)(40-50)(40-60)(40-70)}$$

$$+25 \frac{(55-30)(55-40)(55-60)(55-70)}{(50-30)(50-40)(50-60)(50-70)}$$

$$+34 \frac{(55-30)(55-40)(55-50)(55-70)}{(60-30)(60-40)(60-50)(60-70)}$$

$$+41 \frac{(55-30)(55-40)(55-50)(55-60)}{(70-30)(70-40)(70-50)(70-60)}$$

$$= 12 \frac{(+15)(+5)(-5)(-15)}{(-10)(-20)(-30)(-40)} + 20 \frac{(+25)(+5)(-5)(-15)}{(+10)(-10)(-20)(-30)}$$

$$+25 \frac{(+25)(+15)(-5)(-15)}{(+20)(+10)(-10)(-20)} + 34 \frac{(+25)(+15)(+5)(-15)}{(+30)(+20)(+10)(-10)}$$

$$+41 \frac{(+25)(+15)(+5)(-5)}{(+40)(+30)(+20)(+10)}$$

$$= 12\frac{5625}{240000} + 20\frac{9375}{-60000} + 25\frac{28125}{40000} + 34\frac{-28125}{-60000}$$

$$+41\frac{-9375}{+240000}$$

$$= 12 \times 0.023 + 20 \times -0.156 + 25 \times 0.703 + 34 \times 0.47 + 41 \times 0.039$$

$$= 0.28 - 3.12 + 17.58 + 15.98 - 1.599 = 29$$

No. of students who got 40-55 marks

= No. of students upto 55 marks – No. of students upto 40 marks

= 29 – 20 = 9 students

(4) Parabolic Curve Method (Method of Simultaneous Equation): This method can be applied for interpolating any value of a dependent variable (y) for a given value of an independent variable (x). This method is based on the principle of simultaneous equation. The equation under parabolic curve method is,

$$y = a + bx + cx^2 + dx^3 + \ldots + nx^n$$

This equation should be continued for the number of variables known minus one *i.e.*, x - should be written for upto the power of X^{n-1} where n means number of known values.

For example, if number of known variables are five then x should continue upto the power of four *i.e.*, X^4. Hence, the parabolic curve equation should be,

$$y = a + bx + cx^2 + dx^3 + ex^4$$

Accordingly the parabolic equation would be formed based on the number of known variables. Following are some of the equations based on the known variables.

Number of known variable	*Equations*
2	$y = a + bx$
3	$y = a + bx + cx^2$
4	$y = a + bx + cx^2 + dx^3$
5	$y = a + bx + cx^2 + dx^3 + ex^4$
n	$y = a + bx + cx^2 + dx^3 + ex^4 + \ldots + nx^{n-1}$

The parabolic equation should be solved to get the value for '*a*'. The value of '*a*' is the value for unknown variable.

Illustration 15: *Find out the sales for 1990 through parabolic curve method, from the following data.*

Year	*1988*	*1989*	*1991*	*1992*
Sales (in units)	*175*	*190*	*220*	*260*

Solution: Since only 4 variables of y are known the parabolic curve for the third order can be applied for interpolating the value for 1990.

The equation for the third order is,

$$y_0 = a + bx + cx^2 + dx^3$$

Calculation of values of *a, b, c* and *d.*

X	*Constants*	*Y*
1988	-2	175
1989	-1	190
1990	0	y_0
1991	+1	220
1992	+2	260

We have to determine the values of a, b, c and d. Denoting years by '*X*' and sales by '*Y*' and taking the origin 1990 = 0 we get,

x = –2	–1	0	+1	+2
y = 175	190	y_0	220	260

Here, Y_0 is the value to be interpolated.

Substituting the value of x and y in the equation,

$$y = a + bx + cx^2 + dx^3, \text{ we get}$$

When x = –2 $\quad 175 = a - 2b + 4c - 8d$ . . . (i)

When x = –1 $\quad 190 = a - b + c - d$ . . . (ii)

When x = 0 $\quad y_0 = a$ . . . (iii)

When x = +1 $\quad 220 = a + b + c + d$ . . . (iv)

When x = +2 $\quad 260 = a + 2b + 4c + 8d$ . . . (v)

The value of 'a' would give us the desired result.

Adding equations (ii) and (iv)

$$190 = a - b + c - d$$

$$220 = a + b + c + d$$

$$410 = 2a + 2c \quad \text{. . . (vi)}$$

Adding equations (i) and (v)

$$175 = a - 2b + 4c - 8d$$

$$260 = a + 2b + 4c + 8d$$

$$435 = 2a + 8c \quad \ldots \text{(vii)}$$

Multiplying equation (vi) by 4 and deducting equation (vii) from it.

$$1640 = 8a + 8c \quad \ldots \text{(viii)}$$

$$435 = 2a + 8c \quad \ldots \text{(vii)}$$

$$1205 = 6a$$

$$6a = 1205$$

$$a = 200.83$$

Thus the sales for the year 1990 = 200.83 units

= 201 units

II Extrapolation

Extrapolation means estimation of the value for future period.

Illustration 16: *Extrapolate the production for the year 1996 from the following data.*

Year	*1991*	*1992*	*1993*	*1994*	*1995*
Sales (Rs in '000)	*35*	*42*	*45*	*55*	*70*

Solution: Binomial expansion method can be adopted. The following is the equation for the five known variables.

$$= y_5 - 5y_4 + 10y_3 - 10y_2 + 5y_1 - y_0 = 0$$

X	1991	1992	1993	1994	1995
Y	35	42	45	55	70
	y_0	y_1	y_2	y_3	y_4

$$y_5 - 5y_4 + 10y_3 - 10y_2 + 5y_1 - y_0 = 0$$

$$y_5 - (5 \times 70) + (10 \times 55) - (10 \times 45) + (5 \times 42) - 35 = 0$$

$$y_5 - 350 + 550 - 450 + 210 - 35 = 0$$

$$y_5 - 75 = 0$$

$$y_5 = 75$$

Miscellaneous Illustrations

Illustration 17: *Calculate the value of sales for 1990 from the following data.*

Year	*1988*	*1989*	*1990*	*1991*	*1992*	*1993*
Sales (Rs in '000)	*120*	*·135*	*?*	*143*	*156*	*180*

Solution: Binomial expansion method is suitable for interpolation of the problem.

Year	1988	1989	1990	1991	1992	1993
Sales	120	135	?	143	156	180
	y_0	y_1	y_2	y_3	y_4	y_5

The equation for five known values to estimate an unknown value is,

$$= y_5 - 5y_4 + 10y_3 - 10y_2 + 5y_1 - y_0 = 0$$

$$= 180 - (5 \text{ x } 156) + (10 \text{ x } 143) - (10y^2) + (5 \text{ x } 135) - 120 = 0$$

$$180 - 780 + 1430 - 10y^2 + 675 - 120 = 0$$

$$-10y^2 = -1385$$

$$y^2 = 1385/10 = 138.5$$

Illustration 18: *Estimate the price for 1978 from the following data.*

Year	*1970*	*1975*	*1980*	*1985*	*1990*
Price(Rs.)	*25*	*35*	*47*	*55*	*70*

Solution: Calculation of the differences of y

Year	*Price Rs.*		*Differences* Δ^1	Δ^2	Δ^3	Δ^4
1970	25	y_0				
			10 Δ_0^1			
1975	35	y_1		2 Δ_0^2		
			12 Δ_1^2		-6 Δ_0^3	
1980	47	y_2		-4 Δ_1^2		17 Δ_0^4
			8 Δ_2^1		11 Δ_1^3	
1985	55	y_3		7 Δ_2^2		
			15 Δ_3^1			
1990	70	y_4				

$$x = \frac{\text{Value to be interpolated} - \text{Value at the origin}}{\text{Difference between two adjoining values}}$$

$$= \frac{1978 - 1970}{1975 - 1970} = \frac{8}{5} = 1.6$$

$$y_x = y_0 + x\Delta_0^1 + \frac{x(x-1)}{2!}\Delta_0^2 + \frac{x(x-1)(x-2)}{3!}\Delta_0^3$$

$$+ \frac{x(x-1)(x-2)(x-3)}{4!}\Delta_0^4$$

$$= 25 + (1.6 \times 10) + \frac{1.6(1.6-1)}{1 \times 2} \times 2 + \frac{1.6(1.6-1)(1.6-2)}{1 \times 2 \times 3} \times (-6)$$

$$+ \frac{1.6(1.6-1)(1.6-2)(1.6-3)}{1 \times 2 \times 3 \times 4} \times 17$$

$$= 25 + 16 + (1.6 \times 0.6) + (1.6 \times 0.6 \times 0.4)$$

$$+ \frac{1.6(1.6-1)(1.6-2)}{1 \times 2 \times 3} \times (-6)$$

$$+ \frac{1.6(1.6-1)(1.6-2)(1.6-3)}{1 \times 2 \times 3 \times 4} \times 17$$

$$= 25 + 16 + 0.96 + 0.384 + 0.381 = 42.725$$

Illustration 19: *The marks obtained by students in a class are stated below.*

Marks	0-20	20-40	40-60	60-80	80-100
No. of students	15	20	30	40	55

Find out the number of students who obtained marks less than 65.

Solution: Calculation of differences of y.

Marks x	*No. of students* y		Δ^1	Δ^2	Δ^3	Δ^4
Below 20	15	y_0				
			20 Δ_0^1			
Below 40	35	y_1		10 Δ_0^2		
			30 Δ_1^1		0 Δ_0^3	
Below 60	65	y_2		10 Δ_1^2		5 Δ_0^4
			40 Δ_2^1		5 Δ_1^3	
Below 80	105	y_3		15 Δ_2^2		
			55 Δ_3^1			
Below 100	160	y_4				

$$x = \frac{\text{Value to be interpolated} - \text{Value at the origin}}{\text{Difference between two abjoining values}}$$

$$= \frac{65-20}{40-20} = \frac{45}{20} = 2.25$$

$$y_x = y_0 + x\Delta_0^1 + \frac{x(x-1)}{2!}\Delta_0^2 + \frac{x(x-1)(x-2)}{3!}\Delta_0^3$$

$$+ \frac{x(x-1)(x-2)(x-3)}{4!}\Delta_0^4$$

$$= 15 + (2.25\times 20) + \frac{2.25(2.25-1)}{1\times 2}\times 10$$

$$+ \frac{2.25(2.25-1)(2.25-2)}{1\times 2\times 3}\times 0$$

$$+ \frac{2.25(2.25-1)(2.25-2)(2.25-3)}{1\times 2\times 3\times 4}\times 5$$

$= 15 + 45 + 14.06 + 0 - 0.11 \quad = 74$ students.

Illustration 20: *Calculate the number of students who scored more than 75 marks, from the following data.*

Marks	*No. of students*
Upto 60	*30*
Upto 70	*45*
Upto 80	*50*
Upto 90	*80*
Upto 100	*100*

Solution: Calculation of differences of *y*.

Marks x	*No. of students* y		Δ^1	Δ^2	Δ^3	Δ^4
Upto 60	30	y_0				
			15 Δ_0^1			
Upto 70	45	y_1		-10 Δ_0^2		
			5 Δ_1^1		35 Δ_0^3	
Upto 80	50	y_2		25 Δ_1^2		-70 Δ_0^4
			30 Δ_2^1		-35 Δ_1^3	
Upto 90	80	y_3		-10 Δ_2^2		
			20 Δ_3^1			
Upto 100	100	y_4				

$$x = \frac{\text{Value to be interpolated} - \text{Value at the origin}}{\text{Difference between two abjoining values}}$$

$$= \frac{75-60}{70-60} = \frac{15}{10} = 1.5$$

$$y_x = y_0 + x\Delta_0^1 + \frac{x(x-1)}{2!}\Delta_0^2 + \frac{x(x-1)(x-2)}{3!}\Delta_0^3$$

$$+ \frac{x(x-1)(x-2)(x-3)}{4!}\Delta_0^4$$

$$= 30 + (1.5\times15) + \frac{1.5(1.5-1)}{1\times2}\times(-10) + \frac{1.5(1.5-1)(1.5-2)}{1\times2\times3}\times35$$

$$+ \frac{1.5(1.5-1)(1.5-2)(1.5-3)}{1\times2\times3\times4}\times(-70)$$

$= 30 + 22.5 - 3.75 - 2.19 + 1.64 = 48.20$ i.e., **48 students.**

$\therefore$ No. of students scored more than 75 marks = 100 – 48 = 52.

Illustration 21: *Estimate the production for 1991 and 1994 from the following data.*

Year	*1989*	*1990*	*1991*	*1992*	*1993*	*1994*	*1995*
Production (in tonnes)	*60*	*75*	*?*	*90*	*125*	*?*	*150*

Solution:

Year	1989	1990	1991	1992	1993	1994	1995
Production (in tonnes)	60	75	?	90	125	?	150
	y_0	y_1	y_2	y_3	y_4	y_5	y_6

$$y_6 - 6y_5 + 15y_4 - 20y_3 + 15y_2 - 6y_1 + y_0 = 0$$

$$y_5 - 5y_4 + 10y_3 - 10y_2 + 5y_1 - y_0 = 0$$

$$150 - 6y_5 + (15\times125) - (20\times90) + 15y_2 - (6\times75) + 60 = 0$$

$$150 - 6y_5 + 1875 - 1800 + 15y_2 - 450 + 60 = 0$$

$$-6y_5 + 15y_2 = 165 \quad \text{. . . (i)}$$

$$y_5 - (5\times125) + (10\times90) - 10y_2 + (5\times75) - 60 = 0$$

$$y_5 - 625 + 900 - 10y_2 + 375 - 60 = 0$$

$$y_5 - 10y_2 = -590 \quad \text{. . . (ii)}$$

$$-6y_5 + 15y_2 = 165 \quad \text{. . . (i)}$$

(ii)×6 $\quad 6y_5 - 60y_2 = -3540$ . . . (iii)

(i) + (iii) $\quad -45y_2 = -3375$

$$y_2 = \frac{3375}{45} = 75$$

(ii) $\quad y_5 - (10\times75) = -590$

$$y_5 = 750 - 590 = 160$$

Hence, the estimated production for 1991 is 75 tonnes and for 1994 is 160 tonnes.

Illustration 22: *From the following data estimate the sales for May 1995 through Lagrange's method.*

Month	*January*	*April*	*July*	*October*
Sales (Rs in '000)	*30*	*50*	*75*	*120*

Solution:

	Month x		*Sales* y	
January	1	x_0	30	y_0
April	4	x_1	50	y_1
July	7	x_2	75	y_2
October	10	x_3	120	y_3

x = May 1995 i.e., = 5

Lagrange's formula,

$$y_x = y_0 \frac{(x-x_1)(x-x_2)(x-x_3)}{(x_0-x_1)(x_0-x_2)(x_0-x_3)} + y_1 \frac{(x-x_0)(x-x_2)(x-x_3)}{(x_1-x_0)(x_1-x_2)(x_1-x_3)}$$

$$+ y_2 \frac{(x-x_0)(x-x_1)(x-x_3)}{(x_2-x_0)(x_2-x_1)(x_2-x_3)}$$

$$+ y_3 \frac{(x-x_0)(x-x_1)(x-x_2)}{(x_3-x_0)(x_3-x_1)(x_3-x_2)}$$

$$= 30 \frac{(5-4)(5-7)(5-10)}{(1-4)(1-7)(1-10)} + 50 \frac{(5-1)(5-7)(5-10)}{(4-1)(4-7)(4-10)}$$

$$+75 \frac{(5-1)(5-4)(5-10)}{(7-1)(7-4)(7-10)} + 120 \frac{(5-1)(5-4)(5-7)}{(10-1)(10-4)(10-7)}$$

$$= 30(-0.06) + 50(0.74) + 75(0.37) + 120(-0.05)$$

$$= -1.8 + 37 + 27.75 - 6 = 56.95 \quad \text{i.e., Rs. 56950/-}$$

Illustration 23: *Interpolate the figure of population of a town for the year 1976 from the following data.*

Year	*1960*	*1970*	*1980*	*1990*
Population	*25,494*	*29,003*	*32,528*	*36,070*

(MGU: Section B April '98)

Solution: Newton's method of interpolation can be applied.

Calculation of differences of y.

x	y	Δ_1	Δ_2	Δ_3
1960	25494 y_0			
		3509 Δ_0^1		
1970	29003 y_1		16 Δ_0^2	
		3525 Δ_1^1		1 Δ_0^3
1980	32528 y_2		17 Δ_1^2	
		3542 Δ_2^1		
1990	36070 y_3			

$$x = \frac{1976-1960}{10} = 1.6$$

$$y_{76} = y_0 + x\Delta_0^1 + \frac{x(x-1)}{1\times 2}\Delta_0^2 + \frac{x(x-1)(x-2)}{1\times 2\times 3}\Delta_0^3$$

$$= 25{,}494 + (1.6)(3509) + \frac{(1.6)(1.6-1)(16)}{1\times 2}$$

$$+ \frac{(1.6)(1.6-1)(1.6-2)(1)}{1\times 2\times 3}$$

$$= 25{,}494 + 5614.4 + 7.7 - 0.1 = 31{,}116$$

Illustration 24: *Interpolate the missing figures in the following table of paddy cultivation.*

Year	*1990*	*1991*	*1992*	*1993*	*1994*	*1995*	*1996*
Acres	*60*	*68*	*69*	*70*	*75*	*?*	*82*

(MGU: Section C April '97)

Solution: Binomial expansion method can be applied.

Calculation of the value for 1995

x	y	
1990	60	y_0
1991	68	y_1
1992	69	y_2
1993	70	y_3
1994	75	y_4
1995	?	y_5
1996	82	y_6

$$\Delta_0^6 = y_6 - 6y_5 + 15y_4 - 20y_3 + 15y_2 - 6y_1 + y_0 = 0$$

$$= 82 - 6y5 + 15(75) - 20(70) + 15(69) - 6(68) + 60 = 0$$

$$= 82 - 6y5 + 1125 - 1400 + 1035 - 408 + 60 = 0$$

$$6y_5 = 2302 - 1808 = 494$$

$$y_5 = \frac{494}{6} = 82$$

Acres in 1995 = 82 million.

Illustration 25: *Using binomial expansion method of interpolation, estimate the business done on April from the following data.*

Month	*January*	*February*	*March*	*April*	*May*	*June*
Business done (in '000)	*150*	*235*	*365*	*?*	*525*	*780*

Solution: Calculation of the value for April.

x	y	
January	150	y_0
February	235	y_1
March	365	y_2
April	?	y_3
May	525	y_4
June	780	y_5

$$\Delta_0^5 = y_5 - 5y_4 + 10y_3 - 10y_2 + 5y_1 - y_0 = 0$$

$$= 780 - 5(525) + 10y_3 - 10(365) + 5(235) - 150 = 0$$

$$= 780 - 2625 + 10y_3 - 3650 + 1175 - 150 = 0$$

$$10y_3 = 4470$$

$$y_3 = 447$$

Business done in April = Rs. 447000

Illustration 26: *The expectation of life at different ages of males (for a state) is given below.*

Age (in years)	*20*	*25*	*30*	*35*	*40*
Expectation of life (in years)	*33.0*	*29.8*	*26.6*	*23.5*	*20.5*

Use Newton's formula to estimate the expectation of life at the age of 32. (MGU: Section C April '95)

Solution: Calculation of differences of *y*.

Age	*Expection of life*	*Differences*			
x	*y*	Δ_1	Δ_2	Δ_3	Δ_4
20	33.0 y_0				
		–3.2 Δ_0^1			
25	29.8 y_1		0 Δ_0^2		
		–3.2 Δ_1^1		–0.1 Δ_0^3	
30	26.6 y_2		–0.1 Δ_1^2		0.1 Δ_0^4
		–3.1 Δ_2^1		0 Δ_1^3	
35	23.5 y_3		–0.1 Δ_2^2		
		–3.0 Δ_3^1			
40	20.5 y_4				

$$x = \frac{32-20}{5} = \frac{12}{5} = 2.4$$

$$y_{32} = y_0 + x\Delta_0^1 + \frac{x(x-1)}{1\times 2}\Delta_0^2 + \frac{x(x-1)(x-2)}{1\times 2\times 3}\Delta_0^3$$

$$+ \frac{x(x-1)(x-2)(x-3)}{1\times 2\times 3\times 4}\Delta_0^4$$

$$= 33.0 + 2.4(-3.2) + \frac{(2.4)(2.4-1)(0)}{1\times 2}$$

$$+ \frac{(2.4)(2.4-1)(2.4-2)(-0.1)}{1\times 2\times 3}$$

$$+ \frac{(2.4)(2.4-1)(2.4-2)(2.4-3)(0.1)}{1\times 2\times 3\times 4}$$

$$= 33.0 - 7.68 + 0 - 0.02 - 0.003 = 33.0 - 7.7 = 25.3$$

Illustration 27: *The following table gives the sales of a company for the period 1970 - 76. Find out the sales for the missing year by using Graphic Method.*

Year	*1970*	*1971*	*1972*	*1973*	*1974*	*1975*	*1976*
Sales	*40*	*80*	*120*	*?*	*200*	*240*	*280*

(MGU: Section B September '94)

Solution:

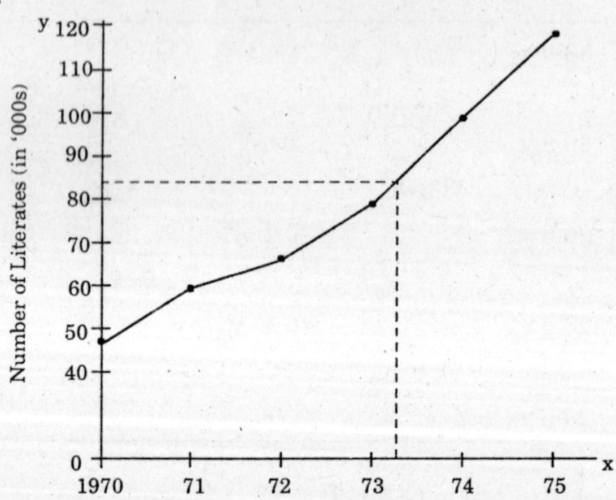

Illustration 28: *Using appropriate formula for interpolation, estimate the number of students who obtained less than 45 marks from the following data.*

Marks	*0-40*	*40-50*	*50-60*	*60-70*	*70-80*
No. of students	*31*	*42*	*51*	*35*	*31*

(MGU: Section B Sep.'92)

Solution: Newton's method of interpolation can be applied.

Calculation of differences of y.

x	f	y	Δ^1	Δ^2	Δ^3	Δ^4
40	31	31 y_0				
			42 Δ_0^1			
50	42	73 y_1		9 Δ_0^2		
			51 Δ_1^1		−25 Δ_0^3	
60	51	124 y_2		−16 Δ_1^2		37 Δ_0^4
			35 Δ_2^1		12 Δ_1^3	
70	35	159 y_3		−4 Δ_2^2		
			31 Δ_3^1			
80	31	190 y_4				

$$x = \frac{45-40}{10} = 0.5$$

$$y_{45} = y_0 + x\Delta_0^1 + \frac{x(x-1)}{1\times2}\Delta_0^2 + \frac{x(x-1)(x-2)}{1\times2\times3}\Delta_0^3$$

$$+\frac{x(x-1)(x-2)(x-3)}{1\times2\times3\times4}\Delta_0^4$$

$$= 31 + (0.5)(11) + \frac{(0.5)(0.5-1)(9)}{1\times2} + \frac{(0.5)(0.5-1)(0.5-2)(-25)}{1\times2\times3}$$

$$+\frac{(0.5)(0.5-1)(0.5-2)(0.5-3)(37)}{1\times2\times3\times4}$$

$$= 31 + 21 - 1.125 - 1.56 - 1.45 = 52 - 4.4 = 47.6$$

= 48 students.

Illustration 29: *Interpolate the value of premium to be paid when the age for the next birthday is 17 by using the Newton's method from the following table.*

Age (Next birthday in years)	*15*	*25*	*35*	*45*	*55*
Premium (Rs.)	*11.1*	*12.6*	*14.3*	*16.1*	*18.3*

(MGU: Section B April '93)

Solution: Calculation of differences of *y*.

x	y	Δ^1	Δ^2	Δ^3	Δ^4
15	11.1 y_0				
		1.5 Δ_0^1			
25	12.6 y_1		0.2 Δ_0^2		
		1.7 Δ_1^1		–0.1 Δ_0^3	
35	14.3 y_2		0.1 Δ_1^2		0.4 Δ_0^4
		1.8 Δ_2^1		0.3 Δ_1^3	
45	16.1 y_3		0.4 Δ_2^2		
		2.2 Δ_3^1			
55	18.3 y_4				

$$x = \frac{17-15}{10} = 0.2$$

$$y_{17} = y_0 + x\Delta_0^1 + \frac{x(x-1)}{1\times 2}\Delta_0^2 + \frac{x(x-1)(x-2)}{1\times 2\times 3}\Delta_0^3$$

$$+\frac{x(x-1)(x-2)(x-3)}{1\times 2\times 3\times 4}\Delta_0^4$$

$$= 11.1 + (0.2)(1.5) + \frac{(0.2)(0.2-1)(0.2)}{1\times 2}$$

$$+\frac{(0.2)(0.2-1)(0.2-2)(-0.1)}{1\times 2\times 3}$$

$$+\frac{(0.2)(0.2-1)(0.2-2)(0.2-3)(0.4)}{1\times 2\times 3\times 4}$$

$$= 11.1 + 0.3 - 0.02 - 0.005 - 0.01 = 11.36 = 11.4$$

Exercise

1. Define Interpolation. State the benefits of interpolation.
2. What is Interpolation? State briefly the different methods of interpolation.
3. Distinguish between interpolation and extrapolation.
4. Define Interpolation. State the procedure for Binomial Expansion Method of Interpolation.

5. Define Interpolation. State the procedure for Newton's Method of Interpolation.

6. Define Interpolation. State the procedure for Lagrange's Method of Interpolation.

7. What is Interpolation? State the procedure for the Parabolic Curve Method of Interpolation.

8. Explain the significance and utility of interpolation and extrapolation. (MGU: Section B April '97)

9. Explain the Binomial Expansion method and Newton's method of interpolation. (MGU: Section B April '94)

10. Find out the sales for 1991 from the following data.

Year	1989	1990	1992	1993	1994
Sales (Rs in '000)	36	47	59	68	85

[Ans: 53.4]

11. Extrapolate the profit for 1996, from the following data.

Year	1991	1992	1993	1994	1995
Profit (Rs in '000)	8	15	25	40	56

[Ans: 63]

12. Find out the number of employed people in a village for the year 1987 from the following data.

Year	1984	1986	1988	1990	1992
Employed	25	37	47	59	78

[Ans: 52]

13. Calculate the number of men getting wages between Rs. 40 and 50.

Wages	20-40	40-60	60-80	80-100
No. of Men	10	25	42	50

[Ans: 17]

14. The wages of workers in a town are stated below:

Wages less than (Rs.)	30	40	50	60	70
No. of workers	45	66	85	100	120

Estimate the no. of workers earning Rs. 45 and Rs. 65.

[Ans: 72 and 108]

15. Estimate the value of y when $x = 125$.

x	50	100	150	200	250
y	120	105	80	60	30

[Ans: 92.11]

16. Calculate the missing value from the following:

Year	1986	1988	1990	1992	1994
Profit (Rs in '0000)	24	31	?	47	57

[Ans: 38.5]

17. Interpolate the production for the month of May 1995, through Lagrange method.

Months	March	June	October	November
Production (in tonnes)	5	12	18	29

[Ans: 12.43]

18. Estimate the advertisement expenses for 1991 and 1994 from the following data through Lagrange method.

Year	1989	1990	1992	1993	1995
Advertisement Expenses (Rs in '000)	320	400	465	600	750

[Ans: Rs. 407,770; Rs. 747,770]

19. Interpolate the number of students who scored below 65 marks through Lagrange method from the following data.

Marks less than	20	40	60	80	100
No. of students	14	39	48	62	70

[Ans: 51]

20. Estimate the production for 1992 by Parabolic curve method from the following data.

Year	1990	1991	1993	1994
Production (in tonnes)	80	130	170	200

[Ans: 153.33]

◆ Chapter 14 ◆

Probability

The probability theory was developed during 17th centry to solve the problems in gambling. The gamblers approached the famous mathematicians in their locality for their gambling problems. Hence the probability theory was developed. The origin of probability is that a French mathematician Blaise Pascal first solved the question, with regard to gambling, raised by a French noble man Antoine Gombauld. Antoine Gombauld is known as Chevaliar De Mere. Pascal discuss the problem raised by De Mere with other French mathematician Pierre de Fermat. This laid the foundation for the theory of probability. This theory got a gradual development during the 18th century. The other contributors for the development of Probability theory are De Moirre (1718), James Bernouli (1713) and Bayes (1768). Mathematicians like R.A. Fisher, Pearson, J. Neyman etc gave further development for the theory.

I Meaning of Probability

In day to day life people are interested in predicting the occurance or non-occurance of an event in future. It is difficult for them to say what will happen in future. Hence they require some theory to determine the chance of happening or not happening an event in future. The theory required for the prediction is called probability theory. Hence, probability is nothing but the prediction of the degree of possibility of occurance or non-occurance of an event. Probability is initially applied in games of chance, like tossing of coin, throwing of dice and playing cards. Now the theory is widely used in solving various managerial problems of companies, Government and social organizations.

Approaches to Probability

There are four important schools of thought on probability. They are,

(1) Classical or a priori approach

(2) Relative frequency or empirical approach

(3) Axiomatic approach

(4) Subjective approach

(1) Classical Approach to Probability: The classical approach of measuring probability is the oldest method. This method is most suitable for gambling situation, since the method had its origin in gambling games. Under classical approach, the probability of an event is the ratio of number of favorable outcomes of an event to the number of possible outcomes.

The character of possible outcomes is that each event is likely to occur.

The probability of occurance of an event A is measured as,

$$P(A) = \frac{a}{a+b}$$

where, a = Number of outcomes favorable to the occurance of A.

a + b = Total number of possible outcomes.

The probability of non occurance of A can be denoted as q(A) and it can be measured as,

$$q(A) = \frac{b}{a+b}$$

where,

b = Number of outcomes not favorable to the occurance of A.

For example, in the throw of a die the probability of occurance of No. 4 is, P(4) = 1/6

Since in the die there is one 4 and the total outcome is 6.

(2) Relative Frequency Approach to Probability: The relative frequency approach to probability was formulated during 1800s by the British Statisticians. This approach is useful in solving problems which could not be solved through classical approach. According to relative frequency approach, the valid procedure for determining the probability is through repetitive experiments. For example, if a coin is tossed the probability of getting head is 1/2 i.e., 0.5. If the coin is tossed repeatedly say, for 10 times we may get 3 heads and 7 tails. Hence the probability of getting head is 3/10 = 0.3. When the number of repetition is increased

to 100 times, one may get head for 42 times. Now the probability of getting head is 42/100 = 0.42. When the repetition is further increased to 500 times, we may get heads for 240 times. Therefore, the probability of getting head is 240/500 = 0.48. It is very close to 0.5. Hence, in practice the probability can be measured accurately through repetitive experiments.

It can be represented as,

$$P(E) = \lim_{n \to \infty} \frac{a}{n}$$

where, a = indicates the number of expected events.
n = indicates total number of experiments.

It means that the accurate probability depends on the greater number of experiments.

(3) Axiomatic Approach to Probability: A.N. Kolmogorov, a Russian mathematician developed the axiomatic approach to probability. According to this approach, the probability of occurance of either of two events is the total of the probability of occurance of each event individually. This approach is applied, when the events are mutually exclusive (disjoint).

For example, if x and y are two mutually exclusive events, then the probability of occurance of either x or y is,

$$P(x \cup y) = P(x) + P(y)$$

(4) Subjective Approach to Probability: Frank Ramsey formulated the subjective approach to probability during 1926. This approach is otherwise called as Personalistic approach to probability.

According to subjective approach, probability may be defined on the basis of the personal judgment of an individual. The personal judgment of an individual depends on evidence and the experience of the individual. For example (i) an individual may judge the probability of coming a bus at 8.30 A.M. as 0.7, on the basis of the punctuality of the bus coming at 8.30 A.M. in previous days. (ii) an individual may judge the probability of his passing the examination as 90% (*i.e.*, 0.9) on the basis of his hard work and the nature of the question papers.

Hence an individual assign probability of occurance of an event for 0 to 1. If he is very sure that an event will occur then he may determine the probability as very close to No. 1. The main limitation of this approach is that the value of probability differs from one individual to other.

Fundamental Concepts of Probability

The important concepts of probability are,

(1) Random experiment
(2) Sample space
(3) Event
(4) Equally Likely Events
(5) Mutually Exclusive Events
(6) Exhaustive Events
(7) Independent Events
(8) Dependent Events
(9) Complementary Events

(1) Random Experiment: Random Experiment is an experiment whose result depends on chance (*e.g.*) tossing of coins, throwing of dice etc. In a random experiment the possible outcomes are known well in advance. The occurance of an event depends upon mere chance.

The experiment conducted to obtain an outcome is called random experiment. (*e.g.*) (i) In the tossing of coin the outcome are head and tail. (ii) In the throw of die the outcome are 1, 2, 3, 4, 5, 6. In a random experiment anyone of these outcome may occur.

(2) Sample space: Sample space means the collection of all possible outcomes. It may also be termed as set of all possible outcomes. The sample space for tossing a coin are head and tail. The sample space of throwing a die are 1, 2, 3, 4, 5 and 6.

Each possible outcome in the sample space is called sample point or element.

(3) Event: Any element or sample point of the sample space is called event. Event may be (i) Simple event and (ii) Complex event. If the event contains one element it is called simple event. If the event is defined by more than one sample point, it is called compound or complex event.

(4) Equally Likely Events: Events are called equally likely events when all the elements of the sample space got equal chance of occurance (or being selected). In the tossing of a coin the head and tail are equally likely events.

(5) Mutually Exclusive Events: Mutually exclusive events mean those event (or events), the occurance of which prevents the possibility of the occurance of other. It means, if one event occur the other event will not occur. When a coin is tossed either head

or tail may occur. Hence head and tail are mutually exclusive events.

(6) Exhaustive Events: Exhaustive events mean that at least one of the events should necessarily occurs. In the throw of a die there exists 6 exhaustive events.

(7) Independent Events: Independent events are those events, the occurance of which do not affect the occurance of other events. Independent events have no influence over the occurance of other events. The occurance of head in a toss of coin won't affect the occurance of head in the second and subsequent tosses.

(8) Dependent Events: Dependent events are those events the occurance of which affect the occurance of other events. For example, the probability of drawing a Queen from a pack of 52 cards is 4/52 i.e., 1/13. In the first draw if the incident happened, and the card is not replaced, the probability of getting another Queen card is 3/51; If the Queen card is not replaced and then the probability of getting a king card is 4/51.

(9) Complementary Events: The non-occurance events are called Complementary Events. If we expect an event x should happen then there are events denoted by 'not x' or x^c. x^c are called complementary events. In the throw of a die, if we expect No. 6 should occur, then the other events *i.e.*, No. 1, 2, 3, 4 and 5 are complementary events.

II Set Theory

Set theory is applied in the modern approach to the probability theory. The important concepts of set theory, applied in the probability theory are stated below.

Set: Set means the collection of well defined and specified elements or objects. (*e.g.*) the books in a library, the students in a class, the employees in a company etc.

Universal Set: The set consisting of all the elements under consideration is called Universal Set. For example, if A is a set and U is the universal set, then every element in A must be in U.

Null Set: The null set or empty set is a set having no element.

Subset: When every element of a set, is also elements for another set, the first set is called the subset of the second set. For example,

Set $A = \{10, 15, 20\}$ and set $B = \{1, 3, 5, 10, 15, 20, 30\}$ are the two sets. Here A is called the subset of B since every element of A is also the elements of B. It can be denoted as $A \subset B$.

Equal Sets: Two sets ar called equal sets when the elements of both the sets are the same.

For example, A and B are equal sets.

When $A = \{3, 4, 8, 9\}$ and $B = \{3, 4, 8, 9\}$.

It can be represented as $A \subset B$ and $B \subset A$.

Functions of Set

The important functions of set are stated below.

(1) Intersection of Set: When two sets are having few common elements, then it is called intersection of sets. In sets, $A = \{4, 6, 8, 10\}$ and $B = \{1, 2, 5, 6, 10\}$ the elements 6 and 10 are common, which are called intersection of sets A and B *i.e.*, $A \cap B = \{6, 10\}$.

It can be written as $A \cap B = \{x / x \in A \text{ and } x \in B\}$.

Intersection of sets can be diagramatically represented as follows.

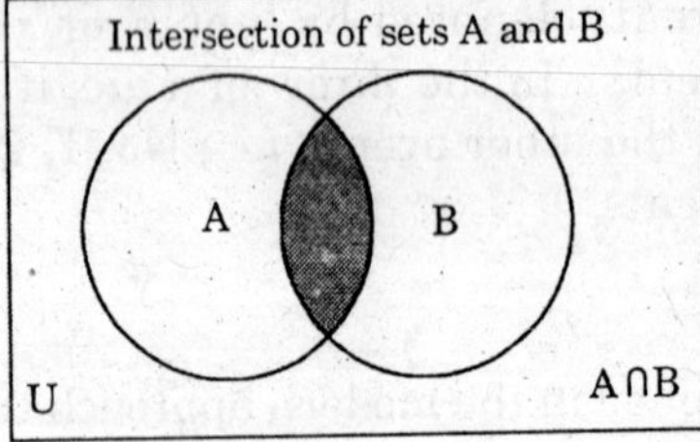

(2) Disjoint Sets: When two sets are not having common elements then the two sets are called disjoint sets.

Example, $A = \{3, 6, 9, 12\}$ and $B = \{4, 8, 10, 15\}$ are two sets. These sets do not have common elements. Hence A and B are called disjoint sets. It can be represented as $A \cap B = \phi$. Where ϕ is a null set. Disjoint sets are represented in the following diagram.

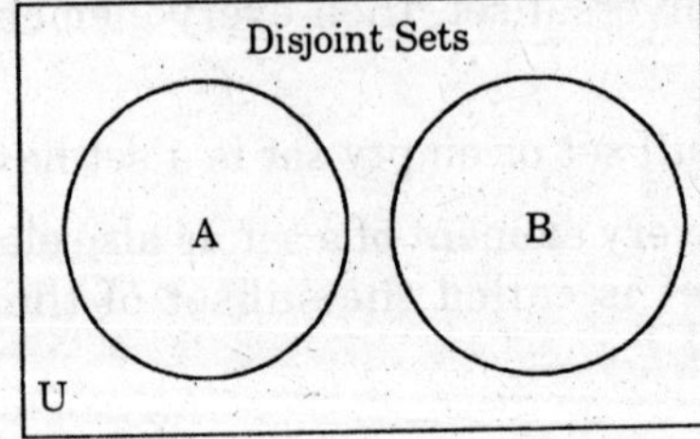

(3) Union of Sets: The set of elements belonging to 2 sets is called union of sets. For example, $A = \{1, 2, 3, 4, 5\}$ and $B = (2, 4, 6, 8, 10\}$. The elements belonging to A and B are 1, 2, 3, 4, 5, 6, 8, 10. They are called Union of sets. It can be written as $A \cup B = \{1, 2, 3, 4, 5, 6, 8, 10\}$. Hence, $A \cup B = \{x / x \in A \text{ or } x \in B\}$.

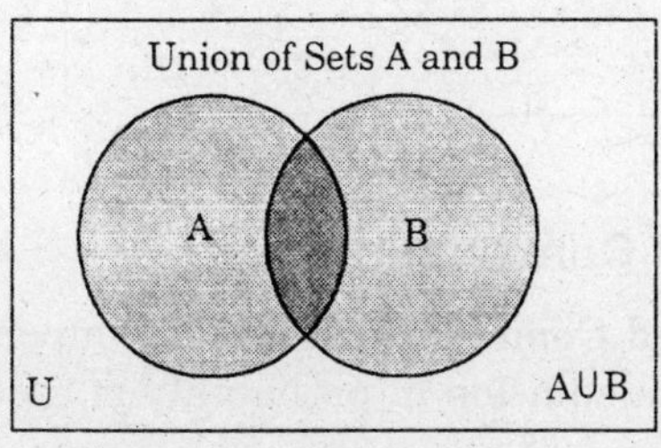

(4) Complement of a Set: Set of all elements of the universe except the elements of a particular set is called complement of a set. If, $U = \{1, 2, 3, 4, 5, 6, 7, 8\}$ and $A = \{2, 3, 5\}$ then the set of the elements 1, 4, 6, 7, 8 is called complement set. It can be written as $A' = \{1, 4, 6, 7, 8\}$. Hence, $A' = \{x / x \in U \text{ and } x \notin A\}$.

Complement of a set is diagramatically represented as follows.

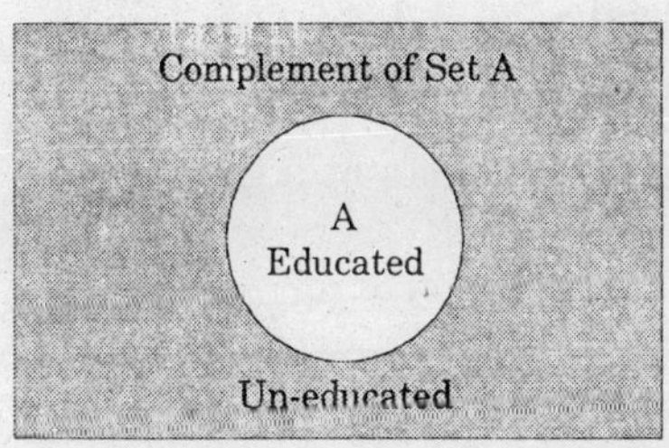

(5) Difference of Two Sets: The set of elements of a set except the intersection elements of the set is called the difference between one set with another set. If $A = \{3, 4, 5, 6, 8\}$ and $B = \{4, 5, 6\}$.

$$A - B = \{3, 8\}.$$

It can be represented as,

$$A - B = \{x / x \in A \text{ and } x \notin B\}.$$

Difference of two sets is shown in the following diagram.

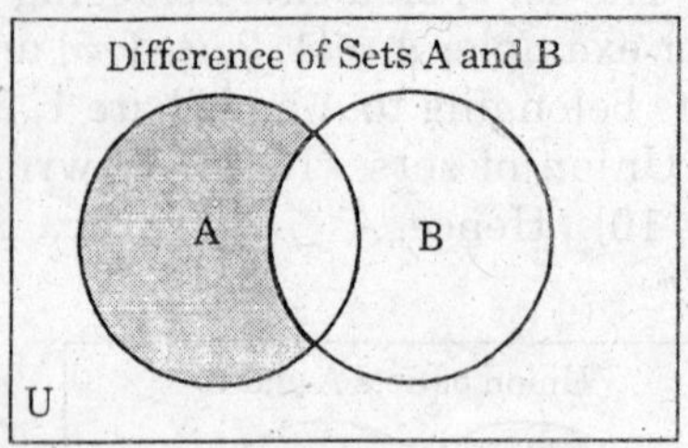

III Permutations & Combinations

Permutations and Combinations are the important counting techniques for the calculation of probability of an event.

Permutation: Permutation means the arrangement of number of objects in a definite order. The number of permutation depends upon the total number of objects and the number of objects taken at a time for arrangement. The formula for calculating permutation is,

$$n\,\mathrm{Pr} = \frac{n!}{(n-r)!}$$

! = Factorial

n = Total number of objects

r = Number of objects at a time

$nPn = n!$

Illustration 1: *Find out the number of ways 6 books in a library can be arranged taking all books at a time.*

Solution: nPn = n !

= 6 ! = 1 × 2 × 3 × 4 × 5 × 6 = 720 times.

Hence, 720 times the 6 books can be arranged.

Illustration 2: *A company received 9 applications for 3 posts. Find out, in how many ways 3 people can be selected for the nine applications.*

Solution: The number of ways 3 people can be selected from the 9 applications is calculated as,

$$n\,\mathrm{Pr} = \frac{n\,!}{(n-r)!}$$

$$9P3 = \frac{9\,!}{(9-3)!} = \frac{9\,!}{6\,!} = 9 \times 8 \times 7 = 504$$

Combinations: Combination is a technique of selection of objects without considering their order.

The formula for calculating combination is,

$$nCr = \frac{n\,!}{(n-r)!\mathrm{r}\,!}$$

$$nCn = 1$$

$$nC_1 = n$$

n = number of objects

r = number of objects taken at a time

! = factorial

Illustration 3: *A basket contains 10 mangoes. In how many ways 4 mangoes from the basket can be selected.*

Solution: The number of ways 4 mangoes from the basket of 10 mangoes can be selected can be calculated as,

$$nCr = \frac{n\,!}{(n-r)!\mathrm{r}\,!}$$

$$10C_4 = \frac{10\,!}{(10-4)!\,4\,!} = \frac{10\,!}{6\,!\ 4\,!}$$

$$= \frac{1 \times 2 \times 3 \times 4 \times 5 \times 6 \times 7 \times 8 \times 9 \times 10}{1 \times 2 \times 3 \times 4 \times 5 \times 6 \times 1 \times 2 \times 3 \times 4} = 210 \text{ ways.}$$

Illustration 4: *A coin is tossed 7 times. Find the probability of obtaining (i) 6 Heads (ii) 7 Heads and (iii) 5 or more Heads.*

Solution: Probability of getting a Head (p) = 1/2

Probability of getting a Tail (q) = 1/2

(i) Probability of getting 6 Heads

$$P(6) = 7C_6 p^6 q^1 = \frac{7!}{(7-6)!6!}(1/2)^6(1/2)^1$$

$$= \frac{7\times6\times5\times4\times3\times2}{1\times2\times3\times4\times5\times6}\times\frac{1}{128} = \frac{7}{128} = 0.055$$

(ii) Probability of getting 7 Heads

$$P(7) = 7C_7 p^7 q^0 = \frac{7!}{0!7!}\times(1/2)^7(1/2)^0 = \frac{1}{128} = 0.0078$$

(iii) Probability of getting 5 or more Heads

$$= P(5) + P(6) + P(7)$$

$$= 7C_5 p^5 q^2 + 7C_6 p^6 q^1 + 7C_7 p^7 q^0$$

$$= \frac{7!}{2!5!}\times(1/2)^5(1/2)^2 + 0.055 + 0.0078$$

$$= \frac{7\times6}{1\times2}\times\frac{1}{128} + 0.055 + 0.0078$$

$$= 0.164 + 0.055 + 0.0078 = 0.227$$

Illustration 5: *Find out the probability of getting (a) Three Heads (b) at least Two Heads and (c) at least 1 Head, when 5 coins are tossed simultaneously.*

Solution: (a) Probability of getting three Heads,

$$P(3) = 5C_3 p^3 q^2 = \frac{5!}{2!\,3!}\times(1/2)^3(1/2)^2$$

$$= \frac{5\times4}{1\times2}\times\frac{1}{32} = \frac{10}{32} = 0.313$$

(b) Probability of getting at least two Heads,

$$P(\geq 2) = P(2) + P(3) + P(4) + P(5)$$

$$= 5C_2 p^2 q^3 + 5C_3 p^3 q^2 + 5C_4 p^4 q^1 + 5C_5 p^5 q^0$$

$$= \frac{5!}{3!\,2!}(1/2)^2(1/2)^3 + \frac{5!}{2!\,3!}(1/2)^3(1/2)^2$$

$$+ \frac{5!}{1!\,4!}(1/2)^4(1/2)^1 + \frac{5!}{0!\,5!}(1/2)^5(1/2)^0$$

$$= \frac{5\times4\times3}{1\times2\times3}\times\frac{1}{32}\times\frac{5\times4}{1\times2}\times\frac{1}{32}+5\times\frac{1}{32}+\frac{1}{32}$$

$$= \frac{10}{32}+\frac{10}{32}+\frac{5}{32}+\frac{1}{32}$$

$$= 0.313 + 0.313 + 0.156 + 0.031 = 0.813$$

(OR)

$$P(\geq 2) = 1 - \left[q^0 + q^1\right]$$

$$= 1 - \left[5C_0 q^0 p^5 + 5C_1 q^1 p^4\right] = 1 - \left[\frac{1}{32}+\frac{5}{32}\right]$$

$$= 1 - (0.031 + 0.156) = 1 - 0.187 = 0.813$$

(c) Probability of getting at least one Head,

$$P(\geq 1) = P_1 + P_2 + P_3 + P_4 + P_5$$

$$= 5C_1 p^1 q^4 + 5C_2 p^2 q^3 + 5C_3 p^3 q^2 + 5C_4 p^4 q^1 + 5C_5 p^5 q^0$$

$$= \frac{5!}{4!\,1!}(1/2)^1(1/2)^4 + 0.313 + 0.313 + 0.156 + 0.031$$

$$= \frac{5}{32} + 0.313 + 0.313 + 0.156 + 0.031$$

$$= 0.156 + 0.313 + 0.313 + 0.156 + 0.031 = 0.969$$

(OR)

$$P = 1 - q_0 = 1 - 5C_0 q^0 p^5$$

$$= 1 - \frac{5!}{5!}(1/2)^0(1/2)^5 = 1 - \frac{1}{32} = \frac{31}{32} = 0.969$$

Illustration 6: *The average percentage of pass in a test paper is 70. Find out the probability that out of a group of 8 students at least 5 passed in the examination.*

Solution: Percentage of pass in the examination (p) = 70% = 0.7.

Hence, $q = 1 - p = 1 - 0.7 = 0.3$

The probability of passing 5 or more students,

$$P(\geq 5) = P_5 + P_6 + P_7 + P_8$$

$$= 8C_5 p^5 q^3 + 8C_6 p^6 q^2 + 8C_7 p^7 q^1 + 8C_8 p^8 q^0$$

$$= \frac{8!}{3!\ 5!}(0.7)^5 (0.3)^3 + \frac{8!}{2!\ 6!}(0.7)^6 (0.3)^2$$

$$+ \frac{8!}{1!\ 7!}(0.7)^7 (0.3)^1 + \frac{8!}{0!\ 8!}(0.7)^8 (0.3)^0$$

$$= 56 \times (0.7)^5 (0.3)^3 + 28 \times (0.7)^6 (0.3)^2$$

$$+ 8 \times (0.7)^7 (0.3)^1 + 1 \times (0.7)^8 (0.3)^0$$

$$= 56 \times 0.005 + 28 \times 0.011 + 8 \times 0.025 + 1 \times 0.058$$

$$= 0.28 + 0.308 + 0.2 + 0.058 = 0.846$$

Illustration 7: *The probability of success in an examination of a village is 0.3. What is the probability that out of 7 students (i) none (ii) one (iii) two and (iv) at least one will be succeed in the examination.*

Solution: $n = 7$

$p = 0.3;\ q = 1 - 0.3 = 0.7$

$$nCr = 7Crp^r q^{n-r} = 7Cr(0.3)^r (0.7)^{7-r}$$

(i) Probability of none success = $7C_0\ (0.3)^0\ (0.7)^7$

$$= \frac{7!}{7!\ 0!} \times 1 \times 0.082 = 1 \times 0.082 = 0.082$$

(ii) Probility of one success = $7C_1\ (0.3)^1\ (0.7)^6$

$$= \frac{7!}{6!\ 1!}(0.3)(0.117) = 7 \times 0.035 = 0.245$$

(iii) Probability of two success = $7C_2\,(0.3)^2\,(0.7)^5$

$$= \frac{7!}{5!\ 2!}(0.09)(0.168) = 21 \times 0.015 = 0.315$$

(iv) Probability of at least one success

= 1 – probability of no success

= 1 – 0.082 = 0.918

Illustration 8: *15 coins are tossed at a time. Find out the probability in a single tossing for the following outcomes.*

(i) less than 5 heads (ii) 12 or more heads

(iii) at least 10 heads (iv) no heads

Solution: Probability of becoming head $p = 0.5$

Probability of becoming tail $q = 0.5$

(i) Probability of getting less than 5 heads

$$P(<5) = 15C_4(0.5)^4(0.5)^{11} + 15C_3(0.5)^3(0.5)^{12} + 15C_2(0.5)^2(0.5)^{13}$$

$$+ 15C_1(0.5)^1(0.5)^{14} + 15C_0(0.5)^0(0.5)^{15}$$

$$= \frac{15!}{11!\ 4!}(0.5)^{15} + \frac{15!}{12!\ 3!}(0.5)^{15} + \frac{15!}{13!\ 2!}(0.5)^{15}$$

$$+ \frac{15!}{14!\ 1!}(0.5)^{15} + \frac{15!}{15!\ 0!}(0.5)^{15}$$

$$= 1365 \times 0.00003 + 455 \times 0.00003 + 105 \times 0.00003$$

$$+ 15 \times 0.00003 + 1 \times 0.00003$$

$$= 0.041 + 0.014 + 0.0032 + 0.0005 + 0.00003 = 0.059$$

(ii) Probability of getting 12 or more heads

$$P(\geq 12) = P_{12} + P_{13} + P_{14} + P_{15}$$

$$= 15C_{12}(0.5)^{12}(0.5)^3 + 15C_{13}(0.5)^{13}(0.5)^2$$

$$+ 15C_{14}(0.5)^{14}(0.5)^1 + 15C_{15}(0.5)^{15}(0.5)^0$$

$$= \frac{15!}{3!\ 12!}(0.5)^{15} + \frac{15!}{2!\ 13!}(0.5)^{15} + \frac{15!}{1!\ 14!}(0.5)^{15} + \frac{15!}{0!\ 15!}(0.5)^{15}$$

$$= 455 \times 0.00003 + 105 \times 0.00003 + 15 \times 0.00003 + 1 \times 0.00003$$

$$= 0.014 + 0.0032 + 0.0005 + 0.00003 = 0.018$$

(iii) Probability of getting at least 10 heads

$$P(\geq 10) = P_{10} + P_{11} + P_{(\geq 12)}$$

$$= 15C_{10}(0.5)^{15} + 15C_{11}(0.5)^{15} + 0.018$$

$$= \frac{15!}{5!\ 10!}(0.5)^{15} + \frac{15!}{4!\ 11!}(0.5)^{15} + 0.018$$

$$= 3003 \times 0.00003 + 1365 \times 0.00003$$

$$= 0.09 + 0.041 + 0.018 = 0.149$$

(iv) Probability of getting no heads

$$= 15C_0(0.5)^{15} = 1 \times 0.00003 = 0.00003$$

Illustration 9: *A basket contains 250 oranges. Out of the total oranges 100 are defective. When 8 oranges are selected at random, determine the probability that,*

(i) at least one is defective (ii) at the most 5 are defective

(iii) all 8 are defective and (iv) all 8 are good

(v) 4 are defective

Solution: Probability of defective (p) = 100/150 = 0.4

Probability of good (q) = 1 – 0.4 = 0.6

(i) Probability of at least one defective is,

$$P_1 + P_2 + P_3 \ldots + P_8$$

or $$1 - q_0 = 1 - 8C_0\ (0.6)^0\ (0.4)^8$$

$$= 1 - 8C_0\ (0.4)^8 = 1 - \frac{8!}{8!\ 0!}(0.00066) = 0.99$$

(ii) Probability of at the most 5 defective is,

$$P(\leq 5) = P_{(0)} + P_{(1)} + P_{(2)} + P_{(3)} + P_{(4)} + P_{(5)} = 1 - \left(P_{(6)} + P_{(7)} + P_{(8)}\right)$$

$$= 1 - \left(8C_6(0.4)^6(0.6)^2 + 8C_7(0.4)^7(0.6)^1 + 8C_8(0.4)^8(0.6)^0\right)$$

$$= 1 - \frac{8!}{2!\ 6!}(0.004)(0.36) + \frac{8!}{1!\ 7!}(0.002)(0.6) + \frac{8!}{0!\ 8!}(0.001)$$

$$= 1 - [0.04 + 0.01 + 0.001] = 1 - 0.05 = 0.95$$

(iii) Probability of all 8 are defective is,

$$P_{(8)} = 8C_8(0.4)^8(0.6)^0 = \frac{8!}{0!\ 8!}(0.001) = 0.001$$

(iv) Probability of all 8 good is,

$$P_{(0)} = 8C_0(0.4)^0(0.6)^8 = \frac{8!}{8!\ 0!}(0.0167) = 0.017$$

(v) Probability of 4 defectives is,

$$P_{(4)} = 8C_4(0.4)^4(0.6)^4 = \frac{8!}{4!\ 4!}(0.0256)(0.1296)$$

$$= 70\,(0.0256)(0.1296) = 0.23$$

IV Theorems of Probability

The theorems of probability are otherwise called as rules of probability or laws of probability. There are two important theorems of probability. They are classified into (1) Addition theorem and (2) Multiplication Theorem.

(1) Addition Theorem of Probability: Addition rules of probability contain two theorems namely (i) Theorem of total probability and (ii) Generalized theorem on total probability.

(i) Theorem of total probability: When events are mutually exclusive this theorem should be applied. If two events A and B are mutually exclusive, then the probability of occurance of either of the events A or B is equal to the sum of the probabilities of A and B. i.e., $P(A \text{ or } B) = P(A) + P(B)$

If $A_1, A_2, A_3, A_4 \ldots A_n$ are mutually exclusive events then the probability of occurance of either of these events is the sum of the probabilities of $A_1, A_2, A_3 \ldots A_n$.

i.e., $P(A_1 \cup A_2 \cup A_3 \ldots \cup A_n) = P_{(A1)} + P_{(A2)} + P_{(A3)} \ldots P_{(An)}$

Illustration 10: *An Urn contains 5 white, 3 red and 7 black balls. Find out the probability of getting a white or black ball in a single draw.*

Solution: Probability of getting a white ball = 5/15

Probability of getting a red ball = 3/15

Probability of getting either a white or red ball

= 5/15 + 3/15 = 8/15

(ii) Generalized Theorem on Total Probability: This theorem should be applied when the events are not mutually exclusive. If A and B are two events not mutually exclusive then the probability of occurance of either A or B is,

$$P(A \text{ or } B) = P(A) + P(B) - P(A \text{ and } B)$$

If A, B and C are three events not mutually exclusive, then,

$$P(A \cup B \cup C) = P(A) + P(B) + P(C) - P(A \cap B) - P(A \cap C) - P(B \cap C) + P(A \cap B \cap C)$$

Illustration 11: *A card is drawn from a well shuffled pack of 52 cards. What is the probability of the card being either red or a jack?*

Solution: The total outcome = 52 (sample points)

Let A be the event that the card is red, then A consists of 26 sample points since there are 26 red cards. B denotes the event that the card is a jack. B consists of 4 sample points since the number of jack cards is 4. Hence, $(A \cap B)$ consists of 2 sample points since there are 2 red jack cards.

$P(A) = 26/52$, $P(B) = 4/52$

$P(A \cap B) = 2/52$

Hence $P(A \cup B) = P(A) + P(B) - P(A \cap B)$

$= 26/52 + 4/52 - 2/52 = 28/52 = 7/13$

Illustration 12: *A box contains 15 balls numbering from 1 to 15. Find the probability that a ball selected at random is a ball with number that is a multiple of 3 or 5.*

Solution: Total sample points = 15

Let A be the event that the ball with number that is a multiple of 3.

So, A has 5 sample points (*i.e.*, 3, 6, 9, 12, 15).

Let B be the event that the ball with number that is a multiple of 5.

So, B has 3 sample points (*i.e.*, 5, 10, 15)

Since A and B has 15 as common sample point, $(A \cap B)$ has one sample point.

$$P(A) = 5/15;\ P(B) = 3/15;\ P(A \cap B) = 1/15$$

Hence, $P(A \cup B) = P(A) + P(B) - P(A \cap B)$

$$= 5/15 + 3/15 - 1/15 = 7/15$$

Illustration 13: *The probability that a contractor will get a building contract is 1/4 and the probability of not getting a road contract is 2/3. If the probability of getting at least one contract is 2/5, find out the probability that he will get either of the two contracts.*

Solution: Let A be the probability of getting a building contract,

i.e., $P(A) = 1/4$.

Let B be the probability of getting a road contract,

i.e., $P(B) = 1 - 2/3 = 1/3$.

Probability of getting both the contract $(A \cap B) = 2/5$.

$P(A \cup B) = P(A) + P(B) - P(A \cap B)$

$$= 1/4 + 1/3 - 2/5 = \frac{15 + 20 - 24}{60} = 11/60$$

(2) Multiplication Theorem of Probability: Multiplication theorem of probability can be applied in two situations. They are,

(i) Multiplication theorem of probability when events are independent and

(ii) Multiplication theorem of probability when events are dependent.

(i) Multiplication Theorem of Probability when events are independent: If two events, A and B are independent, then the

probability that both will occur is equal to the product of the probabilities of these two events.

i.e., $P(A \cap B) = P(A) \times P(B)$

Illustration 14: *Two students A and B are independently solving a problem. The probability of A solving the problem is 4/5 and probability of B solving it is 1/3. What is the probability that both of them will solve the problem?*

Solution: Probability of A solving the problem = 4/5

Probability of B solving the problem = 1/3

Probability of A and B solving the problem

$$= P(A \text{ and } B) = P(A) \times P(B)$$

$$= 4/5 \times 1/3 = 4/15$$

Illustration 15: *A box contains 5 red, 4 black and 3 white balls. What is the probability of getting a white, a black and a red ball.*

Solution: Total outcome = 5 + 4 + 3 = 12

Probability of getting a white ball = 3/12

Probability of getting a black ball = 4/12

Probability of getting a red ball = 5/12

Hence, the probability of getting a white, a black and a red ball

$$= 3/12 \times 4/12 \times 5/12 = 5/144.$$

(ii) Multiplication Theorem of Probability when events are dependent: It is otherwise called as conditional probability. Two events are denoted as dependent events when the occurance or non-occurance of one event in any trial affects the probability of other events in other trial. The probability of occurance of both the events, when events are dependent is stated below.

$$P(A \cap B) = P(A/B)\,P(B) \quad \text{or} \quad P(B \cap A) = P(B/A)\,P(A)$$

Since $A \cap B = B \cap A$, the important property of these two intersection is,

$$P(A \cap B) = P(A/B).P(B) = P(B/A).P(A)$$

Illustration 16: *A bag contains 6 white and 4 red balls. The balls are drawn simultaneously without replacement of the first ball. What is the probability that both balls are of white colour?*

Solution: Total sample points = 6 + 4 = 10

Probability of getting the first white ball $P(A) = 6/10$. Since there is no replacement after the first draw, the probability of getting the second white ball,

$$P(B/A) = 5/9$$

Hence, the probability of getting 2 white balls in the two draws

$$P(A \text{ and } B) = P(A) . P(B/A)$$

$$= 6/10 \times 5/9 = 1/3$$

Illustration 17: *From a well shuffled pack of 52 cards, 2 cards are drawn at random. What is the probability that both of them are Queen cards. Assume that there is no replacement of the card after the first draw.*

Solution: Total outcome = 52

Total Queen Cards = 4

Hence, probability of getting a Queen card in the first draw

$$P(A) = 4/52.$$

Since there is no replacement of the card after the first draw, the probability of getting Queen card in the second draw

$$P(B/A) = 3/51$$

Therefore, the probability of getting 2 Queen cards,

$$P(A \text{ and } B) = P(A) . P(B/A)$$

$$= 4/52 \times 3/51 = 3/663$$

V Baye's Theorem (Rule for the Inverse Probability)

The calculation of unknown, or old probabilities named '*priori probabilities*' from the new probabilities is called '*posterior probabilities*' or '*inverse probability*'. Inverse probability can be calculated through additional information available in the past records. It is one of the important applications of the conditional probability since conditional probability states that the occurance of one event is due to the occurance of a particular event or reason. Inverse probability is derived by a British Mathematician named Thomas Bayes in the year 1763. The rules of the theorem is stated as below.

Let B be an arbitrary event which can only occur in conjunction with one of the n mutually exclusive and exhaustive events, A_1, A_2, A_3, ... An, where $P(B) \neq 0$. $P(B/A_i)$ and $P(A_i)$, (i = 1, 2, ... n) are known.

$$P(A_i/B) = \frac{P(A_i \cap B)}{P(B)} \quad (i = 1, 2, 3 \ldots n)$$

$$P(B) = P(A_1 \cap B) + P(A_2 \cap B) + \ldots P(A_n \cap B)$$

$$\text{Hence, } P(A_1/B) = \frac{P(A_1 \cap B)}{P(A_1 \cap B) + P(A_2 \cap B) + \ldots P(A_n \cap B)}$$

Illustration 18: *Two persons are competing for a manager post in a company. The probabilities that the first and second will win are 0.7 and0.3 respectively. If the first person wins, the probability of opening a new branch is 0.8 and the corresponding probability is 0.4 if the second person wins. What is the probability that the new branch is opened?*

Solution: $P(A_1)$ = Probability of the first person wins = 0.7

$P(A_2)$ = Probability of the second person wins = 0.3

$P(B)$ = Probability that a new branch is opened

$P(B/A_1)$ = Probability that a new branch is opened if the first person wins = 0.8

$P(B/A_2)$ = Probability that a new branch is opened if the second person wins = 0.4

$$P(B) = P(A_1 \cap B) + P(A_2 \cap B)$$
$$= P(A_1).P(B/A_1) + P(A_2).P(B/A_2)$$
$$= (0.7 \times 0.8) + (0.3 \times 0.4) = 0.56 + 0.12 = 0.68$$

Illustration 19: *A company manufactures a product namely X in two of its factories. The factory I manufactures 75% of the product and factory II manufactures 25% of the product. It is found out that factory I manufactures 70 standard products of X out of 100 products of X and factory II manufactures 60 standard products out of 100 products of X. (i) What is the probability that a product X selected at random is of standard quality? (ii) What is the probability that a product X selected at random from factory I is of standard quality? (iii) Also calculate the revised probability.*

Solution: Let $P(A_1)$ = The probability of drawing product X from factory I = 75/100 = 0.75

$P(A_2)$ = The probability of drawing product X from factory II = 25/100 = 0.25

$P(B)$ = The probability of getting a standard quality product of X.

$P(B/A_1)$ = The probability of getting a standard quality product from factory I = 70/100 = 0.7

$P(B/A_2)$ = The probability of getting a standard quality product from factory II = 60/100 = 0.6

(i) The probability of getting a standard product of X from these two factories,

$$P(B) = P(A_1 \cap B) + P(A_2 \cap B)$$
$$= P(A_1).P(B/A_1) + P(A_2).P(B/A_2)$$
$$= (0.75 \times 0.7) + (0.25 \times 0.6) = 0.525 + 0.15 = 0.675$$

(ii) The probability of getting a standard product of X from factory I,

$$P(B) = P(A_1 \cap B) = P(A_1).P(B/A_1)$$
$$= (0.75 \times 0.7) = 0.525$$

(iii) Calculation of Posterior (Revised) Probability,

$$P(A_1/B) = \frac{P(A_1 \cap B)}{P(A_1 \cap B) + P(A_2 \cap B)} = \frac{0.525}{0.525 + 0.15} = \frac{0.525}{0.675}$$

and, $$P(A_2/B) = \frac{P(A_2 \cap B)}{P(A_1 \cap B) + P(A_2 \cap B)} = \frac{0.15}{0.525 + 0.15} = \frac{0.15}{0.675}$$

$$P(A_1/B) + P(A_2/B) = \frac{0.525}{0.675} + \frac{0.15}{0.675} = 1$$

Illustration 20: *There are three persons named X, Y and Z for a General Manager post in a limited company. Their chance of being selected for the post are in the ratio 6 : 4 : 3. If X is selected, the probability that he will introduce a new product is 0.5. The corresponding probabilities of the introduction of the new product,* *are 0.7 and 0.4 respectively if Y and Z are selected. What is the probability that the new product is introduced?*

Solution: Let the probability that the new product is to be introduced $= P(B)$.

$$P(A_1) = 6/13; \quad P(A_2) = 4/13; \quad P(A_3) = 3/13;$$

$$P(B/A_1) = 0.5; \quad P(B/A_2) = 0.7; \quad P(B/A_3) = 0.4.$$

$$P(B) = P(A_1 \cap B) + P(A_2 \cap B) + P(A_3 \cap B)$$

$$= P(A_1).P(B/A_1) + P(A_2).P(B/A_2) + P(A_3).P(B/A_3)$$

$$= (6/13 \times 0.5) + (4/13 \times 0.7) + (3/13 \times 0.4)$$

$$= 3/13 + 2.8/13 + 1.2/13 = \frac{3 + 2.8 + 1.2}{13} = \frac{7}{13}$$

VI Computation of Expected Values

The expected values to be calculated through probability theories, are otherwise called as the calculation of mathematical expectation of the random variable. It can be calculated through the following method.

Let X be a random variable with possible values $X_1, X_2, X_3 \ldots X_n$ with corresponding probabilities $p_1, p_2, p_3 \ldots p_n$ then, the expected value of X,

$$E(X) = p_1x_1 + p_2x_2 + p_3x_3 + \ldots + p_nx_n$$

$$= \sum_{i=1}^{n} p_ix_i, \quad i = 1, 2, 3, \ldots n$$

The expected value is also called by means of x ($\bar{X}$) $E(X^2)$ can be calculated as $\Sigma p_ix_i^2$.

Properties of Expected values of the random variable

The following are the important properties derived from the expected values.

1. The expected value of a constant is the constant itself

   i.e., $E(a) = a$.

2. $E(a + bx) = a + bE(x)$, where a and b are constants.

3. When X and Y are random variables, then

$$E(X \pm Y) = E(X) \pm E(Y)$$

4. When x and y are two independent random variable, then,

$$E(XY) = E(X) . E(Y)$$

Variance of a Random Variable

The variance of a random variable can be calculated as follows.

Let x be a random variable with mean $E(X) = \bar{X}$,

then the variance is,

$$\text{Variance } (X) = E[(X - E(X))^2] - E[(X - \bar{X})^2]$$

$$= (X_1 - \bar{X})^2 p_1 + (X_2 - \bar{X})^2 p_2 + ... + (X_n - \bar{X})^2 p_n$$

$$= (X_1^2 - 2X_1 \bar{X} + \bar{X}^2) p_1 + (X_2 - 2X_2 \bar{X} + \bar{X}^2) p_2$$

$$+ ... + (X_n^2 - 2X_n \bar{X} + \bar{X}^2) p_n$$

$$= (X_1^2 p_1 + X_2^2 p_2 + ... + X_n^2 p_n) - 2\bar{X}(X_1 p_1 + X_2 p_2$$

$$+ ... X_n p_n) + X^2(p_1 + p_2 + ... + p_n)$$

$$= E(X^2) - 2\bar{X} E(X) + \bar{X}^2 \qquad (\text{since}, p_1 + p_2 + ... + p_n = 1)$$

$$= E(X^2) - 2E(X).E(X) + (E(X))^2$$

$$= E(X)^2 - (E(X))^2 = E(X^2) - \bar{x}^2.$$

Standard Deviation of a Random Variable

Standard deviation of a random variable is the square root of the variance of the random variable. It can be derived through the same formula used for deriving variance of a random variable.

Hence, Standard deviation of a random variable is,

$$\text{S.D.} (X) = \sqrt{\Sigma(X^2) - \bar{X}^2} \qquad \text{where } \bar{X} = E(X)$$

Illustration 21: *Find out the expected values of the random variable, standard deviation and its variance when a die is thrown.*

Solution: The random variables for the throw of a die are 1, 2, 3, 4, 5, 6. Hence, the probability of occurance of each value is 1/6.

Hence,

$$E(X) = 1\ .\ 1/6 + 2\ .\ 1/6 + 3\ .\ 1/6 + 4\ .\ 1/6 + 5\ .\ 1/6 + 6\ .\ 1/6$$

$$= 1/6(1 + 2 + 3 + 4 + 5 + 6) = \frac{21}{6} = \frac{7}{2}$$

$$E(X) = \bar{X} = 7/2$$

$$E(X)^2 = 1/6\,(1^2 + 2^2 + 3^2 + 4^2 + 5^2 + 6^2) = \frac{91}{6}$$

Variance (x) $E(X)^2 = \bar{X}^2$

$$= (91/6) - (7/2)^2$$

$$= \frac{91}{6} - \frac{49}{4} = \frac{182 - 147}{12} = \frac{35}{12} = 2.917$$

$$\text{S.D.(X)} = \sqrt{\text{Vari }(X)} = \sqrt{2.917} = 1.708$$

Illustration 22: *Calculate E(X), S.D (X) and variance (X) for the probability distribution.*

No. of heads (X)	*0*	*1*	*2*	*3*	*4*
Probability	*1/16*	*4/16*	*6/16*	*4/16*	*1/16*

Solution: $E(X) = p_i X_i$

$$= 0\times\frac{1}{16} + 1\times\frac{4}{16} + 2\times\frac{6}{16} + 3\times\frac{4}{16} + 4\times\frac{1}{16}$$

$$= \frac{1}{4} + \frac{3}{4} + \frac{3}{4} + \frac{1}{4} = \frac{1+3+3+1}{4} = \frac{8}{4} = 2$$

$$E(X^2) = 0\times\frac{1}{16} + 1^2\times\frac{4}{16} + 2^2\times\frac{6}{16} + 3^2\times\frac{4}{16} + 4^2\times\frac{1}{16}$$

$$= \frac{1}{4} + \frac{3}{2} + \frac{9}{4} + 1 = \frac{1+6+9+4}{4} = \frac{20}{4} = 5$$

Variance $(X) = E(X)^2 - (\overline{X})^2 = 5 - 2^2 = 1$

S.D $(X) = \sqrt{1} = 1$

Illustration 23: *Find out the expected random variable of getting head when a coin is tossed three times.*

Solution:

Probability of getting 0 head $= nC_0 \left(\frac{1}{q}\right)^3 = 3C_0\left(\frac{1}{2}\right)^3 = \frac{1}{8}$

Probability of getting 1 head $= nC_1 \left(\frac{1}{p}\right)^1\left(\frac{1}{q}\right)^2$

$$= 3C_1\left(\frac{1}{2}\right)^1\left(\frac{1}{2}\right)^2 = \frac{3}{8}$$

Probability of getting 2 heads $= nC_2 \left(\frac{1}{p}\right)^2\left(\frac{1}{q}\right)^1$

$$= 3C_2\left(\frac{1}{2}\right)^2\left(\frac{1}{2}\right)^1 = \frac{3}{8}$$

Probability of getting 3 heads $= nC_3 \left(\frac{1}{p}\right)^3\left(\frac{1}{q}\right)^0$

$$= 3C_0\left(\frac{1}{2}\right)^3 = \frac{1}{8}$$

$$E(X) = \frac{1}{8} + \frac{3}{8} + \frac{3}{8} + \frac{1}{8} = 1$$

Illustration 24: *A game is played by a man with the understanding that he will get Rs. 160 for 1 head, Rs. 240 for 2 heads and Rs. 320 for 3 heads, when three coins are tossed at a time. He will not get anything for no head. If the entrance fee for the game is Rs. 200, will he play the game?*

Solution: The man will play the game if he will get more than the entrance fees of Rs. 200/-

$$\text{Probability of getting 0 head} = nC_0\left(\frac{1}{q}\right)^3 = 3C_0\left(\frac{1}{2}\right)^3 = \frac{1}{8}$$

$$\text{Probability of getting 1 head} = nC_1\left(\frac{1}{p}\right)^1\left(\frac{1}{q}\right)^2$$

$$= 3C_1\left(\frac{1}{2}\right)^1\left(\frac{1}{2}\right)^2 = \frac{3}{8}$$

$$\text{Probability of getting 2 heads} = nC_2\left(\frac{1}{p}\right)^2\left(\frac{1}{q}\right)^1$$

$$= 3C_2\left(\frac{1}{2}\right)^2\left(\frac{1}{2}\right)^1 = \frac{3}{8}$$

$$\text{Probability of getting 3 heads} = nC_3\left(\frac{1}{p}\right)^3\left(\frac{1}{q}\right)^0$$

$$= 3C_0\left(\frac{1}{2}\right)^3 = \frac{1}{8}$$

The prize money (X) is $X_0 = 0$; $X_1 =$ Rs. 160

$X_2 =$ Rs. 240; $X_3 =$ Rs. 320

$$E(X) = p_1x_1 + p_2x_2 + p_3x_3 + p_4x_4$$

$$= \left(\frac{1}{8}\times 0\right)+\left(\frac{3}{8}\times 160\right)+\left(\frac{3}{8}\times 240\right)+\left(\frac{1}{8}\times 320\right)$$

$$= 0 + 60 + 90 + 40 = \text{Rs. } 190$$

Since the man is expected to get only Rs. 190 which is less than the entrance fee of Rs. 200, he will not play the game.

Miscellaneous Illustrations

Illustration 25: *Two cards are drawn at random from a pack of 52 cards. What is the probability that it will be (i) two aces, (ii) a diamond and a heart (iii) a king and jack and (iv) a heart and an ace.*

Solution: (i) Total number of cards in the pack = 52

The number of ways of drawing 2 cards in the pack of 52 cards

$$= 52C_2 = \frac{52 \times 51}{1 \times 2} = 1326$$

The number of ways of drawing 2 aces $= 4C_2 = \frac{4 \times 3}{1 \times 2} = 6$

Hence, the probability of getting 2 aces

$$= \frac{4C_2}{52C_2} = \frac{6}{1326} = 0.005$$

(ii) The number of ways a diamond and a heart is drawn,

$$= 13C_1 \times 13C_1 = 13 \times 13 = 169$$

The probability of getting a diamond and a heart is

$$= \frac{169}{1326} = 0.127$$

(iii) The number of ways a king and a jack are drawn,

$$= 4C_1 \times 4C_1 = 4 \times 4 = 16$$

The probability of getting a king and a jack is

$$= \frac{16}{1326} = 0.12$$

(iv) The number of ways a heart and an ace are drawn,

$$= 13C_1 \times 4C_1 = 13 \times 4 = 52$$

$$= \frac{52}{1326} = 0.039$$

Illustration 26: *A bag contains 4 green, 6 red and 3 black balls. 4 balls are drawn at random. What is the probability of getting (i) 2 green 1 black and 1 red balls (ii) All red balls (iii) 3 black and 1 green balls.*

Solution: (i) Probability of getting 2 green, 1 black and 1 red balls,

$$= \frac{4C_2 \times 3C_1 \times 6C_1}{13C_4} = \frac{6 \times 3 \times 6}{715} = \frac{108}{715} = 0.15$$

(ii) The probability of getting 4 red balls,

$$= \frac{6C_4}{13C_4} = \frac{15}{715} = 0.021$$

(iii) The probability of getting 3 black and 1 green balls,

$$= \frac{3C_3 \times 4C_1}{13C_4} = \frac{1 \times 4}{715} = \frac{4}{715} = 0.006$$

Illustration 27: *A box contains 8 yellow balls, 7 blue and 5 green balls. Two balls are drawn at random. What is the probability that the two balls are either yellow or green?*

Solution: The probability of getting 2 yellow balls $= \frac{8C_2}{20C_2}$

The probability of getting 2 green balls $= \frac{5C_2}{20C_2}$

Hence, the probability of getting either 2 yellow or 2 green

balls, $= \frac{8C_2}{20C_2} + \frac{5C_2}{20C_2} = \frac{8C_2 + 5C_2}{20C_2}$

$$= \frac{28 + 10}{190} = \frac{38}{190} = 0.20$$

Illustration 28: *There ar twelve 50 paise coins and eighteen 25 paise coins in a bag. Two coins are drawn out from the bag. What is the probability that a 50 paise coin and a 25 paise coin are drawn when (a) the coin is replaced and (b) the coin is not replaced?*

Solution: (a) $P(A) = 12/30$

$P(B) = 18/30$

$P(A \text{ and } B) = P(A) \times P(B) = 12/30 \times 18/30 = 6/25$

(b) When coin is not replaced,

$P(A \text{ and } B) = P(A) \times P(B/A)$ or

$= P(B) \times P(A/B)$

$P(A) = 12/30$

$P(B) = 18/30$

$P(B/A) = 18/29$ (*i.e.*, if the outcome of first draw is 50 paise coin)

$P(A/B) = 12/29$ (*i.e.*, if the outcome of first draw is 25 paise coin)

$P(A \text{ and } B) = P(A) \times P(B/A)$

$= 12/30 \text{ x } 18/29 = 36/145$

or $P(A \text{ and } B) = P(B) \times P(A/B)$

$= 18/30 \times 12/29 = 36/145$

Illustration 29: *A coin is tossed 5 times. What is the probability that all the five are heads?*

Solution: Let A, B, C, D and E are the events of occurance of heads in 5 tosses.

$$P(A) = P(B) = P(C) = P(D) = P(E) = 1/2$$

$$P(A \cap B \cap C \cap D \cap E) = P(A) \times P(B/A) \times P(C/A \cap B) \times P(E/A \cap B \cap C \cap D)$$

$$= P(A) \cdot P(B) \cdot P(C) \cdot P(D) \cdot P(E)$$

(since all events are independent)

$$= \frac{1}{2} \times \frac{1}{2} \times \frac{1}{2} \times \frac{1}{2} \times \frac{1}{2} = \frac{1}{32}$$

Illustration 30: *A box contains 10 red and 5 green balls. Two balls are drawn one after another. Find out the probability that both balls drawn are red if (i) first ball drawn is not replaced before drawing the second and (ii) the first ball drawn is replaced before drawing the second ball.*

Solution: (i) There are 15 sample points or events in the sample space *i.e.*, 10 + 5 = 15 balls.

Probability of getting first red ball P(A) = 10/15. Since, there are 10 red balls in the box.

Since the first ball drawn is red and is not replaced the sample space reduces to 15 – 1 = 14.

Hence, the probability of getting the second red ball = 9/14.

Therefore, the probability of getting 2 red balls

$$P(A \text{ and } B) = P(A) \times P(B) = \frac{10}{15} \times \frac{9}{14} = \frac{3}{7}$$

(ii) Since the first ball drawn is replaced the occurance of events *A* and *B* are independent.

$$P(A) = 10/15; \ P(B) = 10/15$$

$$P(A \cap B) = P(A) \times P(B) = \frac{10}{15} \times \frac{10}{15} = \frac{4}{9}$$

Illustration 31: *Two cards are drawn from a pack of 52 cards. The second card is drawn without replacing the first card. Find out the probability that (i) the two are Queen cards and (ii) one Diamond card and one Ace card.*

Solution: (i) The probability of drawing a Queen card = 4/52

If the first card is not replaced the probability of getting another Queen card = 3/51

The probability of getting both queen cards, $= \frac{4}{52} \times \frac{3}{51} = \frac{1}{221}$

(ii) The probability of drawing a Diamond card = 13/52

If the first card is not replaced the probability of getting the Ace card = 4/51

The probability of getting a Diamond and Ace card,

$$= \frac{13}{52} \times \frac{4}{51} = \frac{1}{51}$$

Illustration 32: *A card is drawn from a pack of 52 cards. Find the probability that the card is either a diamond or the king of spade.*

Solution: The probability of drawing a diamond card = 13/52

The probability of drawing a king of spade card = 1/52

Hence the probability of drawing a diamond or a king of spade card

$$= \frac{13}{52} + \frac{1}{52} = \frac{14}{52} = \frac{7}{26}$$

Illustration 33: *Three cards are drawn from a pack of 52 cards. Find out the probability that (i) 2 cards are diamond and one card is a king card. (ii) one diamond one king and one spade cards. Assume that the cards and replaced after every draw.*

Solution: (i) The probability of getting 2 diamond cards = 26/52

The probability of getting a king card = 4/52

The probability of getting both 2 diamond and one king cards

$$= \frac{26}{52} \times \frac{4}{52} = \frac{1}{26}$$

(ii) The probability of getting one diamond card = 13/52

The probability of getting one king card = 4/52

The probability of getting one Ace card = 13/52

Probability of getting one diamond, one king and one ace card

$$= \frac{13}{52} \times \frac{4}{52} \times \frac{13}{52} = \frac{1}{4} \times \frac{1}{13} \times \frac{1}{4} = \frac{1}{208}$$

Illustration 34: *Four cards are drawn from a pack of 52 cards without replacement. What is the probability that they are all Queen cards?*

Solution: Probability of getting 1st Queen card = 4/52

Probability of getting 2nd Queen card = 3/51

Probability of getting 3rd Queen card = 2/50

Probability of getting 4th Queen card = 1/49

Probability of getting 4 Queen cards,

$$= \frac{4}{52} \times \frac{3}{51} \times \frac{2}{50} \times \frac{1}{49} = \frac{1}{270725}$$

Illustration 35: *A problem in accounting is given to 3 students A, B and C whose chance of solving it are 2/5, 3/7, 1/4. What is the probability that the problem will be solved?*

Solution: The probability of solving the problem, = 1 – the probability of all of them not able to solve the problem.

The probability of not solving the problems by *A*, *B* and *C* are,

$$=\frac{3}{5}\left(1-\frac{2}{5}\right),\ \frac{4}{7}\left(1-\frac{3}{5}\right),\ \frac{3}{4}\left(1-\frac{1}{4}\right)$$

The probability of all of them not able to solve the problem,

$$=\frac{3}{5}\times\frac{4}{7}\times\frac{3}{4}=\frac{9}{35}$$

The probability of solving the problem $=\left(1-\frac{9}{35}\right)=\frac{26}{35}$

Illustration 36: *The probability of appointment of one of the 4 persons namely A, B, C and D in a company are 1/5, 1/4, 2/7 and 3/4 respectively. The probability that the company earns profit above Rs. 20,000 per month due to their appointment is 1/3, 2/3, 1/5 and 2/5 respectively. What is the probability that the company earns above Rs. 20,000 per month?*

Solution: The probability of earning profit by A's appointment,

$$=\frac{1}{5}\times\frac{1}{3}=\frac{1}{15}$$

The probability of earning profit by B's appointment,

$$=\frac{1}{4}\times\frac{2}{3}=\frac{2}{12}$$

The probability of earning profit by C's appointment,

$$=\frac{2}{7}\times\frac{1}{5}=\frac{2}{35}$$

The probability of earning profit by D's appointment,

$$=\frac{3}{4}\times\frac{2}{5}=\frac{6}{20}$$

The probability that the company earns profit is,

$$= \frac{1}{15} + \frac{2}{12} + \frac{2}{35} + \frac{6}{20} = \frac{28+70+24+126}{420}$$

$$= \frac{248}{420} = \frac{62}{105}$$

Illustration 37: *A coin is tossed 7 times. Find the probability of obtaining (i) 6 Heads (ii) 7 Heads and (iii) 5 or more Heads.*

Solution: Probability of getting one Head $P(1) = 1/2$

Probability of not getting a Head, $q = 1 - 1/2 = 1/2$

(i) Probability of getting 6 Heads,

$$P(6) = 7C_6 \quad p^6 q^1$$

$$= \frac{7\,!}{(7-6)!\;6\,!} \times \left(\frac{1}{2}\right)^6 \times \left(\frac{1}{2}\right)^1$$

$$= 7 \times \left(\frac{1}{2}\right)^6 \left(\frac{1}{2}\right)^1 = \frac{7}{128} = 0.055$$

(ii) Probability of getting 7 Heads,

$$P(7) = 7C_7 \quad p^7 q^0$$

$$= \frac{7\,!}{0!\;7\,!} \times \left(\frac{1}{2}\right)^7 \times \left(\frac{1}{2}\right)^0 - 1 \times \frac{1}{128} - 0.008$$

(iii) Probability of getting 5 or more Heads,

$$P(\geq 5) = P_5 + P_6 + P_7$$

$$= 7C_5 \quad p^5 q^2 + 7C_6 \quad p^6 q^1 + 7C_7 \quad p^7 q^0$$

$$= \frac{7!}{2!\;\;5!} \left(\frac{1}{2}\right)^5 \left(\frac{1}{2}\right)^2 + 0.055 + 0.008$$

$$= \frac{21}{128} + 0.055 + 0.008$$

$$= 0.164 + 0.055 + 0.008 = 0.227$$

Illustration 38: *Find out in how many ways the letters of the word COUNTRY be rearranged.*

Solution: Total no. of letters in the word COUNTRY, $n = 7$

No. of letters taken at a time, $r = 7$

No. of arrangements $= nP_r$

$= 7P_7 = 7\,!$

$= 1 \times 2 \times 3 \times 4 \times 5 \times 6 \times 7 = 5040$

Illustration 39: *Calculate the total number of words to be formed from the letters of the word PROMISE which will begin with the letter 'P'.*

Solution: Total no. of letters in PROMISE, $n = 7$

Since the letter 'P' should remain in the first place the other 6 letters should be rearranged.

Hence, the total no. of such arrangements $= 6P_6$

$= 1 \times 2 \times 3 \times 4 \times 5 \times 6 = 720$

Illustration 40: *How many ways can the letters of the word COMBINE be arranged taking 3 letters at a time? How many of these will contain the letter M? How many will not contain the letter E?*

Solution: Total no. of letters, $n = 7$

No. of letters taken at a time, $r = 3$

Hence, the total no. of arrangements $= 7P_3$

$$= \frac{7!}{(7-3)!} = 7 \times 6 \times 5 = 210$$

No. of arrangements, not containing the letter 'M' $= 6P_3$

$$= \frac{6!}{(6-3)!} = 6 \times 5 \times 4 = 120$$

No. of arrangements with letter 'M' = 210 – 120 = 90

No. of arrangements, not containing the letter 'E'

$$6P_3 = \frac{6\,!}{(6-3)\,!} = 6 \times 5 \times 4 = 120$$

Illustration 41: *How many five digit numbers can be formed with the numbers 1, 3, 5, 7, 8, 9.*

Solution: Total no. of digits, $n = 6$

No. of them taken at a time, $r = 5$

$$6P_5 = \frac{6\ !}{(6-5)\ !} = 1\times2\times3\times4\times5\times6 = 720$$

$\therefore$ No. of total arrangements = 720

Illustration 42: *Find out the total 3 digits odd numbers which can be formed with the help of 3, 4, 5, 6, 7, 8 on the condition that no digit should be used more than once in each number.*

Solution: Total no. of odd numbers = 3 (*i.e.*, 3, 5, 7)

The last place can be filled in $3P_1$ ways.

The remaining 2 places can be filled from the remaining 5 digits.

i.e., in $5P_2$ ways.

The total 3 digit numbers to be formed,

$$= 3P_1 \times 5P_2 = \frac{3\ !}{(3-1)\ !} \times \frac{5\ !}{(5-2)\ !} = 3\times20 = 60$$

Illustration 43: *How many seven digit numbers can be formed from 1, 2, 3, 4, 5, 6, 7 no digit being repeated.*

Solution: Total no. of digits, $n = 7$

Since no digit being repeated, $r = 7$

Total no. of 7 digit numbers = $7P_7$

$$= \frac{7!}{(7-7)\ !} = 1\times2\times3\times4\times5\times6\times7 = 5040$$

Illustration 44: *How many numbers divisible by 5 can be formed from the digits 1, 2, 3, 4, 5, 6, 7.*

Solution: In the given digits, the number divisible by 5 have 5 at the end. Since there is only one 5, the last place can be filled in $1P_1$ way. The remaining 6 digit numbers can be arranged among themselves in $6P_6$ ways.

The total numbers divisible by 5 are,

$$= 1P_1 \times 6P_6 = \frac{1!}{(1-1)!} \times \frac{6!}{(6-6)!}$$

$$= 1 \times (1 \times 2 \times 3 \times 4 \times 5 \times 6) = 720$$

Illustration 45: *How many 5 digit numbers greater than 5,000 can be formed from the numbers 2, 3, 4, 5, 6, 7.*

Solution: The numbers greater than 5,000 is available in digits 5, 6, 7, ($n = 3$)

The first digit can be chosen from anyone of these three digits,

$$= 3P_1 = \frac{3!}{(3-1)!} = 3 \text{ ways.}$$

The remaining 3 digits can be chosen from the remaining 5 digits i.e., $5P_3$ ways.

The number divisible by 5

$$= 3P_1 \times 5P_3 = \frac{3!}{(3-1)!} \times \frac{5!}{(5-3)!}$$

$$= 3 \times (5 \cdot 4 \times 3) = 180$$

Illustration 46: *How many ways can 8 students in a bench can be arranged so that 2 particular students must come together?*

Solution: When two students should come together, then consider total number of students as 6

Total number of arrangements of these 6 = $6P_6$

The two particular students who are coming together can be arranged between themselves in $2P_2$ ways.

No. of arrangements in which 2 particular students must come together,

$$= 6P_6 \times 2P_2 = \frac{6!}{(6-6)!} \times \frac{2!}{(2-2)!}$$

$$= (1 \times 2 \times 3 \times 4 \times 5 \times 6)\ (1 \times 2) = 1440$$

Illustration 47: *An urn contains 5 white and 7 black balls. A second urn contains 7 white and 8 black balls. One ball is drawn at random and put into the second urn without noticing its colour. A ball is then drawn at random from the second urn. What is the probability that it is white?* (MGU: Section B April '98)

Solution:

Probability of drawing a white ball from the first urn, = 5/12

Probability of drawing a black ball from the first urn, = 7/12

Probability of drawing a white ball from the second urn, if the transferred ball is white, = 8/16

Probability of drawing a white ball from the second urn, if the transferred ball is black, = 7/16

The probability of drawing a white ball from the second urn after the transfer of one ball from the first urn.

$$= \left(\frac{5}{12} \times \frac{8}{16}\right) + \left(\frac{7}{12} \times \frac{7}{16}\right) = 0.21 + 0.26 = 0.47$$

Illustration 48: *In how many ways can the word 'MANAGEMENT' be rearranged.* (MGU: Section A April '97)

Solution: Total no. of letters in 'MANAGEMENT' = 10

No. of letters taken at a time = 10

No. of arrangements $n\,\mathrm{Pr} = \dfrac{n!}{(n-r)!}$

$$10P_{10} = \frac{10}{(10-10)!} = 10!$$

$$= 1 \times 2 \times 3 \times 4 \times 5 \times 6 \times 7 \times 8 \times 9 \times 10 = 36{,}28{,}800$$

Illustration 49: *The probability that A can solve a problem is 2/3 and that B can solve it is 4/5. What is the probability that the problem will be solved, if both A and B try.*

(MGU: Section B April '97)

Solution: Probability that the problem will be solved,

$= P$ (at least one solve) $= 1 - P$ (none solve)

$$= 1 - P\text{ (A does not and B does not solve)}$$

$$= 1 - P(A' \cap B') = 1 - P(A') \times P(B')$$

$$= 1 - \left(\frac{1}{3} \times \frac{1}{5}\right) = 1 - \frac{1}{15} = \frac{14}{15}$$

Illustration 50: *An urn contains 8 red and 3 blue marbles. If 2 marbles are drawn at random, find the probability that (i) both are red and (ii) one of them is red and the other is blue?*

(MGU: Section B April '96)

Solution: (i) Probability of getting 2 red marbles,

$$= \frac{8C_2}{11C_2} = \frac{\frac{8!}{(8-2)!2!}}{\frac{11!}{(11-2)!2!}} = \frac{\frac{8 \times 7}{1 \times 2}}{\frac{11 \times 10}{1 \times 2}}$$

$$= \frac{8 \times 7 \times 1 \times 2}{11 \times 10 \times 1 \times 2} = \frac{28}{55}$$

(ii) Probability of getting one red marble and one blue marble,

$$= \frac{8C_1 \times 3C_1}{11C_2} = \frac{8 \times 3 \times 1 \times 2}{11 \times 10} = \frac{24}{55}$$

Illustration 51: *A bag contains 7 white and 2 black balls. Two balls are drawn in succession at random. What is the probability that one of them is white and the other is black?*

(MGU: Section B April '95)

Solution: Probability of getting a white ball $= \frac{7C_1}{9C_1}$

$$P(A) = \frac{7}{9}$$

Probability of getting a black ball $= \frac{2C_1}{9C_1}$

$$P(B) = \frac{2}{9}$$

The probability that one of them is white and the other is black

$$P(A) \times P(B) = \frac{7}{9} \times \frac{2}{9} = \frac{14}{81}$$

Illustration 52: *(a) Explain the theorem of total probability. (b) The probability that a job applicant for the post of an accountant with a post graduate degree is 0.3, that he has some previous experience is 0.7 and the probability that he has both is 0.2. Out of 3000 applicants what number would have either a post-graduate degree or previous experience.* (MGU: Section B April '94)

Solution: (a) Refer the theory portion.

(b) Probability with post-graduate degree $P(A) = 0.3$

Probability with previous experience $P(B) = 0.7$

Probability with both post-graduate and previous experience

$$P(A) \times P(B) = 0.2$$

Probability with either a post graduate or previous experience,

$$= P(A) + P(B) - P(A)P(B) = 0.3 + 0.7 - 0.2 = 0.8$$

∴ Out of 3000 applicants the probable number of applicants with either a post-graduate or previous experience,

$$= 3000 \times 0.8 = 2{,}400$$

Illustration 53: *A bag contains 7 white and 9 black balls. Two balls ar drawn in succession at random. What is the probability that one of them is white and the other is black?*

(Kerala: Section B April '97)

Solution: The probability of getting one white and one black ball

$$= \frac{7C_1 \times 9C_1}{16C_2}$$

$$7C_1 = 7, \quad 9C_1 = 9$$

$$16C_2 = \frac{16!}{(16-2)!\ 2!} = \frac{16 \times 15}{1 \times 2}$$

$$\text{P(One white and one black ball)} = \frac{7 \times 9}{8 \times 15} = \frac{21}{40}$$

Illustration 54: *Two cards are drawn randomly from the well shuffled pack of cards. Find the probability that (i) Both are diamond cards (ii) One is an Ace and the other is a King and (iii) both are not club cards.* (Kerala: Section B April '96)

Solution: (i) The probability of drawing a diamond card = 13/52

If the first card is not replaced the probability of getting another diamond card = 12/51

The probability of getting both diamond cards

$$= \frac{13}{52} \times \frac{12}{51} = \frac{3}{51} = \frac{1}{17}$$

(ii) The probability of drawing an Ace card = 4/52

If the first card is not replaced, the probability of getting a king card = 4/51

The probability of getting an Ace and a King card

$$= \frac{4}{52} \times \frac{4}{51} = \frac{4}{663}$$

(iii) Probability of both are not club cards,

$$= 1 - P \text{ (of both are club cards)}$$

$$= 1 - \left(\frac{13}{52} \times \frac{12}{51}\right) = 1 - \frac{1}{17} = \frac{16}{17}$$

Illustration 55: *A bag contains 4 red, 3 white and 2 black balls. Two balls are drawn at a time. What is the probability that both are either red or white balls?* (Kerala: Section B April '95)

Solution: The probability of getting 2 red balls $= \dfrac{4C_2}{9C_2}$

The probability of getting 2 white balls $= \dfrac{3C_2}{9C_2}$

Hence, the probability of getting 2 red or 2 white balls

$$= \frac{4C_2}{9C_2} + \frac{3C_2}{9C_2} = \frac{4C_2 + 3C_2}{9C_2}$$

$$4C_2 = \frac{4!}{2!\ 2!} = \frac{4\times3}{1\times2} = 6$$

$$3C_2 = \frac{3!}{1!\ 2!} = \frac{3\times2}{1\times2} = 6$$

$$9C_2 = \frac{9!}{7!\ 2!} = \frac{9\times8}{1\times2} = 36$$

$$\therefore\ P\,(\text{2 red or 2 white balls}) = \frac{6+3}{36} = \frac{9}{36} = \frac{1}{4}$$

Illustration 56: *Compute the value of $10C_8$ and $10C_2$. Comment on your computed values.* (Kerala: Section B April '94)

Solution: $$nC_r = \frac{n!}{(n-4)!\,r!}$$

$$10C_8 = \frac{10!}{2!\ 8!} = \frac{10\times9}{1\times2} = 45$$

$$10C_2 = \frac{10!}{8!\ 2!} = \frac{10\times9}{1\times2} = 45$$

$$\therefore\quad 10C_8 = 10C_2$$

Illustration 57: *The following probabilities are to be computed from a well-shuffled pack of cards. (i) The probability of drawing an Ace and Club cards. (ii) The probability of drawing a Heart card and a Picture card. (iii) The probability of drawing a TEN given that a Spade card is drawn. (iv) The probability of drawing either a King or a Queen or a Diamond card. (v) The probability of drawing a Picture and an Ace.* (Kerala: Section C April '94)

Solution: It is assumed that the card is not replaced after the first draw.

(i) $P\,(\text{drawing an Ace and a Club cards}) = \frac{4}{52}\times\frac{13}{51} = \frac{1}{51}$

(ii) $P\,(\text{drawing a Heart card and Picture card}) = \frac{13}{52}\times\frac{13}{51} = \frac{13}{204}$

(iii) P (TEN Spade card) $= \frac{1}{52}$

(iv) P (either a King or Queen or Diamond card)

$$= \frac{4}{52} + \frac{4}{51} + \frac{13}{50} = 0.42$$

(v) P (Picture and an Ace card) $= \frac{13}{52} \times \frac{4}{51} = \frac{1}{51}$

If the card is replaced after the first draw.

(i) P (drawing an Ace and a Club card) $= \frac{4}{52} \times \frac{13}{52} = \frac{1}{52}$

(ii) P (drawing a Heart and Picture card) $= \frac{13}{52} \times \frac{13}{52} = \frac{1}{16}$

(iii) P (TEN Spade card) $= \frac{1}{52}$

(iv) P (either a King or Queen or Diamond card)

$$= \frac{4}{52} + \frac{4}{52} + \frac{13}{52} = \frac{21}{52}$$

(v) P (Picture card and Ace card) $= \frac{13}{52} \times \frac{4}{52} = \frac{1}{52}$

Illustration 58: *In a bag there are 4 white and 10 yellow balls. Two balls are drawn at random. What is the probability that of these two balls one is white and the other is yellow.*

(Kerala: Section B April '89)

Solution: Probability of getting one white and one yellow ball

$$= \frac{4C_1 \times 10C_1}{14C_2}$$

$$4C_1 = 4; \; 10C_1 = 10$$

$$14C_2 = \frac{14!}{(14-2)!2!} = \frac{14 \times 13}{1 \times 2}$$

$$P \text{ (one white and one yellow ball)} = \frac{4\times10}{7\times13} = \frac{40}{91}$$

Illustration 59: *A bag contains 3 red, 2 white and one black balls. Two balls are drawn at a time. What is sample space?*

(Kerala: Section A Sep'93)

Solution: Sample space = $5C_2$

$$= \frac{5\,!}{(5-2)!\;\;2!} = \frac{5\times4}{1\times2} = 10$$

Illustration 60: *From a set of 20 discs numbered 1 to 20, one disc is chosen randomly. Find the probability that the number on it is divisible by (i) 3 and (ii) 5 or 7.* (Kerala: Section B Sep '90)

Solution: Total outcome = 20

(i) No. of discs divisible by 3 = 6

Probability of number on it divisible by 3 = 6/20 = 3/10

(ii) No. divisible by 5 = 4

No. divisible by 7 = 2

Probability of no. divisible by 5 = 4/20 = 1/5

Probability of no. divisible by 7 = 2/20 = 1/10

Probability of no. divisible by 5 or 7 = 1/5 + 1/10 = 3/10

Illustration 61: *Define nPr and nCr. Show that* $nC_r = nC_{(n-r)}$

(Kerala: Section B April '90)

Solution:

$$nP_r = \frac{n!}{(n-r)!}$$

$$nC_r = \frac{n!}{(n-r)!r!}$$

Let $n = 10,\;\; r = 3$

$$10C_3 = \frac{10\,!}{(10-3)!\,3!} = \frac{10\,!}{7\,!\,3\,!}$$

$$10C_7 = \frac{10!}{(10-7)!\,7!} = \frac{10!}{3!\ 7!}$$

$$\therefore \quad 10C_3 = 10C_7$$

i.e., $10C_3 = 10C_{(10-3)}$ or $nC_r = nC_{(n-r)}$

Exercise

1. Define Probability. Explain the classical approach for the calculation of probability.
2. What is Probability? State the addition and multiplication theorems of probability.
3. Explain the different approaches to probability.
4. What are Permutations and Combinations?
5. Define Probability. State the Baye's Theorem of Probability.
6. Explain the following with example,
   (a) Mutually Exclusive Events.
   (b) Dependent and Independent Events. (MGU: Section B April '98)
7. Define Random Variable. (MGU: Section A April '96)
8. What is axiomatic approach to probability? (MGU: Section A April '94)
9. Define Random Variable. What is meant by the expected value of a random variable? Find the expected value of the heads when two coins are tossed. (MGU: Section B April '94)
10. What is Conditional Probability? (MGU: Section A April '93 & Kerala: Section A April '96)
11. Explain with example, the Addition and Multiplication rules of probability. (MG U: Section B April '93)
12. What is a Random Variable? (Kerala: Section A April '97)
13. What are mutually exclusive events? (Kerala: Section B April '97)
14. Define mutually exclusive events of a trial with an example. (Kerala: Section A April '95)
15. State the basic principles of drawing a random sample. (Kerala: Section A April '94)
16. State the addition theorem of probability. What is its importance? State its particular form when the events concerned are independent. (Kerala: Section B April '94)
17. What is an Empty Set? (Kerala: Section A April '89)

18. What are mutually exclusive events? (Kerala: Section A April '89)

19. Define:

(a) Mutually Exclusive Events and (b) Independent Events.

(Kerala: Section A Sep '93)

20. State multiplication theorem of probability. What is the probability of getting at least two heads when three coins are tossed?

(Kerala: Section B Sep '93)

21. What do you mean by equivalent sets? Give an example.

(Kerala: Section A Sep '90)

22. In how many ways can you insert 10 letters in 10envelopes?

(Kerala: Section A Sep '90)

23. Define classical definition of a Probability.

(Kerala: Section A Sep '90)

24. In how many ways two balls can be selected out of five balls.

(Kerala: Section A April '90)

25. Define expectation of a random variable.

(Kerala: Section A April '90)

26. Discuss the basic principles underlying the drawing of random samples. (Kerala: Section B April '90)

27. A bag contains 5 white balls and 3 red balls. Another bag contains 4 white balls and 5 red balls. If one ball is drawn from each bag find out the probability that, (i) both are white, (ii) both are red and (iii) one is white and one is red. [Ans: (i) 5/18 (ii) 5/24 (iii) 37/72]

28. A bag contains 4 green balls and 6 red balls and another bag contains 5 red balls and 3 black balls. If one ball is drawn at random from each bag, what is the probability that both are of the same colour.

[Ans: 3/8]

29. A bag contains 7 red and 4 black balls. Two successive drawings of 3 balls are made in such a way that (i) balls are replaced before the second trial and (ii) balls are not replaced for the second trial. Find the probability that the first draw will give 3 red balls and second draw will give 3 black balls. [Ans: (i) 28/5445; (ii) 7/462]

30. If a card is drawn from a pack of 52 cards, what is the probability of getting either an ace of diamond or king of spades. [Ans: 1/26]

31. Three cards are drawn from a pack of 52 cards without replacement. What is the probability that they are all king cards? [Ans: 1/5525]

32. The probabilities of solving a problem in Mathematics by A, B and C are 1/4, 2/5, 1/2 respectively. What is the probability that the problem will be solved. [Ans: 31/40]

33. The probabilities of promotion of one of three managers A, B and C of a company for the post of Managing Director are 0.4, 0.25 and 0.65 respectively. The probabilities that a new product is launched by three people, if they are appointed are 0.5, 0.8 and 0.6. What is the probability that the new product will be launched by the new Managing Director? [Ans: 0.79]

34. The residents of a city were surveyed to find out the preference of films. 40% of the repondents see English films and 50% of them see Tamil films and 30% of them see both English and Tamil films. Find the probability that a resident selected sees either the English film or Tamil film or both the films. [Ans: 0.6]

35. A candidate attended interviews in 3 companies for the post of a manager. The number of total companies are 25, 30 and 15 respectively. What are the chances of his getting the post at least in one of the company? [Ans: 0.134]

36. A machine will work only when all the four components A, B, C and D are working. The probability of A failing during the month is 0.35, B failing is 0.25, C failing is 0.40 and D failing is 0.30. What is the probability that the machine fails during the month?

[Ans: 0.795]

◆ Chapter 15 ◆

Theoretical Distributions

Distributions which are determined mathematically on the basis of certain assumptions are called Theoretical Distributions. The probability of occurance of events are determined with the help of mathematical calculation. For example (i) the probability of occurance of any number when a die is thrown is 1/6. If the die is tossed 60 times, the probability of occurance of each number is 10 times. (ii) The probability of occurance of Head when a coin is tossed is 1/2. If the coin is tossed 100 times then, the probability of occurance of Head is 50 times and Tail is 50 times. This is called the theoretical distribution. But in practice, there may be variations in the occurance of events. It is not possible to get each number exactly for 10 times when the die is thrown for 60 times. Also it is not possible to get exactly 50 Heads when the coin is tossed for 100 times. Hence, with the help of theoretical distribution, it can be determined that the experiment conducted is biased one or not.

Methods of Measuring Theoretical Distribution

The important methods of measuring theoretical distribution are, (1) Binomial Distribution (2) Poisson Distribution and (3) Normal Distribution

I Binomial Distribution

Binomial distribution was developed by a Swiss mathematician, named James Bernoulli. Hence, it is also called as 'Bernoulli Distribution'. Binomial distribution means a probability distribution explaining the probability of one set of dichotomous alternatives of success or failure of events.

Assumptions

(1) Dichotomous Alternative: Dichotomous alternative means alternative of success and failure. All observations should be classified into two categories, namely,

(i) Those having a particular characteristic - Success

(ii) Those not having a particular characteristic - Failure

(2) Number of trials should be more than one: There should be more than one trial for binomial distribution. In each successive trials there should be dichotomous alternatives, *i.e.*, success or failure.

(3) Probability of success in each trial should be constant: The probability of success in each trial should be constant. The probability of success is denoted by 'p' and the probability of failure is denoted by 'q'.

(4) Independent Trials: All trials are independent. The occurance of an event in the first trial won't affect the 2nd and subsequent trials.

(5) Identical Trials: All the trials should be identical one. There should not be any variations between one trial to another.

Formula for Binomial Distribution

The binomial distribution can be expressed to 'n' items by adopting the following formula,

$$(q+p)^n = q^n + nC_1q^{n-1}p^1 + nC_2q^{n-1}p^2 + nC_3q^{n-3}p^3 + ... + p^n$$

To obtain the frequency of 'N' sets of 'n' trials, the following formula can be applied.

$$N(q+p)^n = N[q^n + nC_1q^{n-1}p^1 + nC_2q^{n-1}p^2 + nC_3q^{n-3}p^3 + ... + p^n]$$

where, p - probability of occurance of an event

q - probability of non-occurance of an event

i.e., $p = 1 - q$ or $q = 1 - p$

Characteristics of Binomial Distribution

(1) The shape and location of binomial distribution changes due to the change in the value of 'p' for a given number of trials 'n'.

(2) When the number of trials are increased, the distribution becomes very close. It may give a bell shaped curve.

(3) If 'np' is an integer, the arithmetic mean and mode of binomial distribution are equal. This would normally happen for a largest probability distribution.

(4) If 'n' is large and 'p' or 'q' is not close to zero, then binomial distribution may be approximately normal distribution, *i.e.*,

$$Z = \frac{\overline{X} - np}{\sqrt{npq}}$$

Illustration 1: *Five coins are tossed 64 times. Find out the number of times (i) 2 heads and (ii) 4 heads will occur,*

Solution: Probability of getting a head p = 1/2

Probability of not getting a head q = 1 - 1/2 = 1/2

Probability of getting heads in *N* trial $= N \ \ nC_r \ \ p^r \ \ q^{n-r}$

(i) Probability of getting 2 heads when 5 coins are tossed 64 times,

$$= 64 \ \ 5C_2 \ \left(\frac{1}{2}\right)^2 \left(\frac{1}{2}\right)^3 = 64 \times \frac{5!}{(5-2)! \ 2!}\left(\frac{1}{2}\right)^5$$

$$= 64 \times \frac{5 \times 4}{1 \times 2} \times \frac{1}{32} = 20 \ \text{ times}$$

(ii) Probability of getting 4 heads,

$$= 64 \ \ 5C_4 \ \left(\frac{1}{2}\right)^4 \left(\frac{1}{2}\right)^1 = 64 \times \frac{5!}{(5-4)! \ 4!}\left(\frac{1}{2}\right)^5$$

$$= 64 \times \frac{5 \times 4 \times 3 \times 2}{1 \times 2 \times 3 \times 4} \times \frac{1}{32} = 10 \ \text{ times}$$

Illustration 2: *Six dices are thrown 729 times. How many times do you expect at least three dices show a five or six.*

Solution: The number of times at least 3 dices are showing a five or six in one throw $p(x \geq 3) = p_3 + p_4 + p_5 + p_6$

$$p = 2/6 = 1/3 \quad q = 1 - p = 1 - 1/3 = 2/3$$

The number of times at least 3 dies showing five or six in 720 throws

$$= 729 \ \ (P_3 + P_4 + P_5 + P_6)$$

$$= 729 \ \ [6C_3 \ p^3 \ q^3 \ + \ 6C_4 \ p^4 \ q^2 \ + \ 6C_5 \ p^5 \ q^1 \ + \ 6C_6 \ p^6 \ q^0 \ ]$$

$$= 729\left[6C_3\left(\frac{1}{3}\right)^3\left(\frac{2}{3}\right)^3 + 6C_4\left(\frac{1}{3}\right)^4\left(\frac{2}{3}\right)^2 + 6C_5\left(\frac{1}{3}\right)^5\left(\frac{2}{3}\right)^1 + 6C_6\left(\frac{1}{3}\right)^6\left(\frac{2}{3}\right)^0\right]$$

$$= 729\left[\frac{6!}{3!3!}\times\frac{8}{729} + \frac{6!}{2!4!}\times\frac{4}{729} + \frac{6!}{1!5!}\times\frac{2}{729} + \frac{6!}{0!6!}\times\frac{1}{729}\right]$$

$$= 729\left[\frac{160}{729} + \frac{60}{729} + \frac{12}{729} + \frac{1}{729}\right] = 729\times\frac{233}{729} = 233 \text{ times}$$

Fitting of Binomial Distribution

According to binomial distribution, the probability of 0, 1, 2, 3, 4, 5, . . . n success would be obtained by the expansion of $(p+q)^n$.

When the experiment is repeated for number of times then, the frequency of success would be,

$$N \times P_{(r)} = N \times nC_r \quad p^r \quad q^{n-r}$$

Where, N means number of times the experiment is repeated; r- is the expected frequency of success; n is the number of outcomes; p is the rate of success and q is the rate of failure.

The binomial distribution for different number of success (i.e., r = 0, 1, 2, 3 ..... n) are shown as follows.

Number of Success (r)	*Expected or theoretical frequency*
0	$N\ q^n$
1	$N\ nC_1\ p^1\ q^{n-1}$
2	$N\ nC_2\ p^2\ q^{n-2}$
3	$N\ nC_3\ p^3\ q^{n-3}$
r	$N\ nC_r\ p^r\ q^{n-r}$
n	$N\ p^n$

Illustration 3: *9 coins are tossed 512 times. What are the expected frequencies of getting heads? Also tabulate the result.*

Solution: Probability of getting a head $(p) = 1/2$

Probability of not getting a head $(q) = 1 - 1/2 = 1/2$

The probability of success (getting a head) in r trial for one toss

$$= 9C_r\,(1/2)^r\,(1/2)^{9-r}$$

Hence, probability of r heads in the toss of 512 times

$$= 512\; 9Cr\,(1/2)^r\,(1/2)^{9-r}$$

Table showing the Expected Frequencies.

No. of heads	*Expected Frequencies* $512\; 9C_r\,(1/2)^r\,(1/2)^{9-r}$	
0	$512 \times 9C_0\,(1/2)^9 =$	1
1	$512 \times 9C_1\,(1/2)^9 =$	9
2	$512 \times 9C_2\,(1/2)^9 =$	36
3	$512 \times 9C_3\,(1/2)^9 =$	84
4	$512 \times 9C_4\,(1/2)^9 =$	126
5	$512 \times 9C_5\,(1/2)^9 =$	126
6	$512 \times 9C_6\,(1/2)^9 =$	84
7	$512 \times 9C_7\,(1/2)^9 =$	36
8	$512 \times 9C_8\,(1/2)^9 =$	9
9	$512 \times 9C_9\,(1/2)^9 =$	1
	Total	*512*

Illustration 4: *8 coins are tossed at a time, for 256 times. Number of heads observed at each throw is recorded and results are given below. Find out the expected frequencies.*

No. of heads at a throw	0	1	2	3	4	5	6	7	8
Frequency	2	6	30	52	67	56	32	10	1

Solution: p - success q - failure

$p = 1/2$; $q = 1/2$; $N = 256$ (Total Frequency)

$n = 8$ (Number of trial)

(1) Expected frequency of 0 head $= N \times q^n$

$$= 256 \times \left(\frac{1}{2}\right)^8$$

$$= 256 \times \frac{1}{2} \times \frac{1}{2} \times \frac{1}{2} \times \frac{1}{2} \times \frac{1}{2} \times \frac{1}{2} \times \frac{1}{2} \times \frac{1}{2} = 1$$

(2) Expected frequency of 1 head $= N \times NC_1 \; q^{n-1} \; p^1$

$$= 256 \times 8C_1 \left(\frac{1}{2}\right)^7 \left(\frac{1}{2}\right)^1$$

$$= 256 \times 8 \times \frac{1}{2} \times \frac{1}{2} \times \frac{1}{2} \times \frac{1}{2} \times \frac{1}{2} \times \frac{1}{2} \times \frac{1}{2} \times \frac{1}{2} = 8$$

(3) Expected frequency of 2 heads $= N \times nC_2 \; q^{n-2} \; p^2$

$$= 256 \times 8C_2 \left(\frac{1}{2}\right)^6 \left(\frac{1}{2}\right)^2$$

$$= 256 \times 28 \times \frac{1}{2} \times \frac{1}{2} \times \frac{1}{2} \times \frac{1}{2} \times \frac{1}{2} \times \frac{1}{2} \times \frac{1}{2} \times \frac{1}{2} = 28$$

(4) Expected frequency of 3 heads $= N \times nC_3 \; q^{n-3} \; p^3$

$$= 256 \times 8C_1 \left(\frac{1}{2}\right)^5 \left(\frac{1}{2}\right)^3$$

$$= 256 \times 56 \times \frac{1}{2} \times \frac{1}{2} \times \frac{1}{2} \times \frac{1}{2} \times \frac{1}{2} \times \frac{1}{2} \times \frac{1}{2} \times \frac{1}{2} = 56$$

(5) Expected frequency of 4 heads $= N \times nC_4 \; q^{n-4} \; p^4$

$$= 256 \times 8C_4 \left(\frac{1}{2}\right)^4 \left(\frac{1}{2}\right)^4$$

$$= 256 \times 70 \times \frac{1}{2} \times \frac{1}{2} \times \frac{1}{2} \times \frac{1}{2} \times \frac{1}{2} \times \frac{1}{2} \times \frac{1}{2} \times \frac{1}{2} = 70$$

(6) Expected frequency of 5 heads $= N \times nC_5 \; q^{n-5} \; p^5$

$$= 256 \times 8C_5 \left(\frac{1}{2}\right)^3 \left(\frac{1}{2}\right)^5$$

$$= 256 \times 56 \times \frac{1}{2} \times \frac{1}{2} \times \frac{1}{2} \times \frac{1}{2} \times \frac{1}{2} \times \frac{1}{2} \times \frac{1}{2} \times \frac{1}{2} = 56$$

(7) Expected frequency of 6 heads $= N \times nC_6 \; q^{n-6} \; p^6$

$$= 256 \times 8C_6 \left(\frac{1}{2}\right)^2 \left(\frac{1}{2}\right)^6$$

$$= 256 \times 28 \times \frac{1}{2} \times \frac{1}{2} \times \frac{1}{2} \times \frac{1}{2} \times \frac{1}{2} \times \frac{1}{2} \times \frac{1}{2} \times \frac{1}{2} = 28$$

(8) Expected frequency of 7 heads $= N \times nC_7 \; q^{n-7} \; p^7$

$$= 256 \times 8C_7 \left(\frac{1}{2}\right)^1 \left(\frac{1}{2}\right)^7$$

$$= 256 \times 8 \times \frac{1}{2} \times \frac{1}{2} \times \frac{1}{2} \times \frac{1}{2} \times \frac{1}{2} \times \frac{1}{2} \times \frac{1}{2} \times \frac{1}{2} = 8$$

(9) Expected frequency of 8 heads

$$= N \times p^8 = 256 \times \left(\frac{1}{2}\right)^8$$

$$= 256 \times \frac{1}{2} \times \frac{1}{2} \times \frac{1}{2} \times \frac{1}{2} \times \frac{1}{2} \times \frac{1}{2} \times \frac{1}{2} \times \frac{1}{2} = 1$$

No. of heads at a throw	*Expected Frequency*
0	1
1	8
2	28
3	56
4	70
5	56
6	28
7	8
8	1
Total	*256*

Properties of Binomial Distribution

The following are the properties of binomial distribution.

(i) It has two parameters. They are number of outcomes (n) and success (p) or failure (q).

(ii) Arithmetic mean = np (iii) Variance = npq

(iv) Standard Deviation = $\sqrt{npq}$ (v) Skewness $(\beta_1) = \dfrac{(q-p)^2}{npq}$

(vi) Kurtosis $(\beta_2) = 3 + \dfrac{1-6pq}{npq}$

(vii) It is symmetrical if $p = q = 0.5$. It is positively skewed if $p < 0.5$ and negatively skewed if $p > 0.5$.

Illustration 5: *State whether the given data related to binomial distribution are consistent or not from the following data.*

Mean is 12 and Variance is 14.

Solution: Mean = np = 12

$$\text{Variance} = npq = 14$$

$$12 \times q = 14$$

$$q = 14/12 = 1.17$$

The value of q should lie between 0 and 1. But the value of q in this distribution is 1.17. Hence the given data are inconsistent.

Illustration 6: *The probability of the defective products from a production line of 5000 products is 12%. Calculate its (a) mean (b) standard deviation (c) skewness and (d) kurtosis.*

Solution: $n = 5000$ $p = 12\% = 0.12$

$$q = 1 - p = 1 - 0.12 = 0.88$$

(a) Mean = $np = 5000 \times 0.12 = 600$

(b) S.D = $\sqrt{npq} = \sqrt{5000 \times 0.12 \times 0.88} = \sqrt{528} = 22.98$

(c) Skewness $(\beta_1) = \dfrac{(q-p)^2}{npq}$

$$= \frac{(0.88-0.12)^2}{5000 \times 0.12 \times 0.88} = \frac{(0.76)^2}{5000 \times 0.12 \times 0.88}$$

$$= \frac{0.5776}{528} = 0.001$$

(d) $\text{Kurtosis}\,(\beta_2) = 3 + \frac{1-6pq}{npq} = 3 + \frac{1-6(0.12\times0.88)}{5000\times0.12\times0.88}$

$$= 3 + \frac{0.3664}{528} = 3 + 0.001 = 3.001$$

Illustration 7: *Find out n, p and q when the mean of a binomial distribution is 99 and standard deviation is 9.*

Solution: Mean $m = np = 99$

Standard deviation $= \sqrt{npq} = 9$

$$npq = 81$$

$$q = \frac{npq}{np} = \frac{81}{99} = 0.82$$

$$p = 1 - 0.82 = 0.18$$

$$n = \frac{99}{0.18} = 550$$

Illustration 8: *Obtain the binomial distribution for which mean is 24 and variance is 6.*

Solution: Mean $= np = 24$

Variance $= npq = 6$

$$q = \frac{npq}{np} = \frac{6}{24} = 0.25 = \frac{1}{4}$$

$$p = 1 - q = 1 - 0.25 = 0.75$$

$$n = \frac{24}{0.75} = 32$$

Hence, the binomial distribution is,

$$(p+q)n = (0.75 + 0.25)^{32} = \left(\frac{3}{4} + \frac{1}{4}\right)^{32} = (1)^{32} = 1$$

Illustration 9: *Obtain the binomial distribution for which mean is 90 and standard deviation is 3.*

Solution: Mean = np = 90

$$\text{Standard deviation} = \sqrt{npq} = 3$$

$$npq = 9$$

$$q = \frac{npq}{np} = \frac{9}{90} = \frac{1}{10} = 0.1$$

$$p = 1 - q = 1 - \frac{1}{10} = \frac{9}{10} = 0.9$$

$$n = \frac{90}{0.9} = 100$$

Hence, the binomial distribution is,

$$(p+q)n = (0.9+0.1)^{100} = \left(\frac{9}{10} + \frac{1}{10}\right)^{100} = 1$$

Illustration 10: *The mean of a binomial distribution is 40 and the standard deviation is 6. Calculate n, p and q.*

Solution: Mean = np = 40

$$\text{S.D} = \sqrt{npq}$$

$$\text{Variance} = npq = SD^2 = 6^2 = 36$$

$$npq = 36$$

$$40q = 36$$

$$q = 36/40 = 0.9$$

$$p = 1 - 0.9 = 0.1$$

$$np = 40$$

$$n(0.1) = 40$$

$$n = 40/0.1 = 400$$

II Poisson Distribution

Poisson distribution was developed by French mathematician Simeon Dennis Poisson during 1837. Poisson distribution is a technique of ascertaining the probability of occurance of an event when there is very rare chance of occurance of an event. It is applied when the probability of non-occurance of an event is impossible to predict. Example, Poisson distribution is applied to test the probability of number of road accidents in a city, number of defective products in a mass production etc. The probability of occurance of an event can be calculated, under Poisson Distribution as follows,

$$P_{(r)} = \frac{m^r \times e^{-m}}{r!}$$

where,

r - indicates expected number of times an event occur.

e - indicates the base of natural logarithms. Its value is 2.7183.

m - indicates the mean of the poisson distribution.

It can be calculated as np. (n = no. of times; p = probability)

The probabilities of occurance of various rare events (no. of success like 0, 1, 2, 3 .... n) according to poisson distribution are given as follows.

$$P_{(0)} = e^{-m} \qquad P_{(1)} - me^{-m} \qquad P_{(2)} = \frac{m^2 e^{-m}}{2!}$$

$$P_{(3)} = \frac{m^3 e^{-m}}{3!} \qquad P_{(4)} = \frac{m^4 e^{-m}}{4!} \qquad P_{(r)} = \frac{m^r e^{-m}}{r!}$$

$$P_{(n)} = \frac{m^n e^{-m}}{n!}$$

where, $P_{(0)}$ is the probability of zero success.

$P_{(1)}$ is the probability of one success.

$P_{(n)}$ is the probability of n success.

m is the mean of the poisson distribution and value of e = 2.71828

Illustration 11: *It is experienced that 4% of the refrigerators manufactured by a company are defective. Find out the probability through poisson distribution technique, that a sample of 200 refrigerators will contain (a) no defective (b) exactly 1 defective and (c) exactly 3 defectives.*

Solution: Probability of defective $p = 4\%$

$$m = 200 \times 4\% = 8$$

(a) Probability of not defective $P_{(0)} = e^{-m}$

$$= 2.71828^{-8} = \frac{1}{2.71828^{8}} = 0.0004$$

(b) Probability of one defective $P_{(1)} = me^{-m}$

$$= 8 \times 0.0004 = 0.0032$$

(c) Probability of three defectives $P_{(3)} = \dfrac{m^3 e^{-m}}{3!}$

$$= \frac{8^3 \times 0.0004}{1 \times 2 \times 3} = \frac{512 \times 0.0004}{6} = \frac{0.2048}{6} = 0.034$$

Illustration 12: *It is known that 2% of blades manufactured by a company are expected to be defective. What is the probability that at most 6 defective blades will be found in a sample of 300 blades.*

Solution: The mean defective blade $m = n \times p = 300 \times 2\%$

$$= 300 \times 0.02 = 6$$

$$e^{-m} = 2.71828^{-6}$$

$$P_{(r)} = \frac{e^{-m} m^r}{r!}$$

The probability of atmost 6 defective blades,

$$P(x < 6) = P_{(0)} + P_{(1)} + P_{(2)} + P_{(3)} + P_{(4)} + P_{(5)} + P_{(6)}$$

$$= e^{-m}\left[1 + m + \frac{m^2}{2!} + \frac{m^3}{3!} + \frac{m^4}{4!} + \frac{m^5}{5!} + \frac{m^6}{6!}\right]$$

$$= 0.0028\left[1 + 6 + \frac{6^2}{2!} + \frac{6^3}{3!} + \frac{6^4}{4!} + \frac{6^5}{5!} + \frac{6^6}{6!}\right]$$

$$= 0.0028\left[1+6+\frac{36}{2\times1}+\frac{216}{3\times2\times1}+\frac{1296}{4\times3\times2\times1}\right.$$

$$\left.+\frac{7776}{5\times4\times3\times2\times1}+\frac{46656}{6\times5\times4\times3\times2\times1}\right]$$

$$= 0.0028[1+6+18+36+54+64.8+64.8] = 0.684$$

Illustration 13: *The past records showed that there were 7 road accidents on an average per month in a locality. What is the probability as per poisson distribution, that in a given month, there will be less than 6 accidents?*

Solution: Mean number of success $m = 7$

$$P_{(n)} = \frac{e^{-m}m^n}{n!}$$

The probability of less than 6 accidents,

$$P(x \le 6) = P_{(0)} + P_{(1)} + P_{(2)} + P_{(3)} + P_{(4)} + P_{(5)}$$

$$= e^{-7}\left[1+7+\frac{7^2}{2!}+\frac{7^3}{3!}+\frac{7^4}{4!}+\frac{7^5}{5!}\right]$$

$$= 0.0009\left[1+7+\frac{49}{2\times1}+\frac{343}{3\times2\times1}+\frac{2401}{4\times3\times2\times1}+\frac{16807}{5\times4\times3\times2\times1}\right]$$

$$= 0.0009[1+7+24.5+57.2+100.04+140.06]$$

$$= 0.0009\times329.8 = 0.2968$$

Illustration 14: *There are 200 mistakes pointed out from 100 pages typed by a typist. Find out the probability that a page contains at least 4 mistakes. Assume poisson distribution.*

Solution: The mean mistakes from 100 pages = 200/100 = 2

$$P_{(r)} = \frac{e^{-m}m^r}{r!}$$

The probability that a page contains at least 4 mistakes,

$$P(n \ge 4) = 1 - P_{(0)} + P_{(1)} + P_{(2)} + P_{(3)}$$

$$= 1 - e^{-2}\left[1 + 2 + \frac{2^2}{2!} + \frac{2^3}{3!}\right] = 1 - e^{-2}\left[1 + 2 + 2 + \frac{4}{3}\right]$$

$$= 1 - (0.1353 \times 6.33) = 1 - 0.856 = 0.144$$

Illustration 15: *Out of the total nuts manufactured by a company o.5 percent became defective. The nuts are supplied in packets of 40. Find out the probability number of packets containing (i) no defective (ii) one defective (iii) two defectives (iv) three defectives (v) less than four defectives and (vi) more than four defective nuts respectively in a consignment of 50,000 packets. Assume poisson distribution.*

Solution: The probability of defective nuts

$$(p) = 0.5\% = \frac{0.5}{100} = 0.005$$

$$n = 40$$

The mean probability of defective nuts

$$= p \times n = 0.005 \times 40 = 0.2$$

The probability of defective nuts as per poisson distribution in 50,000 packets,

$$= 50000 \times \frac{e^{-m} m^r}{r!}$$

(i) Number of packets with zero defective,

$$P_{(0)} = 50000 \times e\text{-}2 = 50000 \times 0.8187 = 40935$$

(ii) Number of packets with one defective nut,

$$P_{(1)} = 50000 \times e^{-m}\, m$$

$$= 50000 \times e^{-0.2} \times 0.2 = 40935 \times 0.2 = 8187$$

(iii) Number of packets with 2 defective nuts

$$P_{(2)} = 50000 \times \frac{e^{-m} m^2}{2!} = 50000 \times \frac{e^{-0.2} \times 0.2^2}{2!}$$

$$= 50000 \times \frac{0.8187 \times 0.04}{2 \times 1} = 50000 \times 0.0164 = 820$$

(iv) Number of packets with 3 defective nuts

$$P_{(3)} = 50000 \times \frac{e^{-m}m^3}{3!} = 50000 \times \frac{e^{-0.2} \times 0.2^3}{3!}$$

$$= 50000 \times \frac{0.8187 \times 0.008}{3 \times 2 \times 1} = 55$$

(v) Number of packets with less than 4 defectives,

$$P(x < 4) = P_{(0)} + P_{(1)} + P_{(2)} + P_{(3)}$$

$$= 40920 + 8184 + 820 + 55 = 49.979$$

(vi) Number of packets with more than 4 defectives,

$$P(x > 4) = 50000 - \left(P_{(0)} + P_{(1)} + P_{(2)} + P_{(3)}\right)$$

$$= 50000 - 49997 = 3$$

Fitting a Poisson Distribution

The expected frequencies as per poisson distribution can be calculated through a short cut method, which has been stated as follows.

$$N(P_0) = Ne^{-m} \qquad N(P_1) = N(P_0) \times \frac{m}{1}$$

$$N(P_2) = N(P_1) \times \frac{m}{2} \qquad N(P_3) = N(P_2) \times \frac{m}{3}$$

$$N(P_4) = N(P_3) \times \frac{m}{4} \qquad N(P_n) = N(P_{n-1}) \times \frac{m}{n}$$

Illustration 16: *Fit a poisson distribution from the following data.*

x	*0*	*1*	*2*	*3*	*4*	*5*
f	*113*	*32*	*21*	*10*	*4*	*2*

Solution: Calculation of mean.

x	*f*	*fx*
0	131	0
1	32	32
2	21	42
3	10	30
4	4	16
5	2	20
Total	$\Sigma f = 200$	$\Sigma fx = 140$

Mean, $$m = \frac{\Sigma fx}{\Sigma f} = \frac{140}{200} = 0.7$$

$$N(P_0) = Ne^{-m} = 200\ e^{-0.7} = 200 \times 0.4966 = 99.3$$

$$N(P_1) = N(P_0) \times \frac{m}{1} = 99.3 \times 0.7 = 69.51$$

$$N(P_2) = N(P_1) \times \frac{m}{2} = 69.51 \times \frac{0.7}{2} = 24.32$$

$$N(P_3) = N(P_2) \times \frac{m}{3} = 24.32 \times \frac{0.7}{3} = 5.67$$

$$N(P_4) = N(P_3) \times \frac{m}{4} = 5.67 \times \frac{0.7}{4} = 0.99$$

$$N(P_5) = N(P_4) \times \frac{m}{5} = 0.99 \times \frac{0.7}{5} = 0.13$$

Total = 199.92 = 200

Illustration 17: *A sample of 150 Air Condition sets are examined to find out the number of defective Sets. The details regarding the number of defectives are stated as below.*

No. of defects	*0*	*1*	*2*	*3*	*4*
No. of sets	*103*	*26*	*15*	*5*	*1*

Calculate the theoretical distribution on the basis of poisson distribution technique.

Solution: Calculation of Arithmetic Mean (m)

X	f	fX
0	103	0
1	26	26
2	15	30
3	5	15
4	1	4
	$\Sigma f = 150$	$\Sigma fx = 75$

$$\text{Mean defects } (m) = \frac{\Sigma fx}{\Sigma f} = \frac{75}{150} = 0.5$$

Calculation of theoretical distribution based on poisson distribution.

No. of defectives X	*Theoretical Frequency Distribution* $N\,P_{(x)}$	
0	$N(P_0) = Ne^{-m} = 150 \times e^{-0.5} = 150 \times 0.6064$	*90.96*
1	$N(P_1) = N(P_0) \times m = 90.96 \times 0.5$	45.5
2	$N(P_2) = N(P_1) \times \frac{m}{2} = 45.5 \times \frac{0.5}{2}$	11.4
3	$N(P_3) = N(P_2) \times \frac{m}{3} = 11.4 \times \frac{0.5}{3}$	1.9
4	$N(P_4) = N(P_3) \times \frac{m}{4} = 1.9 \times \frac{0.5}{4}$	0.2
	Total	*149.96=150*

Properties of Poisson Distribution

The following are the important properties of poisson distribution.

(1) Arithmetic Mean $m = p$ (2) Standard Deviation S.D. = $\sqrt{m}$

(3) Variance = m (4) Skewness $b_1 = \frac{1}{m}$

(5) Kurtosis $b_2 = 3 + \frac{1}{m}$

where, m = mean; p = the mean success in the poisson distribution.

Illustration 18: *Calculate (i) Standard Deviation (ii) Variance (iii) β_1, (iv) β_2 (v) μ_3 and (vi) μ_4 when mean of a poisson distribution is 9.*

Solution: (i) Standard Deviation $= \sqrt{m} = \sqrt{9} = 3$

(ii) Variance = m = 9 (iii) Skewness $\beta_1 = \frac{1}{m} = \frac{1}{9} = 0.11$

(iv) Kurtosis $\beta_2 = 3 + \frac{1}{m} = 3 + \frac{1}{9} = 3 + 0.11 = 3.11$

(v) Third Moment $\mu_3 = m = 9$

(vi) Fourth Moment $\mu_4 = m + 3m^2 = 9 + 3(9)^2 = 9 + 243 = 252$

Illustration 19: *State whether there is consistency in the poisson distribution with mean 15 and standard deviation 4.*

Solution: In the poisson distribution variance is equal to mean *(m)*. In the given distribution variance = 4^2 $(S.D^2)$ *i.e.*, = 16, which is not equal to the mean (m = 15). Hence, the given distribution is not consistent.

III Normal Distribution

The binomial and poisson distribution are based on the discrete probability distribution. But the normal distribution deals with the continuous probability distribution.

The normal distribution was discovered by De Moivre, an English Mathematician in the year 1733.

The normal distribution is an approximation to binomial distribution. When the number of trials or experiment become large the occurance of an event p and non-occurance of the event q tends to be equal. In such a situation the approximation of the events should be taken into consideration. The limiting frequency curve, so obtained is called the normal frequency curve. The curve tends to be normal due to the more number of repetition of experiments.

Hence, a continuous random variable X is said to be normally distributed, if it has the probability density function represented by the equation,

$$p(x) = \frac{1}{\sigma\sqrt{2\pi}} \cdot e^{-1/2((x-\mu)/\sigma)}$$

where, μ - Arithmetic Mean (parameter)

σ - Standard Deviation (parameter)

π - 3.14159 (constant)

e - 2.7183 (constant)

The graph of Normal Distribution will be a bell shaped one which has been stated below.

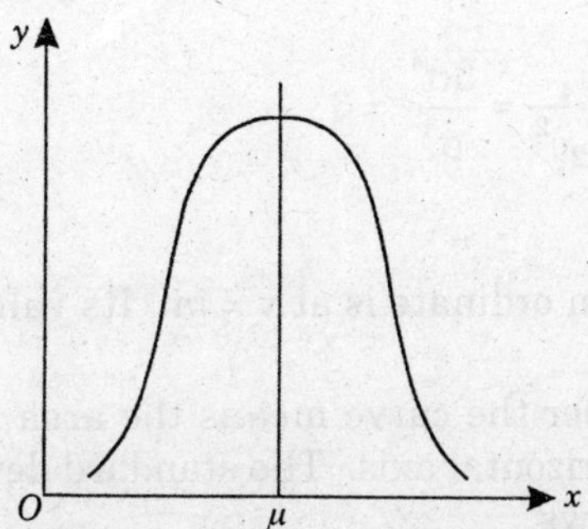

Characteristics of Normal Distribution

The important characteristics of normal distribution are stated below.

(1) The normal distribution curve assumes different shapes based on the different values of m and s.

(2) The normal distribution is a limiting form of binomial distribution when the number of trial is very large.

Properties of Normal Distribution

The important properties of normal distribution are stated below.

(1) The normal curve is perfectly symmetrical about the mean. It is bell shaped. If the curve is folded along the vertical line at the centre the two halves of the curve would coincide.

(2) The mean, median and mode are equal in a normal distribution.

(3) Skewness is equal to zero.

(4) It has only one mode.

(5) The first quartile Q_1 and the 3rd quartile Q_3 are equidistant from median or mean.

$Q_1 = m - 0.67\,\sigma$ $\qquad$ $Q_3 = m + 0.67\,\sigma$

Quartile deviation = $0.67\,\sigma$,

Mean deviation (about mean) = $0.90\,\sigma = 4/5\,\sigma$

(6) All the odd moments about mean are zero

i.e. $m_1 = n_3 = \ldots = 0.$

(7) Kurtosis $= \frac{\mu_4}{(\mu_2)^2} = \frac{3\sigma^4}{\sigma^4} = 3$

(8) The maximum ordinate is at $x = m$. Its value is $\frac{1}{\sigma\sqrt{2\pi}}$

(9) The area under the curve means the area lying between the curve and the horizontal axis. The standard deviation distributes this area as follows.

(i) Mean $\pm 1\sigma$ cover 68.27% area, i.e., 34.135% area will lie on either side of the mean.

(ii) Mean $\pm 2\sigma$ covers 95.45% area i.e., 47.725% area will lie on either side of the mean.

(iii) Mean $\pm 3\sigma$ covers 99.73% area i.e., 49.865% area will lie on either side of the mean.

Standard Normal Distribution

In a normal distribution, the probability of the variate lying between two values can be found out. The number of observations in the interval between two values can also be calculated. For different distributions there exists different means and standard deviations. Hence, the probability curves for different distributions will be different. It requires different tables of area under normal curve. These problems can be reduced if the general variate is converted into a standard normal variate.

The variate is equally distributed about the maximum ordinate (*i.e.*, mean), in the normal distribution. In the standard normal variate, areas to the left of origin corresponds to the probability of negative values of the variate, (*i.e.*, values less than arithmetic mean).

The area to the right of the origin represents the positive values of variate, (*i.e.*, values greater than arithmetic mean). In standard normal variate arithmetic mean = 0 and standard deviation = 1.

Standard normal distribution is denoted as z distribution. It can be calculated as,

$$Z = \frac{X - \overline{X}}{\sigma}$$

The standard normal distribution satisfies the following condition.

$$y = p(x) = \frac{1}{\sigma\sqrt{2n}} \cdot e^{-z^2/2} \qquad (\text{where} - \infty \leq \times \infty)$$

p(x) is called probability distribution. *z* is the standard normal variable with mean = 0 and $\sigma = 1$.

Area under Standard Normal Curve: The area under standard normal curve depends on the mean and standard deviation. The graph of standard normal curve is stated below.

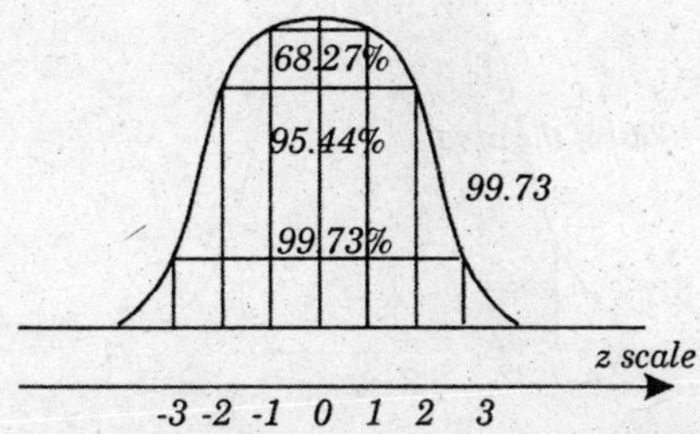

The graph clearly shows that the total area is 1, $x = 0$ and σ– 1. The area under normal curve can be calculated by referring the table corresponding to the calculated value of Z.

Value of z can be calculated as, $Z = \dfrac{X - \overline{X}}{\sigma}$

When X is greater than $\overline{X}$ the area falls on the right side of the curve. When X is less than $\overline{X}$, the area falls on the left side of the curve.

Illustration 20: *Find the are under standard normal curve between Z = 0 and Z = 1.69.*

Solution: The area under standard normal curve for $Z = 1.69$ is 0.4545. It can be represented graphically as follows.

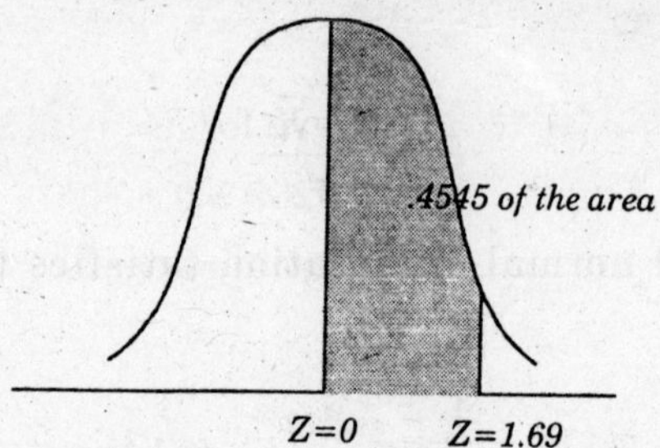

Illustration 21: *Find the area under standard normal curve between Z = 0 and Z = -1.32.*

Solution: The area under standard normal curve for z = -1.32 is -0.4066.

It can be represented in the normal curve as follows.

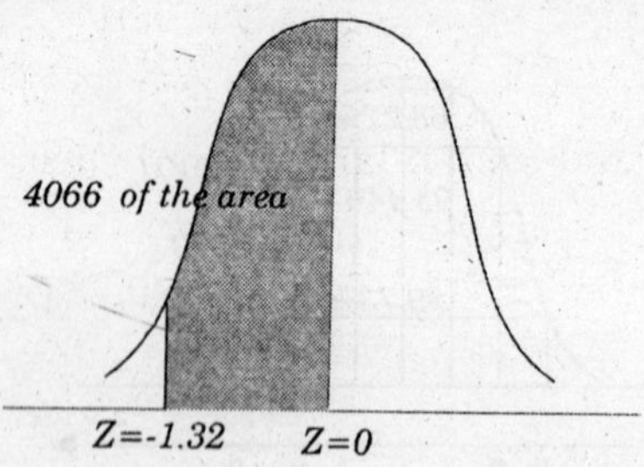

Illustration 22: *Find the area under standard normal curve right of z = 0.45.*

Solution: Area for Z = 0.45 is 0.1736

Area right of Z = 0.45 is,

0.5 – 0.1736 = 0.3264

It can be represented in the normal curve as follows.

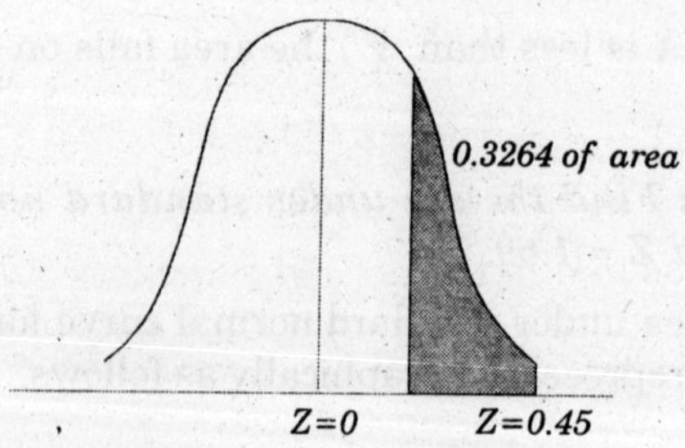

Illustration 23: *Find the area left of Z = 0.95 under standard normal curve.*

Solution: Area under normal curve for $Z = 0.95$ is 0.3289

Area left of $Z = 0.95$ is $0.5 + 0.3289 = 0.8289$ of area.

It can be represented in the normal curve as follows.

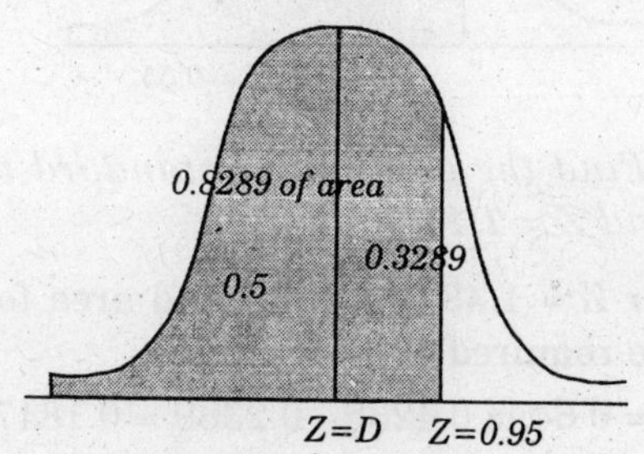

Illustration 24: *Find the area left of Z = -0.72 under standard normal curve.*

Solution: Area under standard normal curve of $Z = -0.72$ is 0.2642.

Therefore area left of Z = -0.72 is 0.5 - 0.2642 = 0.2358

It can be shown in the normal curve as follows.

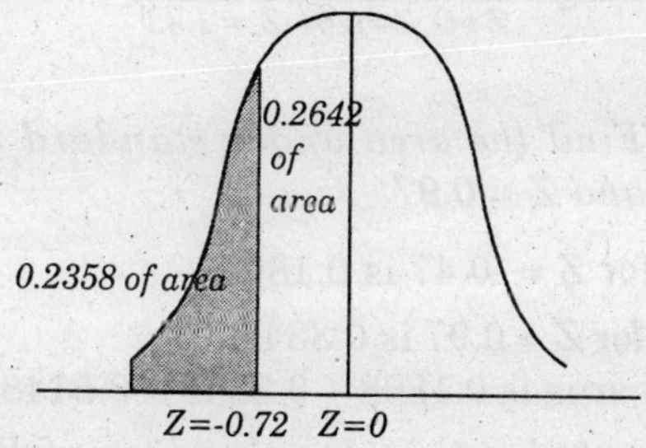

Illustration 25: *Find the area right of Z = -0.55 under standard normal curve.*

Solution: Area for $Z = -0.55$ is -0.2088

Area right of $Z = -0.55$ is $0.5 + 0.2088 = 0.7088$ of area.

It can be represented in the normal curve as follows.

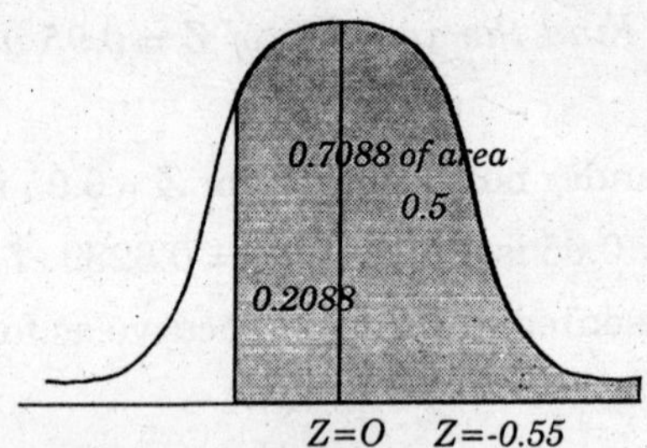

Illustration 26: *Find the area under standard normal curve between z = 0.64 and Z = 1.43.*

Solution: Area for Z = 1.43 is 0.4236 and area for Z = 0.64 is 0.2389. Hence, the required area between,

Z = 1.43 and Z = 0.64 is 0.4236 - 0.2389 = 0.1847.

It can be represented in the normal curve as follows.

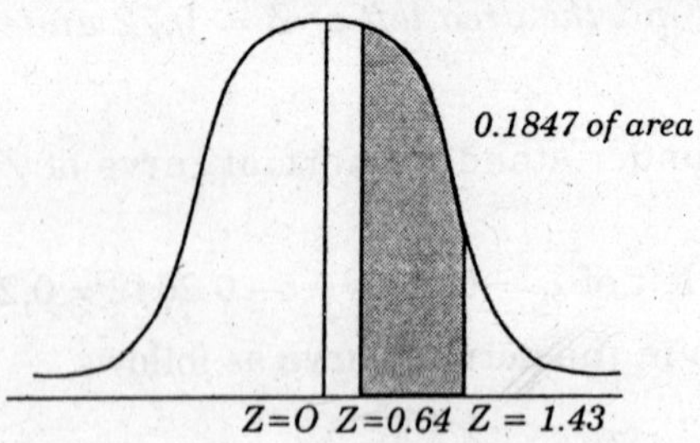

Illustration 27: *Find the area under standard normal curve between Z = -0.47 and Z = 0.97*

Solution: Area for Z = -0.47 is 0.1808

Area for Z = 0.97 is 0.3340

Hence required area is 0.1808 + 0.3340 = 0.5148 of area.

It can be represented in the normal curve as follows.

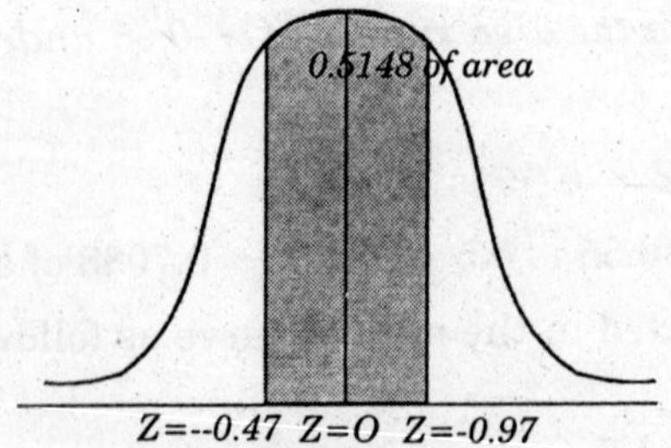

Illustration 28: *The monthly income of 600 people in a village was found to be normally distributed with mean income of Rs. 900 and standard deviation as Rs. 120. Find out, (i) The expected number of persons getting salary above Rs. 1000. (ii) The expected number of persons getting salary between Rs. 600 and Rs. 800. (iii) Number of persons getting salary above Rs. 600. (iv) Number of persons getting salary between Rs. 700 and Rs. 1000.*

Solution: $X = 1000, \quad \overline{X} = 900, \quad \sigma = 120$

$$Z = \frac{X - \overline{X}}{\sigma} = \frac{1000 - 900}{120} = 0.83$$

Area under standard normal curve for Z = 0.83 is 0.2967.

Hence, area for above Rs. 1000 is, 0.5 – 0.2967 = 0.2033

Number of people getting salary above Rs. 1000 is,

$$500 \times 0.2033 = 102$$

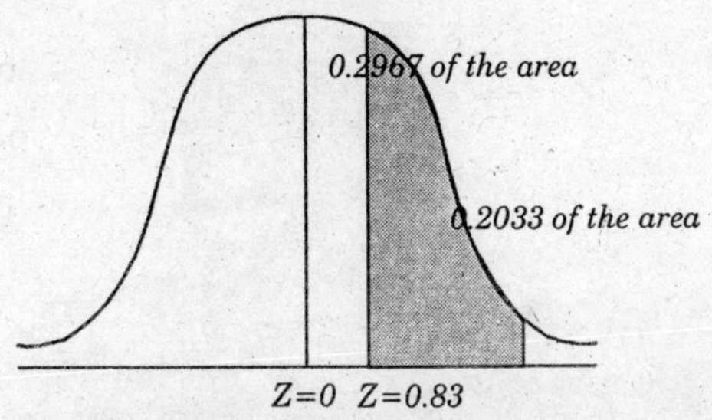

(ii) Number of persons getting salary between Rs. 600 and 800.

Calculation of z for Rs. 500,

$$Z = \frac{X - \overline{X}}{\sigma} = \frac{600 - 900}{120} = \frac{-300}{120} = -2.5$$

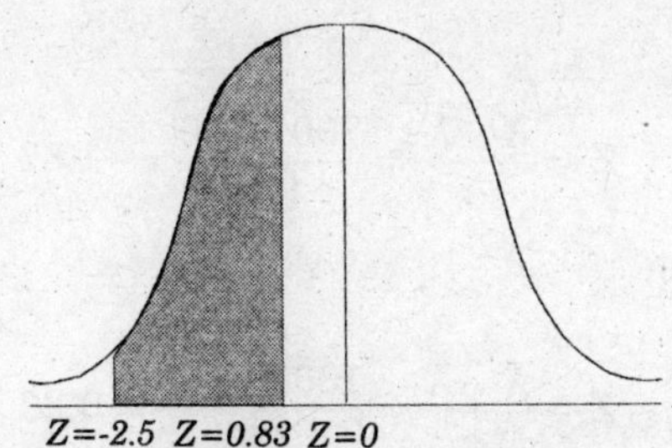

when, $X = 800$,

$$Z = \frac{800 - 900}{120} = -0.83$$

Area when Z = -2.5 = -0.4938

Area when Z = 0.83 = -0.2967

Required area = 0.4938 - 0.2967 = 0.1971

Hence, number of people getting salary between Rs. 600 and Rs. 800 = 0.1971 × 500 = 99

(iii) Calculation of number of persons getting salary of above Rs. 600

$X = 600$,

$$Z = \frac{600 - 900}{120} = -2.5$$

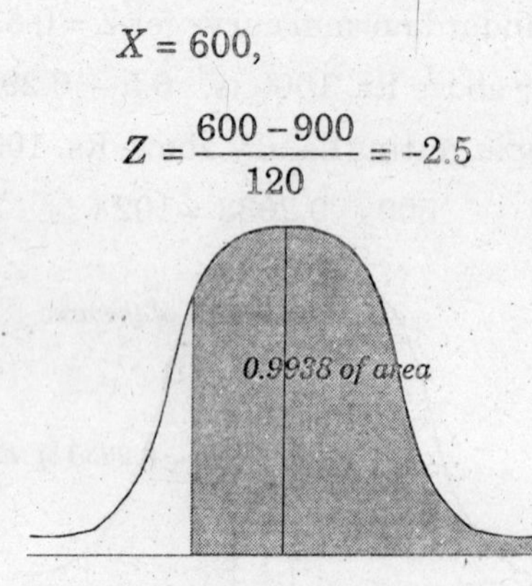

Area for Z = -2.5 is -0.4938

Number of persons getting salary above Rs. 600,

= 0.9938 × 500 = 497

(iv) Calculation of number of persons getting salary between Rs. 700 and 1000

when, $X = 700$,

$$Z = \frac{X - \overline{X}}{\sigma} = \frac{700 - 900}{120} = -1.67$$

when, $X = 1000$

$$Z = \frac{X - \overline{X}}{\sigma} = \frac{1000 - 900}{120} = 0.83$$

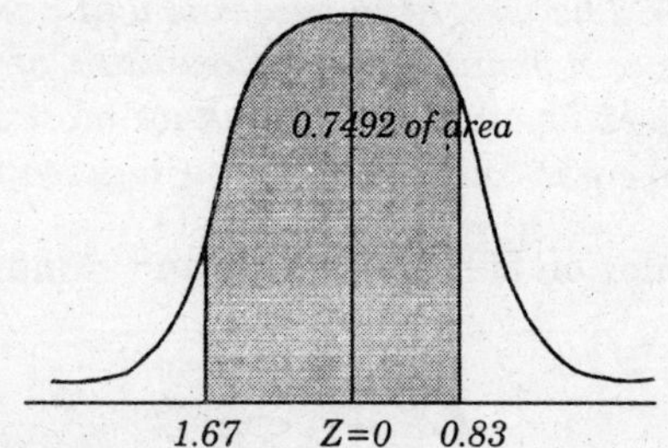

Area for Z = -1.67 is 0.4525

Area for Z = 0.83 is 0.2967

Required area 0.4525 + 0.2967 = 0.7492

Hence, number of persons getting salary between Rs. 700 and

$$1000 = 0.7492 \times 500 = 375$$

Illustration 29: *In a palace 3000 bulbs are installed. If these bulbs have an average life of 1200 burning hours with S.D of 300 hours, what number of bulbs might be expected to fail in the first 800 hours?*

Solution: $X = 800, \quad \overline{X} = 1200, \quad \sigma = 300$

$$Z = \frac{X - \overline{X}}{\sigma} = \frac{800 - 1200}{300} = -1.33$$

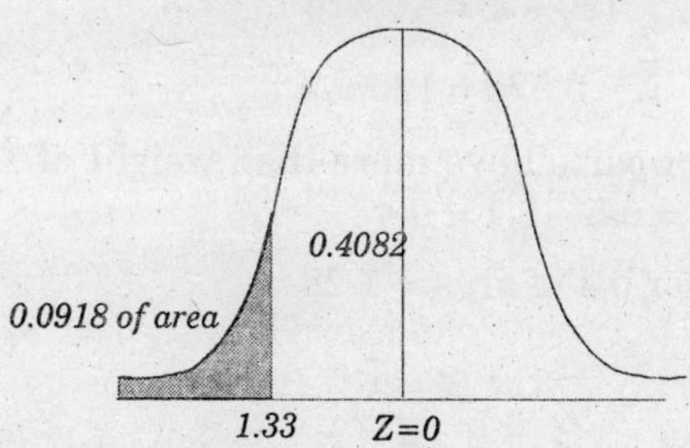

Area for Z = -1.33 is 0.4082

Required area = 0.5 - 0.4082 = 0.0918

Number of bulbs expected to fail in the first 800 hours

$$= 0.0918 \times 3000 = 275 \text{ bulbs.}$$

Illustration 30: *The weight of a component part produced by a factory confirms to normal distribution. 30% of the parts have a weight less than 120 grams and 10% have more than 140 grams. Find the mean weight and S.D of the component part.*

Solution: Calculation of mean weight and standard deviation.

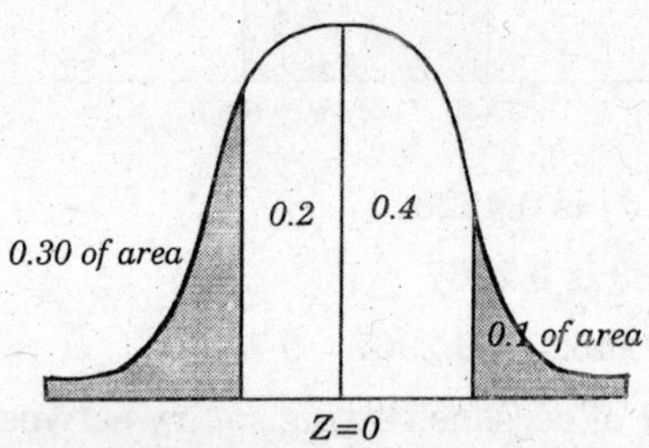

When 30% of the parts have weight less than 120 grams, the required area = 0.5 – 0.3 = -0.2

The value of z for area -0.2 = -0.52

$$Z = \frac{X - \overline{X}}{\sigma}$$

$$-0.52 = \frac{120 - \overline{X}}{\sigma}$$

$$120 - \overline{X} = -0.52\sigma$$

$$\overline{X} - 0.52\sigma = 120$$

When 10% of parts have more than weight of 140 grams, the required area, = 0.5 – 0.1 = 0.4

Value of Z for 0.4 of area = 1.28

$$Z = \frac{X - \overline{X}}{\sigma}$$

$$1.28 = \frac{140 - \overline{X}}{\sigma}$$

$$1.28\sigma = 140 - \overline{X}$$

$$\overline{X} + 1.28\sigma = 140 \qquad \text{. . . (ii)}$$

$$\overline{X} - 0.52\sigma = 120 \qquad \ldots \text{(i)}$$

(ii) – (i) $\quad 1.8\sigma = 20$

$$\sigma = \frac{20}{1.8} = 11.11$$

(i) $\quad X - 0.52(11.11) = 120$

$$\overline{X} = 120 + 5.78 = 126 \quad \text{grams}$$

Illustration 31: *In a distribution exactly normal, 12% of the items are under 50 and 85% of the items are under 75. Calculate the mean and S.D of the distribution.*

Solution: Calculation of Mean and S.D.

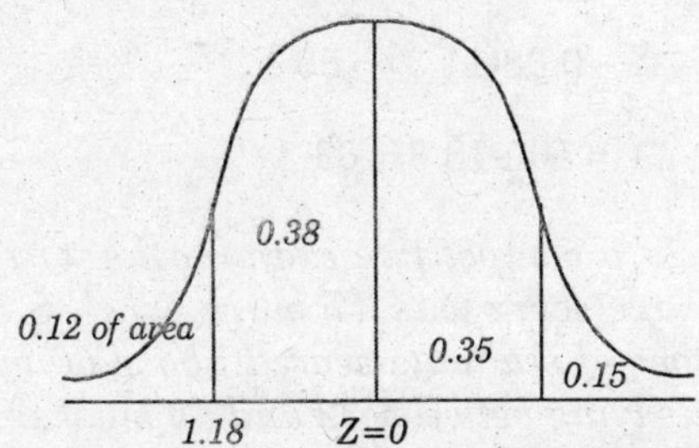

When 12% of the items are under 50, the required area,

= 0.5 - 0.12 = -0.38

Value of z for area -0.38 = -1.18

i.e., $$Z = \frac{X - \overline{X}}{\sigma}$$

$$-1.18 = \frac{50 - \overline{X}}{\sigma}$$

$$-1.18\sigma = 50 - \overline{X}$$

$$\overline{X} - 1.18\sigma = 50 \qquad \ldots \text{(i)}$$

When 85% of items are under 75, required area

= 0.5 - 0.15 = 0.35

Value of Z for area 0.35 = 1.04

i.e.,
$$Z = \frac{X - \overline{X}}{\sigma}$$

$$1.04 = \frac{75 - \overline{X}}{\sigma}$$

$$1.04\sigma = 75 - \overline{X}$$

$$\overline{X} + 1.04\sigma = 75 \qquad \ldots \text{(ii)}$$

$$\overline{X} - 1.18\sigma = 50 \qquad \ldots \text{(i)}$$

(ii) – (i)
$$2.22\sigma = 25$$

$$\sigma = \frac{25}{2.22} = 11.3$$

(i)
$$X - 0.38(11.3) = 50$$

$$X = 50 + 13.3 = 63.3$$

Illustration 32: *In a competitive examination written by 2000 students the average score was 47 marks with S.D 23 marks. Find (i) the number of students scored above 60 marks (ii) the number of students lying between 32 and 55 marks (iii) the value of the score exceeded by the top 100 students.*

Solution: (i) Calculation of number of students, scored above 60 marks.

$$X = 60, \ \overline{X} = 47, \ \sigma = 23$$

$$Z = \frac{X - \overline{X}}{\sigma} = \frac{60 - 47}{23} = \frac{13}{23} = 0.57$$

Area for $Z = 0.57$ is 0.2157

Required area for score above 60 marks,

$$= 0.5 - 0.2157 = 0.2843$$

The number of students scored above 60 marks,

$$= 0.2843 \times 2000 = 569$$

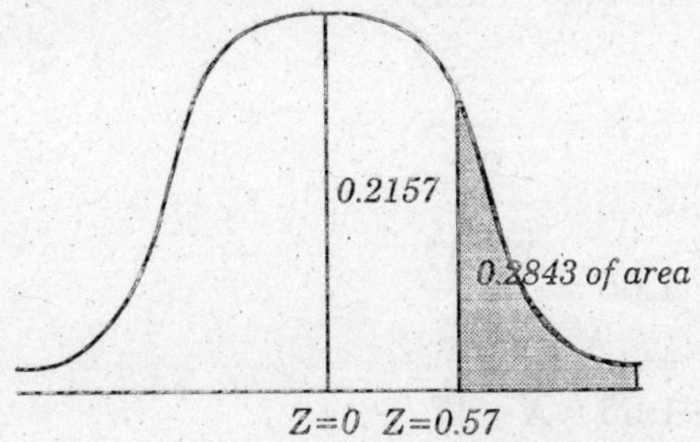

(ii) Calculation of number of students lying between 32 and 55 marks.

when $X = 32$,

$$Z = \frac{X - \overline{X}}{\sigma} = \frac{32 - 47}{23} = -0.65$$

Required area when $Z = -0.65$ is 0.2422

when $X = 55$,

$$Z = \frac{X - \overline{X}}{\sigma} = \frac{55 - 47}{23} = 0.35$$

Required area when $Z = 0.35$ is 0.1368

Total Required area = 0.2422 + 0.1368 = 0.379

Number of students lying between 32 and 55 marks,

$$= 0.379 \times 2000 = 758$$

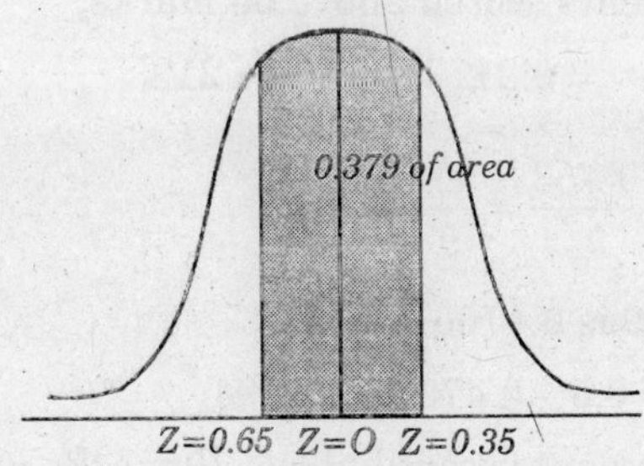

(iii) Calculation of the value of score exceeded by top 100 students

Required area $\times$ 2000 = 100 students

$$\text{Required area} = \frac{100}{2000} = 0.05 \quad \text{i.e., } 5 - 0.5 = 0.45$$

Z value for area 0.45 = 1.65

i.e., $$Z = \frac{X - \overline{X}}{\sigma}$$

$$1.65 = \frac{X - 47}{23}$$

$$23 \times 1.65 = X - 47$$

$$X = 47 + 37.95 = 85 \text{ marks}$$

Illustration 33: *1000 students appeared for a competitive examination. The mean marks was 53 and the S.D was 9. Assume that the marks are normally distributed. Find out (i) the proportion of students scored more than 60 marks and (ii) if in the examination Grade A is given to students scoring more than 70 marks find out the proportion and number of students, receiving Grade A.*

Solution: (i) $Z = \frac{X - \overline{X}}{\sigma} = \frac{60 - 53}{9} = \frac{7}{9} = 0.78$

Area for Z = 0.78 is 0.2823

Required area = 0.5 - 0.2823 = 0.2177

Proportion of students scored above 60 marks,

= 0.2177 × 100 = 21.75%

Number of students scored above 60 marks,

= 0.2177 × 1000 = 218

(ii) $Z = \frac{X - \overline{X}}{\sigma} = \frac{70 - 53}{9} = \frac{17}{9} = 1.89$

Area for Z = 1.89 is 0.4706

Required area = 0.5 – 0.4706 = 0.0294

Proportion of students scored above 70 marks = 2.94%

Number of students scored above 70 marks,

= 0.0294 × 1000 = 29 students.

Normal Approximation to Binomial Distribution: The binomial distribution approximates normal distribution when *'n'* is large and either p or q are not too small. The distribution shoul have both mean and S.D.

i.e., $$m = \overline{X} = np \quad \text{and} \quad \sigma = \sqrt{npq}$$

Steps

(i) In order to calculate *P(a × b)* discrete binomial distribution through continuous normal distribution, the discrete values of a and b are to be converted into continuous by taking *'a'* as, *'a* - 1/2' and *'a* + 1/2'.

Hence, $P(a \leq x b)$ of discrete binomial distribution corresponds to $P(a - 1/2 \leq a + 1/2)$ of normal distribution.

Illustration 34: *Calculate the probability of getting 5 heads in 10 tosses by a unbiased coin by (i) binomial distribution and (ii) normal distribution.*

Solution: $$P(5) = 10C_5 \left(\frac{1}{2}\right)^5 \left(\frac{1}{2}\right)^5 = \frac{10\,!}{5!\ \ 5!}\left(\frac{1}{2}\right)^{10}$$

$$= \frac{6 \times 7 \times 8 \times 9 \times 10}{1 \times 2 \times 3 \times 4 \times 5} \times \frac{1}{1024}$$

$$= \frac{252}{1024} = 0.2461$$

(ii) For calculating the probability through normal distribution discrete value of 5 heads should be made continuous by taking 5 - 1/2 and 5 + 1/2 *i.e.,* 4.5 and 5.5.

$$\overline{X} = np = 10 \cdot \frac{1}{2} = 5$$

$$\sigma = \sqrt{npq} = \sqrt{10 \times \frac{1}{2} \times \frac{1}{2}} = \sqrt{2.5} = 1.58$$

$$X_1 = 4.5, \quad X_2 = 5.5$$

$$Z_1 = \frac{X - \overline{X}}{\sigma} = \frac{4.5 - 5}{1.58} = -0.316$$

$$Z_2 = \frac{5.5-5}{1.58} = 0.316$$

Area for 0.316 is 0.1255

Total area = 0.1255 × 2 = 0.251

The two values in methods (i) and (ii) are very close to each other. The difference will diminish further if the value of n increases.

Miscellaneous Illustrations

Illustration 35: *A box contains 100 oranges. 20 of which are defective. 6 oranges are selected randomly for inspection. Find out the probability that (i) all 6 are defective (ii) all 6 are good (iii) at least 1 is defective (iv) at the most 2 are defective.*

Solution: Probability of defective oranges (p) = 20/100 = 1/5

$$q = 1 - p = 1 - \frac{1}{5} = \frac{4}{5}$$

(i) $P_{(6)} = 6C_6 \left(\frac{1}{5}\right)^6 \left(\frac{4}{5}\right)^0 = \left(\frac{1}{5}\right)^6 = \frac{1}{15625}$

(ii) $P_{(0)} = 6C_0 \left(\frac{1}{5}\right)^0 \left(\frac{4}{5}\right)^6 = \frac{4096}{15625} = 0.2621$

(iii) At least one defective $P(> 1) = 1 - P_0 > 1 - 0.2621 = 0.7379$

(iv) Probability of getting at the most 2 defective

$$= P_0 + P_1 + P_2$$

$$= 6C_0 \left(\frac{1}{5}\right)^0 \left(\frac{4}{5}\right)^6 + 6C_1 \left(\frac{1}{5}\right)^1 \left(\frac{4}{5}\right)^5 + 6C_2 \left(\frac{1}{5}\right)^2 \left(\frac{4}{5}\right)^4$$

$$= \left(\frac{1}{5}\right)^6 [6C_0\, 4^6 + 6C_1\, 4^5 + 6C_2\, 4^4]$$

$$= \frac{1}{15625} [4096 + 6144 + (15 \times 256)] = \frac{14080}{15625} = 0.9$$

Illustration 36: *If the probability of a defective bolt is 1 / 7, find (i) mean (ii) variance (iii) co-efficient of skewness (iv) kurtosis and (v) S.D. Assume that the number of bolts are 700.*

Solution: $n = 600,\ p = 3/7; q = 1 - p = 1 - 3/7 = 4/7$

(i) Mean = $np = 700 \times 3/7 = 300$

(ii) Variance = $npq = 700 \times 3/7 \times 4/7 = 1200/7 = 171.43$

(iii) Skewness $= \dfrac{q-p}{\sqrt{npq}} = \dfrac{4/7-3/7}{\sqrt{171.43}} = \dfrac{1}{7\times 13.09} = \dfrac{1}{91.63} = 0.011$

(iv) Kurtosis $= 3 + \dfrac{1-6pq}{npq} = \dfrac{1-6(3/7)(4/7)}{171.43}$

$$= 3 + \frac{1-1.469}{171.43} = 3 - \frac{0.469}{171.43} = 2.997$$

(v) S.D $= \sqrt{npq} = \sqrt{700\times 3/7\times 4/7} = \sqrt{171.43} = 13.09$

Illustration 37: *State whether a binomial distribution has mean as 9 and S.D as 4.*

Solution: $m = np = 9$

$$\text{S.D} = \sqrt{npq} = 4$$

$$npq = 16;\ \ np = 16/q$$

i.e., $9 = 16/q$

$$q = 16/9 = 1.78$$

$p + q$ should equal to 1. Hence, q should be less than one. Therefore the statement is wrong.

Illustration 38: *0.4% of the blades manufactured by a company are found to be defective. The blades are sold in packets of 10. In a consignment of 40,000 packets of blades. Calculate the approximate number of packets with, (i) No defectives (ii) 2 defectives (iii) At least 3 defectives.* [Given $e^{-0.04} = 0.9608$]

Solution: Probability of defective blade = 0.4% = 0.004

Probability of mean defective in a packet of 10 blades,

$$(m) = 0.004 \times 10 = 0.04$$

$$P_{(r)} = \frac{e^{-m} m^r}{r!}$$

(i) $P_0 = \frac{e^{-0.04} 0.04^0}{0!} = 0.9608$

No. of boxes with no defective blades,

$= 40000 \times 0.9608 = 38{,}432$ boxes

(ii) $P_2 = \frac{e^{-0.04} 0.04^2}{2!} = \frac{0.9608 \times 0.0016}{1 \times 2} = 0.000769$

No. of boxes with 2 defective, $= 40000 \times 0.000769 = 31$ boxes

(iii) $P(\geq 3) = 1 - (P_0 + P_1 + P_2)$

$$= 1 - (0.9608 + \frac{0.9608 \times 0.04}{1!} + 0.000769)$$

$$= 1 - (0.9608 + 0.038432 + 0.000769)$$

$$= 1 - 0.999001 = 0.000999$$

No. of boxes with more than 3 defective,

$= 40000 \times 0.000999 = 40$ boxes

Illustration 39: *The number of bike accidents in a city follows poisson distribution with mean 4. Out of 2000 bike owners, calculate approximately the number of bike owners with (i) no accidents in a year (ii) 3 accidents in a year (iii) more than 2 accidents in a year (iv) at most 3 accidents in a year.* [Given that $e^4 = 0.01832$]

Solution: $m = 4,\ e^m = 0.01832$

$$P_{(r)} = \frac{e^{-m} m^r}{r!}$$

(i) $P_0 = \frac{0.01832 \times 4^0}{0!} = 0.01832$

No. of bike owners with no accident, $= 0.01832 \times 2000 = 37$

(ii) $P_3 = \frac{0.01832 \times 4^3}{3!} = \frac{0.01832 \times 64}{1 \times 2 \times 3} = 0.1954$

No. of bike owners with 2 accidents = 0.1954 × 2000 = 391

(iii) $P(>3) = 1 - (P_0 + P_1 + P_2)$

$$= 1 - \left[0.01832 + \frac{0.01832 \times 4^1}{1!} + \frac{0.01832 \times 4^2}{2!}\right]$$

$$= 1 - [0.1832 + 0.0738 + 0.14656]$$

$$= 1 - 0.23868 = 0.76132$$

No. of bike owners with more than 2 accidents,

$$= 0.76132 \times 2000 = 1523$$

(iv) $P(\leq 3) = P_0 + P_1 + P_2 + P_3$

$$= 0.01832 + 0.0738 + 0.14656 + 0.1954 = 0.4341$$

No. of bike owners with atmost 3 accidents,

$$= 0.4341 \times 2000 = 863$$

Illustration 40: *The number of defective component parts produced in a single shift in a factory are given below.*

No. of faults:	*0*	*1*	*2*	*3*	*4*	*5*
No. of shifts:	*30*	*10*	*20*	*15*	*20*	*5*

Fit a poisson distribution to the data.

[Given that $e^{-2} = 0.13534$]

Solution: Calculation of Arithmetic Mean.

X	f	fX
0	30	0
1	10	10
2	20	40
3	15	45
4	20	80
5	5	25
	$\Sigma f = 100$	$\Sigma fx = 200$

$$\overline{X} = \frac{\Sigma fx}{N} = \frac{200}{100} = 2$$

$$P(r) = \frac{e^{-m} \cdot m^r}{r} \qquad e^{-2} = 0.13534$$

Calculation of Expected Frequencies

x	*Calculation of Expected frequencies*	*Expected frequencies*
0	$\frac{0.13534 \times 2^0}{0!} \times 100$	13
1	$\frac{0.13534 \times 2^1}{1!} \times 100$	27
2	$\frac{0.13534 \times 2^2}{2!} \times 100$	27
3	$\frac{0.13534 \times 2^3}{3!} \times 100$	19
4	$\frac{0.13534 \times 2^4}{4!} \times 100$	9
5	$\frac{0.13534 \times 2^5}{5!} \times 100$	5
	Total	*100*

Illustration 41: *The variance of poisson distribution is 25. Find mean, S.D, skewness and kurtosis.*

Solution: Mean $(m) = np$, Variance $= m$, $m = 25$

$$S.D. = \sqrt{\text{Variance}} = \sqrt{m} = \sqrt{25} = 5$$

$$\text{Skewness} = \frac{1}{m} = \frac{1}{5} = 0.2$$

$$\text{Kurtosis} = 3 + \frac{1}{m} = 3 + \frac{1}{5} = 3.2$$

Illustration 42: *The average number of phone calls per minute in an office between 9 and 10 A.M is 2.3. Find the probability that during one particular minute there will be (i) no phone call at all (ii) exactly 2 phone calls.* [Given that $e^{-2} = 0.13534$; $e^{-0.3} = 0.7408$]

Solution: $m = 2.3$, $e^{-2.3} = e^{-2} \times e^{-0.3} = 0.13534 \times 0.7408$

$= 0.10026$

$$P(r) = \frac{e^{-m}.m^r}{r!}$$

(i) $P_0 = \dfrac{0.10026 \times 2.3^0}{0!} = 0.10026$

(ii) $P_2 = \dfrac{0.10026 \times 2.3^2}{2!} = 0.2652$

Illustration 43: *The mean weekly expenditure of people in a locality is Rs. 500 with S.D Rs. 80. If the expenditure is normally distributed find out (i) the maximum expenditure of those 10% of the people whose expenditure is the lowest; and (ii) the minimum expenditure of those 10% of the people whose expenditure is the highest.*

Solution:

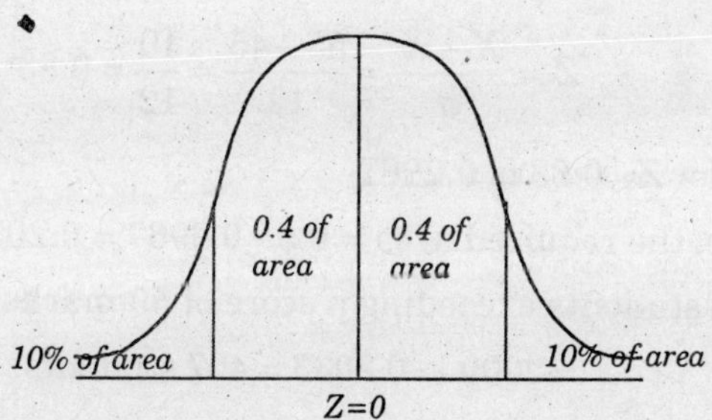

(i) The required area is -0.4 the value of Z for this area = –1.28

$$\overline{X} = 500, \quad \sigma = 80$$

$$Z = \frac{\overline{X} - X}{\sigma}, \qquad -1.28 = \frac{X - 500}{80}$$

$$(-1.28) \times 80 = X - 500 \qquad 102.4 = X - 500$$

$$X = Rs.\ 397.60$$

(ii) The required area is 0.4

Value of z for area 0.4 = 1.28

$$Z = \frac{X - X}{\sigma}$$

$$1.28 = \frac{X - 500}{80}$$

$$1.28 \times 80 = X - 500$$

$$102.4 = X - 500$$

$$X = 500 + 102.4 = Rs.602.40$$

Illustration 44: *In a competitive examination attended by 2000 students, the average mark was 45 with S.D 12 marks. Find (i) the number of students exceeding a score of 55 (ii) the number of students lying between 35 and 60 and (iii) the value of marks exceeded by 200 top students.*

Solution: (i) $\overline{X} = 45, \quad \sigma = 12$

Calculation of number of students exceeding a score of 55 marks.

$$Z = \frac{X - \overline{X}}{\sigma} = \frac{55 - 45}{12} = \frac{10}{12} = 0.83$$

Area for Z= 0.83 is 0.2967.

Hence, the required area = 0.5 - 0.2967 = 0.2033

No. of students exceeding a score of 55 marks,

= 2000 × 0.2033 = 407 students.

(ii) When $X = 35$,

$$Z = \frac{35 - 45}{12} = \frac{-10}{12} = -0.83$$

Area for Z = -0.83, is -0.2967

When $X = 60$

$$Z = \frac{60 - 45}{12} = \frac{15}{12} = 1.25$$

Area for $Z = 1.25$ is 0.3944

Required area = 0.2967 + 0.3944 = 0.6911

Hence, the number of students lying between the score of 35 and 60 marks,

$$= 0.6911 \times 2000 = 1382 \text{ students}$$

(iii) Calculation of the value of marks exceeded by 200 students. 200 out of 2000 means 10% of students. Above 10% of area means above 0.4 area of the normal curve.

Value of Z at 0.4 of area is 1.28

$$Z = \frac{X - \overline{X}}{\sigma}$$

$$1.28 = \frac{X - 45}{12}$$

$$12 \times 1.28 = X - 45$$

$$15.36 = X - 45$$

$$X = 45 + 15.36 = 60 \quad \text{marks}$$

The value of marks exceeded by 200 students = 60.

Illustration 45: *The mean weight of a component part produced by a company is 64 grams with S.D of 4 grams. The maximum and minimum tolerance limit allowed by the company are 61 and 67 grams. Calculate the percentage of defective parts produced by the company. Also find out the number of defective parts in a sample of 1000 parts.*

Solution: The good component parts lie between the weight of 61 grams to 67 grams. The area in normal curve can be calculated by taking $X_1 = 61$ and $X_2 = 67$.

$$Z_1 = \frac{X_1 - X}{\sigma} = \frac{61 - 64}{4} = \frac{-3}{4} = -0.75$$

Area for $Z = 0.75$ is 0.2734

$$Z_2 = \frac{X_2 - X}{\sigma} = \frac{67 - 64}{4} = \frac{3}{4} = 0.75$$

Area for $Z = 0.75$ is 0.2734

Total area for acceptance = 0.2734 + 0.2734 = 0.5468

Hence, Rejection area is 1 – 0.5468 = 0.4532

i.e., 45.32% is the percentage of defective parts manufactured.

No. of defective parts = 1000 × 0.4532 = 453

Illustration 46: *Find the probability of getting 150 heads in tossing a fair coin for 300 times.*

Solution: $p = 1/2$ and $q = 1/2$, $X = np = 300 \times 1/2 = 150$

$X_1 = 150 - 1/2 = 149.5$, $X_2 = 150 + 1/2 = 150.5$

$$\sigma = \sqrt{npq} = \sqrt{300 \times \frac{1}{2} \times \frac{1}{2}} = 8.66$$

$$X_1 = 150 - \frac{1}{2} = 149.5$$

$$X_2 = 150 + \frac{1}{2} = 150.5$$

$$Z_1 = \frac{X - \overline{X}}{\sigma} = \frac{149.5 - 150}{8.66} = -0.058$$

$$Z_2 = \frac{X - \overline{X}}{\sigma} = \frac{150.5 - 150}{8.66} = 0.058$$

Area for 0.058 = 0.0239

Hence, the probability of getting 150 heads,

$$= 0.0239 \times 2 = 0.048$$

Illustration 47: *A multiple choice quiz has 200 problems, each with 5 possible answers of which only 1 is correct answer. What is the probability (using normal approximation to binomial distribution) that sheer guess work yields from 30 to 35 correct answers from 125 problems (out of 200 problems) about which the candidate has no knowledge.*

Solution: $p = 1/5$; $q = 1 - 1/5 = 4/5$, $n = 125$

$$\overline{X} = np = 125 \times 1/5 = 25$$

$$\sigma = \sqrt{npq} = \sqrt{125 \times \frac{1}{5} \times \frac{4}{5}} = 4.47$$

$$X_1 = 30 - 0.5 = 29.5, \quad X_2 = 35 + 0.5 = 35.5$$

$$Z_1 = \frac{X - \overline{X}}{\sigma} = \frac{29.5 - 25}{4.47} = 1.01$$

$$Z_2 = \frac{X - \overline{X}}{\sigma} = \frac{35.5 - 25}{4.47} = 2.35$$

Area for 1.01 is 0.3438, Area for 2.35 is 0.4906

Hence, the probability of getting 30 to 35 correct answers from 125 problems, = 0.4906 – 0.3438 = 0.1468

Illustration 48: *A die is tossed 300 times. What is the probability of getting '5' for 60 times.*

Solution: Probability of getting '5' in one throw (p) = 1/6

$q = 1 - 1/6 = 5/6$, $n = 300$; $\overline{X} = np = 300 \times 1/6 = 50$ times

$$\sigma = \sqrt{npq} = \sqrt{300 \times \frac{1}{6} \times \frac{5}{6}} = 6.45$$

$$X_1 = 60 - 0.5 = 59.5, \; X_2 = 60 + 0.5 = 60.5$$

$$Z_1 = \frac{X - \overline{X}}{\sigma} = \frac{59.5 - 50}{6.45} = 1.47$$

$$Z_2 = \frac{60.5 - 50}{6.45} = 1.63$$

Area for $Z = 1.47$ is 0.4292, Area for $Z = 1.63$ is 0.4484

Hence, the probability of getting '5' for 60 times = 0.4484 – 0.4292 = 0.0192

Illustration 49: *Fit a binomial distribution to the following data.*

X	0	1	2	3	4	5	6	7	8	9
f	6	20	28	12	8	6	0	0	0	0

(MGU: Section C April '96)

Solution: $N = 6 + 20 + 28 + 12 + 8 + 6 = 80$

$n = 9$; Since probability of occurance of the event is not given it is assumed as 1/2.

$$NnCr = N\frac{n!}{(n-r)!r!}P^r q^{n-r} = 80\frac{n!}{(n-r)!r!}\times\left(\frac{1}{2}\right)^9 = 0.156\frac{n!}{(n-r)!r!}$$

Filling of Binomial Distribution

X	$N\frac{n!}{(n-r)!r!}P^r q^{n-r}$	*Theoretical Distribution*
0	$80\times\frac{9!}{9!0!}\left(\frac{1}{2}\right)^0\left(\frac{1}{2}\right)^9 = 0.156\times 1$	0
1	$80\times\frac{9!}{8!1!}\left(\frac{1}{2}\right)^1\left(\frac{1}{2}\right)^8 = 0.156\times 9$	1
2	$80\times\frac{9!}{7!2!}\left(\frac{1}{2}\right)^2\left(\frac{1}{2}\right)^7 = 0.156\times 36$	6
3	$80\times\frac{9!}{6!3!}\left(\frac{1}{2}\right)^3\left(\frac{1}{2}\right)^6 = 0.156\times 84$	13
4	$80\times\frac{9!}{5!4!}\left(\frac{1}{2}\right)^4\left(\frac{1}{2}\right)^5 = 0.156\times 126$	20
5	$80\times\frac{9!}{4!5!}\left(\frac{1}{2}\right)^5\left(\frac{1}{2}\right)^4 = 0.156\times 126$	20
6	$80\times\frac{9!}{3!6!}\left(\frac{1}{2}\right)^6\left(\frac{1}{2}\right)^3 = 0.156\times 84$	13
7	$80\times\frac{9!}{2!7!}\left(\frac{1}{2}\right)^7\left(\frac{1}{2}\right)^2 = 0.156\times 36$	6
8	$80\times\frac{9!}{1!8!}\left(\frac{1}{2}\right)^8\left(\frac{1}{2}\right)^1 = 0.156\times 9$	1
9	$80\times\frac{9!}{0!9!}\left(\frac{1}{2}\right)^9\left(\frac{1}{2}\right)^0 = 0.156\times 1$	0
	Total	*80*

Illustration 50: *Fit a binomial distribution to the following data.*

X	0	1	2	3	4
f	28	62	46	10	4

(MGU: Section C April '95)

Solution: Since the probability of occurance of the event (p) is not given it is assumed as 1/2

$$q = 1 - P = 1 - 1/2 = 1/2$$

$$N = 28 + 62 + 46 + 10 + 4 = 150$$

$$NnCr = N\frac{n!}{(n\text{-}r)!\,r!}P^r q^{n-r}$$

$$150nCr = 150 \times \frac{n!}{(n\text{-}r)!\,r!} \times \left(\frac{1}{2}\right)^4 = 9.375\frac{n!}{(n\text{-}r)!\,r!}$$

Fitting of Binomial Distribution

X	$N\frac{n!}{(n\text{-}r)!\,r!}P^r q^{n-r}$	*Theoretical Distribution*
0	$150\times\frac{4!}{4!\,0!}\left(\frac{1}{2}\right)^0\left(\frac{1}{2}\right)^4 = 9.375\times1$	9
1	$150\times\frac{4!}{3!\,1!}\left(\frac{1}{2}\right)^1\left(\frac{1}{2}\right)^3 = 9.375\times4.$	38
2	$150\times\frac{4!}{2!\,2!}\left(\frac{1}{2}\right)^2\left(\frac{1}{2}\right)^2 = 9.375\times6$	56
3	$150\times\frac{4!}{1!\,3!}\left(\frac{1}{2}\right)^3\left(\frac{1}{2}\right)^1 = 9.375\times4$	38
4	$150\times\frac{4!}{0!\,4!}\left(\frac{1}{2}\right)^4\left(\frac{1}{2}\right)^0 = 9.375\times1$	9
	Total	*150*

Illustration 51: *(a) Give four practical situations where a poisson distribution can be used. (b) If 3% of electric bulb manufactured by a company are found defective, find the probability that in a sample of 100 bulbs exactly five bulbs are defective.* (MGU: Section B April '94)

Solution: (a) Refer the theory part of poisson distribution.

(b) $$P_{(r)} = \frac{e^{-m} m^r}{r!}$$

Probability of defective electric bulbs = 3% = 0.03

Probability of defective bulbs in the sample of 100 bulbs,

$$m = 100 \times 0.3 = 3$$

$$r = 5.$$

$$P_{(5)} = \frac{e^{-3} 3^5}{5!} = \frac{e^{-3} 243}{1 \times 2 \times 3 \times 4 \times 5}$$

$$= \frac{e^{-3} 81}{40} \left(e^{-3} = 0.04979\right) = \frac{0.04979 \times 81}{40} = 0.10$$

Illustration 52: *Fit a normal distribution to the following data.*

Marks:	*10-20*	*20-30*	*30-40*	*40-50*	*50-60*	*60-70*	*70-80*
No. of students:	*4*	*22*	*48*	*66*	*44*	*16*	*4*

(MGU: Section C April '94)

Solution: Calculation of Mean and S.D.

X	*f*	*m*	*d* *m - 45/10*	*d²*	*fd*	*fd²*
10-20	4	15	-3	9	-12	36
20-30	22	25	-2	4	-44	88
30-40	48	35	-1	1	-48	48
40-50	66	45	0	0	0	0
50-60	44	55	1	1	44	44
60-70	16	65	2	4	32	64
70-80	4	75	3	9	12	36
	$\Sigma f = 204$				$\Sigma fd = -16$	$\Sigma fd^2 = 316$

$$\overline{X} = A \pm \frac{\Sigma fd}{N} \times i = 45 - \frac{16}{204} \times 10 = 45 - 78 = 44.22$$

$$\text{S.D} = \sqrt{\frac{\Sigma fd^2}{N} - \left(\frac{\Sigma fd}{N}\right)^2} \times i = \sqrt{\frac{316}{204} - \left(\frac{-16}{204}\right)^2} \times 10$$

$$= \sqrt{1.55 - 0.61} \times 10 = \sqrt{1.55 - 0.006} \times 10$$

$$= 1.24 \times 10 = 12.4$$

Calculation of Area for Normal Curve.

X	$Z = \left(\frac{X - \overline{X}}{\text{S.D}}\right)$	*Area*
10	$\frac{10 - 44.22}{12.4} = -2.76$	-0.4971
20	$\frac{20 - 44.22}{12.4} = -1.95$	-0.4744
30	$\frac{30 - 44.22}{12.4} = -1.15$	-0.3749
40	$\frac{40 - 44.22}{12.4} = -0.34$	-0.1331
50	$\frac{50 - 44.22}{12.4} = 0.47$	0.1808
60	$\frac{60 - 44.22}{12.4} = 1.27$	0.3980
70	$\frac{70 - 44.22}{12.4} = 2.03$	0.4788
80	$\frac{80 - 44.22}{12.4} = 2.89$	0.4981

Fitting of Normal Distribution

X	*Area*	*Theoretical Frequency*
10-20	-0.4774 - (-0.4971) = 0.0227	$0.0227 \times 204 = 5$
20-30	-0.3749 - (-0.4744) = 0.0995	$0.0995 \times 204 = 20$
30-40	-0.1331 - (-0.3749) = 0.2418	$0.2418 \times 204 = 49$
40-50	0.1808 - (-0.1331) = 0.3139	$0.3139 \times 204 = 64$
50-60	0.3980 - 0.1808 = 0.2172	$0.2172 \times 204 = 45$
60-70	0.4788 - 0.3980 = 0.0808	$0.0808 \times 204 = 17$
70-80	0.4981 - 0.4788 = 0.0193	$0.0193 \times 204 = 4$
	Total	204

Illustration 53: *Fit a poisson distribution to the following data and calculate the theoretical frequencies.*

Number of mistakes per page	*0*	*1*	*2*	*3*	*4*
Number of pages on which mistakes occurred	*109*	*65*	*22*	*3*	*1*

(MGU: Section B Sep '93)

Solution: Calculation of Arithmetic Mean.

X	f	fx
0	109	0
1	65	65
2	22	44
3	3	9
4	1	4
	$\Sigma f = 200$	$\Sigma fx = 122$

Arithmetic Mean $\overline{X}$ or $m = \frac{\Sigma fx}{\Sigma f}$

$$= \frac{122}{200} = 0.61$$

$$e^{-0.61} = 0.5434$$

Fitting of Poisson Distribution

No of mistakes	*Theoretical distribution* $NP_{(r)} = N\frac{e^{-m}m^r}{r!}$
0	$NP_{(0)} = 200 \times \frac{0.5434 \times 0.61^0}{0!} = 108.68 \times 1 = 109$
1	$NP_{(1)} = 200 \times \frac{0.5434 \times 0.61^1}{1!} = 108.68 \times 0.61 = 66$
2	$NP_{(2)} = 200 \times \frac{0.5434 \times 0.61^2}{2!} = 108.68 \times 0.186 = 20$
3	$NP_{(3)} = 200 \times \frac{0.5434 \times 0.61^3}{3!} = 108.68 \times 0.038 = 4$
4	$NP_{(4)} = 200 \times \frac{0.5434 \times 0.61^4}{4!} = 108.68 \times 0.006 = 1$
Total	*200*

Illustration 54: *The following are the marks obtained by 492 candidates in a certain examination.*

Not more than	*40*	*marks*	*210*	*candidates*
"	*45*	"	*253*	"
"	*50*	"	*307*	"
"	*55*	"	*381*	"
"	*60*	"	*413*	"
"	*65*	"	*492*	"

Find out the number of candidates who (a) secured more than 45 but not more than 50 marks and (b) less than 48 but not less than 45 marks. (MGU: Section C Sep '93)

Solution: Calculation of Arithmetic Mean and S.D.

X	*m*	*f*	*d=m-47.5/5*	d^2	*fd*	fd^2
Less than 40	37.5	210	-2	4	-420	840
40-45	42.5	43	-1	1	-43	43
45-50	47.5	54	0	0	0	0
50-55	52.5	74	1	1	74	74
55-60	57.5	32	2	4	64	128
60-65	62.5	79	3	9	237	711
		$\Sigma f = 492$			$\Sigma fd =$ -88	$\Sigma fd^2 =$ 1796

$$\overline{X} = A \pm \frac{\Sigma fd}{N} \times i = 47.5 - \frac{88}{492} \times 5 = 47.5 - 0.89 = 46.61$$

$$\text{S.D} = \sqrt{\frac{\Sigma fd^2}{N} - \left(\frac{\Sigma fd}{N}\right)^2} \times i = \sqrt{\frac{1796}{492} - \left(\frac{-88}{492}\right)^2} \times 5$$

$$= \sqrt{3.65 - 0.03} \times 5 = 1.9 \times 5 = 9.5$$

(a) No. of students secured 45-50 marks,

(i) When x = 45 $\quad Z = \frac{X - \overline{X}}{\sigma} = \frac{45 - 46.61}{9.5} = -0.169$

Area under Normal Curve = -0.0675

(ii) When x = 50 $\quad Z = \frac{50 - 46.61}{9.5} = \frac{3.39}{9.5} = -0.36$

Area under Normal Curve = 0.1406

Area for 45-50, = 0.1406 – (-0.0675) = 0.2081

The area is graphically represented as follows.

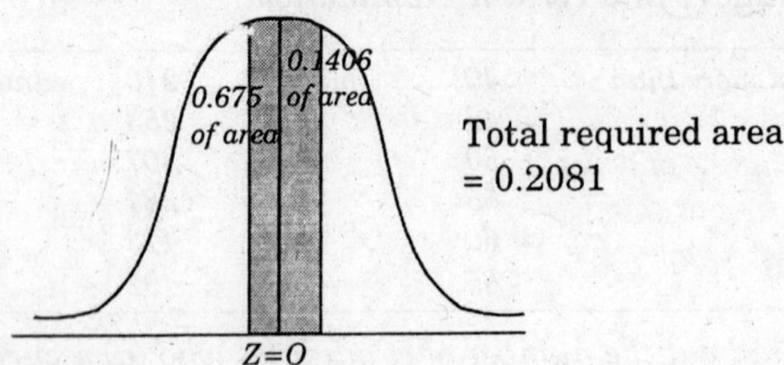

Total required area
= 0.2081

No. of students secured 45-50 marks,

= 0.2081 × 492 = 102 students

Whereas, actual number = 54 students.

(b) No. of students secured 45-48 marks,

(i) When X = 45, Area under Normal curve = -0.0675

(ii) When X = 48,

$$Z = \frac{X - \overline{X}}{\sigma} = \frac{48 - 46.61}{9.5} = \frac{1.39}{9.5} = 0.146$$

Area under Normal Curve = 0.0596

Required area for 45-48 marks,

= 0.0596 - (-0.0675) = 0.1271

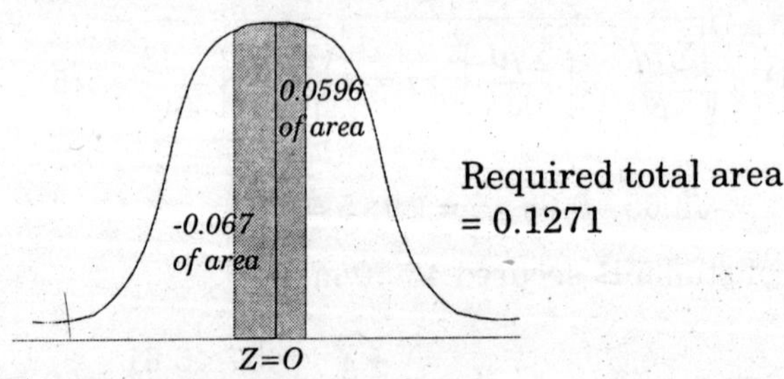

Required total area
= 0.1271

No. of students, secured 45-48 marks,

= 492 × 0.1271 = 63 students.

Illustration 55: *The screws produced by a machine were checked by examining samples of seven. The following table show the distribution of 128 samples according to the number of defective item it contained.*

No. of defectives in a sample of 7	*0*	*1*	*2*	*3*	*4*	*5*	*6*	*7*
No. of samples	*7*	*6*	*19*	*35*	*30*	*23*	*7*	*1*

Fit a binomial distribution and find the expected frequencies if the chance of screw being defective is 0.5. Also find the mean and variance of the fitted distribution. (MGU: Section C April '93)

Solution: N = 128; n = 7;

$$NnCr = N\frac{n!}{(n-r)\;!r!},$$

$p = 0.5 = 1/2;\; q = 1 - 1/2 = 1/2$

Fitting of Binomial Distribution

No. of defective	*N.nCr*	*Theoretical Distribution*
0	$128\times\frac{7!}{7!\,0!}\left(\frac{1}{2}\right)^0\left(\frac{1}{2}\right)^7$	1
1	$128\times\frac{7!}{6!\,1!}\left(\frac{1}{2}\right)^1\left(\frac{1}{2}\right)^6$	7
2	$128\times\frac{7!}{5!\,2!}\left(\frac{1}{2}\right)^2\left(\frac{1}{2}\right)^5$	21
3	$128\times\frac{7!}{4!\,3!}\left(\frac{1}{2}\right)^3\left(\frac{1}{2}\right)^4$	35
4	$128\times\frac{7!}{3!\,4!}\left(\frac{1}{2}\right)^4\left(\frac{1}{2}\right)^3$	35
5	$128\times\frac{7!}{2!\,5!}\left(\frac{1}{2}\right)^5\left(\frac{1}{2}\right)^2$	21
6	$128\times\frac{7!}{1!\,6!}\left(\frac{1}{2}\right)^6\left(\frac{1}{2}\right)^1$	7
7	$128\times\frac{7!}{0!\,7!}\left(\frac{1}{2}\right)^7\left(\frac{1}{2}\right)^0$	1
	Total	*128*

Calculation of Mean and Variance of the Fitted Binomial Distribution.

X	f	fX	$(X-\overline{X})$ $(x-3.5)$	$(X-\overline{X})^2$	$f(X-\overline{X})^2$
0	1	0	-3.5	12.25	12.25
1	7	7	-2.5	6.25	43.75
2	21	42	-1.5	2.25	47.25
3	35	105	-0.5	0.25	8.75
4	35	140	0.5	0.25	8.75
5	21	105	1.5	2.25	47.25
6	7	42	2.5	6.25	43.75
7	1	7	3.5	12.25	12.25
	$N = 128$	$\Sigma fX = 448$			$\Sigma f(X-\overline{X})2 = 224$

$$\text{A.M.} \quad \overline{X} = \frac{\Sigma fX}{N} = \frac{448}{128} = 3.5$$

$$\text{Variance} = \frac{\Sigma f(X-\overline{X})^2}{N} = \frac{224}{128} = 1.75$$

Illustration 56: *The following are the amounts of Income-tax paid by a few businessmen during 1965:*

More than (Rs.)	*500*	*1000*	*1500*	*2000*	*2500*	*3000*
Number of businessmen	*600*	*550*	*425*	*275*	*100*	*25*

Find out the number of businessmen who paid more than 1,200 but not more than 1,500 as Income-tax.

(MGU: Section B April '92)

Solution: Calculation of Arithmetic Mean and S.D.

X	f	m	$(m-1750\ /\ 500)$	d	d^2	fd	fd^2
500-1000	50	750	-2	4	-100	200	
1000-1500	125	1250	-1	1	-125	125	
1500-2000	150	1750	0	0	0	0	
2000-2500	175	2250	1	1	175	175	
2500-3000	75	2750	2	4	150	300	
Above 3000	25	3250	3	9	75	225	
	$N = 600$				$\Sigma fd = 175$	$\Sigma fd^2 = 1025$	

Arithmetic Mean,

$$\overline{X} = A \pm \frac{\Sigma fd}{N} \times i = 1750 + \left(\frac{175}{600} \times 500\right)$$

$$= 1750 + 145.83 = 1895.83$$

$$\text{S.D. } (\sigma) = \sqrt{\frac{\Sigma fd^2}{N} - \left(\frac{\Sigma fd}{N}\right)^2} \times i = \sqrt{\frac{1025}{600} - \left(\frac{175}{600}\right)^2} \times 500$$

$$= \sqrt{1.708 - 0.085} \times 500 = 1.27 \times 500 = 635$$

Calculation of no. of businessmen who paid 1200 - 1500

(i) When x = 1200,

$$Z = \frac{X - \overline{X}}{\sigma} = \frac{1200 - 1895.8}{635} = -1.096$$

Area under Normal Curve = -0.3643

(ii) When x = 1500,

$$Z = \frac{1500 - 1895.8}{635} = -0.62$$

Area under Normal Curve = -0.2324

Area for 1200 - 1500, = -0.2324 - (-0.3643) = -0.1319

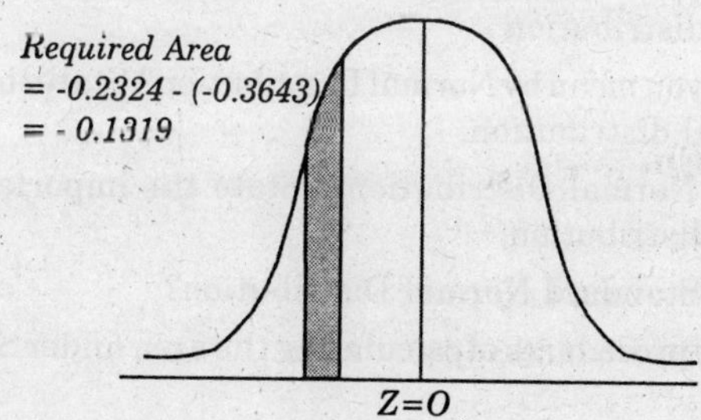

No. of businessmen who paid 1200 – 1500 = 0.1319 × 600 = 79

Illustration 57: *A stock list has 20 items in a lot out of which, 12 are non-defective and 8 defective. A customer selects three items from the lot. What is the probability that all the three items are non-defective.* (MGU: Selection A April '98)

Solution: Probability of non-defective, $p = 12/20 = 0.6$

Probability of defective, $q = 8/20 = 0.4$

or $q = 1 - p = 1 - 0.6 = 0.4$

When 3 items are selected, the probability that all the three are non-defective,

$$P_{(r)} = nCrP^r q^{n-r}$$

$$P_{(3)} = 3C_3(0.6)^3(0.4)^0 = 0.216$$

Exercise

1. Define Theoretical Distribution. State the importance of theoretical distribution.
2. What is Binomial Distribution? State the assumptions of binomial distribution.
3. Define Binomial Distribution. What are the characteristics of binomial distribution?
4. Define Binomial Distribution. What do you mean by fitting of binomial distribution?
5. What is Binomial Distribution? State the important properties of binomial distribution.
6. What is Poisson Distribution? State the objectives of poisson distribution.
7. Define Poisson Distribution. What do you mean by fitting a poisson distribution?
8. Define Poisson Distribution. State the important properties of poisson distribution.
9. What do you mean by Normal Distribution? State the characteristics of normal distribution.
10. What is Normal Distribution? State the important properties of normal distribution.
11. What is Standard Normal Distribution?
12. State the procedures of calculating the area under Standard Normal Curve.
13. Define Theoretical Distribution. Explain briefly the different methods of theoretical distribution.
14. What is a Poisson Distribution?
15. What is a Binomial Distribution? Give a real life example where such a distribution is appropriate. (MGU: Section B April '95)
16. State two properties of a Binomial Distribution. (MGU: Section A April '94)

17. What is Poisson Distribution? State any two uses of poisson distribution. (MGU: Section B April '96)

Binomial Distribution

18. A box contains 200 oranges, out of which 40 are defective. 10 oranges are selected for inspection. Find out the probability that (i) all 10 are good (ii) all 10 are defective (iii) at least 2 is defective (iv) at the most 3 are defective. [Ans: (i) $\frac{1}{5^{10}}$ (ii) $\left(\frac{4}{5}\right)^{10}$ (iii) $1-\frac{1}{5^9}$ (iv) 0.362]

19. Six coins are tossed 6400 times, find the frequencies of distribution of Heads. Also calculate the mean number of successes and standard deviation.

[Ans:

No. of heads	0	1	2	3	4	5	6
Frequency	100	600	1500	2000	1500	600	100

Mean = 3200; S.D = 40]

20. A bag contains 100 oranges, 10 of which are defective. 5 mangoes are drawn with replacement. Find out the probability of getting,

(i) exactly 2 defective oranges (ii) at least 2 defective oranges

(iii) at the most 2 defective oranges.

[Ans: (i) 0.0729 (ii) 0.8146 (iii) 0.99]

21. State whether a binomial distribution has mean as 12 and S.D as 4.

[Ans: No]

22. Find out n, p and q when the mean of a binomial distribution is 192 and S.D is 8. [Ans: n = 288; p = 2/3; q = 1/3]

23. The probability of the defective products from a production line of 2000 products is 10%. Calculate (i) mean (ii) S.D (iii) skewness and (iv) kurtosis. [Ans: (i) 200 (ii) 13.42 (iii) 0.036 (iv) 3.003]

Poisson Distribution

24. Find the probability that at least 5 defective bolts will be found in a box of 400 bolts, if its known that 2% of such bolts are expected to be defective. (It is given that $e^8 = 0.000395$) [Ans: 0.883]

25. A book contains 200 misprints distributed randomly. No. of pages in the book is 100. Find out the probability that a page observed at random contains, (i) at least 2 misprints (ii) at most 3 misprints (iii) exactly 5 misprints

(Given that $e^{-2} = 0.13534$) [Ans: (i) 0.594 (ii) 0.857 (iii) 0.036]

26. If 2% of the component parts manufactured by a company are defective, find the probability that in a sample of 300 parts,

(i) at least 3 defective (ii) none is defective (iii) exactly 4 defectives

(Given that $e^{-6} = 0.00279$) [Ans: (i) 0.93 (ii) 0.00279 (iii) 0.151]

27. In a blade manufacturing company there is 0.3% probability for any blade to be defective. The blades are sold in packets of 10. With the help of poisson distribution, calculate approximately the number of packets containing 3 defective blades in a consignment of 30,000 packets. (Given that $e^{-0.03} = 0.9704$) [Ans: 13 packets]

28. In a company 4% of the blades manufactured are defectives. If the blades are sold in boxes of 100, find out the probability that not more than 5 blades in each box will be defective. [Ans: 0.215]

29. The variance of a poisson distribution is 16. Calculate mean, S.D, skewness and kurtosis.

[Ans: Mean = 16; S.D = 4; Skewness = 0.06; Kurtosis = 3.06]

30. 0.2% of the medicine bottles manufactured by a company are defective. The bottles are packed in boxes containing 200 bottles. The company sold 300 boxes to a drug company. Using poisson distribution find how many boxes will contain, (i) 2 defectives (ii) no defective (iii) at least 2 defective. (Given that $e^{-0.4} = 0.6703$)

[Ans: (i) 16 (0.054 x 300) (ii) 201 (0.6703 x 300) (iii) 282 (0.9384 x 300)

31. The distribution of typing mistakes committed by a typist is given below. Assuming a poisson model, find out the expected frequencies.

Mistakes per page:	0	1	2	3	4	5
No. of pages:	117	63	35	25	8	2

(Given $e^{-1} = 0.3679$)

[Ans: Theoretical distribution is given below.

Mistakes:	0	1	2	3	4	5
No. of pages:	92	92	46	15	4	1]

32. The average number of phone calls per minute in an office between 3 and 4 P.M is 1.74. Find the probability that during one particular minute there will be at most 2 phone calls.

(Given that $e^{-1} = 0.36783$) [Ans: 0.816]

Normal Distribution

33. Find the area under standard normal curve (s.n.c) for the following,

(i) between z = 0 and z = 2.05 (ii) between z = 0.85 and z = 1.95 (iii) between z = 0.33 and z = 1.63 [Ans: (i) 0.4798 (ii) 0.1721 (iii) 0.3191]

34. Using standard normal variate table find the probability that a s.n.v is (i) greater than 0.96 (ii) less than 0.85 (iii) less than -0.74 (iv) greater than -0.4 and (v) less than 2.4.

[Ans: (i) 0.1685 (ii) 0.8023 (iii) 0.2296 (iv) 0.9192 (v) 0.7340]

35. The mean weight of 500 students in a school is 48kg with S.D 7kg. Assuming the weights are normally distributed, find the number of students with weight (i) less than 45kg (ii) greater than 53kg and (iii) between 44kg and 55kg.

36. The mean length of a sample of 500 machine parts produced by a company is 1.35 with S.D 0.3. The tolerance limit of the part is between 1.05 and 1.82. Find out how many machine parts are rejected as defective, if the lengths are found to be normally distributed.

[Ans: 108]

37. The mean weekly income of workers in a factory is Rs. 600 with S.D Rs. 90. If the income is normally distributed find out (i) the minimum income of those 20% of the workers whose income is the highest (ii) the maximum income of those 20% of the workers whose income is the lowest. [Ans: (i) Rs. 675.60 (ii) Rs. 524.40]

38. A fair coin is tossed 100 times. Find the probability of getting 50 heads. [Ans: 0.0796]

39. A multiple choice quiz has 100 questions, each with 4 possible answers of which 1 is the correct answer. What is the probability (using normal approximation to binomial distribution) that sheer guess-work yields from 10 to 20 correct answers for 40 problems (out of 100 problems) for which the candidate has no knowledge.

[Ans: 0.4064]

◆ Chapter 16 ◆

Linear Programming Problems

Linear programming was found out by George Dantzig and his associates during 1947. They invented this technique for solving military planning problems while they are working on a project for U.S. Air Force. Dantzig suggested this approach later on, for solving business and industrial problems.

Linear programming technique deals with the optimization of a function of variables known as '*objective function*' subject to a set of linear equalities and/or inequalities known as '*constraints*'. The objective function may be maximisation or minimisation of a function. (*e.g.*) profit, cost of production etc.

The constraints may be quantity of raw material, production capacity, capacity of machines, market demand etc..

Essentials for a Linear Programming Problem

According to the definition the following are the essentials for a linear programming problem.

(1) There should be an objective function. The objective function may either be maximisation or minimisation. The primary objectives of a company are maximisation of profit or sales and minimisation of cost. Hence, this L.P.P should have an objective function of either a maximisation type or a minimisation type.

(2) There should be minimum two products or activities to form a L.P.P. The quantities of each product should be represented in variables. On the basis of per unit cost or profit a linear equation should able to be formed.

(3) There should be constraints like supply of raw material production capacity, market demand etc. to form a L.P.P. When the resources are in plenty, and there is no problem in selling, then it is difficult to form a L.P.P.

(4) The constraints can able to be represented in linear equations.

(5) There should be a minimum of two constraint equations for a L.P.P.

Formation of Linear Programming Model

The following are the important steps in the formulation of a Linear Programming Model.

Step 1: First of all, determine the key decisions to be made. Represent the key decisions in the form of variables

$$x_1, x_2, x_3, \ldots x_n.$$

Step 2: Determine the objective function and represent it as a linear equation. The objective function may be a maximisation or minimisation. It can be represented as Maximise

$$Z = 5x_1 + 3x_2 + 2x_3$$

Step 3: Find out the constraints. The constraints may be availability of material, production capacity or demand of the product.

Represent the constraints in the form of linear equations.

(e.g.) $3x_1 + 4x_2 + x_3 \leq 60$

$$2x_1 + x_2 + x_3 \leq 26$$

Step 4: Write the feasible alternatives. Feasible alternatives mean alternatives which are physically, financially and economically possible. It can be written as $x_1, x_2, x_3 \ldots x_n$

Illustration 1. *A company manufactures 2 products namely X and Y and sells it respectively for a profit of Rs. 5 and Rs. 4 per unit. These two products are processed by two different machines A and B. The details regarding the processing time for the products and the total capacity per week are stated below.*

Products	*Processing time per unit*	
	A	*B*
X	*2*	*3*
Y	*1*	*4*
Total capacity per week	*40*	*35*

Formulate the above problem into a linear programming problem.

Solution: Formulation of linear programming model

Step 1: Determination of key decisions. Key decision is the optimum production of products *X* and *Y*. The quantity of products *X* and *Y* can be represented as x_1 and x_2 respectively.

Step 2: Formulation of objective function. Since the profit per unit for X is Rs. 5 and Y is Rs. 4, the company has to maximise the profit by producing X and Y.

i.e., Maximise $Z = 5x_1 + 4x_2$

Step 3: Constraint equations to be written. The constraints are the maximum capacity of Machine A and Machine B. Product X requires 2 hour processing time and Y requires 1 hour processing time in Machine A; Product X requires 3 hours processing time and Y requires 4 hours processing time in Machine B. The maximum hour available for Machine A is 40 hours and for B is 35 hours. Hence, the equation can be written as

$$2x_1 + x_2 \leq 40, \quad 3x_1 + 4x_2 \leq 35$$

Step 4: Feasible alternatives can be written as $x_1, x_2 \geq 0$

$\therefore$ The linear programming problem is

Maximise $Z = 5x_1 + 4x_2$

Subject to $2x_1 + x_2 \leq 40$

$3x_1 + 4x_2 \leq 35$

where $x_1, x_2 \geq 0$

Illustration 2. *A company manufactures 3 different products namely X, Y and Z. These three products are manufactured in three different processes namely Process I, Process II and Process III. The maximum processing time available per month for process I, Process II and Process III are 46, 36 and 26 hours.*

Product X requires 20 minutes, 25 minutes and 15 minutes processing time in Process I, II and III respectively. Product Y requires 12, 6 and 16 minutes of processing time in Process I, II and III respectively. Product Z requires 9, 14 and 20 minutes of processing time in Process I, II and III respectively. The cost of production are Rs 7, Rs 10, Rs 11 respectively for products X, Y and Z. Formulate this problem into a linear programming problem.

Solution: Formulation of a linear programming problem

Step 1: The key decision of the company is to determine the optimum production of products X, Y and Z. The quantity of production of X, Y and Z can be written as x_1, x_2 and x_3.

Step 2: The objective function is to minimise the cost of production of these products.

The cost of production of X = Rs. 7; Y = Rs. 10; Z = Rs. 11

Minimise $\quad Z = 7x_1 + 10x_2 + 11x_3$

Step 3: The constraints are the processing time in Process I, II and III which are 46, 36 and 26 hours respectively (*i.e.*, 2760, 2160 and 1560 minutes respectively). The processing time for X, Y and Z are 20, 12 and 9 minutes respectively in Process I. The processing time for X, Y and Z are 25, 6 and 14 minutes respectively in Process II. The processing time for X, Y and Z are 15, 16 and 20 minutes respectively in Process III. Hence, the constraint equations are

$$20x_1 + 12x_2 + 9x_3 \leq 2760$$

$$25x_1 + 6x_2 + 14x_3 \leq 2160$$

$$15x_1 + 16x_2 + 20x_3 \leq 1560$$

Step 4: Feasible alternatives are $x_1, x_2, x_3 \geq 0$

Hence, L.P.P is Minimise $Z = 7x_1 + 10x_2 + 11x_3$

Subject to $\quad 20x_1 + 12x_2 + 9x_3 \leq 2760$

$$25x_1 + 6x_2 + 14x_3 \leq 2160$$

$$15x_1 + 16x_2 + 20x_3 \leq 1560$$

where $x_1, x_2, x_3 \geq 0$.

Illustration 3. *A company produces Television and Radios by using three machines X, Y and Z. The details about the time required for each Television and Radio and the capacity of these machines are stated below.*

Time Requested for		*Maximum Time*	
Machine (in hours)	*Television (in hours)*	*Radio (in hours)*	*Available*
X	*13*	*6*	*360*
Y	*16*	*5*	*400*
Z	*14*	*7*	*260*

The demand for Televisions is 18 and Radios is 70 per month. The profit on Television is Rs 800 and Radio is Rs 160. Convert the problem into a linear programming problem.

Solution: Formulation of L.P.P

Step 1: The key decision is the optimum production of TV and Radios. The quantities of production of TV and Radio are represented as x_1 and x_2 respectively.

Step 2: The objective function is to determine the maximum profit. Profit for TV = Rs 800 per unit and Radio = Rs 160 per unit.

$\therefore$ Objective function is

Maximise $Z = 800x_1 + 160x_2$

Step 3: The constraints are the capacity of Machines. The capacity of machines *X*, *Y* and *Z* are 360, 400 and 260 hours respectively. Another constraint is the demand. The demand for TV and Radios are 18 units and 70 units respectively. Hence, the constraint equations can be written as

$$13x_1 + 6x_2 \le 360$$
$$16x_1 + 5x_2 \le 400$$
$$14x_1 + 7x_2 \le 260$$
$$x_1 \le 18 \text{ and } x_2 \le 70$$

Step 4: Feasible alternatives are $x_1, x_2 \ge 0$

Hence, the L.P.P is

$$\text{Maximise } Z = 800x_1 + 160x_2$$

$$\text{Subject to } 13x_1 + 6x_2 \le 360$$
$$16x_1 + 5x_2 \le 400$$
$$14x_1 + 7x_2 \le 260$$
$$x_1 \le 18 \text{ and } x_2 \le 70$$

where $x_1, x_2 \ge 0$

Illustration 4. *A medicine manufacturing company is producing three different medicines namely A, B and C. It requires 2 hours to prepare 100 bottles of medicine A, 1 hour to prepare 100 bottles of medicine B and 3 hours to prepare 150 bottles of medicine C. Total time available in a week is 40 hours. The raw materials* *available for producing medicine A, B and C are 1500, 2000 and 1000 bottles respectively. The total availability of bottles is 3500. The cost per bottle for medicine A, B and C are Rs 10, Rs 12 and Rs 16 respectively. Convert this problem into a L.P.P.*

Solution: Formulation of L.P.P.

Step 1: The key decision is to minimise the cost of production in the production of the three medicines *A*, *B* and *C*. The optimum quantities of production of these three products are assumed as x_1, x_2 and x_3 respectively.

Step 2: The objective function is the minimisation of the total cost of production. The per unit cost of production for *A*, *B* and *C* are Rs 10, Rs 12 and Rs16 respectively. Hence, the objective function can be written as

$$\text{Minimise } Z = 10x_1 + 12x_2 + 16x_3$$

Step 3: The constraints are the availability of bottles and availability of the maximum hours for production.

Medicine A needs 2 hours for preparing 100 bottles.

Medicine B needs 1 hour to prepare 100 bottles.

Medicine C needs 3 hours to prepare 150 bottles.

∴ For preparing 100 bottles of C requirement of time,

$$= \frac{3}{150} \times 100 = 2 \text{ hours}$$

Hence, the constraint equation is $2x_1 + x_2 + 2x_3 \leq 40$

Another constraint is the availability of bottles which can be written as

$$x_1 + x_2 + x_3 = 3500$$

$$x_1 \leq 1500, \quad x_2 \leq 2000 \text{ and } x_3 \leq 1000$$

Step 4: The feasible alternatives can be written as $x_1, x_2, x_3 \geq 0$

Hence, the L.P.P can be written as

$$\text{Minimise} \quad Z = 10x_1 + 12x_2 + 16x_3$$

$$\text{Subject to} \quad 2x_1 + x_2 + 2x_3 \leq 40$$

$$x_1 + x_2 + x_3 \leq 3500$$

$$x_1 \leq 1500, \quad x_2 \leq 2000, \quad x_3 \leq 1000 \quad \text{where } x_1, x_2, x_3 \geq 0$$

Illustration 5. *The number of units of vitamins A and B present in per Kg of three Foods X, Y and Z are shown in the following table.*

	Vitamin A	*Vitamin B*
X	*12*	*10*
Y	*4*	*6*
Z	*5*	*7*
Daily Requirement	*60*	*40*

The cost per Kg of foods X, Y and Z are Rs 12, Rs 7 and Rs 6 respectively. Formulate a L.P.P on the basis of the optimum spending to achieve the maximum benefit.

Solution: Formulation of L.P.P.

Step 1: The key decision is to determine the optimum spending for the food products *X, Y* and *Z*. Let the quantities of *X, Y* and *Z* be x_1, x_2 and x_3 respectively.

Step 2: Determine the objective function. The objective function is the minimisation of the total cost of spending. It can be written as

$$\text{Minimise } Z = 12x_1 + 7x_2 + 6x_3$$

Step 3: The constraint is the daily requirement of *Vitamin A* and *Vitamin B*. The requirement of *Vitamin A* = 60 units and *Vitamin B* = 40 units. The availability of *Vitamin A* are 12, 4 and 5 units respectively in *X, Y* and *Z*. The availability of *Vitamin B* are 10, 6 and 7 units respectively in X, *Y* and *Z*. Hence the constraint equations can be written as

$$12x_1 + 4x_2 + 5x_3 \le 60 \quad \text{and} \quad 10x_1 + 6x_2 + 7x_3 \le 40$$

Step 4: The feasible alternatives can be represented as

$$x_1, x_2, x_3 \ge 0$$

Hence, the L.P.P is

$$\text{Minimise } Z = 12x_1 + 7x_2 + 6x_3$$

$$\text{Subject to } 12x_1 + 4x_2 + 5x_3 \le 60$$

$$10x_1 + 6x_2 + 7x_3 \le 40 \quad \text{where } x_1, x_2, x_3 \ge 0$$

Illustration 6. *A company which has a monthly budget of Rs 600,000 for advertisement wants to plan its strategy on advertisement in television, radio and newspaper. The per unit* *costs of advertisement in TV, radio and newspaper are Rs 30,000, Rs 10,000 and Rs 6,000 respectively for the nmber of potential customers reached are 150,000, 120,000 and 60,000 respectively for T.V., Radio and News paper. The objective of the company is that at least 20,00,000 exposures should take place among the customers. The amount spent for radio and newspaper advertisement will not exceed Rs 380,000. There should be at least 10 units of radio advertisement and 4 units of TV advertisement. Formulate a L.P.P.*

Solution: Formulation of L.P.P.

Step 1: The key decision of the company is to decide the optimum allocation of fund for advertisement in TV, radio and newspaper. Let the units of advertisement in TV, radio and newspaper be x_1, x_2 and x_3.

Step 2: The objective function is to minimise the cost of advertisement with maximum reach of customers. The objective function can be written as

Minimise $Z = 30{,}000x_1 + 10{,}000x_2 + 6000x_3$

Step 3: Constraints are the reach of advertisement to customers; and the minimum spending to specific advertisement media. These constraints can be written in the form of linear equation as

(i) $150{,}000x_1 + 120{,}000x_2 + 60{,}000x_3 \leq 20{,}00{,}000$

i.e., $15x_1 + 12x_2 + 6x_3 \leq 200$

(ii) $10{,}000x_2 + 6000x_3 \leq 380{,}000$

i.e., $10x_2 + 6x_3 \leq 380$

(iii) $x_1 \geq 4$ (iv) $x_2 \geq 10$

Step 4: The feasible alternatives are $x_1, x_2, x_3 \geq 0$

Hence, the L.P.P is

Minimise $Z = 30{,}000x_1 + 10{,}000x_2 + 6000x_3$

Subject to $15x_1 + 12x_2 + 6x_3 \leq 200$

$10x_2 + 6x_3 \leq 380$

$x_1 \geq 4,\ x_2 \geq 10$ where $x_1, x_2, x_3 \geq 0$

Illustration 7. *A company produces two different products namely A and B and earns profit @ Rs 60 and Rs 50 per unit respectively. Each unit of product A requires 2 hours, 2.5 hours and 3 hours processing time in Process I, II and III respectively. Each unit of product B requires 1 hour, 4 hours and 3 hours processing time respectively in Process I, II and III. The maximum processing time available per week are 47, 39 and 46 hours respectively for Processes I, II and III. Each unit of product A yields 2 units of a by-product C without any extra cost. The profit of product C is Rs 24 per unit. The demand of product C is 15 units per week. If the by-product is not sold the unsold stock should immediately be destroyed and the cost of destruction per unit of C is Rs 4. Convert the problem into a L.P.P.*

Solution: Formulation of L.P.P.

Step 1: The key decision is to maximise the profit in the production of Product *A* and *B* and the by Product *C*. The unsold units of Product *C* can be assumed as *C*'. Hence, let the units of A, B, C and C' are x_1, x_2, x_3 and x_4.

Step 2: The objective function is to maximise the profit in the sales of *A*, *B* and *C* and minimise the destruction cost of C'.

Hence, the objective function is

Maximise $Z = 60x_1 + 50x_2 + 24x_3 - 4x_4$

Step 3: The constraints are the processing time and the demand for Product C. These constraints can be represented as

(i) $2x_1 + x_2 \le 47$ (ii) $2.5x_1 + 4x_2 \le 39$

(iii) $3x_1 + 3x_2 \le 46$ (iv) $x_3 \le 15$

Step 4: The feasible alternatives are $x_1, x_2, x_3, x_4 \ge 0$

Hence, the L.P.P is

Maximise $Z = 60x_1 + 50x_2 + 24x_3 - 4x_4$

Subject to $2x_1 + x_2 \le 47$

$2.5x_1 + 4x_2 \le 39$

$3x_1 + 3x_2 \le 46$

$x_3 \le 15$ where $x_1, x_2, x_3, x_4 \ge 0$

Solutions to Linear Programming Problems

There are two methods to solve the linear programming problems. They are,

(1) Graphic Method and (2) Simplex Method

Graphic Method for Solution to Linear Programming Problems

The L.P.P with only two variables can be solved through graphic method. The following are the steps for the solution to L.P.P by graphic method.

(1) The problem should be converted into a L.P.P.

(2) The inequality constraint linear equations should be converted into equality equations.

(3) In the graph X-axis can be represented with variable x_1 and Y-axis can be represented with variable x_2.

(4) Represent the linear constraint equations in the graph as straight lines. To draw each straight line, values of x_1 and x_2 should simultaneously be assumed as zero. It gives values of x_1 and x_2 for each equation. These straight lines may cut each other.

(5) Identify the feasible region in the graph. The feasible region for maximisation type problems lies within the origin of the graph. It is the region from origin to the straight lines crossing nearest to the origin. The feasible region for minimisation type problem lies above the crossed lines of the graph.

(6) The values of x_1 and x_2 at each co-ordinates of the region can be found out.

(7) The values of x_1 and x_2 at each co-ordinate should be applied in the equation of objective function. The value of Z for each co-ordinate should be calculated.

(8) If the L.P.P is of maximisation type then the highest value of Z among the various values of Z should be the optimum value. Value of x_1 and x_2 for the highest value of Z should be considered as the optimum value of x_1 and x_2.

(9) If the L.P.P is of minimisation type, then the lowest value of Z among the various values of Z shall be the optimum value. Value of x_1 and x_2 for the lowest value of Z should be considered as the optimum value of x_1 and x_2.

Illustration 8. *Solve the following L.P.P by graphical method*

Maximise $Z = 3x_1 + 5x_2$

Subject to $3x_1 + x_2 \leq 21$

$x_1 + x_2 \leq 18$ *where* $x_1, x_2 \geq 0$

Solution: In order to draw graph based on the constraint equations, the linear unequal equations should be considered as equality equations.

Hence, $3x_1 + x_2 = 21$

Assume $x_2 = 0$ $\therefore$ $3x_1 + 0 = 21;\ x_1 = 7$

Assume $x_1 = 0$ $\therefore$ $3.0 + x_2 = 21;\ x_2 = 21$

$x_1 + 2x_2 = 18$

Assume $x_2 = 0$

$x_1 + 2.0 = 18;\ x_1 = 18$

Assume $x_1 = 0$

$0 + 2x_2 = 18;\ x_2 = 9$

Represent the 2 equations in the graph as stated below.

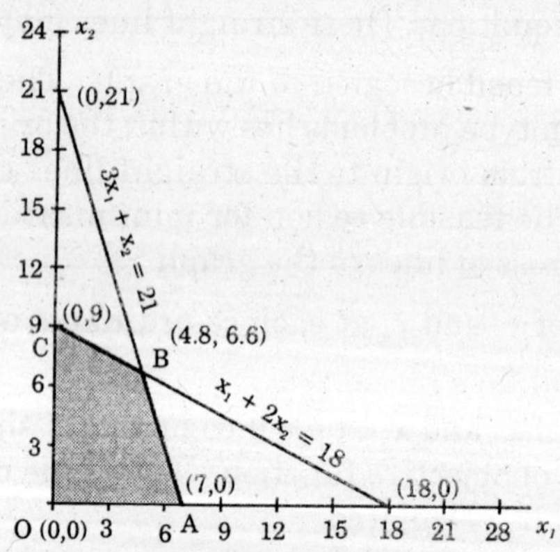

The variable x_1 is represented in X-axis and x_2 is represented in Y-axis.

The linear equation $3x_1 + x_2 = 21$ is represented as AE and $x_1 + 2x_2 = 18$ is represented as CD. Since it is a maximisation type problem, the required area lies in the region $OABC$.

At point O, $x_1 = 0$ and $x_2 = 0$

At point A, $x_1 = 7$ and $x_2 = 0$

At point C, $x_1 = 0$ and $x_2 = 9$

At point *B* value of x_1 and x_2 can be calculated by solving the two intersecting linear equations.

i.e., $3x_1 + x_2 = 21$ ... (i)

$x_1 + 2x_2 = 18$ ... (ii)

(i) × 2 $6x_1 + 2x_2 = 42$ ... (iii)

(iii) – (ii) $5x_1 = 24 \quad \therefore \; x_1 = \frac{24}{5} = 4.8$

(ii) $4.8 + 2x_2 = 18$

$2x_2 = 18 - 4.8;$

$x_2 = \frac{13.2}{2} = 6.6$

Substitute the values in the equation representing the optimal function ($Z = 3x_1 + 5x_2$)

Maximum of *Z* at O = 3.0 + 5.0 = 0

at *A* = 3.7 + 5.0 = 21

at *B* = 3(4.8) + 5(6.6) = 47.4

at *C* = 3.0 + 5.9 = 45

Since the maximum value is at point B the optimal value of $x_1 = 4.8$ and $x_2 = 6.6$.

Illustration 9. *Solve the following L.P.P by graphical method*

Maximise $Z = 2x_1 + 3x_2$

Subject to $3x_1 + 2x_2 \leq 12$

$3x_1 + 5x_2 \leq 15$

$x_2 \geq 2$ *where* $x_1, x_2 \geq 0$

Solution: Let $3x_1 + 2x_2 = 12$ ... (i)

When $x_1 = 0;$ $x_2 = 6$

$x_2 = 0;$ $x_1 = 4$

Let $3x_1 + 5x_2 = 15$ ... (ii)

When $x_1 = 0;$ $x_2 = 3$

$x_2 = 0;$ $x_1 = 5$

$x_2 = 2$ ... (iii)

Represent the above equations in the graph as follows.

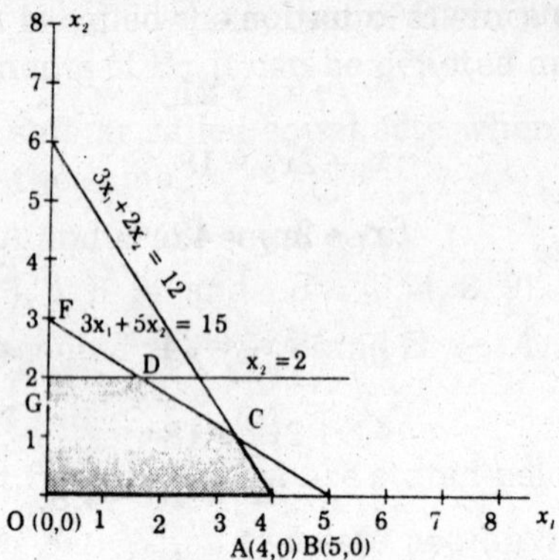

The feasible region is *OACDG*

At point *C*, $3x_1 + 2x_2 = 12$

$3x_1 + 5x_2 = 15$

By solving these equations, $x_1 = 3.3$, $x_2 = 1$

At point *D* $3x_1 + 5x_2 = 15$

$x_2 = 2$; $x_1 = 5/3$

Values of x_1 and x_2 are

At O (0, 0); At A (4, 0);

At C (3.3, 1); At D (5/3, 2); At G (0, 2)

Feasible solutions for maximise $Z = 2x_1 + 3x_2$, are

At *O*, $Z = 2.0 + 3.0 = 0$

At *A*, $Z = 2.4 + 3.0 = 8$

At *C*, $Z = 2(3.3) + 3.1 = 9.6$

At *D*, $Z = 2(5/3) + 3.2 = 9.3$

At *G*, $Z = 2.0 + 3.2 = 6$

Among these feasible solutions point C gives the optimal one.

Hence, the optimum value of $x_1 = 1$; $x_2 = 3.3$

Illustration 10. *Solve the following L.P.P by graphic method*

Maximise $Z = 10x_1 + 7x_2$

Subject to $x_1 + x_2 = 25$, $0 \le x_2 \le 10$, $0 \le x_1 \le 17$, $x_2 \ge 5$,

$x_1 - x_2 = 0$. *Where* $x_1, x_2 \ge 0$

Solution: The equations for graph are

(i) $x_1 + x_2 = 25$, $x_1 = 25$; $x_2 = 25$ (ii) $x_1 - x_2 = 0$,

(iii) $x_2 = 10$; (iv) $x_1 = 17$; (v) $x_2 = 5$

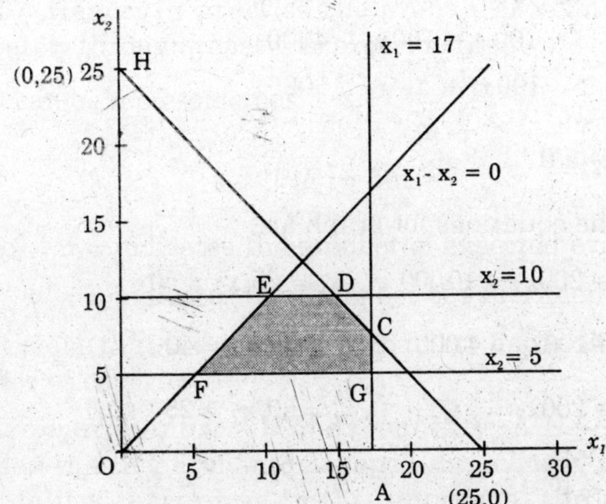

Hence, the feasible region is *FGCDE* x_1 and x_2 are calculated as

At *F*	$x_1 - x_2 = 0$ and $x_2 = 5$; $x_1 = 5$; $x_2 = 5$
G	$x_1 = 17$; $x_2 = 5$
C	$x_1 + x_2 = 25$ and $x_1 = 17$; \ $x_1 = 17$; $x_2 = 8$
D	$x_1 + x_2 = 25$ and $x_2 = 10$
	$x_1 = 15$; $x_2 = 10$
E	$x_1 - x_2 = 0$ and $x_2 = 10$
	$x_1 = 10$; $x_2 = 10$

The feasible solution for Maximum $Z = 10x_1 + 7x_2$ are

At *F*	10.5 + 7.5 = 85
G	10.17 + 7.5 = 205
C	10.17 + 7.8 = 226
D	10.15 + 7.10 = 220
E	10.10 + 7.10 = 170

Hence, the optimal solution is at point *C*.

$\therefore$ Value of $x_1 = 17$ and $x_2 = 8$

Maximum of $Z = 226$

Illustration 11: *Solve the following L.P.P by graphic method*

Minimise $300x_1 + 400x_2$

Subject to $400x_1 + 200x_2 \geq 10000$

$100x_1 + 100x_2 \geq 4000$

$100x_1 + 200x_2 \geq 5000$

Where $x_1, x_2 \geq 0$

Solution: The equations for graph are

(i) $400x_1 + 200x_2 = 10{,}000 \quad \therefore x_1 = 25, x_2 = 50$

(ii) $100x_1 + 100x_2 = 4{,}000 \quad \therefore x_1 = 40, x_2 = 40$

(iii) $100x_1 + 200x_2 = 5{,}000 \quad \therefore x_1 = 50, x_2 = 25$

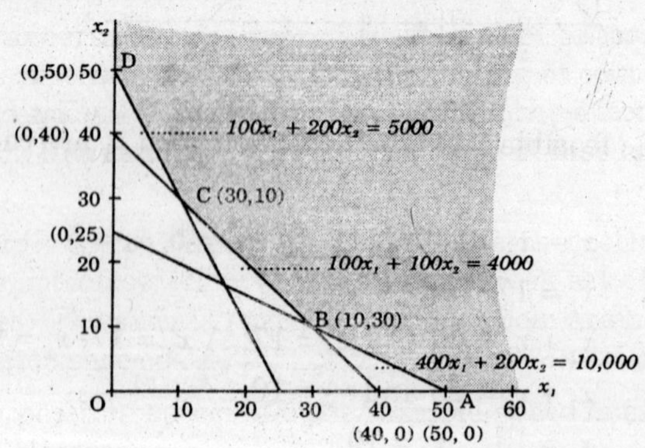

Since the problem is of minimisation type, the feasible area lies above the origin, which is shaded. Hence, the feasible area = *ABCD*

Values of x_1 and x_2

At *B* $\quad 100x_1 + 100x_2 = 4000$ . . . (i)

$400x_1 + 200x_2 = 10000$ . . . (ii)

(i) x 2 $\quad 200x_1 + 200x_2 = 8000$ . . . (iii)

(ii) - (iii) $\quad 200x_1 = 2000$

$\therefore \quad x_1 = 10, x_2 = 30$

At C $\quad 100x_1 + 200x_2 = 5000$ . . . (i)

$100x_1 + 100x_2 = 4000$ . . . (ii)

(i) - (ii) $\quad 100x_2 = 1000$

$x_2 = 10, x_1 = 30$

At A $\quad x_1 = 50, x_2 = 0$

At D $\quad x_1 = 0, x_2 = 50$

Objective function is minimise $Z = 300x_1 + 400x_2$

At A $\quad Z = 300.50 + 400.0 \quad = 15,000$

At B $\quad Z = 300.10 + 400.30 \quad = 15,000$

At C $\quad Z = 300.30 + 400.10 \quad = 13,000$

At D $\quad Z = 300.0 + 400.50 \quad = 20,000$

Since the optimum value of Z is at point C, Optimum value of $x_1 = 30, x_2 = 10$ and $Z = 13,000$

Illustration 12: *A firm manufacturing 2 types of electrical items A and B can make a profit of 20 dollars per unit of A and 30 dollars per unit of B. Both A and B make use of 2 essential components, a motor and a transformer. Each unit of A requires 2 motors and 4 transformers. The total supply of components per month is restricted to 210 motors and 300 transformers. Type B is an export model requiring a voltage stabilizer which has a supply restricted to 65 units per month. How many units of A and B should the firm manufacture per month to maximise its profits? How much is the profit? Formulate the above as a linear programming problem by setting up appropriate constraints and objective function, then answer the question by solving graphically.*

(MGU: Section C April '96)

Solution: Formulation of L.P.P.

1. Let the quantites of the two products A and B be x_1 and x_2 respectively.

Profit per unit of A = 20 dollars, B = 30 dollars.

∴ Objective function is Maximise $Z = 20x_1 + 30x_2$

2. Total supply of component parts,

Motors = 210; Transformers = 300 units.

Each unit of A requires 3 motors and 2 transformers.

Each unit of B requires 2 motors and 4 transformers.

∴ The constraint equations are $3x_1 + 2x_2 \leq 210$

$$2x_1 + 4x_2 \leq 300$$

Product B requires a voltage stabilizer for each unit of production. The supply of the voltage stabilizer is limited to 65 units. The constraint equation is $x_2 \le 65$

3. The feasible alternatives are $x_1, x_2 \ge 0$

Hence, the L.P.P is,

Maximise $Z = 20x_1 + 30x_2$.

Subject to $3x_1 + 2x_2 \le 210$

$2x_1 + 4x_2 \le 300$

$x_2 \le 65$

where $x_1, x_2 \ge 0$

Graphical solution for the L.P.P: The linear equation for graph are

(i) $3x_1 + 2x_2 = 210$

When $x_1 = 0, x_2 = 105$; When $x_2 = 0, x_1 = 70$

(ii) $2x_1 + 4x_2 = 300$

When $x_1 = 0, x_2 = 75$; When $x_2 = 0, x_1 = 150$

(iii) $x_2 = 65; x_1 = 0$

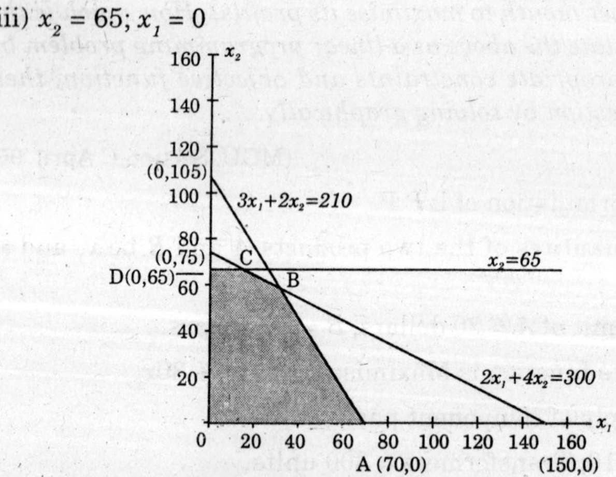

It is clear from this graph that the feasible region is within *OABCD*

Values of x_1 and x_2 are calculated as follows:

At point O $x_1 = 0; x_2 = 0$

At point A $x_1 = 70; x_2 = 0$

At point B in equations $2x_1 + 4x_2 = 300$ . . . (i)

$3x_1 + 2x_2 = 210$ . . . (ii)

(ii) x 2 $6x_1 + 4x_2 = 420$ . . . . (iii)

(iii) - (i) $4x_1 = 120$; $x_1 = 30, x_2 = 60$

At point C in equations $2x_1 + 4x_2 = 300$; $x_2 = 65$

$\therefore\ x_1 = 20$

At point D $x_1 = 0$, $x_2 = 65$

Values of Z: at A $Z = 20x_1 + 30x_2 = 20.0 + 30.0 = 0$

at B $Z = 20.30 + 30.60 = 2400$

at C $Z = 20.20 + 30.65 = 2350$

at D $Z = 20.0 + 30.65 = 1950$

Since optimum value of Z is at point B, value of $x_1 = 30$, $x_2 = 60$, $Z = 2400$

Illustration 13: *Solve graphically the following linear programming problem*

Maximise $Z = 2x_1 + 3x_2$

Subject to $x_1 + x_2 \leq 30$, $x_2 \geq 3$, $0 \leq x_2 \leq 12$, $x_1 - x_2 \geq 0$

$0 \leq x_1 \leq 20$ (MGU: Section C April '95)

Solution: The constraint equations for graph are

(i) $x_1 + x_2 = 30$ $\therefore x_1 = 30;\ x_2 = 30$ (ii) $x_2 = 3,\ x_1 = 0$

(iii) $x_2 = 12,\ x_1 = 0$ (iv) $x_1 - x_2 = 0$

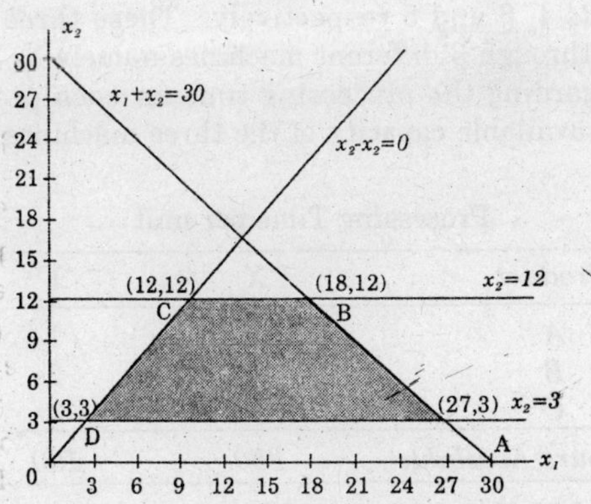

As per the graph the feasible region is within $ABCD$.

The values of x_1 and x_2 on the region *ABCD* are calculated as follows:

At A $\quad x_1 + x_2 = 30$ and $x_2 = 3 \quad \therefore \quad x_1 = 27;\ x_2 = 3$

At B $\quad x_1 + x_2 = 30$ and $x_2 = 12 \quad \therefore \quad x_1 = 18;\ x_2 = 12$

At C $\quad x_1 - x_2 = 0$ and $x_2 = 12 \quad \therefore \quad x_1 = 12;\ x_2 = 12$

At D $\quad x_1 - x_2 = 0$ and $x_2 = 3 \quad \therefore \quad x_1 = 3;\ x_2 = 3$

The feasible solutions for the objective function,

Maximise $Z = 2x_1 + 3x_2$, are stated below.

At *A* $\quad Z = 2.27 + 3.3 = 63$

At *B* $\quad Z = 2.18 + 3.12 = 72$

At *C* $\quad Z = 2.12 + 3.12 = 60$

At *D* $\quad Z = 2.3 + 3.3 = 15$

It is clear from the above solutions that the optimum feasible solution is at point *B*.

Hence, the optimum value of $\quad x_1 = 18$ and $x_2 = 12$

Maximum value of $\quad Z = 72$

Exercises

1. Define Linear Programming. (MGU: Section A April '95)
2. State the procedure for formulating Linear Programming Problems.
3. Define Linear Programming. State the procedure for solving linear programming problem by graphical method.
4. State the merits and limitations of Linear Programming Problems.
5. A company produces three products namely A, B and C and sells for profit at Rs 4, 6 and 5 respectively. These three products are processed through 3 different machines namely X, Y and Z. The details regarding the processing time for each product and the maximum available capacity of the three machines are stated as below.

Processing Time per unit

Product	*X*	*Y*	*Z*
A	2	1	4
B	3	2	5
C	1	3	2
Total Hours Available	*250*	*190*	*175*

The demand for the product *A* is 70 units per month, but products

B and *C* have no marketing constraints. Formulate the above problem into a linear programming problem.

[Ans: Maximise $Z = 4x_1 + 6x_2 + 5x_3$ Subject to $2x_1 + 3x_2 + x_3 \leq 250$; $x_1 + 2x_2 + 3x_3 \leq 190$; $4x_1 + 5x_2 + 2x_3 \leq 175$; $x_1 \leq 70$]

6. A company produces 3 different products, namely A, B and C. These three products are manufactured in three different Machines namely I, II and III. The maximum processing time available for machines I, II and III are 40, 50 and 60 hours per week. Product A requires 6 minutes, 10 minutes and 12 minutes processing time in Machines I, II and III respectively. Product B requires 12, 7 and 14 minutes of processing time in Machines I, II and III respectively. Product C requires 10, 20 and 18 minutes of processing time respectively in Machines I, II and III. The per unit profit for A, B and C are Rs 20, Rs 18 and Rs 15 respectively. Formulate a L.P.P.

[Ans: Maximise $Z = 20x_1 + 18x_2 + 15x_3$

Subject to $6x_1 + 12x_2 + 10x_3 \leq 2400$

$10x_1 + 7x_2 + 20x_3 \leq 3000$

$12x_1 + 14x_2 + 18x_3 \leq 3600$]

7. A company produces two types of Televisions through 3 different processes namely A, B and C. The details regarding the time required for each type of Television and the total capacity of these three process are stated below.

Processes	*Time Required for* *Type I TV (Hrs)*	*Type II TV (Hrs)*	*Maximum Time Available (Hrs)*
A	12	17	260
B	4	7	245
C	10	15	280

The demand for Type I *TV* is 10 per month. The profit on Type I *TV* is Rs 1200 and Type II *TV* is Rs 1500. Convert the problem into a L.P.P. [Ans: Maximise $Z = 1200x_1 + 1500x_2$

Subject to $12x_1 + 17x_2 \leq 260$

$4x_1 + 7x_2 \leq 245$

$10x_1 + 15x_2 \leq 280$

$x_1 \leq 10$]

8. A pharmaceutical company is manufacturing three different medicines namely *X, Y* and *Z*. It requires 3 hours to prepare 500 bottles of x, 2 hours to prepare 500 bottles of *y* and 4 hours to prepare 500 bottles of *Z*. Total time available is 60 hours. The raw materials available for producing medicine *X, Y* and *Z* are for 6000, 4500 and 6500 bottles respectively. The profits per bottle for medicine *X, Y* and *Z* are Rs 7, Rs 6 and Rs 8 respectively. Convert the problem into a L.P.P. [Ans: Maximise $Z = 7x_1 + 6x_2 + 8x_3$

Subject to $3x_1 + 2x_2 + 4x_3 \le 30000$

$x_1 \le 6000, \; x_2 \le 4{,}500, \; x_3 \le 6500$]

9. The number of units of Vitamins A and B present in per Kg of three food products namely *X, Y* and *Z* are shown in the following table.

	Vitamin A	*Vitamin B*
X	11	12
Y	5	4
Z	6	8
Daily Requirement	60	40

The cost per Kg of food product x, y and z are Rs 15, Rs 10 and Rs 12 respectively. Formulate L.P.P.

[Ans: Minimise $Z = 15x_1 + 10x_2 + 12x_3$

Subject to $11x_1 + 5x_2 + 6x_3 \le 60$

$12x_1 + 4x_2 + 8x_3 \le 40$]

10. A company which has a monthly budget of Rs 800,000 for advertisement wants to plan its strategy on advertisement. The company has to advertise in three medias namely Television, Radio and Magazine. The per unit costs of advertisement in TV, Radio and Magazine are Rs 32,000, Rs 11,000 and Rs 10,000 respectively. The number of potential customers reached are 160,000, 120,000 and 80,000 respectively, for TV, Radio and Magazine. The objective of the company is that at least 22,00,000 exposures should take place among the customers. The amount spent for radio and magazine advertisement will not exceed Rs 400,000. There should be at least 12 units of radio advertisement and 6 units of TV advertisement. Formulate a L.P.P.

[Ans: Minimise $Z = 32000x_1 + 11000x_2 + 10000x_3$

Subject to $16x_1 + 12x_2 + 8x_3 \le 220$

$11x_2 + 10x_3 \le 400, \; x_2 \ge 12; \; x_1 \ge 6$]

11. A company produces 2 different products namely X and Y and earns profit @ Rs 17 and Rs 20 per unit respectively. Each unit of product x requires 3 hours, 2 hours and 2 hours processing time in Machine A, B and C respectively. Each unit of product Y requires 2 hours, 2.5 hours and 3 hours processing time respectively in Machine A, B and C. The maximum processing time available are 100, 110 and 90 hours respectively for Machines A, B and C. Each unit of product Y yields 2 units of a by-product Z without any extra cost. The profit for product Z is Rs 12 per unit. The demand for product Z is 40 units. If the by-product is not sold the unsold stock should immediately be destroyed and the cost of destruction per unit of Z is Rs 5 per unit. Convert the problem into a L.P.P.

[Ans: Maximise $Z = 17x_1 + 20x_2 + 12x_3 - 5x_4$

Subject to $3x_1 + 2x_2 \le 100$

$2x_1 + 2.5x_2 \le 100,$

$2x_1 + 3x_2 \le 90, \ x_3 \le 40$]

12. Solve the following L.P.P by graphic method

Maximise $Z = 7x_1 + 5x_2$

Subject to $4x_1 + 3x_2 \le 18, \quad 2x_1 + 5x_2 \le 16$

where $x_1, x_2 \ge 0$ [Ans: $x_1 = 4.5; x_2 = 0; Z = 31.5$]

13. Solve the following L.P.P by graphic method

Maximise $Z = x_1 + 2x_2$

Subject to $5x_1 + 3x_2 \le 19, \quad 3x_1 + 5x_2 \le 21, \quad 2x_2 \ge 7$

where $x_1, x_2 \ge 0$ [Ans: $x_1 = 2; x_2 = 3; Z = 8$]

14. Solve the following L.P.P by graphic method.

Minimise $Z = 3x_1 + 5x_2$

Subject to $2x_1 + x_2 \ge 10, \quad x_1 + 2x_2 \ge 11$

where $x_1, x_2 \ge 0$ [Ans: $x_1 = 3; x_2 = 4; Z = 29$]

15. Solve the following L.P.P by graphic method.

Maximise $Z = 7x_1 + 5x_2$

Subject to $x_1 + x_2 \le 20, \quad 0 \le x_2 \le 7, \quad 0 \le x_1 \le 12, \quad x_2 \ge 4$

$x_1 - x_2 = 0$

where $x_1, x_2 \ge 0$ [Ans: $x_1 = 13; x_2 = 7; Z = 126$]

16. Solve the following L.P.P by graphic method.

Minimise $Z = 5x_1 + 4x_2$

Subject to $x_1 + 5x_2 \geq 50,\ 2x_1 + x_2 \geq 40,\ x_1 + x_2 \geq 30$

[Ans: $x_1 = 10$; $x_2 = 20$; $Z = 130$]

17. Solve the following L.P.P by graphical method.

Minimise $Z = 10x_1 + 6x_2$

Subject to $2x_1 + x_2 \leq 21,\ x_1 + 2x_2 \geq 24$

where $x_1, x_2 \geq 0$ [Ans: $x_1 = 6$; $x_2 = 9$; $Z = 114$]

18. Solve the following L.P.P by graphical method.

Maximise $Z = 5x_1 + 4x_2$

Subject to $10x_1 + 3x_2 \leq 90,\ 5x_1 + 6x_2 \geq 90,\ 0 \leq x_2 \leq 12$

where $x_1, x_2 \geq 0$ [Ans: $x_1 = 6$; $x_2 = 10$; $Z = 70$]

19. Solve the following L.P.P by graphical method.

Maximise $Z = 3x_1 + 2x_2$

Subject to $9x_1 + 5x_2 \leq 45,\ 7x_1 + 5x_2 \geq 42,\ 0 \leq x_2 \geq 7$

where $x_1, x_2 \geq 0$ [Ans: $x_1 = 1.5$; $x_2 = 6.3$; $Z = 17.1$]

20. Solve the following L.P.P by graphical method.

Minimise $Z = 12x_1 + 10x_2$

Subject to $x_1 + x_2 \geq 100,\ x_1 + 2x_2 \geq 120$

where $x_1, x_2 \geq 0$ [Ans: $x_1 = 0$; $x_2 = 100$; $Z = 1000$]

◆ Chapter 17 ◆

Set Theory

A set is a collection of well defined objects. Each object in a set is called element or a member of the set.

Examples: (i) The vowels in the English alphabet (ii) Consumer of a product (iii) Students in a class (iv) Teachers in a college (v) All odd numbers etc.

I Representation of Sets

Sets may be represented in any of the following two ways.

(i) Tabular or Roaster Method and (ii) Rule Method.

(i) Tabular or Roaster Method: Under this method elements of the set should be written in two braces.

Example:

(i) A = The set of numbers multiplied by 5

= {5, 10, 15, 20, 25 ..... }

(ii) B = The set of vowels in English alphabets

= {*a, e, i, o, u*}

(iii) C = The set of positive odd integers less than 15

= {1, 3, 5, 7, 9, 11, 13}

(ii) Rule Method: In this method a general element is used to discribe the elements of the set.

Example:

(i) A = {5, 10, 15, 20, 25 . . . . }

= {*5x / x e N*}, where *N* = the set of all natural numbers.

(ii) B = {*a, e, i, o u*}

= {*x/x* is vowel in English alphabet}

(iii) C = {1, 3, 5, 7, 9, 11, 13}

= {*x/x* is a positive odd integer less than 15}

Types of Sets

1. Finite and Infinite Sets: If the set has a finite number of elements it is called Finite Set. If the number of elements of the set is infinite it is called Infinite Set.

Example:

(i) A = {3, 6, 9, 12, 15} is a finite set.

B = {2, 4, 6, 8, 10, 12 ....} is a infinite set.

(ii) A = {x/x is a natural number < 18, multiplied by 3} is a finite set. B = {x/x is an even number} is an infinite set.

2. Equal Sets: Two sets A and B are called equal sets if both have the same elements. It means, each element of A is an element of B and each element of B is an element of A. It can be represented as $A = B$ If $A \neq B$ it means A is not equal to B.

Example: (i) A = {2, 4, 6, 8, 10}, B = {4, 8, 6, 10, 2} are two sets. These two sets can be called equal sets since both of them have same elements. $\therefore$ $A = B$.

(ii) A = {1, 3, 5, 7, 9} and B = {3, 5, 1, 6, 9} are two sets. These two sets are not equal sets since both of them do not have the same elements. $\therefore$ $A \neq B$

3. Equivalent Sets: Two sets A and B are called equivalent sets when the number of elements in the two sets are equal.

Example: A = {*a, b, c, d, e, f*} and B = {1, 4, 9, 5, 3, 4} are two sets. These two sets are called equivalent sets since the number of elements in these two sets are equal.

4. Singleton Set: A set with only one element is called Singleton Set.

Example: A = {6}, B = {0} C = {x/x is an integer and 6x + 24 = 0}

5. Null Set: A set with no element is called null set or empty set. Null set is represented as ϕ

Example: A = { }

6. SubSet: A set A is called a subset of the set B if every element of A is an element of B. It can be represented as $A \subseteq B$.

Example: A = {6, 9, 2, 5} and B = {1, 2, 3, 4, 5, 6, 7, 8, 9} are two sets. Then $A \subseteq B$ since every element of A is an element of B.

Properties of Subsets

(i) The null set (ϕ) is a subset of every set.

(ii) Every set is a subset of itself.

Example: $A = \{3, 6, 9\}$ $\therefore$ A $\subseteq$ A.

(iii) If $A \subseteq B$ and $B \subseteq C$ then, $A \subseteq C$

(iv) If $A \subseteq B$ and $B \subseteq A$ then, $A = B$.

7. *Disjoint Sets:* Two sets A and B are called disjoint sets if they have no common elements.

Example: $A = \{4, 6, 5, 7\}$ and $B = \{1, 2, 3, 8\}$

These two sets are disjoint sets, since they have no common element.

8. *Universal Set:* If all the sets under consideration in a study are sub-sets of a fixed set, then the fixed set is called universal set. It is denoted by U.

Example: $A = \{a, b, c, d\}$, $B = \{x, y, z\}$

$C = \{a, e, i, o, u\}$, $D = \{l, m, w, x\}$

are considered the subsets of the universal set.

$$U = \{a, b, c, d \ldots y, z\}$$

Venn Diagrams: The representation of sets in the form of diagram is called Venn Diagram.

The universal set is represented by points within a rectangle and other sets are represented by points within circles. A model of Venn Diagram, representing the universal set U and set A is stated below.

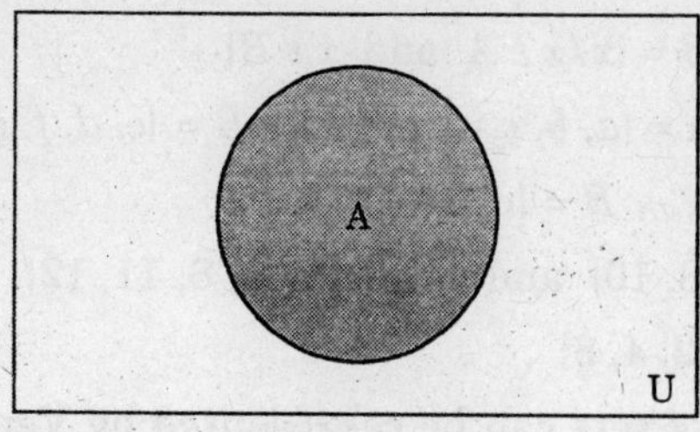

II Set Operations

The important set operations are

1. Union of Sets 2. Intersection of Sets
3. Difference of two Sets and 4. Complement of a Set.

1. Union of Sets: Union of two sets A and B is the set of all elements which belong either to *A* or to *B* or to both A and B. It may be represented as $A \cup B$ and read as "*A* union *B*".

Hence, $A \cup B = \{x \mid x \varepsilon A \text{ or } x \varepsilon B\}$

Example: (i) $A = \{a, b, c, d\}$, $B = \{b, c, e, f\}$

$\therefore A \cup B = \{a, b, c, d, e, f\}$

(ii) $A = \{2, 4, 5, 6\}$, $B = \{1, 2, 3, 4\}$ $\therefore A \cup B = \{1, 2, 3, 4, 5, 6\}$

Union of two sets can be represented by Venn diagram as follows.

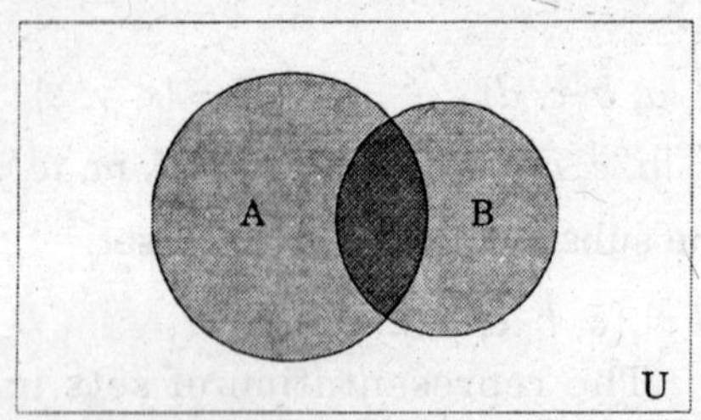

The whole shaded area within two circles is union of sets A and B i.e., $A \cup B$.

2. Intersection of Sets: Intersection of two sets *A* and *B* means set of elements belong to both *A* and *B*. The common elements of sets *A* and *B* are called Intersection of sets A and B. It may be represented as $A \cap B$ and read as "*A intersection B*".

Hence, $A \cap B = \{x / x \varepsilon A \text{ and } x \varepsilon B\}$

Example: (i) $A = \{a, b, c, d, e\}$ and $B = \{c, d, f, g\}$

$\therefore A \cap B = \{c, d\}$

(ii) $A = \{2, 4, 6, 8, 10\}$ and $B = \{1, 2, 4, 8, 11, 12\}$

$\therefore A \cap B = \{2, 4, 8\}$

Intersection of sets can be represented by Venn Diagram as follows.

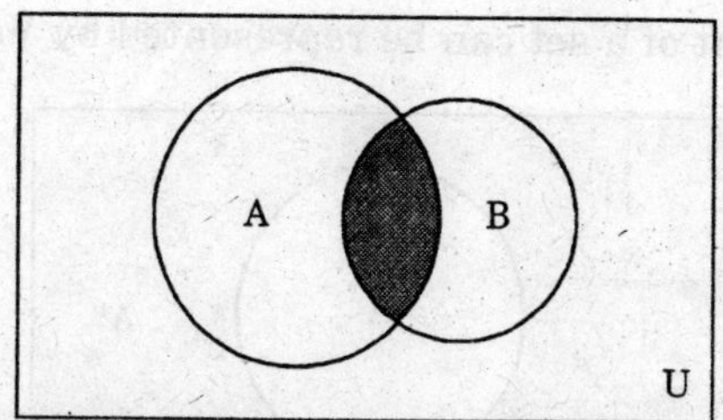

The shaded portion of sets A and B represents intersection of sets A and B i.e., $A \cap B$.

3. Difference of Two Sets: The difference of two set A and B is the set of elements of A which are not in B. Difference of two sets can be written as $A - B$.

Hence, $A - B = \{x / x \varepsilon A; x \varepsilon B\}$

Example: (i) $A = \{a, b, c, d, e\}$ and $B = \{a, c, d\}$

$\therefore A - B = \{b, e\}$

(ii) $B - B = \phi$ (iii) $B' = U - B$

Difference of two sets can be represented by Venn Diagram as follows.

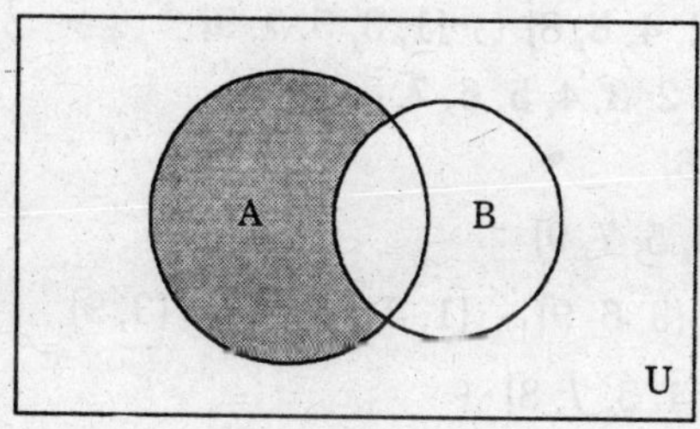

The shaded portion is called difference of two sets A and B i.e., A - B.

4. Complement of a Set: The complement of a set A is the set of all those elements belonging to the universal set, except those elements belonging to A. The complement of A is written as A'

Hence, $A' = \{x / x \varepsilon U \text{ and } x \notin A\}$

Example: (i) $U = \{a, b, c, d, e, f, g\}$, $A = \{a, c, d, f, g\}$

$A' = \{b, e\}$

(ii) $U = \{1, 2, 3, 4, 5, 6, 7, 8, 9, 10\}$, $A = \{6, 7, 8, 9, 3\}$

$A' = \{1, 2, 4, 5, 10\}$

Complement of a set can be represented by Venn Diagram as follows.

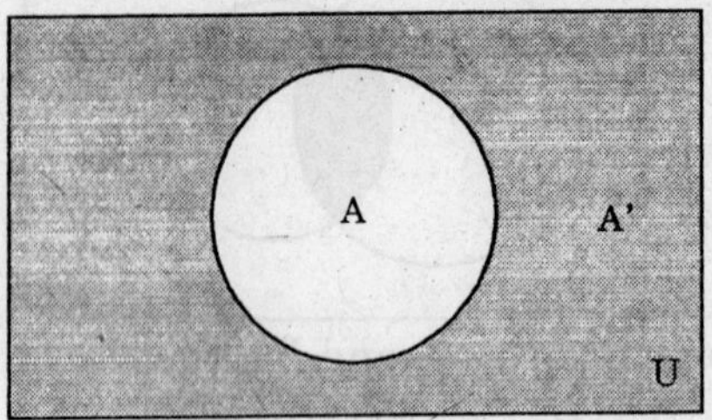

The shaded portion is called complement of a set i.e., A'.

Illustration 1: *If* $U = \{1, 2, 3, 4, 5, 6, 7, 8, 9\}$ $A = \{3, 6, 9\}$, $B = \{2, 4, 6, 8\}$, $C = \{1, 3, 5, 7, 9\}$

find (i) $A \cup B$ (ii) $B \cup C$ (iii) $A \cap B$

(iv) $A \cap B'$ (v) $A' \cap B$ (vi) $(A \cup B)'$

(vii) $(A \cap B) \cup C'$ (viii) $(A \cup B) \cap (A \cup C)$

(ix) $(A \cap B) \cup (B \cap C)$

Solution: (i) $A \cup B = \{3, 6, 9\} \cup \{2, 4, 6, 8\} = \{2, 3, 4, 6, 8, 9\}$

(ii) $B \cup C = \{2, 4, 6, 8\} \cup \{1, 3, 5, 7, 9\}$
$= \{1, 2, 3, 4, 5, 6, 7, 8, 9\}$

(iii) $A \cap B = \{6\}$

(iv) $B' = \{1, 3, 5, 7, 9\}$

$A \cap B' = \{3, 6, 9\} \cap \{1, 3, 5, 7, 9\} = \{3, 9\}$

(v) $A' = \{1, 2, 4, 5, 7, 8\}$

$A' \cap B = \{1, 2, 4, 5, 7, 8\} \cap \{2, 4, 6, 8\} = \{2, 4, 8\}$

(vi) $A \cup B = \{2, 3, 4, 6, 8, 9\}$

$(A \cup B)' = \{1, 5, 7\}$

(vii) $A \cap B = \{6\}$, $C = \{1, 3, 5, 7, 9\}$
$C' = \{2, 4, 6, 8\}$

$(A \cap B)\ U\ C' = \{2, 4, 6, 8\}$

(viii) $A \cup B = \{2, 3, 4, 6, 8, 9\}$, $A \cup C = \{1, 3, 5, 6, 7, 9\}$

$(A \cup B) \cap (A \cup C) = \{3, 6, 9\}$

(ix) $A \cap B = \{6\}$, $B \cap C = \{\ \}$

$(A \cap B) \cup (B \cap C) = \{6\}$

Illustration 2: *If* $U = \{1, 2, 3, 4, 5, 6, 7, 8, 9\}$, $A = \{2, 3, 4, 5\}$ *and* $B = \{4, 5, 6, 7\}$ *Verify that*

(i) $(A - B) \cup (B - A) = (A \cup B) - (A \cap B)$

(ii) $A - B = A \cap B' = B' - A'$

Solution: **(i)** $A - B = \{2, 3, 4, 5\} - \{4, 5, 6, 7\} = \{2, 3\}$

$B - A = \{4, 5, 6, 7\} - \{2, 3, 4, 5\} = \{6, 7\}$

$(A - B) \cup (B - A) = \{2, 3, 6, 7\}$ . . . (i)

$A \cup B = \{2, 3, 4, 5, 6, 7\}$

$A \cap B = \{4, 5\}$

$(A \cup B) - (A \cap B) = \{2, 3, 6, 7\}$ . . . (ii)

It is clear from equation (i) and (ii) that

$$(A - B) \cup (B - A) = (A \cup B) - (A \cap B)$$

(ii) $A - B = \{2, 3\}$ . . . (i)

$B' = \{1, 2, 3, 8, 9\}$

$A \cap B' = \{2, 3, 4, 5\} \cap \{1, 2, 3, 8, 9\} = \{2, 3\}$ . . . (ii)

$A' = \{1, 6, 7, 8, 9\}$

$B' - A' = \{1, 2, 3, 8, 9\} - \{1, 6, 7, 8, 9\} = \{2, 3\}$ . . . (iii)

It is clear from equations (i), (ii) and (iii) that

$$A - B = A \cap B' = B' - A'$$

Illustration 3: *Verify* $A \cup (B \cap C) = (A \cup B) \cap (A \cup C)$ *by Venn diagrams.*

Solution:

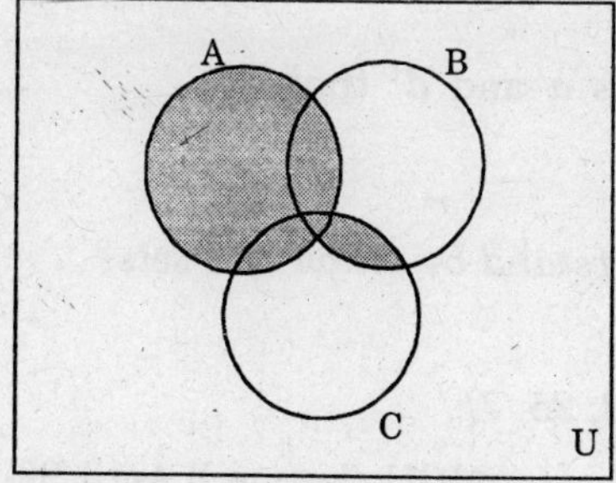

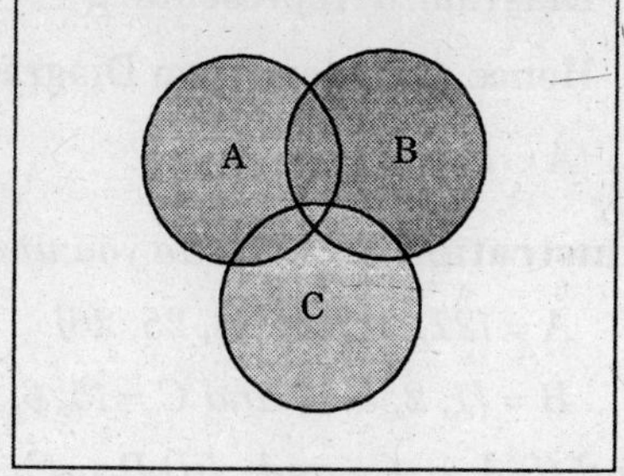

Shaded region in Diagram (i) is same as the region represented by squares in Diagram (ii). Hence $A \cup (B \cap C) = (A \cup B) \cap (A \cup C)$

Illustation 4: *Verify with the help of Venn diagram*

$$(A \cup B)' = A' \cap B'$$

Solution:

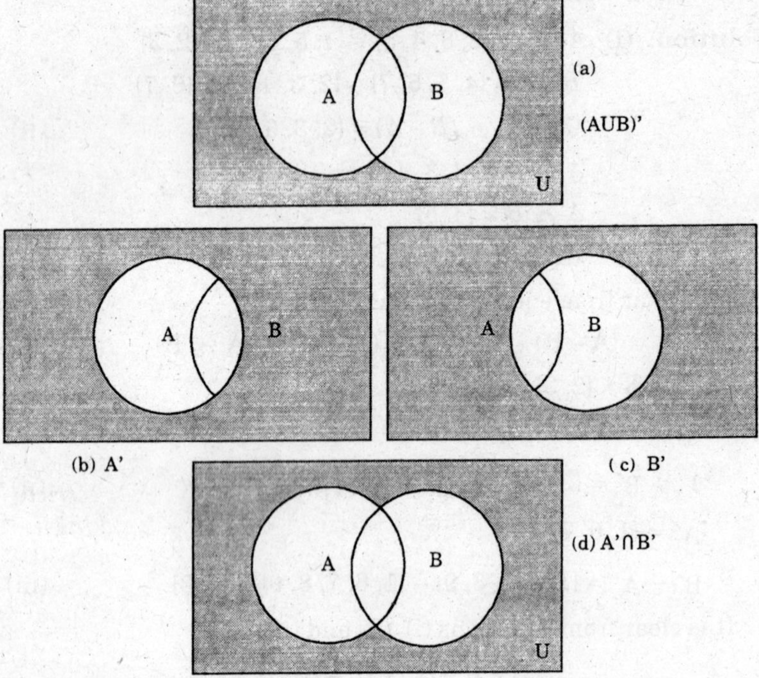

Diagram '*a*' represents $(A \cup B)'$

Diagram '*b*' represents A'; Diagram '*c*' represents B'

Diagram '*d*' represents $A' \cap B'$

Hence, it is clear from Diagrams '*a*' and '*d*' that

$(A \cup B)' = A' \cap B'$.

Illustration 5: *What do you understand by union of 2 sets?*

If $A = \{21, 22, 23, 24, 25, 26\}$

$B = \{1, 2, 3, 4\}$ *and* $C = \{5, 6, 23, 25, 7\}$

find (i) $A \cap C$ *and (ii)* $B \cup C$ (MGU: Section B April '96)

Solution: (i) $A \cap C = \{21, 22, 23, 24, 25, 26\} \cap \{5, 6, 23, 25, 7\}$

$= \{23, 25\}$

(ii) $B \cup C = \{1, 2, 3, 4\} \cup \{5, 6, 23, 25, 7\}$
$= \{1, 2, 3, 4, 5, 6, 7, 23, 25\}$

Illustration 6: *What do you understand by intersection of two sets? If A = {0, 2, 4, 6}, B = {1, 3, 5, 7} and C = {0, 3, 6}. What is (a) A ∪ B (b) B ∩ C* (MGU: Section B April '95)

Solution: (a) $A \cup B = \{0, 2, 4, 6\} \cup \{1, 3, 5, 7\}$
$= \{0, 1, 2, 3, 4, 5, 6, 7\}$

(b) $B \cap C = \{1, 3, 5, 7\} \cap \{0, 3, 6\} = \{3\}$

Illustration 7: *If A = {1, 3, 5, 7, 9}, B = {2, 4, 6, 8, 10} and C = {3, 4, 7, 8, 11, 12}, Show that (i) (A ∪ B) ∪ C = A ∪ (B ∪ C) and (ii) A ∪ (B ∩ C) = (A ∪ B) ∩ (A ∪ C)*

(Kerala: Section B April '97)

Solution: (i) $A \cup B = \{1, 3, 5, 7, 9\} \cup \{2, 4, 6, 8, 10\}$
$= \{1, 2, 3, 4, 5, 6, 7, 8, 9, 10\}$

$(A \cup B) \cup C = \{1, 2, 3, 4, 5, 6, 7, 8, 9, 10\} \cup$
$\{3, 4, 7, 8, 11, 12\} = \{1, 2, 3, 4, 5, 6, 7, 8, 9, 10, 11, 12\}$ . . . (a)

$B \cup C = \{2, 4, 6, 8, 10\} \cup \{3, 4, 7, 8, 11, 12\}$
$= \{2, 3, 4, 6, 7, 8, 10, 11, 12\}$

$A \cup (B \cup C) = \{1, 3, 5, 7, 9\} \cup \{2, 3, 4, 6, 7, 8, 10, 11, 12\}$
$= \{1, 2, 3, 4, 5, 6, 7, 8, 9, 10, 11, 12\}$ . . . (b)

It is clear from equations (a) and (b) that

$$(A \cup B) \cup C = A \cup (B \cup C)$$

(ii) $B \cap C = \{2, 4, 6, 8, 10\} \cap \{3, 4, 7, 8, 11, 12\} = \{4, 8\}$

$A \cup (B \cap C) = \{1, 3, 5, 7, 9\} \cup \{4, 8\}$
$= \{1, 3, 4, 5, 7, 8, 9\}$ . . . (a)

$A \cup B = \{1, 3, 5, 7, 9\} \text{ U } \{2, 4, 6, 8, 10\}$
$= \{1, 2, 3, 4, 5, 6, 7, 8, 9, 10\}$

$A \cup C = \{1, 3, 5, 7, 9\} \text{ U } \{3, 4, 7, 8, 11, 12\}$
$= \{1, 3, 4, 5, 7, 8, 9, 11, 12\}$

$(A \cup B) \cap (A \cup C) = \{1, 2, 3, 4, 5, 6, 7, 8, 9, 10\} \cap \{1, 3, 4, 5,$
$7, 8, 9, 11, 12\} = \{1, 3, 4, 5, 7, 8, 9\}$ . . . (b)

It is clear from (a) and (b) that

$A \cup (B \cap C) = (A \cup B) \cap (A \cup C)$

Illustration 8: *Let S = Universal set = {1, 2, 3, 4, 5, 6, 7, 8, 9, 10} Let A = {2, 4, 6, 8} and B = {1, 3, 5, 9}. What are: (i) $A \cup B$; (ii) $A \cap B$; (iii) A^c; (iv) $A^c \cap B^c$ and (v) $(A \cup B)^c$?*

Solution: (i) $A \cup B = \{2, 4, 6, 8\} \cup \{1, 3, 5, 9\}$

$= \{1, 2, 3, 4, 5, 6, 8, 9\}$

(ii) $A \cap B = \{2, 4, 6, 8\} \cap \{1, 3, 5, 9\} = \{\ \}$ i.e., Null or empty set.

(iii) $S = \{1, 2, 3, 4, 5, 6, 7, 8, 9, 10\}$, $A^c = \{1, 3, 5, 7, 9, 10\}$

(iv) $B^c = \{2, 4, 6, 7, 8, 10\}$

$A \cap B^c = \{2, 4, 6, 8\} \cap \{2, 4, 6, 7, 8, 10\} = \{2, 4, 6, 8\}$

(v) $A \cup B = \{1, 2, 3, 4, 5, 6, 8, 9\}$, $(A \cup B)^c = \{7, 10\}$

Illustration 9: *Explain union and intersection of sets using Venn diagram. If A = {0, 1, 75, 4} and B = {1, 6, 75, 8, 7} find $A \cup B$ and $A \cap B$.* (Kerala: Section B April '95)

Solution: $A \cup B = \{0, 1, 75, 4\} \cup \{1, 6, 75, 8, 7\}$

$= \{0, 1, 4, 6, 7, 8, 75\}$

$A \cap B = \{0, 1, 75, 4\} \cap \{1, 6, 75, 8, 7\} = \{1, 75\}$

Illustration 10: *If A = {1, 3, 5}, B = {2, 4, 6, 8} and C = {2, 5, 8, 0}, find (i) $(A \cup B) \cap (A \cup C)$; (ii) $(A \cup B \cup C)$*

(iii) $(A \cap B \cap C)$ (Kerala: Section B April '93)

Solution: (i) $A \cup B = \{1, 3, 5\} \cup \{2, 4, 6, 8\} = \{1, 2, 3, 4, 5, 6, 8\}$

$A \cup C = \{1, 3, 5\} \cup \{2, 5, 8, 0\} = \{1, 2, 3, 5, 8, 0\}$

$(A \cup B) \cap (A \cup C) = \{1, 2, 3, 4, 5, 6, 8\} \cap \{1, 2, 3, 5, 8, 0\}$

$= \{1, 2, 3, 5, 8\}$

(ii) $A \cup B = \{1, 2, 3, 4, 5, 6, 8\}$

$(A \cup B) \cup C = \{1, 2, 3, 4, 5, 6, 8\} \cup \{2, 5, 8, 0\}$

$= \{1, 2, 3, 4, 5, 6, 8, 0\}$

(iii) $(A \cap B \cap C) = \{1, 3, 5\} \cap \{2, 4, 6, 8\} \cap \{2, 5, 8, 0\}$

$= \{\ \}$ i.e., Null set or empty set.

Illustration 11: *If A = {1, 3, 5}, B = {2, 4, 6, 8} and C = {2, 5, 8, 10}. find (i) $(A \cup B) \cap (A \cup C)$ (ii) $(A \cup B \cup C)$ and (iii) $(A \cap B \cap C)$* (Kerala: Section B April '90)

Solution: **(i)** $A \cup B = \{1, 3, 5\} \cup \{2, 4, 6, 8\} = \{1, 2, 3, 4, 5, 6, 8\}$

$A \cup C = \{1, 3, 5\} \cup \{2, 5, 8, 10\} = \{1, 2, 3, 5, 8, 10\}$

$(A \cup B) \cap (A \cup C) = \{1, 2, 3, 4, 5, 6, 8\} \cap \{1, 2, 3, 5, 8, 10\}$

$= \{1, 2, 3, 5, 8\}$

(ii) $A \cup B \cup C = \{1, 3, 5\} \cup \{2, 4, 6, 8\} \cup \{2, 5, 8, 10\}$

$= \{1, 2, 3, 4, 5, 6, 8, 10\}$

(iii) $A \cap B \cap C = \{1, 3, 5\} \cap \{2, 4, 6, 8\} \cap \{2, 5, 8, 10\}$

$= \{\ \}$ i.e., Empty set or Null set.

Exercises

1. Define a Set. State the different methods of representation of set.
2. What is a Set? Explain briefly the different types of set.
3. What is Venn diagram? Give an example.
4. Distinguish between equal set and equivalent set with example.
5. Write short notes of the following.

   (a) Universal Set (b) Singleton Set (c) Null set
6. If $U = \{1, 2, 3, 4, 5, 6, 7, 8, 9, 10\}$ $A = \{2, 3, 5\}$, $B = \{1, 4, 5, 7\}$ and $C = \{5, 6, 8, 9\}$ find (i) $A \cup B \cup C$ (ii) $A \cap B \cap C$ (iii) $A \cup B$ (iv) $(A \cup B) \cap (B \cup C)$ [Ans: (i) {1, 2, 3, 4, 5, 6, 7, 8, 9} (ii) {5} (iii) {1, 2, 3, 4, 5, 7} (iv) {1, 4, 5, 7}]
7. If $U = \{2, 4, 6, 8, 10, 12, 14, 16\}$ $A = \{2, 4, 6\}$, $B = \{6, 10, 12\}$ and $C = \{10, 12, 14\}$ find (i) $A' \cup B$ (ii) $(A \cup B)'$ (iii) $A' \cap B'$ (iv) $A' \cup C'$ (v) $A' \cap C'$

   [Ans: (i) {3, 5, 6, 8, 10, 12, 14, 16} (ii) {8, 14, 16} (iii) {14, 16} (iv) {2, 4, 6, 8, 10, 12, 14, 16} (v) {16}]
8. If $U = \{5, 10, 15, 20, 25, 30, 35\}$, $A = \{5, 15, 25\}$, $B = \{30, 35\}$ and $C = \{10, 20, 30\}$ (i) $A' \cup B' \cup C'$ (ii) $A' \cap B' \cap C'$ (iii) $(A \cup B)'$ (iv) $(A \cap C)'$ [Ans: (i) {5, 10, 15, 20, 25, 30, 35} (ii) { } (iii) {10, 20} (iv) {5, 10, 15, 20, 25, 30, 35}
9. If $U = \{1, 2, 3, 4, 5, 6, 7, 8, 9, 10\}$ $A = \{2, 5, 7, 10\}$ and $B = \{1, 3, 5, 7\}$, Verify that (i) $(A - B) \cup (B - A) = (A \cup B) - (A \cap B)$

   (ii) $A - B = A - B' = B' - A'$
10. If $U = \{10, 20, 30, 40, 50, 60, 70, 80\}$, $A = \{10, 30, 40, 70\}$, $B = \{20, 30, 40, 80\}$ and $C = \{20, 30, 40, 60\}$, find (i) $A - B$ (ii) $A - C$ (iii) $B - C$ (iv) $A \cup B \cup C$ (v) $A \cap B \cap C$

    [Ans: (i) {10, 70} (ii) {10, 70} (iii) {80} (iv) {10, 20, 30, 40, 60, 70, 80} (v) {30, 40}]

◆ Chapter 18 ◆

Matrices and Determinants

I Definition

A matrix is a rectangular arrangement of number in rows and columns.

The numbers in a matrix are called its `elements'. The elements are of real or complex numbers.

Example: $x = \begin{bmatrix} 2 & -5 \\ 1 & 3 \end{bmatrix}$, $y = \begin{bmatrix} 3 & 2 & 4a \\ b & 0 & -5 \end{bmatrix}$, $z = \begin{bmatrix} 0 & 0 & 1 \\ 0 & 1 & 0 \\ 1 & 0 & 1 \end{bmatrix}$

The elements in x and z are with real numbers and the elements in y are both with real and complex numbers.

Dimension or Order of a Matrix

The number of rows in a matrix is represented with 'm' and the number of columns is represented with 'n'. Hence the matrix can be called $m \times n$ order matrix. The numbers m and n are called dimensions of the matrix.

II Types of Matrices

1. Rectangular Matrix: A matrix with any number of `$m$' rows and `n' columns is called rectangular matrix of $m \times n$ order.

Example: $\begin{bmatrix} 2 & 4 & 5 & 6 & 7 \\ 0 & 1 & 2 & 3 & 1 \\ 4 & 5 & 9 & 6 & 7 \end{bmatrix}$ is a 3×5 matrix.

2. Square Matrix: A matrix with equal number of rows and columns (*i.e.*, $m = n$) is called a square matrix.

Example: $\begin{bmatrix} 3 & 4 & 5 & 6 \\ 1 & 0 & 2 & 5 \\ 2 & 3 & 4 & 9 \\ 1 & 1 & 4 & 1 \end{bmatrix}$ 4×4 $\begin{bmatrix} a_{11} & a_{12} & a_{13} \\ a_{21} & a_{22} & a_{23} \\ a_{31} & a_{32} & a_{33} \end{bmatrix}$ 3×3

In the above example 4 columns and 4 rows are represented; and 3 columns and 3 rows are represented respectively.

3. Row Matrix: A matrix with a single row and any number of columns $(1 \times n)$ is called a row matrix.

Example: $A = [0\ \ 1\ \ 3\ \ 4],\ B = [2\ \ -4\ \ x],\ C = [1\ \ 2]$

A is 1×4 matrix; B is 1×3 matrix; C is 1×2 matrix.

4. Column Matrix: A matrix with a single column and any number of rows $(n \times 1)$ is called a column matrix.

Example: $$A = \begin{bmatrix} 3 \\ 4 \\ 2 \\ 5 \end{bmatrix},\ B = \begin{bmatrix} 4 \\ 0 \\ x \end{bmatrix},\ C = \begin{bmatrix} 2 \\ a \end{bmatrix}$$

Here A is 4×1 matrix; B is 3×1 matrix; C is 2×1matrix.

5. Diagonal Matrix: A diagonal matrix is a square matrix in which all the elements except those on the leading diagonal are zero.

Example: $$A = \begin{bmatrix} 5 & 0 & 0 \\ 0 & 2 & 0 \\ 0 & 0 & -3 \end{bmatrix},\ B = \begin{bmatrix} 3 & 0 \\ 0 & 2 \end{bmatrix}$$

6. Scalar Matrix: A diagonal matrix in which all the diagonal elements are equal is called the scalar matrix.

Example: $$A = \begin{bmatrix} 3 & 0 & 0 \\ 0 & 3 & 0 \\ 0 & 0 & 3 \end{bmatrix},\ B = \begin{bmatrix} 5 & 0 \\ 0 & 5 \end{bmatrix}$$

7. Unit Matrix or Identity Matrix: A diagonal matrix in which each diagonal element is unity (one) is called a unit matrix or identity matrix.

Example: $$A = \begin{bmatrix} 1 & 0 & 0 \\ 0 & 1 & 0 \\ 0 & 0 & 1 \end{bmatrix},\ B = \begin{bmatrix} 1 & 0 \\ 0 & 1 \end{bmatrix}$$

8. Zero Matrix or Null Matrix: A matrix in which every element is zero, is called a null matrix or zero matrix.

Example: $A = \begin{bmatrix} 0 & 0 & 0 & 0 \\ 0 & 0 & 0 & 0 \\ 0 & 0 & 0 & 0 \\ 0 & 0 & 0 & 0 \end{bmatrix}$, $B = \begin{bmatrix} 0 & 0 & 0 \\ 0 & 0 & 0 \\ 0 & 0 & 0 \end{bmatrix}$

9. Triangular Matrix: In triangular matrix, every element above (or below) the leading diagonal is zero. Triangular matrix may be upper triangular or lower triangular.

Example: $A = \begin{bmatrix} 3 & 4 & 5 \\ 0 & 5 & 7 \\ 0 & 0 & 8 \end{bmatrix}$, $B = \begin{bmatrix} 4 & 0 & 0 \\ 3 & 5 & 0 \\ 1 & 2 & 3 \end{bmatrix}$

A is upper triangular matrix and B is lower triangular matrix.

III Operations (or) Algebra of Matrices

The important operations of matrices are as follows.

(1) Equality of Matrices

(2) Addition of Matrices

(3) Subtracting of Matrices

(4) Multiplication of Matrices

(1) Equality of Matrices: Two matrices are said to be equal if they have the same order and all the corresponding elements are equal.

Example: (i) When $\begin{bmatrix} a & b & c \\ d & e & f \end{bmatrix} = \begin{bmatrix} 2 & 3 & 5 \\ 1 & 2 & 6 \end{bmatrix}$

it means, $a = 2$, $b = 3$, $c = 5$, $d = 1$, $e = 2$ and $f = 6$.

(ii) $A = \begin{bmatrix} 2 & 0 & 4 \\ 3 & 6 & 7 \end{bmatrix}$, $B = \begin{bmatrix} 1+1 & 3-3 & 3+1 \\ 2+1 & 3+3 & 3+4 \end{bmatrix}$

Here A and B are equal sets $(A = B)$

(2) Addition of Matrices: The sum of two matrices of the same order is the matrix whose elements are the sum of the corresponding elements of the given matrices.

Example: If $A = \begin{bmatrix} 3 & 2 & 4 \\ 0 & 5 & -3 \\ 2 & 9 & 7 \end{bmatrix}$ and $B = \begin{bmatrix} 2 & 0 & 1 \\ 4 & -2 & 2 \\ 1 & -5 & 4 \end{bmatrix}$

$$A + B = \begin{bmatrix} 3+2 & 2+0 & 4+1 \\ 0+4 & 5-2 & -3+2 \\ 2+1 & 9-5 & 7+4 \end{bmatrix} = \begin{bmatrix} 5 & 2 & 5 \\ 4 & 3 & -1 \\ 3 & 4 & 11 \end{bmatrix}$$

Example: *If* $A = \begin{bmatrix} 2 & 3 & 4 \\ 3 & -2 & 5 \\ 6 & -5 & 4 \\ 2 & 0 & 4 \end{bmatrix}$, $B = \begin{bmatrix} 1 & 1 & 5 \\ 3 & -2 & 4 \\ 6 & 5 & -4 \\ -2 & 1 & 1 \end{bmatrix}$ *Find out A + B*

Solution:

$$A + B = \begin{bmatrix} 2+1 & 3+1 & 4+5 \\ 3+3 & -2+(-2) & 5+4 \\ 6+6 & -5+5 & 4-4 \\ 2-2 & 0+1 & 4+1 \end{bmatrix} = \begin{bmatrix} 3 & 4 & 9 \\ 6 & -4 & 9 \\ 12 & 0 & 0 \\ 0 & 1 & 5 \end{bmatrix}$$

(3) Subtracting of Matrices: Subtraction of the matrices is also done in the same manner of addition of matrices. When the Matrix *B* is to be subtracted from Matrix *A*, the elements in Matrix *B* are subtracted from corresponding elements in Matrix *A*.

Example: $A = \begin{bmatrix} 4 & 3 & 0 \\ 3 & 2 & 7 \\ 6 & 5 & 4 \end{bmatrix}$, $B = \begin{bmatrix} 2 & 1 & 5 \\ 3 & 4 & 6 \\ 5 & 3 & 2 \end{bmatrix}$

$$A - B = \begin{bmatrix} 4-2 & 3-1 & 0-5 \\ 3-3 & 2-4 & 7-6 \\ 6-5 & 5-3 & 4-2 \end{bmatrix} = \begin{bmatrix} 2 & 2 & -5 \\ 0 & -2 & 1 \\ 1 & 2 & 2 \end{bmatrix}$$

Example: $A = \begin{bmatrix} 3 & -2 & 4 \\ 0 & 5 & 3 \\ 2 & 1 & 1 \end{bmatrix}$, $B = \begin{bmatrix} 2 & 3 & 5 \\ -2 & 5 & 6 \\ 1 & 1 & 1 \end{bmatrix}$ *Calculate (i) A + B*

(ii) A – B

Solution: (i) $A + B = \begin{bmatrix} 5 & 1 & 9 \\ -2 & 10 & 9 \\ 3 & 2 & 2 \end{bmatrix}$ (ii) $A - B = \begin{bmatrix} 1 & -5 & -1 \\ 2 & 0 & -3 \\ 1 & 0 & 0 \end{bmatrix}$

(4) Multiplication of Matrices: A matrix may be multiplied by any one number or any other matrix. Multiplication of a matrix by any one number is called a scalar multiplication. One matrix may also be multiplied by other matrix.

(i) Scalar Multiplication of Matrices: If A be any matrix and k, any scalar, then the matrix obtained by multiplying every element of A by k is said to be scalar multiplication. This is denoted by kA.

Example: $A = \begin{bmatrix} 1 & 5 & 6 \\ 3 & 2 & 1 \\ 5 & 6 & 7 \end{bmatrix}$ Calculate $3A$.

$$3A = \begin{bmatrix} 3\times1 & 3\times5 & 3\times6 \\ 3\times3 & 3\times2 & 3\times1 \\ 3\times5 & 3\times6 & 3\times7 \end{bmatrix} = \begin{bmatrix} 3 & 15 & 18 \\ 9 & 6 & 3 \\ 15 & 18 & 21 \end{bmatrix}$$

(ii) Multiplication of one matrix by another matrix: The product of two matrices is defined only when the number of columns of the first matrix is equal to the number of rows of the second.

Let $A = \begin{bmatrix} a_{11} & a_{12} & a_{13} \\ a_{21} & a_{22} & a_{23} \\ a_{31} & a_{32} & a_{33} \end{bmatrix}$ and $B = \begin{bmatrix} b_{11} & b_{12} \\ b_{21} & b_{22} \\ b_{31} & b_{32} \end{bmatrix}$

AB can be calculated since the number of rows in A equal to number of columns in matrix B. Therefore AB can be calculated as follows.

$$AB = \begin{bmatrix} a_{11}b_{11} + a_{12}b_{21} + a_{13}b_{31}, & a_{11}b_{12} + a_{12}b_{22} + a_{13}b_{32} \\ a_{21}b_{11} + a_{22}b_{21} + a_{23}b_{31}, & a_{21}b_{12} + a_{22}b_{22} + a_{23}b_{32} \\ a_{31}b_{11} + a_{32}b_{21} + a_{33}b_{31}, & a_{31}b_{12} + a_{32}b_{22} + a_{33}b_{32} \end{bmatrix}$$

Example: *Find the product of the following matrices.*

$$A = \begin{bmatrix} 2 & 3 & 4 \\ 1 & 0 & 3 \\ 2 & 5 & 1 \end{bmatrix}, \quad B = \begin{bmatrix} 1 & 1 & 0 \\ 2 & 1 & 3 \\ 3 & 2 & 1 \end{bmatrix}$$

Solution:

$$AB = \begin{bmatrix} 2.1 + 3.2 + 4.3 & 2.1 + 3.1 + 4.2 & 2.0 + 3.3 + 4.1 \\ 1.1 + 0.2 + 3.3 & 1.1 + 0.1 + 3.2 & 1.0 + 0.3 + 3.1 \\ 2.1 + 5.2 + 1.3 & 2.1 + 5.1 + 1.2 & 2.0 + 5.3 + 1.1 \end{bmatrix} = \begin{bmatrix} 20 & 13 & 13 \\ 10 & 7 & 3 \\ 15 & 9 & 16 \end{bmatrix}$$

Example: *Calculate AB, when A = [-3, 5, 7] and* $B = \begin{bmatrix} 3 \\ 1 \\ 5 \end{bmatrix}$

Solution: $AB = [-3.3 + 5.1 + 7.5] = 31$

Example: $X = \begin{bmatrix} 3 & 4 \\ 5 & 1 \end{bmatrix}$ *and* $Y = \begin{bmatrix} 3 \\ 2 \end{bmatrix}$

Solution: $XY = \begin{bmatrix} 3.3 + 4.2 \\ 5.3 + 1.2 \end{bmatrix} = \begin{bmatrix} 17 \\ 17 \end{bmatrix}$

Example: *If* $X = \begin{bmatrix} 2 & 4 \\ -2 & 3 \end{bmatrix}$ *and* $Y = \begin{bmatrix} -2 \\ 16 \end{bmatrix}$ *find A, when* $XA = Y$

Solution: Let $A = \begin{bmatrix} a \\ b \end{bmatrix}$

$$XA = \begin{bmatrix} 2 & 4 \\ -2 & 3 \end{bmatrix} \begin{bmatrix} a \\ b \end{bmatrix} = \begin{bmatrix} 2a + 4b \\ -2a + 3b \end{bmatrix}$$

Since $XA = Y$

$$\begin{bmatrix} 2a + 4b \\ -2a + 3b \end{bmatrix} = \begin{bmatrix} -2 \\ 16 \end{bmatrix}$$

i.e., $2a + 4b = -2$ ... (i)

$-2a + 3b = 16$ ... (ii)

(i) + (ii) $7b = 14$

$$b = \frac{14}{7} = 2$$

(i) $2a + 4.2 = -2$

$2a = -10$

$$a = \frac{-10}{2} = -5 \quad \therefore A = \begin{bmatrix} -5 \\ 2 \end{bmatrix}$$

Example: If $X = \begin{bmatrix} 3 & 1 \\ 5 & 2 \end{bmatrix}$ *and XA is a identity (unit) matrix of the order 2×2, find the matrix A.*

Solution: Let $A = \begin{bmatrix} a & b \\ c & d \end{bmatrix}$ XA is an identity matrix with 2×2 order.

$$\therefore XA = \begin{bmatrix} 1 & 0 \\ 0 & 1 \end{bmatrix}$$

i.e., $XA = \begin{bmatrix} 3 & 1 \\ 5 & 2 \end{bmatrix} \begin{bmatrix} a & b \\ c & d \end{bmatrix} = \begin{bmatrix} 3a + 1c & 3b + 1d \\ 5a + 2c & 5b + 2d \end{bmatrix}$

$$\therefore \begin{bmatrix} 3a + c & 3b + d \\ 5a + 2c & 5b + 2d \end{bmatrix} = \begin{bmatrix} 1 & 0 \\ 0 & 1 \end{bmatrix}$$

i.e., $3a + c = 1$ ... (i)

$5a + 2c = 0$ ... (ii)

$3b + d = 0$ ... (iii)

$5b + 2d = 1$ ... (iv)

(i) $\times 2$ $6a + 2c = 2$ ... (v)

(v) – (ii) gives $a = 2$; (i) $3(2) + c = 1$, $\therefore c = -5$

(iii)×2 $\quad 6b + 2d = 0 \quad$ ... (vi)

$\quad 5b + 2d = 1 \quad$ ... (iv)

(vi) – (iv) $\quad b = -1$

(iii) $\quad 5(-1) + 2d = 1$

$$2d = 1+5$$

$$d = 3$$

$a = 2, b = -1, c = -5, d = 3 \qquad \therefore A = \begin{bmatrix} 2 & -1 \\ -5 & 3 \end{bmatrix}$

IV Properties of Matrix Multiplication

(1) Matrix multiplication is associative: If *A*, *B* and *C* are three matrices, and *AB*, *BC* are defined, then

$$A(BC) = (AB)C$$

(2) Matrix multiplication is distributive: If *A*, *B* and *C* are three matrices of proper orders, then

$$A(B + C) = AB + AC \text{ and } (B + C)A = BA + CA$$

(3) Matrix multiplication is in general, not commutative: If A and B are two matrices such that AB and BA are defined, then AB ≠ BA in general.

(1) Matrix multiplication is associative

Example: *If* $A = \begin{bmatrix} 1 & 4 \\ -2 & 3 \end{bmatrix}, \; B = \begin{bmatrix} 3 & 2 & 0 \\ -2 & -1 & 5 \end{bmatrix}, \; and \; C = \begin{bmatrix} 1 & 2 \\ -3 & 2 \\ 0 & 2 \end{bmatrix}$

verify that A (BC) = (AB) C

Solution: $BC = \begin{bmatrix} 3 & 2 & 0 \\ -2 & -1 & 5 \end{bmatrix} \; C = \begin{bmatrix} 1 & 2 \\ -3 & 2 \\ 0 & 2 \end{bmatrix}$

$$= \begin{bmatrix} 3.1+2.(-3)+0.0 & 3.2+2.2+0.2 \\ (-2).1+(-1)(-3)+5.0 & (-2).2+(-1).2+5.2 \end{bmatrix}$$

$$= \begin{bmatrix} -3 & 10 \\ 1 & 4 \end{bmatrix}$$

$$\therefore A(BC) = \begin{bmatrix} 1 & 4 \\ -2 & 3 \end{bmatrix} \begin{bmatrix} -3 & 10 \\ 1 & 4 \end{bmatrix}$$

$$= \begin{bmatrix} 1(-3)+4.1 & 1.10+4.4 \\ (-2)(-3)+3.1 & (-2)10+3.4 \end{bmatrix} = \begin{bmatrix} 1 & 26 \\ 9 & -8 \end{bmatrix}$$

$$(AB) = \begin{bmatrix} 1 & 4 \\ -2 & 3 \end{bmatrix} \begin{bmatrix} 3 & 2 & 0 \\ -2 & -1 & 5 \end{bmatrix}$$

$$= \begin{bmatrix} 1.3+4(-2) & 1.2+4(-1) & 1.0+4.5 \\ (-2).3+3(-2) & (-2)2+3(-1) & (-2)0+3.5 \end{bmatrix}$$

$$= \begin{bmatrix} -5 & -2 & 20 \\ -12 & -7 & 15 \end{bmatrix}$$

$$\therefore \ (AB)\,C = \begin{bmatrix} -5 & -2 & 20 \\ -12 & -7 & 15 \end{bmatrix} \begin{bmatrix} 1 & 2 \\ -3 & 2 \\ 0 & 2 \end{bmatrix}$$

$$= \begin{bmatrix} (-5).1+(-2)(-3)+20.0 & (-5).2+(-2).2+20.2 \\ (-12).1+(-7)(-3)+15.0 & (-12).2+(-7).2+15.2 \end{bmatrix}$$

$$= \begin{bmatrix} 1 & 26 \\ 9 & -8 \end{bmatrix}$$

Hence, it is proved that *(AB) C = A (BC)*

(2) Matrix multiplication is distributive

Example: *If* $A = \begin{bmatrix} 2 & -1 \\ -3 & 5 \end{bmatrix}$, $B = \begin{bmatrix} 2 & 1 & 0 \\ 4 & -3 & 5 \end{bmatrix}$ *and*

$C = \begin{bmatrix} 2 & 1 & 0 \\ -1 & 3 & 4 \end{bmatrix}$ *prove that* $A\,(B+C) = AB + AC$

Solution: $B + C = \begin{bmatrix} 2 & 1 & 0 \\ 4 & -3 & 5 \end{bmatrix} + \begin{bmatrix} 2 & 1 & 0 \\ -1 & 3 & 4 \end{bmatrix} = \begin{bmatrix} 4 & 2 & 0 \\ 3 & 0 & 9 \end{bmatrix}$

$$A\,(B+C) = \begin{bmatrix} 2 & -1 \\ -3 & 5 \end{bmatrix} \begin{bmatrix} 4 & 2 & 0 \\ 3 & 0 & 9 \end{bmatrix}$$

$$= \begin{bmatrix} 2.4+(-1).3 & 2.2+(-1).0 & 2.0+(-1).9 \\ (-3).4+5.3 & (-3).2+5.0 & (-3).0+5.9 \end{bmatrix}$$

$$= \begin{bmatrix} 5 & 4 & -9 \\ 3 & -6 & 45 \end{bmatrix}$$

$$\text{AB} = \begin{bmatrix} 2 & -1 \\ -3 & 5 \end{bmatrix} \begin{bmatrix} 2 & 1 & 0 \\ 4 & -3 & 5 \end{bmatrix}$$

$$= \begin{bmatrix} 2.2+(-1).4 & 2.1+(-1)(-3) & 2.0+(-1).5 \\ (-3).2+5.4 & (-3).1+5(-3) & (-3).0+5.5 \end{bmatrix}$$

$$= \begin{bmatrix} 0 & 5 & -5 \\ 14 & -18 & 25 \end{bmatrix}$$

$$\text{AC} = \begin{bmatrix} 2 & -1 \\ -3 & 5 \end{bmatrix} \begin{bmatrix} 2 & 1 & 0 \\ -1 & 3 & 4 \end{bmatrix}$$

$$= \begin{bmatrix} 2.2+(-1)(-1) & 2.1+(-1)3 & 2.0+(-1).4 \\ (-3).2+5(-1) & (-3).1+5.3 & (-3).0+5.4 \end{bmatrix}$$

$$= \begin{bmatrix} 5 & -1 & -4 \\ -11 & 12 & 20 \end{bmatrix}$$

$$\text{AB} + \text{AC} = \begin{bmatrix} 0 & 5 & -5 \\ 14 & -18 & 25 \end{bmatrix} + \begin{bmatrix} 5 & -1 & -4 \\ -11 & 12 & 20 \end{bmatrix} = \begin{bmatrix} 5 & 4 & -9 \\ 3 & -6 & 45 \end{bmatrix}$$

Since $A(B+C)$ is also equal to $\begin{bmatrix} 5 & 4 & -9 \\ 3 & -6 & 45 \end{bmatrix}$ it is proved that

$$\text{A (B + C) = AB + AC}$$

(3) Matrix multiplication is not commutative

Example: $A = \begin{bmatrix} 3 & 2 \\ -1 & 4 \end{bmatrix}$ *and* $B = \begin{bmatrix} 1 & 4 \\ 2 & 3 \end{bmatrix}$ *prove that* $AB \neq BA$

Solution:

$$AB = \begin{bmatrix} 3 & 2 \\ -1 & 4 \end{bmatrix} \begin{bmatrix} 1 & 4 \\ 2 & 3 \end{bmatrix} = \begin{bmatrix} 3.1+2.2 & 3.4+2.3 \\ (-1).1+4.2 & (-1).4+4.3 \end{bmatrix} = \begin{bmatrix} 7 & 18 \\ 7 & 8 \end{bmatrix}$$

$$BA = \begin{bmatrix} 1 & 4 \\ 2 & 3 \end{bmatrix} \begin{bmatrix} 3 & 2 \\ -1 & 4 \end{bmatrix} = \begin{bmatrix} 1.3+4(-1) & (1.2)+4.4 \\ 2.3+3(-1) & 2.2+3.4 \end{bmatrix} = \begin{bmatrix} -1 & 18 \\ 3 & 16 \end{bmatrix}$$

Hence, it is proved that $AB \neq BA$

Example: If $A = \begin{bmatrix} 1 & -2 \\ -4 & 5 \end{bmatrix}$ *and* $B = \begin{bmatrix} 2 & 1 \\ 1 & 3 \end{bmatrix}$ *Prove that* $AB \neq BA$

Solution:

$$AB = \begin{bmatrix} 1 & -2 \\ -4 & 5 \end{bmatrix} \begin{bmatrix} 2 & 1 \\ 1 & 3 \end{bmatrix} = \begin{bmatrix} 1.2 + (-2).1 & 1.1 + (-2).3 \\ (-4).2 + 5.1 & (-4).1 + 5.3 \end{bmatrix} = \begin{bmatrix} 0 & -5 \\ -3 & 11 \end{bmatrix}$$

$$BA = \begin{bmatrix} 2 & 1 \\ 1 & 3 \end{bmatrix} \begin{bmatrix} 1 & -2 \\ -4 & 5 \end{bmatrix} = \begin{bmatrix} 2.1 + 1(-4) & 2(-2) + 1.5 \\ 1.1 + 3(-4) & 1(-2) + 3.5 \end{bmatrix} = \begin{bmatrix} -2 & 1 \\ -11 & 13 \end{bmatrix}$$

Hence, it is proved that $AB \neq BA$

Example: *If* $A = \begin{bmatrix} 1 & 1 & 0 \\ 2 & -2 & 1 \end{bmatrix}$ *and* $B = \begin{bmatrix} 1 & 3 \\ 2 & 1 \\ -1 & 1 \end{bmatrix}$ *prove that* $AB \neq BA$

Solution: $AB = \begin{bmatrix} 1 & 1 & 0 \\ 2 & -2 & 1 \end{bmatrix} \begin{bmatrix} 1 & 3 \\ 2 & 1 \\ -1 & 1 \end{bmatrix}$

$$= \begin{bmatrix} 1.1+1.2+0(-1) & 1.3+1.1+0.1 \\ 2.1+(-2).2+1(-1) & 2.3+(-2).1+1.1 \end{bmatrix}$$

$$= \begin{bmatrix} 3 & 4 \\ -3 & 5 \end{bmatrix}$$

$$BA = \begin{bmatrix} 1 & 3 \\ 2 & 1 \\ -1 & 1 \end{bmatrix} \begin{bmatrix} 1 & 1 & 0 \\ 2 & -2 & 1 \end{bmatrix}$$

$$= \begin{bmatrix} 1.1+3.2 & 1.1+3(-2) & 1.0+3.1 \\ 2.1+1.2 & 2.1+1(-2) & 2.0+1.1 \\ (-1).1+1.2 & (-1).1+1(-2) & (-1).0+1.1 \end{bmatrix}$$

$$= \begin{bmatrix} 7 & -5 & 3 \\ 4 & 0 & 1 \\ 1 & -3 & 1 \end{bmatrix}$$

Since AB is 2×2 matrix and BA is 3×3 matrix $AB \neq BA$.

Transpose of a Matrix

The matrix obtained by interchanging the rows and columns of a matrix, is called Transpose of a matrix. The transpose of a matrix A is denoted by A^t or A'.

Example: *Find the transpose of the matrix.* $A = \begin{bmatrix} 1 & 5 & 3 \\ 2 & 0 & 6 \\ 4 & 7 & 8 \end{bmatrix}$

Solution: $A' = \begin{bmatrix} 1 & 2 & 4 \\ 5 & 0 & 7 \\ 3 & 6 & 8 \end{bmatrix}$

Example: *Find the transpose of the matrix* $A = \begin{bmatrix} 2 & 3 & 0 \\ 1 & 4 & 3 \end{bmatrix}$

Solution: $A' = \begin{bmatrix} 2 & 1 \\ 3 & 4 \\ 0 & 3 \end{bmatrix}$

Properties of a Transpose Matrix

(i) $(A')' = A$ (ii) $(A \pm B)' = A' \pm B'$

(iii) $(AB)' = B'A'$; $(ABC)' = C'B'A'$ (iv) $(KA)' = KA'$

$$B'A' = \begin{bmatrix} 1 & -5 \\ 0 & 6 \end{bmatrix}\begin{bmatrix} 3 & -1 \\ 2 & 4 \end{bmatrix} = \begin{bmatrix} 1.3+(-5).2 & 1(-1)+(-5).4 \\ 0.3+6.2 & 0(-1)+6.4 \end{bmatrix}$$

$$= \begin{bmatrix} -7 & -21 \\ 12 & 24 \end{bmatrix}$$

Hence, it is proved that $(AB)' = B'A'$

Example: *If* $A = \begin{bmatrix} 3 & 2 \\ 4 & 1 \end{bmatrix}$, $B = \begin{bmatrix} 1 & -1 \\ 0 & 2 \end{bmatrix}$ *show that*

$$(2A + 5B)' = 2A' + 5B'$$

Solution: $2A = 2\begin{bmatrix} 3 & 2 \\ 4 & 1 \end{bmatrix} = \begin{bmatrix} 6 & 4 \\ 8 & 2 \end{bmatrix}$

$$5B = 5\begin{bmatrix} 1 & -1 \\ 0 & 2 \end{bmatrix} = \begin{bmatrix} 5 & -5 \\ 0 & 10 \end{bmatrix}$$

$$2A' = \begin{bmatrix} 6 & 8 \\ 4 & 2 \end{bmatrix},\ 5B' = \begin{bmatrix} 5 & 0 \\ -5 & 10 \end{bmatrix}$$

$$(2A + 5B) = \begin{bmatrix} 6 & 4 \\ 8 & 2 \end{bmatrix} + \begin{bmatrix} 5 & -5 \\ 0 & 10 \end{bmatrix} = \begin{bmatrix} 11 & -1 \\ 8 & 12 \end{bmatrix}$$

$$(2A + 5B)' = \begin{bmatrix} 11 & 8 \\ -1 & 12 \end{bmatrix}$$

$$2A' + 5B' = \begin{bmatrix} 6 & 8 \\ 4 & 2 \end{bmatrix} + \begin{bmatrix} 5 & 0 \\ -5 & 10 \end{bmatrix} = \begin{bmatrix} 11 & 8 \\ -1 & 12 \end{bmatrix}$$

Hence, it is proved that $(2A + 5B)' = 2A' + 5B'$

V Determinants

Determinant is the association of a unique real number with a square matrix. Hence, determinant is possible only for a square matrix.

The determinant of a square matrix A is denoted as $|A|$ or Δ.

Determinant of Square Matrix of Second Order

$$\text{If } A=\begin{bmatrix} a & b \\ c & d \end{bmatrix},\quad |A|=\begin{vmatrix} a & b \\ c & d \end{vmatrix}=ad-cb$$

Example: *Calculate determinant of* $A=\begin{bmatrix} 3 & 5 \\ 6 & 4 \end{bmatrix}$

Solution: $|A|=\begin{vmatrix} 3 & 5 \\ 6 & 4 \end{vmatrix}=3\times 4-6\times 5=12-30=-18$

Determinant of Square Matrix of Third Order

There are two methods to find out the determinants of the Matrix of Third Oder.

They are (i) Laplace Method of Expansion and

(ii) Sarrus Diagram.

(i) Laplace Method of Expansion

$$\text{If } A=\begin{vmatrix} a & b & c \\ d & e & f \\ g & h & i \end{vmatrix}$$

$$|A|=\begin{vmatrix} a & b & c \\ d & e & f \\ g & h & i \end{vmatrix}=a\begin{vmatrix} e & f \\ h & i \end{vmatrix}-b\begin{vmatrix} d & f \\ g & i \end{vmatrix}+c\begin{vmatrix} d & e \\ g & h \end{vmatrix}$$

$$=a(ei-hf)-b(di-gf)+c(dh-ge)$$

$$=aei-ahf-bdi+bgf+cdh-cge$$

Example: Calculate determinant of the matrix, $A=\begin{bmatrix} 3 & 2 & 5 \\ 1 & 4 & 6 \\ 2 & 1 & 3 \end{bmatrix}$

Solution: $|A|=\begin{vmatrix} 3 & 2 & 5 \\ 1 & 4 & 6 \\ 2 & 1 & 3 \end{vmatrix}=3\begin{vmatrix} 4 & 6 \\ 1 & 3 \end{vmatrix}-2\begin{vmatrix} 1 & 6 \\ 2 & 3 \end{vmatrix}+5\begin{vmatrix} 1 & 4 \\ 2 & 1 \end{vmatrix}$

$$= 3(4.3 - 1.6) - 2(1.3 - 2.6) + 5(1.1 - 2.4)$$

$$= 3.6 - 2(-9) + 5(-7) = 18 + 18 - 35 = 1$$

Example: Calculate determinant of the matrix, $A = \begin{bmatrix} 1 & 8 & 4 \\ 9 & 3 & 5 \\ 2 & 6 & 7 \end{bmatrix}$

Solution: Determinant of $A = \begin{vmatrix} 1 & 8 & 4 \\ 9 & 3 & 5 \\ 2 & 6 & 7 \end{vmatrix}$

$$= 1(3.7 - 6.5) - 8(9.7 - 2.5) + 4(9.6 - 2.3)$$

$$= -9 - 8.53 + 4.48$$

$$= -9 - 424 + 192 = -241$$

(ii) Sarrus Diagram: To draw the Sarrus Diagram 3×3 matrix should be converted into 5×3 matrix by adding this first two columns (1 & 2) in the fifth and sixth place.

Example: If $A = \begin{bmatrix} 3 & 2 & 1 \\ 1 & 5 & 7 \\ 8 & 9 & 6 \end{bmatrix}$ then Sarrus Diagram is written as,

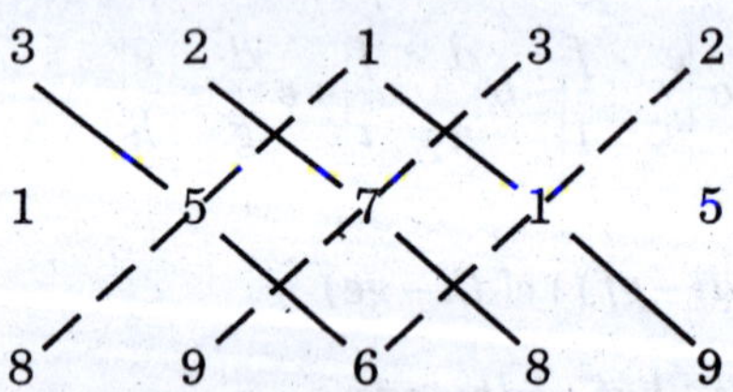

Multiply the terms indicated in the lines Give '+' sign to the figures of the thick lines ($\rightarrow$) and '–' sign to the figures of the dotted lines (.,....). Add all the 6 terms, so obtained to get the Determinant.

Hence, $|A| = (3 \times 5 \times 6) + (2 \times 7 \times 8) + (1 \times 1 \times 9)$

$$-(8 \times 5 \times 1) - (9 \times 7 \times 3) - (6 \times 1 \times 2)$$

$$= 90 + 112 + 9 - 40 - 189 - 12$$

$$= 211 - 241 = -30$$

Example: *Calculate determinant of the matrix,* $A = \begin{bmatrix} 2 & 5 & 0 \\ -1 & 3 & 2 \\ 1 & 4 & 5 \end{bmatrix}$ *by Sarrus Diagram*

Solution: *Sarrus Diagram*

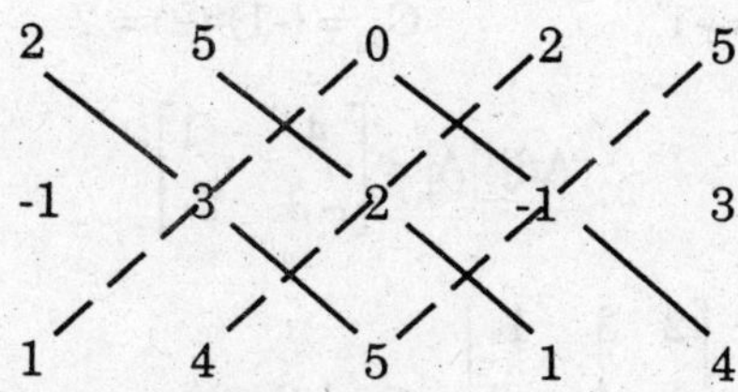

$$|A| = (2\times3\times5) + (5\times2\times1) + 0(-1)(4)$$

$$-(1\times3\times0) - (4\times2\times2) - (5(-1).5)$$

$$= 30 + 10 + 0 - 0 - 16 + 25 = 65 - 16 = 49$$

VI Inverse of a Matrix

Inverse of a matrix is the square matrix of the same order.

All square matrices do not have inverses. Only square matrices which are non-singular have inverses.

The inverse is unique *i.e.*, a given matrix has only one inverse.

Inverse of a matrix is useful in solving simultaneous equations, input-output analysis and regression analysis.

Meaning: For a square matrix *A*, if there exists a square matrix *B* such that *AB* = *BA* = *I*, then *B* is called the inverse of *A* or reciprocal of A. The inverse of A is denoted by A^{-1}.

$$A^{-1} = \frac{1}{|A|} \text{(Adjoint of A)}.$$

Inverse of square matrix exists only if $|A| \neq 0$.

Calculation of Inverse of a Matrix by Adjoint Method

Example: *If* $A = \begin{bmatrix} 2 & 1 \\ 3 & 4 \end{bmatrix}$ *find the inverse of A or* A^{-1}

Solution: $|A| = (2 \times 4) - (3 \times 1) = 3 \neq 0$. Hence, Matrix A has an inverse.

Calculation of Co-factors:

$C_{11} = (-1)^2(4) = 4,$ $\qquad C_{12} = (-1)^3(3) = -3$

$C_{21} = (-1)^3(1) = -1,$ $\qquad C_{22} = (-1)^4(2) = 2$

$$\therefore \text{Adj } |A| = \begin{bmatrix} 4 & -1 \\ -3 & 2 \end{bmatrix}$$

Example: *If* $A = \begin{bmatrix} 2 & 3 & 1 \\ 1 & 4 & -3 \\ 2 & 1 & 1 \end{bmatrix}$, *find the inverse of A.*

Solution: $|A| = \begin{vmatrix} 2 & 3 & 1 \\ 1 & 4 & -3 \\ 2 & 1 & 1 \end{vmatrix} = 2\begin{vmatrix} 4 & -3 \\ 1 & 1 \end{vmatrix} - 3\begin{vmatrix} 1 & -3 \\ 2 & 1 \end{vmatrix} + 1\begin{vmatrix} 1 & 4 \\ 2 & 1 \end{vmatrix}$

$$= 2(4.1 - 1(-3)) - 3(1.1 - 2(-3) + 1(1.1 - 2.4)$$

$$= 2(7) - 3(7) + 1(-7) = 14 - 21 - 7 = -14 \neq 0$$

Hence, Matrix A has an inverse.

Calculation of Co-factors

$$C_{11} = -1^2 \begin{vmatrix} 4 & -3 \\ 1 & 1 \end{vmatrix} = 1(4.1 - 1(-3)) = 7$$

$$C_{12} = -1^3 \begin{vmatrix} 1 & -3 \\ 2 & 1 \end{vmatrix} = -1(1.1 - 2(-3)) = -7$$

$$C_{13} = -1^4 \begin{vmatrix} 1 & 4 \\ 2 & 1 \end{vmatrix} = 1(1.1 - 2.4) = -7$$

$$C_{21} = -1^3 \begin{vmatrix} 3 & 1 \\ 1 & 1 \end{vmatrix} = -1(3.1 - 1.1) = -2$$

$$C_{22} = -1^4 \begin{vmatrix} 2 & 1 \\ 2 & 1 \end{vmatrix} = 1(2.1 - 2.1) = 0$$

$$C_{23} = -1^5 \begin{vmatrix} 2 & 3 \\ 2 & 1 \end{vmatrix} = -1(2.1 - 2.3) = 4$$

$$C_{31} = -1^4 \begin{vmatrix} 3 & 1 \\ 4 & -3 \end{vmatrix} = 1(3(-3) - 4.1) = -13$$

$$C_{32} = -1^5 \begin{vmatrix} 2 & 1 \\ 1 & -3 \end{vmatrix} = -1(2(-3) - 1.1) = 7$$

$$C_{33} = -1^6 \begin{vmatrix} 2 & 3 \\ 2 & 1 \end{vmatrix} = 1(2.1 - 2.3) = -4$$

$$\text{Co-factor of } A = \begin{bmatrix} 7 & -7 & -7 \\ -2 & 0 & 4 \\ -13 & 7 & -4 \end{bmatrix}$$

$$\therefore \text{Adj } A = \begin{bmatrix} 7 & -2 & -13 \\ -7 & 0 & 7 \\ -7 & 4 & -4 \end{bmatrix}$$

Note: $\Big|C_{11} = -1^{1+1} = -1^2;\ C_{12} = -1^{1+2} = -1^3;\ C_{11} = -1^{1+1} = -1^2;$

$C_{13} = -1^{1+3} = -1^4;\ C_{21} = -1^{2+1} = -1^3;\ C_{22} = -1^{2+2} = -1^4;$

$C_{23} = -1^{2+3} = -1^5;\ C_{31} = -1^{3+1} = -1^4;\ C_{32} = -1^{3+2} = -1^5;$

$C_{33} = -1^{3+3} = -1^6\Big|$

Solution for Simultaneous Equations

Simultaneous Equations can be solved with the help of matrix technique on the following two methods.

(i) Co-factor or adjoint method and (ii) Cramer's Rule

(i) Co-factor or Adjoint Method: Let, $a_1x + b_1y = c_1$

$$a_2x + b_2y = c_2$$

are the two simultaneous equations. These equations can be written by matrix technique as,

$$\begin{bmatrix} a_1 & b_1 \\ a_2 & b_2 \end{bmatrix} \begin{bmatrix} x \\ y \end{bmatrix} = \begin{bmatrix} c_1 \\ c_2 \end{bmatrix} \quad i.e., \ AX = B$$

On the following basis the equations can be solved.

$$X = A^{-1}B, \qquad A^{-1} = \frac{\text{Adj A}}{|A|}$$

Example: *Solve completely the following equations by using matrices. 2x + 3y = 12, x + 5y = 12.*

Solution: $2x + 3y = 12,\ x + 5y = 12$ can be written as

$$\begin{bmatrix} 2 & 3 \\ 1 & 5 \end{bmatrix} \begin{bmatrix} x \\ y \end{bmatrix} = \begin{bmatrix} 12 \\ 13 \end{bmatrix}$$

$$\therefore AX = B$$

$$X = A^{-1}B$$

$$A^{-1} = \frac{\text{Adj A}}{|A|}$$

$$|A| = \begin{vmatrix} 2 & 3 \\ 1 & 5 \end{vmatrix} = (2 \times 5) - (1 \times 3) = 7$$

$$\text{Adjoint of A} = \begin{bmatrix} 5 & -3 \\ -1 & 2 \end{bmatrix}$$

$$[i.e.,\ C_{11} = (-1)^2(5) = 5\ ,\ \ C_{12} = (-1)^3(1) = -1\ ,$$

$$C_{21} = (-1)^3(3) = -3, C_{22} = (-1)^4(2) = 2]$$

$$A^{-1} = \frac{1}{7}\begin{bmatrix} 5 & -3 \\ -1 & 2 \end{bmatrix}, \ X = A^{-1}B$$

$$\begin{bmatrix} x \\ y \end{bmatrix} = \frac{1}{7}\begin{bmatrix} 5 & -3 \\ -1 & 2 \end{bmatrix}\begin{bmatrix} 12 \\ 13 \end{bmatrix} = \frac{1}{7}\begin{bmatrix} 60-39 \\ -12+26 \end{bmatrix} = \frac{1}{7}\begin{bmatrix} 21 \\ 14 \end{bmatrix} = \begin{bmatrix} 3 \\ 2 \end{bmatrix}$$

i.e., $x = 3$ and $y = 2$

Example: *Solve the following equations on the bais of matrix technique.* $2x + y + 3z = 19$, $x - 3y + 5z = 13$, $3x + 2y + z = 16$.

Solution: The three equations can be expressed as

$$\begin{bmatrix} 2 & 1 & 3 \\ 1 & -3 & 5 \\ 3 & 2 & 1 \end{bmatrix} \begin{bmatrix} x \\ y \\ z \end{bmatrix} = \begin{bmatrix} 19 \\ 13 \\ 16 \end{bmatrix}$$

$$\text{AX} = \text{B}, \quad \text{X} = \text{A}^{-1}B, \quad \text{A}^{-1} = \frac{\text{Adj A}}{|\text{A}|}$$

$$|\text{A}| = \begin{bmatrix} 2 & 1 & 3 \\ 1 & -3 & 5 \\ 3 & 2 & 1 \end{bmatrix} = 2\begin{bmatrix} -3 & 5 \\ 2 & 1 \end{bmatrix} - 1\begin{bmatrix} 1 & 5 \\ 3 & 1 \end{bmatrix} + 3\begin{bmatrix} 1 & -3 \\ 3 & 2 \end{bmatrix}$$

$$= 2(-3-10) - 1(1-15) + 3(2+9)$$

$$= 2(-13) - 1(-14) + 3(11) = -26 + 14 + 33 = 21$$

Calculation of Co-factors:

$$\text{C}_{11} = -1^2 \begin{bmatrix} -3 & 5 \\ 2 & 1 \end{bmatrix} = 1(-3-10) = -13$$

$$\text{C}_{12} = -1^3 \begin{bmatrix} 1 & 5 \\ 3 & 1 \end{bmatrix} = -1(1-15) = 14$$

$$\text{C}_{13} = -1^4 \begin{bmatrix} 1 & -3 \\ 3 & 2 \end{bmatrix} = 1(2+9) = 11$$

$$\text{C}_{21} = -1^3 \begin{bmatrix} 1 & 3 \\ 2 & 1 \end{bmatrix} = -1(1-6) = 5$$

$$\text{C}_{22} = -1^4 \begin{bmatrix} 2 & 3 \\ 3 & 1 \end{bmatrix} = 1(2-9) = -7$$

$$\text{C}_{23} = -1^5 \begin{bmatrix} 2 & 1 \\ 3 & 2 \end{bmatrix} = -1(4-3) = -1$$

$$\text{C}_{31} = -1^4 \begin{bmatrix} 1 & 3 \\ -3 & 5 \end{bmatrix} = 1(5+9) = 14$$

$$C_{32} = -1^5 \begin{bmatrix} 2 & 3 \\ 1 & 5 \end{bmatrix} = -1(10-3) = -7$$

$$C_{33} = -1^6 \begin{bmatrix} 2 & 1 \\ 1 & -3 \end{bmatrix} = 1(-6-1) = -7$$

$$\text{Co-factor of } A = \begin{bmatrix} -13 & 14 & 11 \\ 5 & -7 & -1 \\ 14 & -7 & -7 \end{bmatrix}$$

$$\text{Adj } A = \begin{bmatrix} -13 & 5 & 14 \\ 14 & -7 & -7 \\ 11 & -1 & -7 \end{bmatrix}$$

$$\therefore A^{-1} = \frac{\text{Adj } A}{|A|} = \frac{1}{21}\begin{bmatrix} -13 & 5 & 14 \\ 14 & -7 & -7 \\ 11 & -1 & -7 \end{bmatrix}$$

$$X = A^{-1}B = \frac{1}{21}\begin{bmatrix} -13 & 5 & 14 \\ 14 & -7 & -7 \\ 11 & -1 & -7 \end{bmatrix}\begin{bmatrix} 19 \\ 13 \\ 16 \end{bmatrix}$$

$$= \frac{1}{21}\begin{bmatrix} -13.19 + 5.13 + 14.16 \\ 14.19 + -7.13 + -7.16 \\ 11.19 + -1.13 + -7.16 \end{bmatrix} = \frac{1}{21}\begin{bmatrix} 42 \\ 63 \\ 84 \end{bmatrix} = \begin{bmatrix} 2 \\ 3 \\ 4 \end{bmatrix}$$

$\therefore x = 2;\ y = 3;\ z = 4$

(ii) Cramer's Rule: Under Cramer's Rule the solution for simultaneous equations can be calculated as

$$x = \frac{|A_1|}{|A|},\ y = \frac{|A_2|}{|A|},\ z = \frac{|A_3|}{|A|}$$

Let $a_1x + b_1y + c_1z = d_1$

$a_2x + b_2y + c_2z = d_2$

$a_3x + b_3y + c_3z = d_3$

then, $A = \begin{bmatrix} a_1 & b_1 & c_1 \\ a_2 & b_2 & c_2 \\ a_3 & b_3 & c_3 \end{bmatrix}$ $A_1 = \begin{bmatrix} d_1 & b_1 & c_1 \\ d_2 & b_2 & c_2 \\ d_3 & b_3 & c_3 \end{bmatrix}$

$$A_2 = \begin{bmatrix} a_1 & d_1 & c_1 \\ a_2 & d_2 & c_2 \\ a_3 & d_3 & c_3 \end{bmatrix} \quad A_3 = \begin{bmatrix} a_1 & b_1 & d_1 \\ a_2 & b_2 & d_2 \\ a_3 & b_3 & d_3 \end{bmatrix}$$

Example: Solve the following equations by Cramer's Rule.

$x + 2y + 3z = 22,\ 2x - y + 2z = 9,\ 3x + 3y + 4z = 32$

Solution: The equations can be expressed as

$$\begin{bmatrix} 1 & 2 & 3 \\ 2 & -1 & 2 \\ 3 & 3 & 4 \end{bmatrix} \begin{bmatrix} x \\ y \\ z \end{bmatrix} = \begin{bmatrix} 22 \\ 9 \\ 32 \end{bmatrix}$$

$$|A| = \begin{vmatrix} 1 & 2 & 3 \\ 2 & -1 & 2 \\ 3 & 3 & 4 \end{vmatrix} = 1\begin{vmatrix} -1 & 2 \\ 3 & 4 \end{vmatrix} - 2\begin{vmatrix} 2 & 2 \\ 3 & 4 \end{vmatrix} + 3\begin{vmatrix} 2 & -1 \\ 3 & 3 \end{vmatrix}$$

$$= 1(-4-6) - 2(8-6) + 3(6+3) = -10 - 4 + 27 = 13$$

$$|A_1| = \begin{vmatrix} 22 & 2 & 3 \\ 9 & -1 & 2 \\ 32 & 3 & 4 \end{vmatrix}$$

$$|A_1| = 22\begin{vmatrix} -1 & 2 \\ 3 & 4 \end{vmatrix} - 2\begin{vmatrix} 9 & 2 \\ 32 & 4 \end{vmatrix} + 3\begin{vmatrix} 9 & -1 \\ 32 & 3 \end{vmatrix}$$

$$= 22(-4-6) - 2(36-64) + 3(27+32)$$

$$= -220 + 56 + 177 = 13$$

$$A_2 = \begin{bmatrix} 1 & 22 & 3 \\ 2 & 9 & 2 \\ 3 & 32 & 4 \end{bmatrix}$$

$$|A_2| = 1\begin{bmatrix} 9 & 2 \\ 32 & 4 \end{bmatrix} - 22\begin{bmatrix} 2 & 2 \\ 3 & 4 \end{bmatrix} + 3\begin{bmatrix} 2 & 9 \\ 3 & 32 \end{bmatrix}$$

$$= 1(36-64) - 22(8-6) + 3(64-27) = -28 - 44 + 111 = 39$$

$$|A_3| = \begin{vmatrix} 1 & 2 & 22 \\ 2 & -1 & 9 \\ 3 & 3 & 32 \end{vmatrix}$$

$$|A_3| = 1\begin{vmatrix} -1 & 9 \\ 3 & 32 \end{vmatrix} - 2\begin{vmatrix} 2 & 9 \\ 3 & 32 \end{vmatrix} + 22\begin{vmatrix} 2 & -1 \\ 3 & 3 \end{vmatrix}$$

$$= 1(-32-27) - 2(64-27) + 22(6+3)$$

$$= -59 - 74 + 198 = 65$$

$$x = \frac{|A_1|}{|A|} = \frac{13}{13} = 1,\ y = \frac{|A_2|}{|A|} = \frac{39}{13} = 3,\ z = \frac{|A_3|}{|A|} = \frac{65}{13} = 5$$

Example: *Solve the following equations by Cramer's Rule.*

$$2x + 3y = 21$$
$$x + y = 8$$

Solution: $$|A| = \begin{vmatrix} 2 & 3 \\ 1 & 1 \end{vmatrix} = 2.1 - 1.3 = -1$$

$$|A_1| = \begin{vmatrix} 21 & 3 \\ 8 & 1 \end{vmatrix} = 21.1 - 8.3 = -3$$

$$|A_2| = \begin{vmatrix} 2 & 21 \\ 1 & 8 \end{vmatrix} = 2.8 - 1.21 = -5$$

$$x = \frac{|A_1|}{|A|} = \frac{-3}{-1} = 3, \qquad y = \frac{|A_2|}{|A|} = \frac{-5}{-1} = 5$$

Rank of a Matrix: The rank of a matrix is the order of the largest square sub-matrix whose determinant is not zero.

Example: *Find the rank of* $\begin{bmatrix} 3 & 2 & 1 \\ 1 & 0 & 5 \\ 3 & 0 & 1 \end{bmatrix}$

Solution: The determinant of $\begin{vmatrix} 3 & 2 & 1 \\ 1 & 0 & 5 \\ 3 & 0 & 1 \end{vmatrix}$

$$= 3(0 - 0) - 2\,(1 - 15) + 1\,(0 - 0) = 28$$

which is not equal to zero. Hence, rank = 3

Example: *Find the rank of* $\begin{bmatrix} 2 & 3 & 5 \\ 4 & 10 & 6 \\ 2 & 5 & 3 \end{bmatrix}$

Solution: The determinant of $\begin{vmatrix} 2 & 3 & 5 \\ 4 & 10 & 6 \\ 2 & 5 & 3 \end{vmatrix}$

$$= 2(30 - 30) - 3\,(12 - 12) + 5\,(20 - 20) = 0$$

Since, the determinant is equal to zero, this rank is not equal to 3. Among the other 2×2 sub matrices determinant of anyone should not equal to zero.

Calculate determinants of anyone of the 2×2 sub matrices,

$$\begin{vmatrix} 2 & 3 \\ 4 & 10 \end{vmatrix}, \begin{vmatrix} 3 & 5 \\ 10 & 6 \end{vmatrix}, \begin{vmatrix} 2 & 3 \\ 2 & 5 \end{vmatrix}, \begin{vmatrix} 3 & 5 \\ 5 & 3 \end{vmatrix}$$

i.e., determinant of $\begin{vmatrix} 2 & 3 \\ 4 & 10 \end{vmatrix} = 2 \times 10 - 4 \times 3 = 8$

which is not equal to zero. Hence, the rank of the number = 2

Example: *Find the rank of* $\begin{bmatrix} 1 & 3 & 5 \\ 2 & 6 & 10 \\ 4 & 12 & 20 \end{bmatrix}$

Solution: The determinant of $\begin{vmatrix} 1 & 3 & 5 \\ 2 & 6 & 10 \\ 4 & 12 & 20 \end{vmatrix}$

$$= 1\,(120 - 120) - 3\,(40 - 40) + 5\,(24 - 24) = 0$$

Hence, the rank of the matrix is not equal to 3.

The determinants of other 2×2 sub matrices.

$\begin{vmatrix} 1 & 3 \\ 2 & 6 \end{vmatrix}, \begin{vmatrix} 3 & 5 \\ 6 & 10 \end{vmatrix}, \begin{vmatrix} 1 & 3 \\ 4 & 12 \end{vmatrix}, \begin{vmatrix} 3 & 5 \\ 12 & 20 \end{vmatrix}$ are all equal to zero.

Hence, the rank of the matrix is also not equal to 2.

$\therefore$ The rank of the matrix = 1

Example: *Find the rank of* $\begin{bmatrix} 2 & 1 & 0 & 4 \\ 1 & 2 & 1 & 0 \\ 4 & 0 & 2 & 1 \end{bmatrix}$

Solution: Since the matrix is of 3×4 order the highest rank can be obtained, only for 3.

Hence, the given matrix can be written as the matrix of 3×3 order, as follows.

$$\begin{vmatrix} 2 & 1 & 0 \\ 1 & 2 & 1 \\ 4 & 0 & 2 \end{vmatrix} \text{ and } \begin{vmatrix} 1 & 0 & 4 \\ 2 & 1 & 0 \\ 0 & 2 & 1 \end{vmatrix}$$

Since, the determinants of the above 2 matrices are not equal to zero, the rank of the given matrix = 3.

Exercises

1. If $A = \begin{bmatrix} 6 & 1 & 3 \\ 2 & -5 & 4 \end{bmatrix}$ find $4A$ **Ans:** $\begin{bmatrix} 24 & 4 & 12 \\ 8 & -20 & 16 \end{bmatrix}$

2. If $A = \begin{bmatrix} 3 & 2 & 5 \\ 1 & -2 & 3 \end{bmatrix}$ and $B = \begin{bmatrix} 1 & 1 & 6 \\ -3 & 2 & 4 \end{bmatrix}$ Calculate (i) $2A + B$

   (ii) $3A - 2B$ **Ans:** (i) $\begin{bmatrix} 7 & 5 & 16 \\ -1 & -2 & 10 \end{bmatrix}$ (ii) $\begin{bmatrix} 7 & 4 & 3 \\ 9 & -10 & 1 \end{bmatrix}$

3. Write the transpose of the following matrices.

(i) $\begin{bmatrix} 1 & 3 & 5 \end{bmatrix}$ (ii) $\begin{bmatrix} 1 & 2 \\ 4 & 5 \\ -3 & 7 \end{bmatrix}$ (iii) $\begin{bmatrix} 3 & 0 & 2 \\ 1 & 1 & 4 \\ 4 & 5 & 6 \end{bmatrix}$

Ans: (i) $\begin{bmatrix} 1 \\ 3 \\ 5 \end{bmatrix}$ (ii) $\begin{bmatrix} 1 & 4 & -3 \\ 2 & 5 & 7 \end{bmatrix}$ (iii) $\begin{bmatrix} 3 & 1 & 4 \\ 0 & 1 & 5 \\ 2 & 4 & 6 \end{bmatrix}$

4. If $A = \begin{bmatrix} 1 & 3 & 4 \\ 2 & 0 & 3 \\ 1 & 3 & 1 \end{bmatrix}$, $B = \begin{bmatrix} 2 & 1 & 1 \\ 3 & 2 & 2 \\ 4 & 1 & 2 \end{bmatrix}$, $C = \begin{bmatrix} 1 & 1 & 5 \\ 3 & 2 & 1 \\ 1 & 5 & 1 \end{bmatrix}$

Calculate (i) $2A + 3C$ (ii) $A + B + C$ (iii) $2A - B + 2C$

Ans: (i) $\begin{bmatrix} 5 & 9 & 23 \\ 13 & 6 & 9 \\ 5 & 21 & 5 \end{bmatrix}$ (ii) $\begin{bmatrix} 4 & 5 & 10 \\ 8 & 4 & 6 \\ 6 & 9 & 4 \end{bmatrix}$ (iii) $\begin{bmatrix} 2 & 7 & 17 \\ 7 & 2 & 6 \\ 0 & 15 & 2 \end{bmatrix}$

5. If $A = \begin{bmatrix} 1 & 3 \\ 2 & -2 \\ 1 & 1 \end{bmatrix}$, $B = \begin{bmatrix} 2 & 1 \\ 3 & 2 \\ 4 & 2 \end{bmatrix}$ find the matrix C. When,

$A + B + C = 0$ **Ans:** $C = \begin{bmatrix} -3 & -3 \\ -5 & 0 \\ -5 & -3 \end{bmatrix}$

6. If $A = \begin{bmatrix} 2 & -1 \\ 3 & 5 \end{bmatrix}$ and $B = \begin{bmatrix} 10 & -2 \\ 0 & 5 \end{bmatrix}$ find X when $A + X = B$

Ans: $X = \begin{bmatrix} 8 & -1 \\ -3 & 0 \end{bmatrix}$

7. If $A-3B=\begin{bmatrix}2 & 3 & -1\\ -3 & 2 & 4\end{bmatrix}$ and $4B-A=\begin{bmatrix}6 & 5 & 7\\ -3 & 6 & 8\end{bmatrix}$ find A and B

Ans: $A=\begin{bmatrix}26 & 27 & 17\\ -3 & 26 & 40\end{bmatrix}, B=\begin{bmatrix}8 & 8 & 6\\ 0 & 8 & 12\end{bmatrix}$

8. If $A=\begin{bmatrix}1 & 3 & -2\\ 0 & 2 & 4\end{bmatrix}$ and $B=\begin{bmatrix}-3 & 2\\ 1 & 4\\ 3 & 1\end{bmatrix}$ find AB and BA. is $AB=BA$?

Ans: $AB=\begin{bmatrix}-6 & 12\\ 14 & 12\end{bmatrix}$; $BA=\begin{bmatrix}-3 & -5 & 14\\ 1 & 11 & -2\end{bmatrix}$; $AB \neq BA$

9. If $A=\begin{bmatrix}2 & -3\\ 1 & 5\end{bmatrix}$, $B=\begin{bmatrix}1 & -1\\ 2 & -2\end{bmatrix}$ find AB, BA, $A'B$, AB'

Ans: $\begin{bmatrix}-4 & 4\\ 11 & -11\end{bmatrix}, \begin{bmatrix}1 & -8\\ 2 & -16\end{bmatrix}, \begin{bmatrix}4 & -4\\ 7 & -7\end{bmatrix}, \begin{bmatrix}5 & 10\\ -4 & -8\end{bmatrix}$

10. Find a and b if $\begin{bmatrix}2 & 5\\ 3 & 1\end{bmatrix}\begin{bmatrix}a & 2\\ 6 & b\end{bmatrix}=\begin{bmatrix}36 & 29\\ 15 & 11\end{bmatrix}$ **Ans:** a = 3; b = 5

11. Calculate determinants for (i) $\begin{vmatrix}3 & 2\\ 4 & 5\end{vmatrix}$ (ii) $\begin{vmatrix}5 & -2\\ 2 & -1\end{vmatrix}$

(iii) $\begin{vmatrix}a+b & 2a\\ a & a-b\end{vmatrix}$ **Ans:** (i) 7 (ii) –1 (iii) $-a^2-b^2$

12. Calculate x when $A=\begin{vmatrix}4 & 2\\ x & 5\end{vmatrix}=0$ **Ans:** $x=10$

13. Calculate x, when $A=\begin{vmatrix}6 & x-1\\ 4 & x-2\end{vmatrix}=0$ **Ans:** $x=2$

14. Evaluate (i) $\begin{vmatrix}1 & 3 & 5\\ -2 & 1 & 1\\ 2 & 2 & 4\end{vmatrix}$, (ii) $\begin{vmatrix}2 & 1 & 1\\ 1 & 1 & 5\\ 3 & 1 & 1\end{vmatrix}$ **Ans:** (i) 2 (ii) 4

15. Solve the following equations by matrix technique.

$$2x + 3y = 5$$
$$4x - 5y = -23$$

Ans: $x = -2,\ y = 3$

16. Solve the following equations by matrices.

$$x - 3y + 4z = -6, \quad 2x + 3y - z = 15, \quad 5x + y + z = 15$$

Ans: $x = 2,\ y = 4,\ z = 1$

17. Solve the following equations by matrices.

$$5x + 4y + 3z = 19$$
$$x + y + z = 5$$
$$2x - 3y + 5z = 32$$

Ans: $x = 3,\ y = -2,\ z = 4$

18. Solve the following equtions by matrices.

$$x - 2y + 10z = 27$$
$$4x + 5y + 3z = 21$$
$$5x - 2y + 4z = 35$$

Ans: $x = 5,\ y = -1,\ z = 2$

19. If $A = \begin{bmatrix} 3 & 1 & 0 \\ 2 & 1 & 1 \\ 3 & 2 & -2 \end{bmatrix}$, $B = \begin{bmatrix} 2 & 1 & 0 \\ 1 & 1 & 1 \\ 2 & 1 & 2 \end{bmatrix}$, $C = \begin{bmatrix} 1 & 2 & 1 \\ 1 & 5 & 1 \\ 1 & 3 & 1 \end{bmatrix}$ show that $A(B+C) = AB + AC$ and $(AB)C = AB(C)$

20. If $A = \begin{bmatrix} 1 & 1 & 5 \\ 2 & 0 & 1 \\ -2 & 1 & 1 \end{bmatrix}$, $B = \begin{bmatrix} 2 & 0 & 4 \\ 1 & 1 & 2 \\ 1 & 1 & 3 \end{bmatrix}$, $C = \begin{bmatrix} 1 \\ -2 \\ 1 \end{bmatrix}$ find a matrix X such that $(3B - 2A)C + 2X = 0$

Ans: $X = \begin{bmatrix} -5 \\ 3/2 \\ -6 \end{bmatrix}$

21. If $A = \begin{bmatrix} 5 & 1 & 5 \\ 2 & 2 & 1 \\ 1 & -1 & -1 \end{bmatrix}$, $B = \begin{bmatrix} 1 & 2 & 1 \\ 3 & 3 & 1 \\ -1 & -2 & -3 \end{bmatrix}$ verity (i) $(A')' = A$

(ii) $(AB)' = B'A'$ (iii) $(A+B)' = A' + B'$

22. Solve the following equations by Cramer's Rule.

$$3x + 5y = 4$$
$$5x + 8y = 6$$

Ans: $X = -2, y = 2$

23. Solve the following equations by Cramers Rule

$$2x + 3y + 4z = 15, \quad x + y + z = 4, \quad 3x - 2y + 5z = 1$$

Ans: $x = -1,\ y = 3,\ z = 2$

24. Find the Rank of the matrices. (i) $\begin{bmatrix} 1 & 3 & 5 & 1 \\ 2 & 0 & 2 & 1 \\ 1 & 1 & 0 & 2 \end{bmatrix}$

(ii) $\begin{bmatrix} 1 & 1 & 4 \\ 2 & 1 & 5 \\ 1 & 5 & 1 \end{bmatrix}$ (iii) $\begin{bmatrix} 1 & 1 & 5 & 5 \\ 2 & 2 & 1 & 1 \\ 3 & 3 & 3 & 3 \\ 4 & 1 & 1 & 1 \end{bmatrix}$

Ans: (i) Rank 3 (ii) Rank 3 (iii) Rank 4

25. Prove that $\begin{vmatrix} 1 & 1 & 1 \\ a & b & c \\ a & b & c \end{vmatrix} = (a - b)(b - c)(c - a)$

(MGU: Section B, April 98)

26. If $A = \begin{bmatrix} 1 & 2 \\ 3 & 4 \\ 5 & 6 \end{bmatrix}$ find a matrix B such that $A + B = 0$

(MGU: Section B, April 97), **Ans:** $\begin{bmatrix} -1 & -2 \\ -3 & -4 \\ -5 & -6 \end{bmatrix}$

27. Using matrices solve the equations

$$x + y + z = 6$$
$$x + 2y + 3z = 14$$
$$-x + y - z = -2$$

(MGU: Section C, April 96), **Ans:** $x = 1$, $y = 2$, $z = 3$

28. If $A = \begin{bmatrix} 1 & 2 \\ -3 & 0 \end{bmatrix}$ find $A^2 + 3A + 2A + 5I$. If I is the unit matrix of order 2 (MGU: Section B, April 95), **Ans:** $\begin{bmatrix} 5 & 12 \\ -18 & -1 \end{bmatrix}$

29. (a) What is inverse of a matrix?

(b) Find the inverse of the matrix. $\begin{bmatrix} 1 & 3 & 3 \\ 1 & 4 & 3 \\ 1 & 3 & 4 \end{bmatrix}$

(MGU: Section C, April '95), **Ans:** (b) = 1

30. Find the value of the determinant. $\begin{bmatrix} 1 & 18 & 72 \\ 2 & 40 & 148 \\ 2 & 45 & 150 \end{bmatrix}$

(MGU: Section B, April '94), **Ans:** –12

31. Solve the system equation.

$$x + y + z = 7$$
$$x + 2y + 3z = 16$$
$$x + 3y + 4z = 22$$

(MGU Section C, April 94). **Ans:** x = 1, y = 3, z = 3

32. Write down the tranpose of $A = \begin{bmatrix} 1 & 0 & 0 \\ 1 & -1 & 2 \end{bmatrix}$ what is the order the matrix got? (MGU: Section A, April 93), **Ans.** $A = \begin{bmatrix} 1 & -1 \\ 1 & 0 \\ 0 & 2 \end{bmatrix}$

33. Find the inverse of $A = \begin{bmatrix} 1 & 2 \\ 3 & 7 \end{bmatrix}$ Hence solve the equation

$x + 2y = 4$ and $3x + 7y = 13$

(MGU, Section B, April 93) , **Ans:** 1, x = 2, y = 1

Appendix I

FORMULAE

Measures of Central value

Arithmetic Mean

Individual Observations: $\bar{X} = \frac{\Sigma X}{N}$

$X = X_1, X_2, X_3,$ etc. ; N = Number of observations

Discrete Series: $\bar{X} = \frac{\Sigma fX}{N}$ (Director method)

$\bar{X} = A + \frac{\Sigma fd}{N}$ (Assumed mean method)

where $d = (X - A)$

Continuous Series: $\bar{X} = \frac{\Sigma fm}{N}$ (Direct method) where m = mid-point

$\bar{X} = A + \frac{\Sigma fd'}{N} \times C$ (Step Deviation Method)

$d' = \frac{(X - A)}{C}$ and C = common factor

Combined Mean: $\bar{X}12 = \frac{N_1 \bar{X}1 + N_2 \bar{X}2}{N_1 + N_2}$

$$\bar{X}123 = \frac{N_1 \bar{X}1 + N_2 \bar{X}2 + N_3 \bar{X}3}{N_1 + N_2 + N_3}$$

Median, Quartiles, etc.

Individual Observations and Discrete Series:

$$\text{Median} = \text{Size of } \frac{N+1}{2} \text{ th item}$$

$$Q_1 = \text{Size of } \frac{N+1}{4} \text{ th item}$$

Continuous Series: $$\text{Median} = L + \frac{\frac{N}{2} - c.f}{f} \times i$$

$$Q_1 = L + \frac{\frac{N}{4} - c.f}{f} \times i$$

L = Lower limit of the quartile class

$c.f.$ = Cumulative frequency of the class preceding the quartile class

f = Simple frequency of the quartile class

i = Class interval of the quartile class

$N = \Sigma f$ i.e., total frequency in a discrete and continuous series

Mode

Containuous Series: $$\text{Mode} = L + \frac{\Delta_1}{\Delta_1 + \Delta_2} \times i$$

where L = Lower limit of the modal class

Δ_1 = difference between the frequency of the modal class and the pre-modal class

Δ_2 = difference between the frequency of the modal calss and the post-modal class

i = Calss interval of the modal class.

or

$$\text{Mode} = L + \frac{f_1 - f_0}{2f_1 - f_0 - f_2} \times i$$

L = Lower limit of the modal class

f_1 = frequency of the modal class

f_o = frequency of the class preceding the modal class

f_2 = frequency of the class following the modal class

i = class interval fo the modal class

Mode = 3 Median – 2 mean [Indirect Method of determining model].

Geometric Mean

Individual observations: $\text{G.M.} = \text{Antilog}\ \dfrac{\Sigma \operatorname{Log} X}{N}$

Discrete Series: $\text{G.M.} = \text{Antilog}\ \dfrac{\Sigma f \operatorname{Log} X}{N}$

Continuous Series: $\text{G.M.} = \text{Antilog}\ \dfrac{\Sigma f \operatorname{Log} m}{N}$

Harmonic Mean

Individual observations: $\text{H.M} = \dfrac{N}{\dfrac{1}{X_1} + \dfrac{1}{X_2} + \cdots + \dfrac{1}{X_n}} = \dfrac{N}{\Sigma\left(\dfrac{1}{X}\right)}$

Discrete Series: $\text{H.M} = \dfrac{N}{\Sigma\left(f \times \dfrac{1}{X}\right)}$

Continuous Series: $\text{H.M} = \dfrac{N}{\Sigma\left(f \times \dfrac{1}{m}\right)}$

(Measures of Variation)

1. Range: Range $= L - S$ where L = Largest Value, and

S = Smallest Value.

$$\text{Coefficient of Range} = \frac{L-S}{L+S}$$

2. Quartile Deviation: $Q.D. = \frac{Q_3 - Q_1}{2}$

$$\text{Coefficient of } Q.D. = \frac{Q_3 - Q_1}{Q_3 + Q_1}$$

3. Mean Deviation:

Individual Observations: $M.D. = \frac{\Sigma|D|}{N}$

Discrete and Continuous Series: $M.D. = \frac{\Sigma f|D|}{N}$

$|D|$ = deviations from median ignoring when mean or median are in fraction the calculations can be simply by applying the following formula:

$$M.D. = \frac{\Sigma mf_A - \Sigma mf_B - (\Sigma f_A - \Sigma f_B)Mcd.}{N} \text{ (from median)}$$

And

$$M.D. = \frac{\Sigma mf_A - \Sigma mf_B - (\Sigma f_A - \Sigma f_B)\overline{X}}{N} \text{ (from mean)}$$

$$\text{Coeff. of } M.D. = \frac{\text{Mean Deviation}}{\text{median}} \text{ or } \frac{\text{Mean Deviation}}{\text{Median}}$$

(in case the deviations are taken from mean)

4. Standard Deviation

Individual Observations: $\sigma = \sqrt{\frac{\Sigma x^2}{N}}$

[where deviations are taken from actual mean i.e., $x = (X - \overline{X})$]

$$\sigma = \sqrt{\frac{\Sigma d^2}{N} - \left(\frac{\Sigma d}{N}\right)^2}$$

[where deviations are taken from assumed mean i.e., $d = X - A$))

Discrete and Continuous Series:

$$\sigma = \sqrt{\frac{\Sigma fd^2}{N} - \left(\frac{\Sigma fd}{N}\right)^2}$$

[where deviations are taken from an assumed mean]

$$\sigma = \sqrt{\frac{\Sigma fd'^2}{N} - \left(\frac{\Sigma fd'}{N}\right)^2} \times C$$

[where step deviations are taken]

$$d = (X - A) \text{ and } d' = \frac{(X - A)}{C}$$

and C = Common factor

Coefficient of Standard Deviation $= \frac{\sigma}{X}$

Coefficient of Variation or $C.V. = \frac{\sigma}{X} \times 100$

$$\text{Variance} = \frac{\Sigma(X - \overline{X})^2}{N}, \text{ or Variance} = \sigma^2$$

$$\therefore \quad \sigma\sqrt{\text{Variance}}$$

$$\text{Variance} = \left[\frac{\Sigma fd'^2}{N} - \left(\frac{\Sigma fd^2}{N}\right)^2\right] \times C^2 \text{ (Continuous series)}$$

Combined Standard Deviation

$$\sigma_{12} = \sqrt{\frac{N_1\sigma_1^2 + N_2\sigma_2^2 + N_1 d_1^2 + N_2 d_2^2}{N_1 + N_2}}$$

$$d_1 = \left(\bar{X}1 - \bar{X}12\right) \quad d_2 = \left(\bar{X}2 - \bar{X}12\right)$$

Standard Deviation of n natural numbers

$$\sigma = \sqrt{\frac{1}{12}\left(N^2 - 1\right)}$$

Skewness, Moments and Kurtosis

Absolute Skewness = Mean – Mode or $Q_3 + Q_1 - 2\,Med.$

Relative Skewness:

(1) Coeff. of $SK = \dfrac{\text{Mean - Mode}}{\sigma}$ (Karl Pearson's Method)

(2) Coeff. of $SK = \dfrac{3(\text{Mean - Median})}{\sigma}$ (when mode is ill-defined)

(3) Coeff. of $SK = \dfrac{Q_3 + Q_1 - 2\,\text{Median}}{Q_3 + Q_1}$ (Bowley's Method)

(4) Skewness based on Moments

$$\beta_1 = \frac{\mu_3^2}{\mu_2^3}, \quad \text{or} \quad \sqrt{\beta_1} = \frac{\mu_3}{\sqrt{\mu_2^3}}$$

Moments

$$\mu_1 = \frac{\Sigma(X - \bar{X})}{N} = 0; \qquad \mu_2 = \frac{\Sigma(X - \bar{X})}{N} = 0,$$

i.e., $\mu_2 = \sigma^2$, or $\sigma = \sqrt{\mu_2}$

$$\mu'_1 = \frac{\Sigma(X - A)}{N}; \mu'_2 = \frac{\Sigma(X - A)^2}{N}, \text{ etc.}$$

Conversion of moments about an arbitrary origin into moments about mean

$$\mu_2 = \mu'_2 - (\mu'_1)^2$$

$$\mu_3 = \mu'_3 - 3\mu'_1\mu'_2 + 2\mu'^3_1$$

$$\mu_4 = \mu'_4 - 4\mu'_1\mu'_3 + 6(\mu'_1)^2\mu'_2 - 3\mu'^4_1$$

Kurtosis

Kurtosis is measured by the coefficient γ_2

$$\gamma_2 = \beta_2 - 3 \quad \text{where} \quad \beta_2 = \frac{\mu_4}{\mu_2^2}$$

(Correlation Annalysis)

(1) Karl Pearson's Method

(a) When deviations are taken from actual means

$$r = \frac{\Sigma xy}{n\sigma_x\sigma_y} \quad \text{Or} \quad r = \frac{\Sigma xy}{\sqrt{\Sigma x^2 \times \Sigma y^2}},$$

where r is the coefficient of correlation

$x = (X - \bar{X})$, $y = (Y - \bar{Y})$ and

N = number of pairs of observattons.

(b) When deviations are taken from assumed means

$$r = \frac{\Sigma d_x d_y - \frac{(\Sigma d_x) \times (\Sigma d_y)}{n}}{\sqrt{\Sigma d_x^2 - \frac{(\Sigma d_x)^2}{n}}\sqrt{\Sigma fd_y^2 - \frac{(\Sigma fd_y)^2}{n}}}$$

where $d_x = (X - A)$ and $d_y = (Y - A)$

(c) Coefficient of correlation in a correlation table

$$r = \frac{\Sigma fd_x d_y - \frac{(\Sigma fd_x) \times (\Sigma fd_y)}{n}}{\sqrt{\Sigma fd_x^2 - \frac{(\Sigma fd_x)^2}{n}}\sqrt{\Sigma fd_y^2 - \frac{(\Sigma fd_y)^2}{n}}}$$

Interpretation of the Pearsonian's Coefficient

$$S.E.\ r = \frac{1-r^2}{\sqrt{N}}, \qquad P.E. r = 0.6745 \frac{1-r^2}{\sqrt{N}}$$

(2) Rank Correlation

(a) $$r_c = 1 - \frac{6\Sigma D^2}{N^3 - N}$$

$D = (R_2 - R_1)$, i.e., different of ranks.

(b) When ranks are repeated

$$r_c = 1 - \frac{6\left\{\Sigma d^2 + \frac{1}{12}(m_1{}^3 - m_1) + \frac{1}{12}(m_2{}^3 - m_2) + \cdots\right\}}{N^3 - N}$$

(3) Concurrent Deviation Method.

$$r_c = \pm\sqrt{\pm\left(\frac{2c - N}{N}\right)}$$

c = number of positive signs after mutiplying d_x with d_y.

Regression Analysis

Regression line of Y on X is given by $Y = a + bX$

Regression line of X and Y is givne by $X = a + bY$

$$Y - \bar{Y} = r\,\frac{\sigma_y}{\sigma_x}\left(X - \bar{X}\right)$$

Regression equation of X and Y

$$X - \bar{X} = r\,\frac{\sigma_x}{\sigma_y}\left(Y - \bar{Y}\right)$$

Regression coefficient of X on Y, i.e., b_{xy} or b_1

$$= r\,\frac{\sigma_x}{\sigma_y} = \frac{\Sigma xy}{\Sigma y^2}$$ (when deviations are taken from actual mean)

Regression coefficient of Y on X, i.e., b_{yx} or b_2

$$= r\frac{\sigma_y}{\sigma_x} = \frac{\Sigma xy}{\Sigma y^2} \text{ (when deviations are taken from acutal mean)}$$

When deviations are taken from assumed means

$$d_{xy} = \frac{\Sigma d_x d_y - \frac{(\Sigma d_x)\times(\Sigma d_y)}{N}}{\Sigma d_y{}^2 - \frac{(\Sigma d_y)^2}{N}}$$

$$d_{xy} = \frac{\Sigma d_x d_y - \frac{(\Sigma d_x)\times(\Sigma d_y)}{N}}{\Sigma d_x{}^2 - \frac{(\Sigma d_y)^2}{N}}$$

$$r = \sqrt{b_{xy} \times b_{yx}}$$

Association of Attribution

Nine-square table

	A	α	Total
B	(AB)	(αB)	(B)
β	(Aβ)	(αβ)	(β)
Total	(A)	(α)	(N)

$$(A) = (AB) + (A\beta)$$
$$(\alpha) = (\alpha B) + (\alpha\beta)$$
$$(B) = (AB) + (\alpha B)$$
$$(\beta) = (A\beta) + (\alpha\beta)$$
$$N = (A) + (\alpha), \quad N = B + (\beta)$$
$$N = (AB) + (A\beta) + (\alpha B) + (\alpha\beta)$$

Methods of Studying Association:

(1) Comparison of observed and expected frequencies method.

Attributes *A* and *B* are called

(i) independent if

$$(AB) = \frac{(A)\times(B)}{N}$$

(actual observation)

(ii) positively associated

$$(AB) = \frac{(A)\times(B)}{N}$$

(actual obervation)

(iii) negatively associated if

$$(AB) < \frac{(A)\times(B)}{N}$$

(actual observation)

(2) Proportion Method.

Attributes *A* and *B* are called

(i) independent if $\frac{(AB)}{(B)} - \frac{(A\beta)}{(\beta)}$

(ii) positively associated if $\frac{(AB)}{(B)} > \frac{(A\beta)}{(\beta)}$

(iii) negatively associated if $\frac{(AB)}{(B)} < \frac{(A\beta)}{(\beta)}$

(3) Yule's Coefficient of Association: $Q = \frac{(AB)(\alpha\beta) - (A\beta)(\alpha B)}{(AB)(\alpha\beta) + (A\beta)(\sigma B)}$

(4) Coefficient of Colligation: $Y = \frac{1 - \sqrt{\frac{(A\beta)\times(\alpha B)}{(AB)\times(\alpha\beta)}}}{1 + \sqrt{\frac{(A\beta)\times(\alpha B)}{(AB)\times(\alpha\beta)}}}$

(5) Coefficient of Contingency: $C = \sqrt{\frac{X^2}{N + X^2}}$ where $X = \Sigma\frac{(O-E)^2}{E}$

O refers to the observed frequencies.

E refers to the expected frequencies.

Index Numbers

(1) Unweighted Methods

(a) Simple Aggregative Method

$$P_{01} = \frac{\Sigma p_1}{\Sigma p_0} \times 100$$

p_1 = Price of the current year

p_0 = Price of the base year

(b) Simple Average of Price Relative Method

$$P_{01} = \frac{\Sigma\left(\frac{p_1}{p_0} \times 100\right)}{N}$$

(c) Geometric Mean of Price Relative Method

$$P_{01} = \text{Antilog}\ \frac{\left[\Sigma \log \frac{p_1}{p_0} \times 100\right]}{N}$$

(2) Weight Methods

(a) Weighted Aggregative Methods

(i) Laspeye's Method: $P_{01} = \frac{\Sigma p_1 q_0}{\Sigma p_0 q_0} \times 100$

q_0 = quantity of the base period.

(ii) Pasche's Method: $P_{01} = \frac{\Sigma p_1 q_1}{\Sigma p_0 q_1} \times 100$

q_1 = quantity of the current period.

(iii) Dorbish and Bowley's Method

$$P_{01} = \frac{\dfrac{\Sigma p_1 q_0}{\Sigma p_0 q_0} + \dfrac{\Sigma p_1 q_1}{\Sigma p_0 q_1}}{2} \times 100 \quad \text{or} \quad P_{01} = \frac{L+P}{2}$$

(iv) Fisher's ideal Method:

$$P_{01} = \sqrt{\frac{\Sigma p_1 q_0}{\Sigma p_0 q_0} + \frac{\Sigma p_1 q_1}{\Sigma p_0 q_1}} \times 100$$

(v) Marshall-Edgeworth's Method

$$P_{01} = \frac{\Sigma(q_0 + q_1)p_1}{\Sigma(q_0 + q_1)p_0} \times 100$$

(vi) Kelly's Method

$$P_{01} = \frac{\Sigma q_1 Q}{\Sigma q_0 Q} \times 100$$

(b) Weighted Average of Price Relative

$$P_{01} = \left(\frac{\Sigma \log PV}{\Sigma V}\right)$$

where $P = \dfrac{P_1}{P_0} \times 100$ and V = value weights, i.e., $p_0 q_0$

Quantity of Volume Index Numbers:

$$Q_{01} = \frac{\Sigma q_1 p_0}{\Sigma q_0 p_0} \times 100$$, when Laspeyre's Method is used.

where Q_{01} = Quantity index.

$$Q_{01} = \frac{\Sigma q_1 p_1}{\Sigma q_0 p_1} \times 100$$, when Paasche's Method is used.

$$Q_{01} = \sqrt{\frac{\Sigma q_1 p_0}{\Sigma q_0 p_0} \times \frac{\Sigma q_1 p_1}{\Sigma q_0 p_1}} \times 100,$$

when Fisher's method is used.

Time Reversal Test: $P_{01} \times P_{10} = 1$

Factor Reversal Test: $P_{01} \times Q_{01} = \frac{\Sigma p_1 q_1}{\Sigma p_0 q_0}$

Circular Test: $P_{ba} \times P_{cb} \times P_{ca} = 1$

Consumer Price Index

(a) Aggregate Expenditure Method

$$\text{Cost of Living Index} = \frac{\Sigma p_1 q_0}{\Sigma p_0 q_0} \times 100$$

(b) Family Budget Method:

$$\text{Cost of Living Index} = \frac{\Sigma PV}{\Sigma V}$$

where $P = \frac{p_1}{p_0} \times 100$ and $V = p_0 q_0$

Analysis of Time Series

Method of Least Squares of Measuring Trend.

The equation of straight line trend is $Y = a + bX$

To determine the value of the constants a and b the following two normal equations are to be solved.

$$\Sigma Y = Na + b\Sigma X$$

$$\Sigma XY = a\Sigma X + b\Sigma Y^2$$

When deviations are taken from the middle period so that $\Sigma X = 0$ the value of a and b can directly be obtained as follows:

$$a = \frac{\Sigma Y}{N}; \quad b = \frac{\Sigma XY}{\Sigma X^2}$$

Second Degree Parabola

The equation of the second degree parabola is $Y = a + bX + cX^2$

To determine the values of the constants a, b and c, the following three nomral equations are to be solved simultaneously:

$$\Sigma Y = Na + b\Sigma X + c\Sigma X^2$$

$$\Sigma XY = a\Sigma X + b\Sigma X^2 + c\Sigma X^3$$

$$\Sigma X^2Y = a\Sigma X^2 + b\Sigma X^3 + c\Sigma X^4$$

When deviations are taken from the middle period so that $\Sigma x = 0$, the values of a, b and c can be ascertained as follows:

$$\Sigma Y = Na + c\Sigma X^2$$

$$\Sigma XY = b\Sigma X^2$$

$$\Sigma X^2Y = a\Sigma X^2 + c\Sigma X^4$$

Interpolation and Extrapolation

Binomial Expansion Method:

$$(y-1)^n = y^n - ny^{n-1} + \frac{n(n-1)}{2!}y^{n-2} - \frac{n(n-1)(n-2)}{3!}y^{n-3} + \cdots$$

Newton's Advancing Difference Method:

$$y_x = y_0 + x\Delta_0^1 + \frac{x(x-1)}{2!}\Delta_0^2 + \frac{x(x-1)(x-2)}{3!}\Delta_0^3 + \cdots$$

where y_0 is the figure to be interpolated and

$$x = \frac{\text{year of interpolation - year of origin}}{\text{time difference between the two adjoining years}}$$

$$x = \frac{\text{year of interpolation - year of origin}}{\text{time difference between the two adjoining years}}$$

Newton's Method for Divided Differences:

$$y_x = y_0 + (x-x_0)\Delta_0^1 + (x-x_0)(x-x_1)\Delta_0^2$$

$$+ (x-x_0)(x-x_1)(x-x_2)\Delta_0^3 + \cdots$$

Lagrange's Method:

$$y_x = y_0 \frac{(x-x_1)(x-x_2)(x-x_3)\cdots(x-x_n)}{(x_0-x_1)(x_0-x_2)(x_0-x_3)\cdots(x_0-x_n)}$$

$$+ y_1 \frac{(x-x_0)(x-x_2)(x-x_3)\cdots(x-x_n)}{(x_1-x_0)(x_1-x_2)(x_1-x_3)\cdots(x_1-x_n)}$$

$$+ y_2 \frac{(x-x_0)(x-x_1)(x-x_3)\cdots(x-x_n)}{(x_2-x_0)(x_2-x_2)(x_2-x_3)\cdots(x_2-x_n)}$$

$$+ \cdots \quad \cdots \quad \cdots \quad \cdots \quad \cdots$$

$$+ y_n \frac{(x_n-x_0)(x-x_1)(x-x_3)\cdots(x-x_{n-1})}{(x_n-x_0)(x_n-x_2)(x_n-x_3)\cdots(x_n-x_{n-1})}$$

where y_x is the figure to be interpolated, x is the value in the series for which y_x is to be interpolated, $x_0, x_1, x_2 \cdots x_n$, are the given values of x-variable and $y_0, y_1, y_2 \cdots y_n$, are the corresponding given values of y-variable.

Appendix II

LOGARITHMS

	0	1	2	3	4	5	6	7	8	9	Mean Differences								
											1	2	3	4	5	6	7	8	9
10	0000	0043	0086	0128	0170	0212	0253	0294	0334	0374	4	8	12	17	21	25	29	33	37
11	0414	0453	0492	0531	0569	0607	0645	0682	0719	0755	4	8	11	15	19	23	26	30	34
12	0792	0828	0864	0899	0934	0969	1004	1038	1072	1106	3	7	10	14	17	21	24	28	31
13	1139	1173	1206	1239	1271	1303	1335	1367	1399	1430	3	6	10	13	16	19	23	26	29
14	1461	1492	1523	1553	1584	1614	1644	1673	1703	1732	3	6	9	12	15	18	21	24	27
15	1761	1790	1818	1847	1875	1903	1931	1959	1987	2014	3	6	8	11	14	17	20	22	25
16	2041	2068	2095	2122	2148	2175	2201	2227	2253	2279	3	5	8	11	13	16	18	21	24
17	2304	2330	2355	2380	2405	2430	2455	2480	2504	2529	2	5	7	10	12	15	17	20	22
18	2553	2577	2601	2625	2648	2672	2695	2718	2742	2765	2	5	7	9	12	14	16	19	21
19	2788	2810	2833	2856	2878	2900	2923	2945	2967	2989	2	4	7	9	11	13	16	18	20
20	3010	3032	3054	3075	3096	3118	3139	3160	3181	3201	2	4	6	8	11	13	15	17	19
21	3222	3243	3263	3284	3304	3324	3345	3365	3385	3404	2	4	6	8	10	12	14	16	18
22	3424	3444	3464	3483	3502	3522	3541	3560	3579	3598	2	4	6	8	10	12	14	15	17
23	3617	3636	3655	3674	3692	3711	3729	3747	3766	3784	2	4	6	7	9	11	13	15	17
24	3802	3820	3838	3856	3874	3892	3909	3927	3945	3962	2	4	5	7	9	11	12	14	16
25	3979	3997	4014	4031	4048	4065	4082	4099	4116	4133	2	3	5	7	9	10	12	14	15
26	4150	4166	4183	4200	4216	4232	4249	4265	4281	4298	2	3	5	7	8	10	11	13	15
27	4314	4330	4346	4362	4378	4393	4409	4425	4440	4456	2	3	5	6	8	9	11	13	14
28	4472	4487	4502	4518	4533	4548	4564	4579	4594	4609	2	3	5	6	8	9	11	12	14
29	4624	4639	4654	4669	4683	4698	4713	4728	4742	4757	1	3	4	6	7	9	10	12	13
30	4771	4786	4800	4814	4829	4843	4857	4871	4886	4900	1	3	4	6	7	9	10	11	13
31	4914	4928	4942	4955	4969	4983	4997	5011	5024	5038	1	3	4	6	7	8	10	11	12
32	5051	5065	5079	5092	5105	5119	5132	5145	5159	5172	1	3	4	5	7	8	9	11	12
33	5185	5198	5211	5224	5237	5250	5263	5276	5289	5302	1	3	4	5	6	8	9	10	12
34	5315	5328	5340	5353	5366	5378	5391	5403	5416	5428	1	3	4	5	6	8	9	10	11
35	5441	5453	5465	5478	5490	5502	5514	5527	5539	5551	1	2	4	5	6	7	9	10	11
36	5563	5575	5587	5599	5611	5623	5635	5647	5658	5670	1	2	4	5	6	7	8	10	11
37	5682	5694	5705	5717	5729	5740	5752	5763	5775	5786	1	2	3	5	6	7	8	9	10
38	5798	5809	5821	5832	5843	5855	5866	5877	5888	5899	1	2	3	5	6	7	8	9	10
39	5911	5922	5933	5944	5955	5966	5977	5988	5999	6010	1	2	3	4	5	7	8	9	10
40	6021	6031	6042	6053	6064	6075	6085	6096	6107	6117	1	2	3	4	5	6	8	9	10
41	6128	6138	6149	6160	6170	6180	6191	6201	6212	6222	1	2	3	4	5	6	7	8	9
42	6232	6243	6253	6263	6274	6284	6294	6304	6314	6325	1	2	3	4	5	6	7	8	9
43	6335	6345	6355	6365	6375	6385	6395	6405	6415	6425	1	2	3	4	5	6	7	8	9
44	6435	6444	6454	6464	6474	6484	6493	6503	6513	6522	1	2	3	4	5	6	7	8	9
45	6532	6542	6551	6561	6571	6580	6590	6599	6609	6618	1	2	3	4	5	6	7	8	9
46	6628	6637	6646	6656	6665	6675	6684	6693	6702	6712	1	2	3	4	5	6	7	7	8
47	6721	6730	6739	6749	6758	6767	6776	6785	6794	6803	1	2	3	4	5	5	6	7	8
48	6812	6821	6830	6839	6848	6857	6866	6875	6884	6893	1	2	3	4	4	5	6	7	8
49	6902	6911	6920	6928	6937	6946	6955	6964	6972	6981	1	2	3	4	4	5	6	7	8
50	6990	6998	7007	7016	7024	7033	7042	7050	7059	7067	1	2	3	3	4	5	6	7	8
51	7076	7084	7093	7101	7110	7118	7126	7135	7143	7152	1	2	3	3	4	5	6	7	8
52	7160	7168	7177	7185	7193	7202	7210	7218	7226	7235	1	2	2	3	4	5	6	7	7
53	7243	7251	7259	7267	7275	7284	7292	7300	7308	7316	1	2	2	3	4	5	6	6	7
54	7324	7332	7340	7348	7356	7364	7372	7380	7388	7396	1	2	2	3	4	5	6	6	7

LOGARITHMS

	0	1	2	3	4	5	6	7	8	9	Mean Differences								
											1	2	3	4	5	6	7	8	9
55	7404	7412	7419	7427	7435	7443	7451	7459	7466	7474	1	2	2	3	4	5	5	6	7
56	7482	7490	7497	7505	7513	7520	7528	7536	7543	7551	1	2	2	3	4	5	5	6	7
57	7559	7566	7574	7582	7589	7597	7604	7612	7619	7627	1	2	2	3	4	5	5	6	7
58	7634	7642	7649	7657	7664	7672	7679	7686	7694	7701	1	1	2	3	4	4	5	6	7
59	7709	7716	7723	7731	7738	7745	7752	7760	7767	7774	1	1	2	3	4	4	5	6	7
60	7782	7789	7796	7803	7810	7818	7825	7832	7839	7846	1	1	2	3	4	4	5	6	6
61	7853	7860	7868	7875	7882	7889	7896	7903	7910	7917	1	1	2	3	4	4	5	6	6
62	7924	7931	7938	7945	7952	7959	7966	7973	7980	7987	1	1	2	3	3	4	5	6	6
63	7993	8000	8007	8014	8021	8028	8035	8041	8048	8055	1	1	2	3	3	4	5	5	6
64	8062	8069	8075	8082	8089	8096	8102	8109	8116	8122	1	1	2	3	3	4	5	5	6
65	8129	8136	8142	8149	8156	8162	8169	8176	8182	8189	1	1	2	3	3	4	5	5	6
66	8195	8202	8209	8215	8222	8228	8235	8241	8248	8254	1	1	2	3	3	4	5	5	6
67	8261	8267	8274	8280	8287	8293	8299	8306	8312	8319	1	1	2	3	3	4	5	5	6
68	8325	8331	8338	8344	8351	8357	8363	8370	8376	8382	1	1	2	3	3	4	4	5	6
69	8388	8395	8401	8407	8414	8420	8426	8432	8439	8445	1	1	2	2	3	4	4	5	6
70	8451	8457	8463	8470	8476	8482	8488	8494	8500	8506	1	1	2	2	3	4	4	5	6
71	8513	8519	8525	8531	8537	8543	8549	8555	8561	8567	1	1	2	2	3	4	4	5	5
72	8573	8579	8585	8591	8597	8603	8609	8615	8621	8627	1	1	2	2	3	4	4	5	5
73	8633	8639	8645	8651	8657	8663	8669	8675	8681	8686	1	1	2	2	3	4	4	5	5
74	8692	8698	8704	8710	8716	8722	8727	8733	8739	8745	1	1	2	2	3	4	4	5	5
75	8751	8756	8762	8768	8774	8779	8785	8791	8797	8802	1	1	2	2	3	3	4	5	5
76	8808	8814	8820	8825	8831	8837	8842	8848	8854	8859	1	1	2	2	3	3	4	5	5
77	8865	8871	8876	8882	8887	8893	8899	8904	8910	8915	1	1	2	2	3	3	4	4	5
78	8921	8927	8932	8938	8943	8949	8954	8960	8965	8971	1	1	2	2	3	3	4	4	5
79	8976	8982	8987	8993	8998	9004	9009	9015	9020	9025	1	1	2	2	3	3	4	4	5
80	9031	9036	9042	9047	9053	9058	9063	9069	9074	9079	1	1	2	2	3	3	4	4	5
81	9085	9090	9096	9101	9106	9112	9117	9122	9128	9133	1	1	2	2	3	3	4	4	5
82	9138	9143	9149	9154	9159	9165	9170	9175	9180	9186	1	1	2	2	3	3	4	4	5
83	9191	9196	9201	9206	9212	9217	9222	9227	9232	9238	1	1	2	2	3	3	4	4	5
84	9243	9248	9253	9258	9263	9269	9274	9279	9284	9289	1	1	2	2	3	3	4	4	5
85	9294	9299	9304	9309	9315	9320	9325	9330	9335	9340	1	1	2	2	3	3	4	4	5
86	9345	9350	9355	9360	9365	9370	9375	9380	9385	9390	1	1	2	2	3	3	4	4	5
87	9395	9400	9405	9410	9415	9420	9425	9430	9435	9440	0	1	1	2	2	3	3	4	4
88	9445	9450	9455	9460	9465	9469	9474	9479	9484	9489	0	1	1	2	2	3	3	4	4
89	9494	9499	9504	9509	9513	9518	9523	9528	9533	9538	0	1	1	2	2	3	3	4	4
90	9542	9547	9552	9557	9562	9566	9571	9576	9581	9586	0	1	1	2	2	3	3	4	4
91	9590	9595	9600	9605	9609	9614	9619	9624	9628	9633	0	1	1	2	2	3	3	4	4
92	9638	9643	9647	9652	9657	9661	9666	9671	9675	9680	0	1	1	2	2	3	3	4	4
93	9685	9689	9694	9699	9703	9708	9713	9717	9722	9727	0	1	1	2	2	3	3	4	4
94	9731	9736	9741	9745	9750	9754	9759	9763	9768	9773	0	1	1	2	2	3	3	4	4
95	9777	9782	9786	9791	9795	9800	9805	9809	9814	9818	0	1	1	2	2	3	3	4	4
96	9823	9827	9832	9836	9841	9845	9850	9854	9859	9863	0	1	1	2	2	3	3	4	4
97	9868	9872	9877	9881	9886	9890	9894	9899	9903	9908	0	1	1	2	2	3	3	4	4
98	9912	9917	9921	9926	9930	9934	9939	9943	9948	9952	0	1	1	2	2	3	3	4	4
99	9956	9961	9965	9969	9974	9978	9983	9987	9991	9996	0	1	1	2	2	3	3	3	4

ANTI-LOGARITHMS

	0	1	2	3	4	5	6	7	8	9	Mean Differences 1	2	3	4	5	6	7	8	9
00	1000	1002	1005	1007	1009	1012	1014	1016	1019	1021	0	0	1	1	1	1	2	2	2
01	1023	1026	1028	1030	1033	1035	1038	1040	1042	1045	0	0	1	1	1	1	2	2	2
02	1047	1050	1052	1054	1057	1059	1062	1064	1067	1069	0	0	1	1	1	1	2	2	2
03	1072	1074	1076	1079	1081	1084	1086	1089	1091	1094	0	0	1	1	1	1	2	2	2
04	1096	1099	1102	1104	1107	1109	1112	1114	1117	1119	0	1	1	1	1	2	2	2	2
05	1122	1125	1127	1130	1132	1135	1138	1140	1143	1146	0	1	1	1	1	2	2	2	2
06	1148	1151	1153	1156	1159	1161	1164	1167	1169	1172	0	1	1	1	1	2	2	2	2
07	1175	1178	1180	1183	1186	1189	1191	1194	1197	1199	0	1	1	1	1	2	2	2	2
08	1202	1205	1208	1211	1213	1216	1219	1222	1225	1227	0	1	1	1	1	2	2	2	3
09	1230	1233	1236	1239	1242	1245	1247	1250	1253	1256	0	1	1	1	1	2	2	2	3
10	1259	1262	1265	1268	1271	1274	1276	1279	1282	1285	0	1	1	1	1	2	2	2	3
11	1288	1291	1294	1297	1300	1303	1306	1309	1312	1315	0	1	1	1	2	2	2	2	3
12	1318	1321	1324	1327	1330	1334	1337	1340	1343	1346	0	1	1	1	2	2	2	2	3
13	1349	1352	1355	1358	1361	1365	1368	1371	1374	1377	0	1	1	1	2	2	2	3	3
14	1380	1384	1387	1390	1393	1396	1400	1403	1406	1409	0	1	1	1	2	2	2	3	3
15	1413	1416	1419	1422	1426	1429	1432	1435	1439	1442	0	1	1	1	2	2	2	3	3
16	1445	1449	1452	1455	1459	1462	1466	1469	1472	1476	0	1	1	1	2	2	2	3	3
17	1479	1483	1486	1489	1493	1496	1500	1503	1507	1510	0	1	1	1	2	2	2	3	3
18	1514	1517	1521	1524	1528	1531	1535	1538	1542	1545	0	1	1	1	2	2	2	3	3
19	1549	1552	1556	1560	1563	1567	1570	1574	1578	1581	0	1	1	1	2	2	3	3	3
20	1585	1589	1592	1596	1600	1603	1607	1611	1614	1618	0	1	1	1	2	2	3	3	3
21	1622	1626	1629	1633	1637	1641	1644	1648	1652	1656	0	1	1	2	2	2	3	3	3
22	1660	1663	1667	1671	1675	1679	1683	1687	1690	1694	0	1	1	2	2	2	3	3	3
23	1698	1702	1706	1710	1714	1718	1722	1726	1730	1734	0	1	1	2	2	2	3	3	4
24	1738	1742	1746	1750	1754	1758	1762	1766	1770	1774	0	1	1	2	2	2	3	3	4
25	1778	1782	1786	1791	1795	1799	1803	1807	1311	1816	0	1	1	2	2	2	3	3	4
26	1820	1824	1828	1832	1837	1841	1845	1849	1854	1858	0	1	1	2	2	3	3	3	4
27	1862	1866	1871	1875	1879	1884	1888	1892	1897	1901	0	1	1	2	2	3	3	3	4
28	1905	1910	1914	1919	1923	1928	1932	1936	1941	1945	0	1	1	2	2	3	3	4	4
29	1950	1954	1959	1963	1968	1972	1977	1982	1986	1991	0	1	1	2	2	3	3	4	4
30	1995	2000	2004	2009	2014	2018	2023	2028	2032	2037	0	1	1	2	2	3	3	4	4
31	2042	2046	2051	2056	2061	2065	2070	2075	2080	2084	0	1	1	2	2	3	3	4	4
32	2089	2094	2099	2104	2109	2113	2118	2123	2128	2133	0	1	1	2	2	3	3	4	4
33	2138	2143	2148	2153	2158	2163	2168	2173	2178	2183	0	1	1	2	2	3	3	4	4
34	2188	2193	2198	2203	2208	2213	2218	2223	2228	2234	1	1	2	2	3	3	4	4	5
35	2239	2244	2249	2254	2259	2265	2270	2275	2280	2286	1	1	2	2	3	3	4	4	5
36	2291	2296	2301	2307	2312	2317	2323	2328	2333	2339	1	1	2	2	3	3	4	4	5
37	2344	2350	2355	2360	2366	2371	2377	2382	2388	2393	1	1	2	2	3	3	4	4	5
38	2399	2404	2410	2415	2421	2427	2432	2438	2443	2449	1	1	2	2	3	3	4	4	5
39	2455	2460	2466	2472	2477	2483	2489	2495	2500	2506	1	1	2	2	3	3	4	5	5
40	2512	2518	2523	2529	2535	2541	2547	2553	2559	2564	1	1	2	2	3	4	4	5	5
41	2570	2576	2582	2588	2594	2600	2606	2612	2618	2624	1	1	2	2	3	4	4	5	5
42	2630	2636	2642	2649	2655	2661	2667	2673	2679	2685	1	1	2	2	3	4	4	5	6
43	2692	2698	2704	2710	2716	2723	2729	2735	2742	2748	1	1	2	3	3	4	4	5	6
44	2754	2761	2767	2773	2780	2786	2793	2799	2805	2812	1	1	2	3	3	4	4	5	6
45	2818	2825	2831	2838	2844	2851	2858	2864	2871	2877	1	1	2	3	3	4	5	5	6
46	2884	2891	2897	2904	2911	2917	2924	2931	2938	2944	1	1	2	3	3	4	5	5	6
47	2951	2958	2965	2972	2979	2985	2992	2999	3006	3013	1	1	2	3	3	4	5	5	6
48	3020	3027	3034	3041	3048	3055	3062	3069	3076	3083	1	1	2	3	4	4	5	6	6
49	3090	3097	3105	3112	3119	3126	3133	3141	3148	3155	1	1	2	3	4	4	5	6	6

ANTI-LOGARITHMS

	0	1	2	3	4	5	6	7	8	9	Mean Differences 1	2	3	4	5	6	7	8	9
50	3162	3170	3177	3184	3192	3199	3206	3214	3221	3228	1	1	2	3	4	4	5	6	7
51	3236	3243	3251	3258	3266	3273	3281	3289	3296	3304	1	2	2	3	4	5	5	6	7
52	3311	3319	3327	3334	3342	3350	3357	3365	3373	3381	1	2	2	3	4	5	5	6	7
53	3388	3396	3404	3412	3420	3428	3436	3443	3451	3459	1	2	2	3	4	5	6	6	7
54	3467	3475	3483	3491	3499	3508	3516	3524	3532	3540	1	2	2	3	4	5	6	6	7
55	3548	3556	3565	3573	3581	3589	3597	3606	3614	3622	1	2	2	3	4	5	6	7	7
56	3631	3639	3648	3656	3664	3673	3681	3690	3698	3707	1	2	3	3	4	5	6	7	8
57	3715	3724	3733	3741	3750	3758	3767	3776	3784	3793	1	2	3	3	4	5	6	7	8
58	3802	3811	3819	3828	3837	3846	3855	3864	3873	3882	1	2	3	4	4	5	6	7	8
59	3890	3899	3908	3917	3926	3936	3945	3954	3963	3972	1	2	3	4	5	5	6	7	8
60	3981	3990	3999	4009	4018	4027	4036	4046	4055	4064	1	2	3	4	5	6	6	7	8
61	4074	4083	4093	4102	4111	4121	4130	4140	4150	4159	1	2	3	4	5	6	7	8	9
62	4169	4178	4188	4198	4207	4217	4227	4236	4246	4256	1	2	3	4	5	6	7	8	9
63	4266	4276	4285	4295	4305	4315	4325	4335	4345	4355	1	2	3	4	5	6	7	8	9
64	4365	4375	4385	4395	4406	4416	4426	4436	4446	4457	1	2	3	4	5	6	7	8	9
65	4467	4477	4487	4498	4508	4519	4529	4539	4550	4560	1	2	3	4	5	6	7	8	9
66	4571	4581	4592	4603	4613	4624	4634	4645	4656	4667	1	2	3	4	5	6	7	9	10
67	4677	4688	4699	4710	4721	4732	4742	4753	4764	4775	1	2	3	4	5	7	8	9	10
68	4786	4797	4808	4819	4831	4842	4853	4864	4875	4887	1	2	3	4	6	7	8	9	10
69	4898	4909	4920	4932	4943	4955	4966	4977	4989	5000	1	2	3	5	6	7	8	9	10
70	5012	5023	5035	5047	5058	5070	5082	5093	5105	5117	1	2	4	5	6	7	8	9	11
71	5129	5140	5152	5164	5176	5188	5200	5212	5224	5236	1	2	4	5	6	7	8	10	11
72	5248	5260	5272	5284	5297	5309	5321	5333	5346	5358	1	2	4	5	6	7	9	10	11
73	5370	5383	5395	5408	5420	5433	5445	5458	5470	5483	1	3	4	5	6	8	9	10	11
74	5495	5508	5521	5534	5546	5559	5572	5585	5598	5610	1	3	4	5	6	8	9	10	12
75	5623	5636	5649	5662	5675	5689	5702	5715	5728	5741	1	3	4	5	7	8	9	10	12
76	5754	5768	5781	5794	5808	5821	5834	5848	5861	5875	1	3	4	5	7	8	9	11	12
77	5888	5902	5916	5929	5943	5957	5970	5984	5998	6012	1	3	4	5	7	8	10	11	12
78	6026	6039	6053	6067	6081	6095	6109	6124	6138	6152	1	3	4	6	7	8	10	11	13
79	6166	6180	6194	6209	6223	6237	6252	6266	6281	6295	1	3	4	6	7	9	10	11	13
80	6310	6324	6339	6353	6368	6383	6397	6412	6427	6442	1	3	4	6	7	9	10	12	13
81	6457	6471	6486	6501	6516	6531	6546	6561	6577	6592	2	3	5	6	8	9	11	12	14
82	6607	6622	6637	6653	6668	6683	6699	6714	6730	6745	2	3	5	6	8	9	11	12	14
83	6761	6776	6792	6808	6823	6839	6855	6871	6887	6902	2	3	5	6	8	9	11	13	14
84	6918	6934	6950	6966	6982	6998	7015	7031	7017	7063	2	3	5	6	8	10	11	13	15
85	7079	7096	7112	7129	7145	7161	7178	7194	7211	7228	2	3	5	7	8	10	12	13	15
86	7244	7261	7278	7295	7311	7328	7345	7362	7379	7396	2	3	5	7	8	10	12	13	15
87	7413	7430	7447	7464	7482	7499	7516	7534	7551	7568	2	3	5	7	9	10	12	14	16
88	7586	7603	7621	7638	7656	7674	7691	7709	7727	7745	2	4	5	7	9	11	12	14	16
89	7762	7780	7798	7816	7834	7852	7870	7889	7907	7925	2	4	5	7	9	11	13	14	16
90	7943	7962	7980	7998	8017	8035	8054	8072	8091	8110	2	4	6	7	9	11	13	15	17
91	8128	8147	8166	8185	8204	8222	8241	8260	8279	8299	2	4	6	8	9	11	13	15	17
92	8318	8337	8356	8375	8395	8414	8433	8453	8472	8492	2	4	6	8	10	12	14	15	17
93	8511	8531	8551	8570	8590	8610	8630	8650	8670	8690	2	4	6	8	10	12	14	16	18
94	8710	8730	8750	8770	8790	8810	8831	8851	8872	8892	2	4	6	8	10	12	14	16	18
95	8913	8933	8954	8974	8995	9016	9036	9057	9078	9099	2	4	6	8	10	12	15	17	19
96	9120	9141	9162	9183	9204	9226	9247	9268	9290	9311	2	4	6	8	11	13	15	17	19
97	9333	9354	9376	9397	9419	9441	9462	9484	9506	9528	2	4	7	9	11	13	15	17	20
98	9550	9572	9594	9616	9638	9661	9683	9705	9727	9750	2	4	7	9	11	13	16	18	20
99	9772	9795	9817	9840	9863	9886	9908	9931	9954	9977	2	5	7	9	11	14	16	18	20

BINOMIAL COEFFICIENTS

n	$\binom{n}{0}$	$\binom{n}{1}$	$\binom{n}{2}$	$\binom{n}{3}$	$\binom{n}{4}$	$\binom{n}{5}$	$\binom{n}{6}$	$\binom{n}{7}$	$\binom{n}{8}$	$\binom{n}{9}$	$\binom{n}{10}$
0	1										
1	1	2									
2	1	3	1								
3	1	4	5	4	1						
4											
5	1	5	10	10	5	1					
6	1	6	15	20	15	6	1				
7	1	7	21	35	35	21	7	1			
8	1	8	28	56	70	56	28	8	1		
9	1	9	36	84	126	126	84	36	9	1	
10	1	10	45	120	210	252	210	120	45	10	1
11	1	11	55	165	330	462	462	330	165	55	11
12	1	12	66	220	495	792	924	792	495	220	66
13	1	13	78	286	715	1287	1716	1716	1287	715	286
14	1	14	91	364	1001	2002	3003	3432	3003	2002	1001
15	1	15	105	455	1365	3003	5005	6435	6435	5005	3003
16	1	16	120	560	1820	4368	8008	11440	12870	11440	8008
17	1	17	136	683	2380	6188	12376	19448	24310	24310	19448
18	1	18	153	816	3060	8568	18564	31824	43758	48620	43758
19	1	19	171	969	3876	11628	27132	50388	75582	92378	92378
20	1	20	190	1140	4845	15504	38760	77520	125970	167960	184756

VALUES OF e^{-m}

$(0<m<1)$

m	0	1	2	3	4	5	6	7	8	9
0·0	1·0000	·9900	·9802	·9704	·9608	·9512	·9418	·9324	·9231	·9139
0·1	·9048	·8958	·8869	·8781	·8694	·8607	·8521	·8437	·8353	·8270
0·2	·8187	·8106	·8025	·7945	·7866	·7788	·7711	·7634	·7558	·7483
0·3	·7408	·7334	·7261	·7189	·7118	·7047	·6977	·6907	·6839	·6771
0·4	·6703	·6636	·6570	·6505	·6440	·6376	·6313	·6250	·6188	·6126
0·5	·6065	·6005	·5945	·5886	·5827	·5770	·5712	·5655	·5599	·5543
0·6	·5488	·5434	·5379	·5326	·5273	·5220	·5169	·5117	·5066	·5016
0·7	·4966	·4916	·4868	·4819	·4771	·4724	·4677	·4630	·4584	·4538
0·8	·4493	·4449	·4404	·4360	·4317	·4274	·4232	·4190	·4148	·4107
0·9	·4066	·4025	·3985	·3946	·3906	·3867	·3829	·3791	·3753	·3716

$(m=1, 2, 3, \ldots 10)$

m	1	2	3	4	5	6	7	8	9	10
e^{-m}	·36788	·13534	·04979	·01832	·00638	·002479	·00091	·000335	·000153	·000045

Note. To obtain values of e^{-m} for other values of m, use the laws of exponents.

Example. $e^{-2\cdot35}=(e^{-2\cdot00})(e^{-0\cdot35})=(\cdot13534)(\cdot7047)=\cdot095374$

AREAS UNDER NORMAL CURVE

Normal probability curve is given by the equation

$$p(x)=\frac{1}{\sigma\sqrt{2\pi}}\ \exp.\left\{-\tfrac{1}{2}\left(\frac{x-\mu}{\sigma}\right)^2\right\},\ -\infty<x<\infty$$

and standard normal probability curve is given by :

$$\phi(z)=\frac{1}{\sqrt{2\pi}}\ \exp.\left(-z^2/2\right),\ -\infty<z<\infty$$

where, $Z=\dfrac{X-\mu}{\sigma}$

The following table gives the shaded area in the diagram *viz.*, $P(0<Z<z)$ for different values of z.

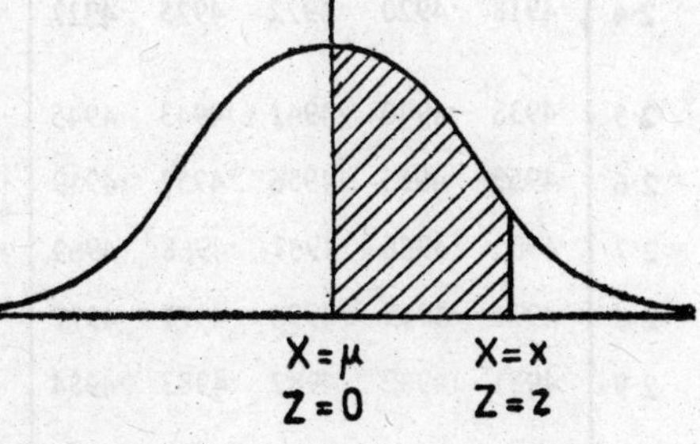

AREAS UNDER NORMAL PROBABILITY CURVE

↓Z→	0	1	2	3	4	5	6	7	8	9
·0	·0000	·0040	·0080	·0120	·0169	·0199	·0239	·0279	·0319	·0359
·1	·0398	·0438	·0478	·0517	·0557	·0596	·0636	·0675	·0714	·0753
·2	·0793	·0832	·0871	·0910	·0948	·0987	·1026	·1064	·1103	·1141
·3	·1179	·1217	·1255	·1293	·1331	·1368	·1406	·1443	·1480	·1517
·4	·1554	·1591	·1628	·1664	·1700	·1736	·1772	·1808	·1844	·1879
·5	·1915	·1950	·1985	·2019	·2054	·2088	·2123	·2157	·2190	·2224
·6	·2257	·2291	·2324	·2357	·2389	·2422	·2454	·2486	·2517	·2549
·7	·2580	·2611	·2642	·2673	·2703	·2734	·2764	·2794	·2823	·2852
·8	·2881	·2910	·2939	·2967	·2995	·3023	·3051	·3078	·3106	·3133
·9	·3159	·3186	·3212	·3238	·3264	·3289	·3315	·3340	·3365	·3389
1·0	·3413	3438	·3461	·3485	·3506	·3531	·3554	·3577	·3599	·3621
1·1	·3643	·3665	·3686	·3708	·3729	·3749	·3770	·3790	·3810	·3830
1·2	·3849	·3869	·3888	·3907	·3925	·3944	·3962	·3980	·3997	·4015
1·3	·4032	·4049	·4066	·4082	·4099	·4115	·4131	·4147	·4162	·4177
1·4	·4192	·4207	·4222	·4236	·4251	·4265	·4279	·4292	·4306	·4319
1·5	·4332	·4345	·4357	·4370	·4382	·4394	·4406	·4418	·4429	·4441
1·6	·4452	·4463	·4474	·4484	·4495	·4505	·4515	·4525	·4535	·4545
1·7	·4554	·4564	·4573	·4582	·4591	·4599	·4608	·4616	·4625	·4633
1·8	·4641	·4649	·4656	·4664	·4671	·4678	·4686	·4693	·4699	·4706
1·9	·4713	·4719	·4726	·4732	·4738	·4744	·4750	·4756	·4761	·4767

(Contd.)

(*Contd.*)

AREAS UNDER NORMAL PROBABILITY CURVE

↓Z→	0	1	2	3	4	5	6	7	8	9
2·0	·4772	·4778	·4783	·4788	·4793	·4798	·4803	·4808	·4812	·4817
2·1	·4821	·4826	·4830	·4834	·4838	·4842	·4846	·4850	·4854	·4857
2·2	·4861	·4864	·4868	·4871	·4875	·4878	·4881	·4884	·4887	·4890
2·3	·4893	·4896	·4898	·4901	·4904	·4906	·4909	·4911	·4913	·4916
2·4	·4918	·4920	·4922	·4925	·4927	·4929	·4931	·4932	·4934	·4936
2·5	·4938	·4940	·4941	·4943	·4945	·4946	·4948	·4949	·4951	·4952
2·6	·4953	·4955	·4956	·4957	·4959	·4960	·4961	·4962	·4963	·4964
2·7	·4965	·4966	·4967	·4968	·4969	·4970	·4971	·4972	·4973	·4974
2·8	·4974	·4975	·4976	·4977	·4977	·4978	·4979	·4979	·4980	·4981
2·9	·4981	·4982	·4982	·4983	·4984	·4984	·4985	·4985	·4986	·4986
3·0	·4987	·4987	·4987	4988	·4988	·4989	·4989	·4989	·4990	·4990
3·1	·4990	·4991	·4991	·4991	·4992	·4992	·4992	·4992	·4993	·4993
3·2	·4993	·4993	·4994	·4994	·4994	·4994	·4994	·4995	·4995	·4995
3·3	·4995	·4995	·4995	·4996	·4996	·4996	·4996	·4996	·4996	·4997
3·4	·4997	·4997	·4997	·4997	·4997	·4997	·4997	·4997	·4997	·4998
3·5	·4998	·4998	·4998	·4998	·4998	·4998	·4998	·4998	4998	4998
3·6	·4998	·4998	4999	·4999	·4999	·4999	·4999	·4999	·4999	·4999
3·7	·4999	·4969	·4999	·4999	·4999	·4999	·4999	·4999	·4999	·4999
3·8	·4999	·4999	·4999	·4999	·4999	·4999	·4999	·4999	·4999	·4999
3·9	·5000	·5000	·5000	·5000	·5000	·5000	·5000	·5000	·5000	·5000